Food & Markets
Proceedings of the Oxford Symposium on Food and Cookery 2014

Food & Markets

Proceedings of the Oxford Symposium on Food and Cookery 2014

Edited by Mark McWilliams

Prospect Books
2015

First published in Great Britain in 2015 by Prospect Books, 26 Parke Road, London SW13 9NG.

© 2015 as a collection Prospect Books.
© 2015 in individual articles rests with the authors.

The authors assert their moral right to be identified as authors in accordance with the Copyright, Designs & Patents Act 1988. No part of this publication may be reproduced, stored in a retrieval system or transmitted in any form or by any means, electronic, mechanical, photocopying, recording or otherwise, without the prior permission of the copyright holders.

ISBN 978-1-909-248-44-1

The illustration on the front cover is of Athinas street and the Municipal Market, Athens in November 1961 (photo by Dimitrios Harisiadis, Benaki Museum Photo Archives). See the paper by Aglaia Kremezi, below.

Design and typesetting in Gill Sans and Adobe Garamond by Tom Jaine.

Printed and bound in Great Britain.

Contents

Foreword
 Mark McWilliams — 9

Plenary Papers

(Re)creating the Irish Farmers Market
 Darina Allen — 11

The Emperor's Plate: Marketing Leftovers in Nineteenth-Century Paris
 Janet Beizer — 15

Symposium Papers

Markets for Mercenaries: Supplying Armies in Sixteenth-Century Germany
 Volker Bach — 35

Are Free Markets Bad for Good Food?
 Julian Baggini — 44

The Merchants of Genoa and the Diffusion of Southern Italian Pasta Culture in Europe
 Anthony F. Buccini — 54

Powerful Scent: The Egyptian Bazaar in Istanbul
 Nihal Bursa — 65

From Nihonbashi to Tsukiji: The Early Years of the World's Biggest Fish Market
 Voltaire Cang — 75

Blood and Sawdust: The Kosher Poultry Racket of New York
 Andrew Coe — 87

Maniva Ecochefs: Forging a New Link between Producers and Consumers in an Organic Street Market in Rio de Janeiro
 Daniel Coelho, Fátima Portilho and Maria Teresa Corção — 96

Food and Markets

Catalan Markets: Constructing National Cuisine and Space through the Market Scene
Venetia Congdon — 104

Markets Boom While Cooking Crashes!
Doug Duda — 114

The Fishmongers of London's Street Markets from the 1840s to the Present
Anastasia Edwards — 124

The Market near Pottery Hill (Testaccio, Rome)
Maureen B. Fant — 135

The Complete History of Food Markets, Abridged
Len Fisher and Janet Clarkson — 147

Food and the Female Body: The Parallel between the Food Market and the Prostitution Market in John Cleland's *Fanny Hill*
Mary J. Gray — 153

The Wroxeter *Macellum*: A Foodway in Every Sense
Christopher Grocock — 163

Local, Super, Super-Local or Local-Super? The Market for Local Food in Edinburgh
Andrew Guest — 177

Twenty-First-Century Meat Markets
Peter Hertzmann — 187

Al Ain Suq – An Enduring Culinary Asset
Phil Iddison — 196

Commonalities and Convergences in World Street Market Food
Bruce Kraig and Colleen Taylor Sen — 206

The Municipal Market of Athens and *Stoa Athanàton* (Immortals' Alley): A Brief Account of Its History, Past and Present
Aglaia Kremezi — 220

Ethical Gastronomy: Organic Food, Markets and Marketing
Jane Levi — 232

Food and Markets

Feeding Dublin: The City Fruit and Vegetable Market
Samantha Martin-McAuliffe — 241

'Fresh' Is Fraught: How Would You Define this Virtuous Word?
Renee Marton — 254

Campo de' Fiori in Rome and the Survival of the Outdoor Market
Elizabeth Minchilli — 265

Flip Dog in the Shad House: Commercial Fisheries Markets and Tavern Culture at Hadley Falls 1730–1880
Elyse Moore — 269

'From Nothing Came Something': Wild Food and its Markets in Industrializing England
Jeanette Neeson — 280

The Fall and Rise of the Canadian Public Market
Lenore Newman — 290

The Identity, Characteristics and Vending of Cucurbit Crops in Israel of Roman Times
Harry S. Paris — 299

Markets in Russia: Back to the Future
Anna Pavlovskaya — 307

Markets, Gender, and Translation in Turn-of-the-Twentieth-Century San Francisco and Southern Vietnam
Erica J. Peters — 319

Going beyond Sights, Smells and Taste: Shared Responsibility for Food Safety at Farmers Markets in the UK
Brigit Ramsingh and Carol A. Wallace — 330

Buying or Selling?
Gillian Riley — 343

The Pilgrimage to *El Babour* – A Functioning Mill in the Nazareth Market
Abbie Rosner — 347

Food and Markets

The Marketplace in Soviet and Post-Soviet Painting: Image Transformation
   Irina Rutsinskaya and Galina Smirnova   355

Eating the Inedible: The Colonial Marketplace at the *Exposition universelle* of 1889
   Kylie Sago   362

Degrees of Freshness: The Contemporary International Market
for Hyperfresh Seafood
   Richard W. Shepro   372

The Hollywood Farmer's Market: Gorgeous Produce, Beautiful People,
a Remarkable Business Plan
   Dan Strehl   384

Markets Under Attack: Rioters and Regulators in Georgian England
   David C. Sutton   388

Markets in Israel: Tradition and Transformations
   Susan Weingarten   399

Foreword

Traditionally the Oxford Symposium on Food and Cookery alternates between broad and specific topics. 2014 was intended to be a year with a tight focus; the theme, Food and Markets, was sandwiched between 2013's Food and Material Culture and 2015's Food and Communication. As the essays in this volume make clear, however, Markets are anything but a narrow subject.

That should not be a surprise: markets arise the moment food is consumed by people who did not produce it. And as soon as there is exchange, it seems, there are rules. What can be sold or traded? By whom? To whom? Under what conditions? Rules allow markets to connect empires, whether Roman, Ottoman, or French, and to resist hegemonic systems, whether by creating alternate supply channels in the Soviet Union or by endorsing Catalan separatism in today's Spain. Market rules both connect local farmers and cooks, whether in rural Ireland or downtown Los Angeles, and enable widespread distribution, whether through twelfth-century Mediterranean trade in dried pasta or the now global trade in fresh fish. Across any distance, rules invite flaunting, and flaunting invites riots, whether over cheese in eighteenth-century Nottingham or over chicken in late nineteenth-century New York.

Regulated markets emerge in unexpected places: to feed soldiers in sixteenth-century Germany, say, or to maximize profits from imperial leftovers in nineteenth-century Paris. Wherever markets spring up, they tend to become inextricably integrated with their surrounding communities, even synonymous with those communities. No wonder that people have worked so hard to save markets under threat – in Athens, in Dublin, in Nazareth – or that people see establishing new markets as a way to revitalize or even create new communities—in Rio de Janeiro, in Vancouver, in Edinburgh. Such high hopes can even inflect larger discussions about the industrial food market in general – hopes that might both be checked by statistics about the dismally small role local markets play in food distribution and be encouraged by what seems like growing consumer demands for higher quality.

During three July days in Oxford, Symposiasts gathered to explore the varied nature, history and potential of markets. The papers gathered here suggest the remarkable range of those discussions as well as the astonishing fluidity of the market concept itself. The way those discussions so easily expanded a specific topic into a broad one represents the best of what's possible in Oxford. As does the collaborative work of the Symposium itself: for their help in preparing this volume, I would particularly like to thank Elisabeth Luard, Ursula Heinzelmann, Peter Hertzmann, Catheryn Kilgarriff, Tom Jaine, and, of course, the many authors included here.

Mark McWilliams
Editor, Oxford Symposium on Food and Cookery

(Re)creating the Irish Farmers Market

Darina Allen

This year's Jane Grigson Memorial Lecture, the traditional Friday night opening event at the Symposium sponsored by the Jane Grigson Trust, was delivered by Darina Allen, the legendary Irish chef, author, television personality and founder of the Ballymaloe Cookery School.

Thank you – it is such an honour to be invited to deliver the Jane Grigson Memorial Lecture. We so loved Jane and regularly cooked from her books at Ballymaloe House and carefully collected her articles from the *Observer Food Magazine* every week. In fact my husband's Christmas present to me in 1971 was a copy of the newly published *Good Things*. I was thrilled and must have cooked everything in that book from cover to cover. I had a clear image of what I imagined Jane would look like from M.J. Mott's drawings and was amazed when I eventually met the much more cuddly real life version.

I still remember the intense excitement when Myrtle Allen came into the kitchens *circa* 1990 to tell us young cooks that Jane and her husband Geoffrey had booked in to Ballymaloe House; I think she was doing research for her cookbook *The Observer Guide to British Cookery*. We put her *Terrine aux Herbes* on the menu and a buttery *Gâteau Pithiviers* on the sweet trolley. She was so sweet and complimentary and pronounced our puff pastry to be much more delicious than hers. Then she confessed that she always had a problem with her pastry and asked whether I could give her a lesson – can you imagine! She returned several times, taught a two-and-a-half-day course at the Ballymaloe Cooking School and just before her untimely passing came with Sophie to a surprise party at Kinoith. How fortunate was I that our paths crossed in life.

Now onto the topic of this lecture – 'Food & Markets'.

The revival of the Irish Farmers Market began in San Francisco of all the unlikely places. I was staying with a friend, Mary Risley who owns the Tante Marie Cookery School. Mary was tremendously excited about a new farmers market that had opened in a parking lot at the other side of town which she insisted we must see, but I had been travelling for over twenty hours and wasn't in the least enthusiastic, nor did I have any intention of being up at 7.30 a.m. However, Mary is even bossier than I am, so she traipsed me across town to see this 'new' market. I've seen lots of markets in France, Italy and Spain, but this was quite unlike any I'd seen before: the stalls were, well, different, so utterly Californian – chic and edgy – and the stall holders were also quite different. Many had been doctors, dentists, lawyers in their 'last life' but had made a lifestyle decision to move to California with the dream of self-sufficiency. Some grew herbs, vegetables and beautiful fruit and flowers; others kept farmyard chickens and heritage pigs so they could have the sort of humanely reared, flavoursome meat they craved. Friends who came to dinner loved it and pleaded to be allowed to buy some. The bread was so appalling in the supermarkets that they baked their own, trial and error at first, but soon leading to wonderful sourdoughs, yeast breads, flat breads.

The US was further down the road of mass production than Europe, so there was a deep craving for real food; out of this desperation was born the farmers market movement.

In Ireland at that time, the supermarkets were well established, and local shops were finding it increasingly difficult to compete unless they became part of the chains. *Circa* 1987 the supermarkets went over to a central distribution system so all the branches were encouraged to order from head office. If they brought more than two per cent of their produce locally, they were actually penalized, so almost overnight local foods disappeared off the shelf even though the general public were largely unaware of the cause. Local farmers and small growers who had traditionally sold their potatoes, cabbages or swede turnips to the shops found themselves turned away. Many a small farmer's production was just too small to justify sending it in on a truck to Dublin for central distribution. There were lots of ludicrous scenarios – e.g. cabbages from a local farmer could be transported to Dublin to the central depot and then arrive back at Shanagarry three or four days later, less fresh and with considerable increase in food miles. The net result of this policy was, on one hand, farmers who could not sell their produce locally, and, on the other, people who could not access fresh local food in season.

In the farmers market in San Francisco – I suddenly had a 'light bulb' moment. If we could re-establish the markets in Ireland, the farmers and food producers could sell directly to the general public. I took lots of photos and came home buzzing with enthusiasm and zeal to tell my mother-in-law Myrtle Allen. She also thought it was a brilliant idea, so we started the first 'new age' farmers market in Ireland on the Coal Quay in Cork on Whit weekend (June Bank Holiday Weekend) in 1997, much to the amusement of the proper 'shawlies' who had been trading there for generations.

The Coal Quay has been a market since the early nineteenth century. My *Simply Delicious* series was on TV at the time, so it caused quite a stir when I set up a stall on the sidewalk with Myrtle Allen and a handful of other producers, many of whom were members of the Cork Free Choice Consumer Group.

Today, over nineteen years later, the Coal Quay Farmers Market continues to trade every Saturday. There are now over 160 farmers markets in Ireland.

In 1999, John Potter Cogan, the head of the Chamber of Commerce in our local town, contacted me in desperation: the local vegetable factory was facing closure – what could we do for the farmers? I suggested a farmers market. The idea of a market was the last thing on earth John expected me to suggest, but he didn't shoot it down even though markets were associated with the 'bad old times' in most people's minds. I had just returned from another trip to San Francisco and had lots of evocative photos. John could see that the

(Re)creating the Irish Farmers Market

re-establishment of a farmers market system in Ireland could have many advantages:
1. Farmers and food producers could sell their produce directly to local people.
2. Farmers and producers could get the full price for their produce to enable them to increase their income and stay on the land that they love in their own parish.
3. People could get local food in season and real traceability.
4. The market would bring positive publicity and food tourists to the town (which it subsequently did, as people would drive forty or fifty miles to come to the market in Midleton on a Saturday morning).
5. It would provide an alternative choice to the supermarket and also a different shopping experience where children could connect with how food is produced.

John sold the idea to the Chamber of Commerce and the Midleton Town Council.

In early 2000, we formed a small committee and decided to launch on Whit weekend. We printed some simple posters with a phone number for interested stall holders to contact, and pinned them up in local shops, pubs, dentists' and doctors' waiting-rooms. The phone started to ring and soon we had a couple of dozen enquiries – we decided on food and fresh herbs only, no crafts. However, storm clouds started to gather as local businesses became concerned that the market would affect their turnover. Rumours were rife, so we decided to call a public meeting to explain the concept. I had figures from the US and the Continent to prove beyond doubt that a successful market raises the turnover of the local businesses by 18–35 per cent on market days. Those with concerns were reassured, and of course this has been proven beyond any shadow of doubt since the market was established. Initially, though, those who were most sceptical were the farmers themselves, but I was positively evangelical about the potential of farmers markets.

In 1991 I wrote a piece for *The Farmers Journal* extolling the virtues of a farmers market, but to my astonishment I got furious letters from farmers who felt I was insulting them by even suggesting such an initiative – 'we'd want to be on our knees to consider selling on a stall off the side of the street like in the bad old times'.

None the less, some, particularly smaller farmers, did see the potential and, although it took enormous courage for them to break ranks, decided to take the plunge. It only took a week or two for them to be convinced by the full retail price in their hand and feedback from grateful customers. One organic beef farmer told me that in all his farming life previously, he had never, ever, received a compliment or a thank-you for his work. The cattle were just herded into a lorry and went to the mart and that was the end of the cycle, but at the farmers market, he was almost reduced to tears the first time a customer thanked him profusely for his delicious mince. He told me that it had taken enormous courage to make the decision to come to the market, but that moment had made it all worthwhile and banished any doubts he might have had.

Another farmer, Willie Scannell, grew beautiful floury Golden Wonder and Kerr

Pink potatoes on his small farm. Traditionally he sold them to the shops in the area, but the central distribution policy meant his market evaporated. His output was too small to go into central distribution, so he was faced with having to consider selling the farm that was his only and chosen way of life. When he saw the Midleton Farmers Market poster in the local pub he decided, much to the amused sniggering of the other lads, that he'd have a go.

He borrowed a green plastic garden table from his sister and her kitchen scales; his till was an old black and gold money box. He arrived in to the market in his rusty van, set up and to his astonishment was sold out of potatoes by 11.00 a.m. The next week he brought in more potatoes and even piled them onto the passenger seat. His tremendous success meant he earned a 'weeks wage' on a Saturday. A year or so later, when Willie was missing from the farmers market two weeks in a row, I enquired where he was and was told that he had gone on a 'continental holiday'. When I asked, 'Where to?' I learned he had gone to 'Cyprus to see how they grow their potatoes over there.' Willie still trades at the market every week. The Midleton Farmers Market will celebrate its fifteenth anniversary on Whit weekend this year.

The Emperor's Plate: Marketing Leftovers in Nineteenth-Century Paris

Janet Beizer

The stuff of imperial banquets and the fare of the lower classes are extreme concepts not usually considered together.[1] And yet they come together in a practice through which food circulated wildly across socio-economic, cultural and imaginary borders over the course of the long nineteenth century.[2] It was not impossible during this period for beggars to eat like the Emperor – or the King or the President of the Republic or the Rothschilds, depending on the year and the milieu – because they might be consuming the very scraps cleared from such privileged tables.[3]

The practice of clearing leftovers from the grand tables of palaces, ministries, embassies and fine restaurants and reselling them to the less privileged as *regrat* or *rogatons* (the most common umbrella terms), *bijoux* and *arlequins* (slang subterms) was common in the nineteenth century and had a special place – a quite literal space – in the market. In the renovated space of the Baltard-redesigned Halles in central Paris, the triage and recomposition of leftovers was done behind the scenes, below ground.[4] In subterranean passages removed from the light of day the remains could be prepared for marketing to the public in a painstakingly refurbished state: the almost intact morsels salvaged for resale at premium second-hand prices, the gristly half-devoured bits re-plated and artfully sauced, recomposed in more or less attractive collages priced accordingly. From here they would be sent up to the pavilion stalls devoted to this specific kind of commerce.[5]

The alimentary history of the underfed is only now being resurrected, piecemeal, thanks to a handful of contemporary historians and their sources in chronicles and novels of the period, many of which are little read or even forgotten (and generally out of print) today. We know a fair amount about the rise of haute cuisine in post-revolutionary France, but the poor left few recipes, and their fare was of little interest to most period chroniclers of gastronomy and fine restauration.[6] It is precisely this gap – of interest, of knowledge, of discourse and, of course, most concretely, of substance – that separated high tables and low (or no) tables, but that also, paradoxically, was responsible for connecting them and for putting into socio-economic circulation a vast array of objects of consumption.

In what follows I will look beyond the already richly preserved corpus of gastronomy as it was codified in nineteenth-century Paris, to the other extreme, the commerce in leftovers, and more specifically, one subgenre: the plate of recomposed table scraps, *l'arlequin*. However, by way of introduction to this trafficking, I must emphasize, if only in passing, how radical were the dichotomies that enabled it. To at least evoke the profound disparities of the Paris food scene, let us consider a small but representative series of polarities. In the first of three examples, we have, on the one hand, Grimod de la Reynière's *Almanach des gourmands* with its recherché counsel – expanded and reinvented each time in the eight editions of the almanac – on where the most discriminating palates might find the highest quality of everything gourmand, from extravagant ingredients, to exquisite restaurant meals, to fine crystal, porcelain and linens; on the other, Pierre Hamp's account of the protest of one outraged beggar, who meets a restaurant kitchen handout of 'ham fat between two rags of gnawed bread' with the cry: 'This is what I get? ... you don't have anything better? You who get to choose your food are lucky. I have to swallow whatever I find, or starve to death.'[7] Or again: let us juxtapose the recipe for 'Le Potage Camerani' (invented on the occasion of an early nineteenth-century dinner for ten eminent gourmets at the elegant Café Anglais), with its stipulation that the chicken liver base be derived from forty fattened chickens killed by electrocution rather than bleeding or strangulation, and the protocol for a rather different preparation of soup, common to multiple soup kitchens catering to the indigent, this one dependent on a stock sourced from the greasy residue of dishwashing skimmed by the kitchen labourers [*les plongeurs*] when they were done with their day's work.[8] And finally, a third apposition: the harmonies of a sumptuous repast prepared with lavish, calculated attention such as Marcel Rouff evokes it ('imagine the intellectual effort, the intuitive genius that will harmonize the products of the earth, the sky and the sea'), or the gentle accords of a well-conducted menu such as Auguste Escoffier conceives it ('to choose ... dishes with discernment, to group them harmoniously and to create, with scattered notes, a sort of delectable orchestration') – contrasted with what Madeleine Ferrières names the 'cacophony of colours and smells', or the dissonances of pot luck borne, in Jacques Castelnau's description, by a ladle emerging 'like a lottery ticket' from a pot of melded remains, with its arbitrary haul of anything ranging from 'a half-devoured chicken thigh [to] a few humble lentils'.[9]

This last example precisely encapsulates the dynamic of the passage from wealth to poverty, privilege to indigence, choice to imposition, aesthetic intention to random consumption that characterizes the particular practice I want to explore in detail in these pages. *L'arlequin* is the alimentary idiom in French for a patchwork of reassembled table scraps generally assumed to be visually reminiscent of the costume of its namesake, the buffoon figure in the *Commedia dell'arte*; on the gustatory, olfactory and tactile levels as well, such food scraps would have been analogous to the garishly mismatched costume fabric of the *Commedia* character. To retain the theatrical and design resonances of the term, and also its later literary and painterly connotations, I will hold to a literal translation, 'the harlequin'.

I'll begin by describing the practice in the dominant discourse of its contemporary historians, journalists and novelists, most often followed by our own contemporaries as well, which represents a perspective I call *degradational* in that it focuses on the ignoble and disgusting nature of the already deteriorating, eventually decomposing second-hand food, and on the Parisian *regrattier*'s business of selling it down the socio-economic chain in increasingly degraded form to a progressively impoverished clientele. A spate of solicitous bourgeois commentators ranging from the late eighteenth century to our time, no doubt priding themselves on their expansive sympathy and pity, have complacently and derogatorily represented the dregs of fine repasts passed down to the dregs of the social order. This discourse typically takes the high voice of overflowing outrage and disgust. In the last part of the essay I will move on to suggest an alternative approach, however, this one constructed upon minor traces also (but more rarely) available in period narratives as well as (but still rarely) latter-day ones, and which I call *aspirational*; this discourse tends more to espouse a subjectivity that is not the author's own, and to represent the practice of eating other people's discarded food as an act that is metaphysically as well as physically motivated; this means approaching hunger in its affective and imaginary regimes rather than only as a somatic imperative. Broadening the concept of hunger and of taste allows us also to thicken our understanding of food in its diversified states, categories and functions, cultural as well as natural, adulterated as well as pure, and to think about eating as an act of potential revolt that puts into question accepted social, political and aesthetic definitions of taste and disgust.

Trickle-down eating

The phenomenon of used food pre-existed the alimentary application of the term *l'arlequin*; Maxime du Camp explains, in 1870, that *arlequins* used to be called *rogatons*, 'but slang has prevailed'.[10] In his late eighteenth-century *Tableau de Paris*, under the entry 'Hideous Dishes' [*Mets hideux*], Louis Sébastien Mercier describes the antecedent to what would become a somewhat better regulated trade in recycled food at Les Halles in the mid-nineteenth century:

> At the bend of the street, in a narrow little stall, what is it I see on these chipped, cracked plates? What are these leftovers that already bear the mark of mould? These remains, rejected by the valets, after touching the mouth of a bishop who thought better of it and switched to another bit, were disdained by the scullions … who sold them to the *regrattiers*, who left them exposed to the air …. In the evening, an indigent soul … descends from his attic to buy these disgusting remains on which the servants have drooled.[11]

Though Mercier's early version of the trade in dinner remains describes the shadiest of food recyclings, concealed in dark alleyways, marginalized in space and time, the cycle announces the very same trickle-down pattern that would remain in place throughout the new century. And as we shall see, the practices he describes, though they become illegal, do not completely vanish during the nineteenth century.

Food and Markets

In the memoir of his early days as pastry and then restaurant chef apprentice (in the late 1880s–early 1890s), Hamp recounts the triage that took place in the kitchens after the diners left:

> From the residues of the cleared plates, the maîtres d' put aside for the harlequin sellers whatever scraps kept a little substance, held on to a semblance of slice or piece. These went to a plate of cold meat for the stalls of Les Halles or cheap restaurants. Whatever was runny or pulpy was given to the beggars to feast on …. After this, the cadaverous remains of sauces and dishwashing, the vomit of drunken diners, the burnt and rotten bits fell into the barrels of [the dishwasher] who watched in jubilation as the viscous level on which he made his small fortune rose …. He sold this to pig farmers …. The food cycle, which began with the vegetable garden, the herd and the flock, ended in the dung heap and the pigsty (pp. 142–43).

Other commentators recount similar kitchen operations that culminate instead in the sale of just such grease and slops and debris to soup vendors and harlequin sellers rather than pig farmers. Castelnau calls harlequin sellers 'the fiercest competitors of dogs, cats, and pigs: they literally take bread from [animal] jaws' (p. 48).

The visual and literary iconography of harlequins in the nineteenth century in fact consistently has consumers vying with beasts for their sustenance. Tales are legion of dishwashers turning a profit by selling off to pig farmers on the sly the dinner vestiges meant for charitable handouts. According to A. Coffignon, the harlequin stands were first providers for 'the good souls that pamper little dogs'; human consumers are listed as secondary clientele.[12] Du Camp specifies that after the choice scraps are snapped up by humans, 'there remains a fair amount of detritus that is difficult to classify'; these dregs lie around waiting for the well-to-do women who cross Paris to buy 'succulent mash' for their 'coddled dogs' or other pets from their favourite harlequin stalls at Les Halles (p. 165). Paintings and photographs of harlequin merchants typically feature a dog crouching beneath the display table, at once naturalist detail and ideological commentary. Written accounts frequently expose a thin conceit on the part of buyer and seller alike that the food is being purchased for a pet at home, though it would be good enough for human consumption, as in the following exchange reported by P.-L. Imbert:

> – I would like a ragoût for my dog.
> – I have exactly what you need: a delicious dish, from the kitchens of M. the Count of the Sylvain Flute. I had some for breakfast, and I'm still licking my fingers. … It's a shame that the dog will be eating it…this is food worthy of a Christian.[13]

The omnibus

Eugène Sue's potboiler novel *Les Mystères de Paris* takes off from a scene in a tavern in which the ex-convict protagonist, Le Chourineur, orders a harlequin and urges his companion to do the same. The dual descriptions of the dish, one from the character's voracious point of view and the other from the novelist's patronizing one, are worth comparing.

> What a dish! God Almighty! What a dish! It's like an omnibus. There's something for all tastes, for those who eat meat and those who don't, for those who like sugar and whose who like spice…Chicken drumsticks, biscuit pieces, fish tails, rib bones, pâté crusts, fried bits, cheese, vegetables, woodcock head, salad. Go on, eat, eat up, la Goualeuse…this is refined food.

Sue, in good editorial form, adds a note to explain the dish, which he evidently deemed too exotic to pass without clarification for his 1842 bourgeois reader: 'A harlequin is a collection of meat, fish, and all kinds of leftovers coming from the cleared tables of the servants of upper-class homes. We are ashamed of these details, but they contribute to the ensemble of such menus.'[14] It is not clear whether his shame is to be attributed to commiseration with the plight of his fellow humans at the bottom of the social hierarchy condemned to consume the relics of the higher orders, or to a potential offence his details might deliver to the taste and sensibility of his bourgeois readers, but it is precisely the carefully crafted ambiguity of his phrasing that begins to demonstrate the hypocrisy of the discourse I call 'degradational'.

Almost all commentators emphasize the 'omnibus' nature of the harlequin and call attention, explicitly or implicitly, to its disgusting nature. Chavette includes the harlequin in his wide-ranging book on restauration in Paris, penultimate in a series of chapters that descends from fine dining to charity hand-outs. He introduces the harlequin by its sinister appearance – 'These strange plates, mysterious amalgams of scraps so diverse that they have been named *harlequins*' – and goes on to detail procedure and composition: 'Restaurant leftovers are sold and carefully picked over for the best scraps, resold as 'jewels' [*bijoux*]. The harlequin is composed of the leftovers of such leftovers! Fish heads, rib bones, bits of lamb leg, pastry crumbs, all this, pell-mell, soaked in twenty different sauces, already four to five days old, waiting for customers in a certain corner of the central Halles' (pp. 109–10).

Imbert describes the completely fortuitous and therefore motley nature of the harlequin and indeed of the whole phenomenon, from consumer to consumed to surface of consumption:

> On plates of all shapes and every dimension we find displayed foods destined for consumers of all classes and even all species: men, dogs, or cats. We see objects whose nature is difficult to determine: bones to which not even the slightest bit of meat adheres; fowl hardly eaten; bits of pastry and of fish mixed in with

fragments of roast beef and of salad. Everything is there, even – too often, alas, for the needy! – that which should not be there! (pp. 114–15)

It is as if commentators were rivalling for the most revolting descriptions possible. Coffignon describes 'pâté crusts, vegetable scraps, half-gnawed legs of lamb, chicken carcasses, fish, a little of everything' (p. 181).

Certainly part of what disturbs about the harlequin is its mixed character, the combining of separate parts that lose identity; but the scandal it provokes is not due only to its jumbled form in spatial display, but also to its combined presentation in time. Pâté and meat bones and pastry heaped together on a plate speak not only to the eradication of separate elements, but to the erasure of course sequencing as well. Du Camp is clear about the violation of temporal structure in his rendition of 'this nameless pile, where hors-d'oeuvre are mixed with roasts, and vegetables, with desserts' (p. 165). The rituals of dining are dependent on sequencing and time, and these formalities are disrupted by the harlequin. In a dramatic example of temporal disordering projected onto the consumer as well, Coffignon paints a portrait of 'Grandma Olden Days' [*la mère Jadis*], who haunts the harlequin stalls by predilection, and injects into every utterance the time marker 'in the olden days'. Roaming the streets of Paris as an old woman, she persistently inserts into the present a past when she was ostensibly one of the beauties of Paris. Working now as an ambulant merchant, she and her words are overtaken by former times of luxurious ease. Choosing her meals from the harlequin display, she recalls and repeats more privileged days of dining on each of the recycled dishes in an original incarnation. Her conversation is a harlequin in time, fragments of different temporal layers juxtaposed, promiscuously cohabiting the same moment (pp. 182–83).

Suzanne attempts to put some order into the disorderly phenomenon, distinguishing between different classes of harlequins destined for different classes of eaters ('choice' harlequins and 'cheap' harlequins). The most expensive portions are also the most highly assorted [*richement assorties*] – no doubt because they are the most highly sorted as well – and the nature of their individual elements is more succulent and more elegant [*recherchée*]. Suzanne offers examples of the finest assortments, going for ten to twelve sous: '[1] a chicken thigh, a lobster claw, a fillet of sole, a dried-up bit of pâté, some pistachio pudding; [2] half a truffled trotter, a slice of galantine, a breaded cutlet, a fish head, a chocolate éclair; [3] some sauerkraut, crayfish in red wine sauce, sautéed rabbit, veal head cheese, a venison fillet, some bits of apple charlotte' (p. 46).

Zola describes the hybrid composition of a lower-end plate: 'Starting at 9 a.m. the plates are displayed in the stalls, prettily made up, dressed and decorated; for three to five sous: scraps of meat, game fillets, fish heads or tails, vegetables, charcuterie, even dessert; cakes barely nibbled and sweets almost whole' (p. 342). His signalling of the artisanal element of the harlequin merchant's work (which requires not merely dishing out, but dressing, decorating, applying cosmetic touches) announces a common motif.

Marketing Leftovers in Nineteenth-Century Paris

The seller as artist

Like Zola and others, Suzanne comments on the artistry necessary to a harlequin seller intent on making her composite wares appetizing to the eyes of those customers who choose to eat remnants of other people's fancy (if used) food instead of buying less extravagant raw ingredients, for much the same price, to be freshly prepared. After the early morning collection by intermediaries (or by harlequin merchants themselves) who contract with various ministries, embassies, fine restaurants and *hôtels particuliers* to pick up pails of leftovers from their kitchens, after the delivery of these dinner remains to the underground sorting areas of Les Halles where they are poured and scraped into large vats, the work but also the craft of the harlequin sellers begins. The labour of sorting through the vats [*les mannes*] filled with mixed ruins of miscellaneous dinners is only the start. She or he must also, most crucially, 'garnish the plates with tact and discernment. … It is no easy matter for the "jeweller" [*la bijoutière*] to dress up her merchandise, add the final touches, divide it among the many plates she has to fill, and arrange all this in such a fashion that it will tempt the eye and the desire of her clients' (p. 46). The harlequin seller is an artisan as well as a merchant. Commentators consistently use verbs such as *habiller*, 'to dress'; *parer*, 'to dress up, deck out, embellish'; *rhabiller*, 'to rehabilitate or dress up'; and *maquiller*, 'to make up, apply cosmetics' to describe the work of *bricolage*, 'cobbling' or 'tinkering', that is the essence of the trade. As Ferrières has suggested, to sell used food is not only to engage in commerce, but also in transformative work; it is to refurbish, to renew, to beautify, to stimulate appetite, to make new things out of old things ['*regratter, c'est aussi rendre plus beau, plus appétissant, faire du neuf avec du vieux*'] (p. 351). Rhetoric writes the harlequin seller as a tailor, a shoemaker, a dresser, a wardrobe mistress, a make-up artist and at times a brothel madam trading in recomposed bodies of food that must be overdressed because they are already overcirculated, overcombined, overmixed, overaged: literally promiscuous objects of desire proffered for public consumption.

In contrast, Suzanne relates, a labourer with many children could feed his entire family economically with another line of goods from the same stall, which also vends, but at a much lower price than the more extravagant mosaics, various ragoûts and stews whose defining meat has disappeared: lamb stew reduced to its potatoes; veal with carrots whose carrots predominate; beef with cabbage condensed to cabbage. Available as well are various stews or soups whose ingredients are so merged as to be almost indistinguishable (p. 46).

Suzanne is not alone among period chroniclers who describe soup sold either by harlequin merchants or by merchants specialized as soup sellers. Soup is the epitome of the harlequin concept: it is the product of ingredients scraped from the bottom of the barrel and the top of the sink, recombined into what is often a rendering into oblivion of the constituent parts. Barbaret describes the soup made by harlequin dealers with what is left after the assembling of harlequin plates:

With the grease skimmed off dirty dishwater allowed to cool and congeal into a crust, supplemented by water, the merchants set bouillon cooking, to which they add the remains of mashed potatoes, some beans, other vegetables, and any crusts of bread they've picked up. … These wares might even be vaguely appetizing for anyone who has not witnessed the manipulations they have sustained. In any case, the consumers of such food are not demanding. … They are usually vagabonds, whose palates have been desensitized by alcohol. (pp. 366–68)

Though Barbaret dismisses the need to cater to the taste of consumers, it is clear elsewhere that the fabrication of soup as well as of plated harlequins is financially commensurate with a work of beautification and ornamentation, not to say disguise. Maxime du Camp and others report on the very specialized tradesman called the 'bouillon bead-maker' (literally, 'the worker who makes eyes in bouillon' [*l'employé aux yeux de bouillon*]). His task was to create the illusion of depth and richness of texture in a very thin bouillon made from such raw materials as we have seen, or, to quote du Camp, from an even more watery base: 'soup drawn from the fountain, and coloured with a bit of burnt onion' (p. 169). Castelnau elucidates the work of this inimitable labourer who must simulate the unctuous depths of complex broth on the dull surface of simple coloured water: 'This precious assistant … takes in his mouth a spoonful of fish oil and blows it out with force while squeezing his lips tightly together. He thereby spreads a kind of mist on the pot. Through the action of this bountiful dew, droplets [*les yeux*] form and transform the flat brownish surface into a lustrous constellation' (p. 51).

The afterlife of the harlequin

The harlequin, as plate or as soup, is one stage in a cycle of recycling. While the practice was more or less regulated and policed in the marketplace by the Second Empire, there were multiple opportunities after the market stalls for reaching outside the law and raising the practice to greater heights of insalubrity, as there were numerous outlets for leftovers prior to or on the sidelines of the market. Jean-Paul Aron has remarked that '[the harlequin] is only the prologue. … The industry of rotting takes as its tenet that nothing be lost. … From vestige to refuse, from refuse to decomposition, the transitions are imperceptible'.[15] To follow the cycle after its 'prologue', to witness some episodes of what may be considered to be the afterlife of the harlequin, we can turn to some period accounts.[16]

Chavette relates the multi-episodic epilogue to the story of foods condemned by the authorities at Les Halles: 'The authorities … order the withdrawal from sale of [food refuse] before it is entirely rotted. But have no fear, these condemned remains are not yet lost. They disappear to outlying areas, far from the purview of the inspectors, to stock the pots of the miserable hovels where poverty feeds' (p. 110). Alternatively, there are the *houillers*, who are traffickers in spoiled food (poultry, game, etc.): food so far gone as to have been rejected by the lowliest of restaurants at the market, and so normally destined for the refuse dump. Instead it is purchased for next to nothing by a *houiller*, who takes it to the outskirts of Paris. There, 'posing as a peasant, he approaches you in the street or under a doorway, with an air of secrecy, to propose cheap game. His merchandise is carefully wrapped "so as not to attract the attention of the police", says the ostensible poacher. The low price convinces you, he passes you the package… and you carry the plague home with you' (p. 111). There is a third scenario offered by Chavette in this survey of deteriorating remains: 'A few years ago, the health services of Les Halles ordered that spoiled fish be carted off to the garbage dumps of [the suburb of] La Villette. One day they arrested some people who for years had been coming after the dump carts left, to refish the fish and resell it on the outskirts of Paris. No comment is needed' (pp. 112–13).

If Chavette makes no further comment, other writers furnish details on the practice of 'making up fish' [*maquiller le poisson*] by infusing blood in the gills of fish no longer fresh. Lobster, crayfish and other molluscs that deteriorate quickly in warm weather were not subject to the same kind of 'freshening up'; instead, the spoiled parts would be simply detached. Any holes or gaping spaces made by the amputations would be 'stuffed with chervil, parsley, or aromatic herbs to mask the ammonia smell given off'.[17]

Coffignon leaves pages that elaborate on the specialized work of oyster resellers, vendors of oysters gone bad and palmed off cheaply by sellers unwilling or unable to sell them to their clients. The resellers, known as 'undertakers' [*des croque-morts*], stock thousands of spoiled oysters in large wooden tubs in large open sheds commonly referred to as 'infirmaries' [*l'infirmerie*]. Here they are set to soak in salt water sometimes dosed with algae. The oyster, dying but not yet dead, has sufficient reflexes remaining to open upon contact with the salt water, to 'drink', and when replete, to close – and to give the illusion of vitality and edibility. 'It will soon die of indigestion,' reports Coffignon, 'but [for a critical limited period] appears fresh to the eye, sounds full and feels heavy' (pp. 219–21). It is no wonder, then, that the consumption of oysters in the nineteenth century begins to be 'democratized', to use Coffignon's term (p. 217).

Hamp's memories of his restaurant apprenticeship include several accounts of the eating habits of those living even below the level of harlequin patrons. The 'moth-eaten' beggars he refers to as *les miteux* come by for handouts the kitchen staff prepares for distribution at appointed hours: 'The maîtres-d' had to clean the cleared plates carefully, scraping off fat parings and sauce dribbles to soften and flavour the dry crusts destined for the teeth of the starving. These damned souls wait[ed] for their disgusting ration each morning, at the very time when the waiters were laying the white tablecloths, setting the crystal and the silver' (p. 143). Hamp further describes a food cycle linking the pinnacle of haute cuisine inexorably to the dung heap, each stage of which is socio-economically determined and strictly hierarchized:

The food served in fine restaurants was passed on from wealthy guests to the clients of stalls that sold bits and pieces, and then on to the wretched of the streets, then on to the institutionalized poor, and finally to the pigs put out to pasture and to fertilize the land. Everyone sought to profit from this traffic where the smallest crumb of bread and the most disgusting drool of sauce had commercial value. (p. 144)

Nature may be but thinly veiled by culture, but culture – economic and political forces – regulates how nature is both determined and determinative.

Nothing is lost

If the harlequin finds its place in an institutionalized (re)cycling of food whose downward path mimics the social ladder, it also is informed by a broad economic mandate of thrift and reuse. Time and again we are reminded by various dictums and declarations in the accounts of food circulation that nothing is to be wasted. As corollary, everything must be done to assure that nothing is discarded, including reconditioning, cosmetic enhancement, savvy marketing and fraud. Though insalubrity and dishonesty were easier to implement away from the surveillance of authorities in the marketplace, commerce at Les Halles was no exception to the rule of salvage and recirculation, and one has the sense that many vendors did whatever they could get away with. 'Nothing is lost in Paris,' Coffignon reminds us, 'at Les Halles less than anywhere else' (p. 151). Butter that fell on the floor would be used for frying (p. 181). Cooking utensils and grills were fashioned from old umbrella ribs by a small tradesman on the edge of Les Halles (Coffignon, p. 260). Discarded butt-ends of smoked cigars were gathered for recycling by another specialized tradesman [*le ramasseur de bouts de cigares*].[18] Du Camp offers the summary judgment that 'all is used in this immense city of Paris, and there is no object too deteriorated, too disdainful, too paltry, to be put to use by some intelligent person.' As illustration, he goes on to narrate the cycle of bread, starting with the used bread sellers (literally, 'crust and crumb sellers' [*les marchands de mie et de croûte*]) at Les Halles. But the story flashes back, for the source of the recycled bread can be traced to school canteens where the boarded children freely waste their bread, throwing it, kicking it 'like pebbles or clumps of dirt' in the schoolyards. These clods of bread, 'covered with dust, stained with ink, damp from puddles, hardened behind trash heaps', are gathered and sold to used bread dealers, who sort the bread. The bits 'still presentable' are dried in the oven and grated, to be used for making croutons or thickening soup. The crusts and crumbs deemed 'too defective' are pulverized in a mortar and used for breading chops. The 'true debris' is 'blackened over a fire, ground into a dark powder, mixed with honey sprayed with a few drops of spirits of mint', and sold as toothpaste (p. 165). Castelnau gives a similar account of the bread recycling industry, adding that the used bread seller's employees charged with bread triage work morning to night in vast sheds, working in teams before 'mountains of bread' to sort the scraps into those still fit for humans and those consigned to feed rabbits (Castelnau pp. 46-47, 49–50).

Zola describes the handling of butter in the cellar of Les Halles. Butter for the poor was composed, like cheap wine, of an amalgam of sources, some turning or already rancid. Once kneaded into a single mass by bare arms buried up to the elbows, the blend would be visually enhanced by the addition of a colourant [*le raucourt*] derived from the annatto tree. If that were not available, carrots or marigolds would do the trick (pp. 330–31). Butter was not the only food artificially coloured. Various kinds of fowl and cuts of pork were 'freshened up'; in fact there was a specialized tradesman called 'the painter of turkey feet' [*le peintre de pieds de dindons*] whose job was to apply a glaze on these appendages so that they would 'appear fresh and red even many days after death' (Castelnau, 46–47). Other sorts of fowl were prepared for sale by various other cosmetic enhancing techniques. Pigeons were force-fed by blowing grain, mouth-to-mouth, then infused with salt water, and killed in their digestive afterglow to present a white and delicate flesh to the consumer (Zola, pp. 392–93). Ducks and chickens were artificially plumped for market by blocking their cloaca with paper and then forcing air into their trachea (Sclaresky, p. 38).

The line separating thrift and enterprise from unsanitary practices and fraud is sinuous, whether within or without the zone of surveillance. Hamp recounts, from his days as a pastry apprentice in the upscale Pâtisserie Laborde, that the owner 'trained us to avoid wasting even a single crumb. We used everything down to the last drop' (p. 62). So it may not be a great surprise that the syrup used for glazing *babas au rhum* was drawn from the 'scum [... of] sugary residues, scrapings of cake icing, meringue left over in the bottom of bowls ... all dumped into five-litre cans. ... When the containers began to overflow due to fermentation, their content was spewed out into a copper pan and cooked to clarification' (p. 62). He also relates the owner's purchase of some very well-priced vanilla beans from a passing sailor ostensibly returning from the Antilles. Upon use, however, it was clear that the vanilla was secondhand: '[these were] old beans soaked in oil to plump them up again and give them lustre, and chemically reinfused with vanilla scent' (pp. 62–63).

Castelnau gives as an example of the increasingly prevalent 'art of reusing leftovers' [*l'art d'accommoder les restes*] – an art that was gradually becoming a bourgeois value, and not just a popular necessity – the 'zester woman' [*la zesteuse*]:

> As soon as she spots a piece of orange or lemon rind, she grabs it greedily. During oyster season she is found prowling around restaurants and bars. ... Her eyes light up when she sees a basket of shellfish. The waiters end up recognizing her, and if she is attractive, they save the precious peels for her. When she returns home, she grates them .... As her business grows, she takes on helpers .... She expands her expeditions from Paris, to France, and then abroad. And the fine powder, sometimes yellow as gold, sometimes copper red, is transformed into lemon extract, orange syrup, and Dutch curaçao. (pp. 51–52)

Echoing the period chroniclers, Castelnau repeats the refrain: 'nothing is lost' [*on ne perd rien*], clearly using the present example to speak not only to avoiding loss, but also, to the potential gains of economy, frugality and entrepreneurial skill (p. 50).

The harlequin eaters

The harlequin finds its place within this general climate of detritus, recirculation and thrift, but also stands out against it as distinctive. It finds its difference in the variegated form we have seen. As I earlier indicated in passing, nineteenth-century commentators, echoed by their successors, tend to assume a direct analogy between Harlequin, that stock figure of the *Commedia dell'arte* immediately recognizable by its stitched-together aspect, and the similarly composed plate of leftovers that came to borrow its name. The naming and the analogy, however, beg to be further considered in terms of their connotations as much as their denotations.

First a brief review of common assumptions about the theatrical harlequin and its avatars. Du Camp expounds: 'Today we call [recycled food scraps] *harlequins*. Just as Bergamasque's costume is made of bits and pieces, [used food sellers'] merchandise is composed of all sorts of goods. They gather the leftovers from sumptuous tables' (p. 165). More succinctly, Chavette explains that the fragments are 'so diverse that they were given the name of *harlequins*' (p. 109). Castelnau depicts even as he disparages the harlequin seller as 'the lowliest of cooks, not even worthy of the name, the person who puts together on a single plate the most assorted dishes; such cuisine resembles the coat of the legendary clown, whence [the plate acquires] the name of that character' (p. 48). Philippe Mellot proposes that 'the remains of meat, fish, or even pastries coming from the cleared tables of great houses are *harlequins*, which no doubt took their name from Harlequin, that comical character whose mottled costume was made of stitched-together patches of green, yellow, red, and blue'.[19]

While the alimentary-vestimentary analogy is apt, I want to argue that it is overdetermined. If the cuisine resembles the pieced-together costume of the legendary character, so too do the clothes of the individual consumers, so too, the physical appearance of each one, and so too, their collective physiognomy. Here is one harlequin client described by Imbert:

> [His clothes are] frayed, wrinkled, crumpled … the buttons are missing in essential places, leaving unjustifiable gaps. Above a shirt collar which on one side disappears under a tie and on the other cascades down limply like a wet dishrag, emerges a round, beardless, florid face, whose eyes, looking in two different directions – the right one downward, the left upward – take on the strangest expression. A few strands of very long hair, meant to hide his premature baldness, float down his back in the most amusing way. His jacket is powdered with dandruff on the shoulders and with lint elsewhere. His pants are not clean; imbedded in the fabric is dog hair (p. 116).

Here is the portrait of another client, 'old Muflard, an aged skinflint who gads about in worn-out, flabby shoes that have lost their shape, and whose clothes, patched together everywhere, recall those of Trichka, the character created by the well-known Russian fabulist Jean Krylof. Trichka chewed off his sleeve cuffs to fill in the holes at his elbows, then his coattails to extend his sleeves' (Imbert, p. 119).[20] A cunning consumer, Muflard (whose name evokes snouts, boors and boorishness) makes the rounds of the harlequin stalls, sampling everything and buying nothing. Imbert, in good physiognomist fashion, marvels at the extent of human gullibility: 'How could the merchants not understand from his costume, from his appearance, and from his way of eating that this man knows all about harlequins!' (p. 122). In both of Imbert's examples, harlequin habits of eating are mediated by harlequin modes of dress which in turn convey a generalized character disorder: a foolishness or petty madness.

More globally, Suzanne comments on the motley horde queuing up for the harlequin stands: 'It is a curious and interesting spectacle to watch the wretched crowd of paupers pressing up around the stalls, minutely inspecting three or four rows of lined-up plates, and making their choice among the unspeakable assortments of dinner debris' (pp. 46–47). He presents two mirror images of harlequin alignments, the plates of assorted debris that are the object of the customers' gaze, and the customers themselves, society's sundry castoffs, comical spectacle for the authorial and lectoral gaze.

Here is Castelnau describing the customers thronging for the 'unimaginable' [*invraisemblable*] harlequin *ragoût* that he has just luridly detailed, and which, more concisely, consists of buckets of food slops and discarded sauces dumped into a pot and heated up together: 'The banquet prepared, the parade of guests begins. They present all that is most pitiable in the human comedy: haggard, emaciated faces, waxen complexions, hunched backs, frail limbs clad in rags, eyes either lit up by revolt or extinguished by resignation' (pp. 48–49). The garbage stew and the human stew are presented as parallel constructs, analogous scenes of mixing, each fit for the other.

And so we begin to see a pattern of determinism characterizing the linked representations of harlequin foods and their consumers. If for Brillat-Savarin it was the case that 'you are what you eat,' the case in hand seems rather to be that you eat what you are.[21] Following a fearful symmetry, the wretched of the earth are fed the wretched remains of the table. As if accomplishing a destiny, the 'moth-eaten' tautologically eat pre-nibbled shreds. The rhetoric and tone of such commentaries make clear that the rags and tatters that cover the harlequin eaters, like the variegated scraps they put in their mouths, are never simply fabric and food, but are always also implicit bearers of greater meaning. Jeremy MacClancy and Helen Macbeth's claims for the double nature of food, 'both "nature" and "culture" … substance and symbol' could easily be extended, *mutatis mutandis*, to clothing.[22] Similarly, the link between clothing tatters and food scraps is not merely circumstantial, not only economic, but also, fundamentally, condemnatory. In the guise of compassion and commiseration we find sanctimony and a presumption of due justice: you eat what you deserve and you deserve what you eat. In a deterministic universe, people who wear mismatched, handed-down clothes swallow oddly combined, handed-down foods. This, I suggest, is because there is something suspect, something potentially disruptive, about those who present a composite exterior, just as there is about those who take in a mottled meal. If to bourgeois eyes, as Ferrières has observed, 'the harlequin [meal] exhibits aesthetic disorder', the consumer cannot be told from the consumed (p. 360). The harlequin plate may evoke Harlequin, but the connection is mediated by the ragtag pauper fool who resembles and assembles both in his or her essentially unbalanced and unbalancing personage.

Patched trousers, asymmetrical collars, clashing colours, dandruff, dog hairs, lint, physical impairments and motley crowds; all are comical, in the commentary of our narrators: unsettling in that what is torn, gnawed, ripped, spotted, patched, sprinkled, stained threatens to destabilize and transgress order and harmony. Negative connotations of the composite can be traced back as far as the Bible, reports Michel Pastoureau: Leviticus prohibits practices of mixing.[23] Throughout the Middle Ages and beyond, the prostitute, the buffoon, the criminal, the disorderly and the mad were consigned to clothes that were striped, streaked, patchworked, gaudily coloured, spotted or otherwise variegated to signal 'the idea of trouble, of disorder, of noise and of impurity'. Such fabrics are visually different, but conceptually or socially alike: 'they translate various degrees of … transgression' (p. 47). And modern occidental culture is still permeated by the medieval scandal of variegation, contends Pastoureau, as by the belief that the solid and the monochromatic are godly while the mottled is diabolical (pp. 13, 40, 99).

In these narratives of Parisian street life, then, the harlequin eaters become harlequins as well, metonymically assimilated to the food they consume, and metaphorically identified with the lineage of Harlequin, the jester, the jongleur, the buffoon, the clown, the servant fool. Each individual case arguably presents itself, too, as a microcosm of the crowd, motley, derisible, socially marginalized, yet basic to the structure of social hierarchy, unstable and potentially destabilizing, and therefore menacing. In both the anecdotes and the rhetoric adopted by most of their chroniclers, as we have witnessed, harlequin eaters provoke a range of reactions including commiseration, benevolence, pity, sanctimony, ridicule, self-righteousness, defensiveness and *Schadenfreude*. Aspiration, inspiration and admiration are less common responses to the consumers repeatedly represented as bottom feeders and cynically described by one author as 'those who make a living by dying of hunger' [*ceux dont la profession est de mourir de faim*], but they do exist, and it is time to attend to them (Castelnau, p. 48).

Savour the harlequins
Du Camp makes clear that there are harlequin consumers who are not simply social victims; some have other options, and patronize the harlequin sellers by election:

Many poor labourers working at Les Halles prefer this odd way of eating to the more substantial but too costly food that they can find in cabarets and cheap restaurants [*les gargotes*]. For two or three sous, they can eat. What is strange is that the vendors have a regular clientele, which they attribute only to the art of the kitchens whose debris they source. A number of well-to-do but miserly people also secretly come to shop there, without ever admitting it; they can be recognized immediately by their anxious and furtive manner; they are mocked, but, since they are paying, never to their face. (p. 165)

Coffignon closes his review of the characteristically revolting components of harlequin plates with the comment that 'there is no lack of avid eyes to survey the display' (p. 181).

Some of these cases are ambiguous; one might assume the draw of the harlequin to be either one of last resort – of money over matter – or of brute hunger. But we approach a different range of accounts where the motivation is more explicitly positive. Portraying a particular patron of the harlequin stalls, Coffignon specifies: 'It is not by need that she visits the harlequin sellers of Les Halles; it is by taste' (p. 183). And Imbert explains: 'The harlequin merchant's clientele is considerable, for many poor people are happy to feed on the same bits as the rich, at a very low price' (p. 116). Such hints of a different kind of motivation for eating other people's food, one that does not depend on physical need, begin to suggest that we look at other kinds of appetite.

There is another side to the story of this 'industry of putrefaction', as Jean-Paul Aron calls it, that needs to be heard (p. 275). It is true that hunger and penury and their exploitation played a fair part in the buying and reselling of prepared food. Who would not, after all, have preferred to be part of the first seating, welcomed among the fortunate diners who had the right of first refusal of the sumptuous excesses of the table? But it is exactly this hunger, understood now in a metaphysical sense, which begins to explain that there were reasons for eating the remains of other people's meals that accompanied and sometimes even transcended brute need.

The allure of socio-economically exotic cuisine in the nineteenth-century imagination responded not only to bodily appetite but also to a hunger for the storied possibilities it opened: its mystique depended upon what Rebecca Spang, in her discussion of restaurants, has called 'the suspicion that somebody else was having a better dinner, a more titillating dalliance, a more exotic bottle of wine'.[24] Taking suspicion here not in its most common sense having to do with a 'conjecture of evil' but in a secondary sense related to the 'imagination of something (not necessarily evil) as possible or likely' (*OED*), I propose that the term is implicitly related to its etymological sense (from the Latin *suspicere*) of 'looking up from below' or 'looking upward': looking on with connotations of admiration and esteem and awe. Just this kind of suspicion abetted not only the institutionalization of restaurants in the nineteenth century, but also the derivative institution of selling food down the socio-economic chain in increasingly deteriorating form. What I propose in place of the degradational discourse we have been following is a reading of harlequin ways of eating that is open to imagination and dreaming. This other way of reading will tease out an aspirational discourse that borrows what we might call an upwardly suspicious voice, along with an upwardly mobile eye. I'll take an extended example from Zola's *Le Ventre de Paris*.

Reading Zola against many of the historical sources – and also against a certain Zola himself – reveals the tonier side of leftovers: the site of fantasy and imagination, they provide, at their best, a royal path to reverie and illusion, a garden of hope and desire, a refuge and an escape. They nourish the spirit more significantly than the body, democratizing the palate as they open the mind's window to imperial palaces. Such is the calculated spiel of the vendors as they market their handed-down fare to the people like a ladder extended from a higher sphere. The appeal of such goods caters to a brand of suspicion that has ties both to desire and gullibility: a kind of pauper's *bovarysme*, to use Jules de Gaultier's word, that opens the space of dreaming in an impoverished world.[25]

My prime reference here is to one of Zola's less admirable protagonists, Mlle Saget, whom I want not to romanticize, not to rehabilitate, but to complicate, perhaps even along with Zola. This 'old bird' – she is a kind of magpie [*une vieille pie-grièche*] – lives on gossip, and, more concretely, on castoff scraps gifted her by the marketplace vendors, supplemented by leftovers she buys from the stalls of harlequin sellers – more by avarice and craftiness than by financial necessity (p. 343). Let's zoom in on Mlle Saget as she lurks before her preferred harlequin merchant, 'who claimed to sell leftovers exclusively from the Tuileries'. So taken is the miserly woman with the myth of the emperor's old food that one day, Zola recounts, 'the saleswoman had talked her into buying a scrap of leg of lamb, claiming it came straight from the plate of the emperor. This slice of lamb, eaten with pride, still appeased the old woman's vanity' (p. 342). Another day, undeterred by a nauseating rancid smell, she buys a plate of cold fried fish and accepts the merchant's lure to return on the morrow: 'Come back tomorrow …. I'll put aside something nice for you. There's a big dinner at the Tuileries tonight' (p. 343). Mlle Saget is a little too settled and a tad too bitter to seek her prince, her Rodolphe who might bear her off to a Swiss lakeside chalet or to a domed city in a forest of lemon trees crowned by stork nests – or even to a ball at the Tuileries, but she, like Emma Bovary, savours symbol before substance when she ogles repurposed table scraps and devours the debris on her plate.

As Jules de Gaultier must have realized when shifting emphasis from psychology to philosophy in his second essay on *le bovarysme*, written ten years after the first, the condition to which Emma lent her name is less personal and pathological than perceptual – metaphysical, even, and hermeneutic.[26] Just so Mlle Saget's upward eating, the emblem of a larger ascending perspective, introduced with her character as a gaze set above and beyond: 'The gable window opened, a little old lady leaned out, looking at the sky, then Les Halles, in the distance' (p. 53). This suspicious eater is the personification of a certain Zolian hermeneutics – open, mobile, capricious – which admittedly is not the one that springs first to the mind of readers of the often didactic

Rougon-Macquart series of novels, but one with which he is certainly flirting well before modernist writers like Colette and Proust and Nabokov moved metamorphic writing centre stage. Transcending the individual perspective of Mlle Saget is the narrative voice given to long descriptions of Les Halles backlit by a seductive rhetoric of flickering, flashing, vacillation, lustre, gleam, shimmering, iridescence, opalescence, phosphorescence, and concretized by metaphors of crystal, mother of pearl, watered silk and the rainbow plumage quickening doves' throats. In another register the metaphors extend to visual juxtapositions such as patchwork, stripes, streaks, collages, stains, clashing colours and patterns; and then further, to pan-aesthetic metaphors of the heteroclitic and the carnivalesque: 'hubbub'; 'chatterings'; 'din'; 'confusion'; 'jumble of merchandise'; 'cacophony of wafting smells'. The visual and conceptual crown of the stunningly unstable carnivalesque is the plate of mismatched leftovers, *l'arlequin*. This cobbled plate is curiously never identified by its common name in *Le Ventre de Paris* (though Zola uses the term freely in other novels); however, only several pages after the extended scene at the used food seller's stall, the unspoken alimentary harlequin is echoed and finally named in a description of the pulsing hub of Les Halles [*le carreau des Halles*], scene of a jumble of animation and vegetation, the entirety of which is framed by 'two kiosks so patched with green, yellow, red, and blue theatre posters that they appeared to be dressed in a harlequin costume' (p. 350).

As countervailing force to the 'upward-looking suspicion' I have tried to draw out in *Le Ventre* from motifs of yearning and desire, associated with an aesthetics of iridescence and mobility, connected in turn to a hermeneutics of openness and indetermination, there is in this novel, to be sure, the more familiar Zolian plot, in the thickest sense of the word, or what we might call 'downward-looking suspicion', of the detective novel variety. It gives rise to thematic designs of spying, hiding and seeking; policing, discipline, knowledge, domination and repression, which play out through a familiar naturalist aesthetics of order, fixity and closure, and are congruent with a hermeneutic approach of determinism and control.[27]

The disordering figure of the *arlequin* – which, I suggest, we begin to consider with Zola's harlequin eaters – dances everywhere on the edges of the nineteenth-century landscape. In *Le Ventre de Paris*, the harlequin introduces a play of lambent lights and colours within otherwise sombre subterranean scenarios of fixed meanings and reductive readings. In the case of Zola, the harlequin is the quixotic knight he sends into the fray to give battle to his own darkest didactic tendencies, to break the clutch of this night and shatter it into day.

Epilogue

Zola is a prologue. From the fumes of his harlequin pots and the scars of his harlequin plates a figure rises to represent the scum but also to transvalue it, intermittently challenging, undermining and transfiguring his dominant voice. But Zola is only the prologue.

Harlequin food, deemed unnatural by the dominant bourgeois culture Zola inhabited, was naturalized by this same culture as the people's base sustenance. In retrospect we might borrow David Gissen's architectural term *subnature* to reclassify it, referring here to a kind of anti-nature: the marginalized 'other, stranger form of nature' – mud, dust, debris, urban waste – disparaged as primitive and vile by social canons.[28]

But canons are always susceptible to inversion.[29] The *Commedia dell'arte* figure – hugely popular in seventeenth- and eighteenth-century France as a lowly trickster and clown – began to be appropriated as rebel and hero in the nineteenth century, by Romantic and then Symbolist writers, and had a similar trajectory in painting. The alimentary harlequin, like its theatrical namesake, underwent an evolution and a revalorization at the hand of certain writers and artists. By the turn of the twentieth century, it was no longer a mere emblem of disgust or at best, of ambivalence (as in Zola), but also a figure of inspiration, agitation and revolt. It served the writers and artists who represented it and often identified with it iconoclastically as a force of provocation and contestation, and, I contend, became a founding figure of modernism. But here begins another chapter.

Acknowledgments

Earlier versions of parts of this material were presented at the Oxford Symposium, the Modern Language Association Convention, the Nineteenth-Century French Studies Colloquium, Amherst College and North Carolina State University. I am grateful to the organizers and the audiences. Thanks also to the librarians of the Bibliothèque Historique de la Ville de Paris, especially Mme Catherine Bernaudat; to the Schlesinger Library staff; to Priscilla Parkhurst Ferguson, Michael Garval, Laure Katsaros, Claire Lyu, Stephanie Sandler, John D'Amico, Kylie Sago, Mark McWilliams, Barbara Wheaton, Carolin Young and the Robert Bacon Fund of the Harvard University Department of Romance Languages and Literatures, for all manner of research assistance and/or conversation.

Notes

1. I use the comparative 'lower' advisedly, because it was not only the lowest classes, the indigent, that formed the clientele for the traffic in alimentary hand-me-downs, but also the petty and even midrange bourgeoisie.
2. I use Eric Hobsbawm's widely accepted term to refer to the period stretching from 1789–1914, from the French Revolution to the beginning of World War I.
3. See, for example, Alfred Suzanne, 'Les Coulisses de la Cuisine: les arlequins,' *L'Art culinaire* (Paris: 1892: Dixième Année), p. 47; Madeleine Ferrières, *Nourritures canailles* (Paris: Seuil, 2007), p. 356; Emile Zola, *Le Ventre de Paris* (Paris: Folio, 2002 [1873]), pp. 341–53. Subsequent references to works cited in the Notes will be given in the text; all translations from the French throughout this essay are mine.
4. Also relegated to subterranean space were such activities as force-feeding pigeons to prepare them to look their plump best upon death, cutting up animal carcasses, plucking chickens, colouring butter – what we might call 'food grooming'.
5. The *arlequins* were sold in Pavilion XII, in the area dedicated to *viandes cuites* or 'cooked meats', which were the most coveted component of plated leftovers, present in greater or lesser degree according to availability and price. They were also dispatched to the regional markets of Paris. The presence of harlequins in the markets (Les Halles and local ones) predated the Baltard Halles, but the ways, means

and legislation of their sale is poorly documented.
6. See Eugène Briffault's chapter 'Des Gens qui ne dînent pas' in *Paris à table* (Paris: Mercure de France, 2003 [1846]), pp. 50–58 for a rare exception.
7. Alexandre Balthazar Laurent Grimod de la Reynière, *L'Almanach des gourmands: servant de guide dans les moyens de faire excellente chère* (Paris: 2012 [1803–1812]) passim.; Pierre Hamp, *Mes Métiers* (Paris: Gallimard, 1929), p. 143. If our sources are to be believed, such a complaint is extremely rare. In any case the reporting of it is exceptional. Far more common are patronizing accounts of the gratitude of the poor for anything at all, along with comments on their lack of discrimination. J. Barbaret, for example, speaks of occasional charitable handouts from harlequin sellers to the truly destitute and starving: 'This composite clump of food was not well presented, but those to whom it was offered didn't look too closely. There was an entire elegy in the silent gratitude they addressed to the gifters. The gift may not have been marketable; in any case … hunger makes stench imperceptible' (*La Bohème du travail* (Paris: Hetzel, 1889), pp. 369–370).
8. Eugène Chavette, *Restaurateurs et restaurés* (Paris: A. Le Chevalier, 1867), pp. 9–10; Barbaret, p. 365.
9. Marcel Rouff, *La Vie et la passion de Dodin-Bouffant, gourmet* (Paris: Editions Sillage, 2010 [1924]) pp. 8–9; Auguste Escoffier, Avant-propos, *Le Livre des menus* (Paris: Flammarion, 1912), pp. 5–6; Ferrières, p. 358; p. 360; Jacques Castelnau, *Les Petits métiers de Paris* (Paris: Astéria, 1952), p. 49.
10. Maxime du Camp, *Paris, ses organes, ses fonctions, et sa vie jusqu'en 1870*, ed. by G. Rondeau (Paris: Moncod, 1993 [1870]), p. 165.
11. Louis Sébastien Mercier, 'Mets hideux', *Tableau de Paris*, ed. by Jean-Claude Bonnet (Paris: Mercure de France, 1994 [1789], 3 vols.), vol. 1, p. 1183.
12. A. Coffignon, *L'Estomac de Paris* (Paris: À la librairie illustrée, ca. 1887), pp. 181–82.
13. P.-L. Imbert, *Les Trappeurs parisiens au XIXe siècle* (Paris: André Sagnier, 1878), pp. 117–19.
14. Eugène Sue, *Les Mystères de Paris* (Paris: Editions Hallier, 1977 [1842]), p. 25.
15. Jean-Paul Aron, *Le Mangeur du XIXe siècle* (Paris: Les Belles Lettres, 2013 [1973]), pp. 274–75.
16. The reader who seeks a summary view may usefully read part of Aron's narrative, with the caution that it is composed of largely unattributed bits of first-hand accounts, lifted from the earlier texts and juxtaposed on Aron's page, as if an in-print imitation of the alimentary composite that is his subject. Ferrières's scrupulously annotated and incisive chapter 'L'Arlequin' in her *Nourritures canailles* (pp. 343–62) is a better starting point.
17. Monique Sclaresky, *Paris si étrange* (Rennes: Éditions Ouest-France, 2005), p. 39.
18. See Jean Paillet's tableau in *Paris qui crie: petits métiers*, ed. by Henri Beraldi, illus. by Pierre Vidal (Paris: Les Amis des livres, 1890), pp. 111–12.
19. Philippe Mellot, *La Vie secrète des Halles de Paris* (Paris: Omnibus, 2010), p. 43.
20. Imbert is referring to Ivan Andrievitch Krylov (1769–1844). The fable, 'Trishka's Coat', or 'Trishka's Caftan', uses the poor peasant's actions as a lesson to be learned about acting rashly in the moment and not thinking through the long term consequences (false thrift, one might say). Trishka actually cut off his various clothing parts; the verb Imbert uses (*rogner*, 'to chew' or 'to gnaw' in English) solders the link between sartorial and alimentary harlequinry.
21. '*Dis-moi ce que tu manges, je te dirai ce que tu es*', Aphorism IV in Jean-Anthelme Brillat-Savarin, *La Physiologie du goût* (Paris: Flammarion, 1982 [1825]), p. 19.
22. Jeremy MacClancey and Helen Macbeth, 'Introduction: How to do Anthropologies of Food', *Researching Food Habits: Methods and Problems*, ed. by H. Macbeth and J. MacClancey (Oxford: Berghahn Books, 2004), pp. 5–6.
23. Michel Pastoureau, *L'Etoffe du diable: une histoire des rayures et des tissus rayés* (Paris: Seuil, 1991), p. 11.
24. Rebecca Spang, *The Invention of the Restaurant: Paris and Modern Gastronomic Culture* (Cambridge, MA: Harvard UP, 2000), p. 234.
25. Gaultier coined the term in 1892 to refer to a state of dissatisfaction, like a latter-day quixotism, in which the subject, prone toward escapist fantasy and day-dreaming, ignores everyday reality and instead imagines being a hero or heroine in a romance (*Le Bovarysme: la psychologie dans l'oeuvre de*

Flaubert (Paris: Editions du Sandre, 2007 [1892])).
26. Jules de Gaultier, *Le Bovarysme: essai sur le pouvoir d' imaginer* (Paris: PUF, 206 [1902]).
27. For an overview of a (negatively valued) suspicious hermeneutics, see Rita Felski, 'Suspicious Minds', *Poetics Today* 32:2 (Summer 2011) pp. 215–34.
28. David Gissen, *Subnature: Architecture's Other Environments* (N.Y.: Princeton Architectural Press, 2009), p.21; pp. 21–26.
29. As Pastoureau maintains, 'any social code is capable of being inverted; any code, to function well, is in fact obliged to be inverted, so that whatever constituted a handicap or a lack at the beginning ends up becoming a benefit' (Pastoureau, p. 10).

Markets for Mercenaries: Supplying Armies in Sixteenth-Century Germany

Volker Bach

Food markets are so ubiquitous across the world that it is easy to think of them as something natural, an automatic product of human civilization that will emerge spontaneously. In fact, they require a great deal of organization and effort to create and are very rarely self-organized. This is often forgotten in their study because so much of the physical and social infrastructure that underpins them is invisible, woven into the fabric of the communities they serve, and thus simply assumed as given. In sixteenth-century Germany, a new form of warfare created a situation in which large-scale food markets needed to be created almost from scratch. With military writers becoming aware of the scale of this challenge, we have a larger body of source material surviving than is usual with such quotidian concerns. This paper is an effort to reconstruct what these markets looked like and what herculean efforts were required to bring them into being.

New armies

In the late fifteenth century, the economics of warfare in Germany changed. Tracing the details of this shift goes beyond the scope of this article, but at the end of it stood a system of mercenary armies based entirely on cash payments. Each individual soldier was under contract either to a mercenary commander or directly to the belligerent government, providing his own weapons and equipment and meeting all necessary outlays from his pay. This was specifically stipulated by the imperial diet of 1507 with the formula *'Sold, Cost unnd Schaden'* (pay, maintenance and damage).[1] Thus, the principal – usually a government or a military entrepreneur – was, at least in theory, entirely absolved from the responsibility of providing equipment, food and shelter for his troops as long as he kept paying them.

Pay was generous, by contemporary standards. A common footsoldier would receive four Rhenish guilders a month, with surcharges if he provided equipment or skills beyond the ordinary. The rate for particularly experienced or well-equipped men was double pay (*doppelsöldner*). Cavalrymen and gunners, too, received multiples of the monthly base rate. Contemporary accounts of how troops were recruited suggest that negotiations on this count could be noisy and protracted, and fraud was common. Infantry troops, *landsknechte*, were also known to negotiate for extra pay before battles or assaults, arguing that such risks were not covered by the base rate. This should not surprise anyone who ever dealt with contractors of any kind, and given their complete dependence on often precarious pay, it is probably understandable. That it was specific to the newly emerging forms of warfare is illustrated by the fact that soldiers in regular employment received a much lower cash stipend, but were entitled to rations and often given clothing and equipment by their employers.

As it turned out, this system did not absolve an army's leaders from the care for their troops' provisioning. The sources clearly show us that wrestling with the mechanics of providing food and drink was a matter of grave concern to commanders, and it may be significant that cash-only recruitment was not adopted by contemporary Swiss or Spanish armies and largely abandoned in Germany by the seventeenth century.

Organizing camp markets

The first thing that strikes us when reading texts about army organization is that it was never enough to simply provide pay. Commanders had to ensure their soldiers would be able to buy food. To do that, ideally the army command would formally organize and police a market. It was possible to provide rations directly, but the practice was problematic. The contemporary military writer Leonhardt Fronsberger suggests that even under siege, men should pay for their rations, though the commander ought to charge them a fair price.[2] It is likely that abuses of such a captive market happened, but the difficulty of supplying armies over longer distances make it unlikely that what profit margins may have existed were large.[3]

Generals were fully aware of the complexity of the task. Lazarus von Schwendi, an officer in the service of the Habsburg emperors, offers this simple calculation to illustrate it: At a consumption of two pounds of bread and one pound of meat, eggs or dairy per man and day, an army of 10,000 men, not counting camp followers, would eat through 2000 hundredweight of bread every day and require 1000 wagonloads every ten days just to meet its demand for basic foodstuffs.[4] This was not an unreasonably large number of troops or an improbable consumption figure. Military writers of the time generally agree on a rate of two pounds of bread daily as a reasonable ration.[5] Even assuming civilian suppliers could provide this quantity under their own steam, organizing and coordinating their effort was a challenge. Fronsberger's account of army organization, though doubtlessly idealized, provides a plausible picture of how this was done, and other contemporary sources bear out his assertions.

Large armies had a senior officer responsible for organizing the flow of supplies, the *proviantmeister* (roughly, master of supplies), who was directly answerable to the general (on the staff, in modern terms). He would not normally purchase any supplies, but arrange for them to be available. This included providing safe conduct to carriers and negotiating exemptions from duties for passing through the hundreds of territories the Holy Roman Empire consisted of, often a complicated diplomatic effort.[6] In some cases, it also required arm-twisting to ensure adequate supplies were in place. For example, we have a surviving letter written by the chancery of Emperor Maximilian in 1499 to the city council of Memmingen in south Germany requiring them to order all shoemakers in the town to produce shoes for sale to the army.⁷ Cities were often the first choice to help resolve logistical difficulties. They held concentrations of capital, skills and transport capacity. Often, there were public or private stockpiles of food, drink and other supplies that the *proviantmeister* could persuade them to part with and bring to prearranged locations. The task of coordinating the delivery must have been enormous, even when neither enemy action not a hostile population interfered.

While smaller armies could make do without a *proviantmeister*, managing their supplies locally, none could function without a *profoss* (cognate with the word provost). The *profoss* was the officer in charge of the camp and specifically its market, charged with keeping the peace and enforcing its regulations. Like the *proviantmeister*, he was a senior officer reporting directly to the overall commander and enjoyed considerable privileges. To enforce his authority, he commanded a force of *steckenknechte* who patrolled the camp, breaking up disturbances and apprehending offenders. He was also in charge of the weights and measures used, another concern that needed addressing in a world of local units and overlapping standards. Each army travelled with a standardized set of weights, containers and measuring rods held in the care of the *profoss* that all merchants had to use. When setting up camp, he was in charge of its layout. In theory, army camps were sophisticated affairs, with a secure water supply far away from latrines and designated places to slaughter animals, a central market, assembly square, defensive works, guarded gates and roads. In practice, things often seem to have been a good deal less organized, though the dangers of poor hygiene were well understood and the use of the *scheißplätz* enforced.

Managing the money in circulation was another logistical consideration for the *profoss*. While the notional pay of the troops was calculated in Rhenish guilders, the men rarely received money in such large denominations. They were typically paid in small silver coins at set, but often negotiable, rates to the guilder.⁸ With hundreds of local coinage issues used in the Empire and many more outside it, an army camp would quickly accumulate a wide array of different coins, adding to the complexity of the task. Presumably, money changers followed the armies, coming under the jurisdiction of the *profoss*, but merchants would still end up dealing with a very mixed cash supply.

Merchants who hoped to sell in the camp needed a licence. This was the responsibility of the *profoss*, who would record names, inspect goods and allow or disallow access. In some recorded cases, goods were marked with their provenance and the name of their owner to ensure that adulteration could be speedily traced to its source. This was a particular concern with beer and wine, major articles of consumption. The merchants had to pay fees for the privilege of selling, either in cash or in kind, a requirement from which pedlars who carried their entire stock on their bodies were exempt. This was probably intended to attract enterprising locals selling their produce, though it must have opened up opportunities for fraud.⁹

Since the purpose of the market was to provide supplies to the troops, affordability was a continual concern. One measure to ensure that prices were not artificially inflated was the ban on buying up goods in large quantities before they reached the market itself, a practice known as *fürkauf*. Similar prohibitions were common in urban markets, but in the case of army camps, they could be enforced by cavalry patrols sent out for that purpose.[10] Some army commands also forbade the sale of captured livestock that could be used to feed the troops outside the camp. Outright maximum prices set by fiat are recorded occasionally, but the practice was discouraged and even specifically forbidden in the articles under which some armies enlisted. Sometimes, the *profoss* would write prices for wine and beer on the casks for all to see, both to head off potentially violent disputes and to keep traders honest.[11]

The rules of the market were backed by the threat of swift and severe punishment. This was unsubtly advertised by a gallows, the first thing that the army would set up when moving into a new encampment. Renaissance Germany believed in the deterrent value of savage punishments, and the army retained a highly paid professional executioner for this purpose.[12] While soldiers were entitled to a form of jury trial according to complex and unique rules, merchants and camp followers were under the direct and often arbitrary jurisdiction of the officers.[13] The need to attract enough supply to the market most likely precluded egregious abuses, but the situation was made very clear.

The image of an orderly camp market, perhaps akin to a modern commissary, understates the pervasive role that the sale of goods and services played in every aspect of army life. Any large body of soldiers depended on a host of camp followers that could easily equal its own number. The Franciscan monk Johannes Pauli wrote in 1520 that 10,000 German troops would bring along 20,000 whores alone, almost certainly an overstatement, but indicative of the scale.[14] An officer known as the *trosswaibel* (roughly sergeant of the supply train) or *hurenwaibel* (roughly sergeant of whores) in contemporary texts was responsible for marshalling them and controlling their movements, a task that cannot have been easy. Many observers at the time noted the picturesque appearance of the army's long tail, and artists rendered it in loving, if perhaps exaggerated, detail.[15] It represented a form of commercial ecosystem in which people of high and low status could make a living. At the low end were poor women who often followed individual soldiers in a kind of domestic partnership, surviving by personal services, occasional prostitution and retailing alcoholic beverages.[16] Higher up the food chain, you would find small merchants, artisans such as shoemakers or armourers, and cooks selling ready-made food. Specialized providers of luxury goods, buyers of loot and wholesale traders occupied the top of the hierarchy. Together with personal servants and paid providers of services, even conservative estimates of the time regard one camp follower for every soldier as a realistic figure. The commercially successful poet Hans Sachs described the disorderly, morally dubious and threatening scene of such a camp in a 1555 broadsheet from the perspective of an outraged, but fascinated respectable citizen. [17]

Supplying the markets

The most important food of the time, and doubtless the one that needed to be provided above all others, was bread. Grain or flour could be carried more easily, but would have been of limited use to the customer base. Hieronymus Bock, a medical writer, mentions a form of simple flatbread prepared on hot stones or baked in the ashes as an expedient in wartime 'as experienced soldiers can tell you well', but it seems unlikely that this was common practice while it could be avoided.[18] Mobile ovens, while mentioned in contemporary sources, are documented very rarely, and hardtack occurs mainly in the context of sea travel.[19] Rather, bread would have been baked in ovens and transported to the market. With spare capacity available from both urban guild bakers and private and communal ovens in rural areas, this was not impossible, but probably required some pressure by the army command. Similarly, convincing city dwellers to part with their often considerable private and public stockpiles of grain would have presented a challenge.[20] High prices alone may have served that purpose, but at a time when bread prices were universally regulated, this seems unlikely. Still, our sources do not tell us whether or how the sale of bread was regulated. A system analogous to that of cities would have presented problems with standardization of loaves from different sources, but nonetheless may have been adopted. Certainly, agents of the army command must have been closely involved with the production and transport of thousands of pounds of bread daily.

While bread or grain had to be carried to the army market in some form of transport, meat could reach it on its own hooves and usually did. Armies were accompanied by herds of cattle whose management and processing was in the hands of butchers travelling with them. They bought livestock where it was available, drove it to the camp and slaughtered it as the market required. Since large herds of beef cattle were driven to German cities from Hungary and Jutland every year, people with the required skills to manage herds would have been available.[21] Civilian butchers were frequently wealthy, and their army counterparts, too, enjoyed high status in the camp market. Especially in times of war, cattle were often sold cheaply by plundering soldiers, and the profit margins in reselling it as meat were no doubt considerable.[22]

Closely related to the butchers, camp markets were served by *sudler*, cooks who sold prepared food by the portion. The word survives in English as sutler, though its meaning at the time was more specific – someone who cooks things in a kettle full of liquid – *sud*. Hans Sachs' poem lists their activities as a cross-section of a heavily meat-based cuisine: 'roasting, baking, seething, brothmaking, with cows, pigs, lambs and geese, with sausages, cabbage, intestines and stomachs'.[23] Such professional providers of cooked meat, the *garbräter*, were a common feature of contemporary urban markets, and it is likely that their main qualification was the butchering and processing of animals. That this skill mattered is evident: Getting the most out of an animal meant stretching supplies and feeding more people. The encyclopaedic 1581 *New Kochbuch* by Marx Rumpoldt lists eighty-three dishes to be prepared from an ox, from lordly roasts to boiled intestine and pickled feet.[24] A surviving anecdote in a fifteenth-century manuscript ascribed to a master cook serving the house of Wurttemberg describes with evident pride how professional cooks could turn a single calf into a variety of dishes fit for a lordly table.[25] Galantine was made from the feet; bread pudding was cooked inside the stomach and oesophagus; the intestines were boiled; the brains were cooked with almonds; the liver was turned into a caul sausage; the blood was used to thicken sauces and a soup; the large muscle parts were roasted or boiled; and small meaty parts were used for galantines, soup or pan dishes. What a *sudler* served may have been less refined, but the basic operations were the same. That armies considered them important is borne out by the fact that the city of Mühlhausen dispatched five cooks, one of them a master cook, to join the rebel army of the peasant war when it allied itself to their cause.[26]

Pictures by contemporary artists show camp kitchens as elaborate affairs, usually centred around one or more large cauldrons, but also including smaller pots standing by the fire or pans managed by individual cooks. Such a setup would have allowed for producing a variety of foods, with meat boiled in the large cauldrons along with puddings and sausages; stock simmered in the standing pots that may also have been used for vegetable or grain side dishes; and organ meats, sauces and deep-fried *krapfen* or other fashionable dainties made in individual pans. Taking into account the fuel consumption, the staff required to tend the fire, and the baggage cart needed to transport the equipment, this would have represented a sizeable capital outlay.

The army's food supply was no doubt supplemented by locals bringing in produce for sale the same way they did on city markets. Eggs, cheese, butter, vegetables and fruit could not be sourced in bulk the way grain could or be herded along like livestock, and the exemption of small-scale vendors from market fees indicates they were welcome. Fuel, clothing, shoes and the many other articles needful for an army at war most likely also entered the camp in a similar fashion, with individual artisans and pedlars bringing in their stock.

We cannot say what share of food was sold ready to eat and how much as raw ingredients, but individuals also cooked for each other on a non-commercial basis. Female camp followers attached to individual soldiers were their domestic as well as sexual partners and prepared food they had bought or looted. They formed temporary families, acquiring household goods and sometimes even having children together. Observers marvelled at their ability to carry the implements of domestic life on their backs over long distances.[27] It has also been speculated that the *rotte*, a self-organized administrative unit of between 6 and 10 men, cooked and ate together.[28] Since some military writers calculate supplies on a per-*rotte* basis, such an arrangement does not seem too outlandish. At the other end of the social scale, senior officers were entitled to employ a cook as part of their retinue drawing regular or even double pay from army coffers.

Food, though, was not the only culinary concern of the soldiers. Drink was at least equally important, and a contemporary proverb said that a soldier, like a pig, expected to be drunk at all times.[29] Beer and wine were carried into camp markets on wagons. Some images show what look like casks on wheels, specialized for that purpose. Vendors, like butchers, paid a fee in kind to the *profoss*, who probably resold it on his own account. Similarly, we know that camp followers bought drink in larger quantities and resold it in individual portions, a small-scale trade that cannot have generated much income, but may have kept them alive in lean times.

How well did it work?

Altogether, this system was very complex, seemingly needlessly so. It seems to have worked, but it is hard to say how well it did. We know very little about the prices that were charged, though the concern over fairness that many contemporary writers expressed suggests that they could be a problem. One surviving record of prices in a camp market during the siege of Metz in 1552 suggests that they were high compared to civilian markets. Applying commonly calculated rations, a soldier on regular pay would have expended three quarters of his income on food.[30] It is difficult to generalize from this set of data, not least because a lengthy siege during autumn and winter might have driven up prices beyond typical levels.

One thing that the camp markets appear to have done well is deliver quality. German mercenaries had a reputation for requiring good and ample food, and Fronsberger warns that any irregularities with their rations in times of dearth would risk mutiny.[31] Records of disputes, which were frequent, rarely mention food as a problem, which suggests the demands of the men in that regard were usually met. However, this was only true as long as a regular supply of cash was on hand to keep the engine running. That was a problem much more frequently, to the extent that the military writer Lazarus von Schwendi lays out how an army can be kept in the field unpaid over long periods of time by substituting payment in kind. This would have represented a breach of contract, and he warns that the more highly paid men who stood to lose more in the exchange would resent it, but the fact that it is suggested points to the difficulties that sixteenth-century governments had with cash flow.[32]

Whatever its advantages and drawbacks, the system of supplying armies through markets died out in the early seventeenth century. Commanders increasingly turned to central supply systems providing uniform clothing, arms and rations, and military food acquired the unenviable reputation it has never been able to shed since. Whether you wish to read this as a parable of the wasteful chaos that results from privatizing essentials or proof that tyrannical governments dislike free-market solutions depends more on modern politics than historical realities. What we are left with, however, is a salutary reminder how complex, fascinating and resilient, but also costly and demanding a system food markets have always been. For those who depended on them for their survival, the answer was control of some kind, whether through market regulations, price controls or central rationing. It is through records of these mechanisms that we often have to try and understand historical markets because they are all that is left.

Notes

1. Quoted in Peter Burschel, *Söldner im Nordwestdeutschland des 16. und 17. Jahrhunderts. Sozialgeschichtliche Studien* (Göttingen: Vandenhoeck & Ruprecht, 1994), p. 177.
2. Leonhardt Fronsberger, *Von kayserlichem Kriegß-Rechten...* (Frankfurt (Main): Sig. Feyerabendt heirs,1596), p. CLI r.
3. Burschel, p. 178 f. writes that many German princes of lesser territories in the sixteenth century systematically developed agriculture, mining and manufacturing in their domains as a profit-making enterprise. Selling their product to armies in the field assured them a ready market.
4. Eugen von Frauenholz, *Lazarus von Schwendi. Der erste deutsche Verkünder der allgemeinen Wehrpflicht* (Hamburg: Hanseatische Verlagsanstalt, 1939), p. 266. The book itself wilfully misunderstands von Schwendi to serve ideological ends, but it remains the only available edition.
5. The most detailed list, provided in a military ordinance by Adam Junghans von der Olnitz printed in 1598, suggests 2 lbs of bread, 1.5 lbs of meat and roughly 3 litres of beer per man per day, with women entitled to 1.5 lbs of bread, 1 lb of meat and 1.5 litres of beer and servant boys to 2 lbs of bread, 1 lb of meat and 2 litres of weak beer. The author additionally lists weekly consumption figures for cheese, bacon and butter, and monthly ones for salt. Various ration estimates of the time are given in Hans-Michael Möller, *Das Regiment der Landsknechte. Untersuchungen zu Verfassung, Recht und Selbstverständnis in deutschen Söldnerheeren des 16. Jahrhunderts* (Wiesbaden: Franz Steiner Verlag, 1976), p. 161 f.
6. Fritz Redlich, *The German Military Enterpriser and his Work Force: A Study in European Economic and Social History*, Vol I (Wiesbaden: Franz Steiner Verlag, 1964), p. 250 f.
7. Quoted in Reinhard Baumann, *Landsknechte. Ihre Geschichte und Kultur vom späten Mittelalter bis zum Dreißigjährigen Krieg* (Munich: C.H. Beck, 1994), p. 45 f. That this was written in the emperor's name indicates how central logistical concerns were to successful warfare.
8. Möller, p. 79 ff analyses the question of pay and coinage in great detail.
9. Möller, p. 160 f. The environs of army camps were regularly patrolled, which probably discouraged fraudulent merchants from storing their goods outside.
10. Baumann, p. 152. Regulations against cornering markets and luring away customers are common in civilian markets of the time.
11. Möller, p. 159 and von Frauenholz, p. 222. This may be an early instance of requiring a visible display of prices rather than an arbitrary maximum.
12. Executioners occupied an odd position in German cities of the time, superstitiously shunned by the populace and often excluded from all polite society, but highly paid. Their craft took on an almost guilded structure, with masters teaching their skill to their sons and passing lucrative positions down in the family. Temporary employment in an army likely attracted those who had yet to find regular employment. For more on them, see Ernst Schubert, *Räuber, Henker, Arme Sünder; Verbrechen und Strafe im Mittelalter* (Darmstadt: WBG, 2007), II.2 passim.
13. Baumann, p. 103 ff. and Möller look into these fascinating traditions in great detail. Soldiers were entitled to a hearing in a regimental court presided over by an officer, but staffed with their peers. The penalties for some infractions were also administered collectively by their comrades, which was considered more honourable than a death at the hands of the executioner.
14. Quoted in John A. Lynn et al., *Women, Armies and Warfare in Early Modern Europe* (Cambridge: Cambridge UP, 2008), p.12
15. Birgit von Seggern, *Der Landsknecht im Spiegel der Renaissancegrahik um 1500–1540* (Bonn: PhD thesis, 2003), p. 474 ff., collects several such images, most famously the pictures in Altdorfer's Triumph of Emperor Maximilian, and provides an analysis of the conventions governing the depiction of soldiers: <http://hss.ulb.uni-bonn.de/2003/0285/0285.htm> [last accessed 29 May 2014].
16. Beate Beate, *Die freien Frauen. Dirnen und Frauenhäuser im 15. und 16. Jahrhundert* (Frankfurt: Campus Verlag, 1995), p. 39 ff. reconstructs this existence on the basis of court files. The resale of beer and spirits acquired from camp merchants was a common source of income.
17. Wolfgang Strauch, Mummplatz, 1555, mit Versen von Hans Sachs (reprint of a woodcut by Hans

Wandereisen), in: Strauss, German Single-leaf Woodcut (note. 27), vol. 3, p. 1066.
18. ...*wie dann die erfarne kriegs leüt wol wissen darvon zu:oreden*. Bock, Hieronymus: *Teutsche Speißkammer*, printed by Wendel Rihel, Strasbourg 1550, p. xliiii v.
19. Fronsberger p. XCII r. refers to copper ovens that could be carried with armies. A picture of an oven on a cart that seems to consist of clay survives in the Richenberger Chronik of the council of Constance dating to the late fifteenth century (A reproduction can be found at <http://www.vinorama-ermatingen.ch/museum/museum/sonderausstellungen/chronik-zum-konzil-von-konstanz.html> [last accessed 27 May 2014].
20. Ulf Dirlmeyer, *Untersuchungen zu Einkommensverhältnissen und Lebenshaltungskosten in oberdeutschen Städten des Spätmittelalters (Mitte 14. bis Anfang 16. Jahrhundert)* (Heidelberg: Carl Winter, 1978), pp. 39–62 gives a good overview of such grain stockpiling. Cities especially in south Germany often maintained public supplies to guard against famine while wealthy individuals similarly laid in stores both to take advantage of low prices and for resale in times of dearth.
21. Ernst Schubert, *Essen und Trinken im Mittelalter* (Darmstadt: Wissenschaftliche Buchgesellschaft, 2006): p. 109 ff. gives an overview of the trade. It was well enough established to create a set of customary rights of way and pasture for passing herds along its routes.
22. Siegfried Hoyer, *Das Militärwesen im Deutschen Bauernkrieg* (East Berlin: Militärverlag der DDR, 1975), p. 138 quotes a 1525 chronicle remarking on very low prices created by a surfeit of looted cattle. On the profit margins of civilian butchers, see Dirlmeier, p. 301 ff. and Schubert, p. 107 f.
23. Quoted after Friedrich Blau, *Die deutschen Landsknechte*, third edition (Phaidon, 1985), p. 143.
24. Marx Rumpoldt, *Ein new Kochbuch / Das ist ein gründtliche beschreibung / wie man recht und wol / nicht allein von vierfüssigen / heymischen und wilden Thieren / sondern auch von mancherley Vögel und Federwildpret / darzu von allem grünen und dürren Fischwerck / allerley Speiß / als gesotten / gebraten / gebacken / Presoln / Carbonaden / mancherley Pasteten und Füllwerck / Gallrat etc. / auff Teutswche / Ungerische / Hispanische / Italianische unnd Französische weiß / kochen unnd zubereiten solle ...* (Frankfurt (Main): printed by Sigmundt Feyerabendt, 1581), p. I. Rumpoldt's magnum opus, now available in a web-based English translation, probably represents the first attempt in German culinary literature to integrate not only specific foods, but all manner of dishes a professional cook might be expected to prepare.
25. *Maister Hannsen des von wirtemberg koch*, trsl. and ed. Trude Ehlert (Frankfurt: Tupperware 1996), recipes 190 and 191. This fascinating treasure trove of German culinary material presumably dating to the 1460s remains untranslated.
26. Hoyer, p. 88.
27. Hans Delbrück, *Geschichte der Kriegskunst: Die Neuzeit* (Berlin: Georg Stilke, 1920), p. 85 quotes an impressive list from a sixteenth-century manuscript that included young children, spare clothing, shoes, tent cloth and poles, and a pan, pot, bowls, spoon, and firewood as a typical load. Articles of war recognized their temporary relationships by assigning the camp wives of deceased soldiers rights to their inheritance, even to the detriment of a legal wife at home if they had children by him, see Baumann, p. 201 f.
28. Matthias Rogg et al., *Landsknechte und Reisläufer: Bilder vom Soldaten. Ein Stand in der Kunst des 16. Jahrhunderts* (Paderborn: Schöningh, 2002), p. 49. Such an arrangement would make sense and was paralleled in many other militaries, but we have little evidence for the practice.
29. *Dan ein landsknecht und auch ein Schwein / Solten tag und nacht nur vol sein* quoted in Rogg, p. 91
30. Möller, p. 161 ff. looks at the data in detail. He suggests that the frequently demanded surcharges were the result of economic necessity as soldiers would not otherwise have been able to survive on their pay. Burschel and especially Baumann disagree with this bleak picture, arguing even a common soldier's pay would have covered necessities.
31. Fronsberger, p. CLVIII v. A contemporary poet quoted in Albert Meinhardt, *Der Schwartenhals. Lieder der Landsknechte* (Heidenheim: Südmarkverlag, 1979), p. 9, sums up the life of the soldier as suffering 'a hard bed for good food'. John Richards, *Landsknecht Soldier 1486–1560* (Oxford: Osprey, 2002), p.50 refers to a Swiss song that mocks the Germans for their extensive camp kitchens. The Swiss armies of the period used a centralized supply system.
32. Quoted in Baumann, p. 89, where the problem is addressed in detail.

Are Free Markets Bad for Good Food?

Julian Baggini

When discussing the rights and wrongs of food production, it's often obvious from the factual content of what is claimed whether it is supposed to be good or bad. Sometimes, however, a statement intended as positive can be read as entirely negative without a single letter or comma being moved. I came across a wonderful example of this recently: 'What a glorious thing the hamburger is. It combines meat, grains, cheese, and vegetables into a simple, delicious package for quick and enjoyable consumption. It seems so easy, yet the efficient production of the hamburger, in all its details, is of infinite complexity. Only the coordinative powers of a market economy could possibly produce it'.[1]

'Only the coordinative powers of a market economy could possibly produce it.' Depending on whether you think the mass-produced hamburger sits at the zenith or nadir of Western civilisation, this statement by Llewellyn H. Rockwell, Jr, president and founder of the Ludwig von Mises Institute, could serve either as a vindication or a condemnation of the market economy.

For many of those interested in and passionate about good food, it might obviously appear to be a condemnation. The hamburger exemplifies how the free market leads to dietary disaster. A free market leads to a race to the bottom, where suppliers compete to provide the cheapest version of whatever product they have to sell. In the case of food that has three main results.

First, maximizing yield on the raw ingredients. That means intensive arable agriculture, fuelled by synthetic inputs such as fertilizer and pesticide. It also means intensive meat, egg and dairy production, with animals crammed into feedlots rather than grazing or roaming on open fields with plenty of space.

Second, maximizing margins on food products. That means economies of scale, choosing mechanized mass-production over artisanal production. It also means using the most easily produced ingredients available, such as corn syrup, soy beans, mechanically recovered meat and palm oil, all derived from the cheapest raw materials.

Third, squeezing producers by buying and selling foodstuffs as commodities on open markets. Instead of negotiating fair prices directly with producers, farmers have to take their products to market, where the price is set by the logic of supply and demand, or sign take-it-or-leave-it contracts with large customers, such as supermarkets, who will use their huge buying power to drive the hardest bargain possible.

Take these three factors together and it seems free markets work to maximize profit at the expense of quality, sustainability, fairness to producers and good conditions for animals. The consequences of allowing market logic to dictate food supply are factory farming, producers of 'commodities' like milk and coffee being paid close to or less than cost price, loss of biodiversity to monoculture mega-farms and heavily processed mass-produced food instead of more wholesome alternatives.

This, at least, is the way it often appears to people who despair of the contemporary food supply system. The arguments used by some campaigners for a better way reinforce the message that market forces are responsible for many of our current ills. Joanna Blythman, for example, has written of the plight of Caribbean banana growers, saying: 'The Windwards cannot possibly compete in a totally free market with intensively grown dollar bananas produced on prairie-like flat plantations offering massive economies of scale.'[2] Blythman is here reflecting the views of other campaigners. In another piece, for example, she quotes Alistair Smith, of the fair-trade NGO Banana Link: 'The "promise" of free trade leads, in practice, to a driving down of prices and squeezing out of smaller producers, forcing down wages and cutting social benefits, more trade union repression, less job security, and increasing damage to the environment and human health.'[3] Blythman also blames free trade for many of Haiti's problems: 'Haiti's now parlous state is also a product of the imposition of free-market trade policies and foreign debt by foreign countries.'[4]

The farmer Troy Roush, who settled out of court with Monsanto after the company accused him of holding back seed, appears to sum up succinctly the logic of the market in the film *Food, Inc.*: 'You have to understand that we farmers, we're gonna deliver to the marketplace what the marketplace demands. If you want to buy $2 milk, you're gonna get a feedlot in the backyard. It's that simple.'[5]

The merits of free markets

This position would appear to be diametrically opposed to that of proponents of free markets, who see the problem with farming as being too much, not too little, meddling with market forces. Way back in 1956, for example, W.M. Curtiss of the free market Foundation for Economic Education had this theory as to why there was a problem with surpluses: 'The surplus exists only because the government has tinkered with the market mechanism. Prices for commodities have been set above where a free market would set them; there is insufficient demand at those prices to move the available supply.'[6] The same basic diagnosis was offered to explain the milk lakes and butter mountains in the EEC during the 1970s.

Then, as now, the solution advocated was liberating the markets. Writing in the *Spectator*, Julian Morris argued: 'Instead of banning exports or providing subsidies, governments should be removing barriers to production and distribution, and letting the market respond effectively to changes in supply and demand. That is the best way to ensure that people are able to feed themselves, now and in the future.'[7]

It is not only governments that are accused of sub-optimizing food production by interfering with the market. Schemes like Fairtrade, which guarantee a fair price to producers and a social premium, are accused of defying market logic. The Adam Smith Institute, for instance, insists Fairtrade means 'its favoured farmers do not have to respect market conditions which might tell others to cut back production in the event of a world surplus'.[8] The *Economist* claims Fairtrade encourages overproduction by 'propping up the price' of commodities.[9]

This appears to be a tricky impasse. On the one hand, it seems undeniable that market forces are responsible for many of the excesses of industrial agriculture. On the other, attempts to manage agricultural production do not have a very good track record. State planning in America and Europe has led in the past to huge surpluses, while state socialism in the Soviet Union and China has led to famine. It might appear that the choice is between the market's race to the bottom or a hubristic attempt to command and control food supply in a way that has never succeeded.

What appears to be an impossible choice, however, often turns out to be a false one. The choice we need to make is not between free markets or some alternative, but between genuinely free markets and laissez-faire anarchy on one side and over-regulated statism on the other.

To see why this is so we need to go back to basics and ask what a free market economy really means. Adam Smith famously characterized the genius of the market with the metaphor of the invisible hand. Supply and demand provide constant self-correcting mechanisms for ensuring that enough of what is needed is produced at a fair price. If supply is plentiful, competition among suppliers drives prices down. If supply is short, prices will rise accordingly. If demand is high, suppliers will meet it, because it represents an economic opportunity to do so. If demand is low, suppliers will bring less to market, and seek out alternatives. Crucially, the collective wisdom of the players in the market is greater than that of any central bureaucracy. There are theoretical explanations for why this is so but the empirical evidence that it is so is too strong to ignore.

Transparency

This does not, however, mean that any regulation of the market amounts to disruption of it. On the contrary, Smith recognized that a genuinely free market requires regulation. First and foremost, in order for the market to work, it is essential that actors in it are prevented from manipulating prices through, for example, organizing cartels. As he famously wrote, 'People of the same trade seldom meet together, even for merriment and diversion, but the conversation ends in a conspiracy against the public, or in some contrivance to raise prices.'[10] Producers can keep prices higher than they need be by artificially suppressing supply or simply agreeing not to undercut each other. OPEC, the oil-producing countries' cartel, has explicitly done just that, by agreeing how many barrels to extract in order to keep the price high.

Cartels are hard to control because they can operate implicitly, without any overt conspiracy. Less noticed is the fact that they can also work to drive down prices artificially. Supermarkets, for example, end up 'competing' on basic food stuffs like bread and milk, selling them sometimes as loss-leaders. This amounts to an implicit agreement to drive down prices to artificially low levels. This matters because it inevitably leads to producers being paid less and less as pressure is put on them to cut prices to protect margins.

Cartels, however, are but one manifestation of what happens if you do not ensure a fundamental feature of genuinely effective markets: transparency. Markets are only efficient if people know what they are buying, how rare it is, what quality it is and so on. That's why markets also require rules to stop producers adulterating foods. If you buy flour that is cheaper than the alternative only because it is not 100% flour, then the market is failing to provide the correct signals to enable you to make the right buying choice.

Maximal market efficiency therefore requires maximal information, and this is often lacking in a food supply chain that is long, complex and opaque. Many people would surely make different purchasing decisions if they knew more about how a lot of cheap food is produced. Imagine, for example, if all meat products were required to make plain the conditions the animals were raised in. In the absence of clear information as to why there is a price difference, when people see one whole chicken selling for £4 and another for £8 it is no surprise that most opt for the cheaper one. The pricier one may be labelled 'organic' or 'free range' but that is seen as a nice, optional extra. If the cheaper one were labelled 'bred for faster growth and earlier slaughter, and raised entirely indoors', suddenly the choice would seem less of a no-brainer.

In the market economy we actually have, of course, there is very little of this kind of transparency. In its place we get quite the opposite: deliberately misleading images on packaging of open fields and weasel words like 'farm fresh', 'British', 'premium', 'butcher's choice', 'traditional' or 'corn-fed'.

This also explains why schemes like Fairtrade are not market-bucking. On the contrary, Fairtrade is a market mechanism par excellence. It involves consumers making choices based on perceived value and requires no price- or supply-fixing. Fairtrade works by doing two things. First, it makes transparent to the buyer the nature of conventional production. Second, it makes transparent how it works in contrast. With this information, the consumer can then choose or not choose to buy the Fairtrade product instead of the alternatives.

Certification schemes are not perfect. Fairtrade has itself come under scrutiny recently after it was reported that although the rules ensure good prices for producers, that does not necessarily translate into better pay and conditions for those they employ.[11] If these criticisms stand up, then they would be a very good reason for Fairtrade to change its rules. But they do not reveal any fundamental flaw in the principle of Fairtrade at all.

Certification schemes are simply a particularly formalized way of providing the consumer with more information so as to make the information they base their buying decisions on more transparent. Understood in this way, they should be seen as market-enhancing rather than market-defying initiatives.

Adam Smith recognized that, left to their own devices, players in the market have every incentive to dissemble, mislead, withhold and manipulate. Proper regulation to ensure transparency is essential to avoid these pitfalls. Contemporary defenders of the free market are guilty of glossing over this, emphasizing the theoretical efficiency of the market while ignoring the political and legal structures which are required to make it work. Genuinely free markets do not operate outside of regulation, but very much within it.

Externalities

There is, however, a second justification for actively managing and regulating markets which could have even more potential to help create a better food system. Orthodox economics accepts that systems must be in place to deal with negative 'externalities'. An externality is a spill-over cost or benefit of an economic activity, passed on to people who did not choose to bear it. An example of a positive externality would be if an area of derelict land were redeveloped into something physically attractive, improving the view for people whose properties looked out over the area, at no cost to themselves. More interesting politically are negative externalities. To give the classic, and perhaps simplest example: if a factory pollutes a river in any way which harms the livelihoods of people who depend on it, that is a negative externality and those who suffer as a result should not be made to pick up the tab for the damage done by the polluter. Likewise if your bar creates noise that disturbs people in their nearby homes. It is standard economic theory, even for die-hard libertarians, that such externalities can and should be charged for.

But is charging for externalities the only way to deal with them? According to the most orthodox economic libertarians, the answer is yes. Whether something is an externality and how great it is all boils down to peoples' willingness to pay. As George Mason University associate professor of economics Bryan Caplan wrote for the Liberty Fund, 'If one thousand people would pay ten dollars each for cleaner air, there is a ten-thousand-dollar externality of pollution. If no one minds dirty air, conversely, no externality exists.'[12]

Nothing seems to describe better Oscar Wilde's description of 'A man who knows the price of everything and the value of nothing'. It is arbitrary to reduce the act of placing value on something to a willingness to pay for it because when it comes to seeking out the good and avoiding the bad, getting out our chequebooks is but one, limited behaviour in the rational actor's repertoire. In the case of pollution, for instance, rather than pay to clean it up, why not just legislate to stop it happening in the first place?

Take, for instance, 2010's Deepwater Horizon oil spill. Who seriously believes that if BP had announced, as soon as the spill started, that it would pay all the costs of cleaning it up and compensation to people who missed earnings, that everything would have been all right? A company had a policy which said that it didn't care about avoiding non-lethal pollution, and only cared about having the funds ready to clean it up, would be considered monstrously irresponsible.

To take the argument even further, no one believes that the way to think about lethal side effects of economic activity is in monetary terms. It is true that when deciding on certain health and safety measures to adopt, cost-benefit analyses do require us to put a cost on a human life. If New York City could spend $1 million on improving road safety or on improving subway safety, we would expect it to spend the cash on whatever will save more lives. But if Ford could reduce the cost of a $10,000 car to $9,500, by making changes that it has good reason to think will lead to even a few more fatal accidents, we do not have to do a cost-benefit analysis to see that this is wrong.

There is a third reason why the purely monetary approach to externalities is inadequate: not all externalities have a measurable economic cost. Take urban uglification. Imagine that a developer wants to construct a building that most people think will make a previously attractive street look horrible. Leave aside for one moment what I consider to be the absurd view that, if one could measure the cost, then the development should be allowed to go ahead, just as long as they pay the tax. Even if we thought that, the real problem is how one would measure the economic cost of that.

The libertarian answer would be by adding up how much what each person who hated the building would pay for it not to be there. But this is not a question I think any sane person could think has anything like a measurable answer. If you came up to me now and said, 'how much would you be willing to pay to replace that ugly building with a beautiful one?' I would simply have no idea. Is this a one-off or a new system of regular payment? If I am to pay my share towards every ugly building I want removed, then would a fair amount be a cent, a dime, a dollar? The thought experiment is crazy: we can't cost the externality in that way. But we don't need to: just make planning law require attention to beauty. It seems quite obvious that if we agree that something is a negative externality and we can just stop it happening by regulation, that is more effective and simpler than trying to cost it.

All economists recognize that negative externalities exist. Only hard line libertarians think that the only way to deal with them is to charge for them. Everyone else thinks that regulation has a role to play too.

In the case of food production, negative externalities include factors such as degradation of the environment, carbon emissions and bad health effects. Such externalities need to be either prohibited, controlled or taxed. It is only because this is not at present happening that unsustainable, unfair food production is viable.

For example, unsustainable arable farming which relies excessively on finite, often fossil-fuel-dependent inputs depletes both the land used and the natural resources required to make it fertile. This creates a negative externality on future generations. If this were taxed, or even prohibited, then it would no longer make economic sense to farm in such destructive ways.

Refusing to pay fair wages or prices to farmers also creates negative externalities. Either governments need to step in to cover the shortfall or people have to pay the price themselves in terms of poor health, poor housing and an inadequate standard of living. If buyers had to pay the full price for food, these externalities would not arise.

It is difficult to think of an objectionable facet of industrial food production that cannot be understood in terms of externalities. Indeed, asking where the externality lies can be a good way of separating legitimate concerns from food snobbery. Take, for instance, the debates about healthy food. If one seriously believes that we should legislate against unhealthy foods, then it must be because they create a social cost that we feel is not acceptable. But if that's the case, what is to be taxed? It is notoriously difficult to answer this question because foods aren't unhealthy, only diets are. Morgan Spurlock made himself ill eating only McDonalds food for a month but he'd have been even sicker if he'd only eaten artisan cheese. It would therefore seem very difficult to justify an obesity tax on McDonalds or chocolate bars if you didn't also apply it to cheese and organic hand-baked cakes as well.[13] Given that, and also that no-one is forced to subsist on an unhealthy diet, the answer to the public health problem is surely to demand more transparency, not to tax or ban 'bad' foods. It is mistaken to think of the bad effects of unhealthy foods as externalities as no one is forced to bear the costs of them.

The not so free food market

If a truly free market should be conducive to a good, clean, healthy, fair, sustainable food supply system, why then does it appear that so many of our current ills are the fault of the market? The short answer is that the current 'free trade' system is very far from a genuinely free market. Many food campaigners know this. For instance, Eric Schlosser, author of *Fast Food Nation*, told an interviewer, 'The people who call me a socialist or a communist really have to deal with the fact that the market isn't working … It much more resembles the Soviet command economy than the kind of thing I'm arguing for.'[14]

The idea that US agriculture is more Stalinist than Hayekian might sound absurd but this certainly fits the picture painted by Michael Pollan, a good example of a writer who never points his finger at 'the market' as the bogey-man. In one of his pieces, for example, he asked why it was that 'a dollar could buy 1,200 calories of cookies or potato chips but only 250 calories of carrots' and '875 calories of soda but only 170 calories of orange juice'. He rightly concluded, 'This perverse state of affairs is not, as you might think, the inevitable result of the free market.'[15] Rather, it was the consequence of the Farm Bill, legislation which subsidizes the production of commodity crops like corn, soybeans and wheat – the principle ingredients of highly-processed manufactured foods. In this way, the current food system not only fails to deal with negative externalities, but, worse, subsidies and import tariffs can actually encourage bad food practices.

Market failures

Although there is much greater compatibility between good, sustainable food production and free market economics, it would nonetheless be naïve to believe that a proper market is all we need. The world is a complicated place, and it is always dangerous to assume that there is one principle or mechanism that can deliver all that is good. The market is an efficient mechanism, but not a perfectly efficient one, and where it fails, it is quite right to try to do something to counter that.

The economist Paul Krugman offers as an example of this the parlous state of British cuisine in the 1970s. Krugman wants to explain why the average Brit continued to eat badly long after good food became more widely available. His answer is that 'by the time it became possible for urban Britons to eat decently, they no longer knew the difference. The appreciation of good food is, quite literally, an acquired taste – but because your typical Englishman, circa, say, 1975, had never had a really good meal, he didn't demand one. And because consumers didn't demand good food, they didn't get it'. This exemplifies a systemic failure of markets, as Krugman notes: 'The whole point of a market system is supposed to be that it serves consumers, providing us with what we want and thereby maximizing our collective welfare. But the history of English food suggests that even on so basic a matter as eating, a free-market economy can get trapped for an extended period in a bad equilibrium in which good things are not demanded because they have never been supplied, and are not supplied because not enough people demand them.'[16]

How should we deal with such problems? It's tricky, but there seems to be a case here for stimulating demand and/or supply if we have reason to think that a good option is not being taken up in sufficient numbers because of bad equilibrium. Long-term subsidies often have unintended consequences and introduce perverse incentives, but at the very least there might be a case for sometimes providing short-term stimuli to try to kick-start change. For example, in 'food deserts' where fresh fruit and vegetables have become almost non-existent, it might make sense to offer stores incentives to stock and promote them, to break the vicious cycle of lack of demand feeding lack of supply which feeds lack of demand.

Whether there is a good solution here or not, the case of 'bad equilibrium' is offered as an example that, although the market may not be the enemy of good food it is often presented to be, nor is it a flawless mechanism for delivering a wholesome, fair food supply. The free market should be embraced only in so far as it delivers the social results we want. Although often presented as an ideology we have to accept or reject wholesale, it is actually no more than a mechanism that we can adopt, more or less adapted, to fit our needs.

Conclusion

Genuinely free markets are not the enemies of a sound food economy. The problem is with under-regulated markets. To some 'regulated market' is an oxymoron, but this is a historical and factual mistake. Free does mean unfettered but free from distortion by manipulation or misinformation. That is why Adam Smith, for example, favoured breaking up monopolies and cartels. Markets need to be regulated in order to be free, fair and sustainable.

In such a market, the final condition necessary is simply that people make their choices in the market in sensible ways. Earlier I quoted farmer Troy Roush saying that 'You have to understand that we farmers, we're gonna deliver to the marketplace what the marketplace demands. If you want to buy $2 milk, you're gonna get a feedlot in the backyard. It's that simple'. I cut the quotation off there, at the point at which I think many people cut off their thinking about how the market works, as some kind of unstoppable driver for cheap, mass-produced rubbish. But Roush continued: 'People have got to start demanding good, wholesome food of us. And we'll deliver. I promise you. We're very ingenious people. We'll deliver.'[17]

An undistorted – which means highly regulated – market is value-free. You only end up with goods at the minimum of cost with the maximum of profit if that's what people demand or accept. If people are prepared to pay a fair price to buy from producers and suppliers that promote values other than mere profit, they will thrive. The market is amoral, not immoral. The values it promotes are nothing other than the values agents in the market decide to put in.

Notes

1. Llewellyn H. Rockwell, Jr, 'Capitalism and the Burger Wars', *The Free Market*, 15.7 (July 1997) <http://mises.org/freemarket_detail.aspx?control=131> [accessed 2 June 2014].
2. Joanna Blythman, 'The Food Chain Is Almost Broken', *The Observer*, 5 June 2011.
3. Joanna Blythman, 'Bent Bananas', *The Ecologist*, 13 January 2009.
4. Joanna Blythman, 'Squalor in Delhi: What Were They Expecting?', *The Sunday Herald*, 26 September 2010.
5. *Food, Inc.*, dir. by Robert Kenner (Magnolia Pictures, 2010).
6. W. M. Curtiss, 'Free-Market Farming: An Economic Remedy for a Political Headache', *The Freeman*, 1 February 1956.
7. Julian Morris, 'How Bad Government Caused the Food Crisis', *The Spectator*, 28 May 2008.
8. Madsen Pirie, 'Misery Wrought by "Fair" Trade', Adam Smith Institute blog, 6 September 2008 <http://www.adamsmith.org/blog/international/misery-wrought-by-'fair'-trade> [accessed 2 June 2014].
9. 'Good Food?', *The Economist*, 7 December 2006 <www.economist.com/node/8381375> [accessed 2 June 2014].
10. Adam Smith, *An Inquiry into The Nature and Causes of The Wealth of Nations*, (1776) <http://www.gutenberg.org/files/3300/3300-h/3300-h.htm> [accessed 14 November 2014] (Chapter 9, Part 2).
11. Christopher Cramer, Deborah Johnston, Carlos Oya and John Sender, 'Fairtrade, Employment and Poverty Reduction in Ethiopia and Uganda: Final Report to DFID', April 2014 <http://ftepr.org/wp-content/uploads/FTEPR-Final-Report-19-May-2014-FINAL.pdf> [accessed 14 November 2014].
12. Bryan Caplan, 'Externalities', *Concise Encyclopedia of Economics* <http://www.econlib.org/library/Enc/Externalities.html> [accessed 2 June 2014].
13. *Super Size Me*, dir. by Morgan Spurlock (Roadside Attractions, 2004).
14. Oliver Burkeman, 'Food Fight', *The Guardian*, 22 April 2006, p. 31.

15. Michael Pollan, 'You Are What You Grow', *The New York Times Magazine*, April 22 2007 <http://michaelpollan.com/articles-archive/you-are-what-you-grow/> [accessed 2 June 2014]
16. Paul Krugman, 'Supply, Demand, and English food', *Fortune*, 20 July 1998, <http://web.mit.edu/krugman/www/mushy.html> [accessed 2 June 2014].
17. *Food, Inc.*

The Merchants of Genoa and the Diffusion of Southern Italian Pasta Culture in Europe

Anthony F. Buccini

Pe-i boccoin boin se fan e questioin.
Genoese proverb

In the past several decades it has become received opinion among food scholars that the Arabs played the central role in the diffusion of pasta as a common food in Europe and that this development forms part of their putative broad influence on culinary culture in the West during the Middle Ages. This Arab theory of the origins of pasta comes in two versions: the basic account asserts that, while fresh pasta was known in Italy independently of any Arab influence, the development of dried pasta made from durum wheat was a specifically Arab invention and that the main point of its diffusion was Muslim Sicily during the period of the island's Arabo-Berber occupation which began in the ninth century and ended by stages with the Norman conquest and 'Latinization' of the island in the eleventh/twelfth centuries. The strong version of this theory, increasingly popular these days, goes further and, though conceding possible native European traditions, posits Arabic origins not only for dried pasta but also for the names and origins of virtually all forms of pasta attested in the Middle Ages, albeit without ever providing credible historical and linguistic evidence; Clifford Wright (1999: 618ff.) is the best known proponent of this approach.

In Buccini 2013 I demonstrated that the commonly held belief that lasagne were an Arab contribution to Italy's culinary arsenal is untenable and in particular that the Arabic etymology of the word itself, proposed by Rodinson and Vollenweider, is without merit: both word and item are clearly of Italian origin. In this paper I address the core question of the basic theory, that dried pasta was invented and diffused by the Arabs from medieval Sicily, a view that is also in my opinion without merit. The historical and linguistic evidence points clearly to there having been an indigenous pasta culture throughout southern Italy, as well as Sicily, and to its diffusion north having been the work of northern Italian merchants, especially the Genoese; indeed, these same northern Italian merchants and later also their Catalan counterparts can be credited with having played a key role in the expansion of pasta consumption both in Spain and North Africa.

The basis of the Arab theory
The basis of the Arab theory of the origins of pasta in the West resides first and foremost

The Diffusion of Southern Italian Pasta Culture in Europe

in the references to pasta products in several cookbooks from around the Arab world before any such texts appeared in medieval Christian Europe; the first such European text appeared only around 1300. The Arabic term *itriyya,* a form of pasta, is attested in texts from the eastern Arab world starting in the ninth century and later also in texts from the western Arab world. The occurrence of related terms in southern Italy already in the Middle Ages, *tri* or *tria,* has then been explained as a result of Arab influence. There is much more to say about *itriyya* than is possible in the space available for this paper, so for now it must suffice to say that the word is unquestionably of Greek origin and appears already in late antiquity as the name of a form of pasta in both Greek and Aramaic sources – the occurrence of the word and item in Sicily and parts of southern Italy with large Greek-speaking populations resident, is more easily explained as reflecting directly Italo-Greek culture and the intermediacy of the Arabs is hardly necessary: when the Arabs brought their *itriyya* to Sicily, they surely found the Sicilians already eating their own *tria* (Romance) and *itria* (Greek). That said, that the Arabs knew and produced and consumed this early form of pasta, *itriyya,* is undeniable, and it is furthermore undeniable that the appearance of the word in the Romance dialects of Iberia is due to Arab agency, where the form appears widely as *alatría/aletría,* with the Arabic definite article fused to the noun.

But there is one textual reference to *itriyya* in Arabic which is regarded as particularly important by those who support the Arab theory: in 1154 there appeared a geography written by Al-Idrisi, a scholar working at the court of the Norman King Roger of Sicily in Palermo, and in that work the author comments on a town near Palermo, Trabìa, where *itriyya* were produced in considerable quantities and thence exported 'to Calabria and other Muslim and Christian lands'. This passage has been taken uncritically as direct proof of the Arabs' role in the development of pasta culture in Sicily and for their alleged invention of dry pasta and its large-scale manufacture. A more superficial interpretation of the text's significance is hard to imagine. First, one notes that while Al-Idrisi's employment at Roger's court certainly reflects an abiding Arab presence in Sicily, the text appears at a point in time more than eighty years after the conquest of Palermo from the Arabs by the Normans and less than 80 years before the removal of the last Muslims from the island. This raises important questions, first about who it actually was in Trabìa who was making what the author refers to in Arabic as *itriyya,* Arabs or 'Italians', and second and more importantly, who it was who had organized the manufacturing and who then was carrying out the export business. These questions are addressed in the following section of this paper.

Perhaps the superficiality of the historical analysis supporting the Arab theory has gone unnoticed on account of the widely perceived strength of the etymological evidence that its proponents have adduced. Indeed, key elements in discussions of the putative Arab role in the spread of pasta in Italy are the etymologies for two early names of pasta. The first of these involves the Italian word *lasagna,* which Rodinson and Vollenweider have argued is a loanword from Arabic, somehow derived from the well-attested medieval Arabic word *lawzinaj*, an almond-paste confection that according to those scholars was cut in rhomboid shapes and became in the European languages both the heraldic term *lozenge* and the culinary term, *lasagna, loseyn*, etc. As mentioned above, however, this theory is, in a word, wrong (Buccini 2013).

The other etymology is more important in that it has direct bearing on the specific question of the diffusion of dried pasta and in this case, food scholars universally embrace an Arabic origin for the word and the item known in Spanish as *fideos* and Italian as *fidelini* etc. Virtually all recent writers on the history of pasta have accepted blindly a bogus etymology for the word which derives it from the Arabic *fidawsh*; the real etymology of the word and its remarkable spread along trade routes will be addressed below.

Al-Idrisi and the pasta of Trabìa

The ninth century AD was a period of extreme turbulence throughout southern Italy, in which there was a general political and socio-economic destabilization due in large measure to attacks from the Arab world, as well as to the related power struggles between all the southern Italian states, namely, the Lombard states of Salerno, Benevento and Capua; the Byzantine region encompassing large sections of Apulia, Lucania and Calabria; and the formerly Byzantine independent territories in Campania of Gaeta, Naples and Amalfi. This period coincides with the period during which the Arabo-Berber forces of Ifriqiya carried out the principal part of their conquest and colonization of Sicily (827–902). During the ninth century and on into the early tenth century, Arab coastal attacks were also carried out along the central and northern coasts of the Tyrrhenian Sea and along the Ligurian Sea, often with devastating effects, as in the sacking of Rome (846) and Genoa (934).

Not surprisingly the Arab predations in Italy provoked responses which manifested themselves in significant developments in the maritime military and associated resources for maritime trade; in addition small Italian states cooperated with increasing frequency to confront and eliminate the Arab threat on and around the Italian mainland and even to carry the fight to Muslim-held lands in Sicily and North Africa. In this regard, a clear turning point was reached already in the second half of the tenth century, by which time the southern Italian states had eliminated not just the Arab raiding bases on the mainland but by and large even the threat of further coastal raids; in these efforts, the Campanian coastal cities – Gaeta, Naples, Amalfi and Salerno – played central roles. To the north, in Tuscany and Liguria, the coastal cities of Pisa and Genoa led the way in developing navies that were superior to those of the Arabs, as evidenced by their string of naval victories in the tenth and early eleventh centuries.

With the elimination of the Arab raids and a reduction in the level of internecine wars, southern Italy achieved a level of stability able to support gradual demographic and economic growth, which manifested itself in the expansion of agriculture to areas that had been depopulated and neglected (marked in some areas by the process of

The Diffusion of Southern Italian Pasta Culture in Europe

incastellamento, Martin 2002: 22) and to an expansion in trade (Wickham 1981: 149ff.). A key role in the growth of trade was played by the already active city of Amalfi, which had long been involved in the movement of luxury goods from Byzantine and Arab lands to the West, but Gaeta, Naples and Salerno, as well as several Adriatic cities in Apulia, also played their parts in the general upswing of mercantile activity. Though there are signs of some modest development of industry (e.g. linen in Naples), agricultural products were the main elements of southern Italian production for export, especially lumber, nuts and other tree materials, wine and grain.

Moving further into the eleventh and early twelfth century, trade intensified between southern Italy and the northern trading centres of Genoa and Pisa, as well as Venice; Genoa was particularly engaged in the south, with regular close ties to the southern trading towns of Gaeta and Salerno. It is noteworthy that Amalfi, long specialized in the movement of luxury goods, began to fade in importance, being eclipsed in this trade by the northern cities. In northern and north-central Italy, with the initial phases of the urbanization and industrialization of the High Middle Ages underway, the agricultural products of continental southern Italy were in great demand to help feed the new concentrations of population, especially in Genoa, a city with hardly any agricultural hinterland of its own. Though the textual evidence for trade in this period is quite fragmentary, it is clear that there was a northward movement of grain along both the west and east coasts of Italy and on occasion we even see evidence of the shipment of grain to Muslim lands from the continental south, for example from Byzantine Calabria to Muslim Sicily in the tenth century (Kreutz 1991: 144–5). Indeed, during the period before the Norman conquest of Sicily in the second half of the eleventh century, there seems to be no evidence whatsoever of the export of grain from that island to Christian lands but rather clear indications that the continental south did have exportable surpluses of grain which were regularly shipped north.

Just as political fragmentation and instability had exacerbated the Arab raids in southern Italy in the ninth/tenth centuries, Muslim Sicily was similarly weakened from within in the eleventh century. In the context of the growing military and economic strength of the Italian states, both the Genoese and Pisans and the increasingly powerful Normans of southern Italy saw Sicily as a vulnerable and attractive place for expansion, leading to the relatively rapid conquest of the island under Norman leadership in 1061–1092, even before they had fully consolidated their control over the southern mainland. And there was little if any lag in time before the northern Italians and most especially the Genoese began to exploit the commercial opportunities that Norman control offered.

There are two key socio-economic aspects of northern Italian participation in the 'Latinization' of Sicily under the Normans. First, as was normal in the Middle Ages, regular trade with a given target city involved the establishment of a merchants' colony there, with its *fondaco*, church and dwellings; thus we find Messina early on fully Christian with a local Greco-Italian population and merchant colonies of Genoese, Florentines and Pisans, as well as Amalfitans and others. In Palermo, already in the early twelfth century, there are similar merchant colonies, and the rapidity with which the Ligurians took on the central position in long-distance trade from Sicily is clearly indicated by the fact that already in 1116 they began to receive privileged legal and commercial status on the island (Abulafia 1977: 62ff.), a development which bespeaks a preceding period of activity and accumulated good-will.

Second, in east-central Sicily we find the establishment of a noteworthy number of agricultural towns – the so-called Gallo-Italic settlements such as Aidone, San Fratello and Piazza Armerina – whose colonists were primarily drawn from western Liguria and neighbouring southern Piemonte, territories under the control of the Aleramici family, to which belonged Adelaide, wife of Count Roger I and mother to the first Norman Sicilian king, Roger II; the initial establishment of these colonies may well date to the period of Adelaide's regency from 1101 to 1112, after her husband's death and before the maturity of Roger II. These colonies filled the dual purpose of exploiting underused land and helping to drive the Sicilian Arabs further to the south and west. The agricultural aspect of these settlements must, however, be viewed in relation to the overarching economic interests of both the Normans and the northern Italian merchants, for it is already in this period that we see the beginnings of a move toward monocultural farming geared toward the production of large quantities of grain and cotton for export (Abulafia 1993: 21ff.). This process is attested in the twelfth century also for the area around Palermo, made capital during Adelaide's regency, as can be seen by the development of the massive land-holdings of Monreale Cathedral, just south of the city (Bercher et al.: 1979). In this context, we should also note the mention of the 'estate of a Genoese' in the province of Palermo from the 1180s, and from the period 1131–1148 there is mention of an estate owned by a Piemontese near Patti on the north coast between Palermo and Messina (Peri 1978: 36). Though Arabs still formed a significant part of the Sicilian population in the period, especially in the west and interior of the island, and Arab merchants still formed part of Palermo's make-up, by the early to mid-twelfth century the northern Italians dominated not only the long-distance trade of Sicilian (as well as southern Italian) goods to northern Italy and elsewhere but they had even insinuated themselves into the local trade of Sicily, as demonstrated by a document in Arabic from about 1150 which shows that a voyage along the north coast of Sicily by Muslim merchants was actually financed by an Italian and likely Genoese merchant (Abulafia 1993: 21).

It is against this socio-economic backdrop that we must read Al-Idrisi's mention of the export of pasta from Trabìa around 1150. Trabìa lies directly on the coast, about 30 km to the east of Palermo, squarely in the part of Sicily that during the first half of the twelfth century was the scene of both agricultural and commercial exploitation by the Genoese. We can be reasonably certain that the actual export of Trabìa's pasta was carried out by the Ligurians and have very good reasons to believe that the production not only of the pasta itself but probably even the grain from which it was made may have been organized by Genoese colonists.

The Diffusion of Southern Italian Pasta Culture in Europe

Commerce in grain, undoubtedly including durum wheat, was not something new to the Genoese arriving in Sicily but had long been part of their commercial activities in continental southern Italy which had begun at least in the eleventh century, when trade between Muslim Sicily and the north did not involve grain. Indeed, during the Norman period itself, according to the *Registrum curiae archiepiscopalis Ianuae* of 1143, the chief points of the grain trade in the south for the Genoese were Messina and Naples, with Salerno playing a key role at times as well (Abulafia 1977: 71ff., Brancaccio 2001: 20ff.). Some of this trade from Campania surely involved transhipment of Sicilian grain but there is no reason to believe that the movement of grain from the continental south (including regions where durum wheat was produced) would have abruptly stopped with the conquest of Sicily. The absence of any linguistic evidence in northern Italian dialects for Arabic involvement in the spread of pasta culture alongside the clear and multiple connexions to southern Italian pasta terminology makes it all but certain that the trade mentioned by Al-Idrisi represented not the introduction of an Arab culinary novelty to the Ligurians, as is generally assumed these days, but rather an expansion of trade in familiar southern products to a new source.

While it is safe to assume that the Arabo-Berbers who conquered Sicily knew pasta before they set out across the sea, it is equally safe to assume that it had already long been familiar to the Greco-Latin Sicilian population they encountered, as it was to the Greco-Latin population of the southern Italian mainland. And the means by which pasta culture – including durum wheat and dried pasta – diffused northward was first and foremost the result of the economic and social interactions of the northern Italians with the southern Italians.

The etymology of *fidê/fideus*

The last major piece of evidence used to support the Arab theory is the etymology of another pasta word that arose in the late Middle Ages, namely, the word that appears in Catalan as *fideus*, in Arabic as *fidawsh* and in Italy as *fidei, fidelini*, etc.

In this case it is noteworthy that the received etymology among food historians today is one that was actually proposed by a distinguished historical linguist and lexicographer, Joan Corominas, but, rather depressingly, it seems many of these food historians have not actually bothered to read Corominas' discussion and an egregious misreading has arisen which is now endlessly repeated in print and on the internet about this word.

Corominas' 1954 etymology of Castilian *fideos* derives the word *fideo/fideos* not directly from Arabic; rather, it was in his view 'a word created in the Mozarabic Romance' (the Romance dialect of Al-Andalus), formed from the verb *fidear* 'to grow, to overflow', which itself was a form built on the borrowed Arabic root *fâḍ* 'grow, overflow' (imperative *fiḍ*). His proposal was intended to address shortcomings of earlier attempts by linguists to explain the family of related words starting from a specifically northern Italian point of origin, to wit: 1) in his view, one cannot derive the Iberian forms from

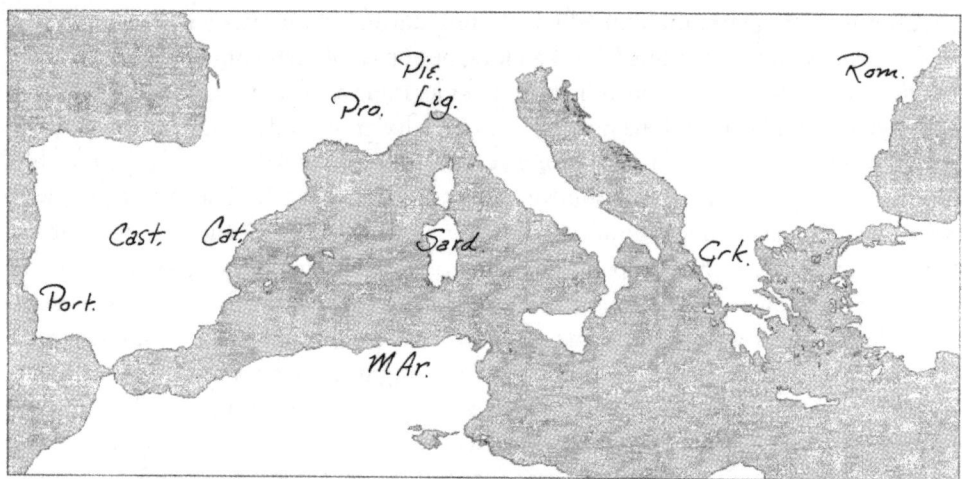

Figure 1. Distribution of basic relevant forms cited in earlier discussions of the etymology (Flechia 1876, Schiaffini 1924, Corominas 1954). Portuguese fidéus, *Castilian* fideos, *Catalan* fideus, *Maghrebian Arabic* fidêuš, fidáuš, *Provençal* fidêous, *Piemontese* fidéi, *Ligurian* fidei, fidê, *Sardinian* findeus, *Greek* φιδές, *Romanian* fideà.

the Italian forms but the opposite is possible; 2) the earliest attestations of the word are from Al-Andalus in the thirteenth century, before the Italian forms are attested; 3) the Arabic forms *fidawsh* etc. are clearly derived from Iberian Romance which Corominas states most plainly: he says of them '[their] phonetic structure proclaims from a mile away their Hispanic or Romance origin'. It is in this last regard that food historians seem to have misread or not read at all Corominas, for it is a commonplace in the recent literature to claim that the Arabic *fidawsh* is original and the basis of all the Romance language forms.

As learnèd as Corominas' attempt to explain the origins of *fideos* is, he missed the mark. First, as others such as Corriente (2008) and Toso (1993) have remarked, his derivation of the word from a marginally attested Ibero-Romance verb meaning 'to grow or overflow' seems semantically quite unsatisfactory as the name for a form of pasta. Second and no less important, Corominas did not examine the Italian evidence carefully and missed the fact that the considerable diversity of related dialect forms in northern Italy is impossible to explain in terms of an imported word from Iberia; and this problem is exacerbated if one considers the southern Italian dialect forms that I bring into the discussion for the first time below. Third, as a general dialectological principle, it is normal to find greater diversity of forms in the original area of an innovation than in areas to which the innovation spreads. Indeed, the complexity of the Italian dialect evidence, alongside the striking similarity across the Iberian and Arabic forms, is problematic for Corominas' position, when we also consider what we know generally about the patterns of trade in agricultural goods and especially of durum wheat and pasta products in the western Mediterranean during the period of the first attestations: in the thirteenth century, when we first find mention of *fidawsh* in two Arabic cookbooks from southern Spain, the general movement of the durum wheat trade was from southern Italy and Sicily first to northern Italy and later also to Iberia and North Africa, and this trade, as discussed above, had originally become a large-scale business in the hands of the Genoese and other northerners in the eleventh century, with the Catalans becoming players in this trade in the late twelfth and thirteenth centuries, particularly after they gained control of Sardinia and Sicily.

In light of my objections to Corominas' etymology, a reconsideration of the Italian evidence is warranted. The only way to account for all the diversity of forms we find in the Italian dialects is to posit as the original base form a southern Italian word *filati*, a word attested throughout southern Italy and Sicily in modern times referring to string-like forms of pasta, in some cases made simply, in some cases with a hole that is formed by means of the use of a reed, piece of wood or a thin metal rod, *un filo di ferro*. In the first case, the action involved in Italian is *filare* 'to make a thread' and the result would be then *un filato*. Similarly the result of using the *filo di ferro* can also be described as *un filato*. Note that this exact use of the verb *filare* and the use of the *filo di ferro* as a pasta-making tool are both attested clearly already in the fifteenth century in the cookbook by Maestro Martino of Como and these turns of phrase are undoubtedly much older than that.

The key step in my etymology involves explaining the relationship between southern Italian *filati* and the range of forms we find in northern Italy. Here it is the hitherto ignored forms of Calabria that are of especial importance. These forms, *filei, fileja, fileda,* are aberrant in their general southern Italian and Calabrian dialectal contexts in that they appear to reflect two sound changes that are generally alien to the region but common in the dialects of north-western Italy, namely, the fronting of the stressed vowel *-a-* to *-e-* and the lenition of the intervocalic *-t-* to *-d-* or even to *-(zero)-*. Indeed, these forms look remarkably like the forms we would expect to see in Genoese or Piemontese dialects of the twelfth century.

An historical explanation readily comes to mind, namely, the aforementioned northern Italian trading colonies in the south, which must have also been established in some of the small port towns of Calabria, such as Tropea (in a zone where the term *fileja* is still current). And in this regard, it should also be mentioned that 'Gallo-Italic' (primarily Ligurian and Piemontese) agricultural communities were established not only in Sicily during the Norman and Swabian periods but also in some parts of the continental south, especially in Calabria and Basilicata; some of these maintained their distinctive northern Italian dialects into modern times, while in some places only isolated lexical reflexes still survive. In any event, it was precisely among these colonists and the northern merchants with whom they were in contact that the southern term *filati* was borrowed into northern-type dialects, in which the word was adapted phonologically, giving rise both to the Calabrian forms cited above and to the form *fidei,* which is the basis for the majority of the later attested forms in north-western Italy and Provence. In this regard, we can explain the *-d-* in northern-type dialects as an adaptation of the strongly articulated and alien intervocalic *-l-* of the southern dialects: intervocalic *-l-* in Genovese during this time was itself reduced to a weak *r*-like sound and ultimately eliminated (Old Genoese *firao* 'filato').

I propose in addition that the remarkable unity of all the Iberian and Arabic forms finds ready explanation through the socio-historical and economic context of the period. Corominas was right that the Arab forms are to be explained as secondary to Iberian Romance forms, but the source he found, along with the proposed half-Arabic etymon, was wrong. The source was surely Catalan, and it would therefore do well to address briefly the Catalan relationship to Italy in this period.

Already in the eleventh century, the Genoese, Pisans and other Italians had commercial contacts with Catalonia, and by the early twelfth century the Genoese in particular had resident mercantile colonies there. In addition, the Italians helped the Catalans in several military campaigns to reconquer lands from the Muslims (Almería, Tortosa, Majorca), and Genoese and other Italian settlers formed a part of the subsequent Christian populations of these areas. The contacts and interactions between the Catalans and Genoese intensified throughout this period (Ferrer i Mallol 2005), and by the beginning of the thirteenth century, 'there was valuable cooperation in the funding of trading expeditions to north Africa, and both Catalans and Italians were active in the grain trade out of Sicily' (Abulafia 1997: 52). Working often together in the thirteenth century, as Dauverd (2006: 46) puts it, 'Catalans and Genoese infiltrated all aspects of commercial life in Sicily.'

The historical and linguistic facts dovetail perfectly. We posit that the Genoese term was borrowed into Catalan in the twelfth century, when the Genoese rendition of *filati* was almost certainly [fidædi]. Borrowed into Catalan in this period and simply adapted morphologically – fitted with the Catalan *-s* plural – the form would give us by well-known and datable sound change ([-d#>-w#] (see Gulsoy 1977); thus [fidæd] > [fidew]) the form attested, *fideus,* which in turn is a perfect source by which to explain the Arab form *fidawsh,* etc.

The contrast between the diversity of Italian forms and the uniformity of Iberian and Arabic forms reflects, in my opinion, the fact that the consumption of these noodles was more restricted in Iberia, more often a question of a commercial product, whereas in northern Italy, it is clear that the family of *fidei* names refers both to fresh, home-made pasta forms, as well as to commercial products. In the context of home use, the tremendous diversity of dialect names in Italy arose naturally.

To sum up, the pasta term *filati* was borrowed from southern Italian dialects into Genoese, possibly as early as the eleventh century (before Sicily was involved) or else in the early twelfth century, leaving traces of the original contact forms in Calabria (*fileja* etc.); the phonologically adapted form, *fidei* etc., spread through the dialects of northwestern Italy but in part as a form of fresh pasta. But the Genoese clearly made a dried, commercial product that bore this name, and as a long-distance trade item it was further diffused throughout the Genoese mercantile empire: to the east it went to their contacts in Greece and on the Black Sea in Romania (see Figure 1), while to the west it spread already in the twelfth century to Catalonia. Subsequently, the adapted Catalan form, *fideus,* spread along their mercantile routes to the rest of Iberia, including Castilian lands (*fideos*) and Moorish Andalusia in the thirteenth century and ultimately also to North Africa (*fidawsh*). We see then that rather than being evidence of diffusion of pasta from the Arab lands to Europe as is universally claimed by food historians these days, *fidawsh* is unambiguous evidence of the exact opposite.

Conclusion

I repeat: I am not claiming that the Arabs did not know pasta in the Middle Ages nor do I deny that they were responsible for the introduction of a form of pasta, *itria* (> Spanish & Portuguese *aletria*) to Iberia. But it is striking that in Iberia, where an Arabo-Berber presence was of vastly longer duration than in Sicily, no pasta culture developed, not even in Andalucía, where Moorish influence was most abiding and deepest: pasta in Portugal and most of Spain has never been more than, at most, a secondary element of the regional cuisines. The one exception in Iberia is the Catalan-speaking lands of the east, precisely the part of Spain which had long-standing political, cultural and, most importantly, economic ties to southern Italy and Genoa in the later Middle Ages. With regard to Sicily then, it makes no sense whatsoever to attribute the existence of a strong pasta culture there to the Arabs, when Sicily shared to a great degree the same Greco-Latin cultural background that existed in continental southern Italy, a place with its own deeply-rooted and old pasta culture from classical times on.

And with regard to the diffusion of pasta culture from its old home in the south of Italy to northern Italy and beyond, the evidence is overwhelming that this movement was the result of the northern Italian merchants' expansion into southern Italy and then Sicily in the eleventh and twelfth centuries. With regard to the specific issue of dried pasta, we find no evidence that the Arabs ever engaged in long-distance trade of this product; rather, the evidence of the socio-economic background of the pasta exports from Trabìa and the linguistic evidence of the development of the word *filati/fidei/fideus* make it quite clear that it was the northern Italians and Catalans, and especially the Genoese, who were the real agents of the diffusion of dried pasta out of its southern Italian and Sicilian homeland.

References

Abulafia, David. 1977. *The Two Italies. Economic relations between the Norman Kingdom of Sicily and the Northern Communes.* Cambridge: Cambridge University Press.

———. 1993. "Southern Italy, Sicily and Sardinia", reprinted as chapter I (pp. 1–32) in: D. Abulafia. *Commerce and Conquest in the Mediterranean, 1100–1500.* Aldershot: Variorum.

———. 1997. *The Western Mediterranean Kingdoms 1200–1500.* London: Longman.

Bercher, Henri, Annie Courteaux, & Jean Mouton. 1979. 'Une abbaye latine dans la société musulmane: Monreale en XIIe siècle.' *Annales, Histoire, Sciences Sociales* 34: 526–547.

Brancaccio, Giovanni. 2001. *'Nazione genovese.' Consoli e colonia nella Napoli moderna.* Naples: Guida.

Buccini, Anthony F. 2013. 'Lasagna: a Layered History.' In: *Proceedings of the Oxford Symposium on Food and Cookery 2012,* Mark McWilliams (ed.), pp 94–104. Totnes: Prospect.

Corominas, Joan. 1954. *Diccionario Crítico Etimológico de la Lengua Castellana.* Berna: Francke.

Corriente, Federico. 2008. *Dictionary of Arabic and allied loanwords: Spanish, Portuguese, Catalan, Galician and kindred dialects.* Boston: Brill.

Dauverd, Céline. 2006. 'Genoese and Catalans: Trade Diaspora in Early Modern Sicily.' *Mediterranean Studies* 15: 42–61.

Ferrer i Mallol, Maria Teresa. 2005. 'I Genovesi visti dai Catalani nel Medioevo.' In: Luciano Gallinari (ed.), *Genova: Una 'porta' del Mediterraneo Pt. 1*, pp. 137–174. Cagliari.

Flechia, G. 1876. 'Postille etimologiche.' *Archivio Glottologico Italiano* 2: 313–384.

Gulsoy, Joseph. 1977. 'El desenvolupament de la semivocal *-w* en Català.' In: *Catalan Studies: Volume in Memory of Josephine de Boer*, pp. 71–98. Barcelona: Hispam.

Kreutz, Barbara. 1991. *Before the Normans. Southern Italy in the Ninth and Tenth Centuries.* Philadelphia: University of Pennsylvania Press.

Martin, Jean-Marie. 2002. 'Settlement and the Agrarian Economy.' In: G.A. Loud & A. Metcalfe (eds.), *The Society of Norman Italy*, pp. 17–45. Leiden: Brill.

Peri, Illuminato. 1978. *Uomini città e campagne in Sicilia dall'XI al XIII secolo.* Roma: Laterza.

Schiaffini, Alfredo. 1924. 'La diffusione e l'origine di *fidelli* "vermicelli" – *fidelini* "capellini".' *Archivum Romanicum* 2: 294–301.

Toso, Fiorenzo. 1993. *Gli ispanismi nei dialetti liguri.* Alessandria: dell'Orso.

Wickham, Chris. 1981. *Early Medieval Italy. Central Power and Local Society 400–1000.* Ann Arbor: University of Michigan Press.

Wright, Clifford A. 1999. *A Mediterranean Feast.* New York: William Morrow.

Powerful Scent: The Egyptian Bazaar in İstanbul

Nihal Bursa

This paper explores İstanbul's Egyptian Bazaar, Mısır Çarşısı, an exuberant spice market that attracts traders and tourists alike. The beauty of its architecture and the inherent romance of the spice trade have combined to make the Bazaar an almost mythical place. This study will consider how the Egyptian Bazaar outlived its original purpose by contributing to the economic activities in this commercially dense area of İstanbul; once a symbol of imperial patronage, the Bazaar has created its own rich social environment with unique commercial practices, behavioural patterns and cultural meanings.

The Egyptian Bazaar is a covered space containing the spice market. It was originally built as part of the Yeni Valide (New Queen-Mother) Mosque complex; its economic activity was considered part of the *waqf*, a charitable foundation based on the Quranic concept of *khayr*, charity, established to support the mosque. The Valide Sultan (Queen-Mother) Mosque complex was initially designed to include a madrasa, a hospice and a caravansary grouped around a monumental Friday mosque.[1] Later, the completed Yeni Valide Mosque included the mosque itself along with the covered bazaar, an elaborate fountain and a tomb. The construction of this complex of buildings was initiated by queen-mother Safiye Sultan in 1597 and it was completed in 1664 by the succeeding patron, queen-mother Turhan Sultan, who was known as a philanthropic queen. The idea was to honour the position of the Valide Sultan, as reflected in the mosque's name.

In the Ottoman Empire, upper-class women often functioned as patrons, particularly for the construction of mosques or madrasas. Towards the end of the sixteenth century, the queen-mother's political power made her especially well positioned to serve as an architectural patron. However, finding and acquiring suitable land for patrons and particularly for lady-patrons to build on was not easy, and as a result many ruling élites chose to build in the less-populated Asian side of İstanbul. At the same time, there was public dissent over the exorbitant cost of such building efforts, which were considered 'a blatant show of prestige' in a city where constructions had reached a saturation point by the late sixteenth century.[2] Given the power of the Valide Sultan, however, only the best location would do for this mosque complex, and the land chosen was among the most valuable in İstanbul: in the Golden Horn, next to the port and close to Topkapı Palace. The cost of acquiring the land confirmed the all-powerful position of the queen-mother, and the mosque endures to this day as a rare representation of women's power.

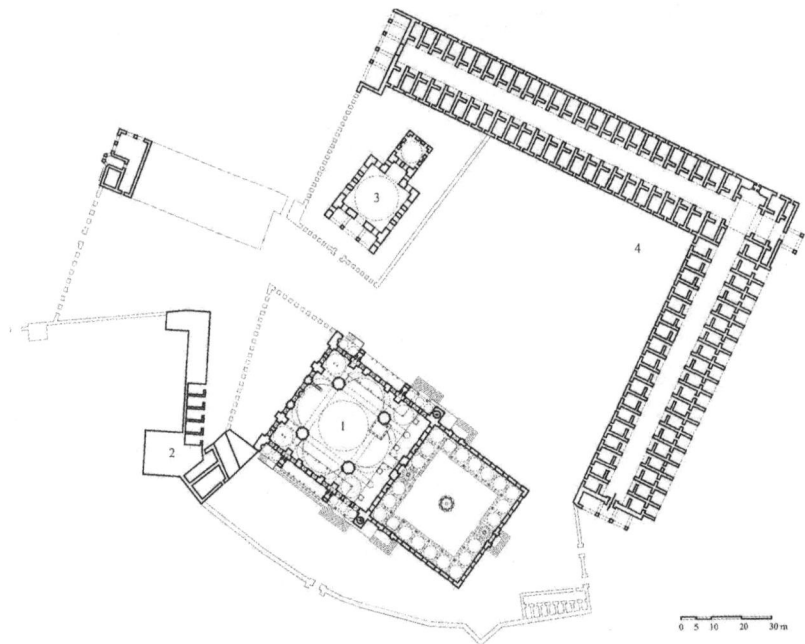

Figure 1. Plan of the Yeni Valide Mosque complex.

Figure 2. Yeni Valide Mosque complex, engraving by G.J. Grelot, c. 1683.

Powerful Scent: The Egyptian Bazaar in İstanbul

Spice market

Located along the waterfront of Eminönü, the 350-year-old Egyptian Bazaar is part of the imposing mosque complex that defines the heart of commerce and trade in İstanbul. Like the mosque itself, the Bazaar was originally named Valide Çarşısı (Queen-Mother Bazaar). During Byzantine times there was a bazaar located on the same site. Facing the port used by ships loaded with spices and aromatics that came from India through Egypt, the bazaar area punctuates this significant trade route. By the completion of Valide Çarşısı, Egypt had been a prosperous Ottoman territory for 150 years. In the sixteenth century, half of the spices that came through Cairo were imported especially for İstanbul and Bursa; from these cities, trade continued to the Balkans and the northern frontiers.[3] In the seventeenth century, after the circumnavigation of Africa by Vasco da Gama and the conquest of Spice Islands by the Dutch, Venice was in crisis, but the merchants of Cairo continued to serve the Ottoman market through the Red Sea, bringing spices, drugs and dyes to İstanbul.[4] The importance of this trade led to the Valide Çarşısı being renamed the Egyptian Bazaar, a reflection of the power of spice.

Although only a single building, the Egyptian Bazaar defines the urban space near the port. That space can be described as a confluence of two plazas bounded by the sea, the L-shaped bazaar building, the mosque, the fountain and the tomb (Figure 1).

Markets were instrumental in creating a sense of urban identity in Ottoman cities. In that respect, the Queen-Mother Mosque complex is one of the prominent examples of Ottoman architecture; it reveals how space was conceived in the Ottoman city, which was linked to the idea of *waqf* and the interrelation of religious and secular space. In fact, until the nineteenth century, there was a wall, beginning at the main door of the Egyptian Bazaar facing the port and encircling the mosque, that served to carefully divide the religious and secular realms (Figure 2). The secular side of the wall was a terminal space for naval merchants and a base for economic activities. The spice market's reliance on naval trade has changed over time; during the twentieth century, the port has become a busy station for public transportation and tourism.

Today, this architectural environment provides a total experience; spice, food and space are all interrelated. Here, spice means more than its materiality; space means more than its physicality. These interrelationships are implied by the roots of the word *port*. The Latin word *portus* denotes a secure place or a landing station; the word describes a geographical configuration.[5] But the Latin root *porta*, which means gate, entrance or transition, implies something beyond geography. Here, Eldem's description of İstanbul through his concept of an interface is also suggestive of the nature of the Egyptian Bazaar. Eldem argues that conceiving of İstanbul as a port is restricting; instead, describing the city as an interface more accurately embraces the city's intertwined realms of power, politics and culture.[6]

An interface occurs when sides come into contact, when boundaries blur or become permeable. The urban space created by the New Queen-Mother Mosque complex attracts both tourists and the inhabitants of İstanbul. Within this complex,

Food and Markets

Figure 3. Vendors outside the Bazaar building.

the Egyptian Bazaar is a popular destination for both groups. There is value created through this exchange and interaction that far exceeds the monetary value of trade. The Bazaar's monumental architecture embodies a human space; the daily routines and rituals of the Bazaar exceed the boundaries of the building. The word *çarşı* helps explain this particular characteristic: the Persian root, *câr-sû*, means crossroads or something which has four directions.[7] This name perfectly delineates the commercial spaces of the crossroads that form a city's centre in eastern cultures. Furthermore, the cities with commercial significance almost always began as settlements at the intersections of trade routes. Since such intersections offer a way of coming together or meeting, they inevitably generate interfaces.

The Egyptian Bazaar creates an interface between different aspects of life in İstanbul. Interactions occur on the basis of trade, but those interactions create relationships and simultaneously develop spaces for socialization. It is no coincidence that the city's first coffeehouse was opened in this vicinity in 1554. When the construction of the whole complex was completed in 1664, this part of İstanbul was already populated with hundreds of coffeehouses. It should also be noted that, besides spice, coffee was one of the major items of trade for the merchants of Cairo and İstanbul.

These interrelated activities and spaces conglomerate around the Bazaar: it acts like a magnet. In addition to the row of shops inside, the L-shaped building is also flanked by shops on the outside. These small shops along the outer walls are symbiotically related

Powerful Scent: The Egyptian Bazaar in İstanbul

to the activities inside the walls, and they, in turn, create new arteries around them full of shops, street vendors and temporary food stations (Figure 3). The whole environment becomes captivating for all.

Architectural space and the guilds

The guilds of spice and textile merchants in the Egyptian Bazaar began to gain power and autonomy in the Ottoman market in the seventeenth century. They formed local resistance against rival Ottoman and foreign merchants.[8] Moreover, the guilds of İstanbul, Cairo and Damascus were all reacting against the demands of the government to use their resources to finance war.[9] French merchants suffered most from the unified Ottoman spice guilds, although they still overcame their British and Flemish rivals to trade spices, herbs, coffee and sugar from their colonial possessions.[10] In İstanbul, commercial life benefited from the cooperation between guilds, and the Egyptian Bazaar served as a concrete architectural embodiment of this economic power.

After two big fires and several renovations, the bazaar building still conflates the sobriety of its noble patroness and the engaging atmosphere of the spice market. From the outside, it is in dialogue with the monumental New Queen-Mother Mosque. Inside, the spatial organization of the Egyptian Bazaar reflects some of the major principles of the Ottoman guild system. This guild system was a continuation of the *Ahî* (*Akhi*) organization which has roots in Muslim mysticism and valued equity, solidarity, forbearance and consideration.[11] Based on these values, Ottoman guilds sought to maintain quality control, standardization, price stability and cooperation rather than competition.[12] These values are encapsulated in the Arabic *esnâf*, which means a class, group or body of people like, in this case, the tradesman and artisans of the guilds.[13]

Throughout its long history, Egyptian Bazaar sustained its power owing much to the commercial union of *esnâf* who identified themselves with these ethical values. Among these, equity and solidarity stand as governing principles visible in the architectural organization of the Egyptian Bazaar. They are evident in the L-shaped plan, articulated in the form of a street with rows of shops on both sides (Figure 4). This type of building, called *arasta*, is widely seen in Anatolian cities where it forms the centre of commerce. The word comes from the Persian root *rāst*, meaning straight or right, which literally describes the physical configuration of the space.[14] The street in the middle acts as the main artery for circulation and as the common space for meeting and interaction. Shops are equal in size and exposure to the main artery. Each shop owner thus has the same opportunity to display goods to customers. Therefore, the concept of equality is embodied in the space itself. On the other hand, *rāst* further means blessed and lucky – the most frequent wish in a bazaar or a market place in Anatolia. In the vernacular language, it implies solidarity as well. Artisans salute each other by saying 'bless your work' which contributes to the unified spirit.

One can easily feel this unified spirit when entering the Egyptian Bazaar today. All of the shops have maximum openings to the main street, and the spices arranged in

Food and Markets

Figure 4. Bird's-eye view of the interior space.

front of each shop extend into the common space. The stalls of adjacent shops visually create an uninterrupted row of open display. Mutual trust and support allows each *esnâf* to watch neighbouring shops during other shopkeepers' brief absences. Commercial interests and social bonds are interdependent here, and the unity among the members of this community of *esnâf* creates its own social culture. Today this community of *esnâf* have a union, the Egyptian Bazaar Tradesmen's Association (EBTA) which was established in 1972.[15] A significant part of this association's aim is to preserve the building of the Egyptian Bazaar and its cultural and historical heritage.

Spicy space

Throughout the history of food, part of the appeal of spice has been that it comes from unfamiliar parts of the world. Therefore, spice has been associated with adjectives like exotic, expensive, unique and luxurious which have contributed to its perceived power from the very beginning. The Western mind often linked spices to 'Paradise' which was believed to be a place in the East.[16] Long trade routes meant high prices that kept spices rare and valued. Longings for faraway places were often gratified by the taste and smell of spices. Between the eleventh and seventeenth centuries, spices dominated the European taste. However, the dishes of Ottoman cuisine were not spicy as the ones in

Powerful Scent: The Egyptian Bazaar in İstanbul

European cuisines during the Middle Ages, Roman dishes in ancient times or Arabic cuisine in the same periods.

In this study, the term spice is used in its extended meaning including herbs and other flavourings.[17] In his *Seyahatnâme* (Book of Travels), the seventeenth-century Ottoman traveller Evliya Çelebi mentions the spices and herbs as flavourings that enrich dishes and serve as medicines.[18] His descriptions of street vendors and spicy cuisines demonstrated that the Palace Cuisine in İstanbul influenced the culinary culture of a much larger area.[19] Notably, the Ottoman Palace was the biggest consumer of the spices in the capital city, İstanbul.[20]

Thus the Egyptian Bazaar still stands as a link to 'Paradise' in the Western mind. It is ironic that the covered market originally meant to serve the needy in the first conceptions of the Queen-Mother Bazaar continues its life as the Egyptian Bazaar which, through its role in the spice trade, creates or redefines the needs of the wealthy today. Spice could be conceived as an agent that turns our desires into needs; in that respect it connotes power. The spice market inspires shoppers and cooks by repeatedly creating – or redefining – need. Within this dynamic process, spice stands as a key phenomenon with historical, cultural and economic significance.

This significance has always drawn visitors to the Egyptian Bazaar, and now its appeal has spread beyond the spice trade. At the very beginning, visitors were mostly Western travellers; now it is a tourist attraction on the itinerary of every visitor to İstanbul. Today, it makes the tourist visit highly efficient by providing various products and experiences in one place. In addition to the spices and herbs which are centre of its trade, there are also textiles, jewellery, ceramics and souvenirs. Most of the foreign tourists prefer to shop in Egyptian Bazaar because they can find all they need in this compact, well-organized place.

This part of İstanbul provides colourful scenes of everyday life in the public, commercial sphere, including sellers and customers, street vendors and beggars. The accounts of curious travelling writers, artists and merchants are full of descriptions of these scenes of Ottoman life. In his extraordinary book published in 1877 after an eighty-day visit to İstanbul, Edmondo de Amicis describes the city vividly. His detailed delineations of the Egyptian Bazaar deserve to be quoted at length:

> At the entrance, you are struck by such a heavy scent of spices. This place is where all the stuff coming from India, Syria, Egypt and Arabia meet; it's the Egyptian Bazaar. All the stuff will turn to powder or essence; will colour odalisques, hands and faces. The perfume will give nice smell to homes, barber shops, bathrooms and beards; calm down the angry pashas, cause the unhappy couples sleep; bring excitement to the smokers; spread the dreams, ecstasy and forgetfulness across the entire city. After a while your head gets heavier, but you cannot get rid off the effects of this heavy and warm atmosphere and strong scent. It follows you to the open air and becomes one of the most memorable moments from the Orient.[21]

Figure 5. A crowded street in the Bazaar.

As de Amicis implies, all kinds of people go to the Bazaar for all kinds of reasons. Unlike the miniature spice corners in supermarkets, people are not here just to buy spices. Instead, they seek the whole experience of the sensual pleasures of the market enclosed by the Bazaar building itself. The spatial characteristics of the architecture contributes to the mythical perceptions of the Bazaar and helps create a unique sense of place.

Although many spices and herbs on the sale in the Egyptian Bazaar can be found in supermarkets, customers often prefer to buy them from the Bazaar. Some of them know that the industrial packages in the supermarket are filled from the same wholesale markets, but they still prefer to visit the Egyptian Bazaar. For the inhabitants of İstanbul who frequent the Bazaar, it is the market where the best quality spices can be bought at reasonable prices. And there is a value in shopping at the centre of trade and commerce, where the wholesalers have been located for centuries. Moreover, the social relations based on reciprocity and trust – similar to farmers markets – still exist there.

The Egyptian Bazaar has its own environment created by the scent of spices and herbs and by the sounds and movement of people. Despite the orderly arrangement of the shops, the visual scene is chaotic, but this chaos contributes to the ambiance, because it occurs around the fundamental simplicity of the architectural idea: the linear repetition of the shops and their symmetrical distribution along the vaulted street space. Densely packed stalls piled up with spices, dry fruits, souvenirs, textiles and ceramics turn this interface into an articulate space (Figure 5). Scents encapsulated in the space mix in a dense microcosm; the powerful scent adds much to lively engagement of the space and makes it more engaging. The environment encourages looking, and looking increases desire. Most importantly, the environment continuously reminds visitors that they are in a space inhabited by humans.

Today, it is amazing to see that while connections to the power of the Egyptian Bazaar's patroness stay in the remote past, the endurance of spice remains overpowering and all-encompassing. This endurance owes much to the continual, extensive web of relations in the spice market which await further research. The Egyptian Bazaar building is currently being restored, but the life there continues vigorously as the Bazaar tries to keep pace with new technologies.[22] Although contemporary consumer culture may have started to substitute the virtual for the real, the powerful scent filling the air cannot be replaced yet.

Notes

1. Gülru Necipoğlu, *The Age of Sinan: Architectural Culture in the Ottoman Empire* (London: Reaktion Books, 2005), p. 511.
2. Necipoğlu, p. 509.
3. Halil İnalcık, *The Ottoman Economic Mind and Aspects of the Ottoman Economy* <http://coursesa.matrix.msu.edu/fisher/hst373/readings/inalcık8.html>, p. 208.
4. Suraiya Faroqhi, *Subjects of the Sultan* (London: I.B. Tauris Publishers, 2000), p. 46.
5. The Turkish name of this district was Emin İskelesi which has become Eminönü in the twentieth century. *Emîn* has Arabic roots meaning secure or reliable person.
6. Edhem Eldem, *Doğu ile Batı Arasında Osmanlı Kenti* (İstanbul: Tarih Vakfı Yurt Yayınları, 2003), p. 155.
7. Ferit Devellioğlu, *Osmanlıca – Türkçe Ansiklopedik Sözlük* (Ankara: 2008), p. 153.
8. Eldem, p. 182.
9. Faroqhi, p. 52.
10. Eldem, p. 201.
11. *Ahî* is an Arabic word which means brother. By the thirteenth century, it had brought artisans and traders together in the form of organized groups and helped the Turks survive commercially against Byzantine artisans and traders in Anatolia.
12. Bursa Araştırmaları Merkezi, *Çarşının Öyküsü: Bursa* (İstanbul: 2011), p. 59.
13. Develioğlu, p. 235.
14. Nişanyan Sözlük <http.nisanyansozluk.com>.
15. The founding principles and aims of the association are 'to establish harmony and solidarity among members and to settle conflict between them, to contribute to the development of national economy, to protect and to pursue the rights of the members before official authorities and third parties, and to have close cooperation with General Directorate of Foundations to protect the characteristics of the Egyptian Bazaar as a historical artifact' <www.misircarsisi.org.tr>.
16. Wolfgang Schivelbusch, 'Spices: Taste of Paradise', *The Taste Culture Reader: Experiencing Food and Drink*, ed. by Carolyn Korsmeyer (Oxford: Oxford UP, 2005), pp. 123–30 (p. 125).
17. Marianna Yerasimos, *500 Years of Ottoman Cuisine* (İstanbul: Boyut Publishing Group, 2005), p. 52.
18. Yerasimos, *Evliya Çelebi Seyahatnâmesi'nde Yemek Kültürü* (İstanbul: Kitap Yayınevi, 2011), p. 71.
19. Yerasimos, *Evliya Çelebi Seyahatnâmesi'nde Yemek Kültürü*, p. 76.

20. For spices used in Ottoman cuisine, see Yerasimos, *500 Years of Ottoman Cuisine*, p. 53; Yerasimos, *Evliya Çelebi Seyahatnâmesi'nde Yemek Kültürü*, pp.72–75; and Christoph K. Neumann, '18.Yüzyıl Osmanlı Saray Mutfağında Baharat', *Soframız Nur Hanemiz Mamur*, ed. by Suraiya Faroqhi and Christoph K. Neumann (İstanbul: Kitap Yayınevi, 2006), pp. 163–70.
21. Edmondo De Amicis, *Constantinople* (Paris: 1883), pp. 95–96.
22. A virtual tour provides a walk through the interior space of the Egyptian Bazaar with 360° views <www.misircarsisi.org.tr>.

From Nihonbashi to Tsukiji: The Early Years of the World's Biggest Fish Market

Voltaire Cang

The Tsukiji Fish Market in Tokyo is the world's biggest seafood market, selling more tons and varieties of fish and marine products than any other food market of its kind. It is one of eleven wholesale markets administered under the Tokyo Metropolitan Central Wholesale Market system, but it is the most famous, and draws hordes of shoppers and tourists who buy from its hundreds of stalls, eat in its sushi counters or witness its early-morning auctions.

The name Tsukiji refers to the area in Tokyo where the market is located. While the name has become synonymous with fish, Tsukiji's association with seafood is relatively recent, as the Tsukiji Fish Market was officially established only in 1923. It was moved from a nearby district, Nihonbashi, after the Great Kanto Earthquake devastated its market in the same year. Indeed, Nihonbashi was Tokyo's central food market and major commercial area for more than three hundred years, having held this position since the establishment of Tokyo, previously called Edo, as the capital of Japan in the beginning of the seventeenth century.[1]

Nihonbashi, literally meaning 'bridge of Japan' [*Nihon*=Japan; *hashi/bashi*=bridge], has since been transformed into Japan's financial hub, with the Bank of Japan (the central bank) and the Tokyo Stock Exchange both headquartered in the area. Money and corporate stocks have replaced fish and daily goods for the trade in today's Nihonbashi.

Nihonbashi has always been an important hub in the life of the capital, and its old market and commercial area has rightfully been scrutinized in much historical research about Tokyo. The bustle on and around the bridge has also been depicted in countless works of art, many from the Edo Period (1603–1867), including famous woodblock prints by the eighteenth- and nineteenth-century artists (Katsushika) Hokusai and (Ando/Utagawa) Hiroshige.[2]

However, most of the research on Nihonbashi as well as majority of the artwork have focused on the period from the late seventeenth century until the present era, after Nihonbashi had already developed into Edo's premier marketplace. Although the birth of the fish market in Nihonbashi has been discussed in earlier research, these efforts have not been extensive and often do not probe the early years of the market's development, before its peak as the commercial centre for the metropolis that was to become Tokyo.

Food and Markets

The paucity of research is mostly due to the limited availability of text and visual records about Nihonbashi in the early seventeenth century, when Edo was formally founded and began its history as the new capital of Japan. Consequently, there is little available information about the early years of the market that developed into today's Tsukiji. This paper will look at this period – the first half of the seventeenth century – in the development of the market in Nihonbashi. In particular, it will discuss and analyse a rare screen painting, the *Edo-zu-byōbu* [Scenes of Edo Folding Screen], especially its detailed illustration of the Nihonbashi market scene, which is the only visual representation of its kind that is of and from this era in Tokyo's history. This illustration will also be briefly compared to another depiction of Nihonbashi found in the *Edo-meisho-zu-byōbu* [Scenes of Famous Places in Edo Folding Screen] that dates from the same period. Through the discussion, the paper aims to provide a description of Tsukiji market's predecessor during its early development and its role in the life and diet of the people in Japan's new capital city.

Birth of the Nihonbashi Fish Market

Several studies in Japanese and a few in English have already outlined the birth of the fish market in Nihonbashi. However, many personalities and events mentioned in these accounts are unverifiable, mainly because the stories – not a few of which include legendary exploits – were initially transmitted through oral tradition. Nonetheless, two works in English, Theodore C. Bestor's book on Tsukiji and Tomioka Issei's series of articles on the Nihonbashi *uogashi* [fish quay] offer succinct and informative accounts of the beginnings of the Nihonbashi fish market, and they comprise the chief sources for the brief summary below.[3] Since both studies refer in turn to another primary source, a nineteenth-century publication in Japanese, *Nihonbashi uoichiba enkaku kiyō* [Bulletin on the origins and development of the Nihonbashi fish market] (Below, Bulletin), this will be referred to as well.[4]

When the warlord Tokugawa Ieyasu entered Edo and took control of the castle in 1590, he was reportedly accompanied by a group of loyal fishermen led by a certain Mori Magoemon from Tsukuda in Osaka. They were no ordinary fishermen; they were rumoured to have also worked for Ieyasu as his spies and/or ninjas.[5] The rumours were founded on the special treatment accorded them: soon after establishing the capital, Ieyasu settled the fishermen on an island in Edo bay and gave them exclusive fishing rights to the area. This island was promptly developed and named Tsukudajima [*jima/shima*=island] in honour of the fishermen's hometown.[6]

Ieyasu was formally appointed shogun by the Emperor in 1603, and as lord of the Edo castle (and leader of Japan), he launched a series of huge engineering and construction projects for the capital's urban development. By this time Mori Magoemon's son, Kyuzaemon, and his fishermen companions had become the official purveyors of fish to the shogunate. Kyuzaemon was later given permission to open a shop near the castle gates, close to a marketplace (Yokkaichi) on the banks of a canal named Dosanburi.[7]

The Early Years of the World's Biggest Fish Market

The Bulletin mentions that Kyuzaemon supplied the fish for the festivities at the birth of Ieyasu's grandson, Iemitsu, born in 1604, and it is thus presumed that Kyuzaemon and his compatriots were already established in their fish businesses by this year. Edo castle was soon expanded and Dosanburi canal was made part of the outer moat, so the marketplace, including Kyuzaemon's shop, was moved to the area near the bridge at Nihonbashi, which had already become the terminal station for travellers to Edo.

In Nihonbashi, Kyuzaemon's fish shop branched out into seven shops, and while they continued to supply the castle with fish, they were also allowed to sell the surplus to the general public. As Edo's population consequently exploded along with the city's booming development and prosperity, the marketplace in Nihonbashi expanded accordingly. While shops that sold clothing and other daily supplies were also established in Nihonbashi, the fish shops dominated and made the most business; the area was eventually called the *Nihonbashi uogashi* [Nihonbashi fish quay].

Tomioka deduces the formal establishment of the Nihonbashi fish market around 1606.[8] Be that as it may, the market at that time could not have been but a few shops selling surplus fish. However, as more and more staff and labourers for the castle and the city's endless construction projects streamed into Edo – increasing the demand for more food – and as transport services and technology for the fish catch and delivery improved, more fishermen and merchants came to be involved in the fish business in Nihonbashi. By 1644, the wholesale and retail businesses of the fish trade was fully centralized in Nihonbashi, and an efficient system of distribution was said to be in place.[9] It is this particular period in the 1640s that coincides with the period depicting Nihonbashi in the *Edo-zu-byōbu*.

Edo-zu-byōbu [Scenes of Edo Folding Screen]

The *Edo-zu-byōbu* (below, *Edo-zu*) is a pair of screens each measuring 162.5 by 366 centimetres, and each consisting of six panels. Edo is seen through golden clouds – made of embossed gold leaf – which frame the different major urban developments, temples and public and private spaces in the capital. Gold leaf is also used for the background, while the scenes and figures are painted in colour and ink.[10] The right screen depicts the north-eastern area of Edo, including the temple areas around Asakusa and Ueno, as well as the castle in the 'little Edo' town of Kawagoe (in present-day Saitama prefecture neighbouring Tokyo). The left screen shows central Edo, with Edo Castle occupying two panels on the upper right part of the screen (and therefore closest to the centre when the two screens are stood on display side by side). Also shown are *daimyō* [warrior lord] estates and the major trade and commercial districts, including Nihonbashi in the second panel from the right, just outside (and illustrated below) the castle gates. Because the left screen depicts the castle and the major urban centres, and has more people (3,131 versus 1,852 figures painted in the right screen), it is considered the more important screen.

The artist is unknown, as the work is unsigned and is painted in combination of

Food and Markets

Figure 1. Scene at Nihonbashi in the Edo-zu-byōbu [Scenes of Edo Folding Screen]. (All images courtesy of the National Museum of Japanese History.)

styles from different traditions; written records about the painting are non-existent as well.¹¹ Concerning the date of its creation, however, an ongoing debate rages: one camp dates it from the early seventeenth century, under the third Tokugawa shogun, while another camp points to a much later period, towards the end of the century and into the eighteenth.¹² (This paper will disassociate itself from the fray.) None the less, there is common agreement that the *Edo-zu* is a portrait of Edo under the third shogun, Tokugawa Iemitsu, who ruled from 1627 until his death in 1653; architectural styles, especially the design and level of completion of the Edo Castle, are dated from Iemitsu's era. Since the painting depicts a prosperous, developed and orderly city and does not show the popular and seedier entertainment districts of Edo, it is also generally presumed that it was commissioned by Iemitsu himself to showcase the accomplishments of his administration.¹³

Now to the portion showing Nihonbashi. Like the other major areas in *Edo-zu*, the location of Nihonbashi is clearly marked, its name written in Kanji (Chinese) characters over the bridge itself (Figure 1). We find a motley selection on the bridge – travellers, street entertainers, vendors, samurai, beggars and at least one monk, among others (Figure 2). On the river's bank are bales of rice in huge piles; just below the bridge are the fishermen (who are deeply tanned) on their boats, delivering their catch in wooden pails to the waiting dealers and vendors (Figure 3).

The market is to the right of the bridge, in the area with nine groups of buildings, each one with an inner courtyard and storehouses. Market stalls face onto the street on the ground floor of the buildings. All the stalls have upper floors – some with turrets – which then served as the shopkeepers' residences.¹⁴

The Early Years of the World's Biggest Fish Market

Figure 2. Detail of the Nihonbashi bridge.

The stalls in the upper section of the market sell vegetables; concentrated in the lower section are the rice dealers' shops, with the rice bales piled just outside their empty storefronts.[15] The main section and central market area is where the fish are. This section is not only the busiest in the Nihonbashi area, but it also the most commercially active in the whole of *Edo-zu*; at this stage in Edo's development, Nihonbashi had become the capital's centre of commerce. By all indications, it had also become the central fish market, as Nihonbashi is the only area in *Edo-zu* that depicts the fish trade. Although itinerant vendors and a few food stalls are shown in other areas of *Edo-zu*, Nihonbashi is the only full-fledged market depicted in the whole work. Indeed, Nihonbashi had become the central food market in Edo, as this was where all the ingredients for the populace's basic diet of rice, vegetables and fish could be procured. By this time, it had already assumed the role of the 'kitchen of Edo' [*Edo no daidokoro*], the nickname that would be given to the area much later.

A closer look at this section of the market in Nihonbashi reveals storefronts with full displays of seafood, shopkeepers and customers in conversation (or perhaps haggling over prices), and different passersby, from vendors to travellers and samurai, and even a musician. In the market stalls, some of the fish are sold dried and hung from the eaves, while most are sold fresh, many placed in seawater tanks. We can mark out certain types of seafood from their colours, shapes and relative sizes. The clams, abalone, squid and octopus are easily identified. Fish that are illustrated in blue can be assumed to include sea bass, bonito/mackerel and sardines, and for those painted in red most are certainly sea bream (Figures 4 and 5).

Sea bream is sold in more than a few stalls, while a number of vendors and at least one customer are carrying it. Its prominence indicates its status in the fish market: Sea bream was a favourite food in Edo castle as well as among the *daimyō* lords and

Figure 3. Fishermen delivering fish at Nihonbashi.

the general populace (when they could afford it or were given permission to consume it).[16] It was prized for its red colour (considered festive and auspicious) and 'majestic' appearance, and was consumed in huge quantities during important rituals and celebratory occasions.[17]

The sea bream symbolized a dramatic shift in food tastes in the Edo era. Until this period in the seventeenth century, carp had been considered the 'king of fish', mostly due to its vaunted place in ancient legend that relates how a carp could be transformed into a dragon once it succeeds in jumping over a waterfall.[18] One could therefore embody the brave and magical qualities of the carp by consuming it. For more practical reasons, however, carp was a more readily available fish. As freshwater creatures, they could be raised and served fresh in the court at Kyoto, the ancient capital which is located inland. Carp was valued so highly that master chefs in the pre-Edo era (and even later) were required to attain skills in cutting and serving it in a variety of ways. One chef's training manual from 1649, the *Shijō ke hōchō shoroku* (Records of the Cuisine of the Shijo House), lists fifty-five ways for cutting and presenting carp, while other fish, including sea bream, are given only ten versions each.[19]

Edo, however, was located near the sea, and Edo castle was easily reached from the shore, whether by foot or through the capital's many canals. Nihonbashi's location just outside the castle moat and its direct access to the Edo bay ensured an abundant and regular delivery of fresh seafood of all kinds, not only from the seas near the bay, but also from different areas around the country. The shogun and his people were soon spoiled for choice. The Nihonbashi market scene depicted in *Edo-zu*, though

The Early Years of the World's Biggest Fish Market

Figure 4: Group of stalls near the bridge at Nihonbashi.

presumably idealized, is at least truthful in its illustrations of the many varieties of seafood available then.

It is also truthful in its prominent depiction of sea bream, since it was also during this era in the reign of the third shogun when a network exclusively for live sea bream distribution was created. In 1628, one year after Iemitsu became shogun, a certain Yamatoya Sukegoro from Nara in western Japan succeeded in monopolizing the sea bream catch in his region, as well as in transporting the fish live in boats equipped with technologically efficient tanks all the way to Edo in eastern Japan.[20] Sukegoro became an immensely wealthy man and retired in Edo, where he was given a residence across the river from the Nihonbashi market.[21]

Aside from the fish, one particular aspect about Nihonbashi market in *Edo-zu* deserves particular mention: we find almost no women in the market area, certainly not among the many shopkeepers, customers or vendors. The only women in Nihonbashi are seen walking near the intersection close to the vegetable stalls: they are in a group of four, two of them wearing veils (called *kasugi/kazuki*, the cloth worn by high-ranking women to cover their faces when they ventured outside), and the other two behind them (presumably their ladies-in-waiting). They look like they are merely passing through, not at all interested in any of the fish (Figure 6).

The absence of women in the main food market of Edo is not an anomaly. In the first place, the kitchens of the shogun and his subjects (the *daimyō* and other retainers) had only male chefs and kitchen managers; they and their assistants constituted the customer base of the fish market.[22] Fishing and business licenses were also granted exclusively to men, so the shopkeepers and fish vendors were invariably male. Such gender imbalance has been faithfully represented in *Edo-zu*'s Nihonbashi market.

Figure 5. Central area of the market in Nihonbashi.

Edo-zu itself is dominated by male figures, which is a reflection of the actual situation in Edo. Especially in its early years, Edo's population was predominantly male, mostly labourers who found work in the city's endless construction and engineering projects. While the *daimyō* did bring their wives (who brought their maids along as well) to Edo, they were also accompanied by hundreds of male retainers and other staff, who were unmarried or left their families behind in their hometowns, thereby further aggravating the gender imbalance.

These retainers and other samurai form the majority of the crowd walking around the Nihonbashi market. Except for one who carries a bird – not fish – in his hand, most of the samurai seem to be in Nihonbashi for reasons other than shopping. We see two of them talking to a shopkeeper in a well-stocked stall at a lower intersection; they are most likely checking market prices for Iemitsu, who was said to have been concerned with food price controls, especially for rice and fish.[23]

Edo-meisho-zu-byōbu [Famous Scenes of Edo Folding Screen]

We briefly turn to the *Edo-meisho-zu-byōbu* (Below, *Edo-meisho-zu*), which also depicts Nihonbashi during the same period, for the sake of comparison. The *Edo-meisho-zu*, like the *Edo-zu*, consists of a pair of folding screens with eight panels each. Each screen measures approximately 107 centimetres in height – considerably shorter than *Edo-zu* and the conventional folding screen – which it makes up for its length, about 488 centimetres each, a third longer than the traditional size.[24]

Like *Edo-zu*, too, it gives a bird's-eye view of the major districts of the capital. Unlike the *Edo-zu*, however, place names are not given in the *Edo-meisho-zu*. However, the

The Early Years of the World's Biggest Fish Market

Figure 6. Detail of the market in Nihonbashi, near the vegetable stalls.

artist utilizes the same conceit for partitioning the areas, that is, golden clouds through which the viewer observes the goings-on in the capital. The right screen of *Edo-meisho-zu* shows the Ueno and Asakusa areas on the farthest end, and traverses through the old district of Kanda toward Nihonbashi, which is depicted on the leftmost panel of the right screen and, thus, positioned in the centre. The left screen has Edo Castle on the rightmost panel, in the upper portion, which again grants it a central place in the work, as we have also seen in the *Edo-zu*. The positions of the Edo Castle and Nihonbashi in both the *Edo-zu* and the *Edo-meisho-zu* clearly attest to their roles as the political centre and the commercial centre, respectively, of the new capital.[25]

As for the Nihonbashi market area in *Edo-meisho-zu*, most of the activity is centred on and around the landmark Nihonbashi bridge. On it we find a similar slice of humanity (and some animals) as in *Edo-zu*: men and women travellers, samurai, labourers, beggars, monks (one sitting in the exact same spot as in *Edo-zu*) and others. The different classes and occupations of the people and their activities speak of the importance of Nihonbashi as the terminal station for travellers to and from Edo, which the artist (also unknown) strove to depict in this work. Under the bridge ply boats loaded with lumber and rice, presumably for unloading at Nihonbashi's banks. On the same spot as in *Edo-zu*, that is, at the foot of the bridge on the side leading to the market, we find again a crew of fishermen delivering their catches to waiting dealers and vendors on the banks. While their boats are full of blue fish (mackerel, perhaps), the fishermen are seen handling the red fish (sea bream, definitely) like precious objects, placing these in individual baskets and handing them over first before the other fish to the men on the banks.

Unfortunately for the present purposes, the fish market in Nihonbashi is invisible: most of it is under golden cloud cover, and the only stalls on view are the ones that sell lacquer ware near the bridge and on the main street. There are no vendors or shopkeepers, either, although there are again people from all walks of life walking on the main street: monks, street entertainers, travellers (one inside a palanquin) and a pair of men dressed like emissaries from the royal court in Joseon (present-day Korea).[26]

The omission of the Nihonbashi marketplace in *Edo-meisho-zu* does not mean that it was not important in the daily life of Edo. It rather emphasizes the different purposes for which *Edo-zu* and *Edo-meisho-zu* were painted: while *Edo-zu* was commissioned mainly to portray the level of urban development in the new capital in the early seventeenth century, the artist/s and patron/s for *Edo-meisho-zu* were more concerned with showing the various lifestyles and occupations of the people flocking the capital.[27] Indeed, there is much more detail in the clothing and equipment of the figures in the latter screen (*Edo-meisho-zu*), and more people involved in pastimes and other forms of recreation than actual work; we see more crowds and activity in the depictions of stage plays, boat parties, picnics, festivals and even fighting scenes. One detail in the Nihonbashi area is telling of this preoccupation with recreation in the *Edo-meisho-zu*: while the fish stalls on the ground floor are not shown, the upper floors are; one room with the sliding doors open is ready to welcome players for the board game of *go*, perhaps for the shopkeeper and his guest.

Conclusion

The different purposes notwithstanding, both the *Edo-zu* and the *Edo-meisho-zu* offer rich and multicoloured depictions of Edo city life in early seventeenth-century Japan. For now, they are the only visual representations of their kind available for Nihonbashi during the period. As a visual text for the market in Nihonbashi, however, *Edo-zu* is more detailed and informative, if not faithful to the actual market scene that developed soon after the establishment of the capital.

Many works on Nihonbashi in relation to its role as the central food market for Edo (as well as predecessor to the Tsukiji Fish Market) lament the scarcity of information for the history spanning its early years. Curiously, not too many studies, if any at all, have referred to the *Edo-zu* as a major source of historical information for Nihonbashi. The present study points to this possibility and the important role of the *Edo-zu* as a reference to fill in the blanks of history, especially with regard to the Nihonbashi market in Tokyo's earliest decades. By this period in its development, as we have seen from the brief discussion above, Nihonbashi was already Edo's fish centre, a role that is now played by Tsukiji for Tokyo and beyond. We can also determine that a system was already in place at this time, which is also the same period when the Japanese diet, especially for those who dictated food trends and tastes, was undergoing some dramatic changes. Further information should be gleaned from a more detailed analysis of the Nihonbashi market scene in the Scenes of Edo Folding Screen, which warrants further study.

The Early Years of the World's Biggest Fish Market

Notes

1. Nihonbashi also served as the terminal station for travellers to Edo. While present-day Tokyo now has several terminal stations located elsewhere, Nihonbashi is still the capital's point zero, as all distances from Tokyo are measured from the Nihonbashi bridge.
2. Japanese names in the main text appear in the traditional order, that is, surname first (Ando), followed by the given name (Hiroshige).
3. Theodore C. Bestor, *Tsukiji: The Fish Market at the Center of the World* (Berkeley: U California P, 2004); Issei Tomioka, 'The History of the Nihonbashi Uogashi: The Birth of the Wholesale Fish Market', *Food Culture*, 14 (2007); and Issei Tomioka, 'The History of the Nihonbashi Uogashi: The Popularity of Fish in Edo', *Food Culture* 15 (2008), pp. 8–14.
4. *Nihonbashi uoichiba enkaku kiyō* is considered the most comprehensive account of the history of the fish market in Nihonbashi (later Tsukiji). It was compiled by an employee of the fish market administrative office in 1889. See Kosaburo Omura, *Nihonbashi uogashi monogatari* [Story of the Nihonbashi Fish Quay] (Tokyo: Seiabo, 1984), p. 14.
5. Tomioka, 'The History of the Nihonbashi Uogashi: The Birth of the Wholesale Fish Market', p. 3. See also Bestor, *Tsukiji*, p. 102.
6. The sea around Tsukudajima has since been reclaimed, and presently it is no longer an island. Although residential towers now occupy much of the site of the former fishermen's establishments, the area is famous as the origin of the *tsukudani* [*ni*=simmer] delicacy, which is seafood and vegetables simmered in sweet soy sauce. *Tsukudani* is now made in many areas in Japan, although it is still one of the more popular food souvenirs bought by visitors to Tokyo.
7. Tomioka, 'The History of the Nihonbashi Uogashi', p. 5.
8. Tomioka, 'The History of the Nihonbashi Uogashi', p. 5.
9. Omura, *Nihonbashi uogashi monogatari*, p. 24.
10. The entire work cannot be reproduced here, but it is available for interactive viewing on the website of the National Museum of Japanese History, at: <http://www.rekihaku.ac.jp/education_research/gallery/webgallery/z_edozu/>.
11. Hiroshi Ozawa and Nobuhiko Maruyama, *Edo-zu-byobu wo yomu* [Reading the Scenes of Edo Folding Screen] (Tokyo: Kawade Shobo Shinsha, 1993), p. 6.
12. Hideo Kuroda, *Edo-zu byobu no nazo wo toku* [Solving the Riddle of the Scenes of Edo Folding Screen] (Tokyo: Kadokawa gakugei, 2010).
13. Makoto Suito and Takashi Kato, *Edo-zu-byōbu wo yomu* [Reading the Scenes of Edo Folding Screen] (Tokyo: Tokyodoshuppan, 2000), p. 170.
14. Turrets generally indicated the wealth of the residence's occupant. In 1649, the shogunate banned their construction in the merchant quarters, which included Nihonbashi. A huge fire, the Meireki conflagration of 1657, had destroyed many buildings with turrets. As such turrets are depicted in the buildings in *Edo-zu* as well as the *Edo-meisho-zu*, the city shown in both paintings (if not the date of the paintings' completion) is dated pre-1657, or much earlier.
15. This area is labelled 'Koami-cho', which then (as now) was part of the Nihonbashi district.
16. Zenjiro Watanabe, *Kyodai toshi Edo ga washoku wo tsukutta* [Edo Metropolis Created Japanese Food] (Tokyo: Nosangyoson bunka kyokai, 1988), p. 33.
17. Naoko Shimaoka, '*Tai*' [Sea bream], '*Tabemono no nihonshi soran*' [Overview of the Japanese History of Food], ed. M. Nishiyama (Tokyo: Shinjinbutsu oraisha, 1994), p. 205.
18. Naoko Shimaoka, '*Koi*' [Carp], '*Tabemono no nihonshi soran*', p.199.
19. Matsunosuke Nishiyama, *Edo Culture: Daily Life and Diversions in Urban Japan, 1600–1868*, trans. by Gerald Groemer (Honolulu: U Hawai'i P, 1997), p. 148.
20. Omura, *Nihonbashi uogashi monogatari*, p. 23.
21. Issei Tomioka, 'The History of the Nihonbashi Uogashi: The Popularity of Fish in Edo', p. 9.
22. Suito and Kato, *Edo-zu-byōbu wo yomu*, p. 132.
23. Suito and Kato, *Edo-zu-byōbu wo yomu*, p. 76.

24. The screens are in the collection of the Idemitsu Museum of Arts in Tokyo, and may be viewed at: <http://www.idemitsu.co.jp/museum/collection/introduction/painting/genre/genre03.html>.
25. Ozawa and Maruyama, *Edo-zu-byōbu wo yomu*, p. 32.
26. Shinzo Ogi and Makoto Takeuchi, *Edo-meisho-zu-byōbu no sekai* [World of the Scenes of Famous Places in Edo Folding Screen] (Tokyo: Iwanami shoten, 1992.), p. 69.
27. Masato Naito, *Edo-meisho-zu-byōbu* [Scenes of Famous Places in Edo Folding Screen] (Tokyo: Shogakukan, 2003), p. 120.

Blood and Sawdust: The Kosher Poultry Racket of New York

Andrew Coe

New York City's public markets have always enjoyed their share of criminal activity, including giving false weight, selling diseased meat and bribing health inspectors. However, large-scale, organized and often violent crime didn't enter the market system until the arrival of masses of poor immigrants from Italy and Eastern Europe in the late nineteenth century. The initial vector for this crime wave, which lasted at least half a century, was the sale of live chickens.

Before 1880, New York's marketplaces stocked a wide variety of poultry, including chickens, turkeys, ducks, geese and all kinds of game birds. Compared with beef and pork, chicken was a relatively minor part of the local diet. Most of the birds were displayed already slaughtered. Only in summer, when keeping meat fresh was more difficult, did butchers bring live birds directly to market. In the early 1880s, large numbers of Jewish immigrants began arriving in New York City; pogroms and other forms of anti-Semitism had driven them out of Russia, Poland, Rumania and other eastern European countries. Many settled on the Lower East Side, where they attempted to rebuild their traditional ways of working, worshipping and eating, while at the same time learning to navigate the local culture. They brought with them the custom of enjoying chicken for dinner every Friday evening at their Sabbath table. They found these birds in the tenement district pushcart markets, like this one on Bayard Street:

> Friday, market-day, is best calculated to reveal all the marked features of this peculiar region. Like the more extensive Jewish quarter east of the Bowery, this street has its itinerant merchants of cheap wares, its open fish stands, and its heaps of wooden cages crammed with tortured poultry, that no old woman fails to pull and squeeze, *en passant*, as if she were judging the merits of some inanimate thing.[1]

After buying a bird, an immigrant housewife would bring it, wings still flapping, to the nearest *shochet*, or kosher slaughterer. After making sure the bird was outwardly healthy, he would slit its throat, bleed the carcass and then examine its bones and internal organs to ensure they were free of defects. Only a kosher bird was fit for the Sabbath table.

Kosher meat has been prepared in New York since its days as New Amsterdam. In 1660, Asser Levy, a Sephardic Jew from Amsterdam, received one of the city's first butcher's licences and eventually operated his own slaughterhouse on the East River.

Food and Markets

He refused to trade in *trefa*, or non-kosher, products; on his death, his estate included a *chalef*, or knife for kosher slaughtering. During the eighteenth century, the city's small Jewish population relied on *shochetim* hired by synagogues to prepare meat and poultry purchased from butchers at the public markets. This led to one of the city's first kosher meat controversies, when Jews discovered market butchers were affixing kosher seals to meat that had not been killed by a *shochet*. Beginning in the 1840s, thousands of Jews escaping revolution and economic uncertainty in Central Europe began to stream into the city, swelling the Jewish population. Many found work as food purveyors, opening beer halls, restaurants, grocery stores and butcher shops selling kosher 'meat, poultry, smoked beef, tongues and sausages'.[2] By 1859, a butcher named Philip Friedman even had his own stand in the Essex Street Market, the largest public marketplace in what was becoming the Lower East Side's *Kleindeutschland*, or 'Little Germany'.

Public market butchers were among the élite of the city's nineteenth-century food system. They earned a comfortable living, celebrated the brotherhood of their trade through elaborate parades and holiday dinners and wielded political power far beyond their numbers. Although markets were overseen by the Department of Public Works, butchers were effectively able to avoid most regulation, thanks to their connection to the corrupt Tammany Hall political machine. In return for generous contributions, Tammany ward bosses helped them bend sanitary rules and block competition. On the Lower East Side, the Essex Street Market's most noted tenant was Martin 'Butcher' Engel, a German-Jewish poultry dealer who became one of the most powerful district leaders in Tammany Hall. He wore a diamond stickpin 'as big as a chestnut' on his shirtfront and on his fingers glimmered diamond rings representing the 'product of a great many barnyards'. By the time Engel retired in 1901, it was estimated that he was worth a half million dollars (over $13 million today). The glitter of his diamonds shone the way for many Jewish poultry dealers that followed.

In the last decades of the nineteenth century, the culture of the Lower East Side changed as masses of Eastern European immigrants crowded into the district's tenements. The vast majority of them were poor. For their Sabbath bird, they couldn't afford the price of an Essex Street Market chicken. However, most of them had grown up in Russian or Polish shtetls where nearly every family kept poultry. They soon began to raise chicken, ducks and geese in their tenement building's backyard or basement, or even their own apartments. This caught the notice of the city's Board of Health, which was then battling to clean up the city's slums:

> The Board of Health has carried on a struggle for some years, with occasional breathing spells for both combatants, against the practice of keeping poultry for sale in the manner practiced by the Polish and Russian Jews. On the plea that their religion requires them to eat only those fowls that have been killed in their sight by a killer authorized under their ritual, they fill the places where they live with chickens, turkeys, ducks, and geese. These poor fowls are huddled together

in coops, or crowded into pens, generally in the basement of the house, and make an incessant noise. The smell, too, from fifty or a hundred geese, is indescribable and intolerable. And yet these people live in an adjoining room, and wonder that any person finds their practice obnoxious. The floor, of course, is covered with excreta of the poultry, and, as the owners have always been used to living in filth, they would never think of cleaning their rooms, unless forced to do so by sanitary authorities.[3]

The Board of Health made it a practice to raid the tenement districts just before Jewish holidays, when everyone was out shopping and the need for birds was greatest:

When the health inspectors, having in charge the poultry branch of this department, come around, there is great excitement, and chickens are put under beds, in barrels, or on the roofs of houses; or they are taken up bodily, coop and all, and carted around the city until the inspector has gone, for he has authority to confiscate all poultry not kept away from the living places of people.[4]

In 1884, the Superintendent of the City Health Department convened a meeting with 17 of the most important rabbis to address the problem. The rabbis responded that, although keeping poultry in unsanitary conditions was contrary to kosher law, strict enforcement of sanitary codes would inflict 'a great hardship on many Israelites, whom religious scruples as to the freshness and general fitness of their poultry, compelled to buy of these middlemen who keep such a line [sic]'.[5] They suggested that the city build a special kosher slaughterhouse where Jews could pick out live birds and be assured that they were properly prepared. The Health Department soon established a kosher slaughterhouse and poultry market on Gouverneur Slip, down by the East Side docks. However, this market could not keep up with the demand for live poultry.

In 1889, the city opened the new West Washington Market, a complex of ten modern brick and terracotta structures built on a pier over the Hudson River at the end of West 12th Street. A parade highlighted the market's opening day, complete with marching bands, gaily decorated carts and over a thousand marketmen marching up Broadway, culminating in a splendid banquet in the structure. A week later, the city's new mayor, Hugh J. Grant, ordered the first investigation of the West Washington Market, over corrupt assignment of market stalls. The backdrop to this was a political power play by Mayor Grant, who was an ally of Tammany Hall boss Richard Croker. An Irish immigrant who had fought his way up from poverty, Croker once bluntly told a journalist: 'Politics are impossible without spoils.'[6] The city's cultured élite might prefer a government that served citizens honestly and without bias, but Croker believed that the city's immigrant masses only understood money and jobs. Grant and Croker were determined to give them their spoils – in this case, jobs at the city's public markets – and line their pockets at the same time. Mayor Grant's West Washington Market investigation impelled many of its targets (all appointees of the previous administration) to flee town in order to avoid indictment, allowing Tammany to appoint its own men as market overseers.

Tammany control was a double-edged sword for market vendors. The downside was that ward bosses, officials and even policemen were constantly after them for 'donations': 'The collector has even made his appearance among the well-to-do merchants of West Washington Market, who are contributing money that Tammany wants to debauch the election, because they fear the vengeance of the police and the other Tammany officials who may interfere with their traffic.'[7] The upside was that allegiance to Tammany had its perks, because the machine controlled not only public market regulators but also many policemen, prosecutors and even judges. This was extremely useful if a group of businessmen wanted to assert control of, say, the live poultry industry. New York State's Donnelly Anti-Trust Act of 1899 prohibited monopolies in 'articles of common use'. But between 1899 and 1906, newspapers printed repeated rumours that a 'chicken trust' was setting prices and trying to drive independent dealers out of business, with Tammany help: 'Tammany city officials are protecting the trust and will not grant a permit to any one to kill chickens unless the person is in the trust. The trust members meet every Monday and fix the wholesale prices that are to be charged for the week. If any member sells at lower than the fixed price he is liable to expulsion.'[8] A group of small dealers complained to the U.S. District Attorney, who agreed there was a violation of anti-trust law. He passed them on to the Manhattan District Attorney William T. Jerome, who claimed he saw no grounds to prosecute. Meanwhile, the newspapers joked:

> John Smith No. 1 stole one chicken. He was sent to jail for thirty days. While there he reformed and became another man. He became John Smith No. 2. John Smith No. 2 organized a chicken trust, took two million chickens as his fee for organizing it and sold the chickens when the market was at its highest. Then he was enabled to endow the jail with a library.[9]

In the two decades after the opening of the market, the city's wholesale live poultry business grew rapidly. Between 1881 and 1910, more than 1.5 million Jewish immigrants arrived in the United States; many settled on the Lower East Side or in Brooklyn or the Bronx. Almost every family purchased at least one live chicken a week. Between 1905 and 1911, the number of train carloads of live poultry arriving in New York City, each carrying as much as 20,000 pounds of chicken, jumped from 2000 to 4000 a year. At the same time, the City Health Department finally managed to rid Jewish slums of most unregulated tenement poultry farms, driving the chicken trade even more securely into the arms of West Washington Market dealers. When the market first opened, it also housed meat and vegetable stalls, liquor dealers and a restaurant; by 1910, the live poultry trade was rapidly colonizing the entire complex, which became known as 'Chicken Village'. Most birds came from the Midwest aboard specially designed freight cars. They arrived at the West Side rail yards and then were hauled by wagon or motor truck down to the West Washington Market. Here, the big commission merchants purchased the birds and then quickly resold them to slaughterhouses and butcher shops, mainly in the city's Jewish neighbourhoods. Operating at the crucial nexus between farmers and New York's retailers and consumers, the commission merchants were in position to control the live poultry industry. They organized the New York Live Poultry Merchants' Protective Association, which in 1906 was recognized as the principal vehicle for the chicken trust:

> This combine regulates the price of live poultry. It not only wants to drive fair men out of business. It not only gets the city to help, through one of its departments, but it gets the Health Department to help…. The slaughter houses, which get permits from the Health Commissioner to kill poultry of everybody, discriminate in favor of the combine, and actually refuse to kill live poultry for the independent dealers.[10]

In 1910, one of those independent dealers turned the tables on the chicken trust.[11] The case began when members of the live poultry association sued a dealer named Barnet Baff for non-payment of bills. When Baff's lawyer learned how the industry operated, he turned around and accused the plaintiffs of conspiring in a trust. He produced affidavits stating that the only way that Baff could buy from the association's dealers was to give them a $1000 deposit and agree to let them fix prices. The association also paid slaughterhouses $100 a week not to kill birds for any dealer blacklisted by the trust. One dealer swore that he heard the association's president tell a meeting of the commission merchants: 'I am now king of the poultry business. I hold in my hand an iron rod. My word is law. My quotations are to be supreme to anybody or any concern that is now in this business. We, brothers, have only to stick together and we will crush anybody or anything that dares to oppose us.'[12]

By then it was common knowledge that the poultry trade was a particularly rough and tumble business. One poultry expert observed: 'I have been astonished at mean business tricks some of these men play on each other, especially in the way of stealing customers and killing trade, and know that in some cases the patrons at both ends of the line have been disgusted when they learned the details of these tricks.'[13] Barnet Baff, however, was apparently fearless. Following his accusations, eighty-six Jewish poultry dealers were charged in state court with 'conspiracy to raise prices and violation of the Donnelly anti-trust law'. The chief counsel for the defence was William T. Jerome, the same man who as district attorney had told the independent dealers that he saw no evidence of a trust. After a tumultuous trial, at which Barnet Baff was the star witness, thirteen of the commission merchants were found guilty. The judge sentenced them to three months in jail and $500 fines, with this admonishment:

> A conspiracy to monopolize and control a food product is a mean and insidious crime stealthily committed usually, if not always, by men who masquerade in the garb of good repute, but in whose breasts the quality of common morality

has been stifled by the most despicable form of greed. It is the kind of crime on which merchants grow fat at the expense of the poor and helpless consumers. The motives which induced these defendants to disregard public interest was selfish aggrandizement regardless of law.[14]

After the trial, the retail price of live chickens dropped more than three cents a pound. However, these convictions did not deter illegality in the wholesale live poultry trade. The thirteen men remained free pending appeal and immediately returned to the poultry trade. They were determined to strike back at Barnet Baff. And he, it turned out, was not afraid of using aggressive business tactics himself. Baff began buying directly from Midwestern farmers, cutting out commission merchants altogether. To process and sell the birds, he also opened his own slaughterhouses or sometimes sold the chickens directly to butchers at a big discount. He even purchased his own fleet of motor trucks to transport the birds. All of this succeeded in antagonizing wholesalers, slaughterhouses and teamsters – in short, the entire wholesale poultry industry. In 1913, they finally saw an opening to attack Baff when *shochetim* discovered something odd about his birds.

When shipments of Baff's poultry arrived at slaughterhouses, workers noticed that the birds were listless and had no appetite, and their crops and stomachs were strangely distended. Upon dissection, they were discovered to be stuffed full of sand and gravel. The commission merchants appealed to the Kehillah, a community council of the city's Jewish leaders, which sent a lawyer named Elias B. Goodman to investigate. He attended a meeting of West Washington Market poultry dealers where the crowd accused Baff of ruining their businesses; a woman named Mrs. Pishkosh shouted that Baff 'ought to be drowned'. Goodman soon discovered how Baff had devised a method for adding weight to his birds. When Baff's chickens were shipped from the Midwest, every rail car had a special compartment for a workman whose job was to make sure that the birds were fed and watered. As the train approached New York, the workman would starve the birds for 24 hours. An hour before the chickens were scheduled to be off-loaded, the worker would mix up a feed of a little corn and grain and a lot of sand and gravel and place it in the birds' feeding troughs. The birds immediately gorged themselves, gaining as much as eight ounces in a matter of minutes – a practice known as 'overcropping'. Goodman estimated that every week New Yorkers were purchasing between 150,000 and 300,000 pounds of sand and gravel with their birds. Goodman and the poultry dealers brought this practice to the attention of Jewish leaders, the Humane Society, the U. S. Department of Agriculture and the news media. Four of the chicken feeders, but not Baff, were arrested and fined. The practice of overcropping, however, continued.

Frustrated at their inability to stop Baff & Son, workers at the West Washington Market resorted to more desperate measures. By now, Baff's many enemies also included the market's 'chicken pullers', a particularly tough breed of men who offloaded poultry from rail cars into coops. In May 1913, they broke into and ransacked one of Baff's stores. Next a chicken puller walked up behind Baff's son Harry and bashed him on the head with a lead pipe. Two months later, Joe Cohen, the so-called 'King of the Chicken Pullers,' paid a local thug named Frank Burke $300 to place a bomb below the porch at Baff's Long Island summer house. Luckily, the fuse had been poorly set and failed to explode.

In the immigrant business world of that era, Joe Cohen's hiring of a gangster to help gain an edge over the competition was not an anomaly but a common practice. Harry W. Newburger, deputy commissioner of police in the reform administration of Mayor Gaynor, commented:

> It is claimed, with much truth, that the small merchant originally in the keen race for a livelihood to which he was subjected in the crowded section, stopped at nothing to destroy his competitor. He hired young men of criminal tendencies, as yet undeveloped, to carry his schemes into effect. Fear of consequences together with the recognition of official indifference sealed the lips of the victim. He retaliated in kind. All forms of oppression were practiced on each other, and the strongest survived. Small associations of employees unable to secure by fair means demands proper or improper, as the case might be, resorted to the use of the gangster to intimidate, blackmail and assault their employers. Employers in return, due to the totally inadequate protection given them by the police, as a matter of self preservation, were forced to pursue similar measures as a means of defense.[15]

In fact, the next front in the war against Barnet Baff was a labour dispute, which began when *schochetim* and other poultry workers on the Lower East Side banded together into the Live Poultry Workers Union and demanded not only a raise but also jobs at the West Washington Market. All the big poultry merchants refused, except Barnet Baff, who signed a contract with the union. The real sticking point was over jobs, because West Washington Market workers were already members of a competing union. One day, two automobiles filled with East Side gangsters, led by one Jack Sirocco, pulled up at the market, looking to put a scare in any worker who wasn't a member of the Live Poultry Workers Union. Sirocco was then a noted gangster-for-hire, adept at everything from running security at six-day bicycle races to breaking heads and strong-arming either side of labour disputes. Joe Cohen claimed that Barnet Baff had hired gangsters in order to further destroy the poultry dealers' business. In retaliation, West Washington Market workers showed up at arbitration meetings with pistols under their coats and displayed them to the East Side opposition. It soon appeared that both sides in this dispute had gangsters under contract: 'During the few days of the lockout or strike, the following characters were seen in or about the Union headquarters, the West Washington Market and Essex Market Court: "Dopey Al," "Cockeyed Meyer," "Long Alderman," "Nigger," several members of the Sorocco [sic] gang and the teamsters huskies of the West Washington Market'.[16]

Food and Markets

Despite the best efforts of the Kehillah to arbitrate, in 1914 disputes worsened between Baff and his competitors. For members of the New York Live Poultry Dealers Association, the last straw was when thirteen of them lost the appeal of their anti-trust conviction and had to report to prison. At a meeting, they decided that they had finally had enough of Barnet Baff. They all chipped into a fund, totalling $5000, to have him murdered. The scheme's planners determined that the perfect venue would be the West Washington Market, where Baff had an office, because 'every one in the marked hated him and not one would lift his finger to frustrate the plot nor ever "squeal" about what might be seen in connection with the murder'.[17] The head of the chicken pullers, Joe Cohen, contacted an Italian saloonkeeper he knew from Harlem and told him what they needed. The bar owner rounded up a team of recent Italian immigrants – not too smart and willing to do anything for money – to do the actual killing. Around 5:50 pm on November 24th, Baff received a mysterious phone call that drew him out of his office. As Baff walked down one of the alleys separating the market buildings, a market worker named Moe Rosenstein, aka 'Chicken Moe,' signalled to the killers that their target was approaching. They stepped out of hiding and shot Barnet Baff point blank through his back, piercing his heart. The gunmen ran past a number of workmen, all of whom claimed they saw nothing, jumped into a waiting car and made their escape.

The Baff murder marked the opening of an era, lasting at least until 1940, when gangsters seized control of New York's city's food industry. As Harry Newburger foresaw, 'Those very instruments of destruction and intimidation so easily encouraged in crime were quick to realize their importance commercially, and the vast possibilities of the game or "graft" as it is called in the underworld.'[18] The city's food 'rackets,' as they became known, began in the public markets. In their earliest years, they were intimately connected with the culture and culinary habits of specific ethnic communities. The kosher poultry racket was entwined with the Jewish population's religious and economic life, while the organization of the Italian artichoke racket followed the practices of the Black Hand, the precursor to the Italian Mafia. By the late nineteen-twenties, however, gangsters became so emboldened that they looked beyond their own communities and close-knit food trades and expanded into the larger market economy. In the early, desperate years of the Great Depression, criminals controlled milk, fish, poultry, bread, fruit and vegetables, jacking up prices when people could afford it least. It was only a concerted attack on municipal corruption and federal prosecution of the gangsters, along with reorganization of the markets, by Mayor Fiorello La Guardia and Special Prosecutor Thomas Dewey, that finally brought the era of New York City's food rackets to an end.

Blood and Sawdust: The Kosher Poultry Racket of New York

Notes

1. Bijur, Nathan, 'Among the Tenements,' *The Jewish Messenger*, New York, 24 April 1885, p. 5.
2. Display ad, *The Jewish Messenger*, New York, 9 April 1858, p. 64.
3. Buck, Albert H., *A Treatise of Hygiene and Public Health* (New York: William Wood & Company, 1879), p. 400.
4. Lawrence, Joshua S., 'The Jews of New York,' *Ballou's Monthly Magazine*, November, 1883, p. 466.
5. 'An Abbatoir For Poultry,' *The American Hebrew*, 8 August 1884, p. 10.
6. Lothrop Stoddard, *Master of Manhattan, The Life of Richard Croker* (New York: Longmans, Green and Co., 1931), p. 77.
7. 'Plain Truths From Moss,' *The New York Times*, 4 November 1898, p. 3.
8. 'A Chicken Trust And A Prune Trust,' *St. Louis Post-Dispatch*, 7 September 1900, p. 6.
9. 'No. 1 And No. 2,' *New-York Tribune*, 21 September 1902, p. 16.
10. 'Cantor Finds A 'Trust,' *New-York Tribune*, 14 December 1906, p. 4.
11. Joselit, Jenna, *Our Gang*, Bloomington: Indiana University Press, 1983, pp. 130–132.
12. 'Poultry Trust Alleged,' *Baltimore Sun*, 9 February 1910, p. 9.
13. 'Produce Dealers' Trust,' *Rural New Yorker*, 21 August 1909, p. 763.
14. 'Poultry Trust Men Get Prison Terms,' New York Times, 17 August 1911, p. 3.
15. Newburger, Harry W., 'The Gangster in Business,' *The American Hebrew*, 8 January 1915, p. 267.
16. Goodman, Elias B., 'The Poultry Situation, the Rule of Gangsters,' September 1913, p. 8, Mayor John P. Mitchel Papers, New York City Municipal Archives, Box 196.
17. 'Cardinale Tells How Baff Was Shot Down by Gunmen,' *New-York Tribune*, June 23, 1917, p. 14.
18. Newburger.

Maniva Ecochefs: Forging a New Link between Producers and Consumers in an Organic Street Market in Rio de Janeiro

Daniel Coelho, Fátima Portilho and Maria Teresa Corção

This paper tries to contribute to studies that analyse new ways to obtain food by promoting short food supply chains and direct sales that bring together small farmers and urban consumers. The main innovation is in analysing the participation of chefs in the relationship between these actors. For such analysis, we turned to the theories of sociology of consumption and economic sociology, choosing as a case study the activities carried out by the Ecochefs of the Instituto Maniva, a non-governmental organization established in 2007 in Rio de Janeiro, Brazil.

The main trends in food consumption point to the promotion of products and productive processes considered 'traditional and authentic', reflecting an idealization of the rural based on the expansion of the urban-industrial system, within which a small farmer is often seen as the main actor in sustainability.

Another strong trend observed in contemporary societies is the search for a 'healthy' diet, as a result of food scandals, increasing chronic cardiovascular diseases, aging populations, widespread fast ways of living, changes in aesthetic body standards in Western societies and the global epidemic of obesity (Flandrin and Montanari, 1998; Wilk, 2006).

In addition, there is a tendency to gourmetization, which means restoring the pleasure of cooking and eating by popularizing fine cooking simultaneously with the promotion of recipes and ingredients.

Protected designation of origin, sustainability, healthfulness and gourmetization are some of the trends informing consumers' actions, competing for space in their dishes (Barbosa, 2009). Such trends are also observed in the action of several social movements organized around food that seek to impact family farming and the organic produce market. Several academic studies have been analysing these movements (Oosterveer and Spaargaren, 2011), emphasizing in general the action of urban consumer groups and their connections to agro-ecology, food safety and family farming. This paper tries to introduce a new element in this scenario, highlighting the support chefs can give to the rural and family farming 'cause' and their role as mediators between farmers and consumers.

Maniva Ecochefs

The Instituto Maniva

In October 2001, while still under the impact of the attack to the Twin Towers in New York, members of the slow food movement gathered in Oporto, Portugal, to award a prize to thirteen initiatives that preserve heritage food from different countries.

The Brazilian chef Teresa Corção was there and something caught her attention: a smiling farmer from Afghanistan walked back and forth with a jar, offering participants a taste of a strange grey paste. This paste was made of poppy seeds, from the same plants being destroyed by American aircraft, destruction that left the farmers who lived on poppy crops without food and work.

Teresa suddenly understood the relationships between food and culture and food and politics. She observed that, as a chef, her work could help improve small farmers' activities and produce in Brazil. After some research, she found a Brazilian food that, although traditionally linked to the people, attracted little gastronomic interest: the manioc. Manioc is a tuberous root of the genus *Manihot*, widely used in Brazilian cuisine, and maniva is the name for the manioc stem. Despite being the most cultivated crop in family farming, manioc was considered a 'poor man's meal'.

Motivated by her passion for Brazilian cuisine and by her experiences in Portugal, Teresa founded the Instituto Maniva (Maniva Institute), aiming at restoring the value of this heritage food. Some chefs joined her, forming the group Maniva Ecochefs, socio-environmentally responsible cooks with a mission to shrink the food production chain in a sustainable way by bringing together producers and consumers. Today, the Instituto Maniva has seventeen Ecochefs.

To accomplish its mission, the Instituto Maniva joined the Circuito Carioca de Feiras Orgânicas (Carioca Circuit of Organic Street Markets), an initiative established as part of public policy to encourage organic food production and consumption, with a total of eleven street markets in different neighbourhoods of the city of Rio Janeiro, Brazil. The Instituto Maniva works in three of these street markets, selling organic *tapioca*, a heritage food made of manioc.

The Parceiro do Agricultor project

The role of chefs as mediators in the relationship between small family farmers and urban consumers and restaurants can be observed in the project Parceiro do Agricultor (Farmer's Partner), developed by Maniva Ecochefs, led by Teresa Corção, in the Circuito Carioca de Feiras Orgânicas do Rio de Janeiro.

In the Jardim Botânico street market, Maniva Ecochefs have a stand next to fruit and vegetable stalls. The Ecochefs buy organic produce directly from farmers and sell food produced with these ingredients, using traditional Brazilian recipes recreated by themselves. In this way, they try to bring together producers and consumers by developing new recipes that value organic family production and consumers' food practice.

Moreover, the project Parceiro do Agricultor locates restaurants near street markets and tries to encourage their owners to buy organic produce directly from farmers. Based

Figure 1. The logo of the project 'Parceiro do Agricultor'.

on their experience, Maniva Ecochefs work with restaurant owners to develop feasible logistics strategies to deliver products to the restaurants. One of their challenges is to make this project economically viable, with a competitive edge for both rural producers and restaurant owners. Aiming at providing better information and guaranteeing the best price and product delivery, the Instituto Maniva has to understand the production skills of rural producers to set prices and determine how products will be delivered to meet the restaurants' needs.

Consuming produce from farms close to major urban centres usually generates a smaller carbon footprint, thanks to reduced energy expenditure in transportation. However, most produce comes from small farms without standardized production. In this changing supply and demand situation, Ecochefs play an important role in shaping consumers' 'taste' for the products offered by small farmers because a chef's opinion can influence consumers.

Chefs are considered to have a legitimate monopoly on 'good taste', conveying credibility and effectively certifying the quality of a product. Consequently, given variable organic production, chefs help balance the relationship between production and consumption, and at the same time help small farmers to sell their production and build consumers 'taste' by promoting new recipes and ways of using seasonal produce.

In this project, it seems chefs, farmers, consumers, and restaurants build a singular 'field'. This field, for Fligstein (2001), would be formed by shared rules and meanings that delineate social relations and determine one's place in these relations. By providing a cognitive structure for these actors, the field orients their interactions and shapes the meanings that will be used to interpret each other's behaviour. The theory of fields thus helps us understand how social orders are created, sustained and transformed in the relationships between farmers, chefs, consumers and restaurant owners.

The logo of the project 'Parceiro do Agricultor' (Figure 1) tries to represent visually the collaboration between farmers, represented by a hoe, and consumers, represented by a fork.

Street markets

Contemporary Brazilian street markets are the result of a long evolution which dates back to their Iberian origins and was redefined in the urban context of the hygienic rationality of the Belle Époque. Today's street markets are often accused of obsolescence because of automobiles and supermarkets. However, street markets persist and offer a singular experience of sociability in public space (Dolzani and Mascarenhas, 2008).

Street markets are part of a broader system of agricultural commercialization responsible for coordinating production, distribution and consumption. With regard to family farming, for example, often insufficient capitalization emphasizes the sales needed to pay for the goods and services consumed by households and to buy the necessary inputs for the next production cycle (Pierri, 2010).

In Brazil, street markets are important weekly events organized by municipalities as a public service for selling local basic produce (Mascarenhas, 1991). In Rio de Janeiro, street markets began in the context of urban modernity at the turn of the twentieth century, during the great urban reform implemented by Mayor Pereira Passos. Gradually, street markets became popular territories and are now present virtually throughout the urban fabric, from wealthy residential areas to distant, pauperized neighbourhoods on the metropolitan outskirts.

Given this relevance, street markets should be a subject for academic consideration and an object of public policy intervention (Sacco dos Anjos et al., 2005). Research on street markets would generate important data for governments to act on by providing relevant information on their function and by strengthening their role in economic activities. Street markets are a much-used resource for regular domestic supply of fresh produce and special products, despite the growing importance of supermarkets. The survival of street markets in this context may indicate that, besides the economic aspect, the cultural and symbolic aspects of a street market are leading characters in consumers' interests. Street markets represent not only a local system of commercialization, but they are also part of a true regional tradition that play a major social role in protecting some marked cultural traits of the city.

Street markets also have additional singular elements not observed in other spaces of commerce. Familial relationships, reciprocal affection, knowledge exchange, price negotiation and customized service are characteristics that consumers value in street markets. Many street markets have a symbolic image linked to the nature and the rural world that blurs the threshold between the rural and the urban, between the end of production and the beginning of consumption (Pierri, 2010).

Organic street markets are spaces to buy food considered healthy. However, what counts as a 'healthy food' is learned cognitively, culturally and ideologically. In her study on organic market consumers, Portilho (2009) shows that the representation of 'healthy eating' is linked primarily to the absence of agrochemicals and food additives, expressed in ideas like 'natural' and 'pure', for example. Moreover, this representation is associated to other attributes, such as a production system understood as 'traditional', which is not harmful to the environment or the small-scale producer.

For Portilho, these representations sum up ideas built on the naturalist demands of the 1960s, which were carried to the following decades as a form of 'resistance to the industrialization processes of food production,' denounced and publicized especially by Rachel Carson in her famous book *Silent Spring*. In this book, Carson denounces the health risks posed by the indiscriminate use of chemicals in agriculture. Although dealing with an extremely technical issue, Carson's book became a best-seller, a landmark of a widespread counter-cultural movement that favours 'natural' or 'organic' products (McCormick, 1992). Dória (2007) remembers that even the *nouvelle cuisine* of the 1970s, with its 'return to the simple' and appreciation for local produce, ended up restoring that ideal, although in a sophisticated way to fulfil the desires of the élite.

Therefore, organic eating emerges as a solution to the anxieties and fears of modern eating generated by new food manufacturing processes and the additives used in them (Goodman et al., 1987). Authors such as Miller (2002) and Warde (2005) remind us that some consumer practices require individual abilities, as well as some degree of devotion and attention to specific behaviours. Consequently, opting for and engaging in organic eating presuppose adherence to some values, the result of a process of initiation and learning, as well as easy access to specialized knowledge and information (Portilho, 2009).

Therefore, street markets are spaces to purchase foods considered 'pure' and to promote shorter food supply chains through direct sales that bring together small-scale rural producers and urban consumers. Portilho (2010) considers organic street markets as 'consumption junctions', an expression coined by Stolle et al. (2005) and Spaargaren (2006) – that is, a location where it is possible to find all actors of the food system: farmers, middlepeople and consumers. Organic street markets can be seen as a complete organism, a meeting place where one can build knowledge, abilities and relationships in a space of face-to-face interaction and trust. Portilho (2010) defines the organic street market as a 'physical, political, affective, and moral organisation; a meeting place that allows for concrete social relationships and exchanges in a circle of social interaction and conviviality, sociability [...], interaction, socialization, association, belonging, and expression of world views, lifestyles, desires, proposals, dreams and utopias' (Portilho, 2010, p. 70). Based on this concept, we tried to examine the participation of chefs in organic street markets as a link between farmers and urban consumers and restaurants.

The politicization of food

Reflecting transformations in global agro-food markets, a broader perception and dissemination of food risks, growing environmental concerns and the politicization of consumption, the political aspect of eating has been spilling into the private, everyday sphere of food consumption (Portilho et al., 2011). For this reason, eating has shifted from a private issue, linked to individual and family preferences, to a topic on the public agenda, with ethical, moral and political dimensions that place on consumers the responsibility for the impact of their choices on their personal health, on the environment and on the lives of small-scale rural producers (Portilho, 2009).

Such dimensions are related not only to the emergence of food ideologies (e.g. vegetarianism, veganism, raw foodism and organic or agro-ecological eating), but also to new forms of food preparation and to the places where food is purchased. Appreciation for the origin of a product can be an expression of the politicization of consumption. According to Barbosa (2009), the politicization of the food market was underlined in the eighties, with the expansion of market certification processes. Today, this type of commerce is widespread, and customers are interested not only in product quality, but also in the need for minimally fair trade. Thus, the organic street market is also an expression of the politicization of consumption, since it tries to mobilize values, people and organizations. Many consumers have been using their power of choice to try and modify market relations, intending to make them fairer. But how can an organic street enter this context called political consumption?

The politicization of consumption means that consuming becomes a practice perceived as a way of participating in a field of debates about what and how the society produces, as well as about the meanings and forms of use of its production. In this context, eating becomes a space for political debates (Portilho and Barbosa, in press).

Daily and home consumption practices have acquired the dimension of a politicized transaction, for they include a perception of the socio-environmental impacts and the power asymmetry involved in production and commercial relations. Signs of such transformations can be seen in the construction of new forms of political action both in the private sphere, by means of 'conscious' or 'responsible' choices, and in the public sphere, by means of consumer movements, consumer cooperatives, labelling systems and participatory certification systems, among other examples. As Portilho and Barbosa (in press) note,

'In political consumption, consumers "lend" their purchasing power to social movements to express their concerns effectively and incisively, at the same time as they increase the possibilities of sanctioning those who run their businesses in an unsustainable and unethical way. Political consumption is a form of collectivizing consumers' individual choices.'

Chefs and farmers

Chefs and small farmers represent the contraposition of two different mindsets: one is urban, with ideals of urban life and a view of eating as an aesthetic process of gustatory pleasure; the other is linked to the rural world and its singularity. Chefs have social status and represent the distinction of refined taste. As for small farmers, in most cases, they are associated with strenuous manual work, lack of social recognition, rudimentary techniques and backwardness. Usually separated, chefs and farmers occupy different spaces in the food chain.

The activities the Ecochefs promote in organic street markets try to take these two actors away from their original social places. Chefs are invited to meet farmers, to know the origins of the raw material of their work and, consequently, promote products and producers, whereas small farmers are called 'gourmets', in an attempt to level the relationship between them.

The Ecochefs took the initiative to create the project Parceiro do Agricultor to bring together farmers and urban consumers. This project is based on a methodology of exchange and innovation in the commercialization network formed by agro-ecological family farmers, consumers, and restaurant owners in the city of Rio de Janeiro. Chef Teresa Corção and the Instituto Maniva, through this project, exemplify the close partnership between these different spheres, which previously had been kept apart. The project helps bring together actors who occupy different fields in the food system, but who are part of the same productive chain, and tries to level their relationships by placing small-scale producers at the heart of the productive chain.

After this project, the Jardim Botânico street market started to be considered an expansion of the 'consumption junction', gathering chefs and restaurant owners, as well as farmers, middlepeople and consumers.

The Maniva Ecochefs place themselves as mediators in this relationship, helping to form the 'taste' of the consumers who attend the street market regularly. They create innovative fillings for traditional *tapiocas*, using products sold in the same street market, to promote a Brazilian heritage food, the manioc, and to encourage consumers to adopt a healthier diet. Moreover, they help to balance the relation between production and consumption and, consequently, help to find a market for the production of small organic farms. Most innovatively, Ecochefs try to attract local restaurant owners to the rural and family farming 'cause' to expand the movement.

References

Barbosa, L. 2009. 'Tendências da alimentação contemporânea', in *Juventude Consumo & Educação*, ed. by J. K. Pacheco and M. L. Pinto (Porto Alegre: ESPM).
Bourdieu, P. 1983. 'Gostos de classe e estilos de vida'. *Bourdieu*. Ed. by R. Ortiz. Trans. by Paula Montero (São Paulo: Ática. Col. Grandes Cientistas Sociais, n. 39).
———. 1984. *Distinction: A Social Critique of the Judgement of Taste*. Trans. by Richard Nice (Cambridge, MA: Harvard UP).
Canclini, N. G. 2001. *Consumers and Citizens: Globalization and Multicultural Conflicts*. (Minneapolis: U Minnesota P).
Dolzani, M. C. S., and G. Mascarenhas. 2008. 'Feira Livre: Territorialidade popular e cultura na metrópole contemporânea'. *Revista Ateliê Geográfico* 2.2 (August), pp. 72–87.
Dória, C. A. 2007. 'A economia política do *terroir*: o estado e a 'magia' do produto'. Seminar 'Pensando o consumo hoje: novas abordagens' (São Paulo: ESPM/CAEPM).
Flandrin, J. L., and M. Montanari. 2013. *Food: A Culinary History*. Trans. by Clarissa Botsford et al. (New York: Columbia UP).
Fligstein, N. 2001. 'Social Skill and the Theory of Fields'. *Sociological Theory* 19.2, pp. 105–25.
Goodman, D., B. Sorj and J. Wilkinson. 1987. *From farming to biotechnology: A theory of agro-industrial development*. (Oxford: Basil Blackwell).
Mascarenhas, G. 1991. 'O lugar da feira livre na grande cidade capitalista: Conflito, mudança e persistência'. Master's thesis submitted to the Post-Graduate Programme of Geography of the Federal University of Rio de Janeiro.
McCormick, J. 1992. *Rumo ao paraíso: A história do movimento ambientalista*. Trans. by Marco Antonio Esteves da Rocha e Renato Aguiar (Rio de Janeiro: Relume-Dumará).
Oosterveer, P., and G. Spaargaren. 2011. 'Organising Consumer Involvement in the Greening of Global Food Flows: The Role of Environmental NGOs in the Case of Marine Fish'. *Environmental Politics* 20.1, pp. 97–114.
Pierri, M. C. Q. M. 2010. 'A feira livre como canal de comercialização de produtos da agricultura familiar'. PCT IICA/MDA – NEAD, 48º Congresso da SOBER, Campo Grande (MS).
Portilho, F. 2005. *Sustentabilidade ambiental, consumo e cidadania*. (São Paulo: Cortez).
———. 2009. 'Sociabilidade, confiança e consumo na feira de produtos orgânicos', in *Consumo: cosmologias e sociabilidades*, ed. by L. Barbosa, F. Portilho, and L. Veloso. (Rio de Janeiro: Mauad X; Seropédica: EDUR), pp. 61–86.
———. 2010. 'Self-Attribution of Responsibility: Consumers of Organic Foods in a Certified Street Market in Rio de Janeiro/Brazil'. *Etnográfica*, 14.3 (October), pp. 549–65.
Portilho, F., and L. Barbosa. in press. 'A adesão à 'causa' rural e da agricultura familiar por consumidores e seus movimentos organizados', in F. C. Marques, M. Conterato, and S. Schneider. *Construção de mercados para a agricultura familiar: desafios para o desenvolvimento rural* (s.l.: s.n.).
Portilho, F., M. Castaneda and I.R.R. Castro. 2011. 'A alimentação no contexto contemporâneo: consumo, ação política e sustentabilidade'. *Revista Ciência e Saúde Coletiva*. Thematic issue 'Alimentação e Nutrição em Saúde Coletiva', 16.1, pp. 99–106.
Sacco dos Anjos, F., W.I. Godoy and N.V. Caldas. 2005. *As feiras-livres de Pelotas sob o império da globalização: perspectivas e tendências* (Pelotas: Editora e Gráfica Universitária).
Spaargaren, G. 2006. 'The Ecological Modernization of Social Practices at the Consumption Junction'. Discussion paper for the ISA-RC-24 conference 'Sustainable Consumption and Society', Madison, Wisconsin, June 2–3.
Stolle, D., M. Hooghe and M. Micheletti. 2005. 'Politics in the Supermarket: Political Consumerism as a Form of Political Participation'. *International Political Science Review* 26.3, pp. 245–69.
Warde, A. 2005. 'Consumption and theories of practice'. *Journal of Consumer Culture* 5.2, pp. 131–53.
Wilk, R. (ed.). 2006. *Fast Food, Slow Food: The Cultural Economy of the Global Food System* (Plymouth: Altamira).

Catalan Markets: Constructing National Cuisine and Space through the Market Scene

Venetia Congdon

Catalonia is an autonomous community in north-east Spain. It has long had a sense of difference from the rest of Spain, demarcated particularly by its own language, Catalan, and other cultural aspects. Until recently, the coexistence of Catalan national identity with Spain seemed possible. But the recent economic downturn, fiscal inequality within Spain and a sense of anti-Catalanism in Madrid has meant that the independence movement has gone from a minority current to a majority view, with 59% of Catalans now in favour of separation. In such a charged environment, culture and the spaces of cultural expression gain a new significance as loci of Catalanism. Markets recorded since the medieval era, such as in my field site of Vic, are seen especially as carriers of a historical tradition. This historical connection is incredibly important for a culinary nationalism like Catalonia's, where claims to national identity are based on historical justifications.

These markets are seen as markers of regional identities within Catalonia. Historically each *comarca* (county) had its own principal market in the main town. These markets, generally held once or twice a week, provided (and still provide) a focus of sociability and an arena of identity construction. This was especially so in the nineteenth century when ideas about national identity were formed. Today, the county markets act as a point of reference and a focus of regional identity. The market is now seen as the place where one can find the produce necessary to cook proper Catalan food, using local ingredients (be they from the county or the rest of Catalonia), and form personal relationships with other Catalans.

A classic demonstration of the importance of markets to Catalan food identity can be seen in a tourist brochure, *Catalonia Is Gastronomy*. Written in Catalan and Spanish, it is aimed at internal tourism within Catalan-speaking areas and from elsewhere in Spain. In the first chapter, we see an image of a modern woman with an old-fashioned wicker basket in the square of Vic, picking out robust, colourful mushrooms and fresh vegetables from a stall. On the page opposite, the introductory text reads, 'Cuisine is geography, history and culture. Tasting the products and enjoying them is synonymous with passing through the customs of a country. We invite you to do gastronomic tourism in Catalonia'.[1] The message could hardly be more obvious. For the Catalan-conscious tourist, food is the best way to experience the nation and its culture, and markets are the principal medium. Hence, this discussion will begin with a brief consideration of

Catalan Markets

the markets held throughout the year in Vic, with a particular focus on the Mercat del Ram and the Mercat Medieval. Next we will consider weekly markets generally within Vic and Catalonia, and conclude with a brief consideration of gastronomic markets in Catalonia as a whole.

Markets in Vic

With a population of 40,000, Vic, the capital of the county of Osona, is an important town in Catalonia, situated seventy kilometres from Barcelona. Agro-alimentary industries are the largest sector, taking up 13% of the employed workforce. Vic is particularly known for its pork and sausage industry, and is home to the Denominated Protection of Origin, *Llonganissa de Vic*. The *llonganissa* is a type of cured sausage produced by seven companies around the city. Vic's unique climate and situation, as well as the region's historic association with pig raising, have given rise to this product.[2]

It is important to recognize too the role of Vic in Catalonia's cultural and nationalist landscape. Vic is seen as one of Catalonia's most Catalanist towns, which helps to explain why so many Catalans recommended that I live there to study any aspect of Catalan identity. Vic has been associated with several important national figures, including Catalonia's national poet, Jacint Verdaguer. Another reason for Vic's importance as a Catalanist centre is related to its foods. *Llonganissa* and various other types of sausage produced in Vic are regarded as some of the most representative products of Catalonia. A recent initiative has also been the candidature of Vic as a UNESCO City of Gastronomy. This has been organized principally by the *Gremi d'Hosteleria* (Hospitality guild), though in late 2014 it was announced that this bid had not been successful. Despite this setback, for Catalans with a sense of national consciousness Vic is a place to visit to experience the Catalan heartland. According to a tour guide who became an important informant, Vic was popular with *turistes nacionals* [national tourists]; for such tourists, who visit Catalan landmarks as a way of exploring their identity, there is 'a real tradition' of visiting Vic.

One of the primary expressions of the city's identity is through its markets. There are two weekly markets in Vic, on a Tuesday and a larger one on a Saturday. Other markets are also held throughout the year. The most important are undoubtedly the Mercat del Ram (Palm Market) held for the weekend of Palm Sunday, the Mercat de Musica Viva (Market of Live Music) in September and the Mercat Medieval (Medieval Market) in December. Other smaller markets, such as antiques fairs, shop sales, craft fairs, etc., are held throughout the year, often to coincide with the major markets or festivals. Like many other towns in Catalonia, the Hospitality Guild has also instituted two *Jornades Gastronomiques*, or gastronomic open days. One, in October, is based on pork and mushrooms, and the other, in February, focuses on *Escudella i Carn d'Olla* (a type of meat and vegetable stew), one of Catalonia's national dishes.

These markets act as a very strong tourist attraction and income generator for the city. Due to its busy schedule of markets and fairs throughout the year, Vic is

Figure 1. Image of Vic market from promotional tourist brochure 'Catalonia Is Gastronomy'. The subtitle in the brochure is 'Flavours of the Earth in Catalan markets'. Taken from Massanes (2010): photo credit Xavier Patau, Generalitat de Catalunya, 2010.

sometimes called the 'City of Markets', a name also promoted in tourist literature. The primary focus of most of these markets is the main square, or Plaça Major. Indeed, an older name for it was *el Mercadal*, which designated its principal function as a market space (from the Catalan *mercat*). As the central square of a town that is part of the Catalan heartland, this space has a symbolic importance in the minds of many Catalans. I lived on La Plaça, and this was seen as proof of a grounded affection and understanding of Catalan culture. I was told I lived in 'the yolk of the egg' (*el rovell de l'ou*), a wonderful food metaphor to express the centrality of the square to Catalans. One can therefore see how the importance of markets held in this space feeds into, and is fed by, nationalist sentiment.

The Mercat del Ram (Palm Market), so called because it specializes in selling the decorative palm leaves given by godparents to godchildren, is without doubt one of the most important markets of Vic, both from an cultural and economic perspective. The chief intention of the market is to act as a trade show and livestock fair, mainly with an agricultural focus but also with an emphasis on food industries (Lactium, one of Catalonia's principal cheese fairs, is held within the Mercat del Ram), and other local businesses. The precise origin of the Mercat del Ram is unknown, but it is certain that there was a fair in existence in the medieval era.

The image of Vic as a city of markets has both been created by and fed into the image of the market in Catalan identity. Vic's strategic location between the sheep grazing pastures to the north in the Pyrenees and the urban market and well-connected port of Barcelona on the coast no doubt contributed to this development. The first recorded instance of a market was in 889, soon after the town was reconquered from the Moors. There are also references to *mercatum* in Vic in 911 and 957.

The first known annual fair in Vic took place in September and was granted royal permission in 1316. In 1528, a May fair was instituted, and then in 1599 two more fairs, all lasting three days. By 1603 there were seven markets throughout the year, some dedicated to particular livestock (e.g. mules or pigs). By 1822, the two main fairs had been standardized to 3 May (the feast of the Holy Cross) and 29 September (Michaelmas), with others of lesser importance interspersed throughout the year. In 1899 three more fairs were proposed, alongside the current ones. Indeed, for much of the nineteenth century there seemed to have been a perpetual fair in Vic. By 1909 however, most of these fairs had already fallen into desuetude, including that of May and September, which had gradually been substituted by the Mercat del Ram since the mid-nineteenth century.[3]

A testament to the reputation of Vic as a market town can be seen in a popular rhyme from the nineteenth century: 'There are the fairs of Catalonia/Much celebrated fairs/ Most that of Vic is the queen/Of the Catalan fairs.'[4] These markets and fairs were a nexus of interactions between rural and urban dwellers, the latter being from either Vic and the surrounding towns or even Barcelona itself. I suggest that the importance of this location in contributing to the development of nationalist ideas should not be underestimated. The rural ideal with its connections to land, earth, homeland and by extension nation could be experienced in this milieu by *excursionistes* (day-trippers), who, like contemporary *turistes nacionales*, saw the experience of travelling through and knowing Catalonia as a nationalist duty. The primary exponent of this rural way of life was the *pagès* (literally 'peasant'), the tenant farmers who brought their produce to market. The most important Catalan writer of the twentieth century, Josep Pla, dedicated a whole book to his interactions with *pagesos*, most of which occur at weekly fairs and markets.[5] For Pla, these markets were a locale in which he could still record vestiges of a national identity that, during the Franco period, seemed in danger of disappearing.

In contrast, Vic's Mercat Medieval (Medieval Market) has only been going about twenty years. It is part of a trend of historical and gastronomic markets that have sprung up in the last three decades. Like many festivals throughout Spain, these have come into their own in the post-Franco era, though in Catalonia they show a renewed confidence in Catalan identity expression. Ironically, many of these festivals have little or no connection with former festivities (mostly banned under Franco), with some exceptions. These are, largely, newly invented celebrations, though town councils are keen to emphasize any link with a past event, however tenuous.[6] For example, the presence of the Mercat Medieval in the weeks leading up to Christmas was seen as a continuation of the markets held in the medieval era at the same time, and the new

Figure 2: Easter Palms at Mercat del Ram (Palm Market) in Vic. Author's personal collection.

event seemed somehow right and proper for that reason. It is possible that the Mercat de Musica Viva, in its twenty-sixth year, was revived for September to recall another defunct market. The use of the word 'market' to denote this festival in this context also plays upon Vic's reputation as a centre of markets.

In the 1990s, the economic potential of these markets as tourist attractions was soon realized. At the same time, promoting internal solidarity through popular festivals was also an aim for many town councils, especially through the joint participation in putting on the spectacle. For example, Vic's group of the *geganters* (giant carriers) spoke warmly of the Mercat Medieval as a place where everyone worked together on their stall to earn a bit of money for their association and could interact with fellow Vigatans and also outsiders from the rest of Catalonia and even further afield.[7]

The *geganters* also referred to the Mercat Medieval as a 'celebration of local food'. Passing through the market, especially in the company of other Catalans, really brings home the truth of this message. A characteristic shared by the Mercat Medieval and the Mercat del Ram is the sheer number of food-related stalls, which take over a large part of Vic's old quarter, and account for about three quarters of the stalls present. In both markets too, buying street food and eating in the street is a central experience, often shared with a group, in the lived participation of these markets. In the Mercat Medieval, which I attended with a middle-aged group, we ate *llardons*, or pork scratchings, the heavy fat coating our mouths. These are a popular snack amongst the older generation in Catalonia, one of many pork-based products. In the Mercat del Ram, another snack, particularly associated with Catalonia, *coca*, sugary flat bread sliced into small pieces and wrapped in greaseproof paper.

Another celebration of local food occurs during the *Jornades Gastronomiques*, or Gastronomic Open Days. These are a fairly recent initiative from the Hospitality Guild. The Mercat del Ram included a gastronomic show from 1984 to 2000, which developed into these two *Jornades Gastronomiques*. The intention was to showcase the restaurants of the city, which each contributed one dish in an attempt to raise awareness of Vic's food scene. Today these open days are based around a series of presentations and tastings held over a weekend in a large tent to one side of the Plaça. A food market is also present in part of the square, and many stallholders give promotional presentations. Indeed, one of the main organizers said that the most important aspect was the market, as it allowed promotion of county products. Despite being a relatively new promotion, he placed these days within the context of continuity, saying, 'there is a tradition of these sorts of [markets in Vic], more or less continuously'.

The choice of theme for the two open days is interesting, since both are foods that my informants listed as typical – even stereotypical – of Catalan cuisine. Pork and mushrooms, the theme for the November event, are foods intimately associated with Catalonia, mushrooms especially due to their connection with foraging and efficiency as well as the fact that they are less popular in the rest of Spain. The other day celebrates the *Escudella i Carn d'olla*, a meat broth that is one of Catalonia's national dishes. Both days play up to Vic's reputation as a Catalanist town. If one had to choose a particular dish to celebrate, then it must be one dear to the hearts of all Catalans, just as Vic as a place is a landmark of the Catalan heartland.

Weekly markets within Catalonia
Walking through a market with a Catalan is an instructive experience for the anthropologist, since through this environment one experiences a whole gamut of associations with food in a particular location and also appreciates the thought process associated with moving through a market from the Catalan perspective. My market guide was an informant who had taken me under her wing as a student in all things Catalan, and visiting the market was part of my education in Catalan identity. By means of an introduction to the market, she said that 'this market is ours. It isn't for tourists; it's for us'.

As we walked, it became clear that food in market stalls was strongly associated with the dishes that these products could make within Catalan cuisine. When my guide saw green and red bell peppers, courgettes and onions, she immediately began describing *Escalivada*, a baked vegetable starter. As we passed another stall selling cabbage, celery, leeks, carrots and potatoes, she described the processes by which she would use these to make a *brou* [broth], which could be perfected with onions, courgettes or pig trotters. Mushrooms of many varieties led to a discussion of the best ways to cook each of these different types. Finally, the presence of a variety of tomatoes near a baker's stall selling *pa de pagès* (literally peasant's bread, now registered as a PGI) brought her to reflect on *pa amb tomàquet*, one of Catalonia's most popular national foods. Tomato is rubbed into bread that is a few days old and has hardened, thus softening it to make it edible; *pa amb tomàquet* embodies an ideal of thrifty use of available resources that is found in other guises in Catalan food culture. For my guide, the market also represented seasonality and local origins, although she admitted that many foods are now brought to the Vic market from further afield due to short growing seasons.

Clearly markets act as touchstones of associations for local and national knowledge amongst Catalans, knowledge which is intrinsically related to identity. In the case of markets, this identity is a culinary identity, as contact with basic foodstuffs generates continual deliberations on the content and processes of Catalan cuisine and its place within national identity. Markets act as locations for these reflections, connecting cuisine, place, and territorial produce.

The image of the weekly market and its produce also appears in contemporary restaurants. There is a popular designation now of restaurants who serve *'Cuina del Mercat'*, or 'Cuisine of the Market'. When asked, chefs normally define this label with explicit reference to the availability of produce in a market and the use of seasonal products. The chef and owner of one of Vic's oldest restaurants, Cal U, defined the phrase: 'It's a bit of following the seasons. What the market offers every season. Also, it's a type of cuisine, a fresh cuisine you could say. Of what you can buy every day, or every three days, and what you can make from it. It's not the cuisine of a product that was certainly stuck in a freezer for three months.'

This explanation brings home quite clearly the importance of fresh ingredients in the idea of *'Cuina del Mercat'*, for which following the seasons is a necessity. There is also an element of chance, change and variety. The availability of so many ingredients, that can be made into such a diverse range of dishes, is in fact another feature of the Catalan culinary identity. I was frequently told that the breadth of Catalonia's recipe collection (*receptari*) is a feature that makes it unique in Spain, specific contrast often being made with Castile and the Basque country, which have a more limited recipe selection.

Related to these concepts is the idea of travel between markets in order to select the best quality products. Another chef who also defined his style as *'Cuina del mercat'* recalled the importance of place where his family went for food. Sometimes they would walk several kilometres to get the best product from a supplier or market they considered of highest quality, be that for bread, meat or even well-water – a practice he described as being both 'sensible and gastronomic'. His restaurant's menu is based entirely on what foods can be found in the markets he and his wife visit each weekend; he particularly recommended the weekly market of Olot (the capital of the county next to Vic), since he thought it had a greater feeling of 'the rural air' than Vic.

This practice of travelling to various markets is important in Catalonia. Seeing other parts of Catalonia, meeting other Catalans, and experiencing the products particular to those areas creates a kind of national consciousness. Unlike Anderson's imagined communities – which can also be seen as applicable to Catalonia – however, these communities are not imagined, but experienced, experienced through market interactions that build a sense of a larger nation.[8]

In Granollers, thirty kilometres from Barcelona, the weekly market is also central to city identity. The most famous establishment is the Fonda Europa, founded 1771 and run by Ramon Parellada. He underlined the importance of the *viatjant*, or travelling sales merchant. These merchants moved from market to market selling their wares. Following a circuit of weekly markets throughout Catalonia, the merchants got to know Catalonia very well, becoming a sort of excursionist embodiment of a Catalan ideal. Ramon's grandfather realized the importance of this group of people, and gave them special promotions. Within thirty years, the Fonda Europa was one of the most successful inns in Catalonia. In order to provide some guaranteed variety for these clients, inns throughout Catalonia, starting with the Fonda Europa, began to offer a set weekday menu, which then entered into popular culture. Sunday was a day for macaroni pasta, or *macarrons* in Catalan; Monday was *escudella*; Tuesday *fideus a la cassola* (a type of short pasta); Thursday the day of rice (*arros*) – at first because Thursday was Granollers's market day, and so a rice dish would use up any leftover ingredients so new ones could be bought. The association between Thursday and rice is still very widespread throughout Catalonia, and even now most restaurants offer a rice dish on Thursday.

Restaurants' eagerness to inform clients about product origins shows another important element central to the idea of markets, that of '*compromís*'. A word that is difficult to translate directly into English, it can mean trust, confidence and a guarantee, and often implies all three. Both consumers and producers remarked that they also liked relationships created through foodstuffs. It was one of trust, but which also has gained new significance in that it is based on the consumption of Catalan products in a politically charged situation. Through using food as the principal form of exchange and basis of a relationship, connections are formulated that act as the basis for the formation of the 'imagined community' in Catalan national consciousness.

One example of this process is the changing associations of '*pagès*' (peasant). Until recently, the notion of being a *pagès* was ridiculed, even despite their idealized connectedness with land. Now, it is seen as almost prestigious to have this connection. I recall several people remarking with pride that one of their children lived '*a pagès*' and grew things for them and their friends. It is now seen as a reasonable career choice, especially in light of the economic crisis that has left many with uncertain employment. Growing or foraging one's own produce and selling the difference can make a tidy sideline; such work gives many a sense of empowerment. Also, this activity was often seen as a way of '*fent país*', literally 'making country', a phrase often used in the context of performing pro-Catalan activities. In this sense, both growing food in Catalonia and also buying that food is a means of '*fent país*' by helping local producers and enjoying the fruits of one's native land.

Gastronomic markets

Catalonia is unusual in that most of its gastronomic markets are based around single food products particular to the region and the season. Examples include mushroom fairs in the autumn and winter months, chestnut fairs for All Saints' Day, citrus fairs (mainly in the south of Catalonia) for December, olive oil picking, pressing and sampling from October to March, cherry and strawberry festivals in the summer, and seafood gastronomic open days on the coast from spring to mid-summer. An example of fairs celebrating specific varieties of products can be found in a town close to Vic, the Market of the Buffet Potato in Orís. It is unknown precisely how many markets of this kind exist throughout Catalonia, since some of these market have lasted for over decades whilst others are more ephemeral.

As briefly touched upon in the context of yearly markets in Vic, Catalan markets are spaces of commensality. The importance of commensality in forming social ties needs no introduction, but in this political context it takes on added significance. We have seen how markets already can act as a focus of national sentiment, through their ability to help in the creation of connections through interaction and travel. Commensality can create kinship, and notions of kinship are crucial to nationalist discourse.[9] Of course, commensality is also central to the experience of a market, through the act of eating in this space. As in the Vic markets, these experiences might be sharing food with fellow participants, buying an on-the-hoof lunch or supper from a stall or just tasting the samples at food stalls.

Pro-independence groups are well aware of the potential of these arenas for promotion. Stalls of many of the main Catalan cultural groups (which now almost entirely have a pro-independence stance) were found in every one of the markets I visited, whether weekly markets or annual events. The use of the national flag on market stalls has become commonplace to denote that the products are Catalan and to guarantee their 'authenticity'. Upon talking to the stallholders who proudly displayed their wares as Catalans, it became obvious that these are an excellent marketing strategy. One told me 'now more than ever before' does he display the flag, thanks to the 'sentimentalism' of the recent generation of Catalans when it comes to national affiliation.

Parting thoughts

This brief exposition by no means covers all the complexities of markets in Catalonia, but it gives a taste of their basic role in the formation of national identity. They are spaces in the landscape of both Catalan food culture and also centres of national identity construction. This is because of the role played by commensality in these spaces, as food and identity come to reflect off each other in these contexts. The result is that food, and the cuisine that results, gains further cultural capital within the construction of Catalan national identity at a complex historical juncture. The markets are also locales where Catalans can experience other places that make up their homeland to gain national awareness by participating in a form of historic continuity (whether real or imagined), and also to come into contact with other Catalans to foster national sentiment and belonging. Time will tell how these multitudinous and multivocal spaces will adapt to the changing situation. What is certain, though, is that if we want to understand a nationalist movement, there can be few better places than a market.

Notes

1. T Massanes, *Catalunya és gastronomia* (Generalitat de Catalunya: Agència Catalana de Turisme, 2010), p. 7. For tour materials in English, see Vic Tourist Office, *Vic + Osona: Visitor's Guide (English)* (Vic: Vic City Council, 2012).
2. Vic is situated on a plain, in the bend of a river, and another famous character of the city is its *'boira'*, or fog. This is seen as such an integral part of the city, that one of the *gegants*, giant figures paraded round Catalan towns on festive days, is a woman dressed in Catalan costume called *'La Boira'*. This moist climate allows the mould to develop on the outside of the *llonganissa* when it is placed in the rafters of the factories to dry, which gives it its unique flavour. Hence a connectedness between place, climate and food – an impression heightened by the odour of the pork industries in the city on some days!
3. S Ponce and M Ramisa, *El Mercat del Ram, la fira de la cuitat de Vic* (Ajuntament de Vic, 2006), pp. 27–29.
4. Quoted in Ponce and Ramisa, p. 27.
5. Josep Pla, *Els Pagesos* (Barcelona: Editorial Selecta, 1952).
6. A M Nogués Pedregal, 'Tourism and Self-Consciousness in a Spanish Coastal Community', *Coping with Tourists: European Reactions to Mass Tourism*, ed. by Jeremy Boissevain (Oxford: Berghan Books, 1996), pp. 56–111; for further examples of this elsewhere in Europe, see *Revitalising European Rituals*, ed. by Jeremy Boissevain (New York: Routledge, 1992) and the other chapters of *Coping with Tourists*.
7. This explanation admittedly contradicted something said by another acquaintance, who claimed that the Mercat was only popular with tourists, mainly from Barcelona, and that locals stayed away as prices were inflated.
8. B. Anderson, *Imagined Communities: Reflections on the Origin and Spread of Nationalism* (London: Verso, 1983).
9. J Llobera, *Foundations of National Identity: From Catalonia to Europe* (Oxford: Berghan Books, 2004), pp. 46–65

Markets Boom While Cooking Crashes!

Doug Duda

Historically, farmers markets developed out of necessity: they served as a primary distribution channel for the agricultural foodstuffs that a post-subsistence economy needed to feed the local population. Shopping at these markets was no more romantic or virtuous than a trip to today's supermarket is for contemporary consumers. Farmers markets were part of the rhythm of a more modern life and integral to its more complex social fabric, with offerings for shoppers in need of one-stop convenience, shoppers focused on religious dietary dictates, budget-conscious shoppers looking for distressed and discounted goods and always – due to the inherently perishable nature of produce and the premium value this confers on freshness – shoppers on the lookout for whatever is new from the farmer, what a French shopper would call *trouvaille*, a lucky find.[1]

In the past century, in many developed countries, the traditional role of the local farmers market has been largely disrupted by industrialized, large-scale distribution systems with superior economies of scale. These regional, national or multinational systems support huge stores offering greater variety of goods sourced more broadly, longer hours, more convenience and, often, cheaper food – all of which are highly attractive to consumers. Even countries with long and deeply embedded market cultures have witnessed the relative eclipse of local farmers markets by hypermarkets that sacrifice the surprise of *trouvaille* in favour of the predictability of something for everyone.

More recently, however, farmers markets in the United States have begun to buck this downward trend: they are booming. Initially sparked by legislation designed to create a new direct-to-consumer channel for local farms, the number of farmers markets has more than quadrupled over the past twenty years, and the dollar value of goods sold directly from farms to consumers has tripled.[2]

While still a minuscule part of the overall US food economy – a mere 0.33% of all agricultural sales in 2012 – farmers markets punch far above their weight in terms of the attention they attract and the cultural symbolism they embody.[3] Politicians and food activists use them to launch campaigns, school children arrive by the busload to learn about nutrition and food and beverage companies study and emulate the products and packaging they find there.

This surge in farmers market popularity is counter-intuitive. The US population has been a notable trend-setter in adopting the very behaviours that put pressure on farmers markets: substituting prepared foods for scratch cooking, allocating less of the food wallet on meals at home and spending dramatically less time on food shopping and preparation. The United States does not enjoy an entrenched farmers market culture or a many-centuries-old distribution system based on local farmers selling their goods to their neighbours. Indeed, it has been almost a century since more than half of the US population lived in rural areas; today, over 80% of the US population is living in or near cities, according to the US Census.[4]

Why, then, is the US experiencing this boom? What factors have combined to help create and expand a local, non-industrialized, non-scalable distribution system? What attracts consumers to these markets despite seemingly contrary economic trends and behavioural patterns? As farmers markets around the world deal with their own challenges from powerful industrialized food distribution systems and changing consumer patterns, what does the US experience imply for food systems throughout the industrialized world?

The surprising US farmers market boom

In 1970, there were only 340 farmers markets in all of the US. By 2013, that number had grown to 8144 – a 2400% increase. The major growth in the number of markets has come in the last eight years, as almost 4000 new markets have been established – presenting the 'hockey stick' pattern of an explosive trend.[5]

Sales of farm-to-consumer food have also tripled during the same time period.[6]

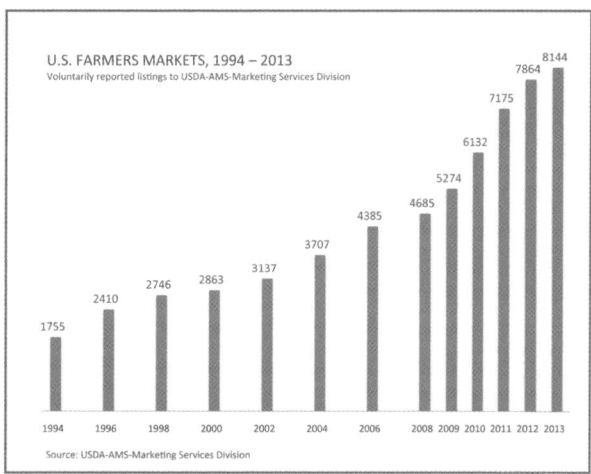

Although farmers markets still represent less than 1% of all agricultural sales to consumers in the US, the rise in both markets and market sales is nevertheless notable, at least initially because it is occurring against the backdrop of agricultural, economic and societal trends that might logically curtail such expansion.[7]

For example, it is axiomatic that healthy distribution channels require healthy suppliers offering a robust and ongoing supply of inventory (in this case, agricultural

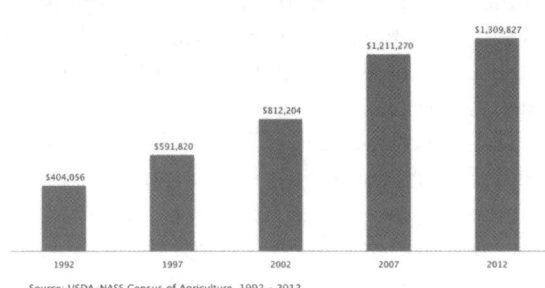

goods) in order to thrive. The US small farm sector supplying the new farmers markets is, however, trending downward: weak, diminishing and unprofitable. In 2012, the average small farm (1–49 acres) generated only about US $38,000 in agricultural revenues and government payments, and 70% of these farms reported a loss.[8] The majority of small-farm owners need to work away from the farm for at least a portion of the year in order to support their families, while continuing to work the farm. Small farms are often under-capitalized, with few resources to call on when bad weather, mounting losses or other misfortunes strike.

These are not new pressures in farm economies, and therefore it is not surprising that small and medium farms have undergone a continual and rather drastic contraction over the past eighty years. From their high in 1935, the number of small farms reached a nadir in 1975 from which they have not recovered. By 1975, the number of small

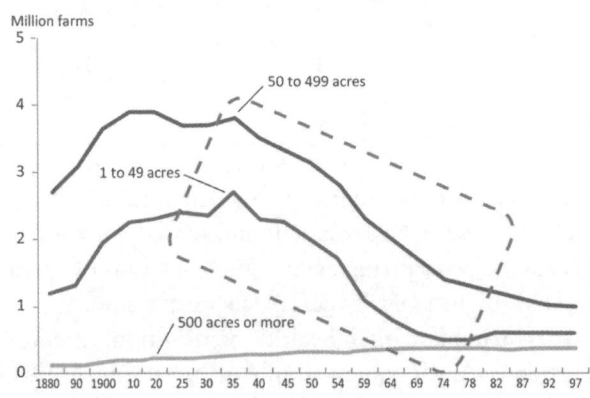

Markets Boom While Cooking Crashes!

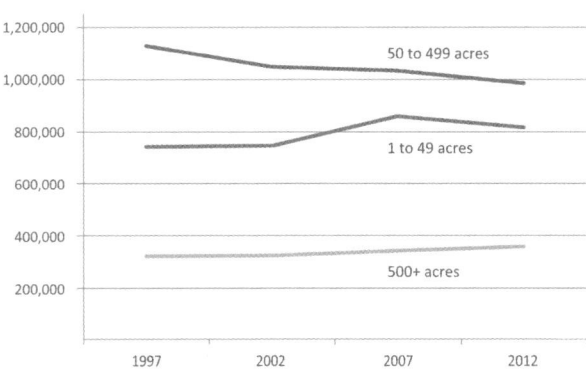

US FARMS BY SIZE, 1997–2012
Number of Acres

farms had fallen by about 80%; nearly 1.5 million disappeared. Medium-sized farms (50–499 acres) followed the same woeful pattern; from about 3.8 million farms in 1935, approximately 2.3 million were lost by 1975. At the same time, 500+ acre farms grew as US agriculture transformed into an industrialized, large-scale system.

This trend is not likely to turn around soon. While it is true that very small farms increased from 2002 to 2007 (adding more than 100,000, or about 15%), they began to fall again from 2007 to 2012, erasing a good portion of their gains.[9] Medium-size farms have continued their downward slide with no gains whatsoever, contracting about 10% from 1997 to 2012.[10]

Structurally, the farm-to-consumer channel appears to be missing one of the critical ingredients for strong farmers market growth – a strong set of suppliers. However, if we interpret this data instead as evidence of a powerful demand-driven – rather than supply-driven – boom, we can begin to account for other agricultural, economic and societal features of the growth in farmers markets that also seem counter-intuitive. The model of a demand-driven boom is consistent with oddities such as high prices for farmers market produce despite the farmer having cut out the middleman; the phenomenon of faster growth in farmers markets than in farmers market sales; and farmers market consumer support for food security, preservation of local artisans and other such issues that imply the need to build local food system capacity.

While it is important to note that there are still almost 1.8 million small farmers in the US – more than enough to supply over 8000 farmers markets even if small farm contraction continues – it is also useful to consider the notion of a boom in search of a product in light of other countervailing behavioural trends involving US consumers' relationship with food, cooking and food consumption.

Consider what farmers markets traditionally offer: raw ingredients for cooking, as well as prepared foodstuffs (e.g. cheese, bread, olives, etc.) that are meant to be part of a meal consumed at home. In the main, their merchandise is centred on locally-sourced fruits and vegetables and other agricultural offerings, with minimal processing and additional preparation. To return to the *sine qua non* of the farmers market experience from the consumers' perspective, the unique potential of the market is to provide the first asparagus of the season, the unexpected wine made from the local fruit, the lucky find of edible *trouvaille*.

Now consider some key prevailing consumer trends:

- *Fewer US households are cooking, and those who do are spending less time doing so.* From 1965–66 to 2007–08, the proportion of women who cooked dropped from about 93% to 68%; this loss was only partially offset by an increase in the proportion of men cooking (from 29% to 42%). The mean time women spent cooking per day has dropped 47 minutes, or 42%, from 112.8 to 65.6 minutes; the 8.3 minutes that men have added to their cooking duties (from 36.7 to 45.0 minutes) does not offset the huge drop in women's cooking time.[11]
- *Fresh food is under-represented in the US diet.* US households spend just 29% of their grocery money on fresh food. In comparison, Europeans spend about 53% of their budgets on fresh food and Asians about 60%, according to a March 2013 report from the Nielsen Company.[12]
- *US households under-consume fresh agricultural products.* As illustrated by the chart below, other than potatoes, Americans significantly underspend on fruits and vegetables versus USDA recommendations. Overall, they use less than 12% of their at-home food dollars on fresh fruits and vegetables, versus the USDA-recommended 40%.[13]
- *More and more food is consumed away from home.* In 1970, about two-thirds of US expenditures on food were on food eaten at home; by 2012 this had dropped to 50%. Real expenditures on food away from home are growing at almost double the rate of food at home.

The negative trends enumerated above certainly create a challenging environment for a farmers market boom, as these markets have been traditionally conceived and executed, and even more so when we think of consumer demand as the primary driver of growth. However, market surveys that describe what people are actually doing at markets suggest interesting ways that challenging trends are being transmuted into farmers market gold.

A 1995 survey of 336 visitors to a market in San Luis Obispo County, California, revealed that more than half of the visitors were not there to shop at all, that both shoppers and non-shoppers listed 'to socialize' as one of their top three reasons to attend the market and that the primary reason non-shoppers attended was 'to eat'.[14]

In 2011, a USDA survey of visitors to its outdoor farmers market in Washington DC, found that more respondents were interested in increasing the number of chef demonstrations than the availability of organic produce at the market, and the desire

Markets Boom While Cooking Crashes!

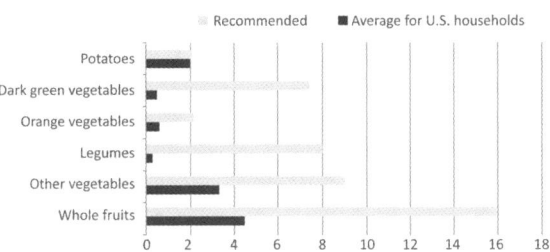

AT HOME SPENDING PATTERNS OF US HOUSEHOLDS
VS. USDA FOOD PLAN RECOMMENDATIONS
Expenditure shares in 1998 – 2006 (Percent)

Source: USDA Economic Research Service calculations using Nielsen Homescan data and USDA, Center for Nutrition Policy and Promotion's Liberal food plan

for greater selection of prepared foods was ranked higher than greater selection of fruits or vegetables.[15]

A fair reading of these and similar surveys is that, alongside the ingredient hunters and home cooks who use farmers markets as they had been used in the past, a substantial number of new farmers market consumers bring majority views about cooking as a spectator sport and the joys of prepared foods to the market, and play a role in shaping future market expansion in such directions.

In light of the discussion above, is the US farmers market experience a positive one to date? Or in the course of negotiating the powerful and inhospitable trends that the markets set out to address, have those trends hijacked the market boom, diluted its power and diminished its possibilities?

Four pillars of the US farmers market boom

Given the relatively brief history of the rise of today's US farmers markets, it is possible for many of the boom's present supporters to identify if not directly remember the specific drivers of progress to date, and appreciate the extent to which the directions for the future represent organic and positive growth. There are four primary drivers.

1) Legislative actions, federal incentives and linkages to other governmental programmes
Legislative support for farmers markets dates back to the mid-1970s with the passage of the Farmer-to-Consumer Direct Marketing Act of 1976, which initially provided $1.5M per year for two years to help expand the number of farmers markets.

It is difficult to understate the political sea change that took place during those years in the wake of President Richard Nixon's resignation following the Watergate scandal. US agricultural policy from 1970 to 1976, under the direction of US Secretary of Agriculture Earl Butz, had clearly favoured large farms. Butz, referred to even then

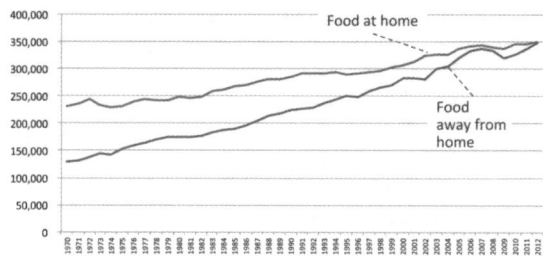

Source: USDA Economic Research Service: ERS Food Expenditure Series

as the father of agribusiness, significantly cut farm subsidies, urged farmers to seek the economies of scale of larger operations and famously often told groups of farmers to 'get big or get out'.[16]

Despite Butz's preferences, other factors made support for the small farmer politically possible in Congress. The 1970s witnessed global oil shock and US bank interest rates shot up to 15%. These two factors rapidly forced many small farmers out of business; in fact, the mid-1970s mark the lowest number of small farmers in the last 125 years. In a country facing, for the first time, a cartel that had the might to control US access to vital energy resources, gaining more control over other strategic resources such as the food supply suddenly gained importance.

From the passage of the 1976 legislation, food was on the table in a new way as a policy issue, and further legislation promulgated organic standards, addressed food labelling and, of particular significance to farmers market boom, bolstered the WIC (Women, Infants and Children) Program that delivered dollars to the markets. The steady stream of support, both financial and political, has been an enduring engine of farmers market growth.

2) Positive societal trends that have acted as a counterweight to aforementioned negative behavioural patterns

The decline of scratch cooking, prevalence of home meal replacement and rise in diet-related health disorders have launched a variety of health initiatives – adopted by the Baby Boomers of the period – that apply continued pressure against negative food habits. As this generation ages and its health concerns grow more acute, these consumers continue the lead role they have played in beginning of the farmers market movement through to the present day.

The belief in the relationship between food and performance, food and behaviour, and diet and remediation has become more widespread over time across all age groups, broadening interest in the farmers market as a site for both better food and more credible information about better food.

The farmers market is also viewed by young people as a place to do well by doing good. Like farm internships and other work experiences that introduce this generation to agriculture and food artisanship, farmers markets have a strong youth presence. Although the market movement is almost forty, it looks and acts younger, moving it safely along to the next generation.

3) The rise of the food culture

Perhaps no growth engine has provided more power to the rise of US farmers markets than the broader food culture that has developed in tandem with the market movement. In April of 1976, alongside the farmers market legislation that year, the Baby Boom generation celebrated the first Earth Day, with its themes of sustainability and conservation. These ideas provided a national platform and public conversation about healthier living, a greener footprint, societal change, new tastes and a deeper connection between individual and community health.

As food historian Warren Belasco documents the period, at best only a large minority of the early self-proclaimed members of the food culture 'were actively engaged in pursuing healthier foods', and when it came to actually buying products that were in keeping with the values espoused at the time, 'estimates rarely ran above 40%, frequently less'.[17]

Nonetheless, practitioners and aspirants together constituted a powerful audience for the marketers of cookbooks, cooking equipment, food television, culinary travel and all other aspects of food lifestyle. If the more recent appearance at food markets of prepared food lovers and non-cooks feels inorganic to the farmers market movement, it is certainly not a new development. The food culture itself, responsible for creating the market for food celebrities, may be the ultimate expression of the impulse toward edible *trouvaille,* and have helped stretch the categories for discovery to every form of food-related experience, far beyond the walls of the kitchen.

4) Intelligent evolution of farmers markets themselves

The final growth driver of the farmers market boom has been the ability and willingness of farmers markets to adapt to their audiences. The embrace of the wants and needs of their customers has resulted in the markets functioning as more than locations for transacting purchases. Like pubs, cafés and other places where previous generations established a sense of community outside of home and work around a stein or a mug, the US farmers market has become a place to be with your kind of people. Ingredient tastings beget demonstrations of recipes beget seating areas for consuming prepared foods and ingredients on premises at the market.

The evolution of the markets has been essential to their survival. As consumer demand has grown for healthier foods, mass market retailers have leapt onto the 'organic/local bandwagon' with both feet. They now dominate the market. In 2010, according to the Organic Trade Association, mass-market retailers (mainstream supermarkets, club/warehouse stores and mass merchandisers such as Walmart) sold 54% of organic food in the US. Natural retailers (such as Whole Foods) accounted for 39% versus 7% at farmers markets.[18]

Looking forward, mass merchants are likely to gain even more share as they seek to capture more of the organic segment, which in 2012 grew by 7.5% over 2011, double the rate of growth in the conventional food segment. What provides the farmers markets with a measure of stability against Walmart, Wild Oats, Target and other price competitors is their ability to compete on experiential benefits, including a sense of community. While weddings at farmers markets event spaces are no longer uncommon, there appears to be little demand for nuptials in the Walmart produce aisle.

Summary

The US farmers market boom began as a government programme focused on helping producers, but its evolution demonstrates the degree to which it has been driven by consumer demand, initially for alternative products, but increasingly for alternative food experiences and lifestyle. Today's culinary *trouvaille* have become as much about nourishing a food culture as the individual consumer.

Notes

1. Helene J. Sinnreich, 'Baluty Market: A Study Of A Food Space', *Food, Culture & Society* 10.1 (Spring 2007), pp. 73–84 (pp.74–77).
2. United States Department of Agriculture – Agricultural Marketing Service – Marketing Services Division, *National Count of Farmers Market Directory Listing Graph: 1994–2013* (2013) < http://www.ams.usda. gov/AMSv1.0/ams.fetchTemplateData. do?template=TemplateS&leftNav=Wholesaleand FarmersMarkets&page=WFMFarmersMarketGrowth&description=Farmers+Market+Growth%5D> [accessed 22 May 2014]; United States Department of Agriculture – Agricultural Marketing Service (D. Tropp), *Why Local Food Matters* (2014), p. 4 <http://www.ams.usda.gov/AMSv1.0/getfile?dDocName=STELPRDC5105706> [accessed 28 May 2014].
3. United States Department of Agriculture National Agricultural Statistics Service, *2012 Census of Agriculture Final Data Release, Released May 2, 2014 at noon* (2014), p. 36 <http://www.agcensus.usda.gov/Newsroom/2014/2012_Census_Final_Data_Release_Webinar.pdf> [accessed 20 May 2014].
4. United States Census Bureau. *1990 United States Census* (1993), p. 5 <http://www.census.gov/population/censusdata/table-4.pdf> [accessed 16 June 2014]; United States Census Bureau, *2010 United States Census* (2012), p. 29 <www.census.gov/compendia/statab/2012/tables/12s0029.xls> [accessed 16 June 2014].
5. USDA, *National Count of Farmers Market Directory Listing Graph: 1994–2013*. 'Hockey stick' growth curves are viewed by market analysts as unambiguous evidence of market acceptance.
6. USDA, *Why Local Food Matters*, p.4. The sharper growth in markets than sales may indicate cannibalization of established farmers markets shoppers by newly opened sites, or may suggest that markets are catering to consumer needs other than shopping.
7. 2012 Census of Agriculture Final Data Release.
8. United States Department of Agriculture (R.A. Hoppe, J.M. MacDonald and P. Korb), *Small Farms*

In The United States: Persistence Under Pressure, Economic Information Bulletin 63 (Washington: Economic Research Service, February 2010), p.27.

9. United States Department of Agriculture – Agricultural Marketing Service. *Facts On Direct-to-Consumer Food Marketing* (2009), p. 3 <http://www.ams.usda.gov/AMSv1.0/getfile?dDocName=STELPRDC5076729> [accessed 28 May 2014].
10. 2012 Census of Agriculture Final Data Release.
11. Lindsey P. Smith, Shu Wen Ng and Barry M.Popkin, 'Trends in US Home Food Preparation and Consumption: Analysis of National Nutrition Surveys and Time Use Studies from 1965–1966 to 2007–2008', *Nutritional Journal*, 12 (April 11, 2013), p. 45.
12. The Nielsen Company, *Why Retailers Are Keeping It Fresh* (March 2013), pp. 10, 13, 15.
13. Nielsen, p.17; USDA, *Assessing the Healthfulness of Consumer's Grocery Purchases* (2012), p. 21. The authors compared Nielsen Homescan data from 1998 to 2006 with the USDA's ideal food consumption plan to point out the disparities between ideal and actual consumption.
14. Marianne McGarry Wolff, Arianne Spitler and James Ahern, 'A Profile Of Farmers' Market Consumers and the Perceived Advantages of Produce Sold at Farmers' Markets', *Journal of Food Distribution Research*, 36.1 (March 2005), pp. 192–201 (p. 196).
15. United States Department of Agriculture – Agricultural Marketing Service. *Results of Dot Survey: USDA Outdoor Farmers Market Survey* (2011), p.12.
16. Michael Carlson, 'Earl Butz Obituary', *The Guardian* 3 February 2008. Unlike US obituaries, The Guardian's version repeats the outrageous racist remark that put Butz on the road to resignation.
17. Warren Belasco, *Appetite for Change: How the Counterculture Took On The Food Industry* (Ithaca: Cornell UP, 1989), p. 190.
18. Organic Trade Association, *2011 Organic Industry Survey* (2011).

The Fishmongers of London's Street Markets from the 1840s to the Present

Anastasia Edwards

In the 1840s, London had 4000 'costermongers' (street-sellers) of fish, who supplied what was then a staple of the diet of the poor. Today, the sight of a fishmonger in London's street markets is rare. This paper will consider the trade of market-based fishmongers in early Victorian London, and then consider the same trade in modern and contemporary London. The principle source for the former is the vast 'cyclopaedia' *London Labour and the London Poor*, by Victorian journalist Henry Mayhew (1812–97), which contains extensive, detailed interviews of London fishmongers in the 1840s.[1] Modern and contemporary sources are interviews with John Wright, born in 1934, whose family have been street fishmongers in Westminster since 1874, and John Norris, born in 1972, the man who took over the stall from Wright in 2010. The paper focuses on anecdotes that illuminate themes such as the shift from mere subsistence to greater profit, and how London fishmongers have viewed themselves and others within the British social order. The approach has been qualitative rather than quantitative. Above all, my aim has been to draw out details and voices of the past in order to give a sense of the broad changes that have taken place in London street markets over the past 175-odd years.

Who were the costermongers?
While there were shops in early Victorian London, these were largely for wealthier citizens. Poor people bought their food, mostly on a daily basis, from the many street markets and ambulatory traders who walked the streets, often plying single wares. In distinguishing shops from street sellers, Mayhew explained that the 'street-seller cries his goods at the head of his barrow; the enterprising tradesman distributes bills at the door of his shop. The one appeals to the ear, the other to the eye'.[2] He also emphasized that unlike shopkeepers, 'costermongers, though living by buying and selling, are seldom or never capitalists. It is estimated that not more than one-fourth of the entire body trade upon their own property' (29).

According to Mayhew, some 50,000 people, or one fortieth of the city's population, made their living in London's streets (6). Of these, some 30,000 were dependent on costermongering for their existence, and 4000 were costermongers selling fish and seafood (4–6). From Mayhew's descriptions, markets were an essential, unavoidable facet of London life. The soul of this vanished phenomenon lives on in films set in Victorian London, such as *Oliver!*, which evoke the sheer mass of people and emotional charge of a street life revolving around petty commerce. The song 'Who will buy?', from *Oliver!*, memorably enshrines the anxieties and voices of costermongers.

In Mayhew, the word costermonger applied to pretty much anyone who sold any food on the streets, whether it be a single item from a barrow or, for the more provident or ambitious, from a stationary stall that sold a few items. According to the *OED*, the word costermonger derives from 'costard', meaning apple, and 'monger', meaning a dealer or trader. While 'costermonger' thus originally meant someone who sold apples in the open street, in London the word came to mean one 'who sells fruit, vegetables, fish, etc. in the street from a barrow'. There are references to costermongers going back to the early 1500s, many of them derogatory. Most well known, perhaps, is Falstaff's line from Shakespeare's *Henry IV Part 2*: 'Vertue is of so little regard in these costermonger times' (I.ii.191 Qo.).

To Mayhew, costermongers appear 'to be a distinct race – perhaps, originally, of Irish extraction – seldom associating with any of the other street folk, and being all known to each other' (6). Indeed, they lived in the same streets, mated with each other (marriage was rare), drank together, engaged in entertainments such as rat-killing, and attended bawdy theatrical performances put on for their benefit. Dressing smartly was a priority, whatever their budget, and four or five London tailors catered exclusively to costermongers. Costermongers also had their own language, back slang, whose principle rule was that words were spoken backwards, although some words were further modified, making them undecipherable even to those members of the public who were wise to the backwards ruse. Thus *Yenep* meant 'penny', but *Cool ta the dillo nemo* meant 'Look at the old Woman' and *Kennetseeno*, 'applied principally to quality of fish', meant 'stinking' (23).

Costermongers selling fish

In Mayhew's London, fish was a major staple of the poor, in part due to the rise of the railways in the 1840s. 'This cheap food, through the agency of the costermongers, is conveyed to every poor man's door, both through the thickly-crowded streets where the poor reside … and through the long miles of the suburbs,' Mayhew explained. 'For all low-priced fish the poor are the costermongers' best customers, and a fish diet seems becoming almost as common among the ill-paid classes of London, as is a potato diet among the peasants of Ireland' (62). So prevalent was fish that its smell never quite left the dwellings of the poor and was sometimes oppressive, especially to those, like Mayhew, who were not as used to it.

To better understand the lives of fish costermongers, Mayhew recommended visiting Billingsgate, London's wholesale fish market since at least the sixteenth century, on a Friday. This was both the 'fast day of the Irish' and the day on which mechanics' wives tended to run out of money and look to buy a cheap fish meal, and so costermongers who usually traded in fruit and vegetables during the week would moonlight as fish sellers on Fridays. Mayhew described the scene as follows:

TABLE, SHOWING THE QUANTITY, WEIGHT, OR MEASURE OF THE FOLLOWING KINDS OF FISH SOLD IN BILLINGSGATE MARKET IN THE COURSE OF THE YEAR:

Description of Fish.	Number of Fish.	Weight or Measure of Fish.	Proportion sold by Costermongers.
Wet Fish.		lbs.	
Salmon and Salmon Trout (29,000 boxes, 14 fish per box)	406,000	3,480,000	One-twentieth.
Live Cod (averaging 10 lbs. each)	400,000	4,000,000	One-fourth.
Soles (averaging ¼ lb. each)	97,520,000	26,880,000	One-fifteenth.
Whiting (averaging 6 oz. each)	17,920,000	6,720,000	One-fourth.
Haddock (averaging 2 lbs. each)	2,470,000	5,040,000	One-tenth.
Plaice (averaging 1 lb. each)	33,600,000	33,600,000	Seven-eighths.
Mackarel (averaging 1 lb. each)	23,520,000	23,520,000	Two-thirds.
Fresh Herrings (250,000 bars., 700 fish per bar.)	175,000,000	42,000,000	One-half.
" (in bulk)	1,050,000,000	252,000,000	Three-fourths.
Sprats	....	4,000,000	Three-fourths.
Eels from Holland } (6 fish per 1 lb.)	9,797,760	{ 1,505,280	One-fourth.
" England and Ireland		127,680	One-fourth.
Flounders (7,200 quarterns, 36 fish per quartern)	259,200	43,200	All.
Dabs (7,500 quarterns, 36 fish per quartern)	270,000	48,750	All.
Dry Fish.			
Barrelled Cod (15,000 barrels, 50 fish per barrel)	750,000	4,200,000	One-eighth.
Dried Salt Cod (5 lbs. each)	1,600,000	8,000,000	One-tenth.
Smoked Haddock (65,000 bars., 300 fish per bar.)	19,500,000	10,920,000	One-eighth.
Bloaters (265,000 baskets, 150 fish per basket)	147,000,000	10,600,000	One-fourth.
Red Herrings (100,000 bars., 500 fish per bar.)	50,000,000	14,000,000	One-half.
Dried Sprats (9,600 large bundles, 30 fish per bundle)*	288,000	96,000	None.
Shell Fish.			
Oysters (309,935 bars., 1,600 fish per bar.)	495,896,000	....	One-fourth.
Lobsters (averaging 1 lb. each fish)	1,200,000	1,200,000	One-twentieth.
Crabs (averaging 1 lb. each fish)	600,000	600,000	One-twelfth.
Shrimps (324 to the pint)	498,428,648	192,295 gals.	One-half.
Whelks (224 to the ½ bus.)	4,943,200	24,300 ½ bus.†	All.
Mussels (1000 to the ½ bus.)	50,400,000	50,400 "	Two-thirds.
Cockles (2,000 to the ½ bus.)	67,392,000	32,400 "	Three-fourths.
Periwinkles (4,000 to the ½ bus.)	304,000,000	76,000 "	Three-fourths.

* Costermongers dry their own sprats.
† The half-bushel measure at Billingsgate is double quantity—or, more correctly, a bushel.

As soon as you reach the Monument you see a line of them, with one or two tall fishmongers carts breaking the uniformity, and the din of the cries and the commotion of the distant market, begins to break on the ear like the buzzing of a hornet's nest. The whole neighbourhood is covered with the hand-barrows, some laden with baskets, others with sacks. Yet as you walk along, a fresh line of costers' barrows are creeping in or being backed into almost impossible openings; until at every turning nothing but donkeys and rails are to be seen. The morning air is filled with a kind of seaweedy odour, reminding one of the seashore; and on entering the market, the smell of fish, of whelks, red herrings, sprats, and a hundred others, is almost overpowering. (64)

The Fishmongers of London's Street Markets

The table gives an idea of the amount and variety of fish that came through Billingsgate throughout the course of the year, as well as how much of each variety was sold by costermongers. (It also indicates how Mayhew's quantitative research skills were more than a match for his qualitative research methods.) Mayhew reckoned that of the fish and seafood that was sold at Billingsgate, one-third was bought and then sold on by costermongers.

Much of the fish that costermongers bought was from 'bummaries', middlemen whom Mayhew said were considered a 'far superior class' to their counterparts in the fruit and vegetable markets, the 'hagglers' (67). Bummaries (a word whose origin was unknown both to Mayhew's informants and to the *OED*) ran the gamut from wholesaler to speculator. While the wholesale green markets only received one delivery per day, Billingsgate would sometimes receive a second delivery, which flooded the market and lowered the price of fish that had been bought in the morning. Bummaries and costermongers might thus be stuck with merchandise, bought in the morning, whose wholesale price had been higher than was the retail price of fish bought from the second delivery (67).

Although the railways had helped make fish become ubiquitous and cheap almost overnight, not everybody felt positively about them. As one veteran street fish seller told Mayhew,

> I have sold 'wet fish' in the streets for more than fourteen years. [… B]efore that I was a gentleman, and was brought up a gentleman, if I'm a beggar now. I bought fish largely in the north of England once, and now I must sell it in the streets of London. … There's a wonderful difference in the streets since I knew them first. I could make a pound then, where I can hardly make a crown now …. I consider that the railways have injured me, and all wet fish-sellers, to a great extent. Fish now, you see, sir, comes in at all hours, so that nobody can calculate on the amount that will be received – nobody. That's the mischief of it; we are afraid to buy, and miss many chances of turning a penny. In my time, since railways were in, I've seen cod-fish sold at a guinea in the morning that were a shilling at noon; for either the wind and the tide had served, or else the railway-fishing places were more than commonly supplied, and there was a glut to London. There's no trade requires a greater judgement than mine – none whatever. (68)

Unlike this informant, most costermongers were illiterate – Mayhew estimates that only one in ten children at the time he was writing had had any schooling – and therefore selling fish provided an obvious (if hard) way to provide basic food and shelter. Mayhew got to know and trust a 'poor shoeless urchin', and gave him the 'trifling' sum of one shilling to set him up as a costermonger selling sprats (70). The boy was thus able to keep himself, his mother, and his sister through the winter on the proceeds of the original shilling.

Mayhew was quick to emphasize that most costermongers, such as this boy, were honest, but his accounts includes tales of the tricks of the trade the costermongers engaged in, such as puffing up the cheeks of cod to make them more appealing. Most contentious of all, perhaps, was the use of 'slang', or false, measurements, whereby the costermonger would find ways to give the customer less than he had paid for (32). One common device was using a measurement vessel with a false bottom, which held a smaller volume of prawns, say, than was apparent to the customer. These accounts are particularly revealing about how fish costermongers saw themselves in relation to others.

One particular costermonger, contemptuous of slangs, was proud of the way he was able to cheat customers using a *true* measure. 'Why, I can cheat any man,' he told Mayhew. 'I manage to measure mussels so as you'd think you got a lot over, but there's a lot under measure, for I holds them up with my fingers and keep crying, "Mussels, full measure! Live mussels!" I can do the same with peas. I delight to do it with stingy aristocrats' (32). Another told Mayhew that even if Prince Albert, Queen Victoria's husband, was to stop him in the street to buy a pair of soles from him, he'd sell him 'a rough pair as any other man – indeed I'd take in my own father' (53). Most often, though, the costermongers, with their shared language that isolated outsiders, seemed to revel in their mutuality and to define themselves in relation to 'aristocrats' (52). 'We never eat eel-pies, because we know they're often made of large, dead eels,' one woman told Mayhew. '*We*, of all people, are not to be had in that way. But the haristocrats eat 'em and never knows the difference' (52).

The costermonger's life was hard, with its low margins and vagaries of supply, and to sell one had to be enterprising and resort to theatricality, if not trickery, through street cries. There are many accounts of costermongers losing their voices temporarily or even permanently. Yet it was a way of life, not just a way of making a living, and a strong source of personal identity. In its own way the 'roving life' conferred a certain freedom, and costermongers became hooked on the constant movement, in the way that someone who is used to regular, intense exercise might miss it if suddenly unable to take it. Mayhew describes one young woman who has been a sprat seller until a rich gentleman took pity on her and offered to train her to become a servant. At first the novelty of her new life was diverting (although, shoeless for much of her life, she found her new boots to be extremely painful). However 'no sooner did she hear from her friends, that sprats were again on the markets, than, as if there were some magical influence in the fish, she at once requested to be freed of her confinement, and permitted to return to her old calling' (44).

Amongst Mayhew informants, there was little talk about the product itself, nor of its provenance. For most costermongers, the seafood they sold was a means towards an end – subsistence. 'My crabs is caught in the sea, in course,' a male costermonger told Mayhew. 'I gets them at Billingsgate. I never saw the sea, but it's salt-water, I know. I can't say whereabouts it lays. I believe it's in the hands of the Billingsgate salesmen' (22).

The Fishmongers of London's Street Markets

THE OYSTER STALL.
"Penny a lot, Oysters! Penny a lot!"
[From a Daguerreotype by BEARD.]

John Wright, London fishmonger (1950s–2006)

John Wright, born in 1934, is the fourth generation of a family of Westminster fishmongers. 'My grandparents were all Victorians,' he says. 'They lived in Dickens' times.' His great-grandfather first took a stall in a street market in the Pimlico neighbourhood of the borough of Westminster in 1876, selling oysters, and operating hansom cabs out of nearby Victoria Station by night. Looking at the picture of the oyster seller published in Mayhew's book, one can forge a vague sense of continuity between what Mayhew describes and what Wright remembers his father telling him of his forebears. One can also see the sartorial pride of the costermongers, an important feature of the Wright family identity.

Pimlico is only a short walk from the Houses of Parliament, Buckingham Palace, Westminster Abbey and Westminster Cathedral. In the 1820s the master builder Thomas Cubitt (1788–1855) had built up vast stucco estates to house wealthy people in Pimlico and nearby Belgravia (houses in the latter have recently sold for around £100 million). While the market has thus served some of the richest and most powerful people (and their housekeepers and cooks) in Britain since the 1840s, it has also served some of the poorest. Pimlico has long been home to vast housing estates housing the poor. Today, some 200 languages are spoken in the borough of Westminster, many of them by first-generation immigrants. (I walk through Pimlico every day, and calculated that on the school run alone, I wave at or say hello to people from at least twenty different countries, many of them recent arrivals to London.) Wright remembers the principal influx of his time to have been Spanish fleeing Franco in the 1930s, as well as Portuguese in search of jobs. Many Spanish and Portuguese settled in the poorer parts of Pimlico, where housing was then cheap and close to London's West End, where many worked in hotels and restaurants.

Until just after WWII, the Pimlico market in which the Wright family traded was on Warwick Way, and extended across three blocks, from Vauxhall Bridge Road to Belgrave Road, about three hundred metres. There were some two hundred stalls, lining either side of Warwick Way, many selling individual items or small ranges of related items. For as long as Wright can remember, and until well into the 1990s, the stall next to his sold only salad. One detail that his father remembers being told by Wright's grandfather was that the market stayed opened late at night, so that working people could buy food on their way home. Hurricane lamps were used to provide light, which recalls Mayhew's accounts of stallholders sticking candles into turnips, and of markets on Saturday nights closing as late as midnight.

During World War II, the market shrank considerably. After the war, Warwick Way was reclaimed as an access road for fire engines, and the market was moved around the corner to Tachbrook Street, only about one-tenth as long as the market on Warwick Way. From then on known as the Tachbrook Street Market, it continued to decline until ten years ago, when only Wright's fish stall, a vegetable stall and a few others remained. In the mid-noughties, Westminster Council invested in the market, encouraging street food stalls to service the hordes of civil servants and others who work nearby. On any given day, half a dozen international food stalls cook up everything from authentic Pad Thai to Palestinian Falafel to Japanese stews.

When Wright was growing up in the late 1930s and early 1940s, his father had two stalls on Warwick way, one selling wet and dry fish, some of which he smoked himself in the flat on their council estate near Westminster Abbey, and one selling shellfish. On weekends, the stalls also sold rabbits, often as many as two hundred. The skins, used for making bowler hats, were often worth more than the meat: a man would come around every week to buy the skins from Wright's father, who would give the proceeds to his wife, Wright's mother, a half-Swedish Garbo-esque beauty. She would then buy a new hat or pair of shoes. The Wright family stalls were two of many more. There were so many fish stalls that Warwick Way was considered informally to be London's second fish market after Billingsgate.

After World War II, during which he was evacuated, Wright started secondary school, but left at the age of fifteen to help his father on the stalls. His job was to deliver standing orders to the canteens of various telephone exchanges, sometimes gruelling work. 'All on the bike I did it, a trade bike, not a van,' he recalls. 'The telephone exchanges all had their own canteens. Mayfair, Sloane, Victoria …. The hard one, of course, was Mayfair, going up around Hyde Park corner …. And it went over! Fish everywhere …. These days I would have been killed.'

In his twenties, promising careers as a pianist, an actor and a theatre director were variously disrupted by financial considerations and illness, and, after his marriage in 1964, Wright gravitated back to the two stalls on Tachbrook Street, working them with his brother. In the face of cheap meat imports from Argentina, trading was tough. 'In the sixties we had to sell *tons* of fish to get a profit,' he recalls:

> Because 70 per cent of it was foreign trade: Spanish, Portuguese, Italian …. But my father wouldn't serve them. He never bought squid or scads anything like that – all the sorts of things that the Spanish bought. Me and brother, in the sixties, we started to sell all this sort of stuff. So *we* changed it as well. And now it's changing again, but it's changing to all this high cuisine, isn't it?

In the 1970s, Westminster Council oversaw the building of a large social housing estate, the Longmoore Estate, part of which included retail premises for a shop on Tachbrook Street. Wright and his wife took on the lease in 1979, and redid the interiors with marble and Italian tiles. 'It cost us a fortune!' he said. As an insurance policy he and his brother kept on the two stalls, which continued to thrive. The shop, although partly obscured by stalls, was a success, attracting royalty, politicians and celebrities. Wright has particularly fond memories of Jennifer Paterson, one of the Two Fat Ladies, for whom he once managed to procure – out of season – a halibut for a dinner she was cooking for 'Charlie' (her nickname for Prince Charles). In 1984, in the face of ever-increasing rents, Wright gave up the shop, which came to house a branch of the high-street chain Holland & Barrett, and focussed his attentions on the stalls.

During all Wright's time as a street fishmonger, he woke up in the earliest hours of each day to commute from his home in Farnham, Surrey, to Billingsgate, to buy fish for the stall and the shop. 'The Old Billingsgate, you had to go down there smart, you know,' he recalls. 'If you didn't wear a tie at the Old Billingsgate, if you weren't smart …. All fishmongers were smart. They all wore hats. I still wear a tie or a bow tie. I couldn't go like this.' He motions to his smart-casual outfit. 'I'd feel terrible.' To illustrate the point further, he shows me a picture of his father, looking like a matinée idol in an elegant suit and hat, with two perfectly combed and dressed young boys, Wright and his brother. The occasion was a day on which Wright's father was taking his sons for a day at the seaside just before the war.

Wright enjoys recalling details of the trade's history, but he warms most to a broader subject. 'I've always been fascinated by the class system,' he says. 'I'm not anti-class at all, but you don't see so much of it now. I was brought up around it.' He explains how the class system manifested itself physically in his family's work on the fish stalls, and still does today. 'First of all, when you're on the stall, you know, you don't hold your hand out for the money,' he explains. 'Did you know that? You wait for it to be tendered. I still hold my hands down until they tender the money to me. That is part of the class system.'

Wright's father had at one point made enough money to be able to afford to send Wright and his brother to the prestigious nearby Westminster School, but did not even bother to apply. 'This was a premier school, and he could have afforded to,' Wright says. 'But being a trader, being trade, there was no way we would get into Westminster School. No way.' He laughs as he recounts the day his brother was given a pass to the Royal Enclosure at Ascot by a resident of the Royal Mews who shopped at the stall. One of their customers at the stalls, who happened to be there on the same day, whispered to her husband, 'What's *he* doing here?'

If the way of accepting money was tightly scripted, there was more freedom when it came to choosing how to sell. Wright emphasizes the importance of being an actor in selling, and has several patters he uses with customers. When one of his colleagues made a mistake with a female client's order, he told her, completely deadpan, 'It was your beauty was the cause of that.' The following is another of his favourite routines:

> I had one a couple of weeks ago. She said, 'I've got a new boyfriend. Well, what can I get him?' She got her fish and everything, and I said, 'Listen, the most important thing …. Do you like Mozart?' She said, 'Mozart?' 'You've got to play the Adagio from Mozart's 23rd piano concerto. If you can get it, he will *melt*.' Another one I do, if a girl and a bloke come up, you obviously know they're together; they're having a dinner party together. Half of them can't cook, you know. You've got to tell them how to cook it and this, that and the other. And I say to the boyfriend, 'Now your job: lay the table, get the candles lit, and *don't forget the Mozart!*

Jonathan Norris, London fishmonger (2010–present)

In 2010, John Wright was one of two remaining market fishmongers on Tachbrook Street. He wanted to retire, but none of his three sons was interested in taking over the business. A young customer of his, John Norris, was 'very bored' by his IT job, and wanted to try something different. After training with Wright, he eventually took over his stall (although Wright still works for him on a Saturday to keep in touch with his old friends in the neighbourhood). If Norris hadn't taken over the stall, it might well have been the end of fishmonger stalls in Tachbrook market, as the other remaining fishmonger eventually retired as well. Norris understands that he is something of a maverick to go back into a dying trade. 'Younger people don't want to do the job,' he says. 'It's not very glamorous. It's very, very hard hours. The amount of people who say,

"My dad used to be a fishmonger…", "My grandfather…." They've all disappeared out of the industry.'

In a few years, Norris has built up an elegant stall that is arguably the main attraction of the market. It is immaculately presented, with smart black and white livery, and it reminds one of some of the few remaining smart fish shops in London. 'If I left it would be a blow to the market,' he says.

Norris is an entrepreneur on a wider scale than Wright and his forebears. He has since started up a successful fishmonger shop in Victoria Park in Hackney, and his goal is to build up a portfolio of five London shops, sell them, and retain the stall on Tachbrook Street which, until recently, was making more in its three days of trading than the shop made in six. Part of his success is knowing his customers and their needs. 'About half my customers are English,' Norris explains. 'Only half. Spaniards are the biggest. Spaniards in the week, Italians on a Saturday, Portuguese the rest of the time.' In addition to the descendants of the original Franco-escapees, 'the new generation [of Spaniards] are bankers' wives.'

While there is a small fresh fish counter at the massive Sainsbury's Market store that is two-minute walk away from the stall, and a smaller Tesco less than a minute's walk away, Norris does not see these as competition. 'You can go to Tesco and get almost anything else,' he says, referring to the fact that many people buy fruit and vegetables from the supermarket rather than the fruit and vegetable store in Tachbrook market. 'Mine's the only stall where you can't walk off and get anything.'

Despite the lack of competition, he is relentless in pursuing quality. He gets only about half of his stock from Billingsgate, and instead has built up relationships with fishermen in places such as Looe in Cornwall, who tweet him about what they have just caught. He describes how he sources his fish:

> There's very little haggling that you'll see me do. I've got the vast bulk of what I call my nice local fish already sitting in the shop in Cornwall. There's still a middle man; they're just based in Cornwall. They're picking out the very best stuff. I'm paying a premium but I know it's absolutely lovely. Everything. There's stuff I cannot get in Billingsgate. The huge hakes on the stall: that's how we've got our huge following of Spanish people.

The market for many traditional fish such as sprats has shrunk or disappeared, although when sprats are in season, Bangladeshi women 'suddenly appear' to buy them to make curries. A small contingent of long-time residents until recently would come to buy jellied eel from Norris, but, as he explains:

> Nobody moans like those customers. So I thought I'm going to make an experiment here. I'm gonna put them up by 50p. That means I could make not even what I'd need to make, but I wouldn't be selling them at a loss. I said to

Brendan, 'The first person who moans, that's going to be the last bowl of this I sell.' The first person who came by I told, 'It's gone up to £3.50 sir.' He said, 'I'm not spending that! You're having a laugh.' ... That was the last bowl I sold, and it'll stay that way. I was basically doing a public service and getting abused for it. Five pounds a kilo [price increase] on Dover Soles and nobody bats an eyelid. Ten pence on jellied eels and you've got a riot on your hands.

Along with jellied eels, the survival of backslang is also under threat. Norris exchanges a couple of words – such as 'ecrips' for prices – with the butcher stall next to his pitch, but doesn't know many more. Indeed, even the word costermonger appears to be obsolete: neither Norris nor Wright were familiar with it.

Conclusion

It became clear to me as I interviewed John Wright and John Norris how much of the history of London's street fishmongers has been lost, and how important a tool oral history can be to food historians.[3] Markets are a rich source of information about food proclivities, prejudices and supply chains, and their traders can shed much light on these phenomena. Many people alive today are vessels for memories told to them by people from earlier generations. Indeed there are still some street-sellers whose grandparents' lives may have overlapped with some of the people whom Mayhew describes, and who might carry with them information, say, that would help to fill in details between Mayhew's time and the end of the nineteenth century. And markets are so dynamic and fluid that interviewing people about what seems quotidian to them (jellied eels?) might soon come to seem historically relevant.

Notes

1. *London Labour and the London Poor* originated as a series of articles written in the 1840s for the *Morning Chronicle* newspaper. The first three volumes were published in 1851, and a fourth volume was published a decade later. This paper has drawn from a facsimile edition of the first volume.
2. Henry Mayhew, *London Labour and the London Poor: A Cyclopaedia of the Conditions and Earning of Those That* Will *Work, Those That* Cannot *Work, and Those that* Will Not *Work*, Volume I: The London Street Folk (London: Frank Cass, 1967) p. 9. Subsequent references are cited in the text.
3. Anyone interested applying oral history to food history should read the following: Máirtín Mac Con Iomaire, 'Culinary voices: perspectives from Dublin restaurants', *Oral History*, Spring 2011, pp. 65–78.

The Market near Pottery Hill (Testaccio, Rome)

Maureen B. Fant

Figure 1. The interior of the old market in Piazza Testaccio a few days before it closed, July 2012.

In July 2012, throughout the Eternal City, tradition-loving hearts broke when one of its most cherished public markets abandoned its ramshackle stalls in Piazza Testaccio (Figure 1) for a sparkling, just-completed construction six hundred metres away. Vendors who remembered riding their parents' wagons to the old market as children were pleased to set up in the bright new quarters with industrial fridges and running water (though some used the expensive move as an excuse to retire). Sentimental shoppers, however, mourned the jolly shouts, the piles of discarded artichoke and *puntarelle* trimmings, the fragrant fish guts by the fountain, that is, the human warmth and comforting squalor of the old market and the sense of being part of the eternal history of *cucina romanesca*.

Two years later, die-hard Testaccio shoppers (and I am one) have become unsentimentally accustomed to the Nuovo Mercato di Testaccio, the New Testaccio

Food and Markets

Figure 2 (left). The shiny new Nuovo Mercato di Testaccio, which opened in 2012. It conceals an interesting archaeological area of markets and warehouses.

Figure 3 (right). Monte Testaccio with Ristorante Checchino dal 1887, a historic restaurant built into the hill in the mid-nineteenth century to take advantage of the perfect year-round cellar conditions.

Figure 4 (left). The former slaughterhouse (mattatoio) of Testaccio was the largest in Europe at the turn of the 20th century. Today, beautifully restored, it houses a museum of contemporary art, university classrooms, and much besides.

Figure 5 (right). Pietro Lombardi's 1927 amphora fountain originally stood in Piazza Testaccio and was moved in the 1930s to Piazza dell'Emporio. It has now been cleaned and returned to its original location. The amphoras, of course, symbolize the Testaccio quarter and Monte dei Cocci.

The Market near Pottery Hill (Testaccio, Rome)

Market, as it is formally known (Figure 2). It's hard to begrudge the hard-working vendors a little comfort and hygiene, but the sense of loss remains acute.

The new structure consists of two buildings, separated by a pedestrian mall, on the corner of Via Galvani and Via Beniamino Franklin. Look to the left as you walk down via Galvani, with the Aventine Hill behind you, and you see an ancient artificial hill formed of pottery fragments, Monte Testaccio (or Monte dei Cocci), and we'll get back to it in a minute (Figure 3).[1] Look straight and observe the so-called ex-Mattatoio, the majestic (in its way) late-nineteenth-century slaughterhouse (Figure 4). But look right, at the new market complex, the putative standard-bearer of all that is good about Roman food, and the first things you see are a sushi restaurant and Roadhouse Grill. Continue to the corner, opposite the ex-Mattatoio, and a glassed-in staircase leads to a three-star hotel. Café tables in the pedestrian area announce that the quarter's venerable epithet, 'working-class', is now definitively obsolete. The newest addition is a snack bar (for want of a better word) called Strit Fud, pronounced 'street food'.

Over the next few pages, we'll have a look both at the archaeological and urban context of the new market, a neighbourhood associated more than any other with the traditional food and food supply of the city, and at the human side of the neighbourhood and its market, drawn largely from my own thirty-some years of shopping there.

******

The Testaccio quarter of Rome lies just within the third-century Aurelianic Walls on the south side of Rome. It is bounded by the Walls on one side, by a bend in the Tiber on two sides, and, on the side that looks toward the centre of Rome, by the Via Marmorata, which runs along the foot of the Aventine Hill (the southernmost of the canonical seven) between the Pyramid of Cestius and the Tiber. The area is fairly vast for a Roman neighbourhood (six hundred square metres), but, thanks to these physical boundaries, has always been somewhat isolated. It has evolved since antiquity from a busy commercial centre and river port to a quasi-rural area with vineyards and fields and space for outdoor events to a virtual workers' ghetto to (in part) a meat-packing district and finally, today, to a gentrified area where the uncool buy groceries in the morning and the hipsters go to clubs in the evening.

As Rome grew, the river port below the Tiber Island became inadequate.[2] The flat expanse of land just downstream, enclosed by the next bend of the river, was the logical place to expand, with warehouses, ship sheds and wholesale markets. This process began in the third century BC. The Emporium, as the principal market was called, is remembered in the present-day toponym Piazza dell'Emporio, at the point where the Via Marmorata meets the Tiber (Figure 5). The excavated remains can be seen from the bridge near the water level well below the street. Wine, wheat, olive oil and other commodities were imported by sea and hauled up the Tiber on barges drawn by oxen which plodded along the riverbank, a three-day journey from Ostia or Portus.[3] The goods were packed in large coarseware jars called amphoras, with two handles (by definition) and a globular or elongated body that tapered into a sturdy pointed foot. The handles were high up on the shoulder or neck, and the foot could be grabbed with the hand, rammed into the ground, or wedged neatly into the hold of a ship, where piles of these amphoras were remarkably stable. Many of the amphoras found in Testaccio bore stamps and painted inscriptions that provide precious insights into where they were manufactured and who owned them. We thus know that about eighty per cent of the imported olive oil came from Spain and about fifteen per cent from North Africa.

Any archaeologist will tell you that pottery is indestructible unless you grind it into powder and blow away its dust. Try to burn a broken, useless pot on the trash heap, and it will just get stronger. Recycling was, as today, an excellent solution. Intact jars were washed and reused or smashed and used in the making of *opus signinum* or otherwise in building construction. But not all the amphoras were (we infer) suitable for recycling, and that is where the story becomes interesting for us. Those that contained olive oil had a problem; the oil would seep into the thick, porous walls and become malodorous. The heaviest jars, those from Spain, which could weigh thirty kilograms empty (and contain seventy kilograms of oil), were hauled off to the disposal area, broken in half and arranged in neat rows. The thinner-walled North African amphoras were broken and the sherds wedged among the others to provide stability. Lime was then poured over all against the smell.

Between the first century BC and the third century AD the pottery mountain was built up until it reached a height of fifty-four metres and a roughly triangular circumference of about a kilometre. Its rather steep profile can be seen on engravings and maps of Rome over the centuries, emerging like a volcano from what is probably the most extended flat area in the hilly city of Rome. Those maps were more inclusive than the guidebooks and tourist material of the twentieth century, which habitually cut off at the Protestant Cemetery and Pyramid, perhaps with a mention of the 'suburban' Testaccio quarter beyond – albeit within the walls, but today gastronomic tourism has put the quarter, literally and figuratively, on the map.[4]

The uses to which the pottery mountain was put during the centuries after the oil jars ceased to be added make a lively story for another day. They included such violent games as pig hurling. At one point the hill was cast as Golgotha for Good Friday commemorations, and a cross still marks its summit. In an archaeological nightmare scenario, in the 1940s it was also used as a dumping place for earth removed from the Circus Maximus.

But the 1600s was when the story of the hill becomes interesting again in the history of Roman food. The cool air that emanated from the hill – a result of the sherds not being packed hermetically – was noticed by owners of the adjacent vineyards, who began to dig *grotte,* caves, for storing wine. In 1870, when Rome became capital of the new Kingdom of Italy, the restricted ownership of the *grotte* was expanded, and the site, unique in all the world, was further dug into for the storage of meat, oil and other foodstuffs. Its exploitation did not stop there. The foot of the hill became populated with barrel makers, blacksmiths, bakers and, later, even a movie-film factory as well as habitations and all kinds of workshops. Aristocrats' wine cellars began to be replaced by popular *osterie*, which would play an important role in the further development of *cucina romanesca*. In the early 1980s, the most conspicuous population in the old hill was auto body shops, but there was also the Scuola Popolare di Musica and numerous trattorias and restaurants, descendants of the old *osterie*.[5] My first solo circumambulation of the hill, about then, was disturbing. Via Galvani was urban enough, but the route quickly came to resemble a rural road with scarcely a living soul – certainly no other visible pedestrians – except those I was sure were lurking in the overgrown vegetation or derelict structures with designs on my purse or person (Figure 6).

******

In its some-three-thousand years of existence, Rome has been characterized more by architectural evolution than by revolution. Although it is not correct to say it has developed without benefit of planning, its many-layered urban fabric, especially in the historic centre, is not the stuff of orderly urban layout and strict zoning.[6] Still, Rome has been altered radically by design a handful times over the centuries. The first of these convulsive moments was the reign of Augustus, who boasted in his *Res Gestae* that he had found a city of brick and left a city of marble. Another was the reign of the Renaissance Pope Sixtus V (r. 1585–1590), and the last was the Fascist era. Since the post-World War II period, the centre of Rome has been protected.[7] Building speculation and urban sprawl do not count since most has taken place mercifully outside the centre, and 'planning' or 'vision' seems conspicuously irrelevant.[8] Much of the building that the world thinks of as Fascist actually took place earlier as part of the Roma Capitale program introduced by the Savoia after Unification. Romans still talk about the grey, rusticated 'Piedmontese' style of public buildings, but they are not important for Testaccio, confirmed as almost a workers' ghetto, given its geographic isolation.[9] Most of the condominium buildings we see today originated as *case popolari,* public housing, and throughout the quarter are vocational schools. Testaccio was supposed to be all about industry. The street names of the spacious new orderly grids were those of Italian giants of invention and technological advancement – Volta and Galvani, Manuzio and Bodoni – but also Beniamino Franklin.

The modern era of Testaccio began with the 1883 Master Plan.[10] It called for the demolition of the old slaughterhouse near the Porta Flaminia (Piazza del Popolo) on the northern edge of town, and the construction of a new one in Testaccio, already exclusively populated by labourers. Housing construction began; public services were still lacking, but hopes were high for the new quarter, which was meant to absorb the various smelly or noisy industries the city needed but preferred not to see. The Plan was nearly derailed by the Torlonia family, which protested that its nearby lands would be placed at risk. Nevertheless, things got under way in 1888 with a handful of buildings,

Food and Markets

Figure 6 (left). Monte Testaccio, a hill made entirely of amphora fragments, has a circumference of about 1 km, and not all of it has yet been gentrified into restaurants and clubs.

Figure 7 (right). Piazza Testaccio, original site of the market, in January 2015, a year and a half after the market closed, ready to start its new life as gathering place of the new, gentrified Testaccio quarter.

Figure 8 (left). Some of todays vendors recall that, after the market closed in the afternoon, the tables of Zi' Elena's gelateria would fill the piazza. Today's it's a small but excellent bar.

Figure 9 (right). Correctly trimmed vegetables (here puntarelle) have always been a feature of the Testaccio market. There are still a few perfectionists maintaining the tradition.

including warehouses, a railway station and the slaughterhouse. Then the bottom fell out of the construction business. The little that had been built fell into the hands of public institutions, and the quality of life in the quarter became dire. In 1905, a local committee was founded for the 'economic and moral improvement of Testaccio'. One of its first acts was the opening of a fruit and vegetable market in Piazza Mastro Giorgio, later called Piazza Testaccio, as a 'meeting place to foster socialization and human relations among the inhabitants of Testaccio'.[11]

And that it became. The market occupied a large square in the middle of a square piazza demarcated by vias Giovanni Battista Bodoni, Luca della Robbia, Aldo Manuzio and Mastro Giorgio and surrounded on four sides by shops, businesses and places to eat, as well as the first residential buildings of the new quarter (Figure 7). Soon neighbourhood personalities emerged and were given nicknames. For years the market was open-air without permanent structures. In the nostalgia-filled days before the big move, one of my vegetable men told me how in the afternoon the piazza would clear out and tables from Zi' Elena's *gelateria* would fill the space. The statuesque Zi' Elena ('Aunt Helen'), known as Zinnona ('well-endowed'), herself was a well-known neighbourhood figure, and her bar is still there (Figure 8). Others recalled how they began their careers in the produce business as children, riding in on their fathers' carts. Liliana Alfonsi, a vendor of an earlier generation – she retired some twenty years ago – told me how her mother sold eggs from a basket in the 1920s. Liliana and her sister, alternating fortnights, shared an excellent stall assisted by their children, but when the sisters retired, the next generation moved on.

It was roofed, for hygiene, in the 1950s, but for the rest of its existence it remained a characteristic Roman market, with lots of yelling and practically no food that did not belong on the typical Roman table. Yes, there was one stall that sold exotic produce, but it closed. The Calabrian stall, still going strong, has expanded at the new market, but Testaccio was the quintessential Roman market, with the best *puntarelle*, artichokes, *broccoletti, rughetta* and other vegetables, as well as plenty of meat (including skinned lamb's heads, tripe and horsemeat) and one whole side devoted to fish, mainly from the Tyrrhenian Sea, which washes the coast of Lazio.

But there was something else going on besides the stasis of tradition. During Testaccio's decades of development, the Aventine Hill too was undergoing some changes. The imposing monasteries that had owned fields and vineyards on the plain around the mountain withdrew, while villas and exclusive apartment buildings for the affluent began to populate the hill. The Aventino became, and still is, one of Rome's most expensive and exclusive neighbourhoods with practically no commerce. All those rich folks, or their maids, had to shop somewhere. By the early 1980s, another phenomenon was under way. The Slow Food movement was around the corner, and affluent young Romans (and not-so-affluent adopted Romans like myself) were rediscovering the old food ways. The drums sent out word that Testaccio was the best of Rome's municipal markets. It was probably true, but they are all good and some

Figure 10. The restored interior of the ex-Mattatoio, as the complex is now known.

Figure 11. Carmelo D'Agostino, famed for his tomatoes-only stall, stayed one extra day in the old market. The city confiscated his tomatoes and imposed a heavy fine.

are larger. Where Testaccio excelled – paradoxically since the neighbourhood was still being called working class – was in the high level of service. You could, and still can, buy, or request, your *broccoletti* already trimmed, your artichokes ready to cook Roman style, your fresh peas and beans freshly shelled.[12] And the *puntarelle*! *Puntarelle*, which has been in the Italian dictionary for only about the last twenty years, are the trimmed stalks of the Catalonian chicory. Today it's rare to find them trimmed properly with a knife – most people use a gadget – and fewer vendors trim them to order, but it used to be common to ask the women to fix you some to be picked up when you'd finished the rest of your shopping. Fortunately, a handful of experts made the move to the new market; many did not (Figure 9).

But back to the 1890s. The new slaughterhouse, the Mattatoio, or, as its inscription states, the Stabilimento di Mattazione, was magnificent, the most advanced in Europe. High above the three arches of its monumental entrance a sculpture group of a winged genius combatting a beef critter ennobles the grisly work within (Figure 10). The complex, which also included the cattle market, employed a huge workforce, the lowliest members of which, the *vaccinari*, received a bonus of meat with their pay, not steaks and chops but offal and tail (and sometimes hides to be tanned).[13] They would take the day's haul across the street to the *osterie* dug into the pottery mountain, where tasty recipes were developed for these humble ingredients. *Coda alla vaccinara*, Rome's flagship dish, stewed oxtail, was named for them, and the various meats, and the cuisine they inspired, were known collectively as the *quinto quarto*, the fifth quarter, a mathematical paradox until you consider that the weight of the entire *quinto quarto* is about the same as that of one of the quarters.[14] Today trattorias all over Rome still offer the *quinto quarto* on their menus, though the mad-cow scare permanently eliminated a number of items, including brains (*cervella*) and spinal cord (*schienale*). The two most durable *quinto quarto* dishes, besides the eternal oxtail, have turned out to be *trippa alla romana* and *rigatoni alla paiata* (or *pagliata*).[15] The former is honeycomb tripe cooked with tomato sauce and flavoured with *menta romana,* a kind of spearmint, and pecorino romano cheese. The latter is short, tubular pasta with tomato sauce and pecorino romano and lengths of intestine of the milk-fed animal, tied into rings to keep the cheese-like milk-solids inside. Guidebooks always like to say that Roman cuisine is all about offal, but what they should actually be saying is that *quinto quarto* cooking is only one of several pillars of the traditional urban Roman kitchen. One look at the Testaccio market, new or old, makes it clear that chicories and brassicas of many kinds, artichokes, zucchini, spinach, tomatoes and other vegetables galore form a considerably greater part of the local diet than meat of any kind, much less tripe.[16]

The Mattatoio closed in 1975 and was mostly abandoned for a good twenty years. Some of its structures were used for a senior citizens' centre (still there), an international centre mainly for immigrants (well before there were noticeable numbers of immigrants in Rome), and other such 'popular' purposes. I myself sat on the ground inside the ex-Mattatoio to hear a concert by Frank Zappa in about 1982. Conditions got worse before they got better, but today the complex houses a branch of MACRO, a contemporary art museum, a university architecture faculty, the Scuola Popolare di Musica, a fair-trade supermarket and much besides. The structure, with its corrals and tracks for moving carcasses around, has been cleaned up and polished and stands as a very beautiful example of industrial archaeology. Renovation of the large refrigeration building next door has begun as well.

The transition from the old market to the new, just across the street from the ex-Mattatoio, was a near comedy of anti-climaxes, with delays for archaeological excavation, incomplete construction, and arguments over what the market vendors considered unfair competition from the farmers market held on weekends in the ex-Mattatoio. Finally the day came. The glass panels in the ceiling of the new building created a stifling greenhouse effect under the July sun, but the atmosphere was festive. Pino and Linda, whose stall had been one of the constants of my years in Rome, had taken a double 'box' (Italian for stall) and had clearly passed the torch to Francesca and Paola, their daughters, who offered exotic fruit and cold drinks to celebrate the inauguration.[17] Many boxes remained unoccupied till after the summer holidays.

Meanwhile back at Piazza Testaccio, a small tragedy was being played out. On opening day, my husband and I had gone to pay our respects to the old market on our way to the new. Carmelo D'Agostino, whose tomatoes-only stall had been finding its way into magazines and blogs the world over but who had decided not to make the move, stood alone at his post in the empty market surrounded by his multiple varieties of tomatoes (Figure 11). We waved, but a sort of bouncer kept us from entering. We later heard that the city had confiscated Carmelo's tomatoes and fined him a large sum. Two years later, his case continues.[18]

Archaeological excavation prior to construction of the new market began in 2005 and lasted till 2009. Back then, when the idea of the new market was fresh and passers-by could admire neat walls of *opus reticulatum* in trial trenches on its site, most vendors grumbled about the proposed change, but Carmelo said he welcomed the idea of selling his tomatoes atop an ancient market. He never explained, at least not to me, why he changed his mind.

It wasn't exactly a market they discovered at the building site but two warehouses, probably for the storage of wine and other liquids.[19] The stratigraphy exposed by the excavations gives an uninterrupted picture of the area from the late republic or early empire (first century BC to first century AD) to modern times. At the beginning a museum was promised beneath the new market. At the moment there is only parking and a rectangular hole in the middle of the market building where a small piece of ancient wall and some pottery on a table (to suggest active archaeological work) can be viewed.

The demographics have changed. The connoisseur food tourists seeking the real Rome have been joined by larger, louder snack-seeking groups. There are more stalls selling higher-end or prepared foods, not unwelcome. There is more junk for sale, but also cute, though incongruous, design thingies. The raw materials are still great. The produce at the burgeoning farmers markets is a tad fresher, and it is practically impossible to find the wild salads from the Roman countryside at Testaccio as we did until eight or ten years ago. The farmers have the edge there too. But the skill with which the vegetables are trimmed and the conversations with the vendors, whether about their health or for an exchange of recipes, remains.

Notes

1. The name Testaccio comes from the Latin *testa,* pottery. Mons Testaceus is thus 'pottery hill,' but the *-accio* suffix in Italian also has connotations of being oversized, disorderly, old and otherwise unattractive. *Cocci* are sherds or, disparagingly, any collection of crockery.
2. A. Claridge, *Rome: An Archaeological Guide*, 2nd edition (Oxford: Oxford UP, 2010), p. 401 ff.
3. Ostia, technically a fluvial port at the mouth of the Tiber, which had constant silting problems, was never really satisfactory. The emperor Trajan built a new port, Portus, with a sheltered hexagonal basin for mooring ships. Its remains, with warehouses and other structures, are near Fiumicino airport can be visited by special permission.
4. Today the maps even mark the Volpetti shop on Via Marmorata where I have been buying bread and cheese since 1980, a small but well-stocked gourmet destination run by two marketing-genius brothers and, now, an Erasmus-scholar son/nephew.
5. At least one body shop remains, on Via Galvani, and is a good spot to catch sight of old Fiat 500 cars. The shop itself is dug straight into the hill with a disconcerting toilet near the street.
6. The emperor Augustus divided the city into 14 Regiones, a name that survives in the *rioni* of Rome within the walls. Outside the centre are *quartieri* and farther still *distretti*, all served by one or more municipal markets in a wide range of sizes. Testaccio is the most recently created *rione* of Rome, number XX. Its symbol is a picture of an amphora.
7. Though that is not the first word to come to mind at the sight of Foot Lockers on charming streets once lined with fashionable emporia or artisans' workshops.
8. Especially the concept of associating parking places and sufficient public transport with large, new residential areas.
9. The style is epitomized by the Palace of Justice on Piazza Cavour, which the Romans still call the 'palazzaccio,' meaning roughly, the big-old-ugly building, which pretty much sums up what they think of the style and how it contrasts with the tawny hues and gentler lines of the rest of central Rome.
10. G. Malizia, *Testaccio* (Roma: Edizioni La Campanella, 2004), p. 55.
11. Malizia, p. 57.
12. The Roman word for trimming vegetables is *capare* – *pulire* or *mondare* in standard Italian. Unlike the Anglo-French way of serving fully armoured artichokes and letting the diners pile refuse on their plates, Romans trim the artichokes carefully before cooking so that nearly everything that goes to the table is edible. The technique is neither simple nor intuitive. *Broccoletti* – broccoli rabe, but so much more delicious – need to be trimmed aggressively yet lovingly of all nasty leaves and most of their stems, but it's not just a matter of hacking off the stringy stems. The women, and some men, who do it right peel and split the remaining stem ends with an artistic, delicate touch. When properly trimmed, the *broccoletti* taste peppery, not bitter.
13. Literally, cow men, also known, more graphically, as *scorticari*, skinners, since that was one of their unpleasant jobs.
14. There is no reason not to believe the claim of the restaurant Checchino dal 1887 to have invented it. The present owners are the fifth generation since the original wine shop dug into the pottery mountain. It is still the best place in town to taste the old flavours.

15. For recipes of these and more, see O. Zanini De Vita, *Popes, Peasants, and Shepherds: Recipes and Lore from Rome and Lazio*, translated by Maureen B. Fant (Berkeley: U California P, 2013). There was joy throughout the land in March 2015 when the European Commission lifted the fourteen-year ban on veal *paiata*. Since the days of Mad Cow, lamb intestines had been used in place of veal.
16. Bread, pasta and pizza are, of course, another sustaining pillar. Although I have not conducted the experiment, I am fairly certain that if you put a Roman on a desert island with one food, he would choose bread – good, chewy, traditional *pane casereccio*.
17. Linda is Testaccio's most skilled trimmer of artichokes the Roman way. Pino died in September 2015, and another pillar of the old Testaccio market fell.
18. In either case, this is a good example of how Italy regularly shoots itself in the foot. With his tomatoes, and the instructional lecture that accompanied every sale, Carmelo did more for educating the public on the subtleties and variety of Italian food than twenty regional governments. He should have been given a medal and a strong incentive to keep up the good work. He had been at the market since childhood, but eventually converted his father's general produce stall to just tomatoes and passed into legend.
19. Preliminary excavation reports (mainly abstracts), in Italian, can be downloaded from the website of the archaeological superintendency of Rome: www.archeoroma.beniculturali.it.

The Complete History of Food Markets, Abridged

Len Fisher and Janet Clarkson

International food markets have become so distorted that 'the luxury tastes of the richest parts of the world [are] being allowed to compete against the satisfaction of the basic needs of the poor'. This is the stark warning of Dr Olivier de Schutter, United Nations Special Rapporteur on the Right to Food, in his final report to the UN Human Rights Council.[1]

How has this situation arisen? de Schutter lays much of the blame on agribusiness. His view is supported by the EU Agricultural and Rural Convention, which argues that 'current food [markets] are efficient only from the point of view of maximizing agribusiness profits and must be radically and democratically redesigned'.[2] 'At the local, national and international levels', says de Schutter, 'the policy environment must urgently accommodate alternative, democratically-mandated visions.'[3]

We argue here that this is a very simplistic approach to the problem, and that to make real progress we need to understand why food markets have evolved as they have. In our rapid-fire talk, presented at the Symposium in picture-postcard fashion, we showed that the evolution of food markets has often been affected by an on-going scenario known as *The Tragedy of the Commons*. This scenario is ultimately responsible for the present condition of food markets, and also for their likely development in the future. In this written version of our talk we describe the scenario, show how it is exemplified in food markets, and explore what (if anything) can be done about it in the future.

The Tragedy of the Commons
The Tragedy of the Commons is a problem that arises when:

- It is in the interest of individuals or groups of people to cooperate with other individuals or groups for their mutual benefit BUT
- where one individual or group do better still by cheating on the cooperation. And so they can UNTIL
- the other individuals or groups use the same logic WHEN
- all of the individuals or groups end up in a worse position than if they had maintained the cooperation in the first place.

The scenario is named after an example proposed by the American ecologist Garrett Hardin in 1966.[4] Hardin used the example of a group of herders grazing their animals on common land. By the logic of self-interest, it would pay an individual herder to add an extra animal to his herd, slightly reducing the average amount of food available for each animal, but still providing an overall gain to that herder. What is sauce for goose is sauce for the gander, however, and if one herder can use this apparently ironclad logic, there seems to be no reason for the others not to do the same. When they all follow the same logic, however, the commons become over-grazed and all of the herders lose out. By following the logic of self-interest, the herders have somehow ended up in a situation where self-interest is the last thing that is being served.

Figure 1. Tragedy of the Commons. Captions by Len Fisher; photograph by Mario Roberto Duran Ortiz (used by permission).

This is not a trivial logical puzzle with an easy solution. It is a deep logical paradox that affects us all in our daily lives, from the maintenance of our relationships to the root causes of international conflict and the preservation of the world's environment and resources.[5]

But what does the Tragedy of the Commons have to do with the problem that de Schutter spelled out? As background to the question, we offer a cartoonishly short synopsis of the evolution of modern food markets, based loosely on historical fact.

We guess that the earliest food 'markets' simply consisted of bartering – meat for grain, for example:

The Complete History of Food Markets, Abridged

But bartering was inefficient, and a new solution was needed:

> **The Daily Caveman**
> 100,000 Years B.C.
> **FORGET BARTERING:**
> Use the amazing new "MONEY"!
> By LEN GRUNT

These methods worked fine if the participants were neighbours and the food was fresh. But trade could be expanded if the food could be preserved for longer periods of time:

> **The Daily Pyramid**
> 2000 Years B.C.
> **FINE DINING**
> By LEN GRUNTANKHAMAN
> Your locusts will last longer if you preserve them in honey!

It was rather easy for traders to cheat, however, especially when the food was in containers and not readily visible. The answer was regulation:

> **The Daily Pyramid**
> 2000 Years B.C.
> **TOUGH NEW PENALTIES FOR UNDERWEIGHT FOOD**
> By LEN GRUNTANKHAMAN
> Cheating traders' ears to be nailed to door!!

Gradually, international trading developed. But the competition introduced new problems:

> **The Daily Pyramid**
> 1800 Years B.C.
> **THE IMPORT DILEMMA**
> By LEN GRUNTANKHAMAN
> Are imported almonds, apples and pears ruining the local date palm industry?

Expanding trade routes brought exotic new species to markets, although local customers did not always know what to make of them:

Food and Markets

> ### DunRoman
> *130 A.D.*
> ### WILD HAGGIS TERRORIZES COLISEUM CROWDS
> *By LENUS GRUNTUS*

With other conquests came yet more food experiences:

> ### The Spanish Sun
> *July 12, 1525*
> ### THIS NEW FOOD IS AMAIZEING!
> *By LEN GRUNTZALES*

Food transport, however, remained a problem. Until the early part of the twentieth century, the solution remained the same as in the times of the ancient Egyptians – to preserve the food in some way so as to prevent bacterial spoilage. This might be done by cooking it, as in ship's biscuits, by drying it, or by pickling, potting or canning it.[6] But then there came a runaway effect as scientists discovered new ways to transport food without the use of preservatives. It was found that meat, and later some fruits and vegetables, could be frozen, or even just chilled, and transported in this state.[7] Controlled atmosphere storage added another dimension, as did fast air transport.[8] Foods themselves could even be altered by selection for characteristics like packability and toughness (never mind the flavour!).

As these foods became more readily available, so expectations as to their availability rose even higher, with suppliers responding to these expectations by applying financial pressure to suppliers to provide yet more food, in greater variety, for less money. This runaway effect (the Tragedy of the Commons in action) was great for consumers at first, but, as more and more people demanded access to these previously exotic foods, production in their place of origin shifted towards them, and fresh local food was squeezed out of the market.

Most of the previously exotic foods whose availability we now take for granted in the West are produced in poorer countries. According to a report by the Food and Agriculture Organization of the United Nations, 'for every one farmer in the developed world, there are 19 in the developing world'.[9] It is these farmers who are being most affected as, with increasing globalization and increasing expectations of availability, corporate profits have become the *sine qua non*.

The Complete History of Food Markets, Abridged

This is just the situation that de Schutter pointed out in his report. A cartoonist has represented it by a shopper looking at a packet and saying, 'The ingredients are listed in order of importance.' 'So what comes after "profit"?' asks his cynical companion.[10]

But it is not agribusiness's search for profit that is the ultimate culprit. It is the inexorable logic of the Tragedy of the Commons, where consumers as well as businesses push for that little bit extra on their own account – cheaper food, more variety, greater availability. If just a few people did it, there would be no problem. When we all do it, the problems rapidly multiply.

Those problems are added to by our expectations of perfection in our food, so that anything not perfect or not immediately used is thrown away – 40% of apples, 24% of grapes, 47% of bakery products, 68% of bagged salads from one British supermarket chain, for example.[11]

Meanwhile, the Tragedy of the Commons played out between nations is producing another disaster that will impact on our future food supplies – global warming. As one of us has pointed out in a recent article, global warming is already affecting farmers in sub-Saharan Africa.[12] It means:

- longer growing seasons, so that pests have more time to proliferate;
- longer rainy seasons, so that roads and other infrastructure suffer more damage;
- ultimately, a diminution of food supplies to the West because of the above factors.

Such consequences leave consumers – and even corporations and governments – feeling powerless. What can we do about it?

An innovative approach by the German company Daimler-Benz suggests one possibility.[13] It all started in 1994, when Mercedes had been trying to sell buses to Ecuador, who wanted them, but simply did not have the money. What it did have was bananas, which it had been selling to the European Union until new regulations made imports from Latin-American companies much harder.

In a brilliant bit of innovative thinking, Mercedes struck a $65m 'buses for bananas' deal, reselling the bananas in Russia and the Far East. The principle was subsequently extended, with honey melons from Honduras and coffee beans from Nigeria in exchange for Mercedes trucks, and dried Colombian pineapples bartered for AEG energy plants.

And so, as we started, we are back to bartering – but with a difference, since this form of bartering could help to provide vital infrastructure support for the countries that are providing us in the West with our food. It is only a first step, but it is a very important one.

To go further requires political will, but above all political and community understanding. The aim of this article has been to provide one essential foundation for the development of that understanding. We are well aware that we have simplified the discussion in the interests of clarity, but clarity, above all, is what is needed for progressive decision-making at this critical time.[14]

Notes

1. O. de Schutter, 'The Transformative Potential of the Right to Food', Final Report to the United Nations Human Rights Council, 24 January 2014.
2. European Union Agricultural and Rural Convention, 'UN Right to Food Expert Demands Radical Change', *ARC2020* <http://www.arc2020.eu/front/2014/03/un-right-to-food-expert-looks-at-broken-food-systems/>.
3. de Schutter.
4. G. Hardin, 'The Tragedy of the Commons', *Science* 162 (1968), pp. 1243–48.
5. L. Fisher, *Rock, Paper, Scissors: Game Theory in Everyday Life* (New York: Basic Books, 2008).
6. S. Shephard, *Pickled, Potted and Canned: How the Art and Science of Food Preserving Changed the World* (London: Simon & Schuster, 2006).
7. J.T. Critchell and J. Raymond, *A History of the Frozen Meat Trade: An Account of the Development and Present Day Methods of Preparation, Transport and Marketing of Frozen and Chilled Meats* (London: Constable & Co., 1912) <http://archive.org/stream/historyoffrozenmoocrituoft/historyof-frozenmoocrituoft_djvu.txt>.
8. D.R. Dilley, 'Historical Aspects and Perspectives of Controlled Atmosphere Storage', *Food Preservation by Modified Atmospheres* (Boca Raton: CRC Press, 1990), pp. 187-96.
9. Food and Agriculture Organization of the United Nations, *Dimensions of Need: An Atlas of Food and Agriculture* (New York: United Nations, 1995) <http://www.fao.org/docrep/u8480e/U8480E01.htm>.
10. Bob Thaves and Tom Thaves, *Frank and Ernest* 8 June 2007.
11. 'Tesco Says Almost 30,000 Tonnes of Food "Wasted"', *BBC News UK* <http://www.bbc.com/news/uk-24603008>.
12. L. Fisher, 'The Effect of Global Warming on Future Food Supplies', *Encyclopedia of Food Issues*, ed. by K. Albala (New York: Sage Publications, 2014), pp. 719–23.
13. J. Eisenhammer, 'Benz Barters Buses for Bananas to Break Trade Impasse', *The Independent*, 21 February 1994.
14. For more detail of the role of game theory in food markets see, for example, Richard J. Sexton, 'Noncooperative Game Theory: A Review with Potential Applications to Agricultural Markets', *Food Marketing Policy Center Research Report 22* (Storrs, CT: University of Connecticut, 1993) <http://www.fmpc.uconn.edu/publications/rr/rr22.pdf>.

Food and the Female Body: Paralleling the Food Market and the Prostitution Market in John Cleland's *Fanny Hill*

Mary J. Gray

In *The Sex of Things: Gender and Consumption in Historical Perspective*, Victoria de Grazia establishes a necessary link between power and consumption, examining the intersection of these themes in relation to women and the market. Because of the power dynamic existing between the consumer and the consumed, de Grazia claims, a 'myriad [of] conflicts over power […] constitute the politics of consumption'. In John Cleland's *Fanny Hill or Memoirs of a Woman of Pleasure*, the power conflicts of consumption emerge within the context of sexual relations, specifically between Fanny and her male clients. Through her various sexual experiences, Fanny partakes in the struggle for power between the consumer and the consumed, experiencing firsthand how the market functions as 'the site where resources derived [… a] form of power' and where 'women figure […] as objects of exchange and consumption'.[1]

In order to analyse the theme of consumption, it remains important to distinguish among the wide variety of contexts in which the word appears. Of these different contexts, two main uses of the word consumption emerge in *Fanny Hill*: gastronomic consumption and commercial consumption. Though both of these forms intermingle, gastronomic consumption serves as the primary focus of this paper. The *Oxford English Dictionary* defines gastronomic consumption as 'the action or fact of eating or drinking something, or of using something up in an activity'. In *The Tropics Bite Back: Culinary Coups in Caribbean Literature*, Valérie Loichot analyses consumption in relation to sex, recognizing consumption as a force that binds sex and food. While physical food gets consumed during the act of consumption, Loichot asserts that the body becomes the metaphorical food of sex; she writes, 'Sexuality … gives us an entryway into articulating the relationship between the consumption of food and the consumption of human bodies'. Because 'the sexual act is often represented in terms of metaphorical eating', the woman or sexual subject metaphorically transforms into the consumable.[2] Though several different points of connection between food and sex exist, the market represents a specific space that showcases the role that gastronomic consumption plays in bridging these two seemingly disparate themes.

In *Markets, Market Culture and Popular Protest in Eighteenth-Century Britain and Ireland*, Adrian Randall et al. analyse the market, beginning with the claim that 'markets of one form or another have occupied a key place in the social, economic and political cultures of all peoples throughout recorded history'. In their eyes, the eighteenth-century market proves crucial to society on many levels; the authors note how 'the market and market place [...] formed a concrete physical location and the centre for community interchange'. While the majority of this interchange was economic, Randall and his co-authors argue that the opportunity for interchange within the market can be of a social or political nature. Although emphasized as a physical space that enables the flow of money, things, people, ideas and connections, 'the market' takes on different meanings depending on the context. While the market exists on the physical level, serving as a commercial space for the sale of food and other products, Randall et al. recognize how 'the eighteenth-century market was not merely a location for economic transaction between buyer and seller' as it also represented 'an abstract agency' or conceptual entity.[3] This conceptual entity of the market proves crucial to an analysis that incorporates both the literal and metaphorical conceptions of the market as a space of consumption.

In *The History of Sexuality: An Introduction,* Michel Foucault dedicates a portion of his argument to analysing the concept of space. He begins by explaining how different sexualities 'haunt [different] spaces', using 'the sexuality of the home, the school, the prison' as examples. Foucault delves further into the intersection of sexuality and space by relating the two to power, describing how the sexuality of spaces 'form the correlate of exact procedures of power'.[4] Like the home, school or prison, the market emerges as a space of sexuality – one in which a power-struggle exists. In accordance with Foucault's connection of sexuality and power in different spaces, Cleland exposes how the purchasing power acquired in the market relates to the sexual power struggle and, ultimately, how consumption enables power. Cleland accomplishes this by creating a scene of power that takes places in an actual market: the Covent Garden market scene with Mr Norbert.

Throughout John Cleland's *Fanny Hill or Memoirs of a Woman of Pleasure*, the market emerges as a space of sexual power. Though diverse markets exist in the novel, Cleland examines the relationship between two specific markets: the physical space of the food market and the conceptual entity of the prostitution market. During Fanny's career as a prostitute, she undergoes a variety of sexual and relational encounters in which consumption emerges as the underlying force of power. Gastronomic consumption constantly operates in Fanny's encounters with her sexual partners, creating multiple parallels between different forms of consumption and different types of markets. Fanny's encounter with Mr Norbert – beginning in the fruit market and extending into the bedroom – encapsulates the parallel between the food and prostitution markets and exposes consumption as the force that links the two. In order to fully highlight the relationship between Fanny's sexual encounters and the theme of consumption, Cleland fills the scenes of Fanny's interactions with her sexual partners with food: the direct presence of food, the constant use of descriptive food-language, the timely occurrence of meals before or after sex scenes and the duality existing between the table and the bed. Through the presence of food in *Fanny Hill*, Cleland establishes consumption as the underlying force of power in the sexual encounters between Fanny and her partners, paralleling the food market and the prostitution market – and, ultimately, the literal consumption of food and the metaphorical consumption of Fanny.

While Fanny's partners exercise power over her through gastronomic consumption, Cleland incorporates another reading of consumption into the text: reverse consumption by which the consumed becomes the consumer. By consistently depicting the vagina as a mouth – the female mouth – Cleland establishes a reverse gastronomic consumption of the male. Through the physical positioning of her body in relation to her sexual partner's and by seeking out sex for the purpose of her own pleasure, Fanny reasserts her agency and exercises power. In so doing, she sexually subjects her partners in the exact way that she has been subjected, achieving power through this reverse consumption. Although Cleland uses consumption as the force that subjugates Fanny, this inclusion of reverse consumption enables Fanny to reclaim and reassert her power.

Gastronomic consumption: the female body as a consumable object

Though the scene occurs far into the novel, the core analysis of this paper begins with Fanny's acquaintance with the rich Mr Norbert in Covent Garden market; the scene serves as an encapsulation of the market as a space of sexual power, paralleling the prostitution and food markets and highlighting how the theme of gastronomic consumption emerges on both a literal and metaphorical level. Fanny's introduction to Mr Norbert transpires during an errand to a fruiterer's shop, during which Fanny experiences an unexpected encounter in the marketplace; she relates how 'whilst I was chaffering for the fruit I wanted, I observed myself followed by a young gentleman'.[5] Amidst Fanny's examination of the food at the fruiterer's market, Mr Norbert simultaneously conducts his own examination of Fanny. After his initial survey of Fanny's person, Mr Norbert 'came to the same basket that [she] stood at, and […] began his approaches' (p. 136). This scene with Mr Norbert in the Covent Garden marketplace serves as a microcosm of the entire novel because, through paralleling the food market with the prostitution market, Cleland creates a second parallel between the literal consumption of food and the metaphorical consumption of the woman. As this market scene encapsulates the principal argument, the analysis begins with this scene and works both backwards and forwards into the novel.

Direct presence of food. The direct presence of food functions as a major vehicle by which Cleland depicts the female as a consumable object. Of the many scenes in which food appears in its physical form, the fruit market scene where Fanny first encounters Mr Norbert serves as the most prominent. Fanny describes how she 'stepped over to a fruit shop in Covent Garden, to pick up some table fruit for myself and the young women' (p. 136). Fanny intends to buy fruit for the purpose of gastronomic consumption, yet as Fanny stands at the fruit shop examining the fruit, Mr Norbert conducts his own examination of Fanny. Like Fanny, Mr Norbert's inspection at the market ultimately relates to the purpose of consumption, though consumption of a much different nature than Fanny's. Cleland draws a parallel between the literal and metaphorical consumptions that will occur: while the fruit will be gastronomically consumed, the female body will be sexually consumed.

The scene at the Covent Garden food market establishes Fanny as the consumed, creating a power dynamic between the consumer and the consumed. This complex power relationship unfolds through Mr Norbert's actions in the fruit market, which substantiate assertions made by de Grazia concerning the 'purchasing power acquired and expended in the market'.[6] Fanny writes how '[Mr Norbert] loaded me with fruit, all the rarest and dearest he could pick out' after 'giving the first price asked for the fruit' (pp. 137, 136). Following his objectifying examination of Fanny's body at the fruit market, this purchase of fruit works to further objectify Fanny because Mr Norbert's purchase of the fruit foreshadows another transaction that will follow: his purchase of Fanny herself. As the purchaser of the consumable, objectified Fanny, Mr Norbert claims power over her, perpetuating the complicated power dynamic between the consumer and the consumed.

Use of descriptive food language. Cleland also highlights consumption's control of the power dynamic between Mr Norbert and Fanny by using language associated with food to characterize Mr Norbert as the consumer and Fanny as the object of consumption. From the moment that Cleland introduces Mr Norbert into the novel, the descriptive language used by Fanny depicts him as a consumer. Mr Norbert's hunger, however, supersedes the gastronomic, physical hunger of the body. Instead, he exhibits sexual hunger. Fanny likens Mr Norbert's sexual hunger to physical hunger, terming this sexual desire 'his strength of appetite' (p. 142). Because Mr Norbert's hunger is of a sexual nature he achieves the appeasement of his hunger through a metaphorical, sexual consumption. Just as the consumption of food satiates physical hunger, Mr Norbert satisfies his sexual desire through the consumption of women.

While Cleland uses food-related language to depict Mr Norbert as a consumer, he exposes how Mr Norbert exercises power over women through his ability to consume them. To illustrate this, Cleland focuses on Mr Norbert's obsession with taking the virginity of his sexual partners. During her elaboration of Mr Norbert's character, Fanny describes Mr Norbert's preference as a 'taste of maiden[s]', which in the eighteenth century alluded to a virgin woman; Mr Norbert's taste for maidens, therefore, equates to having a 'taste' for virginity, a parallel of sexual preference with consumption (p. 165; *OED*). Cleland specifically uses verbs that relate to the act of eating to link Mr Norbert's sexual preference for virgins to his metaphorical consumption of Fanny. Early in her acquaintance with Mr Norbert, Fanny describes Mr Norbert's lustful glut for virginity, claiming that he requires innocence in a woman 'for no other end than to feast [himself] with the pleasure of destroying it' (p. 140). Mr Norbert's desire to 'feast' on Fanny's supposed-virginity illustrates his desire to metaphorically consume her. Through using words closely related to food-language, Cleland creates the illusion of Mr Norbert consuming Fanny's virginity, attempting to exert power over her through sexual consumption.

In the scenes of sexual intercourse between Mr Norbert and Fanny, Cleland illustrates how consumption acts as a force of sexual power. During the initial sex scene in which Mr Norbert believes that he robs Fanny of her virginity, Fanny describes how when 'he saw plainly my thighs, shift, and sheet, all stained with what he readily took for a virgin effusion […] nothing could equal his joy and exultation' (p. 145). The 'idea of a complete victory […] that made [Fanny ...] no longer maid' drives Mr Norbert's sexual actions (p. 146). When Mr Norbert believes that he has achieved this 'complete victory,' he becomes overjoyed from the sense of power he experiences at the thought of devouring Fanny's virginity. Further in the scene, Cleland describes Mr Norbert through a simile, stating that he was 'triumphant and like a cock clapping his wings over his down-trod mistress', a description that serves as yet another testament to Mr Norbert's attempt to exert sexual power over Fanny through his metaphorical consumption of her (p. 146).

The strategic placement of meals in relation to sex scenes. In addition to using food-language in the bedroom scenes with Mr Norbert, Cleland also parallels the literal consumption of food and the consumption of Fanny during sex through his strategic placement of meals within the text, with meals occurring immediately before, directly following, or sometimes even during sex scenes. The strategic placement of meals, though present in a variety of Fanny's relationships, occurs most prominently during Fanny's time as Mr H...'s mistress, beginning at the moment of Fanny's introduction to Mr H... when Mrs Jones 'bring[s] him to drink tea with [them]', a scene which ends with Mr H [...] '[taking Fanny] in his arms, and bore [her ...] to the bed ... having [her] what advantage he pleased' (pp. 64, 67). Within this scene, Cleland sets tea – a form of meal – before the sex scene to precede the sexual consumption that will follow the literal consumption.

Though this first sex scene with Mr H... includes a meal before the sexual act, Cleland later introduces a meal in the midst of Fanny and Mr H...'s lovemaking. After having sex, Fanny writes how 'presently, a neat and elegant supper was introduced, and a bottle of Burgundy, with the other necessaries, were set on the dumb-waiter' (p. 68). While Fanny refuses to eat at first, Mr H... eventually coaxes Fanny to eat 'half a partridge, and three or four glasses of wine', evoking a change in her desires (p. 68). Cleland furthers the meal-sex relationship by writing, 'Mr H... [....] thrust the table imperceptibly from between [them], and bringing his chair to face [Fanny], he soon began […] to lay hold of [her] hands, to kiss [her]' (p. 69). Cleland's inclusion of a meal between two sex scenes not only illustrates a connection between eating and sex but also shows the power dynamic established by the consumption of meals. Just as Fanny's sexual encounters with Mr H [...] include the presence of meals before and during sex scenes, Cleland also incorporates meals immediately after scenes of sex. Following the night's activities, Fanny writes of a brief repose 'but on my first stirring, which was not till past ten o'clock, I was obliged to endure one more trial of his manhood' (p. 72). Immediately following this 'trial,' Cleland introduces a meal: 'about eleven, in came

Mrs Jones, with two basins of the richest soup, which her experience in these matters had moved her to prepare' (p. 72). The immediacy of the meal following the physical act of sex perpetuates the consumer-consumed relationship between Fanny and Mr H [...], ultimately revealing how the gastronomic consumption of meals occurring before, during and after sex parallels the metaphorical, sexual consumption of Fanny that occurs during intercourse.

The dual functionality of the bed and the table. In addition to the strategic placement of meals, Cleland also employs the duality existing between the table and the bed to perpetuate the consumer-consumed relationship. While a bed normally functions for sleeping or sex and a table for eating, Cleland reverses the roles of these two objects. The dual-functionality comes in the ability of these two objects to serve the purposes of both eating and sleeping. The first moment of role reversing occurs after Fanny loses her virginity to Charles. Fanny recounts how 'we spent the whole afternoon, till supper time, in continued circle of love delights, kissing, turtle-billing, toying, and all the rest of the feast', likening the sexual act to a feast (p. 49). This metaphor goes deeper when an actual feast appears in the bedroom: 'at length, supper was served in [...] and sitting down the bed side, we made table and tablecloth of the bed and sheets' (p. 49). In this scene, the bed quite literally transforms into a table in both physicality and function.

While the bedroom scene with Charles illustrates the transformation of the bed into a table, the reverse transformation also occurs later on within the novel. During a brief encounter with a sailor on the streets, Fanny accepts his offer to treat her to a glass of wine. When the pair enter the nearby tavern and immediately commence 'towards the main point', Fanny describes how they 'found no conveniency to [their] purpose, two or three disabled chairs, and a rickety table, composing the whole furniture of the room' (p. 149). As none of the furniture present in the room exactly suites the purpose of sex, the sailor improvises, giving the table the functionality of a bed. Fanny writes how: 'he leads me to the table [...] lays my head down on the edge of it [...] canting up my petticoats and shift' (p. 150). Their sex transpires on the table, metap]horically substituting the act of eating. Rather than the consumption of food, however, Cleland depicts the consumption of Fanny's body by the sailor.

Reverse consumption: the consumed becomes the consumer
In the previous section, the analysis demonstrates how Cleland's use of gastronomic consumption results in the metaphorical consumption of Fanny's body as a consumable object, enabling countless characters to exert power over her. However, as Loichot asserts in her introduction to *The Tropics Bite Back: Culinary Coups in Caribbean Literature*, 'Food [...] can be both the site of lost power and empowerment, depending on its source and its use' (p. x). Like food, consumption enables both disempowerment and empowerment. In *Fanny Hill*, the form of consumption that contributes to empowerment is that of reverse consumption: the process by which the consumed becomes the consumer. Through Cleland's depictions of the female mouth – or vagina –

he highlights how reverse consumption enables the woman to gastronomically consume the male; this reverses the previously established power dynamic of consumption, enabling Fanny to transcend the consumption-driven prostitution market.

Reverse consumption. Through his descriptions of the characters, Cleland highlights the significance of the mouth within his novel. While Cleland spends time analysing the actual mouth, he simultaneously introduces a second type of mouth through his descriptions of the woman: that of the female mouth, or the vagina. Fanny's own depictions of the vagina present the female part as a metaphorical mouth when she writes, 'with one hand he gently disclosed the lips of that luscious mouth of nature' (p. 125). Loichot reinforces the depiction of the vagina as a mouth, stating that 'the vagina is metaphorically presented as a starving mouth' (p. 110). The link between the functions of the mouths, and thereby sex and eating, provides the basis for Loichot's depictions of the woman as a consumer of the male. During 'Sexual Traps,' Loichot asserts 'the woman's body is both things at once […] food eater and food', furthering the depiction of the consuming female through explicitly highlighting the object on which the female feasts: the man (p. 126). Through this new depiction, the 'woman as eater' transforms into 'the man-eater', and though the vagina functions as the vehicle responsible for this reverse consumption, the woman as a whole represents the agent of reverse consumption (p. 133).

Like Loichot, Cleland demonstrates the occurrence of this reverse consumption by depicting the vagina as a mouth that consumes, particularly through Fanny's sexual encounters with Mr H…'s servant. During the scene of Fanny's sexual relations with Will, Cleland's mouth-vagina metaphor demonstrates how Fanny achieves a reverse consumption through the actions of her vaginal mouth. When Fanny seduces Will, she refers to her vagina as 'that part of me I might call a furnace mouth', openly depicting her vagina as a mouth (p. 90). Retrospectively describing her relations with Will, Fanny continues with this metaphor, stating, 'this bred a pause of action, a pleasure stop, whilst that delicate glutton, my nether mouth, as full as it could hold, kept palating, with exquisite relish, the morsel that so deliciously engorged it' (p. 91). Fanny's choice of words – her description of her 'delicate glutton, her nether mouth' – reveal her own desire to sexually consume the male and portray her in the very act of consuming Will's body. Both literally and metaphorically, Will 'was swallowed up' during the sexual act (p. 85). As the regular mouth proves vital in enabling gastronomic consumption, the vagina proves essential to sexual consumption.

Power through reverse consumption. During Fanny's seduction of Will, Cleland exhibits the theme of power throughout the scene, a decision that proves crucial to the analysis of reverse consumption as a power-enabling process. Specifically in the sex scenes with Will, Fanny uses reverse consumption to successfully manifest power over her sexual partner in two ways: through the physical positioning of her body in relation to the men with whom she sleeps and through actively seeking out sex for her own pleasure. Once again, her relations with Will most illustratively exemplify Fanny's exertion of power over a male through the physical positioning of her body during sex. When Fanny describes her own body in relation to Will's, stating, 'I twist my legs round his naked loins [...] and now I had [Will] every way encircled and begirt; and having drawn him home t]o me, I kept him fast there', she demonstrates the physical power that she holds over him; this power results from the sexual positioning of her body in relation to Will's 'begirt' body, mainly through her female mouth consuming Will's body (p. 91). Fanny directly highlights the power her body enables her to exercise when she states, 'the powerfully divided lips of that pleasure-thirsty channel received him' (p. 90). Through these description, Fanny highlights the element of power present during her metaphorical act of consumption of Will.

Power through pleasure. In addition to receiving power through the physical positioning of her body, Fanny also attains power by achieving pleasure. When Fanny declares that her 'pleasure-thirsty channel received him,' she introduces a concept previously foreign to the text: seeking out sex for the sake of her own pleasure. Prior to this scene in the novel, Cleland depicts Fanny as the provider of sexual pleasure, an object for the sexual enjoyment of others. In the sex scene with Will, however, Cleland shows how Fanny actively seduces a man as a result of her desire. During one of her sexual interactions with Will, Fanny declares, 'and now, palpably mistress of any size of man, and triumphing in my double achievement of pleasure and revenge, I abandoned myself entirely to the ideas of all the delight I had swam in' (p. 87); even the terminology perpetuates the connection of pleasurable consumption and power. Through seeking out pleasure, Fanny achieves consumptive pleasure, thereby reversing the power struggle. Just as the literal mouth proves necessary for the gastronomic consumption, Fanny's vagina facilitates her own sexual consumption, achieving both power and pleasure from this reverse consumption.

Conclusion: food for thought

In *A KWIC Concordance to John Cleland's Memoirs of a Woman of Pleasure,* Samuel Coleman and Michael Preston track the occurrence of every word used throughout the novel, ranging from the more basic terms 'become' and 'tea' to less common terms such as 'consummate' and 'appetite'. Despite Cleland's obsession with food and the consumption-centric focus throughout *Fanny Hill,* the actual terms 'food' and 'consumption' are hardly prevalent within the text. For example, 'food' only appears once during the entire novel. Likewise, the term 'consume', even taking into account the several different variations of the verb, only appears in *Fanny Hill* seven times, and the exact term 'consumption' does not appear at all.[7] What the novel lacks in the actual usage of these exact terms, however, it makes up in references and themes. Food and consumption constantly appear throughout the novel, serving to shape the way in which other themes in the novel are analysed.

While the first section initially highlights the objectification – and therefore subjection – of the woman through consumption, the second section addresses how the woman converts consumption into a vehicle of power. Within this analysis on consumption, the empowerment of the woman, specifically of Fanny, is highlighted. A variety of authors substantiate this position. In '"Traffic in More Precious Commodities": Sapphic Erotics and Economics in *Memoirs of a Woman of Pleasure*', for example, John C. Beynon highlights how 'these women [prostitutes] exceed their roles as objects of exchange between men' to claim a form of power over the men with whom they interact. He takes this claim further, stating, 'the prostitutes' awareness of their hyper-commodified status, both as women in a patriarchal society, and, more significantly, as women whose bodies are literally exchanged in a world of trade in pleasures, allows them [...] to exercise a degree of control over these systems'.[8] After recognizing their position as the consumed, the prostitutes reclaim their agency over their consumers, transforming the very force that binds them into one that frees them. Within this transformation, food plays an undeniably crucial role in the power relationship surrounding consumption. Loichot hits directly on this point, declaring, 'Food, therefore, can be both the site of lost power and empowerment, depending on its source and its use' (p. x). While Loichot's scholarship primarily deals with Caribbean literature, the bounds of this assertion and the significance of food and consumption in relation to power and women reach throughout history, from the power structure in Cleland's eighteenth-century London to society today.

Throughout *Fanny Hill*, Cleland routinely incorporates the themes of food and consumption to highlight the power struggle existing between the consumer and the consumed. Although this usage occurs continuously, Cleland specifically utilizes the Covent Garden market scene to serve as a microcosm of the entire novel. While Fanny enters the food market to buy food for her own consumption, she is immediately transported back into the market of prostitution when Mr Norbert pits her as the object of his sexual consumption; though the scene depicts the consuming male's assertion of power over the consumed female – as prevalent throughout the entire novel – Cleland simultaneously includes depictions of the female mouth to demonstrate a reverse consumption whereby the woman reasserts power over the male. Cleland alternates Fanny's position from object of consumption to consumer and back again, yet one major aspect always remains constant: both the loss and the gain of power occur through the relation of food and the female body.

Notes

1. Victoria de Grazia, 'Introduction', *The Sex of Things: Gender and Consumption in Historical Perspective*, ed. by Victoria de Grazia and Ellen Furlough (Berkeley: U California P, 1996), pp. 1-10 (pp. 4, 8, 1).
2. Valérie Loichot, *The Tropics Bite Back: Culinary Coups in Caribbean Literature* (Minneapolis: U Minnesota P, 2013), p. xxxvi. Subsequent references are cited parenthetically in the text.
3. Adrian Randall, Andrew Charlesworth, Richard Sheldon and David Walsh, 'Markets, Market Culture and Popular Protest in Eighteenth-Century Britain and Ireland', *Markets, Market Culture and Popular Protest in Eighteenth-Century Britain and Ireland*, ed. by Adrian Randall and Andrew Charlesworth

(Liverpool: Liverpool UP, 1996), pp. 1-24 (pp. 1, 1, 12, 1).
4. Michel Foucault, *The History of Sexuality: An Introduction* (New York: Vintage, 1990), p. 47.
5. John Cleland, *Fanny Hill or Memoirs of a Woman of Pleasure* (Middlesex: Simon & Brown, 2013), p. 136. Subsequent references are cited parenthetically in the text.
6. de Grazia, p. 8.
7. Samuel S. Coleman and Michael J. Preston, *A KWIC Concordance to Jon Cleland's 'Memoirs of a Woman of Pleasure'* (New York: Garland, 1988).
8. John C. Beynon, '" Traffic in More Precious Commodities": Sapphic Erotics and Economics in *Memoirs of a Woman of Pleasure*', *Launching Fanny Hill: Essays on the Novel and Its Influences*, ed. by Patsy S. Fowler and Alan Jackson (New York: AMS Press, 2003), pp. 3-26 (pp. 14,15).

The Wroxeter *Macellum*: A Foodway in Every Sense

Christopher Grocock

The *macellum* at Wroxeter is a building of particular interest. It is a rarity in the Roman province of Britain, and there have in any case been few really detailed examples of *macellum* sites in the empire as a whole. The building can be seen as the focus of a street market which functioned through at least three centuries.[1] The *macellum* – whose location and plan are shown in Figures 1 and 2 – seems to have been built as part of the major phase of development from the 150s AD onwards and which formed part of the building programme whose main element was the baths and exercise hall.[2]

The classic studies of *macella* and markets in general are those by Claire de Ruyt and Joan Frayn.[3] Of these, de Ruyt's is an exhaustive study of all linguistic literary references to these types of structure, with some discussion about the type of building which comes under the definition of *macellum* and finally a gazetteer of all known sites. Frayn's study also covers the literary and linguistic evidence, but takes the form of a more analytical study of this evidence.

Classical literary references

There are a few references to *macellum* in the *Oxford Latin Dictionary*, where it is defined as (1) 'a provision-market; the provision-merchants, the trade', and (2) provisions sold in the market'.[5] As will be seen from what follows, the most interesting ones come from the comic poets Plautus and Terence, which (arguably) provide just a little social or historical background from Rome in the late second century BC. (All translations are the author's own unless otherwise stated.)

> *1. Plautus,* Amphitruo *1010–12*
> Amphitruo has been looking for Naucrates, a relative of his wife Alcmena:
> 'I've crawled through every piazza, gymnasium and perfume-shop;
> in the bazaar and in the *macellum*, in the wrestling-yard and in the forum,
> in the doctors', in the barbers', in every sacred shrine
> I'm exhausted by looking for him; I can't find Naucrates anywhere.'

Here the obvious point to make, in the comic list of places to look for someone, is the fact that the *macellum* is distinguished from the *forum*, which in ancient republican Rome seems to have been more of a general place for public activity such as banking and negotiation. The same emphasis on specific types of produce is found in the examples which follow, too. In fact, we can identify a number of specialist retail outlets in ancient Rome in addition to the main *forum*: there was the *forum boarium* or cattle

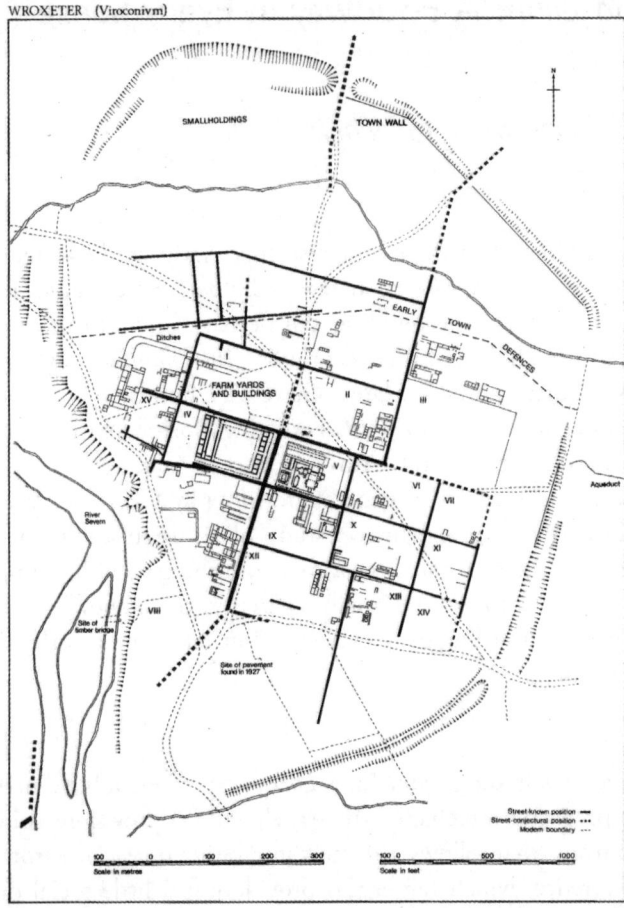

Figure 1. The plan of the mature Roman town of Wroxeter (from J. Wacher, Towns of Roman Britain, figure 165. Reproduced by permission of Batsford/ Pavilion Group Books Ltd.). The macellum *is at the very centre, at the bottom left of insula V.*

market (possibly livestock rather than butchered meat; Varro, *Lingua Latina* 5. 146, Livy 10. 23. 3); the *forum (h)olitorum* or greengrocery (Varro *Lingua Latina* 5.146, Tacitus *Annals* 2. 49); the *piscatoris forum* or fish market (Columella 8. 17. 15) and the *forum suarium* or pig market (referred to in Ulpian, *Digest* 1. 12. 1. 11).[5]

> 2. *Plautus*, Aulularia 373–76.
> Euclio has been shopping for his daughter's wedding:
> 'I come to the *macellum*, I ask for fish; they point out the dear ones;
> lamb is dear, beef is dear,
> so is veal, tuna, pork; everything is dear
> and all the more so as I hadn't any money!'

The list of items which proves to be far beyond Euclio's budget gives us a clear indication of the kinds of produce which could be purchased in the *macellum* at Rome. It is all fish or meat.

The Wroxeter *Macellum*: A Foodway in Every Sense

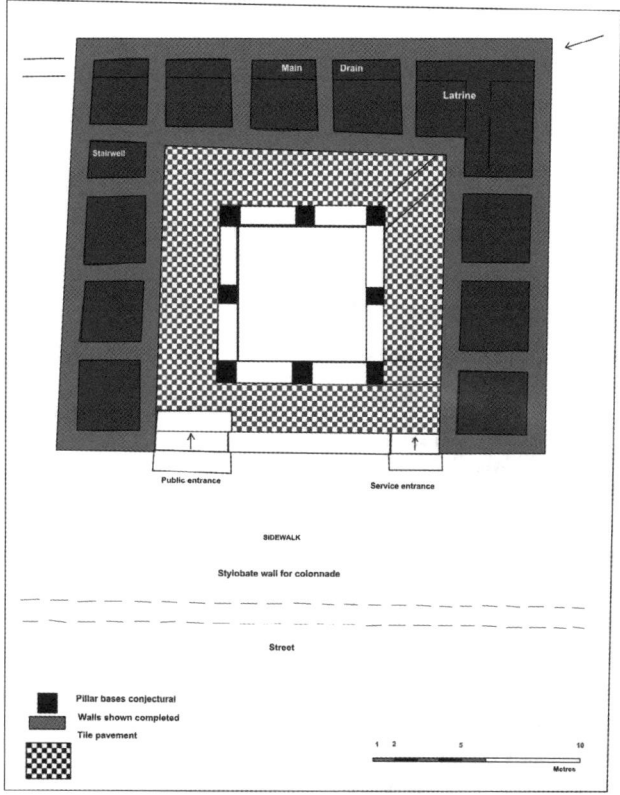

Figure 2. Detailed schematic of the macellum *at Wroxeter (drawn by Sally Grainger, after J. Webster,* The Cornovii, *Duckworth: London, 1975, fig. 25.)*

3. Terence, Eunuchus *255–58*
Gnatho, a 'Parasitvs' or professional hanger-on, is speaking:
'While we were chatting about these things, as bye the bye we came
    to the *macellum*,
there run up happy to meet me all the confectioners,
fishmongers, butchers, cooks, sausage makers, sprat-sellers,
to whom I've done much good whether I was solvent or not, and
    often still do...'

4. Horace, Satires *2. 3. 226–29*
Horace talks of a spendthrift called Nomenclatus, and has a similar list to the one we saw in Terence:
'As soon as this fellow received his legacy of a thousand talents,
he proclaimed that the fruiterer, sprat-seller, poulterer,
perfumer and the unholy crowd from the Tuscan quarter,
the sausage-maker and the wastrels, the whole produce-market
    and the Velabrum[6]
should come to his house in the morning.'

Food and Markets

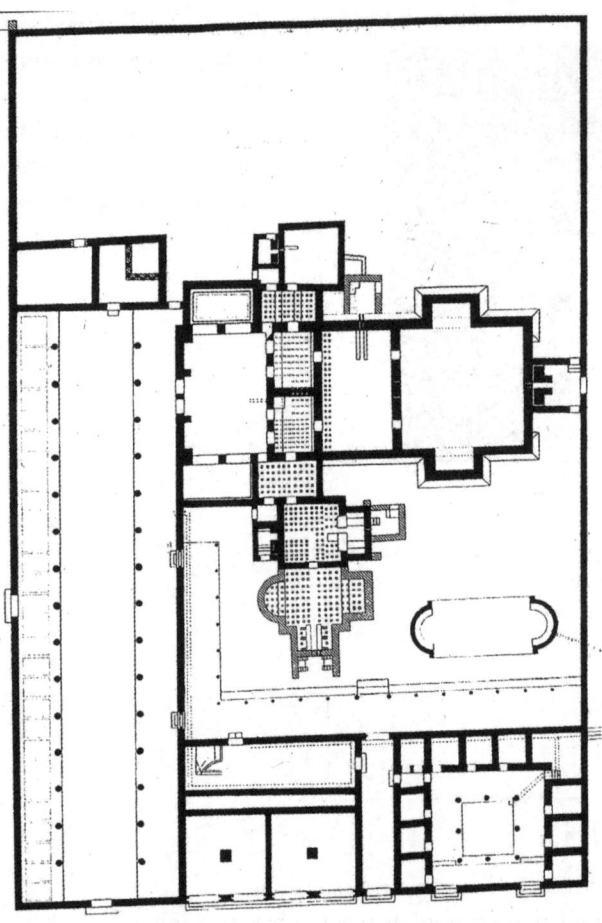

Figure 3. The baths complex at Wroxeter, showing the macellum at the bottom right (drawn by Sally Grainger, after R. White and P. Barker, Wroxeter: Life and Death of a Roman City, *Tempus, Stroud, revised ed. 2002, fig. 46, p. 88).*

Here again we see the *macellum* referred to as the source of high-class luxury goods, which typically meet with opprobrium from Roman authors. Susanna Morton Braund perhaps goes a little too far when she renders the word as 'delicatessen' in her translation of Juvenal 5. 95, but the sense of luxury and good living is certainly implicit in the other depictions of the a *macellum* in literature which we have seen.[7] Similarly Martial refers to 'costly hunger and the *macellum* which brings utter ruin.'[8]

5. Anonymous, Moretum 83

The 'hero' of the poem *Moretum* is described as producing lots of salads and green vegetables such as radish, lettuce, cabbage, sorrel and leeks – all products with a short shelf-life – which he takes into town to sell: 'on market days would carry his bundles on his shoulder into the city to sell them, and would return home from there with an unburdened neck and a heavy purse, scarcely ever with a purchase from the city's *macellum*'.[9] It is possible that the perishables which Simulus produced were sold in a different place – Rome's *forum holitorium* would be a suitable venue – and the poet is stressing that he spends very little on meat, for which – as seems likely from the references in Plautus and Terence – *macellum* was the appropriate source.

6. Pliny the Elder, Historia Naturalis *18. 108*
Pliny looks back in time to an era when households did not have slave-cooks: 'Neither did they keep cooks as slaves, and hired them in the *macellum*.'

The 'macellum' at Wroxeter

So what was a *macellum*? In the archaeological record it usually appears as a square or rectangular structure, with a row of shops or booths arranged around a central courtyard, at the centre of which was a fountain or water source. These varied in size, and although they are found throughout the Roman Empire, they are by no means a ubiquitous feature of all Roman towns.[10]

At Wroxeter, the *macellum* clearly conforms to the general pattern (see Figure 3); constructed as part of the complex which included a bath-house and which occupied an entire *insula* of the town, it comprised twelve booths, four on each of the north, east and south sides. There was a latrine installed in the south-east corner, while the west side, which opened through two entrances on to a main street, took the form of a portico. The *macellum* itself was some 25m x 20m, while the 'shops' were about 3.5m square (see Figure 2). It may well have had an upper floor accessed by a wooden staircase, following the pattern of shops at sites such as Herculaneum or Pompeii.

Wroxeter – the historical context

Wroxeter itself is regarded as one of the *civitas* or tribal capitals which were established in Britain during the period of 'Flavian expansion' after AD 70. Its Latin name was *Viroconium Cornoviorum* or 'Viroconium of the Cornovii'; the Cornovii were a tribe whose territory overlaps much of modern Cheshire and Shropshire. Prior to the Roman occupation, it seems that the area was well-populated and productive – in other words, well-developed as a productive and efficient foodway.[11]

The Cornovii tribe may not have been directly affected by the Roman occupation of Britain until military counter-attacks against the Silures and Ordovices in what is now Wales necessitated the establishment of bases in this area between *c*. AD 60 and 90, before the creation of Viroconium as the capital of the tribe, now organized on Roman lines with an urban centre as its focus.[12] This probably began in the 90s AD, but was given extra impetus during the 120s following Hadrian's visit to Britain. The evidence provided by the archaeology is disputed.[13] At any event Wroxeter's location was a principal reason for its evident prosperity as an urban centre, and its piazza, at 242 ft (74m) by 225 ft (69m), was nearly twice the size of the one found further south at Silchester; the nave of its basilica was about 170ft (52m) and 38ft (11.6m) wide, with side aisles and rooms and either end (see Figures 3 and 4).[14]

Figure 4. The 'Old Work' at Wroxeter. This huge wall joined the basilica to the baths complex (photograph: C. Grocock).

Figure 5. The hypocaust rooms and the 'Old Work' (photograph: C. Grocock).

The Wroxeter *Macellum*: A Foodway in Every Sense

As can be seen from the site plans of Wroxeter, the *macellum* was evidently conceived as a separate, independent structure from the forum proper. It consisted of a square arrangement of booths or shops with a fountain at the centre (the archaeology is not definite but probable). It is interesting to note that there may also have been a *forum boarium* or cattle market on this site as well, in Insula III.[15] This would have been the gathering place for livestock (and perhaps slaughter?) before butchery proper took place at the *macellum*.

The *macellum* construction sequence is summarized by Ellis, with a brief overview by White et al., who term it a 'civic market hall'.[16] It was constructed using a layer of foundation material or 'dump' over the main drain running beneath the east range of rooms in Insula V, and then completed in a series of stages – nine have been identified – using first red and then grey sandstone, and was built as part of the entire complex of edifices in Insula V from the 120s or 130s AD to about AD 150.[17] It had a courtyard surface formed of tiles laid in a herringbone pattern, and a latrine in one corner (see Figures 2 and 7).[18] It was in use from the time of its construction right through to the end of the Roman occupation period and beyond: Ellis comments that 'The success of the Wroxeter building, marked by its refurbishment and evidence for its use late in the fourth century if not in the fifth, might mean that the habits and wealth of an élite among its inhabitants maintained the building in something reasonably similar to its specialized function nearer the centre of the Empire'.

The quantities of animal bone waste found in the Wroxeter *macellum* support the idea that this location was used for similar purposes to those identified in both the literature and from Mediterranean archaeology. A huge collection of animal bone was excavated at Wroxeter – some 900 boxes of it – though it was not sieved, and only large pieces were retrieved. Much came from the infilling of the *natatio*, though much came from the *macellum* and the corridors and areas surrounding it. The vast majority of this was from cattle, with just a few sheep bones.[19] This concurs with bone evidence from Silchester, another civitas capital in the south of the province.[20] It is supported by the statement of Strabo – writing about the pre-conquest period, *c.* AD 20 – that among the main exports of Britain were 'wheat, cattle, hides, hunting-dogs and slaves'.[21]

Of the cattle, few were slaughtered as juveniles (i.e. for veal), and some of the pathologies noted may indicate that mature animals had been used for traction before slaughter. Tooth remains indicate that most were over thirty-six months old. The beef bones show evidence of systematic butchery. Moreover, from horn cores it appears that a variety of cattle were processed at Wroxeter. Sheep seem to have been on the small size by Romano-British standards, and these animals seem to have been slaughtered at three years or more – not as lamb, and not specifically for meat, despite Meddens's comment to this effect. Again, butchery marks were common, and were more frequent from the period of the third and fourth centuries than earlier. There was also a little evidence for pig production at Wroxeter, with animals being slaughtered either at twelve to twenty-four months or beyond four or five years. This largely concurs with evidence from

Figure 6 The south-west range of insula V: the macellum is bottom right (photograph: C. Grocock).

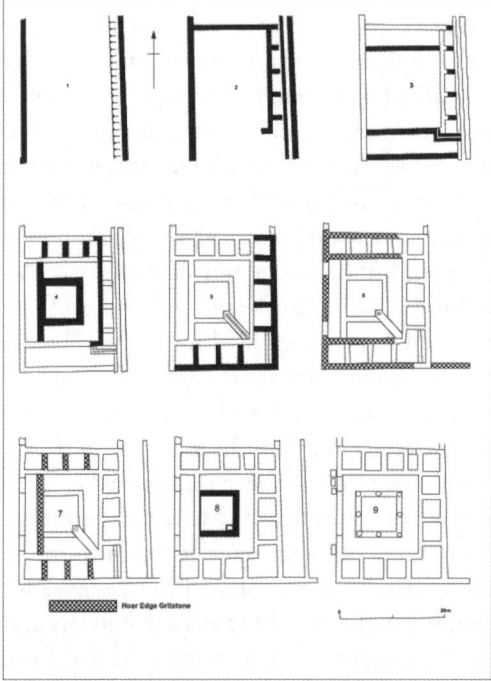

Figure 7. Construction sequence of the Wroxeter macellum, drawn by Sally Grainger, after P. Ellis (Compiler and ed.), The Roman Baths and Macellum at Wroxeter. Excavations by Graham Webster 1955–85, *English Heritage, London, 2000, fig. 3.4.*

Silchester, which shows that animals were slaughtered relatively late.[22] The prevalence of beef production may have been due to the higher fertility of the soils than in other areas.[23] The younger animals are part of a food chain – and their skins were no doubt also processed for leather, as Strabo noted. The presence of older animals may be evidence for breeding stock. It points to the fact that meat processing at Wroxeter was extensive and planned.

In this, Wroxeter may have resembled other Romano-British towns which are thought to have had a *macellum* – Corinium (Cirencester), Verulamium (St Albans), Ratae (Leicester), and perhaps even Coria (Corbridge), where two sides of an extensive building which in its layout resembles a *macellum* have been constructed.

Cirencester (*Corinium Dubonnorum*)

This was a stone building with apparently timber internal partitions:

> a number of pits discovered both inside and outside the building were filled with sawn and cut animal bones, and the building has been interpreted as a meat market or *macellum* (54412). The building may therefore represent a formalisation of pre-existing activity on the site. The *macellum* was extensively repaired to a similar plan in the early fourth century.[24]

It has been suggested that in the fourth century, the site of the *macellum* was redeveloped as the location for a very large building which seems never to have been completed, perhaps due to the development of *Corinium* as a separate provincial capital.[25] This building in Insula II may have been over 57m long by 16.2m wide; 'taken by itself, the building resembled the wing of a forum, and it was suggested that it may have been a *macellum*, a covered market which traded in meat, fish, vegetables and bread'.[26] The size of this construction is significant: 'If the Cirencester building extended as far as Ermin Street a length in excess of 57m would have made for a very large *macellum*, and one on a par with the major towns of the Mediterranean.'[27]

Buildings excavated at Leicester and Cirencester are 'necessarily less certain' as *macella* as they are not fully recovered, but the identification of that at Verulamium is more certain.

Verulamium

Here, it seems that the *macellum* was first built in timber following the destruction of the town in the revolts led by Boudicca in AD 60/61. It burned down in the second quarter of the second century AD and was then rebuilt in masonry. It continued to function until the end of the Roman occupation. The site suffers from being excavated fairly early – before the Second World War, but Rosalind Niblett comments: 'field walking since has recovered quantities of cattle bone and teeth in this area, while a watching brief on a pipe-line trench approximately 120m to the north recorded an enormous dump of animal (mainly cattle) bone in a Roman rubbish pit just outside the town wall.

That cattle were being butchered in third-century Verulamium on a commercial scale was demonstrated by the tips of cattle bone in the upper filling of a pit on the Folly Lane/Oysterfield site. The tips contained bones from the hindquarters of 37 cattle, all showing signs of intensive butchery typical of large-scale meat processing.'[28]

Discussion

To what extent does the *macellum* at Wroxeter indicate a major change in foodways during the Romano-British period? The obvious conclusion is that it was a innovative structure for a pre-Roman society, and that its very existence and function shows the imposition on or acquisition by a Celtic tribe, the Cornovii, of Mediterranean ways of exchange, processing and acquisition of a variety of food products as a result of their contact with the incoming Roman culture. That there was 'change in the air' in agriculture even before the Romans is now becoming clear, and it is also evident that the south and east of Britain by and large saw greater change under the Romans than the north and west did.[29] Wroxeter may represent the edge of this process, for reasons which may have as much to do with its geography and topography as Romano-British politics or the presence of the Roman army; the area seems to have been an 'outlier' in pre-Roman days, with a society organized around a hill fort, as was the norm further to the south-east.

Commenting on the case of Silchester, Claire Ingrem had some necessarily tentative thoughts about the places where cattle were raised in relation to the urban centre where they were processed:

> the extent to which the town was self-sufficient is uncertain, although the presence of very young animals indicates that livestock were raised close by. A number of buildings have been interpreted as barns, cattle stalls and pig sties, whilst pollen analyses indicate that the surrounding land was used for cattle pasture. It is also possible that stock, particularly cattle, were driven to Silchester from rural settlements.[30]

What seems evident at Wroxeter is that a pre-Roman culture in which the land was largely used as cattle pasture was intensively developed, and that pastures of say 20–30 km distant could have been used extensively, and that the roads which lead to Wroxeter could have acted as drove roads, perhaps with appropriate holding pens en route.

Questions such as 'How much livestock was processed through the *macellum* at Wroxeter?' and 'What did this represent in the diet of its inhabitants?' are all *ipso facto* hostages to fortune and open to challenge.[31] This is the overwhelming conclusion of recent studies, though it is equally true that a number of theoretical models have been put forward which can be used to indicate plausible parameters or approximations which are very helpful in achieving a better understanding of the ways in which ancient foodways may have functioned. Roger Bagnall sums up such a theory as 'an interactive model in which every user is free to choose different values for particular variables, and which is created with as plausible a set of values as we can deduce'.[32]

One interesting model, whose ultimate aim was estimating a given area's capacity to support a population, was put forward by Franco de Angelis.[33] This depends to a great extent of the potential for cereal production (as opposed to animal husbandry) of the area in question, and obviously requires a certain amount of value-judgement in identifying or apportioning which areas of land might have been considered appropriate for different uses – using modern maps, historical archives, and archaeological evidence where it is available. The theory put forward by Robin Osborne starts from the assumption that an 'average household' required between three and four hectares of arable land and housed a family of five. Again, careful analysis of an area is needed to try to identify the amounts of arable vs non-arable land within a given distance from the urban centre being studied.[34]

A recent study of the countryside of Roman Britain by Mike McCarthy builds on the idea of regionalism and suggests ways in which modern resources such as maps provided by the Ordnance Survey or the records of the Soil Survey of England and Wales can be used as a broad basis for understanding what the landscape potentials of Britain in ancient times might have been. Assessment of soil groups is one way of assessing land capability; so is height, climate and wetness.[35] Seeing Wroxeter in the context of its landscape, including such features as rivers, roads, other known buildings, and taking into consideration such factors as soil type and height and area of different types of land, was something already undertaken in a fairly simple but illustrative way by Graham Webster, as long ago as 1975.[36] In more recent times Helen Goodchild has shown how the techniques available to scholars such as GIS (Geographical Information Systems) might be used to produce maps which indicate suitability for different agricultural activities.[37] She counters criticism of the use and value of such modelling techniques with a citation from Box and Draper that 'all models are wrong: the practical question is, how wrong do they have to be not to be useful?'

Soil types of the area around Wroxeter indicate the potential of such investigations as a means of understanding how the *macellum* there may have been supplied. The area was part of the wide rolling plain [… which] extends into mid Staffordshire and Cheshire and forms one of the principal lowland interruptions of highland Britain. The Shropshire portion of the plain, like the Staffordshire and Cheshire portions, is interrupted here and there by sandstone hills which do not, however, alter the essentially gentle landscape characteristics which link it with the English midlands …. They are sandy loams, usually greyish brown in colour and well drained. The north-eastern area was fitted for arable in the early modern period as sheep and cattle fattening developed, and the extensive remaining heaths of the north-east and north-west were enclosed at the end of the 18th century when wartime cereal prices brought them into cultivation. The north-east, long retaining its identity as an area of improved heathland … there, in the 1920s and 1930s, dairying spread from the northern part of the plain.[38]

Conclusion

It is possible that meat production was re-organized and intensified as a result of the needs created by the proximity of the Roman army at Chester, though this would hardly have necessitated a *macellum*. Rather, the existence of the building in the town, and the location of the town in the landscape, suggests that intensive animal-rearing – and especially beef (even approaching a level which we might regard as ranching) was developed. Beef formed the backbone, if the reader will excuse the pun, of agriculture in this area, and may well have been predominant in a largely meat-rich diet for the inhabitants of Wroxeter. Claire Ingrem speaks of an 'intensification of cattle husbandry' and a predominance of slaughter at older ages than was the case before the coming of Rome which can be identified not only from Silchester, but also at Winchester and at Continental sites such as Augst and Zwammerdam.[3]

The *macellum* itself is an illustration of a major social and economic change in the region: 'the growth of the flourishing urban culture that was a hallmark of Roman rule would not have been possible without considerable expansion of agriculture and the transfer of wealth from the countryside to cities.'[40] What is certainly true is that a generalized, 'one size fits all' view of production and consumption of foods in the Roman province of Britain have to be replaced by a much more flexible and responsible approach which treats each region on its own merits.[41] Even more important is that older views about the limited spread of villas in Roman-Britain are now being challenged as rural archaeology is carried out more vigorously than in previous times.[42]

Notes

1. P. Ellis (compiler and ed.), *The Roman Baths and Macellum at Wroxeter. Excavations by Graham Webster 1955–85* (London: English Heritage, 2000), p. xiii.
2. Roger White and Philip Barker, *Wroxeter: Life and Death of a Roman City* (Stroud: Tempus, 2002), pp. 89–90.
3. Claire de Ruyt, *Macellum: Marché alimentaire des Romains* (Louvain-la-Neuve: Institut Supérieur d'Archéologie et d'Histoire de l'Art, Collège Érasme, 1983); Joan M. Frayn, *Markets and Fairs in Roman Italy: Their Social and Economic Importance from the Second Century BC to the Third Century AD* (Oxford: Clarendon Press, 1993); a more recent and very thorough study is Claire Hollerman's *Shopping in Ancient Rome: The Retail Trade in the Late Republic and the Principate* (Oxford: Oxford UP, 2012), pp. 159–81.
4. *Oxford Latin Dictionary*, ed P. W. Glare (Oxford: Clarendon Press, 1996).
5. The *Forum Boarium* was at the centre of old Rome, by the Tiber; it is thought that the *Forum Holitorium* lay just to its right (see A. Claridge, *Oxford Archaeological Guides: Rome* (Oxford: Oxford UP, 1998), fig. 112).
6. The area of Rome by the Tiber where markets were situated.
7. Juvenal and Persius, ed. and trans. Susanna Morton Braund (Cambridge, MA: Loeb Classical Library, 2004).
8. Martial, 10. 96. 9, *pretiosa fames conturbatorque macellus*.
9. This possible, and certainly subtle, emphasis escaped me in the brief study of this poem which Sally

Grainger and I did back in 2001: see C. Grocock and Sally Grainger, '*Moretum* – a Peasant Lunch revisited', *The Meal: Proceedings of the 2001 Oxford Food Symposium on Food and Cookery*, ed. by Harlan Walker (Totnes: Prospect Books, 2002), pp. 95–103.
10. de Ruyt, *Macellum*, pp. 285, 301, 326.
11. P. Ellis and R. White, 'Introduction', in Ellis (ed.), *The Roman Baths and Macellum at Wroxeter*, p. 1.
12. John Wacher, *The Towns of Roman Britain* (London: Batsford, 1995), pp. 362–3; he identifies these units as an auxiliary cohort of Thracians, then Legio XIV, and finally Legio XX.
13. Wacher, *Towns of Roman Britain* p. 365; White and Barker, *Wroxeter*, pp. 73–77.
14. Wacher, *Towns of Roman Britain*, pp. 365, 366.
15. R.H. White, C. Gaffney and V.L. Gaffney, *Wroxeter, the Cornovii and the Urban Process. Final Report on the Wroxeter Hinterland Project 1994–1997, vol. 2: Characterizing the City* (Oxford: Archaeopress, 2013), p.97. See now the useful though brief summary by R. White, 'The Wroxeter Hinterland Project: Exploring the relationship between country and town', *The Impact of Rome on the British Countryside*, ed. by D. J. Breeze (London: Royal Archaeological Institute, 2014), pp. 7–11.
16. Ellis, *The Roman Baths and Macellum at Wroxeter*, pp. 86ff.; White, Gaffney and Gaffney, *Wroxeter, the Cornovii and the Urban Process*, p. 99.
17. Ellis, *The Roman Baths and Macellum at Wroxeter*, pp. 87–90, fig. 3. 4.
18. Ellis, *The Roman Baths and Macellum at Wroxeter*, pp. 56–7, figs. 2.52 and 2.53.
19. Beverley Meddens, 'The Animal Bone', in Ellis, *The Roman Baths and Macellum at Wroxeter*, pp. 315–35.
20. Claire Ingrem, 'Animals in the Economy and Culture of Roman Britain: A Case Study from Southern England' *Silchester and the Study of Romano-British Urbanism*, ed. by Michael Fulford (Portsmouth, RI: Journal of Roman Archaeology, Supplementary Series 90,), pp. 184–212, at 208.
21. Strabo, *Geography*, 4.5.2.
22. Ingrem, 'Animals in the Economy and Culture of Roman Britain,' pp.190–2, 204.
23. Cf. A. King, 'Regional Factors in Production and Consumption of Animal-Derived Food in the Roman Empire', paper given at the Roman Archaeology Conference 11/ Theoretical Roman Archaeology Conference 24, in *Programme and Abstracts* (University of Reading, 2014), p. 32.
24. N. Holbrook, '*Corinium Dubonnorum*: Roman *Civitas Capital* and Provincial Capital', *Cirencester: Town and Landscape*, ed. by Timothy Darvill and Christopher Gerrard (Cirencester: Cotswold Archaeological Trust Ltd., 1994), pp. 58–86 (p. 60).
25. Holbrook, '*Corinium Dubonnorum*', p. 75.
26. N. Holbrook (ed.), *Cirencester: the Roman Town Defences, Public Buildings and Shops* (Cirencester: Cotswold Archaeological Trust, 1998), p. 187.
27. For Cirencester, see de Ruyt 1983, 330; the building at Wroxeter, by contrast, measured 25m by 21m.: see G. Webster 1998a, fig 6.17; Holbrook, *Cirencester*, p. 187.
28. Rosalind Niblett, *Verulamium: The Roman City of St Albans* (Stroud: Tempus, 2001), p. 105.
29. Cf. U. Albarella, C. Minniti and S. Valenzuela, 'Was Romano-British Agriculture Innovative? An Integrated Approach to a Complex Question,' paper given at the Roman Archaeology Conference 11/ Theoretical Roman Archaeology Conference 24, in *Programme and Abstracts* (University of Reading, 2014), p. 30.
30. Ingrem, 'Animals in the Economy and Culture of Roman Britain,' pp. 196.
31. See now Alan Bowland and Andrew Wilson (eds.), *Quantifying the Roman Economy: Methods and Problems* (Oxford: Oxford UP, 2009).
32. Roger Bagnall, 'Response to Alan Bowman', in Bowland and Wilson (eds.), *Quantifying the Roman Economy*, pp. 206–09 (p. 206).
33. Franco de Angelis, 'The Foundation of Selinous: Overpopulation or Opportunities?', *The Archaeology of Greek Colonization*, ed. by G. R. Tsetskhladge and F. de Angelis (Oxford: Oxford UP, 1994), pp. 87–110.
34. R. Osborne, *Classical Landscape with Figures* (London: George Philip, 1987). For this and the previ-

ous reference I am indebted to a reading of Alan Greaves, 'Milesians in the Black Sea', *The Black Sea in Antiquity: Regional and Interregional Economic Exchanges*, ed. by Vincent Gabriel and John Lund (Aarhus: Aarhus UP, 2007), pp. 9–21.

35. Mike McCarthy, *The Romano-British Peasant: Towards a Study of People, Landscapes and Work during the Roman Occupation of Britain* (Oxford: Windgather Press, 2013), pp. 27–30 and figs. 2.1, 2.2.
36. Graham Webster, *The Cornovii* (London: Duckworth, 1975), pp. 79–93 and figs. 32, 37 and 38.
37. Helen Goodchild, 'GIS Models of Roman Agricultural Production', *The Roman Agricultural Economy: Organization, Investment, and Production*, ed. by Alan Bowman and Andrew Wilson (Oxford: Oxford UP, 2013), pp. 55–83.
38. 'The Physical Environment', *A History of the County of Shropshire: Volume 4: Agriculture* (1989), pp. 5–20 <http://www.british-history.ac.uk/report.aspx?compid=22839> [accessed 16 May 2014]. See also C.P. Burnham and D. Mackney, *Soils of Shropshire* <http://fsj.field-studies-council.org/media/344453/vol2.1_36.pdf> [accessed 16 May 2014].
39. Ingrem, 'Animals in the Economy and Culture of Roman Britain,' p. 210.
40. Dennis Kehoe, 'State and Production in the Roman Agrarian Economy', in Bowman and Wilson (eds.), *The Roman Agricultural Economy*, pp. 33–53 (p. 35).
41. A. Smith, 'New Light on Romano-Britiish Rural Settlement Archaeology', and J. Taylor, 'Beyond Villa and Farmstead', papers given at the Roman Archaeology Conference 11/ Theoretical Roman Archaeology Conference 24, in *Programme and Abstracts* (University of Reading, 2014), p. 52, 53.
42. Jeffrey Davies, 'Populating a Landscape. Romano-British Rural Settlement in Wales: New Perspectives', paper given at the Roman Archaeology Conference 11/ Theoretical Roman Archaeology Conference 24, in *Programme and Abstracts* (University of Reading, 2014), p. 54.

Local, Super, Super-Local or Local-Super? The Market for Local Food in Edinburgh

Andrew Guest

Where a turnip, or a cabbage or a leek was fifty years ago the only vegetable luxury found on a country gentleman's table, we now see a regular succession of not merely broccoli, cauliflower and pease, but of the more recondite asparagus, seakale, endive and artichoke, with an abundance of early small saladings… The vegetable markets of most towns have within the same period undergone a wonderful improvement […] so that a healthful luxury is now within the reach of all classes.

Mistress Margaret Dods, *The Cook and Housewife's Manual* (Edinburgh, 1826)

Prologue: our changing food

A little over a century after Meg Dods's writings, in 1929, F. Marian McNeill published the first history of food in Scotland, *The Scots Kitchen*. In this she asserts that, although having less soil suitable for cultivation than that of England, and a wetter and colder climate, Scotland was then able to grow forage crops, potatoes, oats, some bush fruits and a great variety of vegetables on a par with the best in Europe.

But by the time of the publication of the second edition of *The Scots Kitchen* in 1963, McNeill was expressing a note of anxiety about Scotland's food. In the preface to this edition McNeill quotes the renowned nutritionist and food policy advocate Lord Boyd Orr: 'Up to the middle of the last century the people of Scotland were eating natural foodstuffs. With the introduction of machinery […] natural foodstuffs have been changed into artificial foodstuffs, with the very substances purified away that the Almighty put there to keep us in perfect health.'[1] McNeill presents these comments as a critique of canning and refrigeration, but by 1963 they could apply also to increasingly industrialized forms of both agriculture and of food retailing, the latter typified by the supermarket which first arrived in the UK in 1951; the comments convey a growing feeling that the health both of the nation's soil and of the nation's body and soul was at risk.

Today the picture has become clearer. Scotland's fine agricultural and horticultural land now produces a range of crops infinitely more limited than in 1929; there is nothing that Meg Dods would recognize as a vegetable market in any of Scotland's towns. And yet, thanks to the supermarket chains that bring in from across the globe an endless variety of fruit and vegetables all year round, you could say that luxury is definitely 'within the reach of all classes'. Whether Meg Dods would deem this a 'healthful luxury' is another matter.

Buying 93% of our food now in supermarkets, and with food markets (both wholesale and retail) having largely disappeared from our cities, we have never been so disconnected from our food and where it comes from. But dissatisfaction with this situation is growing. National surveys report that up to a quarter of consumers are willing to pay more for locally sourced food.[2] In England a consortium of five organizations has just delivered a £5 million National Lottery funded programme *Making Local Food Work*. In Scotland fifty food projects are currently in receipt of over £400,000 from the Scottish Government's new Think Local initiative, and the Scottish Government's discussion document on a new Food Policy for Scotland talks of 'an explosion in the local food movement'.[3]

But what do people mean by 'local food', how much is available and through what kind of markets can it reach us? To simplify a complex issue for the purposes of this paper, 'food' will be considered primarily as vegetables: vegetables are a vital ingredient in our diet, the area around Edinburgh is the key vegetable-growing area in Scotland and vegetables are the simplest form of food for individuals to grow (or imagine growing) themselves. Meg Dods's image of the vegetable market in our towns remains a persistent feature in what many people feel should be a closer relationship between them and their food.

The current situation

Us – the consumers. Convenience is the major driver of how we shop today, brought about largely by demographic changes that accelerated in the second half of the twentieth century, in particular the increase in the number of women working. With more and more people supposedly having less time to shop, or eat, as well as snacking and eating 'on the run', it is convenient for us to do more of our shopping in one place – the supermarket first arrived under the guise of 'the convenience store'. It is convenient for us to buy carrots that have been washed (if not scraped, or cut into ready-to-cook pieces). It is even more convenient to buy a meal that requires no preparation (apart perhaps from putting it in the oven), and the supermarkets make a large share of their profit providing these. It is also convenient to be able to buy a mango, a melon, a tomato, a strawberry or a leek at all times of the year, and we have now come to expect that as normal. When asked whether his customers responded to seasonality, a supermarket manager interviewed for this paper responded, 'It's gone hasn't it? It's down to two [seasons] – warm and cold.' The recent spread of the supermarket chains into town centres in the form of smaller 'convenience' or 'local' stores is an example of their response to their customers' feeling that it was no longer convenient to drive to bigger stores on the edge of town.

The convenience factor on which the supermarkets have played so greatly, and the huge market share which it has now given them, has created consumers who expect to buy the same range of food all year round, mostly in packages, in a brightly lit, scrupulously clean indoor environment. Supported by improved stock control, checkout scanning technology and customer information derived from loyalty cards, it can be said that 'The food industry has moved 180° from being producer driven to being consumer driven…the power in the system is at the retail end'.[4] The growth in ready meals, pre-packed vegetables and the dominance of the consumer as mediated by the retailer has in turn fuelled the industrialization of agriculture, both through the necessity of finding a way to meet the burgeoning all-year-round demand but also through the imposition of different product quality standards (e.g. straight, clean carrots) to meet the higher standards of the retail environment.

Our vegetables – the growers. Fifty-eight thousand tonnes of vegetables (not including potatoes) are estimated as being grown each year in the area around Edinburgh. Although this amount more than meets the estimated annual consumption of vegetables in the same area (although not the much higher recommended dietary intake), only a small fraction of these vegetables, as far as calculations permit, are actually consumed in this area.[5] The only vegetables sold in Edinburgh that with certainty can be traced to having been produced in the same area are those grown by one of the five or six small-scale growers who deliver them in boxes to Edinburgh households, or those sold on a stall at one of the farmers markets in Edinburgh (usually provided by the same growers). These growers are growing in some cases on only five or six acres, although the two bigger ones have farms of 120 to 140 acres (although not all dedicated to vegetables). Taking East Lothian as an example, for this is the prime vegetable growing area not just in the Edinburgh region but in the whole of Scotland, whereas fifty years ago there used to be a multitude of 'market gardeners' growing on an average of between seven and fifty acres and a wholesale market in Edinburgh to which they would bring the bulk of their produce, now the number of small growers can be counted on the fingers of one hand and the wholesale market, having moved out of the centre of the city in 1972, closed *c.* 2000.

Instead, driven by the demand of the supermarkets, the bulk of vegetable growing in East Lothian is concentrated in the hands of two large companies – East Lothian Produce and Drysdale. They grow only Brussels sprouts, cabbage, swedes, parsnips and leeks, on about 1700 acres; almost all of this land is rented from other farmers (potatoes are also grown on a large scale in East Lothian but this is generally a separate business).[6] A vegetable farmer today is also a processor and a packer. Both of these large growers also clean, wash, peel (in some cases also chop), package and label their vegetables before their produce is collected by large refrigerated lorries for delivery to their customers. The grower is also a cold-storage facility: Drysdale can store vegetables for up to two months after harvest so that a steady supply can be delivered to their customers. The bulk of East Lothian Produce's vegetable production goes to six supermarket chains; seventy percent of Drysdale's production is sold to Tesco: all the swedes in seven out of ten of Tesco's UK distribution depots come from East Lothian.

As part of Drysdale's contract to supply sprouts to three Tesco depots, for the four months of the year when they cannot supply sprouts from East Lothian, Drysdale import and process sprouts from Morocco; enough Tesco customers are happy to buy them at three to four times the price of a sprout from East Lothian, and in increasing amounts (1200 tonnes in 2013). Fed again by the convenience factor, sales of prepared vegetables are increasing dramatically. Prepared vegetables 'add value' to a product for the grower – they can charge a supermarket twice as much for a 'peeled' sprout as for a 'conventional' sprout. Highly capitalized businesses, these two growers, and the nature of their relationship to the large supermarket chains in the UK, signify the nature of vegetable growing today.

Where we buy our vegetables – the markets

Supermarkets. Today we buy 93% of our food in a supermarket multiple.[7] The size of individual companies, of the sector as a whole, and the effective aggregation into one industry of growing, processing and selling, gives the supermarkets enormous power not just over growers and suppliers, but also over governments, who love the picture of a private business sector competing to deliver food to people at the lowest possible price. The food manufacturing industry is the largest manufacturing sector in the UK.[8] But while every supermarket store manager or buyer will declare that their company's entire practice is led by their customers, the supermarkets undoubtedly have power over their customers; there is no doubt that our general expectations of the food that we buy and the kind of place we now buy it in has been created by the supermarkets.

The supermarkets say that during the last ten years their customers have been telling them that they want to be able to buy more 'local produce.' Tesco's Head of Local Sourcing Sarah Mackie declared in June 2013 that 'three quarters of our customers are telling us they are buying more local products than a year ago. […]. It's clear that local suppliers have a really important role to play at Tesco and in modern retail.'[9] Tesco was the first chain to create a local sourcing office in Scotland – in 2004. Sainsbury's followed shortly after in 2006, and Scotmid and the Co-op followed in 2011 and 2013. The local sourcing team's role is to find suppliers based in Scotland who can supply products usually in sufficient quantity to be sold into all of their supermarkets in Scotland. The chains claim that a major motivation for this policy is to support local businesses; since distribution depots were set up in Scotland, it is clearly also cheaper for the chains to source as much as they can from nearer these depots.

For the supermarkets, 'local' in Scotland means nothing more local than 'from Scotland'. The lines stocked by a supermarket are laid down by planners and forecasters in the company's head office; some people view the Scottish local sourcing teams as having little real power to influence what the supermarket stocks, and particularly in anything less than every store in Scotland. Given the supposed importance of 'local sourcing' to the supermarkets, it is surprising that the branding of Scottish produce in supermarkets in Scotland is curiously low key. This may reflect the fact that most people who shop in supermarkets are less interested than they say in where the food comes from. However the smaller supermarkets like Scotmid and Aldi have recently started to increase the visibility of their Scottish branding.

The greengrocer. In 1960 people bought 60% of their food in independent retailers.[10] In 2011, this had fallen to 7%.[11] A supermarket local sourcing manager readily admitted that it was the supermarkets that had destroyed the local greengrocer. Only about ten independent greengrocers (shops selling primarily fruit and vegetables) survive in Edinburgh. Since the closure of the Edinburgh Wholesale Market, they have to go to the Glasgow Wholesale Market (still run by the City Council) to get their supplies, unless they order them from the huge international fruit and vegetable wholesaler Total Produce, or from one of the specialist distributors based in England (particularly for 'exotic' fruit and vegetables).[12] Price and variety are the main features of these shops, with information about the produce's origin rarely displayed.

Farmers markets. Farmers markets, which first arrived in Britain in 1997, are usually seen as the key market for local produce, although together with farm shops they probably only account for about 0.5% of food sales.[13] Edinburgh Farmers Market, set up by the City Council in 2000, operates for five hours every Saturday. It can accommodate forty-nine stalls. Of the forty present on 18 October 2014, five were selling fruit and vegetables, seventeen were selling fresh meat, fish or dairy, with the remaining eighteen selling hot food, coffee, drinks, sweets, baking, soap and other 'speciality produce'. The current operators Essential Edinburgh (the City Centre Business Improvement District) say that there is not a queue of farmers wanting stalls at the market, and in fact see a mix of farmers and 'secondary producers' as key to making the market a distinctive shopping experience – as dependent on live music, street food and good coffee as much as on 'farm produce' for its attractiveness as a 'destination'. Seven additional 'farmers markets' (although all do not use the full title) have opened in different parts of Edinburgh in the last five years. Varying in size from between five and thirty stalls with a mix similar to the Edinburgh Farmers Market, six operate on one day each month, and one every week. While they are a welcome alternative place to buy fresh, local food, the continued existence of the smaller ones not in the city centre seems to be vulnerable.

Vicky MacDonald is the co-director of Edinburgh Markets, a social enterprise company which runs one of these markets and in August 2014 (after ten months of negotiation with Network Rail and the City Council) opened a new weekly market in the city's main railway station, although with a licence initially for only one year. Passionate about the benefits of markets both for the character of a city and for a city's local communities, she would love to see people using markets for their regular weekly shop, not just for their occasional dinner party purchases. She describes her existence as a market operator in Edinburgh as having to function in 'the cracks of the city left over from the lucrative development of houses and offices'; she also fears that the City Council's current Market Review will regulate out the smaller, more local markets in favour of the larger commercial markets (often imported *en bloc* from Europe) which will pay the City more in rents and fees. She comments that markets used to be the place you went for 'cheap stuff', but now 'we get that from Poundland'.

Box schemes. Most of the fruit and vegetable growers who sell at Edinburgh's farmers markets also provide food to the city in the form of a weekly box of fruit and or vegetables delivered to individual households. These growers also supply some restaurants and shops, but the box scheme is in most cases their principal market. Five such schemes between them deliver approximately 2000 boxes per week to households in Edinburgh.[14] Whilst all of these schemes are run by people who grow fruit and vegetables within a twenty-five mile radius of the city, only a percentage of what goes into a box on a year-round basis is actually grown by the box provider or other local growers with whom they work. To provide a continuous (and therefore also convenient) service to their customers, like the supermarkets they will source whatever proportion of the box they cannot themselves grow at any point in the year in the form of produce grown elsewhere in the UK, in Europe or further afield. The most 'local' offer that box schemes in the Edinburgh area provide is a box only containing fruit or veg grown in the UK, but the two largest schemes report that only one to two per cent of their customers ask for this particular box. All the box schemes in the Edinburgh area supply only organic produce, implying that how the food was grown matters more to consumers than where it was grown.

What do we mean by 'local'?

What do people really mean when they say that they would like to buy more 'local food'? Although a conversation about 'local food' is generally taken to be one about how far food has had to travel to reach us (with thirty miles being the normal criterion for 'local' in the UK); a more meaningful approach might be to look at the use of the term 'local food' as an attempt to restore to our relationship with food today some of the values that the urbanization of our culture and the industrialization of the production and selling of food have eroded.[15] Until well into the nineteenth century people in many parts of Scotland were completely self-sufficient for their food on what they could grow, hunt or gather around them.[16] In our now largely urbanized culture, where food comes to us as opposed to us having to go and get it, our once close relationship to food still manifests itself in a number of concerns about food, ranging from a greater or lesser degree of individual concern (played on by the producers of cookery programmes and publishers of cookery books) to the healthiness of what we are eating, to the state of the environment that it is being produced in, to the livelihoods of the people that grow or produce it, or to those who cannot afford food. These values also include the desire to grow more of it ourselves, knowing where it comes from, buying it from someone who knows something about it or may even have grown it themselves, rather than just from a check-out assistant or automatic till, or having the pleasure of knowing that it can be grown in our own region or country.[17]

The Market for Local Food in Edinburgh

Research into the marketing of local food has shown that people in particular buy beef and lamb, dairy products and fruits and vegetables from farm shops or farmers markets because (more than any others) those products retain 'a strong link to their farmed form'.[18] This implies that the appeal of food bought locally, and from someone directly involved in its production, is more a matter of confirming the link between food, the kind of place it came from and the person who grew or produced it as opposed to the more abstract 'food miles' notion of how far it has had to travel to reach you.

If these are some of the key values of the relationship we seek with our food, any aspirations for more 'local food', and the markets through which we obtain it, will have to meet criteria that go beyond 'local' in solely physical terms towards notions of community, relationships, resources, connections to the natural world and health.

New markets to supply more local food

Supermarkets. When people in Scotland surveyed by supermarkets and market research companies say that they would like to buy more local food, it appears that at the very most they mean 'food from Scotland'. Given their control over the growing system and their regional distribution systems that are now in place, the supermarket chains are well set up to satisfy that very broad demand, although there is little evidence of the extent to which people are knowingly purchasing food because it is from Scotland. The same definition is also used by some of the independent retailers, and perhaps, given the comparatively small size of Scotland and the pattern of distribution of its food growing and production, there is some sense in defining 'local food' in Scotland as food grown anywhere in Scotland.

But the massive size of the supermarket chains, while seeming to give them an impregnable presence, may also be their Achilles heel, and create opportunities for the smaller chains or the independent sector to provide an offer that is more localized than 'Scottish'. Scotmid is a small co-operative company (194 stores compared to Sainsbury's 1000 plus) with strong ties to its members and to the communities in which its stores are based. Since 2011 its local sourcing manager has developed new relationships with fifty to sixty Scottish suppliers, some of whom only supply to one or two stores. Although much of this supply is of 'ambient' goods (e.g. with longer shelf-life), bread in one hundred of their stores is now supplied by one of nine independent bakers local to the store, and they are beginning to develop local meat suppliers for individual stores as well. They are finding fruit and vegetables more difficult to supply on a more local basis partly as the supply is already so industrialized, and also because issues of maintaining freshness and minimizing waste are harder to solve.

Street markets and box schemes. Although the growth in street markets in Edinburgh over the last five years is positive, the reach of these markets remains limited, and while operating on only a weekly or monthly basis such markets will never be significant outlets for increased sale of fresh fruit and vegetables as turnover of sufficient value cannot be achieved. The creation of a substantial, centrally situated covered market, operating on six or seven days of the week, to sell (on a wholesale or retail basis) the goods of local producers would make a significant difference (and was canvassed by several people spoken to during research for this paper), but there are no signs at present of such a development receiving the backing from the City that it would require. The vegetable box schemes serving the city were badly hit by the recession and although they have recovered they seem to have reached a plateau in terms of numbers of customers. Their businesses are expanding but more through offering a greater range of organic products (e.g. dried foods and flowers) than through increasing the volume of fresh produce sold.

Greengrocers and local shops. Five new food shops, operating on three different models, have opened in Edinburgh during the last six years, perhaps confirming the simple truth that to provide more local food you have to have more local shops. Earthy was set up in 2008 by three partners, one of whom was a small-scale grower and box provider in East Lothian, and now has three shops in Edinburgh which sell a wide range of food sourced as locally as possible and with its origins clearly identified. Deliberately sited in carefully chosen residential locations, Earthy's stores have a mission, in the words of its grower-founder Patricia Stephen, 'to make fruit and veg sexy' and to give people back the delight of 'shopping with their senses'. Earthy now provides a strong retail base for a number of small local producers, and seems to have built a large group of customers who subscribe to their values, with their loyalty paradoxically reinforced by the recession.

The New Leaf Co-op was set up in 2012 by five graduates from Edinburgh University. They took over an existing whole food shop, expanded the range of foods sold, adding in more bread, fruit and vegetables; they also gave the business a more overt ethical and environmental approach; and they make a determined effort to engage their community, their customers and their suppliers in their approach. Set up with the support of private investors and crowd-funding, they are committed, sophisticated and articulate opponents of the monopolization of the food industry by the supermarkets, and their business seems to be reaching its initial targets.

Dig-in Bruntsfield is the first 'community greengrocer' in Edinburgh. Emerging from a meeting in 2011 held to protest at Sainsbury's surreptitious purchase of the local independent delicatessen, the shop opened in May 2014. Setup was supported by the Co-op Hub, the Co-op Group, the City Council Neighbourhood Partnership Fund, and the Plunkett Foundation; £30,000 was also raised from a public share issue. Initial reports say that their turnover is much higher than planned, and that their presence is having a positive effect on other independent shops in their immediate vicinity.

Implications for the future – the wider context of local

If we want our relationship to our food to encapsulate a new range of values we will have to work to make this happen, but the nature of these values – based on health, sustainability, local well-being, community – also provides a justification for the involvement of governments at both local and national level, who should look at the food sector not just in terms of an industry focused primarily on growth, profit and contribution to GDP. Local and national government could make it easier for people to grow a greater diversity of crops, on a smaller scale, preferably on land nearer the city. Cities could make it easier for us to buy this food, through provision of new markets, or more support for independent businesses and through planning and licensing regulations that set limits on the takeover of the centres of cities, as well as the outskirts, by the supermarket chains.[19] Public bodies, in particular schools and colleges and hospitals, could use their purchasing power to lead by example and buy from local producers.[20]

In the middle of the sixteenth century 43% of Edinburgh's merchants were already trading overseas.[21] Global access to food is not going to go away, and it can bring benefits, but if we can make the places that we live in more receptive to the growing of food and to its local distribution we will be able to start to restore a more meaningful connection to our food, on which our health and the health of our environment probably depend.

Acknowledgements

Thanks to the following for their generous contribution of information and ideas towards this paper: Angus Bell, Stephen Brown, Mike Callendar, Ronnie Combe, Oliver Cooper, Mark Farvis, Lindsay Girvan, Graham Hogg, Patrick Hughes, Alison Johnstone, Martin Lowe, Vicky Macdonald, Melanie Main, Alison Muirhead, Ben Lowe, Emma Patterson-Taylor, Tracey Reilly, Cesar Revoredo-Giha, Fiona Richmond, John Saunderson, Patricia Stephen and Peter Thompson.

Notes

1. F Marian McNeill, *The Scots Kitchen* (Blackie & Son Limited, 1929; repr. Granada Publishing, 1979): pp. 6–7.
2. YouGov Sixthsense, Food Provenance, 2012: p. 8.
3. In June 2014 the Scottish Government released *Becoming A Good Food Nation*, a consultation document towards the updating of its 2009 Food Policy. The document takes a broad view of food, encompassing issues of health, sustainability and community. It proposes early action on five key areas: Public Sector Food, a Children's Food Policy, Local Food, Good Food Choices and Continued Economic Growth.
4. Jean Kinsey and Ben Senauer, 'Consumer trends and changing retailing formats', *Amer J Agr Econ* (December 1996): pp. 1187–91.
5. Report compiled by the Edinburgh Local Food Network, 2011, using Scottish Government data of 2009: <http://www.edinburghfood.org/news1/current-projects/could-edinburgh-feed-itself/>.
6. Contrast this to the two hundred varieties grown by East Coast Organics, one of the box-scheme growers in East Lothian.
7. Food Statistics Pocketbook 2013, (DEFRA 2013): p.16.
8. Family Food 2012 (DEFRA 2013): p. iii.
9. Sarah Mackie, 'An Englishman, a Scotsman and a Welshman Walk into a Tesco…', *Talking Shop*, Tesco, PLC <https://www.tescoplc.com/talkingshop/index.asp?blogid=121> [accessed 27 May 2014].
10. One Planet Food, *Our Mutual Food* (Fife, 2010): p. 25.
11. DEFRA, p.16

12. Total Produce is a huge international company which grows, sources, imports, packages, distributes and markets fresh produce through two hundred locations in twenty countries. They supply the major multiples, convenience stores and cash and carry stores as well as the food service and processing industry.
13. *One Planet Food*, p. 25.
14. Averaging four to five kg of produce per box this calculates as some 468 tonnes of fruit and veg delivered by box schemes to Edinburgh every year.
15. The definition of thirty miles as 'local' is used by both DEFRA and the market research and data collection agency Mintel.
16. The Introduction to Catherine Brown's 'Scottish Cookery', 2006, provides a good overview of the development of food culture in Scotland from earliest times to today.
17. In the City of Edinburgh in 2013 there were 2700 people on the waiting list for one of 1266 allotment plots: <https://www.whatdotheyknow.com/request/waiting_lists_for_allotments_358> [accessed 27 May 2014].
18. David Watts, Philip Leat and Cesar Revoredo-Giha, 'Local Food Activity in Scotland: Empirical Evidence and Research Agenda', *Regional Studies*. First published 9 March 2010 (iFirst).
19. Edinburgh is a member of the *Sustainable Food Cities Network*, and is currently working on a Sustainable Food City Strategy '*Edible Edinburgh*'.
20. Food in the public sector is one of the areas for priority action proposed in the Scottish Government's consultation document for a new Food Policy *Becoming a Good Food Nation*. The document states that 'the public sector should champion fresh, seasonal, local and sustainable produce'. Copies of the document can be downloaded from <http://www.scotland.gov.uk>.
21. Information from Oliver Cooper, 'Built on Food, An Archaeology of Edinburgh's 'Intestines'', unpublished dissertation, The University of Edinburgh 2011.

Twenty-First-Century Meat Markets

Peter Hertzmann

Labels may be more important in meat shopping than in any other common consumer purchase. Other than being able to distinguish between ground meat and whole cuts, the average shopper cannot tell the difference between pork and beef, a boneless ribeye and a New York strip, or flank steak and flap meat. Some buyers want to see lots of fat; some want to see a little or none. Some consumers buy strictly by price; others have social agendas that drive their meat-purchase decision.

The cost-conscious buyer is usually happy to purchase meat from their local supermarket. The fact that all the meat is sold on Styrofoam trays and covered with plastic film provides a sought-after convenience. The buyer seems unaware that any less desirable portions of the meat being purchased are either on the reverse side or hidden by labelling. They are unaware that the package they are buying may be back-filled with carbon monoxide gas that keeps red meat looking red for a long time.[1] This same buyer usually wants to be told nothing about how the animal being eaten was raised, slaughtered or butchered.[2] Many go past thinking about animal welfare and do not even want to think that the package they are purchasing contains the flesh of a once-living organism.[3]

Most meat purchases in the United States are made at supermarkets, chain speciality stores or big-box stores. Purchases from small, independent butchers make up a very small portion of the market – maybe not significant from the standpoint of dollars spent, but significant from an emotional level.[4] Independent, artisan butchers respond to the consumer's desire for a perceived quality level, a specialized feeding programme or a desire for 'humane' slaughtering practices. Although independent butchers are a small portion of the retail meat business, major supermarket chains are making adjustments to their marketing practices by adding products that directly address their competition. Some major chains now offer unpackaged meat sold from a meat case and limited custom cutting options in addition to their standard array of pre-packaged meat products.[5] Terms like grass-fed, organic, sustainably raised and antibiotic-free are now routinely found on package labels.[6]

In between the major chain stores and independent butchers are stores like Whole Foods Market and The Fresh Market, both major chains, that feature a butcher counter that sells mostly unpackaged, pre-cut meat. The stores provide the consumer an image similar to what the buying public visualizes as a traditional butcher, but the majority of the product sold from the meat case comes to the store as boxed, pre-cut meat. The counter staff simply has to unbox the meat and arrange it in the case.

Mass-merchandised product labelling is used to describe sources and husbandry methods, usually in general terms to satisfy the requirements of a poorly informed, buzzword-oriented public. The counter staff often seem to know little about the products they are selling, even though most stores have extensive employee training programmes.

Independent butchers are classic niche marketers. Although many butchers offer small grocery sections to support last-minute, dinner-time shoppers, their primary business is selling fresh meat and value-added meat products. They truly are independent butcher shops, and not meat counters inside of larger markets offering one-stop shopping. They generally serve mostly the neighbourhood in which they are located, although they may also be a destination for shoppers that want meat products sold under the particular philosophy of an individual shop.

To outward appearances, individual independent butcher shops all seem to be similar, but when closely observed, they are as individual as the men and women that own and operate them. Customers visiting an independent butcher only see the public side of the meat case. For the most part, they are unaware of time, effort and plain hard work that goes on behind the beautiful display of cut meat.

The butchers

Much of the information contained in this paper is the result of interviews conducted with butchers from five shops located in three major urban areas of the United States and Canada.[7] Although they all can be termed independent, artisan butchers, their shops vary in philosophy and practice. Artisan butchery is a trade plied by individuals that subscribe to some common practices but at the same time interpret these practices in their own individual way. Each butcher has his or her own idea as to the proper meat to source and then how to fabricate the meat into finished cuts for sale to the public.

Most of the butchers interviewed, and in my overall experience in meeting young butchers, came to butchery from the culinary industry. Unlike former times where butchers learned their trade through a formal apprentice programme or from older relatives that were already entrenched in the trade, today's artisan butcher is more likely to come to the trade after first being trained as a professional cook. Often, they initially learned to break subprimals into standard cuts while working in a restaurant. In some cases, the restaurants were purchasing primals or whole carcasses that required fabrication into restaurant portions. For these cooks, the next step was to turn to butchering as a full-time profession where the hours were better and the stress possibly less.

The independent, artisan butchers I interviewed for this paper were in their twenties or thirties. In some of their shops there is an older butcher who brings a different set of experiences to the cutting table. These older butchers may function as both co-worker and mentor to the younger butchers.

Whether young or old, the interaction between the butcher and the customer is almost always at a distance defined by the depth of the meat case. With the occasional exception, it is the rare shop that is set up to allow the butcher and the customer to stand face-to-face without a piece of furniture separating them. Through on-going interactions, it is not unusual for a butcher to become knowledgeable about the customer's eating habits, but it is a rare customer that is familiar with their butcher.

Sourcing

Most artisan butchers have a meat philosophy. Will the meat they sell be organic, humanely raised, free of or never given antibiotics, sustainable, etc.? The list can be quite long. In order to meet their needs, artisan butchers seldom are able their buy stock from wholesale meat suppliers. All of the butchers I talked with have developed supply agreements with a number of independent ranchers.

Cattle need eighteen to thirty months to be ready for slaughter. Younger cattle tend to be smaller and produce less marbled meat. Older animals are larger with better marbling. Older cattle raised strictly for their meat are more expensive to raise so they must achieve a sufficient weight gain during their last year to offset the cost of their feed.

Ranch location can have a large effect on the available type of animal. Coastal grazing lands on the west coast of the United States tend to be sufficiently temperate so that grass grows all year round. Other areas of the west require irrigation, and additional expense, to produce grass through out the year. Still other areas around the country may be covered with snow or susceptible to freezing part of the year. This necessitates moving the cattle to a warmer climate during the winter or augmenting the natural grasses with silage or grain.[8]

These weather- and location-based issues can become a problem for the artisan butcher wanting to offer only 100 per cent grass-fed beef to his or her customers. Although silage is usually made from grass, some butchers do not consider it part of a grass-fed programme and will not offer the resulting meat to their customers. The same is true for grain augmentation, even though grains when properly used for feed in combination with hay do not cause acidosis, the usual complaint with a grain-finishing programme.[9]

Once an animal is ready for slaughter, most ranchers, lacking a slaughtering facility, need to transport the animal to a nearby abattoir. For many, the concept of 'nearby' is moving farther and farther away as the number of abattoirs across the nation continues to shrink. In most cases, once an animal heads to the slaughterhouse, feeding stops, and the animal begins to lose weight. There is also weight loss from the stress caused by the truck ride. The longer the ride, the more expensive it becomes to the rancher.

The typical independent butcher shop will require one to five whole beef carcasses per week. Most of the butchers I talked with choose to receive their beef shipment once a week, preferably on Monday, so initial fabrication can take place when either the store is closed or least busy. The butcher will be committing to fifty to two-hundred and fifty animals a year from a single rancher. Small ranchers need this type of commitment to justify their long-term investment in animals. Butchers will often hedge their bets by purchasing regularly from two beef suppliers. In this way, if one herd is compromised, there will be a fall-back position in place. There is an on-going conversation between the butcher and the rancher as to herd condition and animal maturity in order to monitor short- and long-term planning.

In contrast to cattle, swine reach their slaughtering weight in about six months.[10] Every butcher I spoke with sold pork raised solely from 'heritage' breeds of pig.[11] With some heritage breeds, butchers sometimes prefer to work with animals that are a few weeks shy of maturity in order to reduce the amount of back fat they have to use or toss out.

Pigs are omnivores, and as such, do not live well on grass only. Most independent butchers sell pork that is pasture-raised with the pasture grass being supplemented with organic feed. Some are selling pigs whose diet is supplemented with whey or spent brewers grains. Others are selling pigs that are totally raised by foraging and thus cannot be called organic due to the lack of control of the feed.

Most independent butchers carry lamb all year long, but for some shops lamb is strictly a seasonal item.[12] Terminology regarding lamb age and feed is loosely regulated in the United States. Most commercial lamb is grass-fed with some coarse grain supplements, but independent butchers tend to carry grass-finished lamb that is antibiotic free.[13] To a lesser extent, independent butchers will carry mutton and goats, although it may require a special order or purchase of frozen product.

By and far, the largest selling poultry product available at independent butcher shops is chicken. Turkeys tend to be seasonal, and rabbit, squab, quail, guinea fowl, ducks and geese tend to require a special order. Depending on the farm, the chickens may be free-range or pasture-raised and fed supplemental grain without any antibiotics, growth hormones or animal by-products.[14] Most sell birds that have been air chilled rather than water chilled.[15]

The butcher needs to maintain a good relationship with all of the store's suppliers in order to maintain a proper supply of raw product. Most butchers and their employees have visited the farms where their animals are raised. Some have observed the slaughtering operation. This provides the butchers with the ability to knowledgeably discuss the husbandry of each animal with their customers.

Processing

Once the animal carcasses enter the shop's back door, the work for the butcher begins. Each whole carcass must be fabricated into a series of cuts that fit the shop's sales profile, the season, and the shop's storage and display capability. All of this must take place rapidly but still minimize loss due to spoilage or poor fabrication technique.

Modern butcher shops no longer feature the high ceilings and rail systems of old-time shops. This means that beef carcasses must be delivered to the shop in pieces small enough to be handled and hung. Beef carcasses are generally delivered sawed into eight pieces – two foreleg sections called chucks, two thoracic sections called ribs, two lumbar sections called loins and two hind-leg sections called hips. Hog carcasses are generally split down the middle and delivered as two pieces. Other, smaller animal carcasses are delivered whole. If the offal from the animals has been requested, it is usually packaged separately.

In some cases, beef is delivered as soon as possible after slaughter and sold in that condition. In other cases, it is received dry-aged.[16] In some cases, the meat is received 'green' and dry-aged in the shop itself. Proper dry-aging requires humidity- and temperature-controlled aging rooms, a luxury for most butcher shops. Besides the pluses of aging, increased tenderness and intensified flavour, the butcher needs to contend with the minuses. During aging the meat will lose ten to fifteen per cent of its moisture due to dripping and evaporation. The outer surface will darken and dry. A thin layer of white mould may also form on the surface. The butcher purchases the carcass based on the green weight, and by the time aging is completed the cost per kilo has significantly increased. Generally, only beef is conditioned (aged), but some shops will also condition mutton.[17]

What happens to the meat after it comes through the door is somewhat a function of the shop style and the size of the meat case. The refrigerated meat display case is, from the standpoint of the customer, the centre of the shop. The length of the cases in the shops of the butchers interviewed ranged from a little over a metre (four feet) to greater than eight metres (twenty-six feet). The meat case is a display device more than a storage device. Most use gravity cooling and have no humidity controls.[18] The exposed surfaces of the meat can dry out if left exposed too long. To maintain colour and reduce moisture loss, special paper must be inserted between pieces of meat to prevent contact oxidation. Throughout the work day, the meat case has to be kept appropriately filled, and the contents looking fresh. The butcher from the shop with the longest case said that maintaining the case required the labour equivalent of two man-days each day. This includes filling the case at the start of the day, emptying the case at the end, and wrapping the contents for overnight storage.

Which cuts go into the case is not a haphazard choice. There are seasonal considerations: braising cuts sell better in the winter, and grilling cuts sell better in the summer. Any item displayed in too small a quantity, even if there is more in storage, won't sell well because some customers are reluctant to ask if back stock exists. Items that need to move will be displayed closer to the customer than other items. In a large case, most or all cuts available can be displayed. In a small case, the cuts displayed are more likely to be the most popular cuts or pieces that the shop needs to move before they spoil. A challenge for shops with a small meat case is to get customers to ask for the cuts they desire. Once the customer realizes that the shop cuts to order, this issue is reduced. As one customer said to me, 'I like being able to go into the shop and ask for ground pork or ground turkey, and they do it for me while I wait.'[19] (Not all customers are that patient.) A cut-to-order butcher shop provides a different level of service not obviously available in a shop where most of what is offered resides in the meat case.

A butcher fabricating a whole carcass all at once will work off a real or mental cut sheet whereas one that cuts to order can only prepare the carcass to a point where final fabrication can occur.[20] For the cut-to-order butcher, if a customer requests a rack of pork back ribs, it will not be possible to fulfil a request for rib chops from the same carcass since the cuts are mutually exclusive. In situations like this, the butcher has to be able to engage the customer and suggest alternate cuts.

During the entire fabrication process, the butcher needs to be aware of how much of the product that came in through the back door makes it into the meat case. Besides the mass-reducing water loss that occurs as the meat sits in the walk-in refrigerator, in an environment of customers increasingly requesting bone-out meat cuts, more bone waste is produced. Commercial processors can sell their waste products to other industries, but in most jurisdictions, independent butchers cannot wholesale their waste products. Only the two humerus and the two femur bones on a beef carcass are suitable as marrow bones, so any other bones become waste. Occasionally, an independent butcher will have ethnic clientele interested in the other bones of various animals, such as Asian customers using pig spines for stock. Additionally, some beef tallow can be sold to hobbyist soap makers, and some (pork) leaf fat can be sold to home pie-makers, but this usually does not consume all of this type of waste produced in the shop.

The fabrication of retail cuts yields a certain significant amount of muscle material and small amounts of connective tissue of irregular-sized pieces called trim. Trim results from the cleaning of bones and the tidying of muscle cuts. Trim is not waste. Trim is collected and run through the meat grinder. The resulting ground meat is sold alongside other retail cuts.[21] Some weeks, there will be excess trim to grind, and at other times some whole muscle cuts may need to be added to the trim bucket to fill the current ground meat requirement. Depending on the pricing structure of the butcher shop, this may mean that more expensive meat will now be sold at a lower price.

Another large area of production within the modern, artisan butcher shop is value-added products. Fresh sausages, mostly made from pork and stuffed in natural pork casings, are probably the most common and easiest to produce form of value-added product. Some shops produce cooked-meat products ranging from whole roast cuts to pâtés and spreads. Some shops produced cured and smoked-meat products such as bacon. Dried meat products, such as *salumi,* are often beyond the capabilities of most independent butchers because of the space required for curing and drying and local regulatory issues.

Some of the shops sell meat that is breaded, brined, marinated or cut, seasoned and assembled on skewers. This is a convenient manner to use meat that maybe didn't sell the first day or was in the meat case too long. Other butchers disagree with the practice even though customers welcome the items as timesavers or product improvements.

The handoff

The butcher sits between the rancher and the customer, converting the rancher's products into the products the customer finds desirable. Just as there needs to be a continual dialogue between the butcher and the rancher, there needs to be a dialogue between the butcher and the customer. Some customers welcome a dialogue while others just want to pick up a chop or two and be out the door as soon as possible.

Because the meat prices in an independent butcher shop appear to be significantly higher than the chain supermarket nearby, some observers think that the independents only serve the wealthy. The reality is that most of their customers fall into the middle class and are often local. These customers are seeking particular descriptors for their meat or are seeking a higher level of service than is available in the self-service supermarket or both.

Although one of the butchers interviewed worked in a shop where the customers were generally waited on by counter help, the other shops had direct butcher to customer contact. One said that their butchers spend as much as twenty minutes waiting on a single customer. Some customers bring their recipes in and ask for advice. Some come in and ask the butcher what to fix for dinner! At the shop where the customers are waited on by counter help, much time is spent with the staff to educate them about the meat sources and how each cut should be dealt with in the kitchen.

The biggest customer issue that most of the butchers deal with is a lack of understanding by the customer as to what is meant by all current marketing terms for meat. The customer's definition of grass-fed may not match the reality of the beef being sold as grass-fed. The customer may not understand that very few animals are truly purebred, and that the majority are a combination of breeds.[22] Some common meat terms are regulated, but many are not, and the government definition of a term may not match the consumer's.[23] If the customer is willing to listen, the butcher is able to explain in as much detail as necessary the shop's meat philosophy, which in most cases, will be all the information the customer needs.

Conclusion

Meat-market customers, for the most part, have no idea as to what goes on behind the meat case. The meat case is both a physical and psychological barrier. Besides their normal desire for flavourful, tender and juicy meat, customers require other aspects of the meat they are purchasing to meet their personal lifestyle. Some are interested in breed, feed and other aspects of animal husbandry. Others are only interested how the meat was aged. Most customers would be surprised to learn that the meat they are buying is a result of a continuous dialogue between themselves and their butcher as well as between the butcher and the rancher that raised the animals.

Food and Markets

Notes

1. Carola Grebitus et al., 'Fresh Meat Packaging: Consumer Acceptance of Modified Atmosphere Packaging including Carbon Monoxide', *Journal of Food Protection*, 76 (2013), pp. 99–107.
2. In general, when the term 'slaughter' is used it is assumed to include both killing and evisceration, referred to as dressing, of the carcass.
3. L.E. Mayfield et al., 'Consumption of Welfare-Friendly Food Products in Great Britain, Italy and Sweden, and How It May Be Influenced By Consumer Attitudes To, and Behaviour Towards, Animal Welfare Attributes', *International Journal of Sociology of Food and Agriculture*, 15 (2007), pp. 59–73 (p. 70).
4. The adjectives 'small', 'independent' and 'artisan' are used interchangeably to refer to a free-standing meat shop where whole carcasses are fabricated into retail cuts; Michael Melusky, 'Niche beef products comprise small share of total retail beef sales', *Issues Update 2006* (Beef Check-Off), March–April 2006, pp. 46–47.
5. Note the phrases 'Drop by to meet your neighborhood butcher' and 'Our expert butchers are ready to trim your purchase to your exact specifications' that adorn Safeway's meat and seafood department web page. <http://www.safeway.com/ShopStores/The-Market-SJ-Meat-Seafood.page> [accessed 1 May 2014].
6. Grass-fed is a regulated term: 'Grass and forage shall be the feed source consumed for the lifetime of the ruminant animal, with the exception of milk consumed prior to weaning. The diet shall be derived solely from forage consisting of grass (annual and perennial), forbs (e.g., legumes, Brassica), browse or cereal grain crops in the vegetative (pre-grain) state. Animals cannot be fed grain or grain byproducts and must have continuous access to pasture during the growing season. Hay, haylage, baleage, silage, crop residue without grain, and other roughage sources may also be included as acceptable feed sources. Routine mineral and vitamin supplementation may also be included in the feeding regimen. If incidental supplementation occurs due to inadvertent exposure to non-forage feedstuffs or to ensure the animal's well being at all times during adverse environmental or physical conditions, the producer must fully document (e.g., receipts, ingredients, and tear tags) the supplementation that occurs including the amount, the frequency, and the supplements provided' (*Federal Register*, 72, 199, (16 October 2007), p. 58637). The term 'organic', in the United States, in product labelling is regulated by the United States Department of Agriculture. The rules are highly complex with many exceptions that allow for products that are not fully organic to be labelled as such. To complicate matters, the USDA uses a number of different physical labels, such as '100% organic' versus 'organic', to denote different types of organic products ('Labeling Organic Products', National Organic Program, Agricultural Marketing Service, U.S. Department of Agriculture, October 2012). The definition of 'sustainable', when it refers to meat, can be a bit deceptive. Unlike wild fisheries, the number of animals produced each year is a controlled number. When ranchers describe their cattle, sheep or pigs as being sustainable, they are referring to the ability of the grazing or pasture land to support the herd size without over taxing the land. Antibiotic-free is an unregulated marketing term. It generally means that there were no detectable antibiotics in the animal at time of slaughter. It does not mean that the animal never received antibiotics. The term 'no antibiotics added' is allowed on product labels by the USDA's Food Safety and Inspection Service if sufficient documentation is provided to the Agency.
7. The five butcher shops represented herein and the butchers are: Dave Meli, Executive Butcher, The Healthy Butcher, Toronto, Canada; Tom Mylan, Co-owner and Dear Leader, The Meat Hook, Brooklyn, NY; Monica and Aaron Rocchino, Owners. The Local Butcher Shop, Berkeley, CA; Adam Tiberio, Owner, Adam Tiberio Custom Meats, New York, NY and Angela Wilson, Co-owner and Head Butcher, Avedano's Holly Park Market, San Francisco, CA
8. Silage is made from harvested grass crops using the entire green plant, not just the grain. The plant matter is shredded into pieces about 1.3 cm (0.5 in) long, and spread into even layers on the floor of a silo, out in the field covered by a plastic tarp or baled and wrapped with plastic. Due to the weight of the material, moisture content, and lack of oxygen, the plant material undergoes fermentation to prevent spoilage.
9. Rick Stock and Robert Britton, 'Acidosis', in *Beef Cattle Handbook* <http://www.iowabeefcenter.org/Beef%20Cattle%20Handbook/Acidosis.pdf> [accessed 29 April 2014]. A steer's life can be divided into two phases. During the first, the steer grazes in an open environment, be it farmed pasture or wild

grasslands. Then, in the months before slaughter, the animal may be finished in a closed pen on grain, the most common grain being steam-flaked corn. In a one-hundred percent grass-fed programme, the animal is finished on grass, usually in an open field. Generally, grain finishing will produce a heavier animal in less time.

10. United States Department of Agriculture Economic Research Service, 'Hogs and pork', <http://www.ers.usda.gov/topics/animal-products/hogs-pork/background.aspx> [accessed 29 April 2014].
11. Heritage pork breeds are breeds that do not adapt well to industrial farming. Some common names are Berkshire, Tamworth, Red Wattle, Duroc, Gloucester Old Spot, Yorkshire, Large Black and Mulefoot.
12. Lamb is generally regarded as sheep that is less than one year old.
13. United States Department of Agriculture Food Safety and Inspection Service, 'Lamb from Farm to Table', <http://www.fsis.usda.gov/wps/portal/fsis/topics/food-safety-education/get-answers/food-safety-fact-sheets/meat-preparation/focus-on-lambfrom-farm-to-table/CT_Index> [accessed 29 April 2014].
14. Free-range chickens only have to have access to the world beyond the walls of the hen house. They generally are not forced to leave the hen house, and many never do.
15. Air-chilled 'refers to a specific method used to cool chickens after slaughtering. Most chickens in this country [the United States] are processed by being immersed in ice water. By contrast, air-chilling cools chickens by blasting them with cold air' (Carolyn Jung, 'Great Chicken Chill Debate: Air vs. Water', *Sun Sentinel,* 27 March 2008 <http://articles.sun-sentinel.com/2008-03-27/features/0803250428_1_chicken-air-water> [accessed 29 April 2014]).
16. Initial conditioning of beef muscle starts by storing at 4 °C (38 °F) for a week or so whether vacuum packed, so-called wet aging or simply hung in the cooler, dry aging: 'It takes this long because living muscles protect themselves against autolysis (self-digestion) which might otherwise be initiated by the extreme changes in shape which accompany strong muscle contractions, and because meat cooler temperatures are far below the living body temperatures of mammals and birds.' 'Gourmet conditioning of beef and other intrinsically tough meats is best done with aerobic exposure of primal cuts. It may take up to a month from the time of slaughter, during which time exposed muscle surfaces should become dry, black and lightly dusted with white mould' (Howard J Swatland, *Meat Cuts and Muscle Foods* (Nottingham: Nottingham UP, 2004), p. 39).
17. Mutton generally refers to older sheep. The exact definition may be based on age or denture development. In the United States, the term does not officially exist. According to the Code of Federal Regulations: 'Lamb means ovine animals of any age, including ewes and rams' (*Code of Federal Regulations,* Title 7, Vol. 10, Chap. XI, §1280.111, Lamb).
18. With gravity cooling, the meat case usually has no fans to circulate the air, which would increase the rate of surface drying; Bill Katz, 'Making the "Case" for Conduction Case Cooling', *Contracting Business,* 21 July 2013 <http://contractingbusiness.com/refrigeration/making-case-conduction-case-cooling> [accessed 30 April 2014].
19. Robbin Everson (customer at The Local Butcher Shop, Berkeley, CA), in discussion with the author, 30 April 2014.
20. A cut sheet is a check list of all the possible cuts that can be fabricated from a carcass or primal. It is used to communicate a plan for dividing the meat into retail cuts since many cuts are mutually exclusive.
21. In the United Kingdom and Australia, ground beef is referred to and sold as 'beef mince'.
22. 'The American Angus Association set up the "Certified Angus Beef" brand in 1978. The goal of this brand was to promote the idea that Angus beef was of higher quality than beef from other breeds of cattle. Cattle are eligible for "Certified Angus Beef" evaluation if they are at least 51% black and exhibit Angus influence, which include black Simmental cattle and crossbreds.' There are ten additional criteria, but the point is that even Certified Angus Beef is not purebred ('Angus Cattle, *Wikipedia* <http://en.wikipedia.org/wiki/Angus_cattle> [accessed 2 May 2014]).
23. USDA Food Safety and Inspection Service, 'Meat and Poultry Labeling Terms', <http://www.fsis.usda.gov/wps/portal/fsis/topics/food-safety-education/get-answers/food-safety-fact-sheets/food-labeling/meat-and-poultry-labeling-terms/meat-and-poultry-labeling-terms> [accessed 1 May 2014].

Food and Markets

Figure 1 (left). The market during reconstruction in 1999. Part of the market has been demolished behind the boarding and sales were carrying on in half the normal space. This trading scene shows the vitality and chaos of fish sales.

Figure 2 (right). A social corner in the market: chai *or* gahwa *to be drunk, news and opinions to be exchanged.*

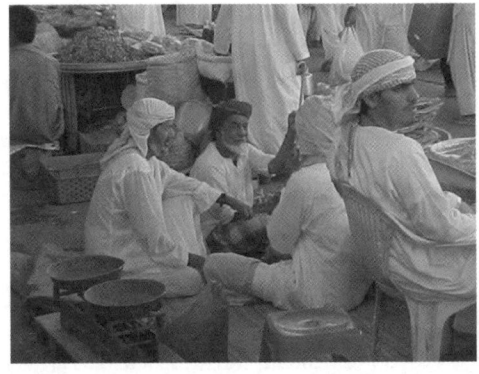

Figure 3 (left). Trader with an Indian threadfish, Alectis indicus, *a member of the jack and trevally family. Large fish specimens are quite common in the market: yellow fin tuna a metre long are regularly available.*

Figure 4 (right). This side alley in the Al Ain suq has some of the character of the dusty markets that I saw when I first worked in the Emirates in 1978. It also displays some traditional craft products such as leef, *palm fibre rope.*

Al Ain Suq – An Enduring Culinary Asset

Phil Iddison

Observation and analysis of traditional food market dynamics can teach us a lot about food marketing generally and also its effects on a more personal scale. These markets do not benefit from mass marketing campaigns and usually rely on word of mouth. They lack an integrated organization and modern management. Despite this they can demonstrate a vitality that makes corporate marketing seem mundane and can also deliver the unexpected. In the case of a fast-developing Gulf state, paying attention to these dynamics reveals the market adapting to development and change.

Al Ain in the United Arab Emirates is the second city within Abu Dhabi Emirate and is the educational, cultural and resort centre for the Emirate. The central *suq* or market area in the city is principally devoted to food sales in the broadest interpretation of this term.[1] It has endured for over sixty years, despite two attempts by the municipal authorities to replace it with modern developments in areas nearer to the administrative centre of the city.[2] It has also survived reconstruction during the late 1990s when some of the structures were renewed around and amongst the traders as they carried on with their business. It continues to be very popular and serves the city community with economy, efficiency and diversity.[3]

The market complex is sited on the northern edge of the Al Ain date palm oasis. This oasis was the principal food reserve of the city and consists of 130 hectares of irrigated date palm gardens with an underplanting of fruit trees and fodder crops. The ruler's fort is located on the eastern edge of the market area and the ruler's palace is to the west of the market. Until the 1990s, the regional camel market was also located just north of the market complex near an old mud brick fort that had become the police post and city jail.

The market's endurance is driven by persistent patronage from a broad spectrum of residents ranging from wealthy nationals looking for date palm pollen to a guest worker collecting ingredients for a fish-head curry. As a result the market presents a developing record of the changes in the city's food requirements and the means by which they are delivered to the population. This ranges from stalls selling livestock feed to the sale of live animals; from trays with bunches of fresh locally grown herbs costing pennies to whole boxes of imported fruit; from great platters of loose fresh dates to anonymous gallon plastic containers of date syrup; from tiny coffee cups to 1000-litre aluminium cauldrons and multi-burner gas rings for wedding feasts, but principally fish, meat, carbohydrates, vegetables and fruit to sustain life on a day-to-day basis.

The development of the market has responded to the changing food cultures and circumstances of the population. In the past there would have been sales of firewood

Food and Markets

Figure 5 (left). A hardware shop on the fringe of the suq selling pressure cookers and a 'small' gas ring.

Figure 6 (right). Camel loin chops from a young beast for sale in the market hall. The thick fat layer was particularly prized.

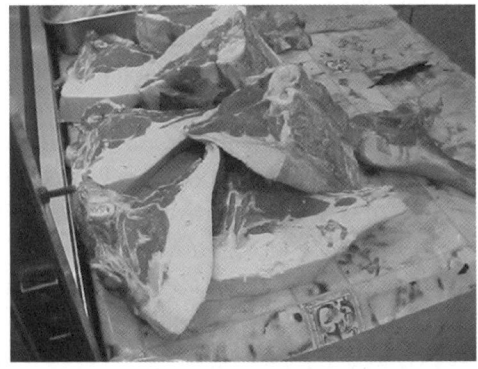

Figure 7 (left). The raised fruit and vegetable stalls in the market hall.

Figure 8 (right). The fresh herb market has twenty odd different herbs for sale in ¼ dirham bunches.

Al Ain Suq – An Enduring Culinary Asset

collected from the hinterland around Al Ain. This and the arisings from date palm culture in the oasis were the principal source of cooking heat before the oil industry by-production of bottled gas took over. This use of fuel wood is still preserved at wedding feasts where the huge cooking cauldrons are fired with acacia wood logs. The resultant taste of the smoke-infused food is still a strongly desired trait.

The Emirati food culture is subject to rapid change. This change concentrates in the young cohorts who have embraced the incoming food cultures and associated social activities. This age-group of nationals is not seen in the *suq*. The Western-style coffee shop is now the meeting place of choice for youth. Coffee was always a key social drink but it was one that was taken in the context of a gift on social meeting. It would be prepared or at least overseen by the host. Coffee as a social drink was embedded in Arabian culture well before the West took to it. The idea of an immigrant barista preparing a formulaic Western version for which you have to pay is at odds with centuries of social tradition. It is therefore heartening to see traditional food knowledge, tastes and products surviving and where necessary evolving in the *suq*.

The market has collective as well as discrete personalities in abundance. In this market buying and selling food is definitely a social affair. The individual personalities of the traders and buyers contribute strongly to the character of the market. There is banter amongst the traders; serious questioning from the buyers; meetings of acquaintances and perpetual movement as people amble or bustle around the market. The clientele is multi-ethnic, based on a swath of cultures from the North African coast to the Philippines. There is a babble of languages, Arabic, Tagalog, Bengali and a minority presence of English which often functions as a common language. All in all this is in stark contrast to the intense corporate character of a modern Western supermarket where people can be perceived to behave more like zombies rather than members of the human race!

The market derives its energy from multiple and disparate inputs. The municipality provides the land, structures and trading licences along with market inspectors to harass the traders and the street cleaning at the end of the trading day. The traders resource the goods; organize their transport and delivery; set up the stalls to display their wares; do their own vocal advertising; negotiate their sales; clear their stalls at the end of trading and go home to repeat the cycle the next day. The customers trawl through the stalls on foot for their essential and elective shopping, perhaps accompanied by a *hamal*, a market porter to collect and carry their purchases. For a city that is totally devoted to the car as personal transport, the *suq* is one of the few locations in the city where the pedestrian is supreme. There is little in the way of mechanization in any of the processes between the bulk delivery truck and the customer's vehicle. It is all down to manpower and the occasional goods trolley. The only exception is the dry goods area that does have a drive-through facility for those collecting sacks of feed or palm leaf sacks of dried dates. The market is open every day of the week and only partially closes on the major Eid holidays.

Food and Markets

Figure 9 (left). Making Omani halwa *from* samn, *starch, spices and rosewater. The process takes up to three hours of stirring in the heated copper cauldron until the consistency demonstrated by the tsunami of* halwa *almost reaching the rim is achieved.*

Figure 10 (right). Traditional products, leef rope, habool, *the waist strap used to climb palm trees, cans of* samn *and more.*

Figure 11 (left). Wild honeycomb of the dwarf Asiatic bee for sale.

Figure 12 (right). Male date palm flowers exposed in the spathe that shrouds them. They will be used for pollinating the flower spathes on the female palms in gardens where there is no male palm present.

Al Ain Suq – An Enduring Culinary Asset

The customers are knowledgeable. For instance none of the fish is labelled, and there will typically be up to eighty species on sale on a particular day. Few goods are priced; the customers know the typical price for a fish such as *shaeri*, emperor fish, and that this price will vary according to the size, freshness and abundance in the market. This can be intimidating on a first visit but you quickly pick up the trading routines: ask the price, politely decline and move on to get more intelligence on price, size and quality from the competing traders, perhaps returning to your first enquiry where the price will not have changed. Customers know the eating qualities of individual species and will often be focussed on a particular choice of fish to purchase. The grouper family is a good example, with four or five recognized grades of eating quality in a family that may be represented by more than twenty individual species with at least five different members available in the market on any one day. Customers closely examine the specimens on sale to assess their freshness and challenge prices accordingly. That said, there is evidence of customer loyalty to traders with an intense exchange of greetings often preceding the discussion on what is the best available choice of the day.

These human scale inputs are characteristic of open traditional markets around the world and are in marked contrast to the hypermarket buying experience that is also now available in Al Ain city. In the hypermarket world a forty-foot articulated truck delivers to a secluded goods entrance at the store; goods are moved around on pallets with powered forklifts; the customer is his own porter with a 'hired' trolley; the food on offer is hygienically and uniformly sealed in plastic packaging; the staff have little interaction with either the food or the customers; and finally at the checkout the barcode reader and the credit card machine stand proxy for the engagement between the customer, the purchased food and the sales staff. No words need to be exchanged.

In stark contrast, the humanity and sociability of a traditional market are its greatest values. Having a multitude of independent traders is the hallmark of a great market. Competition between traders promotes social interaction. The range of available goods can also challenge the hypermarket or shopping mall. It may also produce an extraordinary offering: one day in the *suq as samak* I saw live ducks for sale.

The Al Ain market started out as simple lock-up stores fronting on to open ground.[4] A cloth draped over the goods was enough security for stall keeper to close for an extended lunch. Shop fronts and glazing were added. A purpose-built market hall providing stalls for small traders was added, and as the city developed the surrounding area became streets with blocks of flats above commercial units. Many of these units continue the food theme such as shops selling housewares, spice and coffee grinding establishments and café-style restaurants. None of the market buildings has architectural pretensions; they are all utilitarian structures unlike the mixed-use shopping centres that sprang up elsewhere in the Emirates starting with the Blue Suq in Sharjah in the 1970s. This utilitarian approach is still matched in similar market complexes still in existence in Dubai's Al Ras district, along the creek in Sharjah, in two locations on either side of the creek in Ras al Khaimah and also in Fujairah on the east coast of the

Food and Markets

Emirates. Understandably the core market at these locations is the fish market as fish was a principal and daily staple in the regional diet. Date markets of great antiquity and endurance form a link between the fodder and dry goods markets into which they have now morphed.

One of the city's first supermarkets, the Al Ain Cooperative, was built next to the market and continues to thrive alongside the market trade. In 1994, there were only three Western-style supermarkets in a city of 150,000 people. By 2010, there were at least half a dozen shopping malls and numerous supermarkets.

The Al Ain market is segmented into zones of homogenous food trades in the tradition that is widespread through the Middle East. From the original Al Ain Cooperative store in the west the sequence is:

- a market hall with fruit and veg and the butchers stalls;
- the herb and lime market held in an open area with a shade roof;
- the fish market which is interlaced with more fruit & vegetable stalls and latterly a few grocery shops; there were also some food processing establishments in this area;
- the dry goods market;
- the hardware market;
- the livestock and fodder market, at some distance beyond the bus station and ruler's fort.

This layout dictated my itinerary on regular Friday morning visits from 1995 to 2002 (and the layout remained the same on my last visit in 2010) that invariably followed a regular sequence of activities:

- Park my 4WD in the shade cast by the Al Ain Coop, essential in the 40° C summer heat.
- Walk under the Bengal fig tree and through the market hall. Here the veg traders squat amidst their wares on the raised display platforms, butchers display young camel carcasses hanging in a doorway and porters push trolleys piled with fat-tailed sheep carcasses.
- Check out what was available in the herb and lime market, was there basil for pesto or savory for a roast? Buy 5 limes for a dirham (15p); there were always numerous trays of the small Omani limes.
- Scan the casual traders at the entrance to the *suq as samak* to note foraged food such as *Rumex* or *Caralluma* and the supplies of *regag*. In the spring there were sometimes plants for sale in this area.
- Patrol all the fish stalls with my species checklist in hand to record what was on the benches, collect any unusual specimens, often as a freebie because the fish had no commercial value, and also think about the choice for Friday supper.
- Check the fruit & veg stalls, did anyone have sugarcane, any new yams or green veg available to check out and record?

Al Ain Suq – An Enduring Culinary Asset

Figure 13 (left). A tank of wet salted fish.

Figure 14 (right). National women selling regag *bread.*

- Look out for unusual citrus on the farm traders stalls for marmalade experiments.
- Collect some fresh dates at the *bisr* and *rutab* stages early in the season, perhaps packs of dates with fennel seeds from the Crown Prince's farm later in the season.
- Check if they were making Omani *halwa*, and buy some if it was available in the traditional palm leaf packaging.
- Take photos of the traders selling wild honeycomb from the Asiatic honeybee, *kami* (dried yoghurt), and re-cycled Vimto bottles full of honey, *meshawa*, lime juice or *samn* (clarified butter).
- Look out for the traditional craft products such as food mats and food covers made from date palm leaf. On one occasion there were half a dozen quail sitting in a coop neatly constructed from date palm leaf midrib.
- Observe national men purchasing date palm spathes to pollinate their garden palms.
- Walk through the dry goods area to see what was available in bulk and what was being loaded into pick-up trucks. Here a choice of rice and pulses for human consumption blend into sorghum, millets and other bird feed.
- Watch a customer's personal spice blend being ground in bulk in a grinding establishment. These shops also grind coffee and flour.
- Head back through the hardware *suq*, past camel harness, muzzles and udder covers, pestle and mortars, fearsome knife displays, incense burners and incense. There

were also bundles of *miswak*, the twigs of *Salvadoria persica* which are still used as a natural tooth brush.
- Walk back along my route to see what I had missed or what had been added to the fish stalls as I had walked around. Perhaps collect my fish purchased earlier in the visit.
- Call in the Cooperative Supermarket for their version of *zaatar* croissants and ½ and ¼ kilo bags of spices to top up supplies at home

The sale of salted and dried fish is a marker of changing local food culture. Before motor transport and roads reached Al Ain in the 1960s, the only fish available in the market was dried or salted. Al Ain is located 120 kilometres from the nearest fishing harbour. Dried shark, dried anchovies, *meshawa* and various salted and dried fish were traded.[5] Wet salting of excess tuna was still being done in the Al Ain and Ras al Khaimah fish market in the late 1990s. All these items still appear in the market in the new millennium but trade is modest, being suppressed by the ready availability of fresh fish. The trade is likely to die as tastes move on to the modern alternatives.

In the 1990s there were still several traditional trades associated with food practised in the market:

- the aforementioned fish salting;
- making and packaging Omani *halwa*, a luxury sweetmeat;
- *dibbs* production, date syrup from the sacks of dates that had been stacked for storage in a *madbasa* with channels and collection points for the syrup pressed out of the dates;
- fish gutting and cutting;
- the manufacture of trimming knives used for date palm cultivation, this was located in the livestock market.

The redevelopment of the market in 1999 demolished the facilities of the first three of these trades and they were not reconstructed. Only the fish preparation which complemented the fish sales has survived. However the *halwa* and salted fish products are still on sale. The locally produced trimming knives have been replaced by Chinese imports.

One food trade that is noticeable by its absence from the central market is a traditional bakery. These are distributed round the city, often in the strip malls that developed as housing blocks were constructed. The flat breads, *khubz* and *lavash* baked in *tannur* and dome ovens, come in a variety of forms and are invariably consumed very fresh. This may explain why there is no bakery in the market; they are located near to people's homes.

Another enduring aspect of the market is the presence of various individual traders with selections of 'home' resourced goods. These include prepared food such as *regag* breads or clarified butter, foraged food such as wild honeycomb and unusual crops from smallholdings and abstruse traditional medicinal plants.[6] Many of these traders have a regular pitch and are present throughout the year. Others are seasonal, bringing produce from farms as it became available. They were my main source for the unusual citrus that are grown in the Emirates.

Despite the wealth and range of goods on sale, the Al Ain Market has thankfully not yet become a tourist destination with all that this can imply: visitors who are not customers, photographers rather than buyers and an entitlement to fierce bartering on the assumption that everything is at an inflated tourist price. The development of a 'tourist veneer' is becoming a characteristic of traditional markets worldwide, especially in those countries with a tourist industry that is a major GDP earner.

Up to the departure of the camel market, the central Al Ain market complex was a complete culinary shopping resource providing practically all the traditional food needs of the local population, from the smallest individual snack comprising a handful of dates to the preparations necessary for a wedding feast for hundreds of guests. The broad range of food and related services that are still available ensure its continued viability to feed the city despite the numerous air-conditioned shopping malls and supermarkets that now vie for its trade.

Notes

1. The central market is often referred to locally as the *suq as samak*, the fish market, after its principal and unique sales product.
2. When I arrived to work in Al Ain in 1994 we lived in the Ugdat al Ameriya suburb which was home to the relatively new fruit and vegetable market. This was an imposing modern structure with two water towers, a covered parking level and a whole floor of market stalls. When we visited it we were mobbed by the two market stall holders who were the sole traders in a facility that would probably hold eighty stalls. The residents of Al Ain had definitely voted with their feet and would not use it while the old market in the city centre was thriving. Subsequently a master plan was drawn up by the Town Planning Department for a more complex new market in the Al Jimi area to replace the old market. It was realized that some of the characteristics of the old market, such as the fish stalls, should be replicated in the modern facility. Fortunately this plan never came to fruition. Ironically the redundant Ameriya market building was redeveloped into one of the first modern shopping malls in the city with a Carrefour Supermarket. Once again this did not supplant the central markets.
3. A common sight in the market car park is a pick-up truck leaving the market laden with sacks of dates, a cool box full of fish, sticks of the local small bananas, boxes of imported oranges and perhaps a new gas burner ring lashed on top of this cargo. It would be heading off to a remote oasis community in a valley in the Hajar mountains.
4. The *suqs* in Dubai, Sharjah and Buraimi that I visited in 1978 were still at the lockup stage of development and were constructed of mud brick or breeze block. Around them streets of modern commercial shop units were in use but the *suq* stuck to its ancient form and in some cases have now been reconstructed as 'heritage' attractions for the tourist.
5. *Meshawa* is the traditional local fish sauce made by soaking dried anchovies, a similar process to south East Asian fish sauce production. It has not become a local commercial product; the samples in the market are usually home made in recycled Vimto bottles.
6. The market traders are the only source that I have seen for *regag*. I have seen it baked fresh at heritage festivals but never seen it on sale elsewhere. This bread is used in stews such as *thareed*.

Commonalities and Convergences in World Street Market Food

Bruce Kraig and Colleen Taylor Sen

Worldwide, the most common form of public dining is street food. Generally the term denotes food prepared by a vendor and sold from an open-air stand, cart, truck or market stall. It is prepared quickly from pre-made ingredients, served in timely fashion and consumed on the spot. Other definitions of street food such as vending machines, fairs and festivals greatly expand the number of 'street food' consumers.

The sale of street food is a widespread form of self-employment for the urban unemployed in developing countries. It provides food security to the urban poor, who may not have the resources to prepare their own meal. Many foods are high in carbohydrates and also provide essential nutrients to people who cannot prepare nutritious food themselves. In developed countries, food carts and trucks can be a gateway for trained chefs who do not have the resources to launch a bricks-and-mortar restaurant. In this form, street food has risen from its origins as cheap, common food, to popularity among those interested in new and perhaps more sophisticated tastes. Media attention and sheer mass of diners have changed laws and eating habits in many places. North America and Europe provide especially good examples; for example, Chicago, which banned street food for half a century, now welcomes food trucks.

Street foods are prepared in almost every way known to human beings. The most common techniques are deep-frying, grilling, boiling, roasting and steaming. Street foods fall into several general categories. They can consist of single ingredients, stews and soups, beverages, or they can be stuffed or wrapped. There are only so many ways to cook and prepare foods, so it is natural to see similarities in techniques across the globe. But in looking more closely at world street foods more than superficial similarities emerge.

The specific street foods that are served in a city, region or country are rooted in availability of ingredients and traditional practices which reflect cultural and religious values. Some street foods have become emblematic of their cities: *bhelpuri* in Mumbai, for example, or currywurst in Berlin.

At the same time there are surprising commonalities among street foods in different parts of the world. One reason is the worldwide distribution and adoption of foods following the Age of Exploration, when ingredients such as corn, potatoes, tomatoes, chicken, beef and pork were widely disseminated. Grilled corn, for example, is sold on every continent, while Western sausages such as hot dogs or composed dishes such as pizza appear in cultures to which they were not 'native'.

Commonalities and Convergences in World Street Market Food

Another reason is microeconomic: street foods are prepared in traditional local styles but are based on imported foods and techniques that are elements of world trade and migration. Examples are the Indian street food sandwich consisting of vegetables seasoned with *chaat masala* and coriander but grilled in Western-style bread, or *tacos Arabes* in Puebla, a version of *Shawarma* brought by Lebanese immigrants and served in a slightly thicker than usual wheat-flour tortilla with a *guajillo* sauce. Street food is often the product of deliberate culinary syncretism. A more upscale example is the celebrated Kogo BBQ in Los Angeles that offers such hybrid dishes as spicy pork tacos and kimchi quesadillas.

This paper will explore these convergences and commonalities at several levels, including ingredients, methods of preparation and categories. Our examples come largely from India and North America (especially Mexico), areas that are leaders in the importance and diversity of street food. We give examples of 'hybrid' street foods and ask whether the world is moving to a global street food economy.

Where is street food sold?
Mobile sites
The first street food vendors sold their products from trays, baskets and portable stands. As far back as ancient Mesopotamian civilizations, vendors set up portable stands in primitive bazaars from which people could buy dried dates and fish. So common were serving trays through the history that they are commemorated in the early English nursery rhyme, 'Simple Simon.' Simple trays or baskets hung by a strap from vendors' necks are still universal, such as Turkish *simit* sellers who can be found in every city and town. Baskets evolved into heated or cooled boxes in the United States and, today, ballpark hawkers sell everything from hot dogs and pretzels to peanuts and popcorn to ice-cream and beer from such neck-hung containers.

Vehicles of various kinds became widely used early in historical times. The most basic is a wheelbarrow with a flat, open platform, a device celebrated in the nineteenth-century song about a Molly Malone who 'pushed her wheel barrow through streets broad a narrow crying "cockles and mussels alive alive oh"'. Wooden barrows became pushcarts, either two- or four-wheeled and usually with enclosed food cases. By the nineteenth century many had heating units where food was kept warm or even cooked on the spot. One variation is the pushcart attached to bicycles. Called *tricyclo* around the world, the most famous in the United States were Good Humor ice-cream tricycles that used to be found in neighbourhoods across the country. Pushcarts are the most common form of street food vending, with examples ranging from *thattukadas* in South India to *frietcot* in Belgium and Netherlands and ice-cream carts almost everywhere.

More sophisticated mobile venues appeared when horses were attached to wagons in the last third of the nineteenth century. Usually food was served from a service window on the side of the wagon, often called a 'lunch wagon'. Others were set up as walk-in restaurants with a serving counter. The customers were people working in factories and offices who needed fast service during their short lunch breaks. With the advent of the internal combustion engine, lunch wagons were able to move faster and to more locations. They still serve many working people today, especially in North America.

In recent years, another form of lunch wagon has appeared: food trucks, which resemble delivery vans and are often highly decorated. In North America they serve dishes from every cuisine imaginable: Asian, Mexican, German, African, Jamaican, South American, upscale hot dogs, hamburgers, pizza, cupcakes, cakes and pies and many mixtures. In Europe, food trucks have followed the same trend, usually serving ethnic foods such as North African, Burmese, Nepalese, Indian and others.

Trailers are another portable way of serving street food. One kind is a cart where the vendor stands beside the vehicle making and serving food. The other has cooking or heating and cooling equipment inside with the food served through a window. The larger trailers are commonly seen at seasonal locations such as fairs and at some summer resorts. Virtually all the food served at North American state and county fairs, such as ice-cream stands, corn dogs, caramel corn, cotton candy, saltwater taffy and the many kinds of fried food, come from trailers.

Fixed sites

Street food merges with fast food when it is offered from fixed locations. In Chicago and other North American cities, hot dogs and tacos are sold from fixed stands because of local regulations. The food is served from behind a counter, and the customer goes outside or stands at another small counter to eat it.

Other fixed stands are more rudimentary. European kiosks are located in and around public squares, railway stations and shopping areas. These heavily patronized booths offer everything from sausages, to crepes, fish, breads and sweets. Similar kiosks are common in Asia's cities, especially in popular retail shopping centres. In Mexico and Latin America fixed stands called *fondas* are features of every enclosed market and many retail food stores. These are simple counters with cooking apparatuses behind them on which food is prepared and served. They are among the world's best eateries because the food is almost always fresh and made by experienced cooks using home recipes.

Semi-sedentary-machines

Another very modern and universal kind of public food service place is the coin-operated vending machine. Invented in England in the 1880s, they were adapted to chewing gum dispensers in the United States in the 1890s and soda machines in the 1920s. Modern vending machines usually sell prepackaged industrially-made food such as candy and sodas. However, many are highly sophisticated, especially in Asia which has the world's greatest concentration. These can make items such as hot ramen noodles, rice dishes, fresh French fries and many others, to say nothing of hot drinks such as coffee.

Commonalities and Convergences in World Street Market Food

How is street food prepared?
Equipment and fuel

Street foods are prepared in almost every way known to human beings. Cooking equipment is geared directly to the ways that food is cooked. For instance, deep-frying requires a heavy pot, a high heat source and lots of oil (almost always industrially produced). The same can be said for metal pots, pans and griddles, most of which are made in factories.

Heat sources depend on locally available materials and legal regulations. The earliest heating fuel was wood, followed by charcoal, then coal and kerosene or paraffin. Wood is still used in many parts of the world, in Africa, for instance, either in firepits, ovens or simply set within a circle of stones over which a pot can be set. Charcoal, wood that has been burnt under cover so that the carbon and some ash remain, burns well and is a staple of backyard grilling. It is also widely used to cook street food even in some New York City carts despite smoke pollution regulations. In the seventeenth century, coal began to replace charcoal in England (because England was running out of wood – a resource that was one reason for their colonies in North America). Coal-fired heating units are still used in countries such as China to create very high heat for street food dishes although coal is highly polluting. Kerosene, also known as paraffin, is a liquid fuel refined from petroleum. It was created in the 1850s and eventually became widely popular for food preparation at home, in restaurants and on the street. It is still very popular in India and East Asia for cooking and also in camping stoves around the world. In India, a popular cooking fuel is *gobar*, dried cow dung.

Most purveyors in the Western world use gas, either in its natural state or as propane or butane. Propane gas tanks are universal in portable home gas grills and in street food vehicles. It is relatively cheap and safe and produces high heat depending on the kind of grill used.

Electricity is also used, mainly to run machinery for confection such as popcorn, cotton candy, saltwater taffy, ice-cream and batter mixtures. Modern cold products depend on refrigeration or ice to maintain them. Portable refrigeration was developed in the late early 1930s and made vehicles such as ice-cream trucks popular. These were run from gasoline engines in the trucks. During most of the twentieth century Good Humor, sold from trucks, was the most famous ice-cream company in North America.

The kind of vessels used to cook street food varies by dish and culture. Some examples are:

- woks (*hù* or *guō* in Mandarin, *kuali* in Southeast Asia): used across Asia and everywhere Asian cuisine is made;
- *tawa*: large flat or concave iron pans used for shallow frying bread and meat in India;
- stew pots: used in pan-African and Asian hot pot dishes;
- frying pans: shallower than woks, used for sautéing and lighter frying, such as of south Chinese dumplings;

- flat griddles: used for everything from tortillas to hot dogs and hamburgers;
- grills: in many sizes, and fired by wood, charcoal or gas, used for many skewered meat dishes and vegetables such as corn;
- hot boxes: boxes with heating elements or steam vents beneath them used to heat food such as buns and sausages;
- fryers: electric or propane deep-fryer boxes used to heat oil in which food is cooked.

Ingredients

Most of the ingredients used in world street foods are just that: worldwide in origin, though many are creolized by local adaptation. Consequent upon Euro-African contact with the Americas domesticated plants and animals flowed back and forth across oceans. The histories of these have been written about at length, but the main ones are, from the Old World to the New: cattle, pigs, sheep, goats, chickens, rice, wheat, barley, oats, coffee, sugar cane, citrus fruits, bananas, melons, chickpeas, lentils, sesame, turnips, carrots, radish, brassicas such as broccoli and cauliflower, cabbage, onions, cucumbers, many mustards, rapeseed, olives, raspberries, various wine grapes, apples, peaches, cherries, apricots, pears, figs almonds, cumin, basil and coriander to name a few. In return, from New to Old are: maize (corn), potatoes, sweet potatoes, cassava, peanuts, tobacco, squash, peppers, tomatoes, pumpkins, cacao (the source of chocolate), sunflowers, pineapples, avocados, vanilla and, one of a handful of domesticated animals, the turkey. Many of the ingredients here look like those used in Mexican and Indian cuisines – street fare – all the result of an on-going five-hundred-year process. In its latter stages of world distribution of food commodities, most of these can be found in supermarkets across the globe.

For instance, the taco discussed by Jeffery Pilcher in *Planet Taco* is now a world food. It began as processed maize flatbreads in Pre-Columbian Mexico. It would be hard to imagine street tacos without their Old World additives: beef, pork, chicken and goat cooked in native chile-based sauces made with tomatoes, Old World and New World herbs and spices and vegetables, all mixed with animal fats and topped with European cheeses and perhaps sour cream.

Tacos and other such dishes reflect the actions of world-food introduction, Creolization (cattle for instance morphing into modern breeds), full adaptation (meat running down to even the lowest the social classes) and industrialization and marketing. American mega-chain Taco Bell restaurants have become international with some degree of success or not (in Britain, lately, depending on whether horsemeat has been found in their products).

Techniques

The methods of preparing street foods are similar the world over. However, in poorer countries and regions, economics may place constraints on the type of fuel used. The most basic method is to roast vegetables over charcoal.

Commonalities and Convergences in World Street Market Food

Frying

Fried foods are the most popular worldwide. Fried foods are delicious (everyone loves fat), quick to make and relatively safe if served and consumed immediately. Pan frying requires only a shallow pan in which a small amount of oil or fat is heated and used to cook the food. In deep-frying the food is immersed in hot oil (typically 330–350° F).

Typical fried foods include the ever-popular French fries, or *frites* (Belgium's national street food), *churros* (in Mexico and Latin America) and other fried sweet dough and batters such as funnel cakes and doughnuts, batter-coated and breaded foods like chicken and hot dogs and even fried fruit pies and candy bars. In India, one of the most popular street foods is *chaat*, a generic term for the savoury fried spicy snacks that have a base of crumbled fried dough, wafers or round balls topped with chickpeas, boiled potatoes and a variety of other ingredients, such as tomatoes, yogurt fried noodles, chiles, onions and various chutneys.

Another popular fried food are *pakoras*: chopped onions, potatoes, eggplants, egg or *paneer* coated in a spicy chickpea flour batter. In south India, *vadas* (a deep-fried doughnut-shaped bread made from lentils) and *bondas* are popular snacks, especially in the evening when they are eaten with coffee or tea.

As one nineteenth-century British critic of American food declared, the frying pan is their god. For more than 200 years, Americans have loved fried food. It is everywhere on the food landscape, in most corporate fast food restaurants and in street food. While most portable food carts and stands cannot do deep-frying for technical reasons, food trucks and fair food are loaded with fried products. Of these two types predominate, savoury and sweet. French fried potatoes top the list of favourite deep-fried food, either alone or an accompaniment to another food. Fried chicken might be America's best-known fried meat dish. It can be done in a number of styles, from Chinese to American southern. Buffalo wings is a recent addition, seasoned chicken wings, deep fried, tossed with a spicy hot sauce and served with salad dressing or sour cream. Other popular dishes include fried cheese curds, nachos – fried tortilla wedges swerved with a soft cheese food topping – and, at the Wisconsin State Fair, a bacon and cheese hamburger served between fried Krispy Kreme doughnuts.

Fried stick foods are state and country fair favourites, and can be found on street trucks, as well. Corn dogs are the oldest and best-known fried food on a stick. Dating from at least the 1920s, these are hot dogs, impaled on a stick, dipped in a corn meal batter and then deep fried to a golden brown. At the Illinois State Fair, for example, there a dozen stands, many serving the famous Cozy Dog. Many other savoury stick foods followed including bacon, batter-dipped fish, patty sausage dipped in batter, pizza, macaroni and cheese, pickle slices and battered spam. Nothing escapes the batter bowl.

Sweet fried foods have also long been favourites. Doughnuts in numerous forms, filled and plain, and crullers are sold from street stands and trucks, especially for breakfast. Fried batters, especially funnel cakes (poured into hot oil in strings and served with powdered sugar) and elephant ears (flat, round pastries), appear at almost all fairs and amusement parks. In recent years, Latin American *buñuelos* (fried dough balls) and *churros* (fried dough sticks sprinkled with sugar and cinnamon) have spread to carts, trucks and fairs. Fried Coke is one recent creation, made by mixing coca cola syrup with batter, deep-frying it and pouring more syrup on top of the final product. Sweet stick foods are common in many fairs. Among them are battered deep fried chocolate cake, S'mores, banana splits, fresh fruits, Oreo cookies, Twinkies and candy bars, especially Snickers, Milky Way, Three Musketeers, Reese's Peanut Butter Cups and Tootsie Rolls.

Open Grilling.
Open grills are used the world over to make foods such as *kebabs* – meat and vegetables in skewers – and *satays* in Thailand and other Southeast Asian countries. Sausages are a natural for grills in Europe and the Americas. Vegetables are also cooked, often called 'roasted' as with corn and tomatoes, though roasting means cooking in an enclosed device.

In South Asia, the archetypal grilled food is kebabs. They probably originated in Central Asia where nomads roasted chunks of meat over a fire. Their relative ease of preparation makes them ideal for street food since all that is needed is a grill and wood or charcoal. They are usually served with bread, such as *nan* or *parathas*, and dipping sauces. Spicing can be intense and include garlic, ginger and cloves.

Boti kebabs are chunks of meat marinated in yogurt, spices and herbs, threaded on a metal or wooden skewer and roasted over charcoal. *Kathi kebabs* are *boti kebabs* wrapped in a roti (a soft round wheat bread) and mixed with onions, chiles and sauces. This dish, which originated in a restaurant called Nizam in Kolkata, is typically served wrapped in paper and is a favourite of students.

Seekh kebabs are sausage-shaped kebabs made from ground spiced lamb or goat threaded on long skewers and grilled. *Kakori kebab* and *galouti kebab* are light, delicate kebabs made with meat that is ground extremely fine and whipped.

A kebab that is also popular in Iran and Afghanistan is *shammi kebab* – a disc-shaped patty resembling a hamburger made of spiced ground meat and chickpeas beaten until they are light and airy and lightly sautéed in a pan. *Chapli kebab* (from the Persian word for 'sandal' because of its shape) is a large, flat, round kebab popular in Pakistan, Afghanistan and North India.

Kofta is a generic term for a dish of well-kneaded ground meat mixed with vegetables, grains and other ingredients and formed into balls, patties or sausages. *Koftas* may be grilled, fried, steamed or sautéed. *Pasinda kebab* are long strips of meat marinated in yogurt and spices, threaded on skewers and baked or grilled.

Indian workers returning from the Middle East have introduced *shawarma*. Shaved lamb, goat, or chicken are compressed on a rotating spit, grilled and sliced off as needed. The meat is placed on a flatbread and topped with chutney or ketchup.

Another street food in northern India is *tikka/tikki*, a word that means 'bits' or 'pieces' and takes several forms. Chicken *tikka* consists of pieces of chicken brushed with clarified butter and grilled over coals. *Panir tikki* are cubes of hard cheese marinated in spices and lemon juice, threaded on skewers and grilled. *Alu/aloo tikk*i are small patties made of mashed potatoes, pas, ginger, garlic and other spices sautéed in oil. Sometimes *panir* or chickpeas are added.

Open grills appear in street food venues across the Americas. In the north hamburgers —usually frozen in patties – are staples of fairs, festivals and some food trucks. Sausages are more iconic, especially bratwurst. German in origin, 'brats' are identified with Midwestern states such as Wisconsin and Ohio, both of which have famous festivals such as those in Bucyrus, Ohio and Sheboygan, Wisconsin. Fresh, fat pork sausages are normally boiled in beer and then set on charcoal grills. Set into rolls, they are topped with mustard of various types and onions. Latter day incarnations include hot peppers – a nod to Mexican influence on American food. In Mexico the best-known charcoal-cooked meat is *carne asada* ('grilled meat') or the marinated version, *carne adobada*. Thinly-sliced skirt steaks are quickly cooked on open grills and set into tacos or plated with accompaniments.

Boiling.
Large pots of liquids set over heat sources are prevalent in the street food world. Soups, stews, dumplings, beans and other vegetables are all cooked this way. A great many African dishes are stews cooked in this manner in the open air, as are dumplings made of cassava and other starchy plants.

Momos, steamed dumplings filled with meat or vegetables, originated in Tibet and became popular among hippies and trekkers in Nepal in the 1960s and 1970s. Today they are one of India's most popular street foods, especially among students who enjoy them with a spicy chile sauce.

Few North American street food dishes are stewed, but in Mexico *guisados*, or stews, are among the best of Mexican cooking. Usually, they are made at home by women and sold by them or their families on the street and in *fondas*. The kinds of stews vary from region to region, the differences based mainly on what kinds of chiles are used in the preparation. Meats, such pork, chicken and beef (beef more in the north) and tripe (sliced animal stomach) are usually on the menu. On the coasts, fish, shrimp and octopus are often used for stew. There are also vegetable stews, some with greens, that provide a healthier alternative. Where it is served, a large pot stands on a heat source to keep warm and the vendor scoops out a portion with a big ladle onto a plate or into a tortilla. The *guisado* can be garnished with sour cream, chopped onions, chopped tomatoes and cilantro. This hearty dish often serves as a dinner for people coming home from work.

Roasting

Roasting can be done in ovens, in pits dug in the ground or in the open. Many street foods are pre-prepared by roasting in ovens, and for festivals in many countries whole animals are cooked in pits. Perhaps the best known roasted food is *shawarma* – similar to *gyros* and *doner kebabs* – in which cut meats are compacted on a spit and then roasted before an open flame. In India, the main device for roasting is a tandoor oven.

One of the most universal of all street foods is roasted corn on the cob since it is inexpensive and requires no special equipment to prepare. In India, where it is called *bhutta*, it is associated with the monsoon season. After roasting over hot coals until the kernels start to blacken, the corn is generously sprinkled with a spice mixture that is unique to each vendor, but always includes red chili powder and salt, and then sprinkled with lemon juice. Sometimes the corn is boiled and served with a tamarind chutney.

In Mexico roasting is a time-honoured cooking technique only not necessarily in traditional ovens. *Barbacoa* is another kind of taco often eaten in the morning, especially in market *fondas* where more elaborate cooking can be done. *Barbacoa* is traditionally made by placing a goat or sheep in a pit with heated charcoal, and then cooking it overnight. Alternately, pieces of meat are wrapped in banana leaves or the skin of maguey plant leaves with sauce and cooked. A visitor to almost any large market will be able to enjoy this treat.

Baking and toasting

Typically, baking means cooking in an enclosed oven. In some cases enclosed ovens are used within shops to make street food such as pizza. Mainly, though, street food baking is done on a heated flat griddle. Flatbreads are commonly made in this way, from corn and wheat flour tortillas in Latin America to cheese-filled *gözleme* in Turkey. Toasting can include many sandwiches plus nuts and even insects are roasted and toasted on flat metal sheets. On the Indian subcontinent small portable clay ovens called tandoors are used to bake breads and meat but are rarely used to prepare street food.

Toasting on flat griddles is popular in Mexico. Varieties of open corn-dough based foods are also abundant on the street food scene. Called *sopes* these are small disks of dough baked on a *comal* (flat metal griddle, used in making tortillas) that are topped with different ingredients. The cheapest are bean preparations, sometimes with grated hard cheese on them, or cooked meats with chile sauce, among others. Chopped potatoes and cold salads such as finely diced tomatoes, garlic, onions, peppers and cilantro are among other kinds of *sopes*. *Tostados*, or crisply fried tortillas, can be considered a kind of *sope*.

In North America flat griddles are used for everything from hot dogs – that is, toasted until lightly browned – to griddled sandwiches. The most famous of

Commonalities and Convergences in World Street Market Food

the latter is grilled cheese made from processed American cheese (popularized by Kraft Foods) set between slices of gummy white bread and toasted. Although more popular in diners and lunch counters, grilled cheese sandwiches are made at many fairs.

Steaming

Steaming is often done for dumplings and foods such as hot dogs. A flat sheet or pan with a perforated bottom is set over boiling water so that steam filters upward. Chinese dumplings such as wheat flour buns called *bao zi* are steamed in round bamboo trays and served hot.

Tamales are a steamed and wrapped food that is one of Mexico's greatest food preparations and come in many regional varieties. They are not only eaten on the street, but are served at almost all special occasions, prepared days in advance of the event by women of the household. Tamales are usually called *tamales rojo* (red) when they are filled with shredded pork or beef in a red chile sauce. *Tamales verde* will have similar meats but are mixed with a green, slightly sour and tangy tomatillo sauce. *Tamales dulce* (sweet) are made with dried fruits, such as raisins or berries, fillings and are meant for desserts. Tamales vary by region. In Oaxaca and other southern states larger tamales with red, green and sweet fillings cooked in steamed banana leaves are specialities. Fancier tamales have complex *moles* in them and even the famous *huitlacoche*, a black fungus found on corn. It is no exaggeration to say that 'hot' tamales are a singular identifier of Mexican culture.

Types of street food

Street foods appear in many forms, but can be set into several general categories. Arranging them in such ways is often done by governments so that regulations can be better made and understood. Again, we see both commonalties and differences.

Single-ingredient foods

Single-ingredient foods are the simplest kinds of street food. They are one product unadorned or processed, such as grilled chicken, meats, fish or vegetables. Roasted/grilled corn on the cob is probably the world's most commonly eaten single ingredient food.

Combined ingredients or compound foods

Compounded foods are the most common of street food. They are composed of one or more ingredients made to different textures and flavours in a single dish. Condiments on sausages, hamburgers or tacos are examples. There are several kinds of these foods.

Stuffed

Stuffed foods are ingredients that are processed in some way, usually chopped, mixed with seasonings, forced into an outer covering and then completely encased. A great many street foods fit this category. Among them are sausages – chopped meats in a gut or artificial casing. Some casings can be made of vegetables or leaves; others utilize wheat or corn dough.

Cabbage, grape leaves and flowers such as zucchini are all used to make famous dishes such as *dolma* (Mediterranean stuffed grape leaves), *golubzi* (east European stuffed cabbage) and *flor de calabasa* (stuffed zucchini flowers in Latin America). Corn or banana leaves are also stuffing casings, the most usual dish being the tamale. Green and red peppers and tomatoes are also stuffed but more often served at festivals rather than as street food.

Corn flour dough is used for tamales, *empanadas* and the ubiquitous Latin American *arepa*. Rice flour, sometimes mixed with tapioca starch appears, in almost all *jiao ze* (southern Chinese dumplings) and south-east Asian dumplings. Wheat flour has wider uses, from *bao ze* (northern Chinese steamed dumplings) to Indian *momos* and *samosas,* from Ukrainian German-American *runzas* to Cornish pasties and from East European *pierogis* and *pirozkis* to many Latin American and Spanish *empanadas.* Bean and pea flours are used in Indian dumplings (*muthia*).

The best-known stuffed food is samosa. In the vegetarian version, mashed potatoes, peas, red chili powder, turmeric and other spices are wrapped in a white-flour dough that is formed into little triangles, deep fried and served with coriander or mint chutney. A non-veg version is filled with ground, spiced meat, usually lamb. It may have originated in the Middle East and come to India in the twelfth or thirteenth centuries. Arab cookbooks dating back to the tenth and eleventh centuries call these pastries *sambusak*, a word still used in the Middle East. (It may come from the Arabic *se*, or three, referring to the triangular shape, and *ambos*, a kind of bread)

In North America sausages including hot dogs are the most common stuffed or encased meats and are major street fare. Though hot dogs or *perros calientes* are used in Mexico the tamale is the paradigmatic festival and street food dish.

Wrapped

Likely the most widely consumed complex foods are wrapped. Here, shells of various breads or vegetable leaves are folded around a filling with tops or sides left open. This technique allows flexibility in adding condiments to the food. Anyone who has loaded mustard, onions or other varieties of ingredients on a hot dog knows the method. So popular is wrapping that a whole category of sandwiches called 'Wraps' are now staples of North American dining.

Corn-based flatbreads, tortillas, are among the most popular wrappings, used in everything from tacos to enchiladas. Wheat flour is even more universal. The everyday sandwich, eaten worldwide, is basically a wrap, as is any food served on a bun. Flatbreads such a Middle Eastern *lavash* and pita and Indian *nan*, *chapatti* and *kulcha* serve similar functions. Some breads are yeast-leavened and made in ovens;

others are baked on flat griddles: the Turkish *yufka* is a good example.

Stews and soups

One way to serve many people is by extending a food by cooking it in water. Soups and stews of every variety appear in street food venues and in many, many festivals of every sort. They can be made of meats or meats and vegetables or vegetables and starchy tubers. Usually any soup or stew is accompanied by bread or dumplings – noodles are types of dumplings.

Beverages

People need something to drink with their food, so individual vendors and stands serving freshly made or industrial soft drinks are common in markets. On the Subcontinent, tea stands are ubiquitous, often little more than a single vendor with a small grill, a kettle, a tea pot and cups. In tropical countries, freshly squeezed fruit juices and coconut water are an important source of vitamins and minerals. Aside from beer and wine, alcoholic beverages are not usually supplied by street food purveyors.

Pre-made foods

In the modern industrialized world plenty of foods sold on streets and from vending machines are made in factories. All of them are compounded foods with chemical preservatives and flavourings included. Packaged candies in their considerable profusion are the best examples of industrial snack foods. Small baked cakes, cookies and crackers are others. The most universal of this category are soft drinks. A good many of them are made by international beverage companies that have their brands everywhere. Cola companies are without question the best known.

Hybrid Foods

In the new shopping malls that have sprung up in large and medium-size cities you'll find kiosks selling pizza (even Chicago-style pizza) and hot dogs. Fast food chains such as McDonalds and KFC have opened branches throughout India, adapting their menus to local requirements, including versions without beef or pork and a lot of vegetarian dishes (even Jain dishes, missing onions and garlics). But before the Americanization, Indians created their own versions of Western dishes.

A local version of hamburger, *vada pav/pao*, may be Mumbai's most popular and distinctive street food. (TV chef Anthony Bourdain called it the best thing he ate during his 2007 culinary tour of India.) Mashed, boiled, spiced potatoes coated with a chickpea batter are deep fried, and wrapped in two slices of *pao* — a Western-style white bread of Portuguese origin (the Portuguese occupied nearby Goa until 1955). It is served with dry peanuts and a sweet and sour chutney. *Pav/pao bhaji* is one of the fastest street foods to prepare and a favourite among workers in Mumbai. Leftover potatoes and other vegetables are mashed on a griddle with tomatoes and spices, simmered for a few minutes to form a gravy and then served with buttered Western-style rolls, onions and sliced lemon. Variations are made with cheese, mushrooms, bananas, buttermilk and dried fruits.

A cousin of *vada pao* that is a speciality of the city of Pune is *daabeli*: two buttered toasted buns filled with potato, grated coconut and onions, seasoned with green and brown chutneys and topped with roasted peanuts. *Sev* (nicknamed India's Sloppy Joe) is a thick gravy of potatoes, tomatoes, peas and onions flavoured with coriander and spices and served with Western-style bread. Another hybrid that is a great favourite with students is grilled vegetable sandwich. Slices of cooked beet, cucumber and tomatoes topped with green chutney are served between two slices of toasted Western-style bread with tomato ketchup to taste.

Sandwiches have become ubiquitous, often consisting of slices of white bread toasted on the griddle and filled with sautéed vegetables and cheese. Meat is rarely used. A speciality of Chennai is the *murukku* sandwich, with slices of tomato and cucumber and mint chutney between two crunchy *murukkus* – coiled crispy rounds of rice flour.

Another take on the sandwich invented in Kolkata is the *kathi/kati* roll, invented in the 1930s at a famous restaurant called Nizam's. The original version was made by roasting pieces of meat on skewers, then sautéing them with onions and red chiles, and finally wrapping the meat in a *paratha* with various chutneys and spices. Today *kati* rolls can contain vegetables, egg, chicken or potatoes. They are wrapped in wax paper and eaten on the go. In Kolkata, a legacy of the British is *kabiraj* cutlet, fillets of chicken, mutton or fish coated with egg and fried to form a delicate lacy coating. (The word *kabiraj* is probably an Indianization of the word 'coverage.')

The American hot dog has spread around the world where, as in India, it has been hybridized. Although the form is the same – a sausage in a form of bread – toppings and vary according to local taste, as in Swedish *korv* with shrimp salad or mashed potatoes on it. One might argue that sausages are European in origin, but in today's stands they are modelled on American hot dog stands.

In the United States 'fusion' has become popular. There are two versions of the process. One is creolization of a food; the other is hybridization. Taco Bell and the many 'Americanized' versions of tacos sold in North America is an example for the first. For instance, fried and folded hard taco shells are not Mexican but American, as is ground beef, shredded cheddar cheese and bland tomato sauces.

Hybridized street food was made known nationally in the USA with Mark Manguera and Chef Roy Choi's Los Angeles food truck Kogi BBQ. Fusing Korean and Mexican (called KoMex), they became a sensation. Dishes like tortillas loaded with kalbi and garnished with soy sauce-laced lettuce have been taken across the United States and even back to Korea. There are plenty of other examples of the new fusion dishes that show an ancient disposition to create new dishes out of new ingredients. With the world becoming flat, to cop a phrase, old commonalities are becoming new in highly visible and commercial ways.

Bibliography

Bergerson, Sephi. *Street Food of India* (Delhi: Roli Books, 2009).

Desai, Santosh, 'The Power of Street Food,' *Mother Pious Lady: Making Sense of Everyday India* (New Delhi: HarperCollins India, 2010), pp. 74–77.

Kennedy, Dianna. *The Cuisines of Mexico* (New York: William Morrow Cookbooks, 1989).

Kraig, Bruce and Colleen Taylor Sen. *Street Food around the World: An Encyclopedia of Food and Culture.* Santa Barbara, CA: ABC-Clio, 2013.

Kraig, Bruce and Dudley Nieto. *The Cuisines of Hidden Mexico* (New York, John Wiley and Sons, 1996).

Kraig, Bruce. *Hot Dog: A Global History* (London: Reaktion Press, 2009).

Long-Solis, Janet. 'A Survey Of Street Foods In Mexico City'. *Food & Foodways* 15 (2007), pp. 213–36.

Mukerji, Vimla and Deb. *Street Foods of India* (New Delhi: Roli Books, 2001).

Pilcher, Jeffrey M. *Planet Taco: A Global History of Mexican Food* (Oxford: Oxford UP, 2012).

Public Eating; Proceedings of the 1991 Oxford Symposium on Food and Cookery. Ed. by Harlan Walker (Totnes: Prospect Books, 1992).

Sen, Colleen Taylor. *Food Culture in India* (Westport, CT: Greenwood, 2004).

Soofi, Mayank Austen. *The Delhi Walla Food + Drink* (New Delhi: HarperCollins India, 2010).

Tinker, Irene. *Street Foods, Urban Food and Employment in Developing Countries* (Oxford: Oxford UP, 1997).

The Municipal Market of Athens and *Stoa Athanàton* (Immortals' Alley): A Brief Account of Its History, Past and Present

Aglaia Kremezi

Figure 1. Athinas street and the Municipal Market in November 1961 (Photo by Dimitrios Harisiadis, Benaki Museum Photo Archives).[1]

In Athens, the area around the central food market is one of the few architectural vestiges that remains virtually unchanged from the 1830s, when the city was established as the capital of an independent Greece. Unfortunately, only the municipal market building that houses the fish market and the meat stalls around its perimeter has been restored properly. The privately owned, beautiful old buildings that surround it are part of the market complex that is disintegrating steadily to the point of dereliction. Although some storefronts are shut and others show visible signs of utter neglect, this neighbourhood 'of miracles', as it was once called, is still lively and charming, full of

The Municipal Market of Athens and *Stoa Athanàton*

Figure 2. Athens Central Market, 1910–20 (Benaki Museum Photo Archives)

gems for anybody interested in reasonably-priced, authentic food and old-fashioned kitchen and house utensils.

In this paper I briefly examine the past and present of the municipal market, the area around it, and the imposing building along the market's northern side, called Stoa Athanaton (Immortal's Alley). The building is an integral part of the market, connected with a renovated iron roof that covers the narrow Armodiou street which separates the two buildings.

The market's history

During the last years of Ottoman rule, Athens was nothing more than a small, unimportant town with 1500 houses and 124 churches.[2] Most of its inhabitants cultivated the surrounding fertile fields of Attica and lived in houses built around the Acropolis and scattered *kolones* (columns), the countless remnants of ancient fortifications, temples and arches.

A few years after the creation of the Greek State, in 1830, Otto, royal prince of Bavaria, was appointed first King of Greece by the three Great Powers (Britain, France and Russia). He then chose Athens as his capital to please his father, Ludwig I King of Bavaria, who was a philhellene, a great admirer of classical Greece. The illustrious group of European architects recruited by the young King aspired to design a modern

Figure 3. Illustration from the book Athens from the Nineteenth to the Twentieth Century *(Athens, Melissa Editions 1966).*

city comparable with its glorious past. Although the ambitious city plans changed several times before they were finally realized, the place assigned to the Central Market, although reduced in size, remained roughly where it was originally located, on Athinàs, the street that runs north to south, equally dividing the heart of downtown Athens.

While construction around the area of the future market – on Athinàs, Eolou and Ermou Streets – began booming in 1840s and 'charming and stable mansions' were erected, until 1875 the municipality of Athens was still disputing the exact location of the new market.[3] The funds needed to buy privately owned houses and pieces of land at the site were not yet secured. Finally the Greek government, in its 1877 budget, set aside 30,000 drachmas for the project. But construction still did not start because the Russian-Turkish war was imminent. The municipality decided that it was better to set the money aside for the eventuality of war, if Greece became involved along with other Balkan countries.

The market's construction started in 1878 but stopped the next year because of disputes with the contractor and a lack of funds. Work started again in 1880, with a large loan from the National Bank of Greece, but stopped again, halfway, in 1882, because of disputes with the new contractors – an ongoing curse that infects most Greek public works to this day.

The Municipal Market of Athens and *Stoa Athanàton*

Contrary to the glorious 'Neoclassical Trilogy' of buildings – the Academy of Athens, the National Library, and the University – designed by the Danish architects Theophile and Christian Hansen, the Central Market bears no resemblance to these striking constructions. Although a sketch of the market made by Christian Hansen allegedly exists, no design of the market has been found in his archives.[4] Ioannis Koumelis, a Greek architect from the island of Andros, is cited as the engineer who designed the municipal market of Athens.

Meanwhile, all these years the main market of Athens continued to be the old upper bazaar, a cluster of wooden sheds on the southern foothill of the Acropolis, at the top of Eolou Street, among the ruins of the Roman Agora and the remaining wall of Adrian's library.

In the centre of the bazaar stood Elgin's Tower: a tall construction built in 1811 to house the clock Lord Elgin ceremoniously offered to Athens to show his appreciation for the classical statues, inscriptions and architectural artefacts that he removed from the Acropolis. The upper bazaar was the heart and centre of the old city, the region where people gathered not just to shop but also to socialize. The *Kouseyio* – probably from the French *conseil* (council) – the regional government during the last Ottoman period, was housed in a two-story building in this area.

On the night of August 8th, 1884 a fire destroyed the bazaar's wooden stands as well as Elgin's tower. This accidental event forced the merchants to hastily move their wares to the half-finished municipal market on Athinàs street. The glass roof was installed a few months later in October, along with basement racks and drains. The building was finally completed in 1886. It is estimated that its cost was about half a million drachmas.[5]

The building

A glass and iron structure, along the lines of similar commercial constructions throughout Europe, especially Italy, the building of the municipal market is a symmetrical rectangle forty-five by seventy metres, with a series of arched doorways on the façade; it spans over an atrium eighteen by fifty-eight metres, the largest metal construction in Athens at the time. Its trusses comprise rafters with a double-T section while the tractors and stanchions, with their diagonal braces, are tubular steel rods. They are still in remarkably good condition.[6]

The main building houses seventy-four shops inside and out, and a basement along the rectangular perimeter. At some point between 1902–05 the original glass roof was replaced with a metal one and marble counters were installed. In 1906 a tower with a clock was added at the centre of the roof. The municipality repaired the building in 1981–83; in 1985–86 the façade was restored to its original design and repainted, and non-slip flooring was installed in the fish market, much to my relief.

In 2004 a permanent metal roof was fitted along the three sides of the central building, covering the bordering narrow streets – Armodiou, Filopimenos and Aristogitonos. The

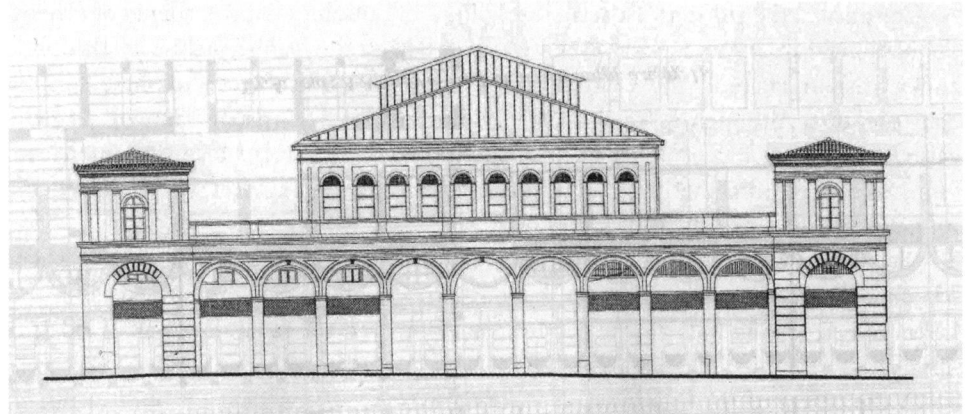

Figure 4. The market's façade designed by Nikolaos E. Thanopoulos.

roof replaced the pre-existing, shabby tin awnings, linking the surrounding buildings to the central construction of the fish and meat market. The extended market complex has side entrances on Sofokleous and Evripidou streets; both these streets house cheese, charcuterie, spice and other food shops.

On the block across from the fish market, on Athinàs street, stood the imposing Varvakeion high school. Ioannis Varvakis, also known as Ivan Andreevich Varvatsi, was a wealthy merchant originally from the tiny Aegean island of Psara.[7] A skilful sailor, he took part in the early, unsuccessful wars of independence. With his ship he played an important role during the Russian–Turkish naval war and showed extraordinary

Figure 5. The permanent metal roof fitted in 2004 along the three sides of the central building covering the bordering streets.

The Municipal Market of Athens and *Stoa Athanàton*

Figure 6. The original Varvakeion High School, in 1867.

courage during the 1770 Battle of Chesma (Çeşme). Catherine the Great of Russia rewarded him with 1000 golden rubles and an authorization for unlimited, duty-free fishing in the Caspian Sea. Varvakis is the one who found a way to preserve and export caviar to Europe in specially created, absolutely waterproof timber boxes.[8] In retrospect, one could say that this fact could link him to the Athens fish market; but in truth the name *Varvakeios,* often used for the municipal market, is a mere reference to the school that was created after his death, with one million rubles he left in his will to promote education for the new Greek state. The original Varvakeion school – still operating in Psychikon today – was demolished in 1944 as this area was destined to be part of the municipal market complex.

The plot was never properly developed, though. During the last renovation of the market an underground parking garage and an elevated square and municipal coffee shop were constructed. It wasn't an inspired design and is said to be partly responsible for the decline of the area. Not visible from the street, the square was attracting drug dealers and their customers all day long, not just at night, the shopkeepers complained. There are vegetable and fruit stalls on the two sides of that block – on Armodiou and Aristogeitonos – while at the opposite side of Armodiou a grocery store selling Polish/Russian food is thriving, as are other ethnic grocery stores in the extended market area.

Food and Markets

The fish market

The fish market in the main municipal building is spectacular. It might not be nearly like Tokyo's Tsukiji or Barcelona's Boqueria, but it is quite large and impressive. One finds here very fresh and reasonably-priced fish and seafood; although recently imported salmon has claimed an important space on the ice-covered marble counters, there are still lots of local and rare fish, like *galeos* (dog fish), much praised since antiquity.[9] Of course these days people are buying mostly fresh sardines and anchovies – considered poor people's fish – for less than four euros a kilo. Others get the miscellaneous small catch that remain on the nets when fishermen separate the breams, groupers, snappers and red mullet that are sold for upwards of twenty-five euros a kilo; the small ones, used for *kakavia* (the Greek fish soup) go for less than five euros a kilo.

When in the 1980s I started to buy my fish, spices and occasionally vegetables and herbs regularly from the market my mother and aunts were genuinely shocked. They told me that the merchants were notoriously unreliable and extremely cunning, almost magicians who managed to replace the fish you had chosen with another, rotten one, in front of your eyes; they would surely cheat while weighing the goods, they said. Strangely, I now hear similar claims even from owners of buildings around the market. I was never cheated, by the way, and always got the best fish and seafood there.

By the time I had my own kitchen, most middle-class and wealthy Athenians were not buying their fish here. Only poor people, who could not afford the steep prices and limited selection of expensive neighbourhood fishmongers, remained loyal to the old market. The poor didn't mind scaling and gutting their fish, a chore undertaken by the fishmongers around Athens. Despite the upscaling – no pun intended – of the fish trade, people who really cared and knew their fish, as well as many restaurant owners and chefs, remained loyal customers. Spyros Korakis, president of the market's fishmongers and well-known to Athenian foodies, is the third generation of his family in shop sixty-eight, midway on the northern side of the hall. His is a very well-kept office, decorated with posters and engravings by Greek painters, rare old photographs of the area, antique telephones and a board where various paper drachmas are nicely pinned. The original wood-carved sign with his grandfather's name is also there. He seemed very busy, all the time answering the phone and filling orders for homes and restaurants around the city, yet he too was complaining that the business was not going well. His son, who wanted to do other, better things, was now obliged to work with him in the market, he told me. He clearly didn't feel any pride or joy that one more Korakis generation was going to continue in the family trade.

Clean Monday, the first day of Lent, a public holiday, has always been the most important day for the fish market. The stands are filled with octopus, calamari and cuttlefish, shrimp, crab, and lobsters, also mussels and the delicious small scallops, all traditionally eaten to mark the beginning of the Lent period, when eating red-blooded animals is prohibited. In the old days the market opened as early as four in the morning; many people who partied the last night of the carnival in Plaka or in downtown homes and bars came straight to the market spreading confetti, often in funny or elaborate costumes, to buy the traditional Lenten food they would enjoy with their friends before getting back home for a few hours' sleep.

Meat and innards

The meat market, spread in stalls all around the fish market hall, was never very tempting, at least since I started to shop here in the early 1980s. After the big renovation, and especially close to the 2004 Athens Olympics, the butchers were obliged to get refrigerated glass cases and stop hanging lamb, kid and chicken carcasses in the open alleys, or displaying pieces of meat on the counters all-day long. The refrigerators were indeed purchased and for a brief time the market's meat alleys started to look less like colourful Arab souks and more like any sterile European or American market. Gradually, though, the refrigerator doors were removed and they became the stage props for the stars of the show: whole carcasses or parts of slaughtered animals reclaimed their old places, hanging from the traditional hooks, while all kinds of butchered pieces were, again, piled on the beautiful old marble counters.

The meat market was always a great place for all sorts of innards and 'inferior' parts of veal, lamb, chicken and pork: tripe and feet, lamb's intestines, liver and kidneys, veal hearts and chicken stomachs, as well as *ameletita* – veal testicles, considered a delicacy in the old days.

Today butchers seem to be hit hardest by the economic crisis. The meat market used to peak around Christmas, as people traditionally buy pork or turkey for the festive table. Again, before Easter, the market would reach its peak, when every family gets a whole lamb or kid to roast on the spit. Recently, even for those sacred days, business hasn't seemed to really pick up. Last year a rumour spread in the city about four, five or six rich ladies who visited the market with their shiny SUVs. They went to some stalls and bought 20,000 (25,000 or even 40,000) euros' worth of turkeys which they distributed to the poor people who happened to be there. The story was repeated on radio shows and blogs, it even made front-page news in some tabloids. Nobody actually saw these ladies; butchers were asking one another where they did their lavish shopping. Journalists couldn't find one who had sold meat to these mysterious benefactors or anyone who received the gift. Even so, the exact same story re-surfaced last Easter, with the ladies buying lamb this time. Still some people insist that it did happen, while others claim that it was a fabrication of some clever butchers who spread the rumour, hoping to attract more people to the market.

As a child, growing up on the outskirts of the city, I visited the area only before Christmas. With my parents we didn't come shopping for food, but to get some new toy, usually a doll at Tsokas, the largest toy store in Athens on Eolou street, behind the fish market. The shop disappeared a long time ago, as the best clothing and other non-food-related shops moved to Ermou Street and later to the posh Kolonaki area. Eolou became a pedestrian street, a bargain shopping area where very cheap clothes, shoes,

Figure 7. Stoa Athanaton has a curved border under the roof and painted panels in dark background between the windows. Bottom right: *Pantopoleion tis Stoas Athanaton (grocery store of the Immortals' Alley).*

linen, gifts and gadgets were sold, often from carts or from baskets on the pavement outside the shops. Few such shops still operate – a Marks and Spencer among them. Storefronts that are not bolted shut have been transformed to coffee shops, bars and restaurants that give new life to the area from midday well until the wee hours of the night.

Stoa Athanaton (Immortal's Alley)

The building along the market's northern side, on Sofokleous street, belonged to a wealthy lawyer named Angelopoulos – no relation to the also-wealthy Mrs Angelopoulos who was very active during the 2004 Olympics. The lawyer was so successful in court that he was nicknamed *Athanatos* (immortal). The building's main entrance (photo top left in Figure 7) in the alley on 17–19 Sofokleous street was called *Stoa Athanaton* (Immortal's Alley) and this came to be the building's name.

This large two-storey mansion was most probably built before the municipal market, but unfortunately I have not been able to locate records or original designs. It is one of the most unusual in that area, where the Neoclassical style dominates. *Stoa Athanaton* has a curved border under the roof and painted panels in dark background between the windows. It has an inside court and once housed several families on the floor above the shops, Mr Altsitzoglou, the administrator and one of the forty-two owners of the building, told me. The shops were always rented to various merchants and were never related to the residents' businesses, Mr Altsitzoglou said.

The pitiful state of *Stoa Athanaton* – similar to most buildings in the area – is not just the result of the latest economic problems. This building has a record number of owners, while other properties have been bequeathed to religious or other non-profit organizations by their departed landlords. Listed as historical monuments, these buildings can only be restored following strict rules. Even for the most vital repairs, like fixing the leaking wooden roof, specific blueprints have to be submitted and approved, passing through considerable red tape, until inspections and permits are granted.

Of course renovating such buildings is terribly costly, and special loans for such purposes are practically nonexistent now; and out of the question for the *Stoa Athanaton*'s many owners who are struggling to pay the latest stiff property tax with almost no income. The first floor is mostly empty and half the ground-floor shops are closed; even the ones that still operate pay considerably reduced rent, if they pay at all. The historic *Pantopoleion tis Stoas Athanaton* (grocery store of the Immortals' Alley), among the stalls of the meat market, is trying hard to survive. A family business since 1957, it was once famous for its great variety of olives, salted sardines and anchovies, pickled vegetables and olive oil from the family farm in the Peloponnese. Although it is often mentioned in food blogs, newspapers and magazines, it has not managed to attract new customers, while the old ones are either dead or too old to travel beyond their neighbourhood supermarket. The owners blame it on the considerably reduced clientele, as do all the merchants in the fish and meat market.

Most merchants pay very low rent for their stalls in the municipal market; the financial department of the municipality informed me that more than half of the market's tenants have not paid rent the last two years. About 30–40% of the people who operated meat, vegetable or fish stalls have abandoned them in the last two years. The auctions to fill the empty spots were unsuccessful, although the prices were very low.

Epilogue

As is often the case in Greece, when elected politicians – mayors or deputies – are involved, decisions and actions are not transparent and may take several years. On one hand, the market is supposed to offer food at low prices, catering to people on a

Figure 8. Poster for the 2012 Athens Opera performance in the market.

limited budget. There are fewer shoppers now than ever, and those who do come spend less; most merchants seem completely resigned and demoralized, not even bothering to remove the dusty Christmas decorations six months after the holidays.

On the other hand, it is obvious that the whole area in and around the fish and meat market is increasingly becoming a tourist attraction. A few renovated old food shops taken over by the younger generation have become very successful gourmet attractions: Elixir on Evripidou street sells all kinds of spices, exotic herbs and teas; Miran, on the same street, the famous producers of *pasturma* (spicy cumin-and-fenugreek-encrusted pastrami) since 1925, has expanded, as the fourth-generation owner has added a few tables and offers tastings of not just the spicy dried beef and sausages, but also camel *pasturma* and a choice of drinks. On Sofokleous street Zouridakis is a new, nicely designed shop that sells fabulous cheeses, homemade pasta, cookies and frozen pies from Crete. People line up to get a taste and buy a piece of the hard and creamy *anthotyro*, or the twenty-four-month aged *graviera* that tastes better than Parmesan and is rarely found anywhere else in Athens. All these shops have websites and Facebook pages. Maybe other merchants could explore similar paths and try to satisfy the changing tastes of the younger consumers who flock the hip Eolou street bars and restaurants, as well as the tourists.

In November 2012, at a time when the whole area was at its worst and people avoided coming here especially after dark, the Athens Opera organized a free performance inside the market: well-known artists sang arias from a stage set where the meat and fish alleys meet.[10] It was a joint effort that tried to bring a different cross-section of the population to this part of the city and also attract a new audience to the opera. It was very successful, attended by 3000 people from all over the city and the suburbs; most had never set foot in the market before and expressed sheer fascination in the Greek social media, the organizers told me. Did this one-time event attract new buyers to the fish and meat market stalls? The results are yet to be determined.

Notes

1. Many thanks to the Benaki Museum's Photo Archives for giving me historic photographs of the market and also to Maria Daniil – architect, MSc in Architectural Conservation (NTU Athens) – for her invaluable help.
2. Κώστα Η. Μπίρη, Αι Αθήναι: από του 19ου εις τον 20ον αιώνα. (Εκδόσεις Μέλισσα, Αθήνα, 1966) [Kostas Biris, *Athens from the Nineteenth to the Twentieth Century*, Athens: Melissa Editions 1966)]; Greek translated by the author.
3. Biris, p. 77.
4. Μαρία Δανιήλ, Η Δημοτική Αγορά και η Ευρύτερη Περιοχή της, *Τα Αθηναϊκά*, έκδοση του Συλλόγου των Αθηναίων, Αθήνα 2002–2003, Τεύχος 108 [Maria Daniil, 'The Municipal Market and Its Surrounding Area', *Ta Athinaika*, vol. 108, 2002–3]; trans. by the author.
5. Archives of the Municipality of Athens, 1938.
6. Νικολαος Ε. Θανόπουλος, Τα Αθηναϊκά Μνημειακά Κτήρια του 19ου και των Αρχών του 20ου αιώνα με Διερεύνηση της Κατασκευαστικής και Στατικής Μεθοδολογίας (1834–1916) [Nikolaos E. Thanopoulos. Imposing Buildings of Athens in the Nineteenth and the Beginning of Twentieth Centuries (1834–1916); Assessment of the Structure and Static Methodology]; trans. by the author.
7. 'Ioannis Varvakis', *Wikipedia* <http://en.wikipedia.org/wiki/Ioannis_Varvakis>; note that in this entry, as in some Greek sources, Varvakis' name is linked with the central market's construction, although he had absolutely no connection with its construction.
8. *God Loves Caviar* (dir. by Yannis Smaragdis (Sony, 2012), a Greek-Russian co-production, relates Varvakis' story.
9. Archestratus. *Fragments from 'The Life of Luxury*, trans. by John Wilkins and Shaun Hill (London: Prospect Books, 2011), p. 57.
10. Video excerpts of the performance are available online: <https://www.youtube.com/watch?v=B7gxhiK8HDE>.

Ethical Gastronomy: Organic Food, Markets and Marketing

Jane Levi

In the process of my broader research into food and utopianism, I often find myself facing some rather uncomfortable self-examination. Measuring the present against a perceived understanding of the past is almost always a dangerous activity, and when dealing with the hopes, ideals and compassionate visions of utopian thinkers it seems all the easier to lose academic objectivity and start taking it all a bit too personally. Longing for my own piece of ground to grow vegetables while assessing the seventeenth-century Diggers' passionate self-sufficiency as they occupied and worked the common land, I find myself asking how it is possible to think dispassionately and unselfishly about the creeping gentrification of the UK allotment movement, itself poor compensation for loss of commons rights. Enjoying wonderful meals and new ingredient discoveries with my similarly interested friends I have to wonder whether the honorific of 'gastronome' really feels like a comfortable label once one is faced with its consumerist heart contrasted with, say, Charles Fourier's compassionate and holistic vision of harmonic 'gastrosophy'. If Keith Taylor was right (as I think he was) to say that most of what we now see as 'progress' began as someone's crazy, utopian dream, then perhaps we do need to ask ourselves some of these uncomfortable questions more often.[1]

Addressing some of the possible drivers for the burgeoning market in 'ethical' foods as represented by the organic products that I frequently buy, this paper investigates the language of ethical consumerism and the utopian origins of organic produce, considering what 'organic' means in Europe today and asks how much of the original meaning is retained within our market-led system. It begins to consider what those meanings might actually be to the producers, consumers and suppliers of those foods, whether there is common ground between them, and how they have developed. To what extent is consumer demand for ethical foods driving markets to supply them, how far are the markets themselves driving consumers to make these choices and what place do policy-makers have in this equation? How much do the users of the market know about what the market really is, and how much choice do they actually have? Is it really possible to evaluate the ethical stance of a market in food, such as that for organic food, once it is established as a worthwhile market?

An ethical language of food
In part, the enquiry begins with language. The ethical gastronome is generally presented as a twenty-first century paragon of virtue, seeking out positive eating experiences

involving 'real' food – food that might, at its most basic level, be described as 'good', 'natural', 'healthy', 'clean', 'fresh', 'local' or 'authentic'. A more considered choice might be based on agricultural technique: is the produce organic, biodynamic, pasture-fed, compassionately or dry-farmed, slow-grown? Further selection could be based on trading practice, from direct supply to fairly traded to co-operative to farmers market. Where in the world did the food come from and what is its carbon footprint? Is it the dietary preference made for vegan, locally-sourced, traditional, omnivorous or free from any number of chemicals or potential allergens? Alternatively the decisive factors might come down to processing: were its ingredients traditionally crafted, stone-ground, wood-fired, cold-pressed, hand-picked? Or is it a super food: pro-biotic, live-fermented? Is the resulting product natural, unfiltered, raw, whole, pure, live, unrefined, fresh, cultured, untreated?

All of these terms seem to imply some kind of definitive meaning, and policy-makers all over the world devote considerable energy to pinning down and protecting such detail. But meaning is slippery, and marketers exploit this slipperiness. At one level, these last descriptors are straightforwardly positive attributes: apart from occasions when the terms are being cleverly inverted to appeal to our desire for safe transgression, most people would run from food described using their opposites – bad, unnatural, unhealthy, unclean, stale, fake.[2] Of course, real choice depends on actual information, even understanding, which would involve far more granular descriptions than the usual reassuring but too general uses of language. Different countries are subject to different labelling standards, but the desire to acquire some virtuous sheen for a product, whether appealing to the consumer's health concerns, ethical preferences or social perceptions – all of which are carefully studied by marketers – is sufficiently strong to compel producers to promote the lack of gluten in a block of butter; the missing trans-fats in a bag of sugar; the healthy, natural nature of a sweetened flapjack. Other modes of this kind of marketing focus on apparent health benefits (such as the idea that the milk helps fight osteoporosis) while neglecting less convenient factors (milk's hormone or fat levels).[3] However they are labelled, there is certainly a strong market for foods that in different circumstances or with different presentation might seem the antithesis of every ethical aspiration, whether dressed in some of their language or not. In our varied marketplace it can be very difficult for the consumer to negotiate the boundaries between the wicked and the righteous.

Development of organic agriculture
Organic agriculture emerged around the 1930s as a response to concerns about the depletion of the soil, built to a great extent on the holistic biodynamic ideas proposed by Rudolf Steiner in 1924.[4] Lady Eve Balfour's popular book of 1943, *The Living Soil*, largely inspired by the work of agriculturalist Sir Albert Howard and nutritionist Sir Robert McCarrison, became one of the founding texts of the Soil Association, established in the UK in 1946 to promote a healthy, organic approach to farming that would increase

people's nutrition and health.⁵ Balfour presented a natural, process-oriented agricultural system based on the use of 'organic' composts or 'humus', opposed to the modern dependence on inputs of so-called 'inorganic' chemical fertilizers. In an organic system, the impact of the farmer should maintain and potentially improve the health of the soil in a 'natural' way that would heal previous damage and prevent further damage in the future, one of the most important responsibilities of the farmer being 'stewardship of the soil'.⁶ Informed by a degree of spiritualism, Balfour saw this ecological mission as atonement for the human failure to understand that self-sufficiency did not mean a focus only on the individual human self:

> If our experience of the last twenty years has not taught us sufficient humility to realize that we are incapable of ordering our lives successfully in a Godless society, then one is tempted to wonder whether as a species we are worth preserving. In every activity, from the management of our soil onwards, we have regarded ourselves as self-sufficient, and in every activity that attitude of mind has led to disaster. ... Human ecology demands that we should think less of our 'rights' and more of our duties to all other living things, including each other. We must start again, with a new and better attitude towards life. Indeed, we must in some cases relearn that life exists.⁷

The principle was that a successful quest for 'methods that encourage and enhance mechanisms that recur in nature' would, by extension, lead to improved human health and nutrition.⁸ The health of the soil translated directly into the health both of the planet and – in the body and spirit – of the individual consumer.

Balfour was deeply influenced by Dr G. T. Wrench's work, in particular *The Wheel of Health*, which not only supported the idea of natural compost fertilizers, but also emphasized the benefits of a 'whole diet'.⁹ For Balfour, too, these ideas were closely tied together. In opposition to the mainstream view that the main problem with food was obtaining sufficient quantity rather than quality, Wrench believed that 'our "faulty feeding" is the cause of disease', suggesting that the blame lay on poor personal choices by people who had lost their natural instincts, and who were now also manipulated by a growing industrialized food and agriculture system.¹⁰ For Wrench, a more traditional and natural diet was the most beneficial to health, and he, like McCarrison and the American soil scientist Franklin H. King, famously found evidence in the story of the apparently remarkable longevity and healthy lives of the isolated Hunza, a people living in a remote valley in the north of what is now Pakistan (close to the borders with Afghanistan, Tajikistan and China). Wrench sought to demonstrate that the Hunza miracle was attributable to their diet, composed of whole, naturally grown grains, vegetables, pulses, unpasteurized dairy products and sun-dried fruits.¹¹ Unlike us, the Hunza remembered that 'a food is a whole thing and should be taken as a whole', skins, peels and cooking water included, and Wrench suggested we should reacquire such knowledge from them.¹² Balfour's work repeats the tale of the Hunza, adding further supporting evidence for the whole-food theory from Britain in the form of anecdotal reports (some apparently from doctors) of dramatically improved health in pregnant mothers and their children who had renounced white bread and (re)turned to whole grains.¹³ Natural agricultural methods and whole foods as better foods combined to produce a message focused on increased nutrition and personal health that in effect elevated 'nature and intuition over science and reason'.¹⁴

Although Balfour and others cited scientists' work in support of their proposals and were well known for their experimental field trials (begun at Haughley in 1939), the mainstream scientific community generally perceived the organic movement as anti-science, while many within the movement itself regarded science with suspicion.¹⁵ In the face of the post-war development of large-scale agri-business and expanding food-processing businesses, the organic message had many opponents, and the combination of their anti-industry and often apparently anti-science messages led them to be dismissed as peddlers of 'muck and mystery'.¹⁶ Balfour had a fundamental objection to the treatment of agriculture as an industry, writing that 'Agriculture *is* a service; it is not, never has been, and never can be an industry'.¹⁷ Protesting the false division set up between 'town' and 'country' interests, she asserted that, since the entire country depended first and foremost on the health of the land, 'Both will eventually prosper or decline in proportion as their joint heritage, the fertility of their soil, prospers or declines'.¹⁸ She therefore proposed that the Ministries of agriculture, health and food should be merged, as each was inextricably linked with the other.

Jorian Jenks, a leading member of the British Union of Fascists and editor of the Soil Association's quarterly newspaper, *Mother Earth*, extended the anti-industry message out along the entire industrial food processing chain, suggesting that 'a fixed idea that foods must be regarded as commodities, articles of commerce which people must be allowed to sell and buy with a minimum of restraint' was to blame for poor eating habits as well as supply and quality problems.¹⁹ Industrially produced foods were said to be subject to a process of 'mutilation and adulteration'.²⁰ The shorter the food chain, or the closer people were to the land and its unadulterated produce, the better.²¹ Jenks called into question the scientific basis of nutritionists' claims that a 'healthy' diet is possible without the use of whole, natural, organic foods, calling their calculations 'not really nutritional science at all, but a combination of chemistry and arithmetic'.²² The two sides were fiercely opposed.

Adopted on a small scale in parts of the US, Australia, New Zealand, UK and elsewhere in Europe during the 1950s, pesticides and other agricultural chemicals led to emerging concerns in the 1960s and 1970s that inspired a differently politicized generation to engage with organic practices.²³ Although many health and agricultural advisors vehemently protested that organic principles were a form of charlatanism, making false health claims designed to trick the vulnerable into unnecessary spending, the movement grew and gained traction throughout the twentieth century: dispensing with what could be described as the more mystical aspects of biodynamic methods, the movement gained supporters and solidified standards.[24] Its development in opposition to the mainstream drive towards agri-business meant that it emerged as a significant influence on many groups in the 1960s and '70s countercultural movements in both the UK and the US.[25] In particular, the ideas that bodily and spiritual health are to be derived from eating whole foods; the association of such foods with 'natural' forms of agriculture and (often) a form of New Age spiritualism; opposition to the industrialization of both agriculture and the food system and to extreme consumerism; and notions of human culpability for despoiling the earth and the resulting obligation to repair the damage became fundamentally associated with movements for social change of many kinds.

Organic food in contemporary Europe

Organic principles as we understand them in the early twenty-first century continue to focus on the idea that there is a direct connection between the way our food is produced and the health of the planet and ourselves, and the market for organic products is now well established. Organic standards are defined in European law, based on the principles of environmental and animal-friendly farming methods: artificial fertilizers are banned and organic animals have high welfare standards (including being free range, with access to fields and defined space requirements).[26] Licensing and certification are required to formally approve and authenticate products as organic, and regular farm and producer inspections maintain the standards. Depending on the country, it is estimated that the European market for organic produce grew between 5% and 30% within the first few years of this century.[27] Now organic produce forms a meaningful component of overall agricultural production: 5.4% of the total utilized agricultural area in the EU in 2012, according to a 2014 Action Plan.

In the 1990s the market for organic food was relatively small, and most purchases took place in health food shops or other specialist outlets like farmers markets. Since 2000, the bulk of sales have shifted to supermarkets, which emphasize reducing the price of organic produce ever closer to that of conventionally farmed produce.[28] What was once a niche marketing idea has moved firmly into the mainstream. Policy makers' attention has accordingly shifted from sceptical examination of fundamental claims to acceptance of the marketplace, and along with that a new focus on the market for and marketing of these products: now 'Public policy pervades all elements of food marketing'.[29] In 2003 the European Commission funded a three-year, €1.8m study called CONDOR (Consumer Decision Making on Organic Products) to understand in detail consumer behaviour and motivations when purchasing (or not purchasing) fresh and processed organic foods in eight EU countries.[30] In July 2008 it launched its ongoing campaign to promote organic farming under the slogan 'Organic farming. Good for nature, good for you'.[31]

Marketing organics

Focused as it is on consumer behaviour, the EU study provides a lot of useful information for those wishing to market organic food. In its detailed interviews with 8400 people, it found that the primary stated motivation for purchasing organic food is one's own health, closely followed by concern for the environment. However, other studies place more emphasis on the individual: 'research indicates that in food choice, environmental friendliness is not a criterion considered to be highly important for most consumers.'[32] Those for whom environmental concerns feature in any significant way are described as 'idealistic consumers', who make more frequent purchases but represent a small segment of the overall market.[33] This kind of consumer was focused on numerous additional positive attributes of organic foods, such as improved taste and naturalness. It was suggested that this group has 'more complicated belief structures, attitudes and values than non-organic consumers', and could be said to have a more complex relationship with moral or principled decision-making.[34] Whereas 'heavy' buyers of organic produce cared about both personal and social factors, personal health was the most important factor for 'incidental' buyers, who also focused more on negatives like higher price and shorter shelf-life, making decisions not to buy on this basis.[35] However, even for these consumers, the survey suggested that the positive moral values associated with participating in activity beneficial to the environment were attributes worth including in marketing messages.[36]

Increasing trust in organic credentials was seen as a key step in making these products more saleable, but the most important factor was availability. In part, this need was satisfied by the survival and growth of brands developed in the 1970s and by the participation of increasingly large-scale businesses in the organic market. The trajectory of Gregory and Craig Sams, founders in 1967 of a small but fashionable vegetarian and organic restaurant in West London, a magazine (*Seed*), a natural food store and an organic food production and packaging company, provides a good illustration of this phenomenon.[37] Their food company became the phenomenally successful Whole Earth brand, while Craig Sams' organic chocolate and ice-cream business, Green & Black's, was purchased in 2005 by Cadbury Schweppes for an undisclosed sum.[38] Another, related, strategy to boost both availability and sales was to increase the number of processed foods certified as organic: 'since this [processed food] represents the majority of sales of food products in parts of Europe, represents higher "added value," and in many parts of Europe is where there is real scope for expansion of the organic market'.[39] In response to questions about whether processed food really represents the 'natural' image that organic food generally projects, it was suggested that these foods would actually be more positively received since 'they are both convenient and do not offend the consciences of environmentally concerned consumers'.[40] The same study found, unsurprisingly, that consumers are most interested in taste, in buying food they like.[41] Put together with the primary association of health with organics – for all consumers – one begins to question the ethics of some food manufacturers' adoption of the organic label. Although one of the EU's main justifications for introducing a Regulation (rather than a less prescriptive Directive) on organic food labelling in 2014 was that a Regulation offered more protection from the possible 'confusion and deception of consumers', a glance at the supermarket aisles shows that the word organic on processed foods is no guarantee of a health benefit to consumers or sound practices throughout the production chain.[42] To some extent, at least, in being adopted into the mainstream and managed by policy-makers as a component of the consumer marketplace, the meaning of 'organic' been subverted to the market's ends.

Organic and biodynamic agriculture developed as a response to concerns about the degradation of the Earth and the health of the humans living on it. Viewing the Earth's soil as living matter, early proponents hoped to restore it to an earlier, purer state. In doing so, humans could be returned to their optimum level of 'natural' health. Food production methods and food supply structures were seen as fundamental means by which messages could be communicated, solutions proposed and action taken. Organic and biodynamic food products remained relatively niche commodities in the UK and the US until the late 1980s, when, Allison James argues, several developments in the wider culture conspired to give organic food or 'eating green' wider appeal.[43] Growing public awareness of environmental and ecological issues (such as global warming) combined with the fear engendered by various food-related health scares to make organic messages appealing to a broader population of consumers – which, in turn, made organics an attractive and potentially profitable market for large producers.[44] Organic's traditional association with individual health as well as planetary health could be turned to the marketers' advantage. In a situation like the UK's BSE crisis, when human 'culture had temporarily lost control over nature', the alignment by marketers of organic methods with what was natural and respectful of traditional ecological boundaries made its message welcome.[45]

While the ready availability of organic and 'whole' products might assist many people in realizing a new pattern of ethical or ecological eating, its association with the very peak of the industrialized food system sits less comfortably with the social vision that informed many of the underlying principles of its early twentieth century origins and the late twentieth century counterculture that championed it. Today, policymakers and consumer marketers alike assert that messages about individual health – rather than planetary health – seem to be most meaningful to the majority of the potential purchasers of these foods. The new place and positioning in the consumer marketplace of organic, whole and health foods meant that it became possible for individuals to participate in this new style of apparently healthier and more ethical eating without converting wholesale to the spiritual or political extremes associated with the movements in their early stages. Only when cleansed of its troubling 'muck and mystery', hippie tarnish and transformative visions was this mode of shopping and eating ready to join the mainstream of twenty-first-century consumer society. We may have made progress, and that might be all that matters – but perhaps in the process we have lost track of the dream.

Notes

1. Keith Taylor, *The Political Ideas of the Utopian Socialists* (London: Frank Cass and Company Limited, 1982).
2. There is a long tradition of associating indulgent, sweet and/or chocolatey foods with ideas of sinfulness. A memorable example of this in the UK is the 'Naughty, But Nice' advertising campaign for cream cakes run by the Milk Marketing Board between 1978 and the mid-1980s, and (perhaps mythically) associated with Salman Rushdie's stint as an advertising copywriter at Ogilvy & Mather. Other products like 'dirty' potato chips attempt to subvert the idea of crisps as unhealthy by acknowledging a negative in the name whilst claiming the positive benefits of a lack of processing; while 'dirty' nachos which use language as license to celebrate their lack of healthiness.
3. Gene R. Laczniak and Patrick E. Murphy, 'Fostering Ethical Marketing Decisions', *Journal of Business Ethics*, 10 (1991), pp. 259–71 (p. 265).
4. The first UK experiment comparing organic and non-organic (conventional) farming methods, the Haughley Experiment, was set up by Lady Eve Balfour in 1939, providing material for her book *The Living Soil* (1943). Lord Northbourne's book *Look to the Land* (1940) coined the term 'organic farming'.
5. Erin Gill, 'New Thoughts on the Failure of the Organic Food & Farming Movement in Postwar Britain', *Annual Conference of the British Economic History Society (2009)* (University of Warwick, 2009) <http://www.eringill.co.uk/conference_papers.html>. It is worth noting in this context that the cooperative Whole Food Society was formed in the same year: see Philip Conford, *The Development of the Organic Network: Linking People and Themes, 1945–95* (Edinburgh: Floris, 2011), pp. 223–25.
6. Julie Guthman, *Agrarian Dreams: The Paradox of Organic Farming in California* (Berkeley: U California P, 2004), p. 120.
7. Evelyn Barbara Lady Balfour, *The Living Soil. Evidence of the Importance to Human Health of Soil Vitality, with Special Reference to Post-war Planning*, rev. edn. (London: Soil Association, 2006), p. 196.
8. Guthman, p. 120.
9. Balfour, p. 135.
10. G. T. Wrench, *The Wheel of Health* (London: C. W. Daniel Company, 1941 [1938]), p. 99; Erin Gill, 'The Impact of the Early British Organic Movement's Anti-Science Bias and New Age Religious Beliefs on Relations with Agricultural Scientists and Policy Makers', *The Environmental Histories of Europe and Japan: September 2010, The Kobe Institute, Kobe, Japan* (Nagoya: Graduate School of Environmental Studies, Nagoya University, 2011), pp. 201–13.
11. Wrench, p. 93–95. The Hunza proved not to have increased resistance to disease, nor to have discovered the secret of longevity. For full destruction of the myth, see Harvey Levenstein, 'Santé-bonheur', *Manger Magique: Aliments Sorciers, Croyances Comestibles*, ed. by Claude Fischler (Paris: Éditions Autrements, 1994), pp. 156–68.
12. Wrench, p. 101.
13. Balfour, pp. 145–51; pp. 136–41.
14. Levenstein, p. 165.
15. This phrase, also used as 'muck and magic', was initially coined by Howard to discredit Steiner's theories in contrast to his own more rational approach to compost: see Gill, 'New Thoughts', p. 2. It is interesting to note that, in common with many words and phrases once used to attack disliked groups, this phrase was first turned on its inventors themselves, and has now been adopted by its intended victims (organic and biodynamic proponents) as a positive affirmation of their activities.
16. Gill, 'New Thoughts'.
17. Balfour, p. 188.
18. Balfour, p. 189.
19. Jorian Jenks, *The Stuff Man's Made Of. The Positive Approach to Health Through Nutrition* (London: Faber & Faber, 1959), p. 188. There is insufficient room here to investigate the links between fascism or extreme right wing politics and organic and other land-based movements, but it is worth noting that

Jenks' circle was an influential group of right-wing rural revivalists, and that he was apparently encouraged to send copies of his books to former 'blood and soil' Nazi Agriculture Minister Richard Walther Darré after the war.

20. Jenks, p. 180.
21. Jenks, p. 185.
22. Jenks, p. 188.
23. See, for example, Rachel Carson, *Silent Spring* (Harmondsworth: Penguin Books in association with Hamish Hamilton, 1965).
24. See, for example, Stephen J. Barrett, 'The Politics of Health Nonsense', *The American Biology Teacher*, 36 (1974), pp. 508–11. Concerns about the ethical behaviour of food marketers continue, with increased awareness about supermarket 'slotting fees' and product dumping. See, for example, Laczniak and Murphy, pp. 259–71.
25. Philip Conford, '"Somewhere Quite Different": The Seventies Generation of Organic Activists and Their Context', *Rural History*, 19 (2008).
26. Soil Association, 'What Is Organic?' (Soil Association UK, 2014) <http://www.soilassociation.org/whatisorganic>..
27. European Commission, 'Organic Farming: European Commission Launches New Promotional Campaign for Organic Food and Farming' (Brussels: European Commission, 2008).
28. Timothy A. Park, 'Assessing the Returns from Organic Marketing Channels', *Journal of Agricultural and Resource Economics*, 34 (2009), pp. 483–97 (p. 483).
29. L.B. Fletcher, 'Evolving Public Policy Issues in Food Marketing', *Journal of Farm Economics*, 45 (1963), pp. 1256–66 (p. 1256).
30. The countries involved were Denmark, Finland, Germany, Greece, Italy, Spain, Sweden and the UK, giving a range from relatively high levels of existing consumption (e.g. Denmark, Sweden) to relatively low levels (Greece, Spain).
31. European Commission, 'Organic Farming'.
32. Richard Shepherd, Maria Magnusson and Per-Olow Sjödén, 'Determinants of Consumer Behavior Related to Organic Foods', *Ambio*, 34 (2005), pp. 352–59 (p. 352).
33. Shepherd et al., p. 352.
34. European Commission, 'CONDOR: Consumer Decision Making on Organic Products', (University of Surrey, 2006), p. 6 <http://www.surrey.ac.uk/psychology/files/condor_brochure-end.pdf>; Laczniak and Murphy, pp. 259–71.
35. European Commission, 'CONDOR'.
36. European Commission, 'CONDOR'.
37. Conford, *Development of the Organic Network*, pp. 230–36; Gregory Sams, 'Gregory's Story', <http://www.gregorysams.com/wholefood-history.html> [accessed 23 September 2014].
38. Ethical concerns raised by this sale (including Cadbury's lack of commitment to Fairtrade) were partly addressed by corporate spokespeople pointing to Cadbury's origins as a Quaker company.
39. Shepherd et al.
40. Shepherd et al., p. 353.
41. Shepherd et al., p. 354.
42. European Commission, 'Proposal for a Regulation of the European Parliament and of the Council on Organic Production and Labelling of Organic Products [...] Repealing Council Regulation (EC) No 834/2007', ed. by DG Agriculture and Rural Affairs (Brussels: European Commission, 2014), pp. 1–73 (p. 8).
43. Allison James, 'Eating Green(s). Discourses of Organic Food', *Environmentalism: the View from Anthropology*, ed. by Kay Milton (London: Routledge, 1993), pp. 205–18, 205.
44. James, p. 213.
45. James, p. 214.

Feeding Dublin: The City Fruit and Vegetable Market

Samantha Martin-McAuliffe

Bananas

Nearly seven years ago, when I first moved to Dublin, Ireland, I was exploring the north inner city centre when I came across a large, eye-catching sign advertising bananas. From a commercial point of view, this sign is exemplary: it consists of a single line of bright yellow sans serif letters emblazoned across a royal blue background. The sign is attached to a warehouse, which is also painted blue, and it juts out over the sidewalk, making it clearly visible from both sides of the street. The warehouse stands just a few blocks from the River Liffey in a neighbourhood of Dublin that is well known for its long-standing connections with the food industry. While it is by no means exceptional to see advertisements for foodstuffs in this area of the city, there is something curious about this one specific sign. It possesses a sort of unpretentious clarity and artless confidence. However, even though it is expressly candid as an advertisement, the sign is not necessarily transparent from a socio-cultural perspective. It is highly abstract, to the point where it seems to signify little more than the potential economic transaction of a commodity. That fact that this particular product is food – literally a form of sustenance – is not much more than an afterthought. And furthermore, by the time any bananas reach this particular warehouse in Ireland, most of the people and places that contributed to their cultivation and production have been anonymized and edited out of the relationship.

It is important to emphasize that this is not so much a criticism, but rather an observation about the progressively widening distance, both in a literal and figural sense, between the city and the productive landscapes that sustain it. This study does not tell the story of bananas, but the banana sign in Dublin is a useful preamble into a discussion about food and the city. Perhaps the main reason that I was initially struck by that advertisement years ago was because it seemed to be a highly abbreviated, even truncated, version of a transaction that I had witnessed just a few minutes earlier during that same pivotal walk.

Around the corner from the fruit warehouse and further east toward the city centre stood a woman hawking bananas out of a large, old-fashioned baby carriage (Figure 1). For a newcomer to Dublin, this was an unusual and striking sight. While street trading is a typical and ubiquitous aspect of cities across the world, it was surprising for me to see fresh produce sold from a pram. Shortly thereafter, however, it became apparent that far from being a lone operator, this woman epitomized a firmly established Dublin convention.[1] A variety of street traders can be found in the city, but perhaps the most

Food and Markets

Figure 1.

Figure 2.

famous are the women who peddle fruit, flowers and other (usually seasonal) items from baby prams.[2] These dealers are often as colourful as the goods they sell, and furthermore, they have an exceptionally long history in Dublin. The legendary status of figures such as Molly Malone, who sold cockles and mussels 'along streets broad and narrow', have been instrumental to their renown.[3]

These two juxtaposed scenarios – an industrial sign advertising bananas and a street trader with her fruit-laden pram – maintain a connection that is at first glance straightforward and unambiguous. Yet this connection also embodies a complex history that not only remains overlooked, but is also, to a large extent, forgotten. What follows here is an account of how this section of Dublin's north inner city was shaped by food. Unsurprisingly, the leading protagonist in this urban story is a landmark Victorian market hall. But, as we shall see, the planning, development and eventual influence of the market building were supported by a diverse set of conditions and circumstances.

Landmark

In 2009, Dublin's female street traders were the subject of a documentary by Joe Lee entitled *Bananas on the Breadboard*.[4] The film carefully traced the traders' role in and contribution to the culture of the city's north side. At numerous points, it emphasized how several families in the street trade had been purchasing their goods from the city's Victorian-era wholesale markets for generations. The largest and most prominent of these wholesale markets is the City Fruit and Vegetable Market, which stands along what is now called Mary's Lane, a busy thoroughfare that runs between Capel Street in the east and Church Street in the west (Figure 2). Dublin's venerable Four Courts, which were designed by James Gandon in 1802, are less than two blocks away to the south-west.[5]

The market hall was built between 1891–92, but it should be noted that its presence gave tangible, architectural permanence to a phenomenon that was already well established by the nineteenth century. Many open or informal markets abounded in this vicinity; some still exist. In fact, this whole area of Dublin is often colloquially referred to as 'the city markets'.[6] If it were possible to suggest that the Fruit and Vegetable Market supplanted a specific earlier market, then the open-air Ormond Market, which was established in the seventeenth century, would be the most likely candidate.[7] Ormond Square, a residential neighbourhood, is situated directly south of the Victorian market hall.

Designed by successive City Engineers Parke Neville and Spencer Harty, the City Fruit and Vegetable Market has a rectangular ground plan that runs north-south and covers some 6000 square meters of internal space.[8] The exterior of the complex is impressive: It has several classically inspired gateways, including an ornate main entrance on Mary's Lane that is flanked by two sets of giant limestone Corinthian columns (Figure 3). Standing atop this gate is a pair of female personifications of Justice and Fair Trade. Such figures are highly apropos given the proximity of the Four Courts,

Food and Markets

Figure 3.

Figure 4.

but their inclusion and monumental size also confer a sense of authority, as if to suggest that the purveyance of food is controlled and orderly. These decorative sculptures and the ethical values they represent are not inherently unusual. For millennia, authorized officials have overseen markets of all kinds, and this is a common component of urban order. However, in the context of nineteenth-century Dublin, the sculptures, as well as other details of the building, can be understood to carry very particular meanings; more will be said on this in a few moments.

The exterior facades of the market building consist of blind arcades (the arches are nearly filled in or blocked) and, in typical Victorian fashion, they are largely composed of red and yellow brick. These two colours play off one another with dramatic effect and are deployed in varying zigzag, crosshatch and chevron patterns throughout the arches. The wall space above the arcade is faced with terracotta panels that are moulded with a floral motif in high relief.[9] In the late afternoon and evening, when building's west side elevation glows with sunlight, the colours and patterns of the façade seem to pulsate with energy (Figure 4).

There are other terracotta details on the exterior of the market that are quite remarkable but which are often overlooked and deserve further attention. Bountiful garlands of fruits, vegetables and foliage are displayed above doorways. In addition, the renowned Dennis Ruabon tile company in Wales provided a series of free-form label stops (the terminations of the arches) depicting produce with largely domestic origins.[10] Bunches of pears, apples, potatoes, parsnips, Brussels sprouts and even fish enliven the perimeter wall of the market (Figure 5). While we today regard these as conventional, even mundane foodstuffs, they were fundamental to the historic food economy and productive landscapes as well as seascapes of Ireland. It would be unfortunate to dismiss the terracotta ornaments as mere quaint embellishments, for they are vestigial reminders of Dublin's ancient and early modern food culture. As such, they are instruments of decorum in the most traditional sense: they signify and articulate what is most fitting, or appropriate, for the ornament of the building. It is also worth noting how these decorative elements refer to different scales of economy. Given the Victorian predilection for the pineapple, it is no surprise that this tropical fruit is present on the wall of the market. Yet besides having symbolic status, the pineapple also speaks to an established, far-reaching food trade. Although we tend to use the terms 'globalization' and 'food miles' in reference to present-day economies, cities have been importing and exporting food across great distances since antiquity.[11] Overall, the terracotta ornaments of the Fruit and Vegetable Market communicate notions of abundance and plenitude. It is as if the entire market was envisioned as a cornucopia incarnate – an expressly symbolic gesture given that Ireland was still very much living in the aftermath of the Great Famine.

While the exterior of the market hall carries a great deal of embellishment, its interior is a model of streamlined efficiency (Figure 6). The use of red and yellow brick continues, but it is relegated to the perimeter wall. The utilization of iron for the

Food and Markets

Figure 5.

Figure 6.

internal structure allowed the entire space to be open, uncluttered and largely free of ornamentation.[12] One could argue that the extensive use of iron allowed the architecture to recede into the background – dematerialize – in order for the 'genuine' ornament to take centre stage: the fresh produce. As such, the terracotta sculptures that decorate the external facades of the market act as promotional advertisements for what one can find inside.[13]

When viewing the market building from Google Earth it is very easy to discern the eight gables (running west-east) that comprise its roof. The main framework of the roof is constructed from the same iron used in the interior of the building; the rest is glass glazing. These two materials – iron and glass – are now so commonplace in the architecture of market halls that they can be considered unremarkable. Yet, like the figures of Justice and Fair Trade, and to some extent even the terracotta ornaments, these building materials carried very specific connotations in Victorian Dublin. It is worthwhile now returning to this topic in brief as it will help illuminate the broader meaning of this particular building. On the one hand, the use of glass and iron for a commercial market hall signified that the city was employing the very latest advancements in structural engineering available at the time. The nineteenth century witnessed the construction of many similar market halls across Europe and America.[14] Such buildings were often heralded as instruments of civic renewal. But, on the other hand, in a political and social sense, architectural technology went hand in hand with changing opinion about public hygiene and sanitation. Dublin was no exception: In the 1880s the Dublin Corporation Market Committee expressed concern over sanitation in the areas surrounding the old Ormond Market.[15] It was believed that this new hall would help sweep away poor conditions and pave the way – quite literally – for an efficient and hygienic food trade.[16]

There is, however, an even larger issue at play here, one that is so plainly evident that it is routinely overlooked: at the time of the Fruit and Vegetable Market's construction, Ireland was still part of Britain. This was certainly not lost on the city officials. At the opening of the hall, the Lord Mayor commented that 'the members of the Corporation [of Dublin] could congratulate themselves on having pushed through this great work and congratulate the citizens on having a market second to none in the Empire'.[17] Although the market was built in Ireland and was largely designed to sell Irish produce, it was in many respects a quintessentially British building.

Roots

The relationship between the Fruit and Vegetable Market and city's street trade has already been mentioned. Certainly, a majority of Dubliners today are aware of how vendors are connected to and reliant upon the market for their livelihood. However, most people are unlikely to realize that when they purchase a bunch of bananas or a punnet of strawberries from a street trader, they are tapping into and participating in an exceptionally ancient tradition of food production and consumption that is rooted in this very section of the city. The area north of the Liffey between what is today Parnell Street in the north-east and Smithfield in the west was one of the nerve centres of pre-twentieth-century capitalism in Dublin. In order to understand this, it is necessary to dig deeper into the situation of the market hall. By this, I do not mean deeper in a symbolic or metaphorical sense, but rather in a very literal way, into the tangible infrastructure of the city.

Instead of understanding the market as a discrete, self-contained entity in the middle of the city, it may be more useful and illuminating to see it as a structure that evolved out of and reflected a complex network of historical trade routes that connected Dublin with Ireland's hinterland and shorelines. The vast, fertile provinces and waterways that originally fed the city have left what may be called a tangible residue. There is a variety of ways through which to see how Dublin still bears the imprint of food. To state this more precisely: the intricate and constantly changing choreography of streets, canals and railways that shaped Dublin emerged directly in response to the city's food industry prior to the twentieth century.[18] As a result, there was a reciprocity between nature and the city that was reflected in the basic structure – the morphology – of the built environment. Most of these urban facilities and conduits still exist today, but we no longer think of them as being connected to food, and much less the vast territories that led to their existence. They are, for the most part, overlooked relics.[19]

Ultimately, it is possible to argue that the Fruit and Vegetable Market was not built on Mary's Lane because the space was simply available. Rather, it was almost predestined to develop here as this location maintains a deep history of food infrastructure. A straightforward way of examining this situation is to reassess Dublin's streets. One only needs to glance at a map of the Fruit and Vegetable Market's neighbourhood to grasp its connections to food. Smithfield, which was mentioned earlier, stands just a few hundred metres to the west. Although now largely devoid of activity, this originally was a thriving open-air marketplace and the heart of Dublin's meat trade. Also nearby is the Old Jameson Distillery, as well as streets with names such as Haymarket and Red Cow Lane. Slightly further afield is the Royal Canal, which was at one time a principal thoroughfare for transporting food throughout Ireland.

Historical maps provide many more evocative details: St Michan's Street, which borders the Fruit and Vegetable Market, was once Fisher's Lane. In fact, it was known as such from at least the 1320s.[20] City records also reveal that there were numerous fisheries in this immediate vicinity well through the early nineteenth century. These have long since vanished, along with their eponymous street name. However, as recently as the 1980s, some of the oldest street traders could remember not only local fisheries, but also a myriad of affiliated businesses, such as stables and piggeries.[21] If we go even further into the archaeology of the city, we find that the north banks of the River Liffey were important grounds for catching fish during the Mesolithic period.[22]

Thus, well before the construction of the market halls, and even before the emergence of the street hawker in the eighteenth century, this place in the city was intrinsically

Feeding Dublin: The City Fruit and Vegetable Market

Figure 7.

connected with food. Put categorically, the roads, streets and squares of Dublin were designed to accommodate and facilitate the transportation as well as the purveyance of food. Although in many cases their names have changed over the centuries, their routes and courses have left an indelible and resilient imprint on Dublin. What is fascinating is the degree to which the deeper identity of these infrastructures has been forgotten by twenty-first-century Dublin. It is as if the population exhibits a collective amnesia toward the city's historic foodways.

Ritual

Apart from the sculptures of Justice and Fair Trade that stand atop the market hall and loom over Mary's Lane, there exists another, much less imposing statue just inside the main entrance. A modern figure of the Virgin Mary, standing upright in a white robe and with folded hands, looks over and across the market hall.[23] She resides in purpose-built transparent box that is fixed directly over the gateway and is illuminated from above by a neon-blue light. Although the average visitor to the markets may easily overlook her, she arguably holds more import and symbolic weight for the traders than her monumental stone counterpoints. Religion, specifically Catholicism, still plays a major role in the life and culture of this neighbourhood in Dublin.

In November each year, the traders and superintendent of the Fruit and Vegetable Market set aside a morning for the 'Market Mass', a traditional Catholic ceremony that interweaves celebration, thanksgiving and the remembrance of past traders. A simple yet plentiful altar is constructed out of fresh produce and flowers in the middle of the hall, and a Capuchin friar from the local parish church of St Michan's at Halston Street leads the ceremony (Figure 7). Notably, he is accompanied by one of the traders, Derek Leonard, who is also a deacon. Members from the community – retired and active stallholders, street traders and their families – gather together to share memories of their lives in the market. Unsurprisingly, the mass is also understood as a memorial, not only for the deceased traders but also more generally for the culture that traditionally underpinned this community for generations. In this year's ceremony the friar described not nostalgia but rather a 'loneliness' for the spirited, confident and sometimes even chaotic vitality that once characterized this neighbourhood. Since at least the 1980s, the north inner city of Dublin has witnessed a dramatic rise in drug-related crime; the recession of 2008–10 brought further economic and social distress to the area. However, well before the 1980s, the Fruit and Vegetable Markets themselves were struggling to address the changing culture of the national and international produce industry. The inner city address and narrow networks of streets surrounding the hall cannot easily accommodate large shipping trucks or lorries.[24] As the produce business migrated to the suburbs, the Fruit and Vegetable Market declined, both in terms of its population and physical condition.

What is remarkable about the annual Market Mass is the ease and informality with which religion and commerce coexist, even if just for one or two hours. During the ceremony the market remains open for business. Some workers take a short break from their shifts to join the congregation for a few minutes. Prayer is briefly interrupted by a passing forklift, and just behind the temporary altar customers shop for plants and flowers. The Eucharist is celebrated while pallets of produce are stacked and transferred between aisles. All of this is extraordinary, but not necessarily surprising. On the one hand, the Fruit and Vegetable Market is situated just a few metres from St Mary's Abbey, which was once one of largest and wealthiest religious institutions in Ireland.[25] Thus, this area of the city has nearly always been a hub of both religion and trade. To some degree, the statue of Mary at the entrance acknowledges and confirms this deep-seated relationship. On a daily basis she stands tacitly in the background, but on certain occasions, such the Market Mass, her contribution to the religious landscape of the city is publicly expressed. Yet, beyond this specific context, it is also important to understand that rituals and markets go hand-in-hand across many cultures. Throughout the world one can find shrines displayed in market halls, sometimes very prominently. Moreover, religious processions commonly weave through marketplaces.[26] This is by no means a modern phenomenon. In the ancient marketplace of Athens, the Agora, an altar of the Twelve Gods stands adjacent to what was once the main thoroughfare and processional route of the city.[27]

Feeding Dublin: The City Fruit and Vegetable Market

Aftermath

Almost all twentieth-century maps covering central Dublin will indicate another large Victorian edifice immediately adjacent to the Fruit and Vegetable Market. Even Google Maps suggests the presence of another similarly sized structure next door to the west. Switching to satellite view or looking at Google Earth will quickly disclose that this space is now a parking lot. Until the late 1990s, this was the home of the City Fish Market, a sister building that was also designed by Parke Neville and Spencer Harty; it was completed in 1897.[28] This building unfortunately did not survive the Celtic Tiger building boom and was demolished to make way for redevelopment at the turn of the millennium.[29] The project never came to fruition.

For most of the twentieth century, the fate of the Victorian market halls on Mary's Lane was tenuous. Several decades ago there were proposals to move the market to the outskirts of the city to make way for modernization projects within Dublin's urban core.[30] This development would have echoed the story of London's famed Covent Garden, a complex that in some respects was ultimately 'saved' but which nevertheless lost its identity as an anchor point in London's food culture. In all likelihood, Dublin's main food market has survived not because of architectural conservation practices but rather due to the seismic shift in the economy over the last decade. Plans to redevelop this entire neighbourhood were shelved for lack of funding. The Fruit and Vegetable Market is now a recognized and protected historic structure.

When I first visited the markets in 2008 the Victorian hall was in dire need of restoration and largely unused. In fact, its fruit and vegetable vendors were conspicuous by their absence. The complex, which had opened to great fanfare in 1892, steadily declined to become an obsolete relic of a food economy that no longer existed. By 2010 only a handful of wholesale dealers remained in business; in the last two decades the majority have given up the fight against large supermarket retailers. However, change is now afoot once again. Under the auspices of an indefatigable superintendent, the building began a renovation programme in 2012, 120 years after its inauguration. The city is now intending to redevelop the entire premises as a mixed retail and wholesale market, which is set to open in 2015. The surviving wholesale vendors will relocate to the western side of the market hall and will continue to serve not only local shops and restaurants, but also the traditional street vendors who have relied on the market for over a century. The rest of the building will be refurnished to accommodate a wide variety of retailers, including cheesemongers, butchers and bakers in addition to traditional greengrocers. These vendors will be accommodated in permanent stalls that can be individually closed and shuttered.[31]

Arguably, a key reason why the Fruit and Vegetable Market is now on the threshold of revitalization is the fact that Dublin's food economy has come full circle. When the market was established it was supposed to feed a population of approximately 250,000 residents, most of whom lived within the two canals that ring the city. Now, of course, the population of the city centre has more than doubled, and yet there is a rising public consciousness of the value of local produce. Remarkably, this relic of an early-modern food culture is set to become the cornerstone for the renewal of placehood. This will be instrumental in the development of a new, twenty-first-century foodscape, which re-grounds the city, both in a literal and metaphorical sense.

Notes

1. On the whole, there is a dearth of academic discourse regarding the history and culture of street vending in Dublin. See 'The Pram Wars', *Dublin Review of Books*, <http://www.drb.ie/blog/dublin-stories/2012/11/19/the-pram-wars> [accessed 9 November 2014]. See also Barry Kennerk, *Moore Street: The Story of Dublin's Market District* (Dublin: The Mercier Press, 2012).
2. For a photographic portrait see, Susan Weir, *Dublin's Working Prams* (Dublin: Susan Weir, 2012).
3. Sean Murphy, 'Who Was Molly Malone?', *History Ireland*, 2 (1993), 39–41.
4. *Bananas on the Breadboard*, dir. by Joe Lee. The film can be viewed at: <http://joelee.ie/portfolio/bananas-on-the-breadboard/> [accessed June 28 2014]. One retired stallholder from Moore Street, Ms. Annie Dillon, told the author that her family has retained its produce stand for ninety-eight years; it is now run by her niece (Annie Dillon, personal interview, 14 November 2014).
5. Edward McParland, 'The Early History of James Gandon's Four Courts', *The Burlington Magazine*, 122 (1980), pp. 727–33.
6. For example, Dublin City Council refers to this entire area as the City Markets. See <http://www.dublincity.ie/main-menu-services-planning-urban-development-plans-framework-development-plans/city-markets> [accessed November 11, 2014].
7. Colm Lennon, *Irish Historic Towns Atlas, no. 19, Dublin, part II, 1610 to 1756* (Dublin: Royal Irish Academy, 2008), p.3. See also Niall McCullough, *Dublin: An Urban History* (Dublin: Anne Street Press, 1989).
8. Christine Casey, *The Buildings of Ireland: Dublin. The City within the Grand and Royal Canals and the Circular Road with the Phoenix Park* (New Haven, CT: Yale UP, 2005), pp.100-101.
9. For the terracotta see, Susan Keating, 'Chromatic Delights: Dublin's Terracotta Buildings in the Later Nineteenth Century', *Irish Architectural and Decorative Studies, the Journal of the Irish Georgian Society* 4 (2001), pp.142–69.
10. Casey, p.101.
11. For an excellent discussion of ancient food miles, see Carolyn Steel, *Hungry City* (London: Chatto and Windus, 2008) pp. 72–75.
12. The internal, structural ironwork was supplied by John Lysaght of Bristol. The decorative ironwork than can be seen in the gates and arches was provided locally by McGloughlin Bros. See Dublin Corporation, *Report of the Markets Construction Committee*, 6 December 1892.
13. It is interesting to compare this kind of representation with the advertisement for bananas that is described at the beginning of the essay. Arguably, both are fulfilling the same essential purpose: to promote and advertise a commodity. However, the sign marketing bananas, which of course has a much later twentieth century date, is so streamlined that it is almost an abridgment of the semiotic equation.
14. A good overview is provided by James Schmiechen and Kenneth Carls, *The British Market Hall: A Social and Architectural History* (New Haven, CT: Yale UP, 1999).
15. Dublin Corporation Reports, *Report of the Markets Committee*, 24 August 1886. For an excellent discussion of the slum culture that was endemic to this area of Dublin, see Jacinta Prunty, *Dublin Slums, 1800–1925: A Study in Urban Geography* (Dublin: Irish Academic Press, 1998).
16. See also, Samantha L. Martin-McAuliffe, 'The Ethics of Giving and Receiving: A Study of the Iveagh Markets, Dublin', *Portraits of the City: Dublin and the Wider World*, ed. by Gillian O'Brien and Finola O'Kane (Dublin: Four Courts Press, 2012) pp. 175–90.

17. *Irish Times*, 7 December 1892.
18. See Samantha L. Martin-McAuliffe, 'On the Possibility of a Re-emergent Landscape in Dublin, Ireland', *Emerging Landscapes: Between Production and Representation*, ed. by Davide Deriu, Krystallia Kamvasinou, and Eugénie Shinkle (Farnham, England: Ashgate, 2014), pp . 135–146.
19. Martin-McAuliffe, 2014, p.137.
20. C.T. M'Cready, *Dublin Street Names: Dated and Explained* (Blackrock, Co. Dublin: Carraig Books), p. 37. See also Paul Clerkin, *Dublin Street Names* (Dublin: Gill and MacMillan, 2001), p. 158.
21. Kevin Corrigan Kearns, *Dublin Street Life and Lore: An Oral History* (Dun Laoghaire, Co. Dublin: Glendale, 1991), p.60.
22. M. McQuade and L. O'Donnell, 'Late Mesolithic Fish Traps from the Liffey Estuary, Dublin, Ireland', *Antiquity* 81 (2007), pp. 569–84.
23. This statue replaces an earlier example that dated from the 1950s and which was lost during renovations of the Market hall in the 2000s (Joe Crosbie, personal interview, 27 February, 2012).
24. 'Dublin Fruit Market "should be moved": Survey Team Finds It Inefficient', *The Irish Press*, 6 February, 1975. The article names traffic congestion as one of the largest problems facing the Market.
25. St Mary's Abbey is clearly indicated on John Speed's Map of Dublin from 1610: see H.J. Lawlor, 'The Foundation of St. Mary's Abbey, Dublin', *The Journal of the Royal Society of Antiquaries of Ireland* 16 (1926), pp. 22–28.
26. For example, in Ambleside (Cumbria, England), the annual rushbearing festival procession passes through the town's marketplace.
27. See Laura M. Gadbery, 'The Sanctuary of the Twelve Gods in the Athenian Agora: A Revised View', *Hesperia* 61 (1992), pp. 447–89. See also Walter Burkert, *Greek Religion: Archaic and Classical* (Oxford: Blackwell, 1985).
28. Douglas Bennett, *Encyclopedia of Dublin* (Dublin: Gill and MacMillan, 1991), p. 75. For the closure, see Tim O'Brien, 'Fish Market Closes: Council Calls it a Day on Dublin's Inner City Market', *Irish Times*, 6 May, 2005.
29. Edel Morgan, 'Fish Market Sale to Open Way for Area's Revamp', *Irish Times*, 25 May 2005.
30. See above, note 24.
31. Olivia Kelly, 'Plans for Historic Dublin Market to be Lodged Next Month', *Irish Times*, 26 February 2014.

'Fresh' is Fraught: How Would You Define this Virtuous Word?

Renee Marton

When we think of food markets, we often visualize heaps of colourful fruits and vegetables, leafy greens, baked goods and all manner of prepared foods, artfully displayed. Meats, jams, eggs, pasta and fish are also in evidence. Even though they are often behind a barrier, we still see and evaluate them. It is difficult to imagine this tableau without the word 'fresh' coming to mind, but what does 'fresh' specifically refer to?

Farmers markets, usually by legal requirement, sell recently harvested, slaughtered or prepared comestibles, usually without any middlemen between farm and consumer. Degrees of ripeness, moistness, seasonality and short shelf-life are part of the 'fresh' panoply of assumptions: fruits and vegetables are at or near their sensory peak, and other products the best that they can be. As for meat and fish, the consumer assumes that slaughter was recent, even if these foods are frozen when brought to market. Another presupposition is that these foodstuffs are safe to consume; this assumption is based on time since harvest or slaughter and 'best practices' handling by farmers and farm personnel. If we have questions, we have our senses to rely on, as well as being able to talk to knowledgeable personnel. Microbiological questions don't ordinarily arise because the newness factor is perceived as a gateway to a healthy choice. A definition of 'fresh' under these conditions might include: recent harvest or slaughter, highest seasonal quality, ripe, nutritious, safe to eat, a short shelf-life (not including frozen items) and tampered with as little as possible, especially raw foods – what I will call 'best-edible'. In the nineteenth and early twentieth centuries, the cost of such foodstuffs was often reasonable because of an abundance of farms and farmers. The whole idea of farmers markets, as specialized places where one could get really 'fresh' foods, as they exist today (in the US), did not return to the public sphere until industrial agriculture was well established. Today, farmers markets are still relatively rare, and their foods often are more expensive than the same or similar foods found at the supermarket. This will probably be the case for many years in the US, as farmers market sales currently represent two per cent of US food sales. Just as allotments still exist in Britain, urban farming allotments are slowly beginning to be promoted in the US. This is a long-term movement, and won't take a big bite out of industrial farming for a number of years.

The word 'preserved' or 'cured' includes in its meaning 'safe to eat' and high quality, just as 'fresh' does. Raw pork becomes 'cured ham'. Cured refers to the absence of toxins that would cause someone to become ill after consumption. Salting, sugaring or peppering, drying and/or smoking, fermenting or using brine: each technique is an effective means of reducing the bacterial count to safe (or safe enough) levels. Equally important, these methods are valued because the flavour, texture, appearance and tradition of foods being preserved in particular ways have become the gastronomic capital of different cultures. While we do not consider such foods 'fresh' in the sense I described in the first paragraph, we do consider them safe to eat and high quality within their category. Should we call them 'freshly preserved'?

Farmers markets are increasing in number (especially in wealthier and wealth-building countries), although I am focusing here primarily on the US. The global marketplace, while expanding consumer choice and the customer base, is simultaneously shrinking thanks to the rapidity of modern travel, the chill chain and food processing technologies. As foodstuffs are shipped all over the planet, how is 'freshness' maintained in the global marketplace? Is this the same 'freshness' that I described earlier? Giant farms, food processing factories, packaging plants, wholesale food markets and superstores: these are the primary food producers, transporters and sellers today. For example, Walmart, the largest supermarket in the US, is responsible for almost twenty-five per cent of food sales in the country. Boxed, vacuum-sealed and/or frozen provisions pass through huge warehouse/stores, similar to airline hubs. Much of what we consume is transported to wholesale markets, sometimes repackaged or re-treated in some way, and shipped to supermarkets, restaurants, hospitals, schools and other institutions. Is it reasonable to call these foods 'fresh' in the same way the word is used at the farmers markets? Thanks to Country of Origin Laws (in the US), we can at least find out something about provenance, but not everything we want to know. While the spinach may be from China, we don't know how long it took to get from the farm to the exporter, nor how long the travel time was to bring it to the American marketplace, nor what treatments the spinach received so as to last longer than it otherwise would. Perhaps we should call this 'freshly delayed'?

Consumers cannot generally use wholesale markets, so 'freshness' and our traditional quality checks, both sensory and verbal, are unavailable. 'Trust' is now an issue, and with 'trust', transparency becomes supplemental knowledge the consumer needs in order to make a good choice. 'Fresh' now has a value added component: 'trust' in purveyors. And 'trust' leads directly to 'source' or 'origin'. Recent increases in foodborne illness outbreaks, added to issues of provenance and quality control, require an increased level of scrutiny that may eventually lead to a more precise legal definition of 'fresh' than the current definition, which varies so wildly that it is not worth going into here. Modern methods of food preservation allow foods to be trucked, shipped or flown anywhere. The criteria we have used to evaluate our food purchases for hundreds of years no longer fit the paradigm in which we find ourselves. The customary standards for evaluating 'freshness' are not so readily apparent. Canned and frozen foods that remain frozen until consumer purchase are usually not problematic. But what is one to do about 'Fresh Frozen Fish', signage I saw recently at my local upscale supermarket. Perhaps we could call this 'freshly defrosted fish'?

Food and Markets

To repeat some old news: cities are growing, pathogens are evolving, food-processing protocols are changing and food miles are so long that transport and storage are included in the food safety model. I have not mentioned allergens, and suffice it to say that if everything were labelled honestly and completely, information would be accessible so consumers could avoid allergenic products. That might necessitate a pamphlet attached to each food item – something that is unlikely to happen anytime soon. And what about organic fruits and vegetables? And is organic is related to 'freshness'? It depends on your point of view. Grass-fed beef may be presumably from farmers with a more humane approach to their animals, but does that also mean that the grass has not been sprayed with insecticides, even organic ones? Fish illustrate the problems in a more complex way, at least in the US. There are no organic standards for fish in the US, but there are in Canada. So it is quite possible – I have seen this – to see a sign stating, 'organically raised fish' in a US market. Explanation: the fish comes from Canada. Is the fish 'fresh'? And what would that mean, anyway?

When applied to meat and fish, the word 'ripe' usually implies the onset of rankness, so we must use other defining words and concepts, such as date since slaughter. Perhaps meat should have a label stating: slaughtered on a specific date, at a specific location. Then we could say 'freshly slaughtered'.

Strategies to bring foods (both plants and animals) from very large farms to the consumer involve delaying tactics as the foods speed through processing plants, and travel via trucks, rail, ships and planes to wholesale markets, superstores and institutions. This periodically means that boxed food spends time on loading docks, in the open air and at a level of temperature and humidity that promotes spoilage. Delay – at least at the wrong temperature – is the enemy of 'fresh'.

Thomas Friedman, a columnist for the *New York Times*, suggested that four words no longer have any meaning: 'privacy', 'local', 'average' and 'later'. I would like to add 'fresh' to the list. No doubt there would be broad resistance to this idea, because 'fresh' has such a positive connotation, even with contemporary encumbrances. And even at farmers markets, 'fresh' is not quite as simple as it seems, since perishability is a commodity in which quality declines over time. Some examples that complicate matters in defining 'fresh' include beef that is aged for several weeks before consumption to tenderize it and alter the flavour, or bluefin tuna and other fish, which must go through rigor mortis before being edible.

Efficiencies in food processing result in money saved – not only for the food processor, but also for the consumer. In the US we spend eleven per cent of our disposable income on food purchases (compared to western Europe, where food comprises upwards of twenty per cent). Economies of scale in agribusiness mandate policies and implementation of those policies to keep costs down. In these industrial scenarios, the word 'fresh' is often used to offset negative industrial imagery (confined animals, older foods, loss of flavour/texture, lower quality). Yes, these foods are safe to eat, but at a cost. 'Fresh' apples from New Zealand? Isn't that an oxymoron? 'Fresh' fish from Chile (farm raised)? Beef from Argentina (not frozen, but vacuum sealed)? Happy cows (cows that eat grass and can roam) produce better cheese; so say the California dairy ads. Pasteurization is controversial in some quarters. The US Department of Agriculture considers pasteurized milk 'fresh', as do most consumers. Raw milk supporters believe that the only 'fresh' milk is unpasteurized. Irradiation is controversial, even though it has been approved by the US Food and Drug Administration since the 1960s. Does the word 'fresh' belong anywhere near the word irradiation? Some strawberries are irradiated; is 'fresh' acceptable to describe them? It depends. Consumers are afraid of irradiation, so 'fresh' irradiated strawberries might leave a consumer perplexed. If we accept irradiation, confusion may decrease, but perhaps another word is necessary, rather than 'fresh'. After all, if both treated and untreated strawberries are 'fresh', how can we tell the difference? Currently in the US, irradiated foods sold at shops and markets must have the Radura symbol, but this requirement does not apply to restaurants or processed foods, according to the EPA. Perhaps we might say 'freshly' irradiated?

The explosive growth of bagged salads since the 1990s has made convenience a top priority when shopping for 'fresh' salad greens, despite the use of Modified Atmosphere Processing (the use of different gases to delay deterioration) in the packaging. Convenience trumps 'best-edible' most of the time. Fresh Express, the largest US producer of bagged salads, uses a breathable plastic bag, without which the greens would not last through storage and transport. Are these greens 'fresh' in the same way that a head of lettuce that I cut up myself is 'fresh'? Perhaps 'freshly bagged' would do the trick?

We have broader definitions of food safety today, hardier microorganisms to worry about, more high-risk eaters, a larger middle class in our own and in developing countries (to which we export goods) that have increasing 'freshness' demands and an approach to food safety presumably based on prevention rather than treatment after the fact. Hypermarkets, such as Costco and Walmart, cross the divide between wholesale and retail, as they sell large quantities of goods that come straight from the factory or wholesaler, but are open to some degree of viewing by the consumer. And what about 'organic' markets? Some 'fresh' fruits and vegetables, and certain meats, are organically raised, within legal guidelines, but those guidelines themselves are widely contested by industry and activists alike. It is confusing at best.

Food markets are like layer cakes: they look beautiful as you walk around (in addition to farmers markets, think of Whole Foods, or Harrods Food Court), but you make assumptions about what is 'fresh' and safe within those layers.

Market templates

Our first model is the farmers market, or green market, where there is a relationship of trust between consumer and farming personnel. This permits 'fresh' to have a relatively clear definition.

In wholesale markets, however, you do not actually go to the market yourself. Whom do you trust? How do you know what is 'fresh' when many thousands of items are delivered, altered in some way and re-routed daily, through a phone or online order? In this second template, the relationship is with a middleman – if that – for the procurement of provisions. There may be trust, but it is based on prior history with that purveyor, and is minimally personal. You already know that what you purchase is not the 'freshest' it can be because it has been stored for some time and travelled a distance to get to you. But you need it, and it is satisfactory. With extended time come multiple 'fresh' and food safety issues, which you do not worry about unless something obvious is wrong. There is history here also, as these methods are not themselves associated with major food problems (there are exceptions) other than 'freshness'.

Providing increasingly large cities, and their consuming institutions (schools, residential buildings, hospitals, etc.) with safe foods is part of a multi-tiered system in which transparency and provenance are as important as the provisions. Expanding product lines, including imports and exports, make sourcing and oversight difficult to manage well. Storage and transportation add another layer of potential food contamination, whether accidental or deliberate. 'Fresh' has a different meaning in this second template. Produce and fruit may be unblemished, boxed or packaged and transportable, but unripe and treated to ripen later. Cucumbers are waxed, tomatoes are sprayed with ethylene and salad greens are dipped in a chlorine bath. Meat may be vacuum-sealed, or sprayed to look red, so it is difficult to judge quality, colour, aroma, etc. – the criteria we usually use to judge 'freshness'. Fish and shellfish are often frozen at sea and defrosted (possibly more than once): are they 'fresh'? Food safety protocols are critical in these markets and in processing plants. The question remains: is using a Hazard Analysis Critical Control Point (HAACP) plan – one prevention-based approach in the US – a viable way to change the definition of 'fresh'? As automation within food factories increases, personal hygiene becomes less worrisome, but our link to the land becomes more and more distant. And it is that link that has much to do with definitions of 'fresh' and freshness.

Vertically integrated food companies are yet another template in our layer cake comparison. Trust here is corporate. These companies generally have admirable HACCP and food safety records. 'Fresh' has a third meaning here, as manufacturing goals with tight deadlines mitigate the freshness factor for an end-product that varies from less processed (bananas) to highly processed (tomato sauce).

Farmers markets
Daily or weekly farmers markets and Community Supported Agriculture plans sell locally sourced produce, fruit, meat, fish, dairy and artisanal products (honey, cured meats, pickles and preserves). Legal requirements to be a registered participant in a farmers market make it relatively simple to feel secure about what is 'fresh' and safe to eat, in the old sense of newly harvested or slaughtered and uncontaminated (even if that

'Fresh' is Fraught

Figure 1. Green Market, Oxford

means there are 'organic' pesticides being used). In this model, farmers and freshness are almost synonymous. Food safety issues are easy to track because this system promotes transparency through a positive attitude towards maintaining pristine products and short travel distances. These factors mitigate many food safety issues. Just as in olden days, you talk to your farmer, or at least to someone who comes from the farm. This look/see approach usually works through verbal, tactile and visual vigilance. This is not a perfect system (most causes of foodborne illness are invisible), but you may look, smell and even touch the varied foodstuffs in ways that cannot take place at a supermarket, much less a wholesale market. You can see if the radishes are really firm and still have soil on the roots. Turnips appear in many varieties, all with their greens still attached. Apples, if you are in New York or Washington State, come in multiple colours, shapes and flavours. And they even smell good, too, something that does not usually happen at a supermarket.

Distance from farm to market, storage of product, scale of the business – this model does not involve long distances or gigantic quantities. Sales at farmers markets are contingent on a general assumption of procedural transparency and openness regarding food safety issues. There are food safety problems, but they are by and large contained because of the size of the businesses and the speed and ease of reporting a problem. Also, the lag time for the growth of foodborne microorganisms is such that the level of risk is considered low, generally. Farmers markets and CSAs are on the rise.

Food and Markets

Total annual sales at US farmers markets are estimated to be one billion dollars, according to the Agricultural Marketing Resource Center. As a comparison, however, the Hunts Point Cooperative Market in New York, the largest wholesale market in the world, processes three billion dollars in food product value annually – at this one market. Is it fair to compare farmers markets and wholesale markets? Yes, because the word 'fresh' is used to describe the same products at each kind of market, yet I would say these products are worlds apart in terms of what is 'fresh'.

******

Occasionally, when farmers markets have fruit or produce that has not sold that day, the farmers sell them to a store or other secondary retailer/wholesaler. The steps in this process begin to mimic some of the problems that plague the industry in general, albeit on a much smaller scale. A head of romaine lettuce picked at the farm on Sunday will be displayed on Monday, outdoors, under a tent, at the farmers market. That head of lettuce will be pristine for much of the day (if misted with water or kept out of sunlight). We would call this a 'fresh' head of lettuce. The fact is that no one would even bother to use the word 'fresh' – it is totally obvious. If the lettuce does not sell by late afternoon on Monday, the farmer may sell it to the nearest supermarket, which refrigerates it for the night and displays it on Tuesday. Depending on how the lettuce is stored, and whether it comes into contact with prepared foods and/or raw meats and fish, the risk of contamination has just risen. Contact in either direction will be problematic. In the meantime, quality decreases: before being refrigerated, the lettuce has been left at room temperature for several hours. Refrigeration keeps our head of romaine in fairly good shape, even if some outer leaves are browning. Quality, nutritional value, firmness and flavour are decreasing as time passes. A supermarket employee removes the brown leaves, and the price is reduced to encourage a sale. Is this lettuce still 'fresh'? Partially, but it is no longer pristine. Is it still safe to eat? Possibly, if well washed by the consumer. If the romaine lettuce has not been sold by Wednesday, it is cut up and used in the Prepared Foods department, where it is added to the 'Chicken Salad Special', made by an employee whose training protocols include wearing gloves when preparing ready-to-eat food. Why do we care about this? The lettuce was safe for consumption while at the farmers market (after being washed). By the time the lettuce arrives at the supermarket, this assumption can no longer be made. By Thursday, the chicken salad, which was made with other leftovers besides the lettuce, will be on Special Sale and sold with a sticker on the container indicating that it should be consumed that day (if the chicken salad does not sell, it will be thrown out at the end of the day). At this point, the potential for cases of foodborne illness in high-risk populations is something to be very concerned about, if not a legal requirement for the store. Populations at high risk for foodborne illnesses include the elderly (an increasingly large group), infants and toddlers, persons with chronic medical conditions, pregnant women and people with organ transplants. Where does 'fresh' fit into this scenario? It does not, even though the

'Fresh' is Fraught

Figure 2. Hunts Point Cooperative Market.

word is bandied about because we all respond so well to it: fresh Romaine lettuce for Caesar salad (Wednesday)? Or Freshly Prepared Chicken Salad (Thursday)? Take your pick. Or take your chances. But if it says 'fresh', you are more likely to purchase it.

Wholesale markets and big box stores

In the middle of our continuum are wholesale markets – usually in or near cities – that have often been in existence for fifty or more years. These markets have evolved in terms of the 'built environment', the number of products sold, and in terms of how foodstuffs are packed and unpacked, transported, sorted, stored and otherwise handled. At Hunts Point Cooperative Market in New York, lengthy loading docks, filled with boxed, canned, frozen, bagged and packaged foods in huge quantities, abut giant warehouses. In the meat market (one of three markets at Hunts Point), most beef arrives pre-cut, boxed and vacuum packed. Stacked boxes are kept in refrigerated warehouses (often after sitting on the loading docks for a while) or refrigerated trucks (when there isn't enough room in the warehouse). The beef itself is a deep reddish brown colour within the plastic packaging. Oxygen removal allows the beef to last long enough to reach the customer. Just as with a human kidney transplant, the meat 'pinks up' once the plastic is removed, and the beef is left to recover in open air. The off-putting aroma also recedes and eventually you find yourself with beautiful red beef that smells good too. Still, would we call this meat 'fresh'? Some would. I would not. The beef ages within the packaging, and thanks to normal enzymatic action tenderness results; also, no 'bugs' can get into the beef from outside, which might not be true if the beef were unprotected and left exposed to the elements. It probably tastes good, but is this 'fresh' beef? How about 'freshly vacuum sealed'?

A conflict has arisen: how to keep foods in 'best quality' condition, and keep them safe for travel, storage and appeal. Schools, hospitals, prisons, restaurants and supermarkets use wholesale markets or big box retailers like Costco and Walmart for their purchases. With wholesale markets, delivery systems are in place, pricing is negotiated regularly, quantities needed are large and HACCP systems are routine. For example, at the Fulton Fish Market, another of the three markets in Hunts Point, delivery trucks must now park in a 'clean room' where they are cleaned and sanitized to keep 'bugs' at bay. Drivers and other workers wear booties and use other forms of chemical and barrier protection.

Outbreaks of foodborne illness usually come from farms where produce is harvested and packaged (as in the 2006 *E. coli* O157:H7 outbreak in Michigan schools), or beef processors (one hamburger may contain beef from hundreds of cattle, of which one animal might be ill) or food handlers (personal hygiene is the primary issue, though this problem does not get enough press). Other self-contained facilities, such as schools, hospitals, cruise ships and prisons, suffer regular outbreaks of foodborne illness. More virulent strains of salmonella poisoning, such as the Heidelberg variant found in poultry at Foster Farms that sickened more than four hundred people, need more stringent oversight. Cruise ships and norovirus outbreaks are practically synonymous today.

What does any of this have to do with 'fresh' foods? Everything. Crowding of farm animals, increasing resistance of humans to antibiotics given to factory farm animals, the time taken (long enough to get bacteria or other microorganisms to high enough levels to cause illness) to get products to market and different storage conditions – all contribute to an increased likelihood of food poisoning. As for prepared foods on a buffet, such as one might find on a cruise ship, they may have been 'fresh' when first placed on the buffet, but this quality disappears quickly if time and temperature controls are not maintained. Add to that everyone breathing over the displays and you just might lose your appetite.

Vertically integrated companies

A different example is Paradise Tomato Kitchens. As Frederick Kaufman has pointed out, Paradise supplies large pizza chains like Domino's and Pizza Hut with uniformly consistent tomato sauce for the billions of pizzas eaten annually in the US (and in Europe and Asia as well). Domino's sells more than one million pizzas per day, and Pizza Hut sold two million during the Super Bowl alone. Often, to save on fuel for transport, the processing facility is located near the farm. And tomatoes are bred to fit into the factory processing them. Should the word 'fresh' be on the jar labels, as in 'made with fresh tomatoes' rather than 'processed tomatoes'? Perhaps 'formerly raw' would work, but then again, saying 'raw tomato' in a tomato sauce might confuse people, since the tomatoes are pasteurized.

Variability – whether in shape, aroma, colour, feel or taste, one of the intrinsic characteristics of a 'fresh' fruit or vegetable – does not come into play at these companies. Vertically integrated companies sell their products to food manufacturers and processors, wholesalers and big box stores that further process them, whether by incorporating them into their own prepared foods (frozen lima beans in butter sauce or filet of sole stuffed with crabmeat), or unpacking, rewrapping and shipping processed foods (unripe papayas or frozen pancakes) to other locations. Even seemingly harmless methods are needed for large amounts of foodstuffs in storage. Icing broccoli heads delays bud softening – for a while. With bananas, ethylene gas pumped into the storage room or directly into the truck promotes ripening. Storage space and time, and transport truck and time, have both become potential food safety hazards. While HACCP plans are standard in processing plants and in the field, trucks are recent entrants into the food safety pantheon, and not everyone is on-board yet. 'Freshness' has a rather different definition in this situation. The bananas and broccoli will be weeks old before you buy them, and the use of ethylene gas to encourage ripening and ice to delay spoilage add to the complexity of the idea of 'freshness', and, by extension, food safety. If you put an apple into a paper bag with a banana, the banana will ripen faster than it otherwise would have because the apple naturally gives off more ethylene gas than does the banana. Is all this 'fresh'? Yes, although not the way it would be at a farmers market. What happens when you spray a truckload of tomatoes with ethylene because you have picked them when they are green, so they will travel well and ripen slowly on the voyage to the processor? Does the same analogy work? Not really, because the goals of the manufacturer are not the same as that of the farmer. Neither are the procedures for achieving those goals. Are Paradise's tomatoes still 'fresh' when they get to the factory? Yes and no. Again, perhaps 'unripe and as yet unprocessed' would be a more accurate description. This might work for a factory, but not for a consumer.

We need a new definition of 'fresh'.

Bibliography

Agricultural Marketing Resource Center. 'Farmers' Markets'. Agricultural Marketing Resource Center, 2015 <http://www.agmrc.org/markets__industries/food/farmers-markets>.

Booth, Michael and Jennifer Brown. *Eating Dangerously: Why the Government Can't Keep Your Food Safe… and How You Can*. Lanham, MD: Rowman and Littlefield, 2014.

Brown, Cheryl and Stacy Miller. 'The Impact of Local Markets: A Review of Research on Farmers Markets and Community Supported Agriculture (CSA)'. *American Journal Agricultural Economics* 90.5 (2008). pp. 1296–1302.

Desrochers, Pierre and Hiroko Shimizu. *The Locavore's Dilemma: In Praise of the 10,000-Mile Diet*. New York: Public Affairs, 2012.

DeVille, Nancy. *Death By Supermarket: The Fattening, Dumbing Down, and Poisoning of America*. Fort Lee, NJ: Barricade Books, 2007.

Food Inc.: A Participant Guide: How Industrial Food is Making Us Sicker, Fatter, and Poorer–And What You Can Do About It. Ed. by Karl Weber. New York: Public Affairs, 2009.

Friedman, Thomas L. 'Four Words Going Bye-Bye.' *New York Times*. 20 May 2014 <http://www.nytimes.com/2014/05/21/opinion/friedman-four-words-going-bye-bye.html> [Accessed 24 May 2014].

Gopalan, Radha. 'Sustainable Food Production and Consumption: Agenda for Action'. *Economic and Political Weekly* 36.14/15 (14–20 April 2001). pp. 1207–1225. <http://www.jstor.org/stable/4410484> [Accessed: 17 May 2014].

Hewitt, Ben. *Making Supper Safe: One Man's Quest to Learn the Truth about Food Safety*. New York: Rodale, 2011.

Kaufman, Frederick. *Bet The Farm: How Food Stopped Being Food*. Hoboken, NJ: John Wiley and Sons, 2012.

Mittal, Anuradha. 'The New Face of Agriculture: Alternative Models to Corporate Agribusiness'. *Race, Poverty and the Environment: Reclaiming our Resources: Imperialism & Environmental Justice* 11.1 (Summer 2004). pp. 71–73. <http://www.jstor.org/stable/41554437> [Accessed: 18 May 2014].

Nestle, Marion. *Food Politics*. Berkeley: U California P, 2002.

Nestle, Marion. *Safe Foods: Bacteria, Biotechnology and Bioterrorism,*. Berkeley: U California P, 2003.

Remaking the North American Food System: Strategies for Sustainability. Ed. by C. Clare Hinrichs, Thomas A. Lyson. Lincoln, NE: U Nebraska P, 2007.

United States Environmental Protection Agency. 'Labeling'. *Radiation Protection*. <http://www.epa.gov/radiation/sources/food_labeling.html> [Accessed 18 May 2014].

Campo de' Fiori in Rome and the Survival of the Outdoor Market

Elizabeth Minchilli

If there is one quintessential image that people have of food and Italy, it is the open-air market, filled with farmers hawking their apples and oranges, fishmongers slapping around sea bass and squid, and butchers hacking off huge *bistecche* to wrap up in a rough piece of brown paper to take home for the family meal. Unfortunately, these days, this image is more likely to be seen in a trip to the cinema for a Fellini revival rather than in a cobblestoned piazza. For better or (usually) worse, the open-air market that was the mainstay of shopping in Italy for hundreds of years has changed drastically in the last three decades.

One place this image still survives is Campo de' Fiori in Rome. While it is a market that many love, it is also a market that many love to hate. The market has undergone radical changes in the last thirty years, but never the less survives. This is only thriving open-air market left in the historical centre of Rome. The changes at Campo de' Fiori have affected other open-air markets throughout Italy and have resulted in many cases in their demise. What makes Campo de' Fiori different from the rest? What has it done to reinvent itself to adapt to a changing clientele, while at the same time featuring some of the best produce in Rome? The Campo de' Fiori market is often dismissed by the food community as being either too commercial, too touristy or too expensive. Even though all of this may be true, it still remains an open-air market where Romans do their daily shopping. I believe this topic begs examination as an example for the survival of other open-air markets in the centre of historic cities.

Campo de' Fiori translates into English as Field of Flowers, and today's visitors assume that the name refers to the fact that the north end of the piazza is taken over by flower stalls. The name, however, has nothing to do with this new development but is most likely a reference to the fact that until recently – a few hundred years ago – the area was an open space: a field of flowers. Like many piazzas in Rome, Campo de' Fiori was never formally planned as a square, but developed organically with the construction of palaces from the fifteenth century onward.

The area around Campo de Fiori was always commercial and many of the smaller streets in the neighbourhood take their name from various trades: *Giubbonari* (tailors) which is still predominantly filled with clothing stores; *Chiavari* (key makers); *Baullari* (chest makers) where there are still two stores selling luggage, etc. In the seventeenth century the piazza was the scene of executions, including the most famous: the burning of Giordano Bruno in 1600.

Food and Markets

The current food market dates from the latter half of the nineteenth century when, in 1869, a daily fish and vegetable market was established. It was previously held in Piazza Navona.

Throughout the late nineteenth and twentieth centuries Campo de' Fiori was a thriving market, one of the largest in the historic centre of Rome. While each of Rome's various *rioni*, or neighbourhoods, had their open markets, the one located in Campo de' Fiori was the biggest.

The big changes in the market began in the 1950s and had to do with the changing population in the historic centre of Rome. The market, up till then, had catered to a local population. The neighbourhood was densely populated and many of the warren-like apartments were home to extended families. The multi-million-euro apartments of today were then a series of one-bedroom flats that could easily have hosted families numbering up to eight to ten people and often more. The restored buildings that we see today in Rome's centre were virtual slums in the 1950s and those that could afford to move out of Rome's centre did so, to the areas that now ring the *centro storico* and were built up during the post-war boom. As the markets on the periphery of Rome began to grow, those in the centre began to fade.

One of the more recent and larger changes to affect the markets in the centre of Rome was the change over from the lire to the euro. Up until 1999 there were relatively few supermarkets in Rome. Some small Italian chains had supermarkets in the suburbs of Rome, but there was no real competition in the historic centre. This situation changed with the introduction of the euro which made it much easier for the big chains of northern Europe to move in. Not only did they open mid-sized supermarkets right in the centre of town, but they also bought up small-scale grocery stores and replaced them with mini-market stores offering not only dry goods, but also fruits and vegetables.

By this time, of course, Italian shopping habits were also changing drastically due to shifting family structures. With women entering the workforce and few extended families still under one roof, there was no longer a *nonna* at home, doing the daily shopping for the entire family. Instead, it became much more likely that the entire family would shop together on the weekends, and favour the more convenient, and certainly less expensive, supermarkets with lower prices and longer hours than the open-air markets that used to be the only option.

From 1999 onwards, then, open-air markets in the centre of Rome became a dying breed. Street markets near the Trevi Fountain, the Spanish Steps and the Colosseum grew smaller each year until they finally disappeared. And even though Campo de' Fiori still survived, it too had grown smaller and was barely holding on.

The first stalls to go were those selling meat. Then the last fish stalls finally closed. Each year there would be a few less fruit and vegetable stalls, until, about eight years ago, there was more open space in the piazza than there were stalls.

And then things started to change. New stalls began to take the place of those long since gone. There was a new vitality to the square, but unfortunately it was not the food stalls that were opening, but stalls aimed at a new breed of customer: tourists. The new stalls were easily identifiable since they stocked things like sun hats, t-shirts and other items most likely made in Asia.

At the same time an interesting thing began to develop. The fruit and vegetable stalls that had managed to survive began to adapt to the changing clientele. Most of the fruit and vegetable stalls in Campo de' Fiori today are owned and operated by the same families that have been there for generations. The most industrious of these vendors decided that to be able to continue to survive doing what they were doing, they needed to market directly not only to tourists, but to the new inhabitants of the historic centre: the wealthy.

Roman domestic real estate is among the most expensive in Europe. Apartments in the *centro storico* can be sold for up to 12,000 euros a square metre, with apartments often selling for incredible sums. As a result, vendors began to sell produce aimed at those to whom price didn't really matter. And so the best wild mushrooms, baby strawberries and hand picked wild greens began to show up. Imported lemon grass from Thailand, blue potatoes from Peru and rhubarb from England were for sale.

The fruit and vegetable stalls not only began to thrive, they expanded. One of the most industrious grew from one small space overseen by his parents to today occupying almost a quarter of the square.

The produce these stalls were selling could compete with supermarkets because it was not only of such a high quality, but also often available only at this market. Prices were high, but that didn't matter to the new and wealthy clientele.

Yet the produce vendors were still missing out on the other half of the equation: tourists. About four years ago the first 'food' stalls aimed primarily at tourists began to show up. At first selling small bags of 'Campo de' Fiori Spice Mix' the stalls soon grew to include such brightly coloured, dubious products as violin-shaped bottles of pink limoncello, anatomically-shaped multi-coloured pasta and balsamic and truffle everything – all immediately recognizable 'food' that tourists could easily take back home as edible souvenirs.

It is very easy to be disdainful of these 'food' stalls, which now take up about a third of the real estate at Campo de' Fiori. Their products are barely edible and many I suspect are not even Italian. But investigation into the ownership of these stalls provides a deeper understanding of what exactly is going on.

The stalls themselves are manned mostly by Pakistani men. But these are not the owners. The owners of these stalls are the very produce vendors who have always been there, and are still selling some of the highest quality produce in Rome. As it turns out, the stalls aimed at tourists are subsidizing the stalls that are selling produce to locals.

Today the market is not only thriving, it is so crowded that some days it is difficult to make one's way through the stalls. The open market at Campo de' Fiori has become one of the top sites in Rome to visit, ranked high on Trip Advisor. While tourists are filling up their baskets with lime green limoncello and multi-coloured pasta, locals are able to buy real food, and in fact some of the best produce in the centre of Rome. Does this example provide a sustainable solution for other cities? As both tourists and local customers begin to be willing to pay a premium for local and organic food, can we hope that the vendors will soon start catering to this market? It's unclear what the future holds for the outdoor market in Italy, but at least for the time being the vendors at Campo de' Fiori have found one solution.

Flip Dog in the Shad House: Commercial Fisheries Markets and Tavern Culture at Hadley Falls 1730–1880

Elyse Moore

In 1733, the first recorded retail purchase of thirty Connecticut River shad (*Alosa sapidissima*) for a penny apiece at Northampton, Massachusetts launched a fishery industry that continued through the industrial development of the mid-nineteenth century.[1] Commercial fisheries along the Massachusetts reach of the Connecticut during the spring migratory runs of salmon and shad supported an associated tavern culture at riverside communities that shared the river's historical moment of prosperity. By 1801, as many as fourteen fishery wharves below the Great Hadley Falls, a natural sixty-foot cataract in the river between Northampton and Springfield, landed, salted and shipped between 15,000 and 20,000 pounds of shad daily, at five to ten pence a pound. Present-day shad fisherman and author of *The Founding Fish*, John McPhee, declares that the location, known today as South Hadley Falls, was possibly the best shad-fishing location in New England.[2] Connecticut River shad were prized for their sweet flesh, and sought after at New York City's Fulton Market. Shad fisheries from Haddam to Hadley were situated in a unique locus that had the capacity, as a food source, to both sustain the local population and serve the growing Atlantic markets. The business of shad fishing complemented the seasonality of the valley agricultural rhythms, and was absorbed into the established tavern culture where the fishermen found a homely meeting place for their planning, marketing, socializing and sharing of profits.[3] One, Craft's Tavern in Ireland Parish, was home to the western Massachusetts Connecticut valley's fisheries commerce.

The Connecticut River

The Connecticut River flows in a general southerly direction, 410 miles from its source at the four Connecticut Lakes Region of Quebec and northern New Hampshire. It continues along the border between Vermont and New Hampshire, and through the western counties of Massachusetts and Connecticut, where it empties into the Long Island Sound, near the eastern tip of Long Island.[4] The surface of First Connecticut Lake is about 1,600 feet higher than the level of the Atlantic waters of the Sound. Ocean tides meet the river waters twelve miles north of Hartford, Connecticut, sixty miles from the ocean. The name originates from the French translation of the native Mohegan word, *quinni-tuk-ut*, which refers to the land 'beside the long tidal river'.[5]

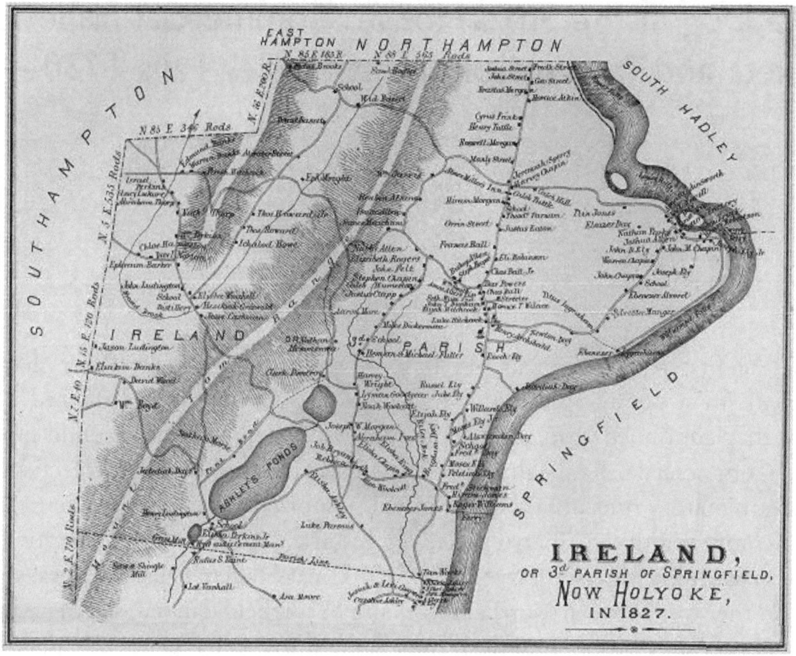

Figure 1. Connecticut River at Ireland Parish, c. 1827 (Wistariahurst Museum Archives, Holyoke Collection).

In the early seventeenth-century days of European settlement, native Pocumtucks of Deerfield were the first to negotiate arrangements to preserve and exercise tribal fishing rights. As early as 1687, the English proprietors from the eastern Massachusetts Bay Colony town of Dedham had pursued their interest to claim and settle Pocumtuck tribal lands in western Massachusetts. John Pynchon was 'empower[ed] to contract with those said Indians for the buyeing out of all their claime in the premises'.[6] A local Podunk tribal representative deeded the land to the English settlers with contingency usufruct rights to 'reserve Liberty of fishing for ye Indians in ye Rivers or waters & free Liberty to hunt Deere or other Wild creatures, & to gather Walnuts chestnuts & and other nuts things &c on ye commons'.[7]

Within twenty years, the Commonwealth of Massachusetts had exerted its own authority over the taking of inland fish. One law, dated 1709, prohibited the erection of 'wears [sic], hedges, fishgarths, stakes, kiddles, or other disturbance or incumbrance', that prevented the 'passage of fish in their seasons'.[8] In spring, salmon, shad and alewife passed from the ocean to the upper reaches of large rivers to the shallows of tributaries or ponds to cast their spawn. Hatchlings grew in the nutrient-rich river waters before making the return migration back to ocean waters for several years to grow to maturity. The spawning and migration cycles brought hundreds of thousands of food fish up the river each season, and many early settlers along its banks chose homesteads based, at least partially, on the richness of the fishing grounds.[9]

Flip Dog in the Shad House

Figure 2. Illustration in The History of Hampden County *(Springfield: Century, 1902).*

Additional inland fisheries laws also required owners and occupiers of mill-dams or other dams to allow 'sufficient water passage round, through, or over such dams for the passage of such fish or their young spawn in the season of their going down such rivers or streams on penalty of forfeiting the sum of fifty pounds for every offence'.[10] Beginning in 1812, the state legislature negotiated a long list of laws and resolutions regulating the damming of rivers to ensure the continued availability of food fish, and to prevent the destruction of fisheries on the Connecticut and other rivers throughout the Commonwealth.

The shad-fishing season

The fishing season for the migrating shad typically began between mid-April and early May. And by the third week of June, the season was over. Though most shad fall in the two- to five-pound range, the world record eleven-pound four-ounce shad was taken in at South Hadley Falls in 1986. Nineteenth-century records were more about volume and pricing than individual fish weights; the *Springfield Republican* regularly reported the size of the daily catch and fluctuations in pricing.

A bony fish, with an intricate skeletal system that often defies dressing, these 'inside-out porcupines', as they were known in the Pocumtuck tribal translation, were nonetheless prized for their sweet, rich flesh.[11] They make a delicious smoked fish – known as planked shad – so called because the dressed and butterflied fillets are nailed to soaked oaken or other hardwood planks, and arranged, cut-side out, facing an outdoor open fire, to cook slowly and allow the wood-smoke flavours to permeate the flesh.

Shad was not always considered fashionable fare. Indeed, for early settlers, eating shad was an indication that a household lacked the competence to produce enough pork for the family's annual consumption. But the people of the eastern American river valleys grew to love shad, in spite of its boniness, for its flavour and its keeping-qualities as a salt fish. And for some, the spring migration season represented a natural resource with significant entrepreneurial prospects. For a period of nearly a hundred years, before the 1849 building of the hydropower dam at South Hadley Falls, shad was the region's only commercial fishery. In the present market, shad is among those historical regional food sources enjoying a resurgence in availability and popularity. As river clean-up projects create more favourable habitats and niche markets, shad is valued as an artisanal food of primary historical relevance.[12]

In the early nineteenth century, the abundance of shad seemed inexhaustible. Every spring, massive schools of Atlantic shad would try to make their way up their natal rivers, through constructed fishways and over natural falls, including the natural thirty-foot Hadley Falls waterfall. The little hamlets of Ireland Parish and South Hadley's Canal Village, 80 miles from the Atlantic, would turn into a city of guesthouses, taverns and open-air camping to accommodate fishers on both sides of the river during the two-month fishing season.

The region's agricultural communities were accustomed to an annual spring hiatus for fishing excursions to the Great Falls to net their annual supply of fish. From April to June, people came from many miles to fish at the falls where 'the most plentiful supply could be netted'.[13] As many as 1500 horses were said to have been drawn at one time up on the river banks a day or two after the fish had begun to run. The Emerson Bates Inn at South Hadley Falls was 'filled with fishermen; and farm houses on the east and west shores alike lodged the thrifty householders who came to secure their supply of salmon or shad to salt down'.[14]

In his *History of Hadley and South Hadley Falls*, Sylvester Judd's interview with two elder statesmen of the Hadley Falls shad fishing industry has found its way into the Connecticut River historiography, lending an authentic voice to the evolving historical understanding of relationships among industrial development, natural resources and the region's social and economic traditions of agriculture and community. Joseph Ely and Justin Alvord shared details of the life of the river and its people, as much as the story of commercial fisheries. Judd recounts the Ely and Alvord story of the abundance of shad at Hadley Falls:

Shad were caught in seines below the falls and in scoop-nets on the falls. Boats were drawn to places on the rocky falls, fastened and filled with shad by scoop-nets; then taken ashore, emptied and returned. A man in this manner could take from 2000 to 3000 shad in a day, and sometimes more, with the aid of a boatman. These movements required men of some dexterity. There were some large hauls of fish at the wharves below the falls. The greatest haul known was

Figure 3. Craft's Tavern, c. 1902 (Wistariahurst Museum Archive, Holyoke Collection).

3500, according to Ely, and 3300, according to Alvord [...]. The river seemed to full of shad at times in some places, and in crossing it, the oars often struck shad. Ely and Alvord, like other old men, related that fishermen formerly took salmon from the net, and let the shad go into the river again, but not in their time; and that people in former days were ashamed to have it known that they ate shad, owing in part to the disgrace of being without pork. Alvord sold thousands of shad after the Revolution for three coppers each.[15]

By the time Judd published the *History of Hadley* in 1863, the retail price for shad had risen as high as fifty cents apiece.[16]

In addition to scoop nets, some fishermen employed the draw-seine fishing method: a net weighted at the bottom and buoyed at the top, and dragged along a section of the fishing ground to maximize the catch in areas where fish were abundant. The Ireland Parish fisheries used the Danish seine in the fishing ground below the Hadley Falls. The nets were payed out from a boat that boatmen poled around the middle of the river, describing a large oval. The captain directed the proceedings from his vantage point at the boat's stern, the apex of the operation. Seiners took their places every few feet around the 300 foot oval of fishnet, guiding its progress into the madness of a migrating school of shad, to ensure that neither the base nor the floats of the net were hung up. Nets full of fish would come ashore at the appointed wharf location, where the next group of men jumped into action, shovelling the catch into barrels. Finally, the barrels would be gutted or salted and loaded onto horse- or oxen-drawn carts, or onto flat-bottomed barges, ready for distribution.

Figure 4. Flipdog and glasses. Alice Morse Earle, Stage-coach and Tavern Days, *Macmillan and Company, 1900.*

Craft's Tavern

As in most New England fishing ports, a tavern's participation in the fisheries business on the west bank of the Connecticut River at Hadley Falls helped to create the necessary environment that allowed these small businesses to meet an expanding market beyond the three western Massachusetts counties that subsistence fishing had formerly served. While many shad-run fisherman and entrepreneurs did work independently, the Hadley Falls and Ireland Parish fisheries companies' organized approach increased their substantial profit by good planning, aggressive pursuit and a division of the strenuous labours for the duration of the short season.

The Hadley Falls fisheries companies, led by such men as Joseph Ely, Justin Alvord, Alonzo Converse, Corey Smith, Warner and Pierce and Jed Day, enlisted ten to twenty or more fishermen to their ranks to haul thousands of seine-netted shad daily. Salted and packed shad, preserved and shipped in barrels, increased their collective return, and situated Hadley Falls in a growing market. The market had grown to include wholesale and retail businesses in Boston and New York, but also the provisioning of West Indies slave colonies. The physical labour of long days in the river and on the shore, fishing, preserving and loading barrels of fish reaped more than shared profits. The fishermen found the congenial atmosphere of centrally located taverns much to their taste. They drank sweetened rum that the international fishing trade brought back on return trips from the Indies. Local inns and taverns served as the weekday meeting house for the local merchant and transportation community, where fishermen, teamsters, salesmen and travellers alike gathered to conduct business and share food and drink.

Commercial fishers in early-century Hadley Falls favoured Craft's Tavern with their patronage. A little more than a mile above the falls in Ireland Parish, the inn and tavern at the northernmost parish of West Springfield was acclaimed for its excellent food and communal pitchers of flip.[17] Chester Craft had purchased the tavern in

Flip Dog in the Shad House

1832 from its original owner, Abner Miller. Craft's Tavern was located along the main north-south stage route, midway between the more populated cities of Northampton and Springfield. The main stage route connected Hartford and Springfield with early nineteenth-century Connecticut River trading centres of Deerfield and Greenfield, and as far north as Bellows Falls, Vermont. Craft's was also the mail depot for the community and its general store, in addition to its central operation as public house, licensed victualler and stable for teamsters' horses.

Nineteenth-century historians Charles Warner and Clifton Johnson evoke the behind-the-scenes tavern culture during the late winter months at Craft's. Teamsters and stagecoach drivers from all over Hampden County pushed their wagons and coaches hard to make the hospitable tavern in the north corner of West Springfield's Ireland Parish before supper. A woman known simply as 'Aunt Patty' was the celebrated tavern cook, and owned the tavern's reputation for its delicious and plentiful food, hot biscuits and candlelight pre-dawn breakfasts.[18] Generous pitchers of hot flip wafted their rum-and-spice steam through the parlour where a bright fire welcomed tavern guests. On a chosen night in late winter, while snow still lay on the ground and ice prevented any river navigation, the committee that planned the spring shad-fishing harvest arrived to join their company.

It doesn't take much to imagine the tavern scene where, in the kitchen, Aunt Patty mixed a full measure of cream into half a dozen cracked eggs for the next batch of flip as soon as she heard the snowy stomp of the latest horse and oxen teams labour past the tavern entrance towards the stable. She would add about a pound of sugar and a bit of mixed Jamaican spice to the eggs and whip the mixture to a froth before adding a quart, more or less, of Santa Cruz rum. Then she would add three-quarters of a measure of ale from her measuring jug to the mix, and set the pitcher on the warming shelf by the hearth. Chester would come out from behind the bar and, from the glowing coals, pull out the flip dog, a sort of salamander iron used only for one purpose: the heating of the tavern's hot beverages. He'd plunge the red-hot iron into the pitcher until all was nearly boiling, and another steaming pitcher of flip would be on its way around the tables.

The hot and heady New England tavern concoction called flip was a slightly sweet, rum, ale and spice beverage heated to a caramelized froth with the wrought iron flip dog. Flip was the winter house-beverage of pretty much every tavern in the west counties, and indeed, throughout the region. The citizenry had developed a taste for it, and every publican had a special recipe. At Craft's, there were no hand-blown, etched flip glasses, featured in some of the more urban roadhouses. Each guest drank his draught straight from a stoneware pitcher.[19] The communal beverage, passed from man to man, was a tavern ritual and an ancient convention. As fishermen drank their flip, they decided who would captain the boat, who would mend the nets, who would work the nets in the water, how much salt would be needed to pickle and preserve the catch – and who would sell the flip and cigars at the shad-house.

During the fishing season, flip followed the fisheries to one shad-house where local schoolmaster Chester Chapin took an annual leave of absence from his duties at the academy, invested in a puncheon of rum and a deep supply of cheap cigars, and, with stove, pitcher and flip dog, set up a concession at a rude wooden bar in a little corner of the riverside shad-house. There Chapin took a busman's holiday, making and peddling flip and cigars to 'those who found themselves in some need of refreshment', and repeating the oft-told fishing lore of his day.[20] Commercial crops of high-quality tobacco grew in the fertile alluvial fields along the river; and the smoke of abundant, locally rolled cigars filled the air near the fisheries wharves during the fishing season.

The market

The informality of the late-winter fisheries' meetings at Craft's Tavern belied the broad reach of the bags and barrels of fresh and salt fish that were processed and embarked from the humble shad-houses of Ireland Parish and South Hadley. Local marketplaces of rural Massachusetts were first to receive their share. According to Judd, an estimated one-third of a typical river-valley household's foodstuffs came from fresh and salt fish.[21] Sole proprietors delivered to market towns throughout the valley, as far away as Williamsburg and Ashfield in the west, and Belchertown in the east. They came to the Falls on horseback with one or two sacks to fill and returned each day. In the early nineteenth century, shad sold for a penny a piece. As dams were built across the river in the late eighteenth century, the 'number of shad diminished, and […] increased the value to six to nine pence and then a shilling'.[22] By 1850, the prices had risen to forty pence per shad, and men had ceased to purchase a barrel of salt shad for their families' summer use.[23] By the 1880s, the price had reached twenty cents a pound for shad – no longer sold by the piece.

Flat-bottomed river barges and steamships, loaded with the bulk of the catch, embarked from South Hadley Falls and headed south through the Enfield locks and canals, toward Hartford and the deep-water ports near the mouth of the river. There the catch would be transferred to sloops (and later the railways) that provisioned the wholesale fish markets at the coastal cities of Boston and New York. As early as 1736, Connecticut River shad was being sold in Boston. At that time, shipping by sloop was the preferred method of transport. New York *Market Book* and *Market Assistant* author, Thomas DeVoe, praised Connecticut River shad as the best, 'known by their superior size, length, square-shaped back […] a fatter fish'.[24] New York's Delmonico's Restaurant featured an almond oil-roasted Connecticut River shad, served with shad roe croquettes and a ravigote sauce.[25] Properly dressed prepared shad and the roe from the migrating females were (and are still) a spring delicacy. Shad sold at New York retail markets in the 1850s for twenty-five cents a pound.

A report from the 1801 *Morse's Geography* claimed one company's net profit for the season's catch was $4800. By this time, shad prices had risen from the long-held price of a penny a piece to six to eight pence. By 1840, rail service to the Connecticut valley

Flip Dog in the Shad House

opened up commerce to the New York market where shad sold for ten to twenty cents apiece. A fish seller in 1847 could earn as much as ten dollars a day, or the modern equivalent of about $2500. Warner and Johnson characterized the shad fishery as a 'mine of wealth' in the old village days, before the dam, and 'he was a lucky man who owned a share in it'.[26] But the railways that brought Connecticut River shad to the New York market also created the infrastructure improvements that attracted industrial development.

By 1847, the *Hampden Freeman* reported that a salesman named George C. Ewing, from the Fairbanks Scale & Company of St Johnsbury, Vermont had organized a group of Boston venture capitalists and obtained a charter from the Massachusetts Legislature in the winter of 1847–1848 under the relicensed Hadley Falls Company. The company's plan was to build a dam across the Connecticut River, between Ireland Parish and South Hadley Falls village on the east. Ewing was appointed as land agent for the Hadley Falls Company, and began the task of acquiring riverfront farmland on the Ireland Parish flats. The newly formed development company also purchased the land and business of the Locks and Canal works in South Hadley that had been facilitating passage of riverboat traffic since 1796. The Hadley Falls Company, backed by Boston investors, secured the water rights with the purchase of a total of 1,100 acres on both sides of the river in 1848, and immediately began the design and building of the largest dam in the country. After a failed initial effort that sent $40,000 worth of timber and building materials down the river in a spectacular disaster, a second dam was successfully completed in 1849. The commercial fisheries market did not survive the river's transformation.

In 1866, in what may be regarded as the last nineteenth-century attempt to restore food fish to river, then-governor John Andrew of Massachusetts appointed fisheries biologist and Harvard environmentalist Theodore Lyman to the newly formed state Commission of Inland Fisheries. Under Lyman's stewardship, first as secretary and then as director, Massachusetts enforced long-standing laws that required dam owners to build and maintain fishways to prevent any obstruction from inhibiting the passage of migrating fish in the Connecticut.[27] The response of the growing Connecticut valley capitalist lobby was to promote the repeal of laws that affected uninterrupted use of water diverted for industrial power, to ignore legislation, and to pay the fines. As Boston Associates pushed the dam and canal system forward to support the building of industrial manufacturing on the hayfields of Ireland Parish in the newly chartered city of Holyoke, city planners pushed for the continuous use of Connecticut River waterpower.[28] A few fish, they said, were not sufficient to stall the progress. The best intentions and spirit of pre-environmentalist legislation failed to protect the fisheries.

Yet, this legislative forum proved to be the beginning of the long-term responsibility for preservation and sustainable access to the Connecticut River fisheries. The pre-industrial riverine culture that dominated the spring economy between winter and summer agricultural pursuits has re-emerged in the artisanal markets and festivals that support the restoration of the American shad to the river. Though neither shad nor rum would be completely eradicated from the markets along the river, and though the surge of hydro-powered paper and cloth manufacture in the city of Holyoke usurped the primary character of commercial fisheries, the history of generations-old ties between food and drink that shaped life along the Connecticut River remains part of the rich history of Connecticut valley foodways. Craft's Tavern and the foodways that it sustained help us to understand the emergence and development of Atlantic world fisheries in the inland food system, of local and sustainable food resources, and something about the cultural relationships that help food markets to expand and thrive. Without those cooperative meetings and discussions held at Craft's Tavern by the fishermen of Hadley Falls, the uniquely American story of shad would be a very different tale.

Figure 5. Hound-handle stoneware pitcher. Alice Morse Earle, Stage-coach and Tavern Days, *Macmillan and Company, 1900.*

Flip

Keep grated Ginger and Nutmeg with a fine dried Lemon Peel rubbed together in a Mortar. To make a quart of Flip: Put the Ale on the Fire to warm, and beat up three or four Eggs with four ounces of moist Sugar, a teaspoonful of grated Nutmeg or Ginger, and a Quartern of good old Rum or Brandy. When the Ale is near to boil, put it into one pitcher, and the Rum and Eggs, etc., into another: turn it from one Pitcher to another till it is as smooth as cream. To heat plunge in the red hot Loggerhead or Poker. This quantity is styled One Yard of Flannel.[29]

Flip Dog in the Shad House

Notes

1. Sylvester Judd, Lucius Manlius Boltwood and George Sheldon. *History of Hadley, Including the Early History of Hatfield, South Hadley, Amherst and Granby, Massachusetts, by Sylvester Judd...also Family Genealogies by Lucius M. Boltwood* (Northampton: Metcalf and Company, 1863), p. 314.
2. John A. McPhee, *The Founding Fish* (New York: Farrar, Straus and Giroux, 2002), p. 25.
3. John T. Cumbler, *Reasonable Use: The People, the Environment, and the State: New England 1790–1930* (Cary, NC: Oxford UP, 2001), p. 13.
4. Connecticut River Watershed Council (CRWC), 'Watershed Facts' http://www.ctriver.org/river-resources/about-our-rivers/watershed-facts/> [accessed 1 May 2014].
5. W. DeLoss Love, 'The Navigation of the Connecticut River', *Proceedings of the American Antiquarian Society*. Oct 1903, Vol. 15 Issue 3, pp. 385–441 (p. 387).
6. Harry Andrew Wright, *Indian Deeds* (Pocumtuck Valley Memorial Association), pp. 61–62 qtd. in Margaret M. Bruchac, 'Revisiting Pocumtuck History in Deerfield: George Sheldon's Vanishing Indian Act', *Historical Journal of Massachusetts* 1–2 (2011), p. 30.
7. Wright qtd in Bruchac, p. 30.
8. Massachusetts, *A Collection of the Laws of Massachusetts Relating to Inland Fisheries, 1623–1886*, ed. by Secretary of the Commonwealth (Boston: Wright & Potter Printing Co., 1887), pp. 7–8.
9. Josiah Gilbert Holland, 'Holyoke', *History of Western Massachusetts*, Vol. II (Springfield, Mass.: Samuel Bowles and Company, 1855), pp. 70–77; Judd, *History*, p. 305; *A History of Hampden County Massachusetts*, ed. by Alfred Minot Copeland, Vol. One (Springfield, MA: Century Memorial Publishing Company, 1902), p. 94.
10. Massachusetts, p. 10.
11. 'American Shad', *The Ark of Taste*, Slow Food USA, 2014 <http://www.slowfoodusa.org/ark-item/american-shad> [accessed 8 April 2014].
12. Atlantic States Marine Fisheries Commission, 'Connecticut River American Shad Sustainable Fishing Plan' (2012), p. 1.
13. Constance McLaughlin Green, *Holyoke, Massachusetts: A Case History of the Industrial Revolution in America* (New Haven CT: Yale UP, 1939), p. 10.
14. Judd qtd. in Green, p. 11.
15. Judd, p. 308.
16. Judd, p. 308.
17. Charles Forbes Warner and Clifton Johnson, *Picturesque Hampden: 1500 Illustrations* (Northampton, MA: Picturesque Publishing Company, 1892), p. 9.
18. Warner and Johnson, 9.
19. Warner and Johnson, 7.
20. Warner and Johnson, 10.
21. Sylvester Judd Manuscript, Forbes Library. Northampton, Mass., 'Hadley'.
22. Judd, p. 307.
23. Judd, p. 307.
24. Thomas DeVoe, *The Market Assistant, Containing a Brief Description of Every Article of Human Food Sold in the Public Markets of the Cities of New York, Boston, Philadelphia, and Brooklyn* (New York: n.p., 1867), p. 201.
25. Charles Ranhofer, *The Epicurean* (New York: C Ranhofer, 1894), p. 458.
26. Warner and Johnson, p. 16.
27. Massachusetts, p. 238, sect. 8.
28. John T. Cumbler, 'The Early Making of an Environmental Consciousness: Fish, Fisheries Commissions and the Connecticut River', *Environmental History Review* 4 (1991), p. 73.
29. Alice Morse Earl, *Stage-coach and Tavern Days* (New York: Macmillan and Company, 1900), p. 111.

'From Nothing Came Something': Wild Food and its Markets in Industrializing England

Jeanette Neeson

24 July 1782 'Whortle-berries ripen.'
27 June 1788 'Met a cart of whortel-berries on the road.'
13 July 1792 'Whortle-berries are offered at the door.'[1]

The abundance of wild food plants found in eighteenth- and early nineteenth-century English markets is almost too rich to imagine. Sea kale gathered from English beaches supplied the tables of the south and south-west. Bath asparagus travelled to markets in Bath and Bristol from copses and banks across Somerset, Gloucestershire and Wiltshire. Cranberry bogs served the markets of north Lincolnshire and its neighbours. Whortleberries, cranberries and cowberries appeared in Manchester markets. Even in London, nettles and watercress became soups and salads, spring tonics and tea. And across the length and breadth of the country wild-gathered foods such as these, and many more, were sold in markets.

These markets were both urban and rural but they did not always take the shape of designated and regulated physical spaces – market*places*. Often markets in wild foods, particularly in those that were most perishable, were local, even door to door. In villages the sellers were those who had gathered the produce, often women and children, servants, young men and women.[2] Or they were specialists like the trufflers described by Gilbert White ('Two *truflers* came with their dogs to hunt our hangers, & beechen woods in search of truffles.'[3]). Sometimes they gathered to order: when Earl Fitzwilliam wanted his favourite mushroom ketchup in September 1705 he sent word to his steward in Northamptonshire: 'I forgot in my last to say that my wife and I wished Mrs Pendleton to pickle up for us as many mushrooms as she can get, if it's a right season to do them in, and likewise to pickel a great many cucumbers which either Mrs Pendleton or Mrs Bull may do, but for the mushrooms we depend upon Mrs Pendleton.'[4]

Buyers were usually neighbours, local farmers, the gentry – people whose custom could be relied upon from season to season. In these circumstances intermediaries in the form of retailers were few; instead, markets in wild foods occurred in every transfer or exchange that took place between households. Even offering gifts of wild food could imply a market since few gifts, particularly of food, required no return, or implied no obligation.[5]

So what were these foods and what happened to them in the century of England's industrialization and urbanization? Evidence from the authors of eighteenth- and nineteenth-century natural histories, journals, floras, herbals, receipt books and *Reports* to the Board of Agriculture suggests that the sale of berries, mushrooms, wild greens and nuts flourished into the late eighteenth century but declined thereafter. Consider, for example, the three wild fruits brought most often to Gilbert White in the Hampshire village of Selborne in the later eighteenth century: whortleberries, cranberries and wood strawberries.[6]

Whortleberries or bilberries: (blaeberries, hurtleberries, whinberries)[7]

White noted the whortleberry season in his journals three times: in July 1782 as they ripened, in June 1788 when he met a cart of them on the road, and in July 1792 when they were offered at his door.[8] None of this was particular to White or to Selborne, many other writers described the gathering, selling and eating of whortleberries (aka bilberries) across England from East Anglia through the Midlands to the West Country, and from the southern heaths to the highlands of Scotland. In many counties they had their own local names.[9] In the West Country 'whorts' were common enough to require their own verb: to gather whortleberries was to be 'out a whorting' or to 'go a whorting'.[10] In late seventeenth-century Staffordshire the diarist Celia Fiennes described the bilberry harvest in Sir Charles Wolseley's park near Tamworth as an unbreakable custom:

> its a Large parke 6 miles round full of stately woods and replenish'd wth red and fallow deer, one part of it is pretty full of Billberryes wch thrives under ye shade of ye oakes, its a black berry as big as a large pea and are Ripe about Harvest. There is a very ill Custome amongst them, now not to be broken, when they are ripe. The Country Comes and makes Boothes and a sort of faire ye outside of ye parke and so gather ye berries and sell ym about ye Country.[11]

In Nottinghamshire a few decades later the physician-botanist Charles Deering saw them on Nottingham Lings where gorse gatherers grubbed them up before they could ripen, but there was a 'great Plenty of them in my Lord Biron's Park at Newstead, eight miles from Nottingham'. Ripe in June, the berries had 'a pleasant Tartness and are very cooling'.[12] There were still more of them in Sherwood Forest, as there were in other woodlands in other counties.[13] Philip Miller in *The Gardener's Dictionary* distinguished northern bilberries from southern whortleberries and thought that both grew best in 'never cultivated' places, not gardens, thus the 'poor inhabitants' of both regions gathered and sold them 'in the Markets for Tarts etc.'[14] Half a century later, in the 1780s, Charles Bryant also saw them gathered and carried to market for sale to be eaten in tarts 'and other devices' or 'raw with cream and sugar'.[15]

In the 1700s, then, these berries grew in almost every British and Irish county.[16] But in the 1790s William Withering offers evidence of a change: he says that in the Midlands both children and game liked them. He describes no other markets there.[17]

In the following decades whortleberries probably fell victim to the combined forces of a number of things: expanded game-keeping (which increased competition for their consumption and discouraged access), intensified furze-gathering and burning (which destroyed their wires), heath-land development or the end of bracken-cutting (which reduced their habitat) and the availability of imported cranberries (which took their place in larger markets).[18] They did not disappear, but they survived best where heaths survived too – in parts of the West Country, the north, Scotland, Staffordshire, Surrey – and they survived there as a regional speciality, no longer a widely available national commodity.[19] So they appeared at Manchester markets in the 1850s, and a century later Dorothy Hartley noted the rights that apportioned access to villagers and gypsies on northern moors.[20] But Charles Johnson, writing in 1862, described their decline in the south. They no longer came to London from the Surrey heaths. They were found, he said, 'in some heathy districts' where they were eaten by the locals. Everyone else now ate imported Baltic cranberries.[21] In the twentieth century, Henslow and Hall found whortleberries sold in the north, where Hall described them as 'a delicacy for some'; Geoffrey Grigson noted their use in Ireland and Scotland but not England and Richard Mabey describes their consumption in the West Country.[22] Even in the north burning the moorland to prepare grazing for sheep and grouse reduced the bilberry crop after 1800.[23]

Cranberries[24]

The boggy equivalents of the heath-loving whortleberries were the indigenous cranberries – the 'moss berries' of the northern moors and 'fen berries' of the Norfolk and Lincolnshire fens. They grew on wet lowland as well as upland, including the mires of Woolmer Forest, from which women occasionally brought berries to White's door, often unripe.[25] Charles Bryant said he preferred them to bilberries. They were 'collected in large quantities by the country people, who carry them to market-towns for sale'. Like whortleberries they were turned 'into tarts, or eaten raw with cream and sugar', but when dried and bottled they could be kept from year to year.[26]

East Anglian fenlanders may have learned the skill of harvesting their wild cranberries early in the eighteenth century from growers further north.[27] In Cumberland two to four thousand pecks found their way to the market at Longtown for five or six weeks every season and from there they travelled to London.[28] By 1813 Arthur Young thought the cranberries growing on Lincolnshire's common East Fen supplied all the adjacent counties. They were 'so plentiful' he wrote 'that one man has got nine score pecks in a season'.[29] Sir Joseph Banks rowed Young across the East Fen to see how he had made his own cranberry bog; Banks, being Banks, grew a new variety: '*V. macrocarpa*' – the American cranberry.[30]

Cultivable (in some varieties) and valuable enough in the north to be listed in some farm leases, it would be wrong to think that cranberries were either wholly wild or always free for the taking, or that they were eaten only by humans – birds ate cranberries too, and so did cows.³¹ But they were a substantial crop growing on fens, marshes and common wastes across the country and, like whortleberries, they began to disappear from markets in the early nineteenth century. In 1814, George Walker illustrated his *Costume of Yorkshire* with a 'Cranberry Girl', whose moor-gathered fruit was superior, he thought, to all imports: 'The oxycoccus or cranberry, is well known as a species of vaccinium, and grows plentifully upon the moors in the north of England. For many years it has been held in such estimation for pastry, [sic] that it is regularly brought to market like other fruit.' But he went on to say that 'Cranberries of larger size and more beautiful appearance are imported from Russia and America, but their flavour is much inferior to those grown in England'.³²

In the United States the commercial management of cranberry bogs began early in the nineteenth century and imports of American cranberries into Europe followed soon after.³³ By the 1830s enclosure and drainage in Lincolnshire had brought cranberry sales there to an end: 'Not long since', George Don wrote in 1834, 'cranberries from Lincolnshire and the north west corner of Norfolk were sold in the streets of Norwich by cart-loads; but the extensive enclosures in many parts have destroyed and drained their native bogs.'³⁴

At mid-century Johnson noted that the country people gathered the berries 'in considerable quantities' in the north, and in the mountain bogs of South Wales, but elsewhere 'modern agricultural improvements' had 'banished the Cranberry'. Londoners bought the more abundant and prolific Baltic cranberries instead. For commercial purposes, and for garden cultivation, Johnson recommended the American cranberry *V. macrocarpa* which he had seen growing in Flintshire – the variety that Banks had grown in the Lincolnshire fens half a century earlier.³⁵

The twentieth-century history of cranberry gathering is one of local survival and national decline: in 1917 Cameron located the indigenous cranberry on the border between England and Scotland, in 1939 Hill thought it was rare and in 1981 Mary Briggs wrote that gathering and selling Sussex cranberries had come to an end within living memory.³⁶ Today the mires of White's Woolmer Forest and nearby Shortheath Common (protected as an SSRI) shelter the largest colonies of *V. oxycoccus* in southern England.³⁷

Wood strawberries³⁸

The relatively fragile wood strawberries probably travelled less far from home than cranberries and whortleberries, which is perhaps why Joseph Miller saw them more often 'at the Table than in the Shops'.³⁹ Nevertheless, in 1790 James Sowerby thought that 'most woods and thickets produce them', and in Gloucestershire he ate them for dessert 'gathered out of the woods' every day.⁴⁰ In Selborne it was the children who brought them to White's door, where they received a warm welcome, for White mentioned this berry more often than any other.⁴¹ Every year he looked forward to 'Strawberry time', watched the crop ripen, and recorded its quality and quantity. Although hawkers sold several cultivated varieties of strawberry in Selborne, and White grew his own garden 'Scarlets', they were only a pleasant alternative to the wild fruit; they did not take its place. This taste for the wood strawberry was not unusual. Throughout the eighteenth century, and well into the nineteenth, writers prized it for its flavour and for its health-giving properties. It was wholesome, familiar and increasingly cherished as the most English of wild berries.[42]

In Selborne the crop was regular but it was not always plentiful. In 1785 White mourned 'not one mess of wood strawberries brought this year'. But the crop was better in 1787, and in the late '80s and early '90s the recently cleared parts of the beech hanger were a prolific source of supply. White thought that regular felling would ensure that this continued; and he described how good strawberry locations were named, remembered and anticipated:

> When old beech-trees are cleared away, the naked ground in a year or two becomes covered with straw-berry plants, the seed of which must have lain in the ground for an age at least. One of the *slidders* or trenches down the middle of the hanger, close covered over with lofty beeches near a century old, is still called *strawberry slidder*, though no strawberries have grown there in the memory of man. That sort of fruit, no doubt, did once abound there, & will again when the obstruction is removed.[43]

In 1790, the first year after the trees were felled, the supply was 'prodigious' and lasted six weeks. In 1791 there were enough wild strawberries to make jam.[44]

While White noted the supplies of wild strawberries he also noticed the growing sales of new American varieties of cultivated strawberry. His own Scarlets and the indigenous Hautboy were superior, but threatened.[45] So too was the supply of wild strawberries. The enclosure of woods made getting them more difficult, as did the employment of more gamekeepers and the increase of game.[46] The new enclosures of fields with double hawthorn hedges may have offered new supplies because strawberries liked the rough ground of the spaces in-between.[47] But access to these new spaces may have been difficult: no farmer wanted his new-planted hedges broken. In these circumstances farm servants may have taken the place of local children as gatherers, at best.[48]

Conclusion

The decline of markets in wild food is no surprise. We don't need the evidence set out here to know that people in the past bought wild-gathered foods and that they no longer do this to any comparable extent. What we don't know is when this change occurred, why it happened, and what it meant. Readers of autobiographical memoirs and other histories of village life of the late Victorian or Edwardian period might well conclude that eating wild food was as normal then as ever before. But the evidence presented here suggests that the gatherings they describe were survivals from the past, not the seasonal, regional and national norm they once were.[49]

The indigenous wild component of urban diets in early nineteenth-century England may have declined first.[50] At the same time formerly national markets became regional. Rural communities may have continued to enjoy and exchange a greater variety of resources but even in the countryside fewer wild plant foods were gathered and sold than before: even rural families could not escape the domestication of the food they ate. In 1862 Johnson regretted the ignorance of wild greens shared by poor town and rural populations alike, and rejoiced in the recent cultivation of watercress which provided an alternative for town dwellers.[51]

So the end of gathering wild food has a history as particular as any other. In England between the eighteenth and the mid-nineteenth century industrialization, urbanization, agricultural 'improvement' and the development of game-keeping all reduced the extent of land over which gathering took place; and imports or domesticated plants took the place of some indigenous wild berries. At the same time notions of land ownership also changed, reducing the access of children, women and gypsies to the remaining uncultivated space.[52]

To assess the loss we need to know what gathering meant in the first place. Perhaps some of its significance lay in the social relationships it may have enabled. As these relationships grew they may have reduced the social distance that often accompanied wage labour, unemployment and poor relief. This should be seen in the context of other social mediators, particularly shared access to commons for grazing or fuel, and the right to glean.[53] Like them, the sale of wild foods reduced a woman or a child's dependence on a husband or a father's wage. But *more* than access to grazing, fuel or gleaning, the ability to gather and sell wild foods to neighbours of higher social status could build mutuality, even a sense of reciprocal obligation.[54] When the gatherers were children who would grow to adulthood in the same village their early gathering may have established a continuing connection. In short, these markets in wild food may have been more than a way to make a living in a world in which waged work was becoming hard to find; they may have offered sociability too.

The exchange of goods is a central part of all social relations. The exchange of food may be the most significant of all these exchanges. Understanding this allows us to see 'markets' in food as social spaces in which the exchange of goods is more than economic. Instead these markets define and sometimes strengthen human relationships. When the goods exchanged include foods gathered for nothing save the cost of the time spent gathering then 'from nothing came something': the market for edible wild plants empowered those who often had nothing else to sell.

Notes

1. *Journals of Gilbert White*, ed. Walter Johnson (London: Routledge & Sons, 1931; rpt. Cambridge, MA: MIT Press, 1971), pp. 209, 311, 408 (hereafter *Journals*); also see pp. 106,189.
2. E.g. *Journals*, 15 August 1784: 'Women bring cran-berries, but they are not ripe'; July 28 1790: 'Children gather strawberries every morning from the hanger where the tall beeches were felled in winter 1788'; 22 July 1791: 'Children bring wood-strawberries in great plenty'; though men hunted truffles and brought mushrooms to White's door on 15 April 1791: 'A man brought me half a dozen good mushrooms from a pasture field! a great rarity at this season of the year!'
3. *Journals*, 23 October 1783.
4. Northamptonshire Archives Office: Fitzwilliam (Milton) Correspondence: letter 389 F(M)C 1416, London, 1 Sept. 1705. Also Fitzwilliam to Guybon F(M)C 1007, London, 19 August 1697: 'My wife hopes Mrs Bull has taken up her bees before this; if not, she desires it may be done out of hand and wishes Mrs Pendleton to pickle her some mushrooms, at least a peck.' For wild mushrooms in mushroom ketchup and pickle see Elizabeth Hirst [& others], Medical and Cookery Receipts 1684- [c. 1725], Wellcome Institute for the History of Medicine Library Western Manuscript 2840.01, pp. 142, 156. On gathering to order see J. Oakes and M.P. Morris, 'The West Indian Weedwoman of the United States Virgin Islands', *Bulletin of the History of Medicine* 32 (1958), p. 164.
5. Gareth Stedman Jones, *Outcast London: A Study in the Relationship between Classes in Victorian Society*, rev. edn. (London: Oxford UP, 1992), p. 251.
6. Other edible wild-gathered fruits in the sources consulted were blackberries, sloes, bullaces, medlars, juniper berries, raspberries, elderberries, crab apples, cherries, red and black currants, gooseberries, barberries.
7. Philip Miller, '*Vitis Idaea*: The Bilberry or Whortleberry-bush', *The Gardener's Dictionary Containing the Methods of Cultivating and Improving the Kitchen, Fruit and Flower Garden. As Also, the Physick Garden, Wilderness, Conservatory, and Vineyard Wild Foods of Britain* (Dublin: S. Powell, 1732); Geoffrey Grigson, *Vaccinium myrtillus L* (vice-counties: 102, H 40), *The Englishman's Flora* (London: J.M. Dent & Sons, 1955; repr. 1987); '*V. myrtillus*', *The Oxford Companion to Food*, ed. by Alan Davidson (Oxford: Oxford UP, 1999).
8. *Journals*, 24 July 1782; 27 June 1788; 13 July 1792.
9. Grigson lists local names in 22 English counties (p. 262).
10. Francis Grose, *A Provincial Glossary; with a Collection of Local Proverbs, and Popular Superstitions*, 2nd edn. (London: S. Hooper, 1790); William Holloway, *A General Dictionary of Provincialisms Written with a View to Rescue from Oblivion the Fast Fading Relics of By-Gone Days*, 2 vols (Lewes: Baxter & Son., 1839).
11. Celia Fiennes, *Through England on a Side Saddle: In the Time of William and Mary* (Cambridge: Cambridge UP, 2010), p. 136; on Cannock Chase, see William Pitt, *General View of the Agriculture of the County of Stafford* (London: T. Wright, 1796), p. 215.
12. G.C. Deering, *Catalogus Stirpium…or, A Catalogue of Plants Naturally Growing…about Nottingham* (Nottingham: George Ayscough, 1738), p. 229.
13. Ben Cowell, 'Parks, Plebs and the Picturesque: Sherwood Forest as a Contested Landscape in Later Georgian England, 1770–1830', *Forest History. International Studies in Socio-Economic and Forest Ecosystem Change. Report No. 2 of the IUFRO Taskforce on Environmental Change*, ed. M. Agnoletti and S. Anderson (CABI Publishing: 2000), p. 201; Brian Waters, *The Forest of Dean* (London: J.M. Dent & Sons, 1951), p. 98.
14. Miller, 'Vitis Idaea: The Bilberry or Whortleberry-bush'; the nurseryman James Gordon agreed that cranberries, bilberries and whortleberries would not grow in gardens, although he had cultivated the American cranberry *V. macrocarpa* in 1760 (*The Planters', Florists', and Gardeners' Pocket Dictionary* (Edinburgh: printed for the author, 1774), p. 37); Lady Charlotte Murray, *The British Garden. A Descriptive Catalogue of Hardy Plants, Indigenous, or Cultivated in the Climate of Great-Britain*, vol. 1 (Bath and London, [1799]), p. 312). However in 1748 Peter Kalm noted that 'Mr Collinson of Peckham,

London' had raised *V. oxycoccus* 'in a damp and mossy pot' (*Kalm's Account of his Visit to England on His Way to America in 1748* (London and New York: 1892), p. 68). In 1800 seeds of the 'Great wortleberry' (and the common and American cranberry) could be bought (Russell, Russell and Willmott, *A Catalogue of Garden, Grass and Flower Seeds, Trees, Shrubs, Herbaceous, Green-House and Hot-House Plants, sold by Russell, Russell, & Willmott* (London: T. Plummer, 1800), p. 20). In the same year all three plants grew in the Dublin Botanic Garden (Royal Dublin Society, *Catalogue of Plants, &c. &c. in the Dublin Society's Botanic Garden, at Glasnevin* (Dublin: Graisberry & Campbell, 1800–01), p. 17).

15. Charles Bryant, *Flora Dietetica: or, History of Esculent Plants, Both Domestic and Foreign* (London: B. White, 1783), p. 173.
16. Grigson, pp. 262, 20: in the1950s the vice-county distribution was 102, H40.
17. William Withering, *An Arrangement of British Plants*, 3rd edn., vol. 2 (Birmingham: printed for the author, 1796), p. 370.
18. For the ubiquity of black grouse and appetite for whorts, see C[harles] Pierpoint Johnson, *The Useful Plants of Great Britain: A Treatise upon the Principal Native Vegetables Capable of Application as Food, Medicine, or in the Arts and Manufactures. Illustrated by John E. Sowerby* (London: W. Kent, 1862), p. 163; for moor game, see Witherin, p. 370 and L.C.R. Cameron, *The Wild Foods of Great Britain: Where to Find Them and How to Cook Them* (London: George Routledge & Sons, 1917), p. 5. For development, see Alan Everitt, 'Common land', *The English Rural Landscape*, ed. by Joan Thirsk (Oxford: Oxford UP, 2000), p. 223; N. Symes and J. Day, *A Practical Guide to the Restoration and Management of Lowland Heathland* (London: RSPB, 2003), pp. 15–19; James Parry, *Living Landscapes. Heathland* (London: The National Trust, 2003), pp. 49–53; Laurie Forsyth, 'Tiptree Heath. Its History and Natural History', *Essex Naturalist* 3 (London: Essex Field Club Publications, 1978), pp. 6–7, 12. For bracken, see Symes and Day, p. 215. On furze-burning, see Johnson, pp. 68–69; Nigel Webb, *Heathlands* (London: Collins, 1986), pp. 47–8. For imports, see George Walker, *The Costume of Yorkshire Illustrated by a Series of Forty Engravings, being Facsimiles of Original Drawings with Descriptions in English and French* (Leeds: Robinson & Son, 1814), 'Cranberry Girl' and Johnson, p. 163.
19. Anne Pratt, *The Flowering Plants, Grasses, Sedges, and Ferns of Great Britain, and Their Allies the Club Mosses, Pepperworts and Horsetails*, vol. 3 (London: F. Warne & Co., 1873); G. Henslow, *The Uses of British Plants. Traced from Antiquity to the Present Day. Together with the Derivation of their Names* (London: Lovell Reeve & Co. Ltd, 1905), p. 110; Jason Hill, *Wild Foods of Britain* (London: A & C. Black, 1939), p. 43; Dorothy Hartley, *Food in England* (London: Macdonald & Co., 1954), pp. 429–30; Richard Mabey, *Flora Britannica* (London: Sinclair-Stevenson, 1996), pp. 162–63.
20. Leo Hartley Grindon, *Grindon's Manchester Flora* (London: William White, 1859); Hartley, pp. 429–30.
21. Johnson, p. 163.
22. Henslow; Rev. Charles Hall, *Wild Flowers in their Haunts* (London: W.H. and L. Collingridge, Ltd, [n.d 1914–18]), p. 74; Grigson; Mabey, pp. 162–3.
23. Oliver Rackham, *The History of the Countryside* (London: J.M. Dent & Sons, 1986), p. 321.
24. Grigson, p. 262: Cranberry (*Oxycoccus palustris* Pers.): Vice-counties 76, H 34. For *Vaccinium oxycoccus*, see also William Arnold Bromfield, *Flora Vectensis being a Systematic Description of the Phænogamous or Flowering Plants and Ferns Indigenous to the Isle of Wight* (London: William Pamplin, 1856); Johnson and Pratt; and *V. oxycoccus* and *V. vitis idaea* in Davidson. Currently *V. oxycoccos* (*Online Atlas of the British and Irish Flora*). Gilbert White, *The Natural History of Selborne* (London: Thomas Bensley, 1789; repr. London: Penguin Books, 1977), p. 211: '*Vaccinium oxycoccus*, creeping bilberries, or cranberries – in the bogs of *Bin's-pond*; *Vaccinium myrtillus*, whorts or bleaberries, – on the dry hillocks of *Woolmer-Forest*'. For cranberries confused with whortleberries at James Hillard's trial, see *Old Bailey Proceedings Online* 21 Sept. 1846 (t18460921-1863).
25. *Journals*: 17 August 1782; 15 August 1784; 9 July 1788; 25 July 1789; Parry, p. 91.
26. Bryant, p. 174. Also Jane Grigson, *Jane Grigson's Fruit Book* (New York: Atheneum, 1982), pp. 140-41.
27. Arthur Young, *General View of the Agriculture of the County of Lincolnshire* (London: G. Nicol, 1813;

repr. New York: Augustus M.Kelley, 1970), p. 263; Trevor Bevis, *Wide Horizons. Hard Graft for Old-Time Fenmen* (March, Cambridgeshire: the author, [1994]). The degree to which the cranberries were transplants is moot: 'A principal part of the East Fen which appertained to this parish of Friskney was denominated the Mossberry or Cranberry Fen from the quantities of cranberries which grew upon it in its wild and uncultivated state' (Edmund Oldfield, *A Topographical and Historical Account of Wainfleet and the Wapentake of Candleshoe, in the County of Lincoln* (London: Longman, Reese, Orme, Brown, Greer etc., 1829), p. 55).

28. John Lightfoot, *Flora Scotica or, a Systematic Arrangement, in the Linnaean Method, of the Native Plants of Scotland and the Hebrides* (London: B. White, 1777), p. 203; Thomas Pennant, *A Tour in Scotland, and Voyage to the Hebrides* (Chester: John Monk, 1774 ed.), p. 93.
29. Young, p. 263. A peck is a unit of dry volume: if cranberries and tomatoes share a similar volumetric weight a peck of cranberries would weigh about thirteen pounds. Thus two to four thousand pecks would amount to thirteen to twenty-six tons.
30. Don, p. 858. Now *V. macrocarpon*. Mabey, p. 164.
31. Cumbria Record Office, Kendal: Wilson of Dallam Tower, Milnthorpe: WD D/D 6/65 (1780-1843): farm leases at Foulshaw include peats and cranberries, see White, p. 208; on their vulnerability to moor-grouse, see John Aikin, *A Description of the Country from Thirty to Forty Miles Round Manchester* (London: Stockdale, 1794), p. 474.
32. Walker, p. 33.
33. *V. macrocarpa* was domesticated earlier; it was raised in Lincolnshire c. 1813 (above); and in the US c. 1816: Miro Cernetig, *Toronto Globe and Mail* 13 October 1997, p. A2; and Cape Cod Cranberry Growers Association <http://cranberries.org>.
34. George Don, *A General System of Gardening and Botany. Founded upon Miller's Gardener's and Botanist's Dictionary*, vol 3 (London: C. J. G. & F. Rivington, 1834), p. 858.
35. Johnson, pp. 164–65; Don, vol. 3, p. 858. Miller thought domestication impossible but in 1748 Pehr Kalm noted that Mr Collinson of Peckham had raised *V. oxycoccus* 'in a damp and mossy pot' (p. 68); both it and the 'Great Whortleberry' were listed for sale in Russell, Russell, & Willmott, p. 20. Pratt noted the continuing sale of cranberries in Cumberland, Cheshire and Staffordshire; elsewhere imports reigned: Pratt, pp. 355-57.
36. Cameron, p. 99; Hill, p. 57; Mary Briggs, 'Sussex Medical Plants', *Pharmacological Historian* 11.3 (1981), pp 2-4.
37. Woolmer Forest: <http://www.sssi.naturalengland.org.uk/*citation/citation_photo/1004188.pdf*>.
38. Grigson, *Fragaria vesca L.*: vice-counties 112, H 40, pp. 152-53.
39. Joseph Miller, *Botanicum Officinale; or a Compendious Herbal: Giving an Account of All Such Plants as are Now Used in the Practice of Physick. With their Descriptions and Virtues* (London: E Bell, 1722), p. 203; on fragility, see Mabey, p. 187.
40. James Edward Smith, *English Botany; or, Coloured Figures of British Plants, with their Essential Characters, Synonyms, and Places of Growth. To which will be Added, Occasional Remarks*, vol. 22 (London: James Sowerby, 1790–1813), p. 1524.
41. White, pp. 311, 334, 336, 339, 363, 364, 386, 388, 407, 432.
42. Pratt, pp. 194–99.
43. White, 19 July 1789; see also Mabey, p. 187.
44. White, 22 July 1791.
45. White, 1 July 1791; nor was the new variety a match for the indigenous Pine or Drayton though marketed as such.
46. Harry Hopkins, *The Long Affray. The Poaching Wars in Britain 1760–1914* (London: Secker & Warburg, 1985), pp. 7, 40–42, 234, 264, 280; J.M. Neeson, *Commoners: Common Right, Enclosure and Social Change in England 1700–1820* (Cambridge: Cambridge UP, 1993), p. 184.
47. Grigson, p. 152
48. Nathaniel Dale, *The Eventful Life of Nathaniel Dale, with Recollections & Anecdotes Containing a Great*

Variety of Business Matters, &c., as Occurred in the Life of the Author ([Kimbolton]: the author, [n.d. 1871], p. 88: 'My Favourite Girl' describes women farm servants gathering wild strawberries; I thank Dr Robin Ganev for this reference.

49. Everitt, p. 214.
50. Joan Thirsk, *Food in Early Modern England. Phases, Fads, Fashions 1500–1760* (London: Continuum Books, 2006), pp. 225–26.
51. Johnson, pp. 30–31.
52. Bob Bushaway, *By Rite: Custom, Ceremony and Community in England 1700–1880* (London: Junction Books, 1982), p. 242; Neeson, chap. 1, esp. pp. 46–52.
53. Jane Humphries, 'Enclosures, Common Rights, and Women: The Proletarianization of Families in the Late Eighteenth and Early Nineteenth Centuries', *Journal of Economic History* 50 (1990), pp. 17–42; Peter King, 'Customary Rights and Women's Earnings: The Importance of Gleaning to the Rural Labouring Poor, 1750–1850', *Economic History Review* 44 (1991), pp. 461–76; Neeson.
54. Mary Douglas and Baron Isherwood, *The World of Goods: Towards an Anthropology of Consumption,* rev. edn (London: Routledge, 1996).

The Fall and Rise of the Canadian Public Market

Lenore Newman

Palaces of food

Granville Island Public Market in Vancouver, Canada is very photogenic. Tourists snap photos of the gleaming fish and oven-fresh bread, and art students from the nearby Emily Carr University take studied shots of stacks of rare and perfect fruit. About twelve million people visit the market each year, half of whom are tourists to the city, making Granville Island the most visited attraction in the city. The thousands of photos of the market taken each year testify to the health and popularity of public markets in Canada. After nearly vanishing in the early post-war period, the Canadian urban public market has enjoyed a strong renaissance, correlated with a revitalization and repopulation of major urban cores. Seen as popular and valuable additions to urban neighbourhoods, these markets are sites of culinary encounter where one can explore new and interesting foods and sites of commensality where even solo diners can eat together with other market-goers. However, these markets draw a different demographic from the earlier Canadian markets where good value for money was the dominating narrative; they have become hubs for an élite gastronomy and the promotion of an emerging Canadian cuisine that dovetails with a broader rise in Canadian nationalism. As sites where the twin narratives of local food and exotic imports play out side by side (and often together on the same plate), public markets tell us less about what Canadians actually eat than they say about the created culinary identity that we wish to present to the world.

The twenty-first-century urban public market is about much more than food. These markets have become important urban destinations for local residents and tourists; they cater to a crowd interested in both the culinary delights on offer and the spaces themselves. Benjamin Coles wrote that markets are 'places of places', an astute way to describe the many levels of activity occurring in a market; they are a study in microgeography, and extremely spatially dense. Coles also, in a rather tongue-in-cheek way, describes Borough Market in London as simply feeling 'markety', a property that emerges out of the riot of activity and visual stimulation found in a busy market.[1] Canadian public markets share this deep sense of place; there is a specific set of complex experiences that make up urban public markets. These spaces are for the most part wildly successful, and can and do act as sites of revitalization and gentrification within urban neighbourhoods.[2]

Canada's public market spaces have followed a pattern of decline and resurgence that has been mirrored across North America's cities, though my own research would suggest the resurgence has been somewhat stronger even in Canada than it has in the US. The marketplaces of today draw upon ancient roots; as noted by Biesenthal, the market is a central component of human city-building.[3] She describes hieroglyphs in tombs at Sakkarah that depict scenes that would be at home in today's markets, including taboos against selling light bushels or shoddy goods. Canada's markets draw directly on the tradition of the market town in the fifteenth century, when almost every major British and French centre hosted market days, and great halls were erected, often with public funds, to host sellers. As Helen Tangiers argues in her seminal work on market spaces, the activity of buying and selling food has shaped our cities and towns for centuries, and continues to do so.[4] Even when market spaces are private, Tangiers argues that they function as quasi-public arenas. She describes the market experience as having a unique spirit and character, qualities that no other form of food retailing has yet been able to match. The supermarket might excel at basic provisioning; the public market provides an encounter with the cities we live in.

The first Canadian markets were founded in cities such as Halifax, Montreal and Toronto where there were garrisons to feed, but by the beginning of the twentieth century most cities had established public markets. Considered an element of public infrastructure, Canada's market spaces often served double duty as public focal points; the hall above Marché Atwater in Montreal could hold ten thousand people and was the site of key public debates during the mid-twentieth century.[5] Canadian public markets of the period included resale as well as direct sales by farmers, often from trucks or carts in the squares and streets surrounding the market buildings. Each of the most popular markets in Canada follows a distinct and memorable pattern of architecture. Atwater is housed in a grand (and very expensive at the time) art deco building with an imposing clock tower, while St John, one of the oldest markets, is designed with a roof that evokes the sense of being under a great overturned boat. Byward Market in Ottawa dominates a district of narrow streets; a popular market treat in winter is found outside the buildings at the syrup shacks where men in flannel shirts pour hot maple sap onto basins of snow to make maple toffee. St Lawrence in Toronto, a great imposing space, incorporates a building that once served as a meeting place for city council. Granville Island occupies repurposed industrial spaces with high ceilings and smoky dark wood beams; drinking coffee in the waterfront courtyard at the market gives the impression of sitting in the city's living room. These markets are just as impressive behind the scenes; St John is built on a slight incline so that the floor can be washed with a fire hose, and St Lawrence has giant freight elevators that delve into a warren of cold-storage cellars. A good market is like an iceberg, with the public elements hiding what is really an intricate node in global chains of provisioning.

That these public spaces exist at all was not inevitable; North American market spaces experienced a stunning decline during the nadir of urbanism that occurred after the Second World War. Though Canada did not experience the extremes of urban depopulation that devastated some cities in America, suburbanization and standardization dominated urban planning. This trend can be traced to earlier movements; Charles Mulford Robinson, one of North America's first well-known urban planners, felt markets were dirty and obsolete, and by 1910 he was arguing strongly that food was outside the scope of urban planning. He created some very tidy – but very hungry – urban landscapes; this attitude was typical of the City Beautiful Movement.[6] Markets enjoyed a light resurgence during the war years, but in the 1950s and 1960s many Canadian cities lost their markets as supermarkets on the suburban edge dominated provisioning; in 1968, for example, Montreal's mayor Jean Drapeau and his council attempted to close Montreal's six publicly owned (and profitable) markets. The media at the time reported that council felt 'the large urban market has had its day and is no longer viable'.[7] A future without public markets seemed inevitable; Biesenthal describes the resurrection of the public market as completely surprising. However the markets that returned were not, for the most part, the markets that had vanished, even when they were located in the same buildings (Atwater, for example, was saved, but now serves a very different clientele). The food on offer and the central experience of the markets is very different.

Food as art: the new age of the urban market

The resurgence of the public market in Canada began in the early 1980s, and mirrored a similar movement in the US, which is well documented.[8] In contrast to the public market as a strictly local shopping venue, the public market emerged as a must-see tourist destination and a site for experiencing regional cuisines and exotic flavours. Moreles captures this feeling of renewal in his study of Chicago's Maxwell Street market, which he felt served social, political and economic ends and contributed to quality of life.[9] He argues, 'markets are liminal places where social rules or expectations are suspended or replaced in favour of a variety of experiences inclusive of trade but also where identities are explored and non-economic agendas are promoted.' He lauded the market for its perceived spontaneity, as a destination in a pedestrian landscape, as a safe and vibrant space with a unique rhythm.[10] These spaces appeal to what Holloway and Kneafsey describe as an emerging 'food élite' that uses consumption to help frame identity.[11] This group is perhaps best captured in the works of Zukin, who was one of the first writers to focus on the new interest in the urbane. In her book *The Naked City*, she claims that the tastes of the urban consumers – for lattes and organic food, as well as for green spaces, boutiques and farmers markets – define the modern city. For these groups, food is the new art.[12]

In order to better understand the role of the public market in the lives of the new urbane Canadian I have spent five years studying public markets in Canada's major cities. The methodology for this study was a longitudinal investigation of urban food spaces modelled after the public space work of William Whyte,[13] who used observation and photography to examine the use of public squares in New York City. A similar, broadly phenomenological method described as topography or 'place-writing' has been used by Coles in a study of Borough Market in London; capturing spaces that are at

The Fall and Rise of the Canadian Public Market

heart full of sights, sounds, smells and tastes is always incomplete at best, but certainly is supported by repeated visits, long observation and the use of photography.[14] I did also eat a fair amount of food, and borrowed kitchens near the markets so that I could experience what it was like to shop at the markets in advance of preparing a meal. In my observation of St Lawrence Market in Toronto, Byward Market in Ottawa, Marché Atwater in Montreal and Granville Island in Vancouver, I found the new revitalized market to serve three roles in the life of the city. Far from just being places one can buy food, Canada's urban markets are sites of encounter, spaces of commensality and leaders in the creation of national culinary identity.

The market as encounter

The market is a site of encounter between nature and culture, between producer and consumer; it also serves as a site where the exotic is introduced to the established. This is not surprising, given the intrinsic nature of food, which Cook and Crang describe as a liminal substance that stands as a bridge between the human and the natural world and the inside and the outside.[15] In many ways the encounter is a defining feature of a globalized age; we are besieged with newness, with exotic experience that then becomes incorporated into our daily lives. Food is seen as a novel and low-risk encounter, in part due to its intrinsically incremental nature; we can try a new food with little risk beyond a moment of unpleasant taste or a few hours of indigestion.

The idea of the encounter has emerged as a defining feature of our age. As Merrifield argues, we can understand urbanity through the myriad sorts of contingent interaction that define urban society.[16] In this, Merrifield is inspired by the later writings of Louis Althusser, who considers history as emerging from the multiplicity of encounters that define it.[17] Building upon this work, Merrifield argues that urban society is the drama of the encounter, a process that can be understood as 'a collectivity of comings together, of sheer *co-presences* defining their singular object, the becoming-objective of the world'.[18] The sights, tastes and ideas associated with urban society create the individuals who encounter them, making identities always contingent. That a market comes complete with a rich array of sounds and smells intensifies the experience and does much to commit it to memory.

Canada's public markets are rich in encounter. In St Lawrence Market in Toronto, I found rare Canadian foods such as pickled spruce tips from the Arctic and local delicacies such as ice wine, which is heavily marketed as 'Canada's gift to the world' – even though, strictly speaking, the Germans made it first. The market is also a source of luxury goods such as caviar, truffles and unusual cuts of meat. St Lawrence also is the home of the peameal bacon sandwich that led to the association of the label 'Canadian' being associated with peameal or back bacon, an association that is particularly strong in the northern US, but puzzles us north of the border. In Montreal, Marché Atwater has done much to re-establish the idea of eating in season, featuring unusual local foods such as ground cherries and fiddleheads.[19] Atwater also highlights preserves, and one of my more memorable market meals involved savoury bottled spiced pears poached in wine and served on fresh meringue, along with a sampling of the Quebec cheeses available at the market. At St John Market, one can sample the dried dulse of Grand Manan Island, a rough and rocky fortress that rises from the tidal flats of the Bay of Fundy. The dulse is crisp and salty, and works well as a seasoning in salad, though when I visited Grand Manan I learned that the local teens toast the dulse with a lighter until it takes on the flavour of popcorn.

To the north in Ottawa at Byward Market one can find the original home of the beavertail donut, which is a doughy disk shaped like its namesake's tail. Tourists can purchase a variety of beavertail-branded goods in the market, and when Barack Obama stopped in Byward Market specifically to eat a beavertail donut on 19 February 2009, it made national news. There was a certain level of general good feeling that the American president would take the time to stand in the snow and eat one of our beavertails. At some level he was sharing a commensal moment with the nation, and a certain pride in our title as the world's most prodigious donut eaters.

Commensality, or meet me at the market

The commensality of the market is largely tied to the nature of these spaces in Canada; save for an excellent market in Quebec City that is almost entirely aimed at the cook, almost without exception urban public markets in Canada highlight a large amount of prepared food designed for eating on the spot, and contain ample space to sit. The term commensality literally means eating at the same table, but a wider definition proposed by Sobal & Nelson is that commensality is eating in the company of other people.[20] As Pierre Van den Berghe notes, we are food-sharing animals, and use food to establish, express and consolidate societies – a glue creating a society out of a loose collection of individuals.[21] However, what is particularly interesting about those who take a meal at a Canadian public market is that they were often observed to be eating on their own, and even when they were in a group people at the market would often buy food from different stalls and only then eat at one table. Markets provide a chance for people to eat separately together, thus taking advantage of each other's company with little or no requirement for lasting social entanglement.[22] I observed this behaviour in multiple markets across Canada. At Marché Atwater the bakery and surrounding sitting area was very well used by patrons lingering and chatting over pastry and a coffee, particularly in winter, when the markets play the role of a town square. This behaviour was observed in the Forks market in Winnipeg as well; market vendors often joined in the chatter, and the warm steamy market hall, filled with the smell of frying pierogis and hot Saskatoon berry pie, contrasted starkly with the bitter cold outside. At the Halifax market, patrons jockey for tables that overlook the activity of the harbour as they enjoy fresh lobster rolls.

Commensality at Canadian public markets, however, is not entirely open to all. Price points at most public markets are significantly upscale, and the sharing of food that occurs there is encompassed with controlled boundaries of income level that has grown increasingly stark. Bell and Valentine note that communities are as much about exclusion as inclusion. Food is one way that boundaries get drawn and insiders and outsiders distinguished.[23] This exclusion is not usually overt at the public market; just as Burnett found in her study of restaurant gentrification in Vancouver, Canada, price point is enough to control who gets to walk through the door.[24] Control over who sells in Canada's public markets rests with the management, allowing for the price points to be kept high; the offerings are curated to appeal to those interested in food, not price. As most markets are quasi-public spaces, more overt control often lurks behind the scenes in the form of on-site security, but its presence is rarely seen.

The market and national culinary identity

In addition to acting as sites of encounter and of commensality, markets can act as sites of identity formation, particularly with respect to regional and national cuisines. As Lisa Heldke notes, cuisines are not static entities that remain unchanged over time;[25] they are constantly generated dialectically by a nation's people. This is also true of nations in general; as argued in Benedict Anderson's *Imagined Communities,* the idea of a national identity is a new concept, and nationalism a cultural artefact, even though he sees 'nation-ness' as the most universally legitimate value in the political life of our time.[26] The role of an imagined national cuisine in the creation of a national identity has been explored in depth in the literature; Priscilla Ferguson describes national cuisine as part and parcel of the nation state that emerged in the West during the nineteenth century, and as a case in point, Wilk's exploration of Belizean cuisine shows how regional dishes can be enlisted in a project that codifies practices as a characteristic of the whole, where an invented shared culinary experience food is a potent symbol of personal and group identity.[27] Canada's cuisine is as elusive as Canada's national identity, which has historically faced the challenges of a small population spread across a large landmass, diverse and conflicted founding groups and one of the world's highest immigration rates. It is hard to argue that Canada's cuisine existed in any real sense before the centennial of 1967 and the accompanying world's fair in Montreal, for which a cuisine was in effect invented.[28] The idea of a Canadian cuisine remained elusive; Jacobs, for example, notes that although Canadian cuisine has proven difficult to define, it combines the use of native ingredients with techniques and recipes that originated elsewhere.[29] Canadian cuisine has also been described as one shaped by regions, climate and cultural groups.[30]

My attempts to tease out Canadian cuisine have taken me across the country to sample dishes as varied as Newfoundland's boiled Jigg's dinner to Thunder Bay's Persian donuts to the Canadian Creole that dominates Vancouver's food landscape, which spans everything from blueberry lassi and butter chicken poutine to sushi made with smoked salmon and cream cheese. There are several food writers who have attempted to define Canadian cuisine through narrative and recipe; Webb's *Apples to Oysters* reflects the primacy of ingredients and the regional sweep and role of wild foods and *Pemmican to Poutine* follows similar themes of fresh, regional and wild foods.[31] My own experience of Canada's cuisine is an idea of food defined more by properties rather than by signature dishes; Canadian cuisine has proven to be highly seasonal, embraces wild ingredients, is highly multicultural, favours ingredients over recipes and draws heavily on regionalism. If Canada can be said to have national ingredients, these include rhubarb, maple syrup and salmon; these ingredients and the traits listed above aren't just present in Canada's urban markets, they are actively reinforced there. Our markets celebrate Nova Scotia apples, fresh lobster and other seafood, maple in all of its forms, wild blueberries, spring fiddleheads (which at St Lawrence were nestled with the very regional Ontario wild leeks), Alberta beef, luxurious ice wine and, on the Pacific coast, an endless supply of salmon.

It may be famous for its salmon, but Granville Island Public Market in Vancouver is a space of encounter, commensality and identity creation, and is unusual both in its large size, high popularity with both tourists and locals and its place as a modern market opened in a city with almost no history of public market spaces. Vancouver is a young city, born of resource extraction and gold rushes; a first market hall erected in 1889 lasted only ten years in an area where, as Biesenthal describes, residents made do with canned goods and the wares of farmers who sold door to door or out of the back of trucks.[32] Though there was a general sense that the city didn't need a space dedicated to the trade of market goods, the city most certainly needed public gathering space. The locals might not have chosen a market, but in the 1970s, with waterfront industry in sharp decline, the federal government saw an opportunity to clean up a brownfield, open up the waterfront and enliven the city's culinary scene all at once. Johnson called the city a 'meat and potatoes' place, but that was about to change.[33]

Granville Island was developed shortly after the redevelopment of Seattle's Pike Place Market and followed the same model of creating a destination location in the city. Granville Island public market opened in 1979 on its namesake, a disused industrial island, to almost immediate success. Karen Johnson described the city as a frontier town that had almost no food culture to speak of at the time. The market introduced the city to fresh bagels, to cappuccino and to fresh flowers.[34] This encounter with the new and exotic continues at the market today. A stroll through the market sheds this winter turned up Canadian caviar at the Longliner (from farm-raised sturgeon in Sechelt, BC), which is also known for its vacuum-packed smoked salmon prepared for air travel. At South China Seas importers, I have found Australian finger limes, fresh shiso leaves and young ginger. These exotics tend to show up in local restaurants; shiso mohitos were popular last year. Masa Shiroki makes Canada's only local sake at Granville Island, and has begun using rice grown nearby in the Fraser Valley.

Granville Island has emerged as a particularly strong site of identity building through national cuisine. Smoked salmon has been a large part of the market since opening day, but it is also a good place to find maple syrup, which isn't as prevalent in the west as elsewhere in the country. The Canadian brand is stressed in the market, a trend that has accelerated since the opening of the Edible Canada shop and bistro. The bistro is one of many places offering poutine, a French fry, cheese curd and gravy concoction that has spilled out of Quebec to become a national food, and this last winter they also offered to Vancouverites Newfoundland cod and brewis, a mixture of salt cod, hardtack and molasses that is a Newfoundland favourite rarely found away for the north-east coast. The bistro offers a very scripted expression of Canada, however; most of the dishes, even the eastern ones, carry a note of California cuisine to suit west-coast tastes.

Conclusion

Though it has been said that no place 'epitomizes city life on the west coast so much as Granville Island', geographer David Ley is a little more circumspect when he states that Granville Island is the quintessential public space in the postmodern city.[35] Canada's public markets entered the twentieth century as essential pieces of urban infrastructure, nearly vanished and then emerging again with greater appeal but with perhaps less innocence. They are helping to generate an idea of a national Canadian cuisine, spurred in part by the rise of Canada as a petro-state (rising fortunes have driven the market for luxury foods) and a shifting of power from the traditional eastern heartland to the western regions. Whether this national culinary discourse will last remains to be seen, but it does seem certain that markets will remain critical sites of encounter where new and exotic foods appear and where new products can be introduced with little risk to the people most likely to be culinary adventurers. They have emerged as public spaces, where people can go to socialize, enjoy a meal or even just commune with the city. Rising inequality threatens to keep many people excluded from the modern market, however. As quasi-public spaces, markets highlight certain elements of Canada's cuisine to the world, but not everyone is invited to the feast.

Notes

1. Benjamin F Coles, 'Making the Market Place: A Topography of Borough Market, London', *Cultural Geographies* (2013), p. 65.
2. For the Canadian context, see Lenore Newman, Ann Dale, and Chris Ling, 'Meeting on the Edge: Urban Spaces and the Diffusion of the Novel', *Spaces & Flows: An International Journal of Urban & Extra Urban Studies*, 1 (2011), pp. 1–14.
3. Linda Biesenthal and J Douglas Wilson, *To Market, to Market: The Public Market Tradition in Canada* (Toronto: PMA Books, 1980), p. 6.
4. Helen Tangiers, *Public Markets*, (New York: Norton, 2008), p. 9.
5. Lenore Newman, 'Neige Et Citrouille: Marché Atwater and Seasonality', *Cuizine: The Journal of Canadian Food CulturesCuizine:/Revue des cultures culinaires au Canada*, 3 (2012). pp. 1–10.
6. Gregory Alexander Donofrio, 'Feeding the City', *Gastronomica* 7,4 (2007), pp 30–41.
7. Brian Stewart, "Closing of Atwater Market Confirmed", *Montreal Gazette,* (September 24th, 1968), p. 3.
8. See, e.g., Thomas K Tiemann, 'Grower-Only Farmers' Markets: Public Spaces and Third Places', *The Journal of Popular Culture* 41 (2008), pp. 467–487.
9. Alfonso Morales, 'Public Markets as Community Development Tools', *Journal of Planning Education*

and Research, 28 (2009) , pp. 426–440.
10. Alfonso Morales, 'Marketplaces: Prospects for Social, Economic, and Political Development', *Journal of Planning Literature* 26 (2011), p. 6.
11. Lewis Holloway and Moya Kneafsey, 'Reading the Space of the Farmer's Market: A Preliminary Investigation from the UK', *Sociologica Ruralis,* 40 (2000) , pp 285–299.
12. S. Zukin, *Naked City: The Death and Life of Authentic Urban Places,* (Oxford: Oxford UP, 2009) , p. 4.
13. William Whyte, *The Social Life of Small Urban Spaces* (Washington, DC: Conservation Foundation, 1980).
14. Benjamin Coles, 'Making the market place: a topography of Borough Market, London', Cultural Geographies 21 (2014) pp. 515–523
15. Ian Cook and Philip Crang, 'The World on a Plate Culinary Culture, Displacement and Geographical Knowledges', *Journal of Material Culture* 1 (1996) , pp. 131–153.
16. Andy Merrifield, *The Politics of the Encounter: Urban Theory and Protest under Planetary Urbanization* (Athens: U Georgia P, 2013).
17. Louis Althusser, *Philosophy of the Encounter: Later Writings, 1978–87* (London: Verso, 2006).
18. Merrifield, p. 56.
19. Newman, 'Neige Et Citrouille'.
20. Jeffery Sobal and Mary K Nelson, 'Commensal Eating Patterns: A Community Study', *Appetite* 41 (2003), pp. 181–190.
21. Pierre L Van den Berghe, 'Ethnic Cuisine: Culture in Nature', *Ethnic and Racial Studies* 7 (1984), pp. 387–397.
22. Lenore Lauri Newman and Katherine Burnett, 'Street Food and Vibrant Urban Spaces: Lessons from Portland, Oregon', *Local Environment* 18 (2013) , pp. 233–248.
23. David Bell, *Consuming Geographies: We Are Where We Eat,* (Psychology Press, 1997).
24. Katherine Burnett, 'Commodifying Poverty: Gentrification and Consumption in Vancouver's Downtown Eastside', *Urban Geography* 35 (2014), pp. 157–176.
25. Lisa M Heldke, *Exotic Appetites: Ruminations of a Food Adventurer* (New York: Routledge, 2003), p. xix.
26. Benedict Anderson, *Imagined Communities: Reflections on the Origin and Spread of Nationalism* (London: Verso, 2006).
27. Priscilla Parkhurst Ferguson, *Accounting for Taste: The Triumph of French Cuisine,* (U Chicago P, 2006); Richard R Wilk, "Real Belizean Food': Building Local Identity in the Transnational Caribbean', *American Anthropologist* 101 (1999), pp. 244–255.
28. For a detailed exploration of this process, see Rhona Richman-Kenneally, 'The Cuisine of the Tundra: Towards a Canadian Food Culture at Expo 67', *Food, Culture, & Society* 11 (2008), pp. 287–313.
29. Hersch Jacobs, 'Structural Elements in Canadian Cuisine', *Cuizine: The Journal of Canadian Food Culture* 2 (2005), pp. 1–14.
30. Dorothy Duncan, *Canadians at Table: A Culinary History of Canada,* (Toronto: Dundurn Press, 2006).
31. M. Webb, *Apples to Oysters: A Food Lover's Tour of Canadian Farms,* (Toronto: Viking Canada, 2008); Suman Roy and Brooke Ali, *From Pemmican to Poutine: A Journey through Canada's Culinary History,* (Toronto: The Key Publishing House, Inc., 2010).
32. Biesenthal and Wilson, p. 139.
33. K. Johnson, *Granville Island,* (Vancouver, Dreamica, 2010), p. 150
34. Johnson, p. 65.
35. David Ley, *The New Middle Class and the Remaking of the Central City* (Oxford: Oxford UP, 1997), p. 7.

The Identity, Characteristics and Vending of Cucurbit Crops in Israel of Roman Times

Harry S. Paris

Cucurbits have been popular fruit vegetables since time immemorial. The cucurbits so familiar in markets of the developed world today are assumed by the uninitiated to be identical to those existing in classical times. However, the cucurbits enjoyed by the peoples of Mediterranean civilizations of 2000 years ago were different taxonomically or otherwise lacked traits that are critical to large modern marketing chains, which are based on adaptation to long-distance shipping.

There are five cucurbit crops that are of global distribution today. These are cucumbers (*Cucumis sativus* L.), melons (*Cucumis melo* L.), watermelons (*Citrullus lanatus* (Thunb.) Matsum. & Nakai) and squash and pumpkins (*Cucurbita* L. species). Cucumbers and squash are elongate fruits that are consumed immature. The melons that are most familiar today, including the cantaloupes (*Cucumis melo* Cantalupensis Group) and muskmelons (*Cucumis melo* Reticulatus Group), as well as watermelons and pumpkins, are round fruits that are generally consumed when ripe.

Images and literature from provinces of the Roman Empire show a different array of cucurbit crops. Specifically, only four cucurbit food crops from three species can be identified. The most familiar of the cucurbits to Roman subjects were the very long-fruited snake melons (*Cucumis melo* Flexuosus Group) (Paris, 2012). The other three familiar cucurbits were the more-or-less round dessert melons (*Cucumis melo* Adana Group), dessert watermelons (*Citrullus lanatus*) and bottle gourds (*Lagenaria siceraria* (Mol.) Standl.) (Janick et al., 2007). There were three distinct cultivars of bottle gourds, a long-fruited one for eating, and a large one and a small one for use as vessels and other purposes. Cucumbers, which are native to India (de Candolle, 1886; Bisht et al., 2004; Sebastian et al., 2010), diffused into Mediterranean lands after the fall of the Roman Empire, during the Dark Ages (Paris et al., 2012a). Squash and pumpkins, which are native to the Americas (Whitaker, 1947), were introduced during the European Renaissance (Paris et al., 2006).

The wild ancestors of the cucurbit crops typically have small, spherical fruits. Melons, *Cucumis melo*, which have an Asiatic origin (Sebastian et al., 2010), diffused westward to Africa prior to recorded history. It is not known when they were selected by people for longfruitedness, a trait advantageous for the consumption of the immature fruits, but elongate melons were illustrated in ancient Egypt and have been identified as the *qishu'im* which the ancient Israelites, after their exodus from Egypt, longed for during their journey through the Sinai Desert (Numbers 11:5) (Feliks, 1968, p. 166;

Janick et al., 2007). Round melons, eaten when ripe, were stated by Pliny (*ca.* 77 CE) to be a new introduction into Roman lands. Bottle gourds, *Lagenaria siceraria*, are native to southern Africa (Decker-Walters et al., 2004), became widely dispersed even overseas and were used by humans in the Americas at least 10,000 years ago (Kistler et al., 2014). Watermelons are native to Africa (Rubatsky, 2001; Mujaju et al., 2011; Welman, 2011). Wild and primitive cultigens of watermelons typically have watery but hard, pale-colored or white, insipid or bitter flesh. Watermelons are identified in depictions in Egyptian tombs (Janick et al., 2007). The *avattihim* of the Bible (Numbers 11:5) are watermelons (Feliks, 1968). It is not known when and where sweet watermelons were first isolated and selected.

The snake melons, bottle gourds, watermelons and dessert melons were known, respectively, as *qishu'in* (or *qishu'im*), *delu'in*, *avattihim* and *melafefonot* in three codices of Jewish Law that were compiled in Israel during the time of the Roman Empire (Janick et al., 2007). The first of these codices is the *Mishna* (Redaction), which was compiled in the latter half of the second century and completed *ca.* 200 CE. The *Mishna* consists of six 'orders' or volumes each of which is divided into seven to twelve tractates for a total of sixty-three. The *Tosefta* (Supplement), which was compiled approximately a century later, is organized much like its predecessor and has a mostly similar text, but nonetheless has many statements that are not found in the *Mishna*. The last of these codices is known as the *Jerusalem Talmud* even though, like the *Mishna*, it was compiled in northern Israel. This last codex, which was completed around 400 CE, consists of text very close to that of the *Mishna*, as well as much additional rabbinical commentary and analysis. These three works have been reproduced electronically and can be conveniently viewed, studied and compared at Mekhon Mamre. Much of the discussion concerning the edible-fruited cucurbits is found in the tractates named *Kil'ayim*, *Ma'asrot* and *Terumot*, which deal with planting, tithing and contributions, respectively. From these discussions, it can be inferred that the snake melons, bottle gourds, watermelons and dessert melons were offered for sale locally, apparently at roadsides of agricultural homesteads and nearby village and town marketplaces. These cucurbits, too, were presented for prospective customers in different ways that were dictated by their different traits. All four of the cucurbits were ill-adapted for long-distance transport, due to their short shelf-life or fragility.

The *qishu'in* (snake melons, *Cucumis melo*) were the cucurbit mentioned most often in the codices of Jewish Law, undoubtedly a reflection of their widespread use (Paris, 2009; Paris, 2012). These *qishu'in* could be used fresh, cooked or pickled. The esteem for them is underlined in a later writing, composed in what is now central Iraq, known as the *Babylonian Talmud* (*ca.* 600 CE), which relates that Rabbi Yehuda the President, compiler of the *Mishna*, always had *qishu'in* on his table to honour his guests. The tractate on tithing indicates that the *qishu'im* were to be tithed either after (1) they underwent rubbing off of their hairs, a process which had a special name, *piqqus*, probably derived from the ancient Greek *pekos* (soft hairs), allowing for immediate

Cucurbit Crops in Israel of Roman Times

Figure 1. A pile of snake melons, Cucumis melo *(Flexuosus group), offered for sale at Faisal's Market, Nahariyya, Israel, 17 April 2014. (Photograph by the author.)*

consumption (Lieberman, 1955), or (2) they were gathered in a pile, for sale (*Mishna, Ma'asrot* 1:5, *Tosefta, Ma'asrot* 1:5, *Jerusalem Talmud, Ma'asrot,* 1:5) (Figure 1).

Evidently, snake melons were produced by small growers who ate some of their produce at home. Most of the produce, though, was gathered together, for vending, in a pile. The rabbinical commentary of *Ma'asrot* 1:4, page 4a, in the *Jerusalem Talmud* even has a special word for this pile, *paqqesusiyya*, confirming that this must have been the common way that snake melons were marketed. Being extremely long, the snake melons were a 'brag-patch' home garden crop, but their extreme length often resulted in their being twisted. Moreover, their juiciness together with their long, thin shape imparted fragility, and must have rendered them rather difficult to transport without breaking. These *qishu'in* were highly perishable, too, being fit for contribution for only one day after harvest (*Tosefta, Terumot* 4:5). Today, around the Mediterranean and in the Middle East, the snake melons, known in Arabic as *faqqous*, are still widely grown for home use and local markets, but extremely long specimens are not common in wholesale markets.

The *delu'in* (long-fruited, young bottle gourds, *Lagenaria sicararia*) are mentioned together with the *qishu'in* in the same passage on tithing (*Ma'asrot* 1:5). Young bottle gourds are also softly hairy and thus also had to undergo *piqqus*, rubbing off of the

Figure 2. A pile of young bottle gourds, Lagenaria siceraria, *offered for sale at Faisal's Market, Nahariyya, Israel, 17 April 2014. (Photograph by the author.)*

hairs, before eating. They too were gathered in a pile for sale (Figure 2), at which time they had to be tithed.

They also had a shelf-life of only one day (*Tosefta, Terumot* 4:5). In these passages as well as others in the codices of Jewish Law, for example *Mishna Kil'ayim* 3:4, *Shabbat* 9:7, *Terumot* 8:6; *Tosefta Kil'ayim* 2:13, *Makhshirin* 3:3; *Jerusalem Talmud Kil'ayim* 3:4, *Terumot* 2:1, *Shabbat* 10:2, *Shevi'it* 1:5, when the *qishu'im* and *delu'im* are mentioned together, the *qishu'im* are mentioned first. Apparently, the *delu'in* were not as widely consumed or as highly esteemed as the *qishu'in*. Unlike the *qishu'in*, the *delu'in* had to be cooked before they were eaten. An analogous situation occurs between two popular modern cucurbits. Cucumbers can be eaten fresh or processed and, in the Far East, are also cooked. Summer squash have to be cooked before being eaten. Both vegetables are popular, but cucumber is more widely consumed than summer squash.

The *avattihim* (watermelons, *Citrullus* sp.) were to be tithed when they were gathered (*Ma'asrot* 1:5). Like snake melons and bottle gourds, young watermelon fruits are covered with soft hairs but, like them, as the fruits grow and mature, the hairs tend to slough off. The use of the word *piqqus*, rubbing off of hairs, would thus have been inappropriate for mature cucurbit fruits and, clearly then, watermelons were not consumed immature, but only as mature, ripe fruits, like almost everywhere today.

The watermelons could also be tithed after they underwent *shilluq* which, in common usage, means blanching or boiling and so this word has been understood by modern commentators as indicating that watermelons were dipped into hot water after harvest (Feliks, 2005 p. 65). Indeed, hot water dipping has been shown to extend the shelf-life of melons (*Cucumis melo*) (Fallik et al., 2000). However, the word *shilluq* has a rarely used, second meaning, slicking (Even-Shoshan, 2003, p. 1908). The great twelfth-century scholar Maimonides, in his *Commentary on the Mishna* (*ca.* 1168), explained that *shilluq* meant smoothing of the fruit by hand (*yahliq beyado*) to get rid of the *zihuv*, yellowing, on it (Qafah, 1963). Apparently, *shilluq* was intended to clean off the dust that had accumulated on the fruit during the month-long period of its growth and development in the rainless Middle Eastern summer. This polishing of the fruits would certainly have made for a more attractive product. After harvest, watermelons were not offered for sale in a pile. Instead, they were laid out, one-by-one, in a *muqze* (*Mishna, Ma'asrot* 1:5) for which there was also a special word, *shallequqiyya*, in the *Jerusalem Talmud* (*Ma'asrot* 1:4, page 4a). In contrast, modern watermelons are often trucked, stacked on one another (Rushing et al., 2001). It seems strange, then, that these large fruits would be laid out for sale rather than stacked, as this arrangement would be a waste of space. However, these watermelons may well have differed in a critical characteristic from the ones produced today for long-distance shipping. Maimonides explained that if watermelons were stacked they would crush one another (Qafah, 1963). Some modern cultivars of watermelon, especially those developed in the Far East for home gardens and small growers, share a recessive gene which confers explosive rinds (Wehner et al., 2001). Furthermore, intensive breeding for improved rind toughness, to adapt the fruits to long-distance shipping, was conducted during the twentieth century (Parris, 1949). If the watermelons of Israel and neighbouring lands had explosive or merely tender rinds, they indeed would best have been marketed in a *muqze*, laid out one-by-one, rather than stacked.

The *melafefonot* (dessert melons, *Cucumis melo*) are often mentioned together with the *avattihim* (watermelons). When considered together, the *avattihim* almost always precede the *melafefonot (Mishna, Ma'asrot* 1:4, *Terumot* 8:6; *Tosefta, Kil'ayim* 1:2, 2:11, *Ma'asrot* 1:5, *Pesahim* 1:8; *Jerusalem Talmud, Demay* 2:1, *Kil'ayim* 1:2, *Ma'asrot* 1:3, *Terumot* 8:6), the one exception being in regard to their seeds, for which one rabbi explained that the seeds of the *melafefonot* are subject to tithing because they are eaten and the seeds of the *avattihim* are exempt because they are only for planting (*Jerusalem Talmud, Ma'asrot* 1:2, p. 2b).

Despite their often being mentioned together in the Jewish texts, the watermelons and melons are seen to differ conspicuously in several ways. First, no indication is given as to whether, like watermelons, the melons were to be laid out in a *muqze* or stacked. Second, the *Tosefta* (*Ma'asrot* 1:5) indicates that the *melafefonot* did not have to be tithed *'ad sheya'alan min hayora*, which most commentators have understood to mean 'until they are lifted out of the vessel of boiling water', an astonishing interpretation parallel to the often misunderstood need for watermelons to undergo blanching. The *Tosefta*, though, was not fully edited. This passage makes complete sense if it is assumed that the weak letter *alef* dropped out of the word *yora*; its restoration would result in the reading *'ad sheya'alan min haye'ora* [pronounced ha-ye-o-ra], 'until they are lifted out of the field of ripening fruits'. Analogously, figs ripen successively over the course of the summer season and waves of ripening fruits are referred to as *meruyyot* (*Jerusalem Talmud*, *Ma'asrot* 1:2, p. 3b), and the harvesting of them would be *ye'uru* (Feliks, 2005, p. 55). Melons are similar to figs in that their fruits ripen in two or three waves over the course of the harvest period (McGlasson and Pratt, 1963). The ripe fruits in a field of melons were all too obvious to the farmer because of their colour change from green to yellow and their spontaneous detachment from the connecting stem, phenomena first recorded by Pliny in regard to the *melopepones* (Janick et al., 2007). In contrast, watermelons have no such readily visible indicators of fruit ripeness (Rushing et al., 2001). Third, the *melafefonot*, like figs and table grapes, if taken to more a distant locality because of the need to fulfil the obligation of contributions, were apt to lose their quality and decay *en route*; the decayed produce was to be discarded in an appropriate place (*Tosefta, Terumot* 1:18). The *melafefonot* could be contributed for only three days after harvest (*Tosefta, Terumot* 4:5). In contrast, there was no limitation on the number of days after harvest that watermelons could be contributed. Apparently, the watermelons of that era, like modern watermelons, remained in good condition for a longer period of time (Rushing et al., 2001). Fourth, the watermelons, but not the melons, are mentioned together with common, juicy and typically sweet fruits eaten raw when ripe, the *te'enim* (figs), *eshkol* (cluster of table grapes) and *rimmonim* (pomegranates), in regard to exemptions from tithing (*Mishna, Ma'asrot* 2:6, 3:9; *Jerusalem Talmud, Ma'asrot* 2:4, 3:4). Evidently, the watermelons of the first centuries CE in Israel were typically sweet, just like the figs, table grapes and pomegranates, but the melons did not belong to this category. The *melafefonot* were likely melons from a cultivar or cultivars of the Adana Group, which typically have soft, pleasant but rather thin, mealy and insipid flesh (Cizik, 1952). The sweet dessert melons that are so familiar and prized today are derived from the region of Khorasan in Central Asia, and dispersed westward during the medieval period (Paris et al., 2012b).

To conclude, the array of cucurbits that were familiar to Mediterranean peoples of Roman times is not identical to that which is so widely appreciated today. Snake melons, which were the most widely consumed cucurbit in Israel and other Mediterranean lands, have been largely replaced by cucumbers. Bottle gourds have been replaced by summer squash. Watermelons remain very popular today, but modern cultivars have tough rinds, allowing them to be shipped long distances. Dessert melons are popular today, too, having much-improved fruit-flesh quality than the melons that had been available in Mediterranean lands during Roman times. The growers back then did not have the benefits of modern transport, refrigeration and packaging technologies that greatly extend the geographical range of distribution and shelf-life of their produce.

Given their short shelf-life and fragility, the cucurbits not could be shipped over a journey that would last more than several days. All of the produce had to have been locally grown and could not be transported to distant locations without desiccating, decaying, or breaking *en route*. The cucurbit produce must have been limited in its distribution largely to roadside stands and market stalls of nearby villages and towns. The long, immature fruits of snake melons and bottle gourds were each vended as a pile of fruits. The round, mature watermelons had to be laid out individually to avoid splitting.

Acknowledgements

I have searched and studied the *Mishna*, *Tosefta* and *Jerusalem Talmud* through the gracious on-line service of Mekhon Mamre (http://www.mechon-mamre.org). Generous financial support for research on cucurbit crop history was donated by the Lillian Goldman Charitable Trust (New York).

References

Bisht, I.S., K.V. Bhat, S.P.S. Tanwar, D.C. Bhandari, K. Joshi and A.K. Sharma. 2004. 'Distribution and Genetic Diversity of *Cucumis sativus* var. *hardwickii* (Royle) Alef. in India', *Journal of Horticultural Science and Biotechnology* 79: pp. 783–91.

Cizik, B. 1952. *Ozar ha-Zemahim [Treasury of Plants]* (Herzliyya: B. Cizik).

De Candolle, A. 1886. *Origin of Cultivated Plants* (New York: Appleton), pp. 264–66.

Decker-Walters, D.S., M. Wilkins-Ellert, S.-M. Chung and J.E. Staub. 2004. 'Discovery and Genetic Assessment of Wild Bottle Gourd [*Lagenaria siceraria* (Mol.) Standl.; Cucurbitaceae] from Zimbabwe', *Economic Botany* 58: pp. 501–08.

Even-Shoshan, A. 2003. *Millon Even-shoshan: Mehuddash u-Me'udkan Lishnot Ha'Alpayim [Even-Shoshan Dictionary: Renewed and updated for the 2000s]* (Tel Aviv).

Fallik, E., Y. Aharoni, A. Copel, V. Rodov, S. Tuvia-Alkalai, B. Horev, O. Yekutieli, A. Wiseblum and R. Regev. 2000. 'Reduction of Postharvest Losses of Galia Melon by a Short Hot-water Rinse', *Plant Pathology* 49: pp. 333–38.

Feliks, J. 1968. *'Olam ha-Zomeah ha-Miqra'i [Plant world of the Bible]* (Ramat Gan: Massada), p. 166.

Feliks, J. 2005. *Talmud Yerushalmi Massekhet Ma'asrot, Perush u-Vi'ur. [The Jerusalem Talmud Tractate Ma'asrot, Annotated Critical Edition.]* (Ramat Gan: Bar-Ilan UP), pp. 64–65.

Janick, J., H.S. Paris and D.C. Parrish. 2007. 'The Cucurbits of Mediterranean Antiquity: Identification of Taxa from Ancient Images and Descriptions', *Annals of Botany* 100: pp. 1441–57.

Kistler L., A. Montenegro, B.D. Smith, J.A. Gifford, R.E. Green, L.A. Newsom and B. Shapiro. 2014. 'Transoceanic Drift and the Domestication of African Bottle Gourds in the Americas, *Proceedings of the National Academy of Sciences of the United States of America* 111: pp. 2937–41.

Lieberman, S. 1955. *Tosefta Kifshuta [Tosefta Simply Explained]* (New York: Jewish Theological Seminary of America), pp. 227–29, 666–72.

McGlasson, W.B. and H.K. Pratt. 1963. 'Fruit-set Patterns and Fruit Growth in Cantaloupe (*Cucumis melo* L. var. *reticulatus* Naud.), *Proceedings of the American Society for Horticultural Science* 83: pp. 495–505.

Mujaju, C., A. Zborowska, G. Werlemark, L. Garkava-Gustavsson, S.B. Andersen and H. Nybom. 2011. 'Genetic Diversity Among and Within Watermelon (*Citrullus lanatus*) Landraces in Southern Africa', *Journal of Horticultural Science and Biotechnology* 86: pp. 353–58.

Paris, H.S. 2009. 'Faqqous: A Melon that Resembles Cucumber—An Ancient Crop in Israel', *Haqla'e Yisra'el* 39: pp. 65–66.

Paris, H.S. 2012. 'Semitic Language Records of Snake Melons (*Cucumis melo*, Cucurbitaceae) in the

Medieval Period and the "piqqus" of the "faqqous"', *Genetic Resources and Crop Evolution* 59: pp. 31–38.

Paris, H.S, M.C. Daunay, M. Pitrat and J. Janick. 2006. 'First Known Image of *Cucurbita* in Europe, 1503–1508', *Annals of Botany* 98: pp. 41–47.

Paris, H.S., M.C. Daunay and J. Janick. 2012a. 'Occidental Diffusion of Cucumber (*Cucumis sativus*) 500–1300 CE: Two Routes to Europe', *Annals of Botany* 109: pp. 117–26.

Paris, H.S., Z. Amar and E. Lev. 2012b. 'Medieval Emergence of Sweet Melons, *Cucumis melo* (Cucurbitaceae)', *Annals of Botany* 110: pp. 23–33.

Parris, G.K. 1949. 'Watermelon Breeding', *Economic Botany* 3: pp. 193–212.

Qafah, Y. 1963. *Mishna 'im Perush Rabbenu Moshe Ben-Maymon, Maqor we-Tirgum* [*Mishna with Interpretation by Our Rabbi Maimonides, Source and Translation*] (Jerusalem: Mossad Harav Kook), vol. 1, Seder Zera'im, p. 322.

Rubatsky, V.E. 2001. 'Origin, Distribution, and Uses', *Watermelons, Characteristics, Production, and Marketing*, ed. by D.M. Maynard (Alexandria, VA: ASHS Press), pp. 21–26.

Rushing, J.W., J.M. Fonseca and A.P. Keinath. 2001. 'Harvesting and Postharvest Handling', *Watermelons, Characteristics, Production, and Marketing*, ed. by D.M. Maynard (Alexandria, VA: ASHS Press), pp. 156–64.

Sebastian, P.M., H. Schaefer, I.R.H. Telford and S.S. Renner. 2010. 'Cucumber and Melon Have Their Wild Progenitors in India, and the Sister Species of *Cucumis melo* is from Australia', *Proceedings of the National Academy of Sciences of the United States of America* 107: pp. 14269–73.

Wehner, T.C., N.V. Shetty and G.W. Elmstrom. 2001. 'Breeding and Seed Production', *Watermelons, Characteristics, Production, and Marketing*, ed. by DM Maynard (Alexandria, VA: ASHS Press), pp. 27–73.

Welman, M. 2011. *Citrullus lanatus* (Thunb.) Matsum. & Nakai <http://www.plantzafrica.com/plantcd/voteplant.php>.

Whitaker, T.W. 1947. 'American Origin of the Cultivated Cucurbits', *Annals of the Missouri Botanical Garden* 34: pp. 101–11.

Markets in Russia: Back to the Future

Anna Pavlovskaya

This paper looks at modern Russian markets as centres of food trade. It traces the historical roots of current markets, explores the peculiarities of Soviet-era markets, discusses changes that took place in the decades following Perestroika, evaluates the outlook for market trading in Russia and gives special consideration to features unique to Russian markets.

Food markets have always played an important role not only in the country's food supplier, but also in its culture. The modern Russian language has three words to describe places for retail trade: *rinok* (market), *bazar* (bazaar) and *yarmarka* (fair). The words *rinok* and *bazar* are synonyms and can be used interchangeably, with *bazar* most commonly referring to trade in the open air; however, where open trade has been replaced by covered stalls, the word still applies through habit. The word *yarmarka* is used in connection with seasonal sales; the authorities of many large cities have recently started to endorse so-called weekend fairs, which display product samples for business people. In Russia the word has retained its original significance of large markets, where small producers sell different goods, including food.

Markets have always played a special role in Russian life. A historical overview suggests that many seemingly modern phenomena originated in the distant past. In a country as large as Russia, regular countrywide trade was unfeasible for centuries. Under such conditions market trading, often spontaneous, provided for local exchange. More importantly, even in big cities like Moscow, markets and fairs were a common way of conducting business. This explains why the shopping arcades that adorn many of Russia's oldest towns look very much like market stalls.

For many centuries, and until the middle of the twentieth century, Russia was a peasants' country, which still shapes Russian market culture. For the Russian peasant, visiting markets was a special occasion. In many Russian fairy tales, intrigue starts with a visit to the market. The tales imply that it is possible to get anything there – even the Little Scarlet Flower that will help the Beauty to find her Beast, or the feather of Finist, the Brave Falcon, that again will help the young heroine to find her betrothed. So the very idea of a Russian market includes a sense of possibility and exuberance – and abundance too, ever dear to the Russian soul: even if you came for a horse collar, it was nice to walk along the multi-coloured rows of stalls heaped up with goods you have little need for. Interestingly enough, in the eighteenth century landowners tried to restrict peasants' visits to the market, claiming that it diverted them from their work and 'depraved' them.[1]

Food and Markets

Figure 1 (left). Interpersonal relations are very important for the Russian market: mother and daughter, sellers from Ryazan region.

Figure 2 (right). Private 'road business': tea with pies.

Figure 3 (left). Private kitchen gardens are a good supplement to modest Russian pensions.

Figure 4 (right). Meat in abundance at a Russian market.

Markets in Russia: Back to the Future

In the past, trade in Moscow was carried out in the present Red Square. It was later moved a few blocks away to *Kitay-gorod*; in the middle of the sixteenth century, the stone-built *Gostiny Dvor* (Merchant Yard) was constructed, and tradesmen were directed to relocate there. At first, merchants refused to abandon their wooden stalls, but 'the Terrible tsar ordered his oprichniks to drive out the merchants from the square with whips .... The measure worked'.[2] Elsewhere, wooden stalls continued to be used for centuries. The arrangement of these stalls and the trading manner that developed there resembled a large eastern bazaar even in Moscow. In the nineteenth century, one Muscovite, N.V. Davidov, recalled: 'Asia was in the air: it seemed as if you were in the eastern caravanserai. Yes, the covered bazaars of Smyrna and Constantinople are very similar to the city stalls of Moscow'.[3]

Moscow fairs, especially loud and cheerful before major holidays, astonished the visitor with displays of abundant goods. As far back as in the fifteenth century, Contarini, an Italian diplomat, described a Moscow autumn market set up on the frozen Moscow river:

> At the end of October the river which flows through the city freezes over; stalls for different goods are constructed on it, and all the bazaars take place there, while almost nothing is sold in the city. This is done because the place is considered to be less cold than any other: it is anchored by the city at each bank and protected from the wind. Every day a large quantity of grain, beef, pork, wood, hay and other essential products are displayed on the ice. The goods never cease during the winter.[4]

Such fairs became festivals, the main Russian attractions of the year. Parents brought their marriageable daughters, and young men came to see them and be seen. With more entertainment than anywhere else, fairs brought people from many parts of Russia to communicate and exchange news.

This tradition continued into Soviet times. The 1949 film *Kuban Cossacks* is set at an autumn fair that features not only bright stalls groaning with goods but also swings and roundabouts, cinemas and sideshows, horse racing and dancing. The fair was a meeting place for people from different collective farms. Here girls met their loves, women gossiped, men drank, and the elderly discussed the news. Amid the socializing, traders made deals. Such has been the ideal of a Russian market to this day, and market day very often is the main occasion to see people and to show oneself and one's family. Fairs that accompany popular holidays like New Year, Easter or International Women's Day, still celebrated widely around Russia, are full of people in their best clothes.

Despite this popularity, trading and traders have always been looked upon with some sort of disdain in Russia, an attitude that continues despite merchants' support for charity and the arts. In the nineteenth century, for example, merchants spent great sums building churches, opening hospitals and schools (not for their own workers, but for the poor) and making generous donations to charities. Their children and

Food and Markets

Figure 5 (left). Selling sweets in a Moscow park. (All photographs by the author.)

Figure 6 (right). Saturday market in the provincial town of Tarusa.

Figure 7 (left). Russian staples: potatoes and cabbage.

Figure 8 (right). Russian staples: potatoes, onions and cabbage.

grandchildren used their fortunes to promote art and culture: they gathered splendid collections, financed local crafts, set up theatres and endorsed young talented artists. Thus, the famous Tretyakov Gallery appeared in Moscow through the sponsorship of Pavel Tretyakov, from a famous merchant dynasty, while the Moscow Arts Theatre was founded by the celebrated Stanislavsky, again from a distinguished merchant dynasty, with the support of another Moscow merchant, Savva Morozov. But Russian literature and culture often proclaimed that 'money cannot buy happiness', and this idea is deeply rooted in the Russian mind. As a result, this suspicious attitude towards wealth still lives on in mercantile Russia today: wealth brings envy, hostility, but not respect or status. This often pains so-called 'new Russians', who hope to win the respect of others.

One of the most prominent features of Russian entrepreneurship was the dominant role of commerce, which boosted the development of industry, and not the other way round. The majority of Russian businesses started from trading, accumulated capital and only then began to invest in manufacturing. Even after industrialization, Russian rural residents often had to go to towns to shop at fairs, markets and bazaars. The trend, to a great extent, continues today.

During the Soviet period, large city markets offered goods which could not be found in stores, such as Asian spices, southern vegetables and mutton (which was oddly never available in those times). Demand for such items was low, and prices high. In smaller provincial towns, markets played almost the same role as in the nineteenth century: they were the main centres of food supply.

One of the most interesting cultural aspects of food markets in modern Russia is their surprising traditionalism. Culturally (though not economically, which is quite different), markets remain reminiscent of Soviet and Tsarist times and, in some aspects, even of ancient Russia. A tendency to keep old traditions appeals to both customers and sellers. Although government administration is trying to change markets' structure and organization – to build new covered buildings, to establish strict control over food products, to regularly check vendors' documents, etc. – these changes are met with constant customer accusations of state attempts to destroy the traditional market system. The internet is overflowing with nostalgic reminiscences of a mythic time when food at markets seemed more natural, ecologically safe, mostly locally produced (former Soviet Republics are considered to be 'local' as well) and tasty. It is natural to idealize past times – the grass was greener and the sun was brighter – but in this case the inclination of Russians for their traditional markets has deeper roots. The idea of a food market (and the idea very often differs from reality) appeals to the Russian cultural tradition and, if I may use this term, to Russian national character.

In Russia, we still have different types of places selling food, all of them more or less equivalent to the English 'marketplace': food markets, bazaars and food fairs. They differ mainly in size, which is reflected in an old Russian proverb: where two people meet is a market, three a bazaar and seven a fair. In modern Russia, markets fall into several types:

Figure 9: A good butcher is always ready to help.

Figure 10: Fermented cabbage is the main source of vitamins in Russia.

Figure 11: Caucasian Shashlik a'la Russe.

Figure 12: Conference dinner in Siberia, with food from a local market on the table.

- Indoor city markets: uniformly organized with adequate equipment, these offer the same range of goods as supermarkets seven days a week throughout the year.
- Permanent markets in large urban centres: wooden stalls, open seven days a week, offer both local and non-local food; locals often sell produce on the fringes of the market area.
- Markets in small towns: run one day a week, these offer local and non-local items; locals, often elderly people, are usually found on the fringes.
- Weekend fairs: organized by municipal authorities in Moscow and other major cities, these feature both local and non-local producers.
- Village roadside stands: these offer seasonal specialities from local producers, though sometimes wholesale dealers masquerade as such traders because locally grown food is in special demand.
- Fairs: organized by local authorities, these festive, seasonal events, sometimes with a special theme, offer more entertainment than shopping.
- Spontaneous mini-markets along highways and at road junctions: these spring up to meet particular needs.

To understand the place and role of food markets in modern Russia, it is important to see how Russia is supplied with food today. Three zones can be identified: the first one includes large cities and their environs, where more and more supermarkets open each year; the second encompasses small towns and large villages which have retained small trade in both speciality and convenience stores; the third group is made up of places where people rely on subsistence farming to provide themselves with basic food items and only occasionally purchase limited amounts of things they cannot produce.

In each of these zones markets have different, sometimes opposing, significance. In the third group markets are often the only place for food shopping. In the Soviet times attempts were made to open food stores in all the remote areas of the country, but without state subsidies the system soon fell into decay, and a lot of shops were closed down.

People who live in these places rarely shop in the nearest centres. Some live on potatoes, cabbage and onions from their own household plots, and spend their money only on salt and drinks for special occasions. Even people in less remote villages often see little reason to extend their range of products by planting various vegetables.

In the second group, markets are vital for the supply of goods which cannot be found in a store (often meat, almost always fish and imported fruit and vegetables). In small towns markets are a sort of weekend destination, providing an opportunity to socialize. People dress up when they go shopping to the market and often make it a family occasion. In rural areas markets are often the only source of income for residents who sell produce from their household plots, for example pensioners and stay-at-home mothers.

Food and Markets

Typical of the markets in this second group is the town market of Tarusa in Kaluga region. An old Russian town on the picturesque Oka river 135 km from Moscow, Tarusa has become very popular among the Russian artistic élite; it is trendy to have a vacation house in Tarusa and to spend weekends there. The life of the locals, though, is similar to that in other small towns all over Russia.

On Saturdays markets are set up in Tarusa. Like everywhere, most of the goods on sale are produced in China. One may, of course, come across locally made barrels, shapeless socks knitted by old women and bunches of green birch twigs for Russian baths. The same can be said of food products: the fruit and vegetables come from Caucasus and Asia (or the Netherlands, it can be difficult to tell), just like elsewhere in Russia.

But these goods are sold by bold local women, sometimes helped by young, sluggish Eastern men. Suspicious women shopping in Tarusa feel the tomatoes and enquire: 'Where from?' The shy young man lingers and looks at his partner searchingly. She reacts immediately: 'What do you mean? They are local, they are from Tarusa'. The same goes for everything, including bananas. Surprisingly, the shopping women buy everything – feeling content, as if they had a choice.

There is a fine selection of meat brought from the neighbouring farms. Muscovites buy a lot of meat to make *shashlik* (skewered grilled meat); the locals bargain for every bone. For some reason there is no poultry, for which Tarusa used to be famous. And, hidden among the imported goods, people sell local vegetables, milk, greenery and pickles, perching themselves in inconvenient spots on boxes and homemade tables.

Still, the markets in towns like Tarusa are lifesaving. Here people exchange news and buy food for the week, and especially for holidays. Some, especially the elderly, have an unusual chance to make some money from their home-grown vegetables.

In larger towns and cities, markets for the affluent are strikingly different. The prices here are usually higher than in supermarkets, but the range of goods offered is wider. Despite the fact that giant international stores like Auchan and Metro have opened in Moscow over the past decade, the choice of fresh food is often limited. It is also universally believed that food from the market is more 'natural' and healthier.

In large towns and small villages, the most popular foods at the markets are the simplest: simple food is at the heart of Russian cuisine. In the sixteenth century Michalon Litvin, a Lithuanian, pointing out the difference between what he saw as uncivilized Russians and civilized Lithuanians, reached the unexpected conclusion that Russian simplicity is better for one's health:

> They [the Muscovites] do not accept spices to such an extent that even during Easter meals not only common people, but even the nobility and their leader, who has seized our fortresses and is now counting them arrogantly, are content with such seasoning as grey salt, mustard, garlic, and the bearings of their soil. During the feast at the Duke's table there might be some pepper served raw in

separate bowls, but nobody touches it. The Lithuanians eat overseas delicacies and drink various wines, thus getting all sorts of diseases.[5]

In his novel *Anna Karenina*, Leo Tolstoy describes celebrates simple peasant fare, as in this description of a meal during the summer field work:

> Any uneasiness before the landlord was long gone. The muzhiks were getting ready for their meal. Some were washing themselves, the young men were bathing in the river, and others were fixing a place to rest, undoing their bread bags and uncorking their jugs of kvass. The old man crumbled some bread into a cup, mashed it with his spoon, poured some water, cut some more bread and having added a pinch of salt started to pray, facing the East: "Well, barin, have some of my turya," he said, kneeling before the cup. The turya had such a delicious taste that Levin changed his mind about going home.

For a nobleman like Levin such food was, of course, a novelty, but having worked alongside his peasants, having made an effort to put himself in their shoes, he fully appreciated the taste of peasant food.

Poverty has often been seen as the reason for the simplicity of Russian food, and of course not everyone could afford variety and extravagance. But the main point is that simplicity was a guiding principle: it is not that one 'couldn't afford', but rather that one 'didn't want'.

This desire for simplicity came under attack during the Stalin's rule. A famous culinary book entitled *The Book of Tasty and Healthy Food*, first published in 1939, stigmatized the peasant simplicity of the people's taste and propagandized the success of Soviet food production. A section titled 'To Nurture New Tastes' critiqued the limited popularity of salt-water fish, tinned crab meat, and Roquefort cheese. Similarly, '[a]sparagus, artichokes, Brussels sprout and Savoy cabbage, … chestnuts, champignons, eels, oysters, small game, etc. have undeservedly been forgotten.'[6]

Such efforts, though, failed to change the Russian love of simple fare. Despite the pull of fine cuisine, the distinction of 'civilized' dining, even modern urbanites with refined tastes remain nostalgic for the simple fare of their childhoods, for the peasant dishes of the national past. After Perestroika Russia was flooded with new food products. Many people, especially the intelligentsia and those who could travel (still a very small minority of five to ten per cent), tried new foods from asparagus to avocados to exotic fruits and seafood. But the vast majority of the population remains loyal to traditional products, bought from markets or, even better, grown at home.

These traditional tastes celebrate foods like fermented cabbage and pickled cucumbers, potatoes – thought to have saved a starving nation during the Second World War – tomatoes, spring onions, herbs, meat and poultry, all of which are sold in abundance at Russian markets. Many of these foods are also available in supermarkets, but often in more limited varieties and at higher cost. Some things – like the wild mushrooms and berries craved by Russians – can only be found at markets, unless one has time to forage for them.

Markets also provide the ingredients for the national dishes of the former Soviet Republics that have become so popular in Russia. Promoting such dishes was once government policy during the Soviet era: *The Book of Tasty and Healthy Food* proclaims that 'Soviet cuisine is made up of traditional dishes: Russian pies, Ukrainian *borscht*, Uzbek *pilau*, Georgian *shashlik*, Armenian *tolma*, Azerbaijan *piti*, as well as many other superb national dishes and starters of all the peoples of our country'.[7] While actively promoted in propaganda celebrating the unified Soviet state, these dishes have enriched Russian cuisine. Thus *shashlik* – with meat cubed, marinated, skewered and cooked over coals – from Caucasus became a Russian national dish as well, and large amounts are consumed during weekends and at country houses (*dachas*).

Markets cater to the desire for such foods. For example, markets are the best source for the spices, rice, walnuts, dried fruit, herbs such as coriander and basil, alycha (cherry plum), vine leaves for dolma, mutton and legumes – beans, lentils, chickpeas –which make up the basis of Caucasian and Central Asian cuisines that have become popular in Russia and are celebrated by newcomers from the southern regions and the former Soviet Republics.

The main reasons that Russians buy food at markets, according to a recent poll conducted mainly in large cities (although in many aspects it is universal) are:

1. Market products are traditionally seen as more natural, pure and healthy; their quality is thought to be higher than that of the goods from stores (especially because there are very few specialized shops in Russian towns, and most of them have been replaced by general food stores).
2. Greater choice and variety, including ethnic food, which cannot be easily found in supermarkets, although they do make an effort to cater for local preference; some products, including such basics preferred by Russians as duck, goose, and turkey, usually can only be purchased at the market.
3. A possibility to sample food is also important, as well as a possibility to bargain. Many enjoy the game of bargaining, particularly if they can beat down the price.
4. Interpersonal relations between customer and vendor are very important. The experts advise: 'at the market choose the butcher, not the meat.' Regular customers have their 'own' sellers, who can supply special products, extend credit, and offer advice about freshness or incoming deliveries. In small towns, some sellers even put aside meat offcuts and bones to give to old customers who can no longer afford them.
5. Multicultural character is important. The market is the meeting place for different cultures. A famous nineteenth-century fair in Nizhniy Novgorod took this to extremes, including not only a huge Orthodox cathedral but also a mosque, an

Armenian church, and a special space for tea trade built in a Chinese style. Ideally the marketplace remains a place for peace and multicultural harmony, but too often it has become a place of interethnic conflicts.
6. Markets are places where staple Russian foods, including those of former Soviet Republics that have integrated deeply into Russian food culture, can be bought. Locally produced food is preferred.
7. The main delicacies from different Russian regions, such as sturgeon, crab, red and black caviar (despite the official ban black caviar is still sold 'under the counter'), many kinds of fish from Lake Baikal, etc., are only available at markets. The attitude towards fish in Russia is complicated: the majority of the population has always preferred meat; during the Soviet times efforts were made to establish a taste for fish. However, now good fish is more expensive than the best meat, and herring has become an everyday meal, and holidays feature fish delicacies like salmon and red caviar.

Despite the continued preference for markets in Russia, there are problems. The biggest is re-trading; it is an open secret that most of the market goods come from producers who supply them to stores as well, so the myth about purity and freshness is often just that – a myth. The majority of market traders buy from resellers who deal in everything from sugar and vegetable oil to yoghurts and cereals. Some traders are representatives of local or far-off farming enterprises (these usually sell meat, fruit and vegetables). A small proportion is made up of private traders who sell produce grown on their private plots or traditional land resources (especially greens, berries, mushrooms and root crops).

In addition, the traditionally negative attitude to trading and traders persists even today. It is particularly noticeable in relation to people of Caucasian and Asian nationalities, who often own large trading businesses but are sometimes subject to discrimination. Lately, such dealers have tended to hire local residents to sell their goods, as locals are viewed as more trustworthy.

Finally, markets are hotbeds of crime, especially in large Russian cities. This has been the case for centuries, and quite often in Russian history crime prevention started with the 'cleansing' of the markets.

Today many officials draw attention to food markets, claiming that they no longer serve a necessary purpose and need to be replaced by modern store trade. But this seems to go against the opinions of the people, who still consider markets an essential part of Russian gastronomic culture. Despite state attempts to restructure and modernize Russian markets, to replace them with modern stores, markets still survive in their traditional old forms because they appeal to people's preferences and remain an important part of Russian gastronomic culture.

Notes

1. *An Outline of Russian Culture in the Eighteenth Century*, ed. by B. Rybakov, vol.1 (Moscow: Moscow State UP, 1985), p. 218
2. I.A. Slonov. *Trade in Moscow* (Moscow: Tonchu, 2006), p.104
3. Slonov, p. 104.
4. Giosafat Barbaro and Ambrogio Contarini, *Barbaro and Contarini in Russia* (Moscow: Nauka, 1971), p. 158.
5. Michalon Litvin. *On the customs of Tatars, Lithuanians and Muscovites* (Moscow: Moscow State UP, 1994), p.73.
6. *The Book of Tasty and Healthy Food* (Moscow: Pishchepromizdat, 1954), p. 38.
7. *The Book of Tasty and Healthy Food*, p. 38.

Markets, Gender and Translation in Turn-of-the-Twentieth-Century San Francisco and Southern Vietnam

Erica J. Peters

What makes a farmers market work? Like any kind of market situation, it requires sellers and buyers, and a meeting of the minds between them. Buyers and sellers need to reach agreement regarding product and price. I argue that such agreements are most readily reached when people coming to the market, whether to buy or sell or both, feel they share a common language and common experience. Efforts to establish farmers markets have often stumbled when there was not enough of a shared language and shared food culture to create these agreements.[1] Some recent authors focus on trade-offs between economic interests and social/community-building interests.[2] Others hold out hope that curiosity about other foodways may sustain a market's business.[3] In contrast, this paper suggests that building on an existing sense of community and shared experiences may provide a more robust environment for economic exchange.[4]

By comparing two different gendered market cultures on opposite sides of the Pacific Ocean – the male-dominated Colombo produce market in turn-of-the-twentieth-century San Francisco and the female-dominated country markets in the same period in southern Vietnam – this paper examines how vendors and customers took pleasure in sharing the market space together. Based on contemporary newspaper accounts and published reports, I argue that same-sex interactions made communication and haggling easier and more enjoyable, facilitating the purpose of the markets from both an economic and a social perspective. Further, I show that as Saigon developed into the urban centre of southern Vietnam, structural forces generated a new largely male culture of customers and vendors, despite Vietnam's long-standing traditions of female-dominated markets.

Women in country markets in southern Vietnam

In the nineteenth century, Vietnamese village life was roughly segregated by gender. That was especially true at country markets, where women overwhelmingly predominated as both buyers and sellers. Each woman usually arrived at market with baskets full of goods to sell and went home at the end of the day with her baskets full of goods purchased from other vendors. Vietnamese women had long played a major role in trade, inspiring current debates over whether they had more autonomy than early-modern women in other Asian countries.[5] During the nineteenth century, however, day-to-day male violence may have increased women's preference for trading only with other women.

When the American John White was exploring trade relations in the southern region in 1824, he noted that 'every man is a soldier, [while] the commercial operations are performed by the women'.[6] When he visited a market outside Saigon, he noted that the vendors were all women, 'each one the focus of her own little domain' (219). He heard some of the older women complaining loudly as soldiers seized some of their best goods to bring back to a high-ranking official's household: 'This, we afterwards found, was a common and universal practice [...]. We had frequent opportunities to notice that poor old women were the victims of their extortion, while young girls were passed by with a smile or salutation' (228). The region had been in an extended civil war a quarter century before, and there was still a great deal of civil unrest – hence the general militarization of Vietnamese society, and the impunity of these men grabbing what they wanted in the marketplace without paying for it.

Forty years later, when the French invaded southern Vietnam, again they noticed only women in the markets. Rumours of French soldiers coming to abduct local women regularly emptied out these southern markets during the years of French conquest, though each time the women soon returned to make their necessary exchanges. Men faced their own dangers on the road, as they were liable to be impressed as soldiers or unpaid labourers if away from the safety of their village. Large groups of women thus walked together to market, or rowed to riverine markets, during these troubled times.[7]

Gabrielle Vassal was the English wife of a French army doctor stationed for a few years at the Pasteur Institute of Nha Trang, a good-sized southern Vietnamese town with about three thousand inhabitants. In 1910 Vassal described her observations of market day in Nha Trang. In a nearby village, a Vietnamese woman prepared to go to the market. Before setting out, she handed her infant to her own mother, and took up her baskets full of dried fish.[8] Vassal noted that mothers occasionally brought their infants to market, balanced in one of the baskets they carried on poles over their shoulders. But the preference was to leave young children at home with their grandmother or another older woman. Older girls came to the market, to help and to learn the ropes:

> Going to market is certainly the favourite occupation of the Annamese girl and woman. She likes the independence of the day spent in the company of her acquaintances and friends from other villages, and above all she rejoices in the opportunity of exercising her cunning over a bargain [...]. In the smallest transaction she concentrates all her energies to make every *sapek* [small coin] she can, and if she is able to introduce a rotten mango among the good ones that she is selling to a cook, or persuade her friend to give her another handful of rice for nothing, she absolutely glories in her astuteness and business capacity. She will always ask twenty cents for a coconut when she is willing to take five, and it is only when the would-be customer is in the act of leaving [...] that she will lower her price.

> Not that I often go to the market. The spectacle of all these women sitting on the ground with their goods spread on the bare earth does not induce appetite, nor is the smell agreeable, with all the dried fish, *nuoc-mam* [fish sauce] and *choum-choum* [rice liquor]. The noise, too, is appalling. None of the women stop talking for a single minute, and to be heard above the conversation going on close to them they have to employ the full force of their lungs. (95)

The women were not divided into vendors and consumers; the same woman who sold mangos or coconuts might be buying fish to take back to her village. Women arrived in the morning with baskets full of goods to sell, and left with baskets full of goods to carry back to the village – or sometimes a squealing pig caged in a special lattice-work basket, slung on a pole between two women. The woman Vassal followed brought back food for her own household but also replenished the stock of lentils, beans and betel leaves for Grandmother to sell out of their house during the day.

In her description, Vassal stressed the absent men: 'At the market the only masculine forms to be seen are those of the Europeans' cooks who are catering for their next meal. Except for these men and an occasional child whom a mother has been unable to leave behind, the market is entirely given up to women' (96). Male guards, tax inspectors, and occasional unruly bands of soldiers ventured into the markets under French colonialism, as they had before as well. But male vendors were very rare, and the first regular male shoppers were men who cooked for European households.

Women at market were not free from social strictures. Common sayings reminded them of their duties to their families. A late nineteenth century proverb recommended women not delay on their way to market: 'Aunt, whether you go to market or not, the market will still be crowded.'[9] If she went earlier she would presumably find better deals; the proverb also promoted a sense of anticipation, looking ahead to the excitement of circulating in a crowd. Around the same time, the poem 'Advice from a Mother to her Daughter,' provided more detailed instructions for women in the marketplace:

> Do not talk too much, you will sound like a fishwife […]. Go early to market for the best food. Check what others are paying for each item, so as not to spend too much. Buy ingredients your parents enjoy, but do not forget food for the servants as well. When buying fish, examine the gills; when buying gourds and squash, check them carefully to see if they are fresh, and buy some onion to cook them with. Watch out for thieves and vagabonds, and avoid disputes […]. And above all, when you return from market, do not spoil your younger brothers and nephews by giving them treats.[10]

If those words echoed in women's heads while they shopped, perhaps that explains why Vassal heard them speaking so much and so loudly – to drown out the echoes of their families' instructions and enjoy the marketplace as a space of female sociability and relative independence.

Food and Markets

Figure 1. Saigon's main market (1882). Courtesy Charles le Myre de Vilers Collection of the French Consulate in Ho Chi Minh City.

Men in Saigon's urban market

The situation in Saigon's urban markets was completely different. Saigon was a new city, which developed into a major urban centre after the French took over southern Vietnam in the 1860s. The markets on the outskirts of the city remained female-dominated for decades, as they had been when John White visited in 1824. In the city proper, however, a new class of male buyers and sellers emerged.

Many of them were male Chinese immigrants, drawn to the Saigon region for its economic opportunities. Chinese merchants had been significant participants in south-east Asian trade networks at least since the Manchus overthrew the Ming dynasty in the seventeenth century. By the nineteenth century these Chinese men were embedded in south-east Asian commerce, supplying farmers with loans and buying their crops for resale and export throughout the region. They often married local women, gaining access to their networks of commercial relationships. And when Europeans arrived in force, the Chinese took on the role of translating between the new arrivals and the local population. This combination of language skills and commercial networks made the Chinese likely participants in Saigon's multilingual marketplace.

Chinese men also had strong culinary reputations. Upper-class households in Saigon, whether Vietnamese, Chinese, or French, prided themselves on hiring Chinese chefs. This provided another connection to the marketplace, as one's Chinese chef was entrusted with the kitchen budget each day, so he or his underlings could select ingredients at the market. Those families or restaurants that could not afford Chinese chefs usually hired Vietnamese male chefs, whether because of a preference for men or because Vietnamese women were somewhat wary of the colonial urban culture.

All these new male buyers called forth new male vendors who could speak their respective languages, make them feel comfortable and explain any new ingredients. As a consequence, Saigon's food markets became a largely male space. In 1887 Arthur Delteil provided a detailed report on this new market in Saigon, noting that the whole city was only about a quarter-century old: 'Today there are quais, a market, and the town center, where [in 1859] there was just a vast swamp.'[11] The market was established along one of those new quais. Delteil described four large covered halls, although an image from 1882 (Figure 1) seems to show five or six halls. This was the city's main market, with areas set aside for fish, poultry, meat, produce, handicrafts and stalls offering ready-to-eat food.

Fish vendors sold river fish, mud-coloured and unappealing to French eyes. They also sold deep-sea fish such as tuna, sea bream and anchovies, and offered 'excellent oysters,' 'delicious crabs,' 'large shrimp' and lobsters 'as good as we can get in Europe' (63). Poultry included ducks, capons, pigeons, peacocks, guineafowl, snipe and quail. For produce, Delteil noted bananas, mangos, mangosteens, cucumbers, cabbages and asparagus, as well as various kinds of lettuce. Butchers offered mostly pork, but also wild rabbit, boar and some beef, for European tables.

Delteil reported that the market was crowded with Chinese and Vietnamese 'of both sexes,' doing their marketing but also eating prepared foods right then and there (62). Delteil was fascinated with the stalls selling fried rice, white rice, rice porridge, noodles, spring rolls, pastries and gelatinous treats. Shoppers squeezed in around the displays, and chose from among ten or twelve dishes at each stall. One man wrapped shrimp and bean sprouts in what Delteil called a little 'omelet'; meanwhile an old woman made 'crepes' without a frying pan: 'She took a piece of dough and laid it on two little forked sticks, which she then manipulated cleverly over the stove. At every second I felt that the dough would escape and fall into the fire, but not at all …. It puffed up, and took on such a golden color as it cooked, that I very much wanted to try it' (64). In the evening, the area around the market was filled with tables and lit with cheerful lanterns. The city's residents came to enjoy the cooler night air, to socialize and to feast on the delicious street food.

This was a vastly different kind of market than the ones in the countryside. Open from early morning until late at night, Saigon's urban market buzzed with curious visitors. It was a place to try new dishes and new ingredients. In 1824 Saigon had been a small town; now it was a city of 35,000 people. Saigon's urban market was a social zone for vendors and shoppers, both men and women, of varying ethnicities: Chinese, Vietnamese, Khmer, Tamil, Malay, European as well as people of mixed heritage. Soldiers had less leeway to harass women or seize their goods than they had had sixty years earlier when John White was there. Pidgin dialects emerged to provide a way

Figure 2. Colombo wholesale market (1910s). Courtesy, California Historical Society.

for people to communicate, but the atmosphere was very different from a single-sex country market.

Unlike Vassal, Delteil did not mention the noise of rambunctious negotiations. His descriptions of the prepared foods laid out for buyers' selection suggests that people were simply pointing to what they wanted rather than having detailed conversations about the dishes and ingredients or trying to negotiate a better price. He observed specifically that people went there to see the sights and do their marketing: 'One never sees fights there' (65). Given the wide range of people of different backgrounds, not to mention colonial tensions, a fight might quickly turn deadly. It was best to keep the atmosphere light and the transactions straight-forward and professional.

San Francisco's Colombo Produce Market

After it opened on Front Street in 1876 (Figure 2), San Francisco's Colombo wholesale produce market was known for being an exclusively male space – and for its raucous haggling, mostly in Italian. Men were the ones both buying and selling in that marketplace. Male market gardeners arrived with produce and went home with their wagons empty. Their counterparts were also mostly men; they arrived with empty carts, and by seven a.m. these commission merchants, peddlers, grocers or chefs had bought the fruits and vegetables they would either resell to stores or San Francisco's housewives, or cook up themselves in restaurant and hotel kitchens. Vendors spoke various Italian dialects, and preferred to negotiate with other Italians, such as prominent commission merchant A.P. Giannini, who later went on to found the Bank of Italy, and later still took over the Bank of America.[12]

Women showed up only after the selling had finished, to pick up scraps from the market floor. These poor women were not customers, and got no explanation of which produce was ripe or how to use each ingredient. San Francisco housewives did hear about the wares, second-hand, from the peddlers who shopped the Colombo market and then carried produce up the city's steep hills. Each housewife had a relationship with a particular peddler, Irish, Italian, or Chinese, whom she trusted to deliver fresh fruits and vegetables to her doorstep. She might bargain with him herself, or she might have her Irish or Chinese cook do so. But women in turn-of-the-century San Francisco did not go down to the produce market to haggle with male vendors.

A reporter at the Colombo market in 1892 described the arrival of the Italian truck gardeners, with their 'repelling aroma of garlic [and] cigarettes'. Shortly after midnight they arrived at the market, with their carts loaded down with cabbages, carrots, beets, leeks, turnips and more. After unloading, the drivers shared a glass of wine or black coffee at a local bar: 'they are ever chatting as friends and no spirit of business rivalry is displayed.' Then the customers arrived, notably 'the fat chefs of the Italian restaurants'. Vendors greeted these buyers warmly, 'as if two old friends'. And they chatted with them in Italian:

> The blending of these voices – basso, orotund, tenor and sepulchral basso profundi – sung out in the merriest of moods, gives to the place an air of an impromptu opera bouffe. The basso 'points with pride' to his tomatoes, or in gutteral notes sings the praises of his carrots [...] and the tenor seems sorry that he has been interrupted in his melodious plaint as to the esculent qualities of his beets.

Other customers came by a little later in the morning; these were mostly other European immigrants or Chinese men. Now vendors would call out in broken English: 'Cabbages, all good!' or 'Beets, vera nice!' At this point, the bargaining changed from a light-hearted conversation among friends: 'The bargaining is fierce and close, for neither trusts the other...The remnants that [even] the Chinese do not buy are swept up into heaps for the scavengers' carts.'[13]

Ten years later, a similar story. The reporter, Harriet Quimby, even called it 'The Italian Market', and relied on the same musical metaphor:

> The dialect of these sons of the soil has a musical cadence difficult to describe [...] it may be the diet of garlic, for I have heard it said that the latter is excellent for the voice [...]. By sunrise, the stock is almost gone and the floor [...] is

covered ankle-deep with crisp cabbage leaves, carrot and turnip tops [...]. The men sit about on crates and while they eat their bit of breakfast they amuse themselves by watching the basket and sack bearers, men, women, and children, who come to get their day's stock of vegetables from the miscellany on the floor.

As in 1892, these scavengers got to pick through what was left when the real buyers were done for the day. But this time the *Chronicle* reader got a fuller description of these scavengers:

Down from Broadway and Vallejo street come the women – sometimes two or three in a group. Short skirts showing white-stockinged ankles – some with typical peasant dress, others with half American garb, but nearly all wearing large gingham aprons – scatter throughout the market [...]. As if they were gathering cranberries on the marsh these women stoop and turn over the mass of leaves, taking out a carrot here, a turnip there, sometimes finding a whole bunch that has been overlooked or neglected. Into the basket or sack they go. A bunch of lettuce, a piece of dill or perhaps a handful of summer savory, all fresh and crisp, are tucked carefully away and the finder continues the search.

Quimby asked a gardener if anyone gave the women any trouble, taking food for free: 'Nobody seems to care,' he answered, 'for they do not come early enough to be much in the way.' On Saturdays, children came instead of their mothers to pick up the leftover vegetables, chattering together in large groups, running through the market 'like so many chickens, eating raw carrots and turnips as they would apples'. Quimby noted that occasionally an adult man would come to gather scraps, but he would look 'sheepish', embarrassed to be there doing women's work, and he would leave as quickly as he could. By eleven a.m. the leftovers had been picked over, the truck gardeners were well on their way back to their farms and the garbage men were sweeping up.[14]

A few years later, it was still the same situation. A reporter named Alberta Bancroft went to the market at six a.m., thinking to arrive in the thick of the transactions, only to discover that at that hour most of the men were already finishing up their sales. Still, the all male environment was intoxicating to her. On the street, 'big horses, tall wagons [...] and men, men everywhere'. By the wholesale produce market, she saw 'men seething to and fro, sidewalks crowded with crates and boxes'. The atmosphere put her in an excellent mood:

I never was so enthusiastic over things to eat in my life; everything looked so good; everything smelt so good. There were currants and strawberries and loganberries by the crate. There were bunches of bananas that topped your hat. There were pineapples and baby watermelons and grown up cantaloupes and tiny new pink and white apples and cherries and rhubarb and asparagus by the ton [...].

Then there were the men. Such a strapping, handsome lot. Such red cheeks and black eyes. And so marvelously good natured. They were all madly anxious to tell anything any one might have a fancy to ask them; and they all seemed to consider everything such a huge joke. 'Gangway for the lady!' bellowed an apple-faced, black-eyed young scamp several stories up on a fruit wagon, as I paused before a formidable array of men armed with hand trucks.[15]

Bancroft was definitely an unusual person at the market, quite amusing to the vendors, with her gender, her reporter's questions and her eager appreciation for both the produce and the male producers.

After an hour or so, she reported, the Colombo Market was strewn with scraps of produce, mostly cabbage leaves, lettuce leaves and bits of cauliflower:

'A gypsy woman, black shawl over her head and two heavily laden aprons about her waist, was hungrily looking about for more [...]. A lady with a sailor hat ornamented by a bedraggled and indignant plume was foraging in another corner [...]. It was 7:30, and the early morning glamour was gone.'

Like the other, earlier observers of the wholesale market district, she was struck by the gendered aspect of the market. And like them, she also commented on the language she heard there: '[Besides] a smatter of German and a jabber of Chinese … the babel of speech was caused by those ruddy, handsome, kinky-haired "Dagos," and was unintelligible.'[16]

In this urban market, like in Saigon, the gendered nature of the market was not absolute, nor was the language exclusive. But the transactions went most smoothly between men who shared a language, and that was usually Italian. Italian vendors especially liked drinking with other Italian vendors. They liked doing business with Italian customers and looked forward to those interactions. They saw non-Italian men – especially the Chinese – as interlopers, who should come later in the morning in order to avoid disrupting the musical nature of the commerce among countrymen. And women should come last of all – the Italian men 'amused themselves' watching poor women forage for some scraps to thicken a soup. That was not even commerce, since no money changed hands.

Conclusion

Such interactions – congenial haggling – between people who shared a gender and a language were a key part of the experience in certain turn-of-the-twentieth-century food markets. Sharing a gender as well as a vocabulary helped put people at ease and encouraged the making of mutually desirable deals. And this was markedly true in San Francisco's urban environment when Italian men connected with each other by excluding other men and a whole city's worth of women from their bonds of fellowship.

Food and Markets

When studying produce markets it is important to keep in mind the question of farm labour. Recent authors have noted that farmers markets encourage customers to believe they are buying direct from the person who cared for the crop. For instance, when Christie McCullen worked as a part-time vendor at a market in Davis, California, she was often mistaken for a farmer, farmer's daughter, or farmer's wife. Not only did customers conflate vendors with growers, but they also romanticized farm work: 'Farming's not an easy job...[Farmers] use their hands and use their physical labour to feed us.'[17] These customers create a fantasy that they and their families are fed and nurtured by the white person in front of them, erasing the experience and expertise of the non-white labourer.[18]

In Vietnam's country markets, where vendors were also buyers, these women each had a solid understanding of the material realities of planting, tending, harvesting and bringing goods to market. But in the urban markets of Saigon and San Francisco, customers varied in their awareness of who was actually growing their food. Some came from farming families themselves, and shared that experience and knowledge-base with the vendors. Over time, however, visitors to the Colombo Market in San Francisco began to treat the person in front of them more as a living symbol of the farm than as a simple participant in a complex food distribution system. When reporters called vendors 'sons of the soil', or described vendors' pride in their tomatoes, or compared their red cheeks to tasty apples, they contributed to the illusion that markets can give buyers access to cheerful, well-fed farm labourers – what Margaret Gray has called the 'idealized, agrarian vision of soil-and-toil harmony on family farms'.[19] Labour and capital played an increasing role in agriculture, and yet both were hidden from consumers at twentieth-century urban farmers markets. As Jane Pyle already noted four decades ago, the farmers market is 'stoutly defended by those who see in it old-fashioned virtues of individuality and direct connection with Mother Earth'.[20] In the twentieth century, city residents might come to market for the fantasy of face-time with a farmer as much as for the goods on offer.

Notes

1. Alison Hope Alkon, *Black, White, and Green: Farmers Markets, Race, and the Green Economy* (U Georgia P, 2012), pp. 43–44, 124, 136, 146–49; Michael Mikulak, *The Politics of the Pantry: Stories, Food, and Social Change* (McGill-Queen's UP, 2013), pp. 14–19; Margaret Gray, *Labor and the Locavore: The Making of a Comprehensive Food Ethic* (U California P, 2013), pp. 10–12, 74–79; Jenrose Fitzgerald, Lisa Markowitz and Dwight B. Billings, 'Not Your Grandmother's Agrarianism: The Community Farm Alliance's Agrifood Activism,' *Transforming Places: Lessons from Appalachia*, ed. by Stephen L. Fisher and Barbara Ellen Smith (U Illinois P, 2012), p. 218.
2. David Connor, Kathryn Colasanti, R. Brent Ross and Susan B. Smalley, 'Locally Grown Foods and Farmers Markets: Consumer Attitudes and Behaviors', *Sustainability* 2:3 (2010), pp. 742–56.
3. Rachel Slocum, 'Thinking Race through Corporeal Feminist Theory: Divisions and Intimacies at the Minneapolis Farmers Market', *Social & Cultural Geography* 9:8 (2008), pp. 849–69, esp. 864–65.
4. C. Clare Hinrichs, 'Embeddedness and Local Food Systems: Notes on Two Types of Direct Agricultural Market,' *Journal of Rural Studies* 16 (2000), pp. 295–303.
5. George Dutton, 'Beyond Myth and Caricature: Situating Women in the History of Early Modern Vietnam', *Journal of Vietnamese Studies* 8.2 (Spring 2013), pp. 1–36.
6. John White, *A Voyage to Cochin China* (London: Heinemann, 1824), pp. 261; subsequent references are given in the text.
7. Paulin François Alexandre Vial, *Les premières années de la Cochinchine, colonie française* (Paris: Challamel, 1874), 2, p. 254; Henri Ludovic Jammes, *Souvenirs du pays d'Annam* (Paris: Challamel, 1900), pp. 279–82; Henri Mouhot, *Travels in Siam, Cambodia, and Laos, 1858–1860* (Oxford: Oxford UP, 1992), 1, p. 227; M. J. Silvestre, 'Rapport sur l'esclavage,' *Excursions et reconnaissances* 2:4 (1880), p. 138.
8. Gabrielle Vassal, *On and Off duty in Annam* (London: Heinemann, 1910), pp. 90–98; subsequent references are given in the text.
9. J.M.J., *Notions pour servir à l'étude de la langue annamite* (Tân Đinh: Impr. de la Mission, 1878), p. 306.
10. 'Advice from a Mother to her Daughter', *Bulletin de la Société des Etudes Indo-Chinoises de Saigon* 1888 (1er Semestre), pp. 20–21, 25–29.
11. Delteil, *Guide du voyageur à Saigon: Un an de séjour en Cochinchine* (Paris: Challamel, 1887), p. 59; subsequent references are given in the text.
12. Compare to Maria Laura Viteri, 'The Buenos Aires Central Wholesale Market (BACWN): A Case of Multiple Power', *International Journal of Sociology of Agriculture and Food* 16:2 (2009), pp. 54–69, especially 65–67.
13. 'The Colombo Market', *San Francisco Chronicle* 5 June 1892, p. 21.
14. Harriet Quimby, 'Free Vegetables in the Italian Market,' *San Francisco Chronicle* 31 August 1902, p A1.
15. Alberta Bancroft, 'What One Woman Saw in the Wholesale Market District Before Breakfast Time,' *San Francisco Chronicle* 18 June 1905, p. 6.
16. Bancroft.
17. Christie McCullen, 'The White Farm Imaginary: How One Farmers Market Re-fetishizes the Production of Food and Limits Food Politics', *Food as Communication: Communication as Food*, ed. by Janet M. Cramer, Carlnita P. Greene and Lynn M. Walters (New York: Peter Lang, 2011), pp. 217–34 (p. 230).
18. McCullen, pp. 218–26; Gray, pp. 22–25, 77; Julie Guthman, *Agrarian Dreams: The Paradox of Organic Farming in California* (U California P, 2004), pp. 51–53.
19. Gray, p. 2.
20. J. Pyle, 'Farmers Markets in the United States: Functional Anachronisms,' *Geographical Review* 61:2 (April 1971), pp. 167–97 (p. 197); See also Todd Holmes, 'Farmer's Market: Agribusiness and the Agrarian Imaginary in California and the Far West' *California History* 90:2 (2013), pp. 24–41.

Going beyond Sights, Smells and Taste: Shared Responsibility for Food Safety at Farmers Markets in the UK

Brigit Ramsingh and Carol A. Wallace

'The sense of smell, like a faithful counsellor, foretells its character.'
Jean Anthelme Brillat-Savarin (1755-1826)[1]

'In the 1960s, people would go to a butcher and smell meat to see how fresh it was [...]. Nowadays so much is pre-packaged, people don't have the same experience of smelling food.'
Chris Smith (2013)[2]

'Eyeballing or sniffing food is not a reliable way to assess its safety. Spoilage bacteria, which cause a deterioration in smell or appearance, are different from those that make you sick. You could eat food spoilt by these microorganisms and feel fine. Equally, a hamburger teeming with *E coli* might smell great.'
Dr Luisa Dillner (2012)[3]

With all apologies to Brillat-Savarin and other sensory zealots, there are many myths and conflicting advice that remain abundant with regard to food safety. Indeed, food is and should be a sensory experience and enjoyed accordingly via the nostrils and eyes as well the mouth – hence a key attraction of farmers markets is that they enable closer contact and connection with the food itself as well as with the food vendors. Many researchers and foodies alike promote the role of farmers markets in establishing a bond between producer and consumer; how this cooperation adds value and how the consideration of taste and choice among consumers can be a matter of class and social distinction.[4] But whilst wandering the stalls of farmers markets, inhaling the aromas of pork pies, artisanal cheeses and fresh herbs, no one likes to think about the dangers that may lurk within these products. The reality is, however, harmful bacteria have a way of creeping in to unexpected places and, in spite of Brillat-Savarin's faithful counsellor, the senses of smell, sight and taste are not enough as tests for consumers or vendors to gauge the character or safety of market products. As many food safety experts warn, farmers markets can be sources of harmful, odourless, unseen and tasteless bacteria such as *E.coli* O157:H7, salmonella and campylobacter, not only in foods such as beef, pork, lamb, chicken, turkey, game, fish, shellfish, raw milk and eggs, but also in vegetables and fruit that have not been labelled as ready-to-eat and especially vegetables that are visibly dirty.[5] Good practices to prevent foodborne contamination should be a high priority and shared responsibility since recently published results from the Food Standards Agency's (FSA) Biannual Public Attitudes Tracker show the top three food safety issues of concern for respondents were food hygiene when eating out (36%), the use of additives in food (26%), and food poisoning such as salmonella and *E.coli* (26%).[6]

This paper aims to expand on the notions of the food market not only as a sensory and social experience, but also ideally as a *safer* experience. Recent literature suggests that environmental issues in the United States and food scares in Europe have been significant drivers in the growth of farmers markets, since these markets are believed to offer a higher amount of information through direct contact with producers.[7] Whilst this re-connection between producers and consumers is a positive step, there is a perception within the local-food movement that locally grown produce is safer and carries less risk than commercially grown products.[8] One common misconception is that produce grown on a small-scale farm is automatically safer because it does not travel long distances or come from a large industrial-sized farm; however, regardless of scale, the same risks apply to how fresh produce is grown, how raw products are handled and how ready-to-eat products are produced.

In order to mitigate these potential hazards, in recent years many scholars have identified the importance of establishing what Griffith has called a positive 'food safety culture' – defined as 'the aggregation of the prevailing, relatively constant, learned, shared attitudes, values and beliefs contributing to the hygiene behaviours used within a particular food handling environment'.[9] Moreover, it has been recognized that food safety should be a 'shared responsibility' among producers, processors, retailers, *food service providers*, and the public.[10] In other words, because food is produced, processed, distributed, sold and cooked – essentially handled or under the care of many people before it is eaten – blame and accountability for its safety is also shared along this continuum of stakeholders, from 'farm-to-fork' or 'gate-to-plate'. This paper aims to reinforce the important relationship of the food market to food safety and to consumer health protection.

With these concepts in mind, this paper will characterize the resurgence of interest in farmers markets in the UK since the mid-1990s, what some have described as a 'harbinger of the second industrial revolution' alongside parallel developments in food safety and consumer health protection.[11] It will thus examine the recent past and current state of farmers markets in the UK especially in terms of their food safety facilities, practice, education training and culture and the legislative and institutional structures that support and govern them, such as the National Farmers Retail and Market Association (FARMA), the National Association of British Market Authorities (NABMA) and the work of the Food Standards Agency (FSA).

Although the history of markets in the UK could arguably span hundreds of years, this paper provides an historical overview of food safety guidelines amidst the recent resurgence of farmers markets in the UK since the first was held in Bath in 1997.[12] It will build upon narratives which examine the historical and cultural contexts which have led to the resurgence of farmers markets and other 'alternative food networks' as key institutions in the trend towards less industrialized agricultural systems.[13] It will outline current considerations for food safety at farmers markets and propose actions to establish and evaluate food safety facilities, practices and education/guidance requirements at farmers markets. In this way the paper will consider support needs for farmers, vendors and consumers to help make the concepts of 'shared responsibility' and food safety culture a reality along the continuum from farmer to market to home kitchen.

The resurgence of farmers markets in the UK

The resurgence of farmers markets in the UK has its origins in the mid-1990s. As recently as five years ago, however, in 2009, they were seen to be under threat in the wake of the 2008 economic downturn. By 2011 several factors came into play which suggested that UK farmers markets are indeed recovering, growing stronger and 'making a comeback'.[14] This period of renewed interest can best be examined through the work of key organizations like NABMA and FARMA against the backdrop of several high-profile food safety scares that marked the late 1990s and early 2000s in the UK and worldwide. In comparison, Brown suggests that the trend of renewed interest in farmers markets in the US occurred in the 1970s and 1980s, approximately twenty years earlier than the same resurgence in the UK.[15]

The 1990s UK renaissance of farmers and local markets is not necessarily a widespread phenomenon among industrialized countries. In fact many Western nations (for example Italy, France and Germany) did not see as great an interruption in the emphasis on local and fresh farm-produced food. The UK 'interruption' is perhaps better characterized as an 'eclipse' in the form of large supermarkets growing to dominate food retailing in the late twentieth century. Although some supermarkets emerged earlier, their widespread popularity only grew in the 1960s due to British postwar food rationing.[16] Meanwhile, although 'American-style' supermarkets did emerge in Italy, France and Germany, for various reasons there existed much greater continuity of focus on markets and small-and medium-sized food retail businesses, which could often remain even larger food outlets such as supermarkets and hypermarkets developed.[17]

Some of the characteristics of this 'second industrial revolution' and the rise of what Renting and Banks have called the search for 'alternative food networks' include the conservation of resources and values; a means of bonding between producer and consumer; an increase in value of this exchange; a sense of belonging, engagement, and character and in some cases an improvement on taste of the produce.[18] However, at the same time serious food safety crises prompted a renewed interest in a search for 'alternative food networks' and a rallying cry around the farm-to-fork/gate-to-plate mantras, not just from consumers and producers but also among public health institutions.

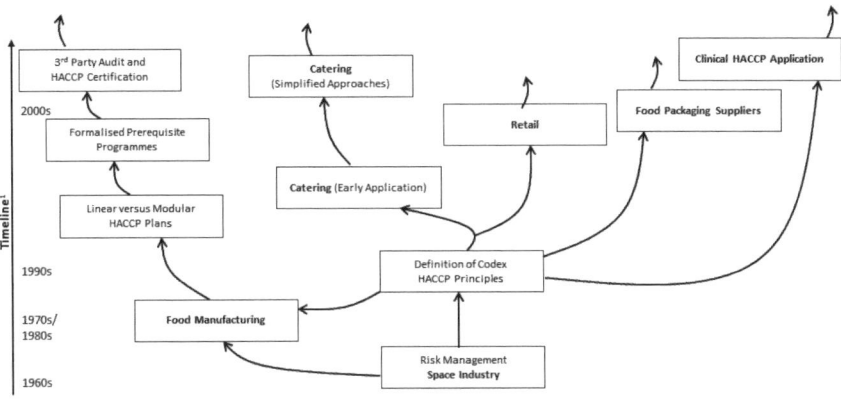

Figure 1: The Evolution of HACCP. (Adapted from: Wallace, CA. 2014. 'Editorial: HACCP-based Food Safety Management Systems – great in theory but can we really make them work in practice?' Perspectives in Public Health, 134 (4) pp. 188-190.)

The UK was hit by several high-profile food safety crises in the last thirty years, which contributed toward increased surveillance, regulation (both within the UK and the EU) and the advent of the Food Standards Agency in 2001. Bovine Spongiform Encephalopathy (BSE) emerged as a problem in cattle from the mid-1980s, resulted in the first human death from its human form, variant Creutzfeld Jakob Disease (vCJD) in the mid-1990s and led to a worldwide ban on British beef exports. During this time period, there were also some particularly dramatic and devastating local outbreaks such as the 1996 *E.coli* O157 outbreak in Scotland, in which twenty-one people died, and later the 2005 *E.coli* O157 outbreak in South Wales in which there were 157 cases, mostly children, with one death of five-year-old Mason Jones. These major outbreaks were attributed to poor food handling practices which led to cross contamination of the ingested products.[19]

In response to these tragedies, recommendations not only in the UK but also at the EU pointed toward the need to adopt food safety management systems such as the hazard analysis and critical control point system (HACCP), which was formally endorsed by the Joint FAO/WHO *Codex alimentarius* committee in 1993.[20]

The hazard analysis and critical control point system (HACCP) is an approach to food safety management through the identification and control of hazards that might occur in foods. HACCP was developed as part of the food supply project for the US manned space programme when the National Aeronautics and Space Administration (NASA) asked the Pillsbury Company to help design the system. The concept was launched publicly to the food industry in 1971. The evolution of HACCP throughout the food industry and beyond is shown in Figure 1, and, although the principles of HACCP were further developed to become the internationally agreed approach endorsed by the UN's *Codex alimentarius* in the 1990s, the methods for HACCP application are still based on the original approach. Although the principles of HACCP have been defined for many years, various sectors of the food industry still struggle with making it work in practice.[21]

At this time the WHO was also promoting its 'Healthy Cities' project, which included a key theme of 'Healthy Marketplaces'.[22] A network was established along with a pilot project for assessing markets in these cities. The project, currently in phase VI (2014–2018), is based on a HACCP approach to market management. It identified four main areas of concern/sources of food contamination in a market setting: 1) Food becomes unsafe during primary production and/or transport which is then brought into the market without inspection or control; 2) Food becomes unsafe in the market due to improper food handling, preparation and/or storage; 3) Food becomes unsafe in the market due to poor infrastructure and environmental conditions; 4) Food becomes adulterated and/or is misrepresented in the market leading to adverse health, nutritional or economic consequences for the consumer. Although this strategy was 'aimed more at urban markets', it was also intended to apply to the context of rural markets.[23] However, whilst application of the four-pronged strategy will help to address the food safety concerns related to production and markets, the consumer element of the food safety continuum still needs to be considered with respect to food becoming unsafe due to improper food handling, preparation and/or storage in the home.

Farm and market associations in the UK

It is difficult to trace exactly where and when the first farmers market emerged during this new wave of interest; however, several sources (including the market in question itself) identified Bath as the first farmers market to arrive on the scene in the autumn of 1997. By 1998, an estimated 250 operated in England and Wales.[24] By 2005, approximately 400 farmers markets existed in the UK, which suggests a steady growth of this sector.[25] Most recently this number has been reported to have doubled to 800, and, at the time of writing, the number of Love Your Local Markets (LYLM) participating in the LYLM fortnight is listed at 917, although this number is likely to include both traditional local markets and farmers markets.[26]

The transient and sometimes 'pop-up' nature of local and farmers markets make it difficult to trace exactly how many are in existence at one time, also marred by the 'lack of consistency in classification', 'incomplete descriptions' and 'loss of data'.[27] In the UK and Europe recent studies have attempted to classify and define markets into several different areas. In the UK, there have been two national surveys, the Rhodes Survey in 2004 and more recently the Retail Markets Alliance survey in 2009 *Market 21*; this latter survey reported 605 'farmers markets' in the UK, apart from other categories of 'country markets' and 'traditional retail markets' (see Table 1).[28]

Table 1. Total Farmers, country and retail markets in the UK: breakdown by Government Office Region (GOR) (Adapted from: Smith, 2009 as quoted in Markets 21: A Policy & Research Review of UK Retail and Wholesale Markets in the 21st Century. The Retail Markets Alliance.)

GOR	Total	Traditional Retail Markets	Farmers markets	Country Markets
Eastern	237	107	78	52
East Midlands	169	94	48	27
London	193	144	47	2
North East	70	48	14	8
N. Ireland	24	15	6	3
North West	222	158	48	16
South	77	37	40	--
South East	303	124	102	77
South West	283	101	100	82
Wales	170	86	42	42
West Midlands	172	101	42	29
Yorks. & Humberside	159	109	38	12
TOTALS	2079	1124	605	350

This resurgence of interest in farmers markets is reflected in the relatively recent establishment of FARMA, which came about in a 2003 merger between the Farm Retail Association and the National Association of Farmers Markets.[29] FARMA independently verifies farmers markets in the UK, awarding the Farmers Market Certification for those establishments that sell fresh produce from the area defined as 'local' to that market and that meet the following criteria: 1) the principal producer or a representative directly involved in the production process, or a member of the family, must attend the stall; 2) all primary, own produce sold must be grown, reared, caught, etc., by the stallholder within the defined local area; 3) all secondary, own produce must be brewed, pickled, baked, smoked or processed by the stallholder using at least one ingredient of origin from within the defined local area and that ingredient must be substantially altered – e.g. the sale of home-made cottage pie made from beef reared by the stallholder in the defined local area; 4) information should be available and publicized to customers at each market about the rules of the market and the production methods of the producers.[30] These criteria clearly limit the producers who can participate and products that can be sold at a farmers market meeting the FARMA Certificate. While 250 farmers markets have earned this certificate, the larger number of farmers markets reported in Table 1 indicate that some markets are not applying for certification and/or do not meet these criteria. Clearly all farmers markets are not the same in terms of connecting the producer and the consumer.

More broadly speaking, two additional organizations with overlapping mandates are also involved in supporting markets selling farm produce. The National Market Traders Federation (NMTF), which has been around since 1899, provides direct support from a business trading perspective most notably through its *First Pitch Programme*. The *First Pitch Programme* is a start-up scheme and provides funding, training and tailor-made advice to applicants as well as networking and educational events such as 'Market Masterclasses'.[31]

NABMA, in existence for over 90 years, helped to draft the *Industry Guide to Good Hygiene Practice: Markets and Fairs Guide* (discussed in detail below). NABMA's priority is to 'raise the standards in markets management'.[32] With this in mind, in 2014 NABMA launched training in the form of a Diploma in Markets Administration in cooperation with Manchester Metropolitan University. Although there are no explicit food safety elements to the course, it speaks to popularity of local markets.

Rising once again from the ashes

Almost as soon as this presumed 'harbinger of the second revolution' and 'phoenix from the ashes' was declared, farmers markets were quickly named as being under threat of extinction by 2009, at least in the UK.[33] The 2008 economic crisis brought the markets under threat: a survey conducted by the Retail Manufacturers Association in 2009 suggested that farmers markets were operating at a loss, could not compete with supermarkets and were in danger of becoming extinct.[34]

However, like a phoenix rising (again) from the ashes, thanks in part to the championing of British celebrity chefs such as Hugh Fearnley-Whittingstall, James Martin and Jamie Oliver (among many others) who consistently espouse the value of local produce and Mary Portas who endorsed the importance of the UK's high streets and markets and recommended the creation of a 'national market day', there was again a renewed focus on farmers and local markets.[35] This emphasis also sparked the idea for the *Love your Local Market* (LYLM) Campaign supported by NABMA. The 'LYLM fortnight' which ran in May 2014 has attracted many participants and raised awareness via social media – so many markets attempted to register their events on the first day that the LYLM website crashed.[36] It appears that markets are on the rise again and building momentum with a great deal of support. But what about renewed interest in food safety at these events?

In spite of these positive developments, recent reports suggest that contamination still does occur at alarming frequency at various outdoor events in the UK. For example, a recent study by the Health Protection Agency (HPA) of large scale events in the UK showed that over a seven-month period, 1662 samples (collected at 153 events) showed

8% of the food samples and 27% of water samples were of unsatisfactory quality, with 1% containing potentially hazardous pathogenic bacteria.[37] Although there have been improvements, food safety must continue to be on the agenda as a shared responsibility among producers, vendors and consumers.

Food safety laws and guidelines for farmers markets in the UK and the EU

During the 1990s, many recognized that the approaches to food safety in the EU were diverse and inconsistent and that there was a need to harmonize requirements to provide basic principles for all EU food law. The UK Food Safety Act was introduced in 1990 with a statutory obligation to handle food intended for human consumption in a controlled way. Meanwhile, a few years later, the European Council announced a Directive on the hygiene of foodstuffs in 1993 (Directive 93/43/EEC), recognizing that by the free movement of foodstuffs across the internal European market, the hygiene of foodstuffs in all stages of preparation, processing, manufacturing, packaging, storing, transportation, distribution, handling and sale to consumers must be ensured to protect human health. In 1995, the UK tried to implement the EU-level directives on the hygiene of foodstuffs by issuing other regulations to add clarity, including the Food Safety (General Food Hygiene) Regulations and the Food Safety (Temperature Control) Regulation.

These two regulations led to industry guidelines for markets and fairs that were promulgated through various local authorities in the form of the *Industry Guide to Good Hygiene Practice: Markets and Fairs Guide*.[38] Developed in collaboration with NABMA and the Environmental Health Officers at Sheffield Council, these guidelines are still widely in circulation today, albeit distilled down into more succinct form on many council websites as the original document is now out of print. The *Industry Guide* provided guidance on how traders should carry out a hazard analysis, identify critical control points and ensure that safety controls are in place, maintained and reviewed. It gave examples of this process for various businesses such as greengrocers grocers, butchers, ice-cream vendors, delicatessens and fishmongers, and explained what vendors should do to comply with the 1995 Food Safety Regulations, outlining best practices in terms of transport, storage, cross-contamination, prevention, personal hygiene, temperature control and food hygiene training. The guidelines also included information on services, layout, water supply, washing facilities, equipment, drainage, refuse and sanitary accommodation, and they provided examples of acceptable surface finishes for walls, vertical frameworks, floors, ceiling covers and food contact surfaces in mobile and temporary premises such as outdoor stalls or tents one finds at farmers markets. It also advised vendors on the risks associated with giving away free samples and providing cooking demonstrations, as well as the risk associated with animals – either consumers' pets along for the day or farm animals which feature as a petting zoo or other animal-based attraction in the vicinity. Issues to do with the 'vagaries of the UK climate' were also discussed in terms of how weather might affect vendors' ability to protect their food from wind, dust and insects.[39] As such, this document provided a detailed best-practice guide that, if implemented, would help to manage food safety effectively and protect consumer health.

Although many of these principles in the guidelines remain relevant, the food safety legislative scene in Europe changed quite a bit in the 2000s with the creation of the EU General Food Law (EC No. 178/2002) which also outlines the establishment of the European Food Safety Authority, or EFSA.[40] A few years later, the so-called EU 'Hygienic Package' set of regulations came into force in the mid-2000s as a more comprehensive and horizontal approach to legislation within the EU.[41]

By way of response in the UK, in 2006, the 1995 Food Hygiene Regulations were revised as The Food Hygiene Regulations (England, Scotland, Wales, Northern Ireland) to meet the requirements of the EU 'Hygienic Package'. Schedule 4 (i.e. Temperature Control Requirements) of the Food Hygiene Regulations 2006, implemented by separate but similar legislation in England, Wales, Scotland and Northern Ireland, remade the majority of the requirements from the 1995 regulations. Although these UK regulations have in fact been updated to reflect EU law of mid-2000s, it seems the guidelines for markets and fairs have not been updated accordingly, an oversight given the resurgence of farmers markets. The 1995 guidance remains useful, as legislative changes were not so substantial to make it invalid; however, given updated legislation and the out-of-print full guide, the time is now appropriate for updating the document. According to NABMA there is no planned update to these industry guidelines at the moment, and, because vendors who fall under the category of farmers market are under the jurisdiction of FARMA, it might be appropriate for that organization to be involved. This need suggests a clear division between the farmers markets and traditional markets in terms of organizational support, even if they all get lumped in together in campaigns or research studies.

Instead, one finds the 1995 *Industry Guide to Good Hygiene Practice: Markets and Fairs Guide* is still referred to, in some cases distilled into simple leaflet form for farm vendors (see Figure 2). These leaflets are not intended to be exhaustive but instead cover some of the basic areas of storage, preparations, basic hygiene and sources of further information. The leaflets tend to distinguish between 'high risk foods' (e.g. meat, dairy and fish products) and 'low risk foods' such as 'cakes and jams'.[42] Vegetables and fresh produce are not often mentioned as possible sources of contamination, in spite of growing reports in the UK, Europe and North America of incidents of food contamination linked to these foods. For example, the WHO reported that in the UK between 1996 and 2006 there were a total of 88 reported outbreaks with more than 3435 known cases of illness relating to fresh fruits and vegetables; more recently, in 2011, the Advisory Committee on the Microbiological Safety of Food (ACMSF) stated that in the UK between 2008 and 2010, there were 531 cases of reported illness relating to the consumption of fruits and vegetables, including one death.[43]

Food Safety Guidance For Farmers' Market Traders

How this Leaflet will help you

This leaflet will explain how to meet the food safety laws that apply to you while trading at a farmers' market. It covers the basic areas that apply to typical farmers' market stalls that prepare, handle or sell (including giving free samples) food or drink, whether open or wrapped. To make it readable and straightforward to understand, it is not a detailed guide - but you should find information here about how to obtain further advice on some of the more complicated food safety issues.

Farmers' markets are the subject of routine checks by food safety officers from your local Environmental Health and Trading Standards Department, who may visit you on the day a market is held. The farm or other premises from which you operate may also be subject to inspection.

Figure 2. Food Safety Guidance for Farmers' Market Traders (Canterbury City Council website https://www.canterbury.gov.uk/media/254612/farmers-market-guidance.pdf [Accessed May 2014].)

There is great variation among the guidance available to vendors on farmers markets' websites, ranging in several pages of text to a few bullet points. Some mention where food hygiene training courses/certificates can be obtained if desired or required and link directly to the FSA website, whereas others have more limited information (further information may be available to registered vendors that is not visible on public websites).

More recently, in 2012, the FSA in Scotland produced a *Food Safety and Labelling Guide for Farmers Markets in Scotland*, a revision of an earlier 2005 edition called *The Farmers Market Manual*. It is accompanied by an easy-to-use, pared-down leaflet called *Selling at a Scottish Farmers Market: The First Steps* which provides specific information on compliance with Regulation 852/2004 on the hygiene of foodstuffs, Regulation 853/2004 specific hygiene of foods of animal origin, and, in relation to temperature control, the Food Hygiene (Scotland) Regulations 2006. The new composition and labelling section provides guidance on general and product-specific labelling requirements. Interestingly, a new addition to this guidance document is the identification of raw vegetables as possible hazards as sources of cross-contamination, for example: 'Vegetables and fruit that have not been labelled as ready-to-eat and especially; vegetables that are visibly dirty'. Another key addition/update is a section on allergens and practices on how to reduce the risk of contamination as well as on labelling within the context of a farmers market setting.[44] No formal standardized and updated equivalent guideline currently exists in England, Northern Ireland or Wales.

Beyond sights and smells at farmers markets in the north-west

Armed with this knowledge of the UK farmers market scene, its waves of resurgent popularity, the existing laws and guidelines, what's next for farmers markets and food safety? How does a vendor or consumer go beyond the sights and smells and taste of food to assess food safety in a farmers market? Currently it is very difficult to answer these questions. Whilst vendors and consumers might look to general levels of cleanliness in and around the stalls to give a measure of confidence, this type of assurance is not enough, as indicated by Sherriff Graham Cox in the fatal accident inquiry following the 1996 *E. coli* O157 outbreak in Lanarkshire: 'I have no doubt Mr John Barr liked a clean shop and maintained a clean shop. What he failed to do was to maintain a safe shop and the main ingredient of his failure was ignorance of the requirements which would produce that result.'[45]

As discussed above, the resurgence in farmers markets, whilst perhaps mirroring the updating of food safety legislation, has not been accompanied by provision of up-to-date guidance to achieve the necessary food safety standards throughout the UK. This area needs to be addressed to allow development of shared responsibility and food safety culture through each link in the food supply chain. Our ongoing research with farmers markets in north-west England aims to assist in identifying potential barriers and providing guidance towards implementing stringent food safety standards to establish a positive food safety culture at these establishments. In this way, we hope to contribute to the shared responsibility for public health protection, ensuring that the unseen and unsmelt risks do not overcome the positive experiences of the sights and smells of the farmers market.

Notes

1. Jean-Anthelme Brillat-Savarin, The Physiology of Taste; or, Transcendental Gastronomy, trans. by F. Robinson (Philadelphia: Lindsay and Blakiston, 1854), p. 64.
2. Vanessa Barford, 'Should you smell your food?' *BBC News Magazine* 10 January 2013 <http://www.bbc.co.uk/news/magazine-20971347> [Accessed May 2014].
3. Luisa Dillner, 'Dr Dillner's health dilemmas: should you stick to the use-by dates on food?' *The Guardian* 17 June 2012 <http://www.theguardian.com/lifeandstyle/2012/jun/17/use-by-dates-on-food> [Accessed May 2014].
4. L.Samuel, 'Food Bonds Two Communities', *The Progressive* 67.7 (2003): p. 16; R. Lawson, 'Creating value through Cooperation. An investigation of farmers markets in New Zealand.', *British Food Journal* 110.1 (2008), pp.11–25; P. Bourdieu, *Distinction: A Social Critique of the Judgement of Taste*, trans. R. Nice (Cambridge, MA: Harvard UP, 1979) and C. Weatherell, A. Tregear, and J. Allinson, 'In search of the concerned consumer: UK public perceptions of food, farming and buying local', *Journal of Rural Studies* 19 (2003), pp. 233–44.
5. Food Standards Agency, *Food Safety and Labelling Guide for Farmers Markets in Scotland* (2012).
6. Food Standards Agency, *Biannual Public Attitudes Tracker, November 2013* (2013).
7. G. Feenstra, 'Creating Space for Sustainable Food systems: Lessons from the Field', *Agriculture and Human Values* 19 (2002), pp. 99–106; I. Szmigin, S. Maddock and M. Carrigan, 'Conceptualising community consumption: farmers markets and the older consumer', *British Food Journal* 105.8 (2003), pp. 542–50; R. Vecchio, 'European and United States Farmers Markets: Similarities, Differences and

Potential Developments', *113th EAAE Seminar: A Resilient European Food industry and Food Chain in a Challenging World* (Crete: Chania, 2009); Weatherell, Tregear and Allinson.

8. M. Pollan, *The Omnivore's Dilemma: A Natural History of Four Meals* (New York: Penguin, 2006); J. Smithers, J. Lamarche and A.E. Joseph, 'Unpacking the Terms of Engagement with Local Food at the Farmers Market: Insights from Ontario', *Journal of Rural Studies* 24 (2008), pp. 337–50.
9. C. Griffith, K.M. Livesey and D.A. Clayton, 'Food Safety Culture: The Evolution of an Emerging Risk Factor?', *British Food Journal* 112.4 (2010), pp. 426–38
10. M. Nestle, *Safe Food: The Politics of Food Safety* (Berkeley: U California P, 2010). p. 1.
11. J. Guthrie, A. Guthrie, R. Lawson and A. Cameron, 'Farmers Markets: The Small Business Counter-Revolution in Food Production and Retailing', *British Food Journal* 108.7 (2006), pp. 560–73.
12. K. Spiller, 'It Tastes Better Because … Consumer Understandings of UK Farmers Market Food', *Appetite* 59.1 (August 2012), pp. 100–07.
13. M. Renting and J. Banks, 'Understanding Alternative Food Networks: Exploring the Role of Short Food Supply Chains in Rural Development', *Environment and Planning* 35 (2003), pp. 393–411; Vecchio; L.M. Hamilton, 'The American Farmers Markets.' *Gastronomica* 2.3 (2002), pp. 73–77.
14. J. O'Connell, 'Can Britain's Food Markets Make a Comeback?' *The Guardian* 12 May 2014.
15. A. Brown, 'Counting Farmers Markets', *The Geographical Review* 91.4 (October 2001): pp. 655–74.
16. A.R. Bailey and J. Hamlett, 'Reconstructing Consumer Landscapes: Self-Service Britain', *Local History Magazine* 115(September/October 2007), pp. 24–26.
17. E. Scarpellini, 'Shopping American-Style: The Arrival of the Supermarket in Postwar Italy.' *Enterprise & Society* 5.4 (December 2004), pp. 625–68; R. Poole, G.P. Clarke and D.B. Clarke, 'Growth, Concentration and Regulation in European Food Retailing', *European Urban and Regional Studies* 9 (2002), pp. 167–86.
18. D. Suzuki and H. Dressel, *Good News for a Change: Hope for a Troubled Planet* (St Leonards: Allen & Unwin, 2002); Lawson; C. Steel, *Hungry Cities: How Food Shapes Our lives* (London: Vintage, 2013); Spiller.
19. J.M. Cowden, 'Scottish Outbreak of Escherichia coli O157, November-December 1996', Euro Surveillance 2.1 (1997), p. ii–134 and H. Pennington, *Report on the Circumstances Leading to the 1996 Outbreak of Infection with E.coli 0157 in Central Scotland, the Implications for Food Safety and the Lessons to be Learned* (Edinburgh: The Scottish Stationary Office, 1997); H. Pennington, *The Public Inquiry into the September 2005 Outbreak of E.coli O157 in South Wales* (London: Queen's Printer and Controller of HMSO, 2009).
20. Codex Committee on Food Hygiene. *Guidelines for the Application of the Hazard Analysis Critical Control Point (HACCP) System*, WHO/FNU/ FOS/93.3 II (Geneva: World Health Organization, 1993); C.A. Wallace, W.H. Sperber and S.E. Mortimore, *Food Safety for the 21st Century: Managing HACCP and Food Safety Throughout the Global Supply Chain* (Oxford: Wiley-Blackwell, 2011).
21. C.A. Wallace, 'Editorial: HACCP-based Food Safety Management Systems – Great in Theory But Can We Really Make Them Work in Practice?', *Perspectives in Public Health* 134.4 (2014), pp. 188–90.
22. World Health Organization, *The WHO Healthy Cities Project* <http://www.euro.who.int/en/health-topics/environment-and-health/urban-health/activities/healthy-cities/who-european-healthy-cities-network> [accessed May 28, 2014].
23. G.G. Moy, 'Healthy Marketplaces: An Approach for Ensuring Food Safety and Environmental Health', *Food Control* 12 (2001), pp. 499–504.
24. Renting and Banks.
25. J. Grant, 'Farmers Markets: A Phoenix from the Ashes – A Viable Shopping Experience?', *Proceedings of the 4th Global Conference on Business and Economics*, Oxford, 26–28 June 2005.
26. O'Connell; Love your Local Market (LYLM) <http://loveyourlocalmarket.org.uk/> [accessed May 2014].
27. Brown.
28. K. Zasada, *Markets 21: A Policy & Research Review of UK Retail and Wholesale Markets in the 21st*

Century, The Retail Markets Alliance of the National Association of British Market Authorities (November 2009) < http://www.nabma.com/?action=download-pdf&file=4dd6419ec9584_markets-21-report.pdf>.

29. National Retail and Farmers Market Association (FARMA) <http://www.farma.org.uk/> [Accessed May 2014].
30. National Retail and Farmers Market Association (FARMA).
31. National Market Traders Federation (NMTF), *A Century of Service* (1999) <http://www.nmtf.co.uk/mt/centenary/#/1/> [Accessed May 2014].
32. National Association of British Market Authorities <http://www.nabma.com/> [Accessed May 2014].
33. Grant; O'Connell.
34. Zasada.
35. See, e.g., the River Cottage (<http://www.rivercottage.net/about/meet-hugh/> [Accessed May 2014]), *James Martin's Food Map of Britain* (<http://www.bbc.co.uk/food/programmes/b03bhng2> [Accessed May 2014]) or (focusing just on fish) Episode 1 of *Jamie Oliver's Jamie's Fish Suppers* on Channel 4 (<http://www.channel4.com/programmes/jamies-fish-supper/episode-guide> [Accessed May 2014]); Mary Portas, 'The Portas Review: An Independent Review into the Future of Our High Streets' (2011).
36. Love your Local Market (LYLM).
37. Willis,C, N. Elviss and J. McLauchlin, Health Protection Agency, 'Follow-up Study of Hygiene Practices in Catering Premises at Large Scale Events in the United Kingdom' (London: Health Protection Agency, 2013).
38. *Industry Guide to Good Hygiene Practice: Markets and Fairs Guide*: *Food Safety (General Food Hygiene) Regulations 1995, Food Safety (Temperature Control) Regulations 1995* (London: Chadwick House, 1995).
39. Worsfold, D. 2003. 'Food safety at shows and fairs.' *Nutrition and Food Science*, Vol. 33 No. 4, pp. 159–164.
40. *Regulation (EC) No 178/2002 of the European Parliament and of the Council of 28 January 2002 laying down the general principles and requirements of food law, establishing the European Food Safety Authority and laying down procedures in matters of food safety.*
41. *Regulation (EC) 852/2004 on the hygiene of foodstuffs; Regulation (EC) 853/2004 laying down specific hygiene rules for food of animal origin; Regulation (EC) 854/2004 laying down specific rules for the organisation of official controls on products of animal origin intended for human consumption; Regulation (EC) 882/2004 on official controls performed to ensure the verification of compliance with feed and food law, animal health and animal welfare rules.*
42. Canterbury City Council, *Food Safety Guidance for Farmers Market Traders* <https://www.canterbury.gov.uk/media/254612/farmers-market-guidance.pdf> [accessed May 2014].
43. Caroline Goodburn and Carol A. Wallace, 'The Microbiological Efficacy of Decontamination Methodologies for Fresh Produce: A Review', *Food Control* 13.2 (August 2013), pp. 418–27.
44. Food Standards Agency, *Food Safety and Labelling Guide for Farmers Markets in Scotland* (Edinburgh: 2012).
45. G.L. Cox, *Determination by Graham L. Cox, QC, Sheriff Principal of Sheriffdom of South Strathclyde Dumfries and Galloway into the E. coli 0157 fatal accident inquiry* (Sheriffdom of South Strathclyde, Dumfries and Galloway: 1998).

Buying or Selling?

Gillian Riley

The comely young woman in the painting by Vincenzo Campi, *The Fruitseller*, is strangely passive. She is not crying her wares, but sits holding up a bunch of grapes in a hieratic posture, surrounded by baskets and bowls of fruit and vegetables. The background is more of a rural idyll, with fruit pickers at work in a pleasant countryside, than an urban market scene. No buying, no selling. Simply an array of produce, like the chilled cabinet of a posh supermarket, with items from all seasons in their frigid perfection, the asparagus and fresh young peas of early spring alongside the mulberries and root vegetables of autumn.

This painting, executed in northern Italy in the 1580s, may have been for clients who enjoyed genre scenes by artists in the Low Countries. There the buying and selling was quite vigorous, but these everyday scenes also contained a load of symbolism, and their interpretation has become an academic growth industry. The difficulties and complexities of deciphering a still life or genre scene should not be underestimated, but they do have to be taken with a pinch of salt. What might seem obscure to us was clear and obvious to painters and their clients, who did not need help in interpreting the artists' work. They already knew what was going on. Proverbs, sayings, books of doggerel verse embodying folk wisdom and dreary platitudes, with woodcut illustrations, Bible stories and old wives' tales, were all common knowledge. You could commission a painting and put it on your wall, and enjoy it for the pleasurable sight of things to eat, expensive possessions and bright colours, while taking on board the moral or symbolic content as well.

Campi's fruit and vegetable stall is a celebration of Italian produce throughout the year, from the peas, broad beans, cherries and apricots of early summer, to the cabbages, mulberries and nuts of autumn. The luxury items, asparagus and artichokes, are isolated in the bottom left-hand corner, a contrast to the homely cabbages at the bottom right. Asparagus was a luxury in the 1580s, but later became mainstream. We can see a crop being harvested in the late fifteenth century in the *Tacuinum Sanitatis*, where peasants in straw hats prepare bundles of the shoots. Several copies of the *Tacuinum* have survived: this fifteenth-century health handbook was derived from an earlier Arab manual, with descriptions of most edible things and various other factors which influence health, and it is likely, from the brilliance of the illustration and the condensed nature of the text, that they were the equivalent of coffee table books, luxury artefacts for the rich, rather than medical manuals for specialists. The images of everyday life, with elegantly attired gentry and wholesome peasantry, pretty rural scenes and modern townscapes, were the work of Giovannino de' Grassi and his workshop; they give us delightful details of foodstuffs, cooking and eating, even in this idealized social setting.

Castelvetro, a century later, was telling the English about the massive cash crops produced by improved agriculture in the Veneto. The loggia of Agostino Chigi's villa, now known as the Farnesina, has artichokes and asparagus among the plants and fruit celebrating local and exotic produce. Aldrovandi's visual record of the natural world includes a rare monkey holding up a luxurious globe artichoke. By the mid-seventeenth century Giovanna Garzoni immortalized them in her work, with one painting showing different varieties of artichoke. Back in the Low Countries we see asparagus on market stalls and in kitchen scenes, and the final tributes to Dutch horticulture are the plump bundles glowing with a mellow buttery light by Adriaan Coorte in the late seventeenth century.

Murals in the Castello at Issogne show local market stalls selling fruit and vegetables, and we get glimpses of local produce on sale in the *Tacuinum* where a peasant woman has lined up a crop of leeks, or takes a trayful of spinach to market on her head.

Market scenes by Aertsen and Beuckelaer show a similar profusion of basic and luxury vegetables, often with symbolic meaning, which need not obscure the wealth of information in them about local and imported produce. We do need to be aware of the implications here: did the Netherlands really produce bunches of grapes in the same profusion as in Campi's northern Italy? His modest fruit seller holds a bunch of grapes up not just as an invitation to buy, but as a symbol of virginity in a virtuous maiden, and fruitfulness within marriage for a modest housewife. Some of Aertsen's vegetable stalls are full of possible double meanings, with huge cabbages like rotund pregnant bellies, and phallic gourds and cucumbers often in obscene postures. Plant historians at Wagenigen have studied the varieties of produce, and learnt a lot about Dutch agriculture of the time, unimpeded by an angst-ridden search for symbols. Wttwael uses a market woman selling apples as a vehicle for much moralizing: a crafty old crone offers a rosy apple to an apple-cheeked chid, whose mother reproachfully points out the blemishes on the fruit – a moral tale as well as a typical market scene, with the three ages of woman and the corruption of innocence or the worm within causing the fruit to rot. There is more symbolism in Beuckelaer's fruit and vegetable stall, one of four paintings of the four elements, with a fish stall, fruit and vegetable seller, a poultry seller and a kitchen scene depicting mainly meat.

Meat stalls in markets figure in the *Tacuinum Sanitatis*. The different kinds of meat, the creature it comes from and the nature of the product, offal, extremities, prime cuts, are all displayed on stall or in shops, with butchers at work and interacting with their customers, as one might have seen in a north Italian town at that time. Maestro Martino tells us in his recipes to cut hard pork fat into little dice, and here we see a pork butcher doing just that for a customer. We see another man leaving the shop with a whole side of bacon. Another vendor slices liver and offal; heads, feet, unmentionable innards are all there in the *Tacuinum* as they would have been in real life.

Buying or Selling?

A century later Pieter Aertsen painted several versions of a butcher's shop. Brilliant research into the circumstances of its execution has been done that explains the extremely complex story behind the choice of subject and many of the details in it. The butchers' guild, local real-estate shenanigans, small town politics and demographic unrest all play a part, but we are still able to take at face value the details of the butcher's wares, his sausages, white and black puddings, tarts and various joints of meat. The dramatic composition and bright colouring are so seductive that the painting has an immediate impact regardless of its complex origins. People appear only in the background, where a possible Bible story is juxtaposed with some lewd behaviour.

Aertsen's contemporary Joachim Beuckelaer chose to paint meat and fowl by the time they had got into the kitchen; his kitchen scene, the element Fire in a series of four paintings, shows meat in the hands of some strong, competent women, and hanging up waiting to be dealt with.

Annibale Carracci painted two versions of a more sombre shop, with butchers at work in the unglamorous tasks of cutting up carcasses. There is little decorative effect, but much helpful detail.

Goya painted meat on a butcher's slab, a horrifying reminder of the slaughter of a living thing, massacred to assuage our greed, perhaps a reminder of the horrors of the Peninsular War depicted in his engraving *Tanto y mas*.

Artists enjoyed the challenge of conveying the ephemeral beauty of freshly caught fish, either straight off the boat or on a market stall. The cod and plaice of the North Sea can be seen on Dutch market stalls on a chill winter's day, with snow on the ground but fresh cod on the slab, with the fall-back position of salt cod hanging from a hook in one corner. A wind-blown corner of the fish market in Amsterdam was painted by De Witte showing his landlady and her small daughter, cheeks and hands red in the cold wind which tears at the awning, in the fading light of a wintry afternoon. It is a relief to get to the warm south, where Giuseppe Recco and Ruoppolo painted many scenes of freshly caught fish, lined up on the shore, each one identifiable in its moment of maximum freshness. Some of these artists were employed by patrons in Tuscany and Liguria, and one can discern in some of their work the recipes made from them, as when at the end of the day the unsold bits of the catch are boiled up with red wine, garlic and plenty of *peperoncino* to make the celebrated *cacciucco* of Livorno.

Some artists showed the serious business of choosing and pricing a purchase, and the next stage, the ingredients of a meal plonked on the kitchen table, waiting to be cooked, like the two sea bream in a Meléndez still life, joined by a cord through the gills, about to be fried in olive oil in a huge iron pan, and dressed with a sauce of bitter orange and garlic, all lined up in the painting.

Fowl both wild and farmed are displayed in shops and markets. Scenes in the *Tacuinum* reflect the importance of the poultry yard in the domestic economy of northern Italy, where the *rezdora* or female head of the household, reared chickens, pigeons and rabbits for their value as a cash crop as well as ingredients. Loarte's *Poultry*

Food and Markets

Vendor shows a woman selling fowl and eggs. Beuckelaer depicts the element Air as a poultry market, with a variety of birds, and the banter and tensions of the scene made clear (dead birds can signify libidinous behaviour; caged birds might remind both market woman and client of their subordinate status). Goya again admonishes us that his dead turkey is a figure of grief and sorrow, not a delicious ingredient.

Jan Steen portrayed a baker and his wife at the moment when the horn was blown to tell the neighbourhood that the bread is out of the oven, and the display is still typical of artisan bakeries in the Netherlands. Before that we have an image from Issogne of the pie-maker alongside the butcher who provided the filling for his wares. Breads of different kinds appear in the *Tacuinum* but sweetmeats, pastries and tarts figure more in still lifes than market scenes.

On the whole it seems that images of shops and markets can be looked at along with kitchen and genre scenes, larders, tables laid for a meal and still lifes, to give us information about ingredients and how they were prepared, but the evidence for a transaction, some hard-nosed buying and selling, is more hard to come by.

The Pilgrimage to El Babour – A Functioning Mill in the Nazareth Market

Abbie Rosner

'All roads lead to the wheat mill.'
Palestinian *fellah* saying

The Holy Land under the centuries of Ottoman rule was relatively isolated from developments taking place in other parts of the world, due to strict limitations on the presence and status of foreigners. In the largely rural landscape of the Galilee, at the western edge of the Fertile Crescent, growing wheat was a central occupation of the *fellaheen* (farmers) living on and off the land, as it had been since the agricultural revolution. By the mid-1800s, however, with the Empire sliding into decline, numerous reforms were enacted which opened the gates to foreign powers eager to establish footholds as close as possible to the holy sites.[1] Along with Jerusalem, the Galilee town of Nazareth, revered as the site of the Annunciation and the childhood home of the Holy Family, was at the top of the Western expansionist agenda.

Nazareth in the late nineteenth century was as much a commercial centre as a pilgrim destination. Several churches in the city, built, razed and rebuilt over the centuries, served the region's Christian communities as well as foreign pilgrims. But the Nazareth marketplace attracted its own clientele, drawn from the local urban population and the mainly Muslim *fellaheen* and Bedouin living in the surrounding villages. Five different caravanserais served merchants and travellers passing through the city, and the *Khan el Basha*, located across from the Basilica of the Annunciation, was Nazareth's commercial heart.

In and around the *khan*'s walled courtyards, Nazareth's merchants offered a broad array of goods and services for urban and rural patrons. Here one could purchase fabric, shoes and housewares, as well as spices, sugar and confections. Tradesmen sold and repaired agricultural tools and equipment, and the city's cutlers were renowned for the quality of their knives. The Brides' Market supplied jewellery, fabric, clothing and other wedding accessories.

Because bread was synonymous with sustenance for city dwellers, villagers and travellers alike, wheat was a basic market commodity, and a supply of flour was as essential as water. Such was the importance of wheat that it served as currency, for payment of rent or wages, as taxes to the Ottoman authorities, tithes to religious institutions and debts to merchants.

Even as the industrial revolution was transforming food production in other parts of the world, in Ottoman-era Palestine, wheat cultivation and processing, with its rituals of sowing, harvesting, threshing and milling, had changed little over the millennia. Milling grain for family consumption was commonly, and laboriously, performed on stone hand querns. Yet to produce larger quantities, and for those who could afford it, the arduous work of milling grain to produce flour was outsourced to commercial mills operated by animal, water or even wind power. 'All roads lead to the mill', goes the traditional Palestinian *fellah* saying, attesting to a journey that was embedded in a wheat-centric world order.

The Babour mills

Among the Europeans headed to Palestine was a small group of Germans intent on establishing a spiritual presence in the Holy Land, calling themselves the Temple Society (*Tempelgessellschaft*).[2] The first official Templer delegation arrived in Haifa in 1868, hoping to create a settlement in Nazareth. Unable to purchase enough land in the city to meet their needs, the Templers eventually set down roots in Haifa, Jaffa, Jerusalem and several small agricultural communities. Yet their original plan took into account the need for a reliable supply of flour, and among the first things the Templers did was assign one of their members to establish a mill in Nazareth. In spite of the fact that he was a shoemaker by profession, Melchior Wagner, a German who left a religious colony in Bessarabia to join the Templers in the early 1870s, took the job.[3]

Wagner had a large stone house built for his family on a hill above the city centre, with room in the basement for a treadmill and a stable of horses to run it. Yet Templers in other parts of Palestine had begun importing industrial equipment from Germany, and soon Wagner upgraded his mill with a steam-engine to turn the stones – most probably the first motor-driven mill in Nazareth. The mill's local clientele called it a '*babour*' derived from the term 'vapour', which it generated. The Wagner's *babour* placed labour-saving motor power for the first time at the disposal of the local community, while preserving the ritual of the trip to the mill.

The potential of the steam mill caught on quickly. A survey of Nazareth's population by occupation, conducted by a German visitor to the city and published in 1890, lists nine millers, five working in steam mills.[4] A map of Nazareth from an 1897 Baedeker guide shows three mills in the city, the 'German Mill' on one side of the city, and two others, one a steam mill, near Mary's Well on the other.[5]

Prior to WWI, Melchior's eldest son Johannes was taken out of school to replace his aging father in running the mill, which eventually became known as the 'Johannes Babour'. During the war, the mill was commissioned almost exclusively to supply the Turkish forces with flour, with only one day a week allocated for the needs of the civilian customers.

When triumphant British forces occupied Nazareth at the end of the war, Johannes was interned as a prisoner of war and Melchior was forced out of retirement to continue to provide what had become a vital service. Melchior died in 1922 and, according to Johannes' granddaughter, the last living relative who still remembers the mill, the mill house was sold to an order of nuns around 1936. By the end of WWII, the last of the Templers were deported from Palestine by the British for their political affiliation with the Third Reich. Most of them, including many of the Wagners, eventually settled in Australia.

Without the Johannes *Babour*, customers still had access to the city's second steam mill. Set in a grand Ottoman style structure built of golden local stone with massive, vaulted ceilings, the mill, which became known simply as '*El Babour*', was purchased from its German owner by Jarjoura Kanaza, a Nazareth resident. When WWII broke out, Jarjoura's grandson and namesake recalls, the mill was requisitioned by the British army, and the millers received detailed instructions on the percentage of each grain to be mixed into their flour.

The 1948 war that led to the establishment of the State of Israel, with its destruction of Arab agricultural villages and appropriation of agricultural land, set into motion a process which effectively put an end to traditional Palestinian agrarian society in the Galilee. The small number of *fellaheen* fortunate enough to maintain ownership of at least part of their land selectively adopted modern agricultural techniques and continued to cultivate wheat and other traditional crops for the local Arab market, at the periphery of Israel's large scale, cooperative agro-industry.[6] But for many thousands of others who lost their lands and homes entirely, Nazareth became their city of refuge.

Wheat in Galilee Arab cuisine

The Arab citizens of Israel have been an ethnic minority in Israel for almost seventy years, and their foodways, as sociologist Liora Gvion has observed, share certain characteristics with those of ethnic minorities that have settled in foreign countries.[7] One such characteristic is the desire to limit the extent to which the dominant society has access to the minority's cultural capital. Yet unlike the far-flung migrants who may have difficulty obtaining their traditional foods, Arab-Israelis remain in their native geographic sphere and retain access to its local products. Indeed, Galilee-Arab cuisine still gives prominence to wheat products and other local ingredients, and it is difficult to imagine a meal in an Arab home that doesn't include bread and/or a dish featuring bulgur or *farike* (roasted green wheat). Many of these staple foods are produced within the Arab sector and are distributed in channels that almost exclusively serve the Arab-Israeli market.

In certain rural Galilee-Arab communities, it is still relatively common to purchase wheat in grain form from local growers.[8] To maintain the inventory of flour in a household's pantry, a measure of grain is periodically taken to one of the small commercial mills that operate in certain Arab cities and towns. The fresh, whole-wheat flour produced from local, hard wheat varieties is particularly suited for baking the flat breads that are traditional in this region. These mills also sell freshly milled flour from locally grown wheat to customers seeking a more convenient, local product.

Wheat purchased from local suppliers can also be boiled and dried at home to produce bulgur, and then brought to the mill for processing into the coarse and fine grinds for different culinary applications. The coarse grind is commonly matched with lentils and caramelized onions to make the Galilee version of *mejadra*, and the finely ground bulgur is combined with parsley and lemon juice when preparing *tabbouleh*, or used to make the crispy coating for seasoned ground meat in *kubbeh*.

In the spring, some local farmers still produce *farike*, harvesting the green ears of wheat by hand and roasting them over an open fire. Then the roasted grain is sold to local customers. *Farike*, like bulgur, is divided into coarse and fine grinds, where the former is generally used for a pilaf-like side dish, and the latter to enrich and impart its distinctive smoky flavour to *farike* soup.

Purchasing wheat from the farmer not only gives the consumer control over the quality of the product, but over the form and timing of its processing as well. It also retains the ancient and eminently local relationship between the field, farmer, miller and consumer. These locally grown and processed wheat products, as anyone who is used to them will attest, are fresher, healthier and tastier than anything on the supermarket shelf.

In fact, most of the flour consumed in Israel is an anonymous, foreign commodity milled in large industrial facilities from wheat that is mainly shipped to the Middle East either from the FSU or the US. Even as interest in local, healthful eating in Israeli society is blossoming, the possibility of (and awareness of the possibility of) acquiring and milling locally grown wheat remains largely within the Arab sector.[9]

El Babour: a functioning mill

Throughout all the tectonic shifts that transformed Galilee Arab society in the last century, the *El Babour* mill has continued to serve its local clientele. Today, it is run by Jarjoura and Tony Kanaza, the grandsons of its first Nazarene owner. Now both in their forties, the two grew up in the shadow of the massive milling machinery, and maintaining this Nazareth institution is the central concern in their lives.

The brothers' earliest memories are imbued with the thin layer of white powder that once covered every surface of the mill. As children, they recall the steady stream of customers who came to the mill, leaving their donkeys and camels tied up in the small walled courtyard. They remember the mill as a place where people from different villages could meet, catch up with news and even find prospective spouses. While waiting for their turn at the mill, which during peak periods could take hours or even days, customers would sit and talk. 'The rich landowner and the *fellah* who owned nothing wore the same clothes and spoke eye to eye about the farming that occupied them both,' Jarjoura recalls. During times of war, when a larder full of flour was the most security a villager could hope for, Tony and Jarjoura's father would remain at the mill for weeks at a time.

The mill was outfitted to supply a variety of grades, from the finest flour to the coarsest animal feed. For bulgur and *farike*, a mechanical sifter, built by a local carpenter, separated fine and coarse grain from the chaff, and expanded the milling services offered. But Tony remembers how the *fellaheen* women often opted to sift their grain by hand, sitting on the floor and wielding large round wooden sifters.

One of the Kanaza brothers' favourite stories is about a *fellah* from the nearby town of Kufar Kana, who would send his young worker on a donkey every two days with sacks of bulgur to be milled, relying on the animal to reach his destination and return home safely. That same boy eventually came to work at *El Babour*, and wanting to surprise his employer one day, he decided to mill some of their own grain himself, not realizing until it was too late that a stash of gold jewellery had been hidden in that particular sack.

Tony and Jarjoura's father made a major investment to upgrade the original *babour* to operate on electricity. Yet the larger political and socio-economic realities in the country were impacting the Nazareth market in ways that affected the mill as well. The expansion of commercial – and milling – options outside of Nazareth diverted many of its clients. And two successive Intifadas deterred pilgrims and tourists from visiting the city, sending the market into a serious decline from which it is now recovering.

As the other mills in the city closed down shop, Tony and Jarjoura were intent on breathing new life into *El Babour*. They retired the flour-milling machinery and filled the vast spaces with colourful sacks of grains, pulses, seeds and spices from and for the local Arab market, and shelves of crafts and spice mixtures for tourists. On the walls, they displayed traditional Palestinian farming and cooking implements, including a dried goat skin for churning milk and several sets of basalt hand mills. Yet, as tourist groups inspect the colourful Armenian pottery and the array of pastel sugared almonds and roasted chickpeas, beyond their view, in the building's back courtyard, *El Babour* continues to offer milling services to its local clientele.

Passing through a massive room where the old flour mill stands silent and disassembled, a door leads out into that same outdoor walled space where pack animals once waited for their owners. There, lined against the wall, stands an impeccably maintained array of milling, roasting and processing machines. In between them, tarps are spread across the stone-paved floor on which locally grown sesame, colourful herbs and spices dry in the sun. An old well, now dry and covered, serves as a work surface.

On any given day, customers will arrive at the mill with bulgur, *farike* or other products to be milled. During spring, which is *farike* season, a steady stream of customers make their way to the back courtyard carrying sacks of the roasted grain – much of it purchased from suppliers in the neighbouring village of Mashad, which is one of the centres for *farike* production in the Galilee.

Two elegantly dressed young Nazareth women bring a pillowcase full of *farike*, and the small child with them watches wide-eyed as the mill's young worker pours the grain into the hopper of a compact, electric mill and flips the switch. The milled wheat is then taken to the same wooden mechanical sifter that has been operating here for over fifty years, and which would earn a place of honour in any agricultural museum. The sifter starts to whir, sending the coarsely ground grain out of one chute, the finely ground out of another, and the chaff from a third. The entire process takes about ten minutes.

Another customer arrives, this time an older woman from the Bedouin village of Z'bidat, who bought a few kilos of wheat and has asked for it to be ground in order to prepare '*jerisha*', which she describes as a dish that combines the ground wheat, yoghurt, spices and a little meat. She has the worker adjust the mill several times, evaluating the grind each time, until she is satisfied with the consistency.

The same set of milling machines are used for bulgur, although the hard, parboiled grains take significantly longer to mill than the soft, green *farike*. An older woman from the nearby town of Yaffia comes with her teenaged granddaughter, bringing two large sacks of bulgur she has prepared from wheat she purchased in a nearby town. Taking labour and associated costs into account, the imported Turkish bulgur is certainly more economical. Yet clearly, for this customer, the ability to engage in a process that begins with the transaction with the farmer and continues at the mill before ending at the table, all under her watchful eye, is more compelling than factors of economics or convenience.

A middle-aged man from Nazareth explains to me that the sack of *farike* he has brought to be milled is a '*seah*' – a measure of grain that is mentioned in the Bible and today is the equivalent of about five kilos. One of his brothers purchased several sacks of *farike*, and distributed the grain among the heads of families. 'When you get your grain straight from the farmer, you know that it is clean and fresh,' he continues.

When I ask customers why they still make the ritual journey to *El Babour*, even though everything is easily available at any store, one after another, they patiently explain what for them is obvious. They prefer to buy locally grown wheat and mill it because it is superior in terms of its culinary qualities and health benefits as well.

In addition to wheat, *El Babour* mills other local products for its customers, including *zaatar* (*Origanum syriacum*), the local herb at the base for the eponymous spice mixture, which is a standard ingredient of Galilee Arab cuisine.[10] Spring is also *zaatar* season and a woman from Nazareth in her fifties brings a bag of dried *zaatar* leaves in one hand, and a plastic soda bottle full of locally grown sesame seeds in the other. The mill worker pours them both into the hopper of a tall, noisy machine, which emits a crumbly, fragrant powder, accomplishing in seconds what once required patient and time-consuming rubbing of the leaves by hand through a sieve. While commercial *zaatar* mixtures are readily available, making one's own mixture, as this customer assures me, is still considered well worth the effort.

Another customer, a young man in his thirties with his small daughter, waits as Jarjoura pours a small bucket of nigella seeds through a different mill. The milled black seeds, he explained, are used to make a traditional Palestinian *ketzah* cake. Once that is finished, Jarjoura hands his worker a sack of dried corn kernels and another of wheat, and sends him to grind them into chicken feed for yet another customer.

A Functioning Mill in the Nazareth Market

On a Friday morning, Jarjoura stands behind the counter on which a tray holds a small pot of freshly brewed black, Turkish coffee. Men of all ages come in, and he pours each of them a cup, as they exchange a few words, pay for their purchases, and continue, some to Friday prayers in the White Mosque in the market, others to the back courtyard carrying sacks of grains and herbs. One customer purchases a kilo bag of local, freshly milled whole-wheat flour. 'This flour has soul', he tells me, sipping the last drop of coffee and heading on his way. Even now, the mill clearly retains its social function.

Some of the men linger in the back office, next to the chimney of a large stone oven that now stands cold but once served the cooking needs of the entire neighbourhood. Tony laughs when he tells the story of a woman who sent her pot to the local oven. Before leaving home, the woman, who was known for her stinginess, would string all the pieces of meat together like beads on a chain, so that when the owner claimed his payment for the cooking services – a portion of the pot – he wouldn't be able to extract the best part.

Meeting at the mill

While *El Babour* is featured in most guidebooks, its thriving milling operation remains largely beyond the perception of the city's foreign and Israeli tourists. In fact, the disparity between what outside visitors to Nazareth observe, and that of the city as experienced by its own, is not new. Even before Edward Said's polemic on the pitfalls of Orientalism, the Galilean As'ad Mansur felt compelled to publish his own history and guide to Nazareth, *Tarikh al Nasira* (The History of Nazareth) in 1924, reflecting a proud local perspective and intending to refute the erroneous, ethnocentric and patronizing accounts written by European and American clergymen, archaeologists and missionaries.[11] Among its distinguishing features, *Tarikh al Nasira* was also the first biographical dictionary of Nazareth, in which Mansur accounted for every resident of the city, not as a number or by profession, but by name and family origins. Sadly, this invaluable resource is accessible only to readers of Arabic.

For any visitor to a foreign city, gaining insight into the local culture is a challenge, and Nazareth, with its extra burden of religious narrative, is no exception. Yet, not far, but worlds away from the churches, shopping malls, congested throughways and tourist trails, the *El Babour* courtyard offers a fascinating opportunity to see local Nazarenes perpetuating one of the most ancient rituals of this land, and to meet Tony and Jarjoura Kanaza, the last remaining millers in Nazareth.

Acknowledgements

Special thanks to Tony and Jarjoura Kanaza, Dr Norbert Schwake, Ghada Boulos, Atef Fahoum, Dr Nakhle Bishara, Muhammad Abu-Rabieh, Dr Maha El-Taji Daghash, Dr Miryam Sivan and the many *El Babour* patrons who generously shared with me their knowledge.

Notes

1. On the period of Ottoman decline, see Yael Buchman, *Pashas, Fellaheen and Pirates: A Window into Life in Eretz-Israel in the Sixteenth to the Eighteenth Century*, in Hebrew trans. by the author (Hotzaa Yeda Aretz, 2013); Yehoshua Frenkel, 'Between Mongols and Ottomans: Nazareth in the Mamluk Period' *Nazareth History & Cultural Heritage*, ed. by Mahmoud Yazbak and Sharif Sharif (Nazareth: Municipality of Nazareth Academic Publications, 2013); and Benjamin Z. Kedar, 'Nazareth in Two Accounts of the Late Ottoman Period', also in *Nazareth History & Cultural Heritage*.
2. For the Temple Society, see Y. Ben Artzi, *The Physical Structure of Templer Settlements and their Place in the Eretz Israel Landscape: 1869–1914*, in Hebrew trans. by the author (Jerusalem: Yad Itzhak Ben Zvi, 1990); Alex Carmel, 'A Note on The Christian Contribution to Palestine's Development in the 19th Century', *Palestine in the Late Ottoman Period – Political, Social and Economic Transformation*, ed. by David Kushner (Jerusalem: Yad Izhak Ben-Zvi, 1986), pp. 302–08 and 'The German Settlers in Palestine and their Relations with the Local Arab Population and the Jewish Community, 1868–1918', *Studies on Palestine During the Ottoman Period*, ed. by Moshe Ma'Oz (Jerusalem, The Magnes Press, 1975), pp. 442–65; Paul Sauer, *The Holy Land Called – The Story of the Temple Society* (Melbourne: Temple Society Australia, 1991); and Alexander Scholch, Alexander, *Palestine in Transformation – 1856–1882* (Washington, DC: Inst. For Palestine Studies, 1993).
3. From correspondence between the author and Heide Dryburgh, great-granddaughter of Johannes Wagner (3 April 2014–7 May 2014) and from a speech given by Isolde Ruff at the Bentleigh Frauenverein in April 2007.
4. G. Schumacher, 'Das jetzige Nazareth', *Zeitschrift des Deutschen Palästina-Vereins* (1878–1945) Bd. 3 (1890), pp. 235–45.
5. Karl Baedeker, *Baedeker's Palästina und Syrien* (Leipzig, Karl Baedeker, 1897), p. 275.
6. The British and the Israelis both extended agricultural services to the Arab farming sector, encouraging them to adopt modern crop varieties and farming techniques. For discussions on the extent and impact of these efforts, see, e.g., Isaac Arnon and Michael Raviv, *From Fellah to Farmer – A Study on Change in Arab Villages* (Rehovot, Settlement Study Centre, 1980) and Charles S. Kamen, *Little Common Ground – Arab Agriculture and Jewish Settlement in Palestine, 1920–1948* (Pittsburgh: University of Pittsburgh Press, 1991).
7. Liora Gvion, *Beyond Hummus and Falafel: Social and Political Aspects of Palestinian Food in Israel*, trans. by David Wesley and Elana Wesley (Berkeley: University of California Press, 2012). The Arab citizens of Israel make up about 20% of Israel's population and about 50% of the population of the Galilee. While Arab citizens of Israel generally identify themselves as Palestinian, the Galilee is home to at least one Arabic-speaking group, the Druze, whose members may not consider themselves as Palestinian. To add further potential for confusion, the Palestinians living in the Palestinian Authority and their foodways are beyond the scope of this paper. For these reasons, the terms Arab, Arab citizens of Israel and Israeli-Arabs are used in this paper, with no intention of diminishing the Palestinian identity.
8. The characterization of milling practiced in Galilee Arab society will be the subject of a future study. For more on wheat in general, see W.R. Akroyd and Joyce Doughty, *Wheat in Human Nutrition* (Rome: Food and Agriculture Organization of the United Nations, 1970).
9. An article about the flour mill in Kufar Kana was recently published in the Israeli newspaper *Haaretz*: Ronit Vered, 'Flour Power and the Goof Loaf', *Haaretz* English Edition, 26 December 2013.
10. Wild *zaatar* was declared an endangered plant by the Israel National Parks Authority and picking it is punishable by fine. In the meantime, cultivated *zaatar* is now a readily available commodity, and I have even seen one "pick your own" field of cultivated *zaatar* not far from Nazareth.
11. Nabil Matar, 'Writing Back: As'ad Mansur and *Tarikh al-Nasira*, 1924', in *Nazareth History & Cultural Heritage*, ed. by Mahmoud Yazbak and Sharif Sharif (Nazareth: Municipality of Nazareth Academic Publications, 2013), pp. 155–69.

The Marketplace in Soviet and Post-Soviet Painting: Image Transformation

Irina Rutsinskaya and Galina Smirnova

On 11 October 1931, the government of the USSR declared a complete ban on private trade. Private stores were nationalized, and entrepreneurs and traders of the NEP epoch were disenfranchised, banished to Siberia or imprisoned in camps. From then until the end of the 1980s, there existed only one legal form of private commerce: the so-called 'collective farm marketplace', which was the space for small-scale retail trade. The given name was a Soviet euphemism as the goods on sale in the marketplace were not those grown by collective farms, but those produced in the private gardens of the farmers and the town-dwellers who managed to produce bumper harvests at their *dachas* (600 square metres of land rendered by the State).

For many Soviet people, marketplaces became the only way to survive a supply deficit. Understanding the situation, the State permitted their existence: they allowed for space in cities, built the pavilions and established strict controls. There existed many instructions, regulations and limitations for sellers; in some years, for example, the sale of flour and bread was prohibited. Suits were filed for frivolous and sometimes absurd grounds. The Soviet media worked hard creating propaganda to paint a negative image of the private trader: the idea that these people were thieves, profiteers and enemies of the Soviet system was proliferated across the society. In this kind of paradox, marketplaces existed in the Soviet Union for more than fifty years, which was reflected in language, literature and arts.

Therefore, it is interesting to consider how the marketplace was depicted by Soviet and post-Soviet painters. Works of art preserve images of the past by providing us with vivid pictures of its spaces, of people's behaviour and of other elements of that epoch's everyday culture. Of course, painting can capture visual information, but more importantly it can convey people's attitudes to the depicted event and its society's stereotypes, antagonisms and prejudices.

Since the beginning of the seventeenth century, the image of the marketplace has been quite common in European painting. And it was only in the second part of the nineteenth century that these images became popular in Russian painting. Two approaches are clearly defined: the critical approach, which reflects the marketplace as a space of social injustice; and the picturesque approach, which creates bright visual patterns providing joyful and colourful effects.

Food and Markets

Although Critical Realism became the mainstream in Russian visual arts in the second part of the nineteenth century, the marketplace was more often the subject of admiration than condemnation. Russian painters depicted festivities vividly and colourfully, highlighting people's joy and happiness, as in Boris Kustodiev's *The Marketplace* (1910).

During the Soviet period, interest in the topic remained strong, which might seem surprising considering the State policy to abolish all forms of private trade. While researching the subject, we studied about 130 paintings, most of them not by well-known painters. In these so-called 'second-class paintings', usually created by provincial artists, it is not the artistic value that is of primary importance. These works reveal not only the personal vision of the artist but also common views, judgements and stereotypes existing in society at that time.

Before referring to the analysis of these works by Soviet artists it is worth mentioning that there are three main ways of depicting scenes of the marketplace in European art. Applying terms from photography and cinematography, we can identify these three ways as close-ups, medium shots and long shots based on the distance from which the artist chooses to portray the object. The most vivid examples of the close-ups are Frans Snyders' masterpieces. Although called 'marketplace scenes' they are more like sumptuous still lifes. In *The Fishmonger* (1657), for example, Snyders concentrates on the depiction of the shop boards with goods on them while the canvas itself tells a story about nature's bounty. A man appears in these pictures only to clarify the context in which all these loads of foodstuffs appear. While such close-ups are full of poetry, solemn hymns to nature and metaphors of prosperity and well-being, medium shot compositions mostly depict daily routine, demonstrating human interaction, negotiations and specific marketplace elements, as in Frans Josef Luckx's *At The Vegetable Market* (1843). Long shots are used by the artist when they want to show the marketplace as a picturesque element or a moving human crowd (e.g. Balthazar Nebot's *Covent Garden Market*, 1737). The ways of depicting reality refer to different artistic genres: still life, genre painting and town/city landscape. However, it is possible for the genres to overlap: for example, in the background of the marketplace one might see scenes of ordinary life.

The medium shot is the most popular way of depicting reality in European arts, which makes sense because this method provides the painters with limitless opportunities to fix human types and show methods of communication within certain frames and environments.

Studying the mass of Soviet painters' works from the 1920s to the 1980s, however, the first thing that captures our attention is the abundance of panoramic views. The artists seem to observe the space of the marketplace from a distance, not willing to get closer to it. And it is not only the interest in creating abstract pictures that makes them refuse to enter and reveal the marketplace area: this approach to reflecting reality allows the painter to show the marketplace itself, along with people moving chaotically within it, like a bright impressionistic canvas distant from the scene with little concentration on detail. One of the consequences of – or possibly the reason for – this approach, is the absence of portraits of traders in the pictures. Before the Revolution of 1917, portraying merchants, market traders and different types of people was of great interest for the painters. However in the post-Revolutionary period, an image such as 'the Soviet private trader' could not exist. Socialist Realism required praising and glorifying the person portrayed. The portraits had to present not only individuality but reflect the professional and social status of a person: Soviet teacher, Soviet miner, Soviet deputy. Proud members of the Socialist Society! There was no possibility to create images in such an exalted manner of a banished group.

The Soviet press used to call marketplace sellers 'profiteers', 'swindlers', 'pilferers'; Soviet power fought them stubbornly. Article number 107 of the Criminal Code of the RSFSR (1926) on agricultural products speculation led to the imprisonment of thousands of people involved in trade. There was nothing illegal if a person living in the south of the USSR grew a rich harvest of fruit in a warm climate and sold it single-handedly in the north. But if the same person sold not only his own but also his neighbour's harvest or, worse, bought and resold products of a few suppliers, he became a criminal. Under Soviet law only those growing goods themselves had the right to sell them in the marketplaces. All middlemen were considered criminals; the process of buying up and selling agricultural or other goods with the aim of profit could result in imprisonment for two to seven years, along with the confiscation of the entire property.

Consequently, there were collective farmers, pensioners, people on leave and others in the agricultural sector who sold goods in the marketplaces during their free time; but all these people were under the watchful eye of the State. When suspected to be selling too much one was checked immediately and punished administratively. It quite often occurred that a collective farmer, in order to sell his own harvest, needed a certificate granted by the head of the *kolkhoz* to prove the origin of the products, but the duty of a *kolkhoz* member was to sell goods to procurement centres where the prices were not profitable. Surprisingly enough, even under these circumstances there still existed people who brought goods to the marketplaces, but Soviet citizens, brought up on USSR propaganda, treated them with suspicion.

In this situation, it was not possible to make a marketplace trader the main character of a work of art. But how could an artist portray the marketplace itself without any sellers? Soviet painters came up with endless ways to solve this predicament. One of them was to make the marketplace space itself the centre of the composition, replacing individuals with a crowded area filled with indistinguishable personages.

Nevertheless, if a painter decided to enter the marketplace's environment, to get closer to shop boards and traders he had to think of some ways out of the dilemma. For example, they used compositions with only buyers seen in the foreground. In Alexander Pushnin's *In The Marketplace* (1960), consumers hurrying away home with hands full of goods. Somewhere in the background are counters and sellers preoccupied with something. One watches them from a distance, seeing only their backs or half-faces. Consumers, happy citizens of the Soviet country, march proudly towards the viewers. We can see each detail of their fair images, but we can hardly notice the people who supplied them with the goods they carry. By no means could the sellers be the centre of the painting or its meaning.

Even when painting a sales desk, the artist never depicted the buying and selling process itself. Close-up images of traders and buyers show them gossiping, flirting, discussing abstract topics, anything not relating to the commodity, as in Fedot Sitchkov's *Kolkhoz Marketplace* (1936). The painters shamefully avoided any depiction of haggling, examination of products or money exchange. As a result the very function of the marketplace, its meaning and purpose, became hidden and concealed. This approach correlated with the State's approach to the matter: in official Soviet documents, the sale of agricultural production was called 'exchange between city and village'. Such vague language reflected the government's desire to speak as little as possible about private trade that was considered to be 'the remnant of the bourgeois past'.

To avoid unwanted emphasis on the market itself, the artists often turned to the depiction of the road to or from the market: subjects like 'The Way to the Marketplace' and 'The Way Back from the Marketplace' are quite common. You can hardly find such subjects in pre-Revolutionary Russian arts, but by using them Soviet painters were able to show the marketplace without depicting it. They kept the entire process of buying and selling outside the picture, far away, beyond one's vision. The spectator notices only the preparation or the result of the case. Mostly the paintings on the theme of 'The Way to the Marketplace' depicted sellers carrying their goods to the marketplace, as in Hsar Gassiev's *To The Marketplace* (1973), but to guess the topic one had to read the title of the picture. Before arrival at the marketplace, the seller acted as a common Soviet toiler or a peasant, the role accented in the picture. The carried merchandise was shown quite shamefacedly, but the volume of agricultural goods was never emphasized.

Paintings showing 'The Way Back from the Marketplace' were devoted to consumers. The painters seemed not to be ashamed of placing heavy bags into people's hands, as in Konstantin Britov's *Back from The Marketplace* (1985). The painters themselves seemed unaware that their works traced the route of the harvest from producer to consumer excluding the selling process. There is another key detail in these pictures: when depicting the way to marketplace and back, painters felt freer in choosing ways of artistic expression. Characters could be tired, cheerful, thoughtful or amorous, as in Piotr Konchalovskiy's *Way Back From The Marketplace* (1926); the landscape could be shown at night-time, during the winter or filled with rain, as in Andrei Kotzka's *From The Marketplace* (1969).

In the marketplace itself, however, the weather was always depicted as fine and warm, the sun was shining, people (with rare exceptions) were calm, joyful and satisfied as in Alexander Pushnin's *In The Marketplace* (1960). The marketplace was considered

The Marketplace in Soviet and Post-Soviet Painting

a social space where, due to the requirements of Socialist Realism, people and weather alike should be positive.

As mentioned before, still life played an important role in European art depicting marketplaces. As a rule, however, there were no close-up views of shop boards in Soviet art. Spectators had no opportunity to admire a single fruit or to examine produce in detail; they could only view a stall from a distance, as in Mikhail Volodin's *Collective Farm Marketplace* (1973). These were signs of profusion but no visual evidence. In an environment where people of many regions of the country used ration cards to obtain their food supply, where indeed people had no idea what profusion meant, it was difficult to portray it.

In 1949, famous Soviet film producer Ivan Pyryev presented his masterpiece, *The Cossacks of Kuban*. The film became the enduring symbol of Soviet embellishment of reality through its mythic portrayal of the wealthy life of a Soviet village. The action took place in the marketplace in Kuban. The shop boards full of goods captivated the audience. In reality, people in the country were starving during this period; a lot of cities were still in ruins after the cruel war. In this lean time, it was impossible to get enough fruit and vegetables for shooting; the film makers had to make a great number of plaster casts to portray the desired profusion. Stalin liked the film; having seen it, as the legend said, he pronounced: 'As I can see, the situation in agricultural sphere in our country is not so bad'. This was how the State presented the model of depicting the marketplace: with sun, joy, songs, happiness and ostensible prosperity. The paintings of Stalin's period often correspond with the images from *The Cossacks of Kuban*. It seems that the counters are full of the fakes of a mythic abundance, as in Anna Cherednitchenko's *In The Marketplace* (1947).

Taking into account the huge territory of the USSR, we might expect that visual art would reflect regional peculiarities as there were obvious differences both in the population's ethnography and in the types of the products on sale. It makes no sense to compare poor marketplaces in the north of the USSR with those in the south. But Soviet art levelled these obvious differences. Judging by the pictures, one could barely guess where the action took place. It was somewhere in Central Russia, in a nondescript Russian city. The titles of these pictures offer no precise information and do not provide exact place names; instead the marketplace was generalized: *To the Marketplace; In the Marketplace; In the Marketplace Square; In the Market; Marketplace*. Only the depictions of Central Asian and Ukrainian markets possessed regional peculiarities. There artists seem captivated by the national flavour, the brightness of the southern sun, by exotic surroundings and distinctive characters (e.g. Oganes Tatevosjan, *Market in Fergana*, 1929).

Statistical analysis of the paintings devoted to the Soviet marketplace indicates a surge in interest in the topic in the 1930s, 1960s and 1970s. These periods coincide with those when the Soviet State proclaimed policies to 'satisfy the vital needs of the Soviet people'.

Surprisingly, there are few scenes devoted to the marketplace in the paintings of the 1920s. It was the period of the New Economic Policy; the relatively high freedom in the economy and the boom in the commercial sphere had to attract painters' attention. But this didn't happen because of avant-garde trends in the twentieth century; these artists were full of revolutionary enthusiasm and ready to solve universal problems, not to depict everyday life and daily routine. In the 1930s, a new trend – Socialist Realism – led artists to respond to the call of the Soviet power to 'reflect Soviet reality' in their works. The number of pictures depicting marketplace scenes increased, but such works were often regarded as second-class: portraits of Soviet leaders and depictions of workers' heroic deeds won the top prizes. Nevertheless, many painters yielded to the temptation to depict the bright and colourful life of marketplaces. Even taking into account existing limitations and antagonisms, Soviet art still reflects the flavour of its epoch, visualizes the realities of life in that period and reveals its contemporaries' attitude to these realities.

The post-Soviet period in Russian history has been filled with staggering economic and ideological changes. One of the fundamental changes was the rebirth of private property and the market. These changes were painful for the community as they affected daily life and basic social existence. Private traders, who used to be criminal offenders and were contemptuously labelled 'profiteers', became an everyday reality.

In the 1990s Russia suffered an economic crisis during which the population thought only of survival. For both buyers and sellers, private trade became an escape. People had large amounts of depreciated money while the counters of State stores were empty. For many years the State had been in charge of supplying the country with products; under new realities it was unable to fulfil this duty. The citizens of the country took matters into their own hands. They cultivated land around the cities and planted potatoes, carried goods from one part of the country to another, or even from abroad, for sale. A new term was coined: 'a shuttle-trader', which referred to people who went to buy goods in Greece, Turkey or Poland, carried these goods in their own luggage and then sold them in the marketplace. Former engineers or teachers started selling goods. Small marketplaces arose spontaneously near underground stations, along country roads, by bus stops. It became impossible to despise or to denounce this activity: the entire country was involved in it.

It is little wonder then, that during the post-Soviet period the marketplace has remained vital for many Russian artists. There are no more limitations requiring the concealment or euphemistic exaggeration of the Soviet era; new realities are invading art. The State is no longer in control of topics, subjects, characters or style of artistic works. Consequently, there is no longer a single way to depict the marketplace. On the one hand, for example, many contemporary artists emphasize the levelling tendencies of globalization, showing marketplaces in every part of the country obtaining the same kind of goods. Peaches, watermelons and melons are no longer a distinctive feature of the Central Asian and of the Ukrainian markets, but also typical of those in Siberia. On the other hand, other artists accentuate the unique surroundings and character of each marketplace. The church or some other conspicuous object is positioned by the marketplace to highlight its location. Geographic names have begun to appear frequently in titles: *Marketplace in Zdemirovo; Kalitnikovskiy Market; Marketplace in Omsk; Market Day in Torzhok*.

Nowadays, Socialist Realism is no longer an obligatory trend that painters have to follow in the USSR; artists are free to express their values and ideas freely in any suitable manner. The marketplace topic inspires the artist to express emotions in colours. The variegated and noisy sphere inspires the creation of bright and abstract compositions with often little attention to detail. As a result, exultant and optimistic paintings have been created, as in Nikolai Komarov's *Summer Breathing* (2012). Other painters tend to simplify forms, like Vladimir Lubarov in his *Winter Marketplace* (2008). With pathos and seriousness left in the Soviet past, new intonations including irony, mockery and sometimes even nostalgia are appearing.

One of the most vivid acknowledgements of change in these works is a new focus on the seller, who is now often the main character of the paintings. A significant number of images are being painted that could be called 'marketplace portraits'. They focus on the seller as an individual, with a psychological state and a mood that worries the artist. Most of these sellers are women. Old and young, cheerful and sad, they stand at the shop counters close to the painter, who analyses their faces and carefully fixes the details. It seems that the marketplace area is a feminine space. In Soviet Russia many people were ashamed of selling goods that they had fairly cultivated themselves. Therefore, the main sellers in the marketplaces were elderly women, which was reflected in Soviet paintings. Men bought commodities but didn't often sell them. During the post-Soviet period, private trade stopped being shameful but the practice remains: even nowadays most of the traders in the marketplaces are women, as we see in Vladimir Yanaki's *Generous Autumn* (2006).

In the work of Soviet painters, figures of buyers prevailed while sellers appeared, if at all, in the background. In post-Soviet art the situation is the opposite. It sometimes seems that there are no buyers in the compositions at all, as in Anastasiya Lobanova's *Autumn's Gifts* (2012), the portrait of a private trader that reflects her double treatment of the attitude to the marketplace, to new values, and to a new way of life that has existed since Perestroika. Two models of behaviour and self-expression of people belonging to two epochs are fixed together: 'two Russias', a new one and an old one. In one picture, Georgiy Kichigin's *Bazar In Omsk* (2004), elderly women are frozen in silence, suggesting static rigidity and unnaturalness. In another, Tatjana Potvorovova's *A Fishmonger* (2010), we see girls and young women behaving dynamically, happily and harmoniously. One part of the community is still true to the Soviet ideals and does not share new life modes and strategies; the other part feels absolutely free in the new market environment. During the Soviet period the marketplace was a kind of phantom. Nowadays the market has turned into a complicated world to be depicted through the visions of current Russian painters.

Eating the Inedible: The Colonial Marketplace at the *Exposition universelle* of 1889

Kylie Sago

Food and the colonial marketplace

The construction of a space at the *Exposition universelle* of 1889 in Paris devoted entirely to the exhibition of the colonies – an innovation in the World's Fair model – resulted in a concentrated marketplace of colonial products. Food mediated the encounter between the imperial power and its domains overseas, and exotic culinary practices were continuously highlighted to suggest the difference between Hexagonal France and its territories in North Africa, south-east Asia and the Caribbean. Food figured prominently in anthropological exhibitions of colonial subjects eating, where perceived primitiveness or savageness emphasized 'otherness' and reiterated the need for the 'civilizing mission' of French imperial intervention.[1] In the context of these imperialist displays of colonial food practices, commentary published in contemporary guides and newspapers anxiously considered the implications of European visitors' participation in this marketplace of food items and spectacles. The possibility of consuming inedible objects – ranging from contaminated dishes to lingering traces of cannibalism – represented a persistent worry for visitors to the Exposition, who tasted fruits grown on colonial soil, sampled products like wine and bread and sat down to eat in restaurants for 'authentic' dining experiences. Paradoxically, the fascination with and demand for exoticized displays of colonial consumption betrayed an avid thirst for the colonies, even as insistent expressions of disgust reinforced the desperate desire to establish distance between the colonizer's and 'other' eating practices.

The central *Palais des colonies* at the *Esplanade des Invalides* on Paris's Left Bank was surrounded by twelve individual (and architecturally elaborate) structures representing French territories, as well as six replica villages populated by colonized peoples. Restaurant spaces for visitors could be found in the Café Maure of the Algerian Pavilion, the Tunisian Café-Concert and pastry shop, the Annamite pavilion and the Javanese restaurant and refreshment bar. Exotic flavours of the colonies were embodied in the agricultural products displayed and available for purchase in marketplaces: figs, dates, bananas, pineapples, oranges, almonds, pomegranates, coconut and the like.[2] Van Troi Tran theorizes that the emphasis on importable products (rather than prepared dishes) in reviews and guides to the *Esplanade* demonstrates the Exposition's prioritization of presenting the commercial possibilities of the empire over care for the individual visitor's gustatory experience of colonial cuisines. The tension between highlighting the economic purpose of the colonies through the exposition of their agricultural products and catering to visitors' desires for entertainment demonstrates the dual function of the colonial exposition, which existed, as Tran suggests, to educate French citizens on the empire while it entertained them. Laurier Turgeon further proposes that the edifying goals of the colonial exhibition served to justify imperialism: 'The intercultural encounter is presented as a means to augment one's consciousness and comprehension of the Other and serves as a moral principle legitimizing geographical consumption.'[3]

Eating the inedible

In the context of the *Exposition universelle*, food products and cultural practices of consumption became powerful markers of identity, as well as expressions of progress of the culture from which they originated. The agricultural products at the *Esplanade* allowed visitors to taste the fruits of France's colonial earth, but the ubiquity of these flavours led visitors to the colonial exposition to lament the inevitable loss of the exoticism that first constituted their appeal. The Tunisian pavilion, in particular, drew critics' attention for the predictability of the agricultural products available for purchase. Maurice Brincourt describes that just outside of the Café-Concert of the Tunisian pavilion, 'one finds a few more kiosks and small pavilions, where couscouss [sic] (a ragoût of sheep) is made, pottery and fans are sold, as well as the inevitable dates, coconuts and slices of pineapple served in their juice'. Théodore Lindenlaub's description of the marketplace (*souk*) of the Tunisian pavilion echoes both Brincourt's disappointment in the repetitive produce, listing the 'ordinary delicacies – alas, too ordinary! – of the exotic displays: slices of pineapple in their juice, date paste, groups of bananas impudently peeled, coconuts carved as faces of black men'. While the banality of the exotic seems to constitute a regrettable loss in the opinion of Brincourt and Lindenlaub, Turgeon suggests that '[r]endering these products commonplace represented a way to domesticate and desacralize them, and to radically alter their original meaning in order to express their appropriation even more forcefully'.[4]

As these exotic flavours became progressively normalized due to their pervasiveness at the *Esplanade*, visitors to the colonial exhibition sought out even more dramatic examples of foreign cuisine to satisfy their appetite for the unfamiliar. Instances of eating practices perceived as primitive or savage – the pinnacle of which would be eating the inedible – are increasingly evoked in guides and commentaries on the Exposition, and the identification of these practices marked as 'other' presented a way to express (and construct) difference between European visitors and the colonial subjects on display. In some cases, the uneatable is evoked in reaction to methods of preparation that could result in contamination of the food; in others, the reaction is inspired by unpalatable ingredients, ranging from dog meat to the threat of cannibalism. European commentaries on the colonial eating practices at the Fair employ expressions of disgust in response to these foreign culinary customs as a way to highlight the alterity of the colonial subjects.

The emotional, affective experience of disgust, as psychologist Paul Rozin suggests, evolved out of the body's mechanism of rejecting foreign substances threatening bodily harm (vomiting), to also include metaphorically purging concepts or ideas harmful to the individual (especially reminders of animal nature or mortality). Disgust differs fundamentally from distaste as a rejection of substances on the basis of their conceptual offensiveness, rather than a simple question of unpleasant taste or texture. Disgust, however, does not function exclusively at the level of the individual; the essential concept of the expulsion of offensive or dangerous items can be applied to the social body, as well. In this way, disgust works as a powerful social cement, providing a cultural mechanism of grouping people with similar tastes and permitting them to reject those whose practices – alimentary or otherwise – violate their principles. Additionally, the expression of disgust creates a shared social space based precisely on the exclusion of a certain group or practice from a given social body: 'sharing and comparing disgust reactions can be the source of a social bond or attraction that distinguishes the ingroup from the outgroup.' As a mechanism to designate the boundaries between the interior and exterior of a cultural group, disgust proves a useful, if graphic, way to consider difference and reject the Other in favour of maintaining one's own 'taste'. As disgust finds its evolutionary roots, as Rozin suggests, in the reversal of the physiological process of taking food into the body, it remains a particularly relevant mode of evaluating food items and their moral implications; to this effect, anthropologist Wulf Schiefenhövel suggests that '[f]ood customs of other cultures are very often evaluated on the crude basis of the disgust mechanism'.[5]

At the *Esplanade des Invalides*, the inedible – and expressions of disgust that its consumption provokes – is sometimes invoked for reasons of sanitation, both metaphoric and literal; the potential contamination of food raises issues for European consumers. In *Purity and Danger,* Mary Douglas famously defines dirt as 'matter out of place', indicating that 'dirt is essentially disorder' within a culturally constructed system. A function of the specific order that it violates, dirt 'exists in the eye of the beholder' and, like disgust, is a marker of group identity. To this effect, the evocation of dirt in the food at the Exposition gestures as much to conceptual contamination as to the possible pathogenic consequences of unsanitary food. As Douglas suggests, however, not all experiences of anomaly are displeasing. A comment from Paul Bluysen published in *Paris en 1889: Souvenirs et croquis de l'Exposition* demonstrates the paradoxical belief that food prepared in the colonial exhibition was feared to be contaminated, and therefore inedible, but was possibly even more delicious precisely because – and not just in spite – of this: 'Do you enjoy couscous? You will find it in the different cafés of the *Esplanade*. It is prepared by hands that are perhaps not very white, but it is said this only adds to its flavour.' The *double entendre* of the quotation associates the colour of the hands preparing the food and the compromised sanitation of the prepared dish, lumping race and dirt together in an accumulation of difference that plays to imperialist associations of exoticism and savagery. The implied disgust expressed in reaction to the double contamination of the dish – its preparation by a colonial subject and its contact with dirt – may be attributed to the prevailing Western belief that 'you are what you eat'. In this case, the adage could be expanded to read, 'you are what your food has touched'. Eating food prepared by a colonial subject, very different in appearance from European visitors to the *Esplanade*, may play on fears of racial mixing or cultural atavism; the dirt present in the dish contaminates it, precisely, with the inedible.[6]

The disgust inspired by the potential presence of dirt in the couscous (which Bluysen only implies rather than overtly affirms) hinges on the identification of dirt as a substance inappropriate for consumption (recalling Douglas' definition of 'matter out of place'). From a Western point of view, dirt is taken for granted as a non-food item, despite its widespread consumption and despite the fact that eating earth does not necessarily pose a risk to the body. The long-standing Western denigration of consuming dirt may represent associations with indiscriminate eating and unsanitary conditions, and implied in this, proximity to animals.[7] Cătălin Avramescu argues that squalor, and the notion of foodborne illness, gained momentum over the eighteenth and nineteenth centuries as motifs of unacceptable eating practices; as an expression of extreme otherness, contaminated or unhygienic food even came to replace the previous associations of alterity and cannibalism (which, however, linger in the European imagination and find expression in the context of the World's Fairs).[8] At the *Exposition universelle*, as Tran suggests, great care was taken – and a very public show of it made – to establish and maintain European standards of hygienic conditions in the exhibition spaces occupied by colonial subjects.[9]

The preoccupation with the ingredients and preparation of food served at the colonial exhibition – especially in restaurant spaces of the Fair – demonstrates an uneasy attention to the potential implications of European visitors' consumption of dishes prepared by natives of the colonies. In the *Revue de l'Exposition Universelle de 1889*, Léon de Fourcourd distinguishes between food preparation in the Javanese village for the villagers (that is, colonial subjects who inhabited the space for the duration of the exhibition) and for the visitors to the restaurant: 'In another cabana near the entrance to the village, yellow cooks prepare the same food, but with more finesse, for service in the restaurant. It is only spiced ground meat, poultry with pepper, strips of dried venison, eggs covered in seasoning […], without counting the entremets.'[10] The Javanese cooks are again described in terms of the colour of their skin, a marker of their alterity that gestures to the otherness of the dish and its potential contamination, if all the implications of the racial notation are pursued. The fears that the European visitor will participate in eating the inedible are attenuated, however, by the quotation's specification that the food destined to be served in the restaurant, although fundamentally the same as the food that nourishes the natives, is cooked with 'more finesse' and in a wholly separate space. The visitor to the *Esplanade* can therefore partake of an authentic meal without worry.

In addition to the process of food preparation, much attention is given to ingredients used in restaurant spaces, and especially those marked as offensive – if not wholly inedible – by Western standards. Similar to the evocation of the contaminated couscous, in descriptions of meats ranging from dog to human flesh, the expression of disgust which attempts to establish difference between European and 'other' practices cannot help but also betray a sense of curiosity, fascination and attraction to these examples of extreme, caricatured exoticism.[11] Camille Debans, in *Les coulisses de l'Exposition: guide pratique et anecdotique*, recommends (with hesitation) the food at the Palace of Annam and Tonkin at the *Esplanade*: 'I could not say if the cuisine will be to your liking, but if you do not fear a piece of raw pork or if, out of curiosity, you would like to try a bite of dog, you can risk it. There is never a dull moment when you seat yourself to dine in the Tonkin manner and with the ingredients familiar to the children of Annam.'[12] Serving the pork uncooked represents a primitive manner of presenting the meat, both exciting and dangerous in its strangeness. Claude Lévi-Strauss identifies a universal 'culinary triangle' comprised of the raw, the cooked and the rotted, according to which 'the cooked is a cultural transformation of the raw, whereas the rotted is a natural transformation'. The pure raw or the rotted would represent examples of the inedible (although sometimes processes of decomposition are harnessed and controlled by a culture to create food products); even food items left uncooked are not in the condition of 'pure rawness', as 'only certain foods can really be eaten raw, and then only if they have been selected, washed, pared or cut, or even seasoned'.[13] Lévi-Strauss notes, however, that the boundaries of the culinary triangle shift between cultures; the precise definitions of raw, cooked and rotted are not universal. Debans's commentary demonstrates this fluidity, as the rawness of the pork in the Palace of Annam and Tonkin represents an acceptable food item for a given culture, but one dangerously close to the category of the pure raw from the perspective of another. Despite the reservations of the recommendation of the raw pork or bits of dog found in the dishes in the restaurant, Debans's statement ultimately amounts to a challenge to the reader of the article; he appeals to the courage of the visitor to the *Esplanade* to participate in an eating practice whose very authenticity carries with it, significantly, the assurance of relative harmlessness.

Even more thrilling than the prospect of dishes from Annam and Tonkin, the preparation of beef in the Kanak village titillates in its proximity to cannibalism. Paul Arène, in his article, '*Les Cuisines exotiques*' in the *Revue de l'Exposition universelle de 1889*, takes his readers on a dream-tour of the restaurant spaces at the *Esplanade des Invalides*. Stopping at the Kanak village representing New Caledonia, the guide Monselet beckons his guests:

– Come in, *messieurs*. We are now with the Kanaks.
– The cannibals!
– I esteem, after so many other inhuman cuisines, that we will dine in their agreeable company on the most succulent of stews.
– Oh, horror! So this was your surprise?

But, as Monselet continued to smile maliciously, a guard assured us and explained that the Kanaks, a people of good taste and accessible to progress, renounced anthropophagy and henceforth preferred beef even to the most appetizing of their enemies killed in war. Besides, thanks to the ancient experience of a people for whom the idea of cuisine is inseparable from the values of bravery and glory, they cook the meat superiorly.

The lid was removed from a boiling pot and a delicious odour filled the air.
– Taste it!
We did so.[14]

Just as the perceived racial and sanitary contamination of the rice prepared in the Javanese restaurant contributed to its deliciousness, the proximity of the beef's preparation to cannibal consumption adds to, rather than detracts from, its delectable flavour. It is as close to the cannibal experience as the visitor to the Exposition can venture without violating the highest of Western eating taboos, maintaining enough distance to avoid actually eating the inedible while still managing to profit from the proximity of the act to the most succulent of sins.

As these quotations from Bluysen, Fourcourd, Debans and Arène suggest, the European visitor's implicated participation in colonial eating practices is problematic, and especially so when the act in question approaches or constitutes eating the inedible. A sense of exotic authenticity is necessary to establish the sense of a real cultural encounter and anthropological experience, as the Exposition sought to do, and as visitors demanded. Despite the insistence on disgust inspired by the presence of dirt or dangerous meats in colonial dishes, as well as the associations of savagery and barbarity they raised, such 'primitive' foods came to be expected in the restaurant spaces of the World's Fair. In the periodical, *L'Avenir du Tonkin à l'Exposition*, the article '*Variétés: Les restaurants exotiques de l'Exposition*' portrays the disappointment of a man from Marseille at the perceived westernness of the Annamite restaurant: 'I expected to be served by little Annamites! There are so many at the Exposition, and it would be so original! A waiter came, a real devilish braggart. I asked him for the Annamite menu – oh the disappointment! One had to choose between a lamb chop with steamed vegetables and a Bercy steak. Between beef and sheep, not even buffalo!'[15]

The central question for the food marketplace became how to preserve the claim of authenticity and the thrill of participating in taboo eating practices without actually putting the European subject in the position of experiencing disgust at their own consumption. This 'self-disgust' would be precarious for the identity of the European visitor, for (as Rozin's definition implies) it would entail self-repulsion and even self-rejection. Problematically, the very aspects of a given dish that verge on the disgusting or inedible – the alterity of its chef, the contamination in its preparation, and the acceptability of the ingredients – made it exotic and highly attractive. The colonial exposition sought balance between the extremes of a culinary marketplace unacceptable to visitors due to the too-drastic alterity of its eating practices, or a sterile dining experience that ignored European fantasies of the exotic. Partaking of so-called authentic consumption practices required the construction and careful maintenance of a certain distance between the visitor and the colonial subject, which took the form of several simultaneous strategies. The imperialist gaze of these and similar commentaries to the Fair proclaims fundamental difference by calling attention to racial hierarchies and indications of a culture's relative advancement as represented by its culinary arts. The evocation of disgust – provided it is directed toward the Other – serves precisely this effect. Separation might also occur in a more literal sense, such as in the different food preparation areas as in the Javanese village; these preserve the authenticity of the colonial display while purportedly raising standards of hygiene to render European consumption acceptable. Finally, ingredient substitutions (of beef for human flesh) insist on the difference between cannibal practices and the 'succulent' recipes served at the Fair, which nevertheless still evoke the bravery and glory of a violent culinary past. This constant and multivalent establishment of just enough difference between eating practices that inspire insurmountable disgust and those displayed at the colonial marketplace of the *Exposition universelle* of 1889 made it so that products consumed by Europeans were no longer properly inedible, but just barely so.

Problematic incorporation

As visitors purchased and tasted the fruits of colonial labour, this act of consuming the colonies represented a rehearsal of the incorporation of territories into the imperial body, the nourishment from which can be considered physically, economically and politically for the imperial power. Consuming products of the colonies, whether in terms of importable agricultural goods, of restaurant dishes or even of the visual consumption of colonial spectacles, displays the imperial power dynamics that animate the *Esplanade des Invalides*. As many scholars have suggested, the anthropological expositions deeply reflected the imperialist perspective of a colonial power that insisted on Western superiority by emphasizing the primitiveness of the reaches of its empire. Despite the anthropological and even ethnographic pretensions of the colonial exhibition, the cultures of France's colonies were not objectively placed on display at the World's Fairs; rather, a biased, imperial perception of these cultures, firmly anchored in hegemonic discourse, was presented to the public.[16] The presentation of colonial eating practices at the Parisian Fair of 1889 therefore lent itself to the rehearsal of the superiority of imperial France, both culinary and, by extension, moral. The market dynamics of the *Esplanade des Invalides* further reinforced this power by placing the European visitor in the dominant position of economic control, positing the colonized person and their eating practices not only as products to be consumed (on the scale both of the individual and of the empire), but also to be changed to better conform to European taste.

This very hierarchy of imperialist domination is undermined, however, by the metaphor of incorporation that figured so prominently in these colonial displays, both in terms of the literal ingestion of food products happening at the *Esplanade des Invalides* and the metaphoric cultural and economic consumption of colonialism to which they gestured. The identification of eating practices clearly marked as 'other' and the disgust they potentially inspired served to reinforce a conceptual model demarcating France from its Others. Furthermore, the disgust evoked by the commentators on the Exposition insisted on the capacity to reject those practices and cultures that proved too fundamentally different for successful imperial incorporation. The idea of incorporation is not without internal inconsistencies, however, as Maggie Kilgour suggests in *From Communion to Cannibalism: An Anatomy of Metaphors of Incorporation*: 'The idea of incorporation [...] depends upon and enforces an absolute division between inside and outside; but in the act itself that opposition disappears, dissolving the structure it appears to produce.' When the colonial product is internalized, boundaries between 'eater and eaten' blur 'as the law "you are what you eat" obscures identity and makes it impossible to say for certain who's who'; this applies equally for the metaphoric incorporation of imperialism as for the fruits, pastries and dishes literally consumed by visitors to the *Exposition*. Turgeon adds that the body is transformed by that which it incorporates; rather than it effecting a change in the material it brings within its bounds, it cannot help but become what it eats.[17] The eventual banality of the once-exotic flavours at the Exposition demonstrates precisely this transformation; as the foreign is internalized, it loses its sense of unfamiliarity and becomes part of the culture.

In the context of incorporation of the colonies into the economy and culture of France, the desire to construct the colonies as Other in order to affirm cultural superiority and justify colonial involvement resulted in a spiralling search for increasingly dramatic expressions of alterity in eating practices. The *Exposition universelle* of 1889 represented the paradoxical environment that expressed both incorporation and difference, where, as it blurred lines between Hexagonal France and its territories overseas, the expression of disgust allowed European visitors to insist – however ineffectually – their ability to reject that which threatened or offended.

(Inedible) food for thought

The inedible is again invoked if an item not only cannot do bodily good by providing nutrition, but furthermore threatens bodily harm. The taboo of consuming uneatable objects is especially evident in the Aïssaouas' evening show at the Café Maure in the Algerian pavilion, where performers would carry out acts of self-mutilation in a spiritual trance – including piercing their lips, cheeks and arms; walking or laying on a sword; and eating glass, rocks, hot coals and living scorpions – purportedly without feeling pain. In reactions to this spectacle, the emphasis on the primitiveness of this practice reveals an imperial violence – a metaphoric cannibalism, even – that proves deeply problematic for justifications for the colonial endeavour. In other words, the immense popularity of this spectacle of eating the inedible could not help but betray the aggressive appetite of those who participated as paying spectators. Even more than the evocation of contaminated food or the gesture towards the past cannibalism of the Kanak people, the spectacle at the Café Maure used the tropes of savagery and violence in its portrayal of colonial eating, which the reciprocal (and deeply contradictory) cannibalism of colonialism sought to suppress.[18]

The taste of the colonies made available at the *Exposition universelle* of 1889 provided French visitors the opportunity to explore their desire for the exotic – a desire which commentaries on the spectacle at the Café Maure and other culinary practices at the *Esplanade des Invalides* demonstrated to be highly ambivalent. Desire was accompanied by disgust, and attraction coupled with aggression, as the imperial power negotiated its identity and relationship to the territories it had absorbed into its empire. At the Parisian Fair of 1889, food provided a framework to explore the implications of colonial consumption, as well as a vocabulary to express the pleasure and anxiety surrounding the incorporation of the foreign and exotic into the imperial body. As borders between the Self and Other were explored, drawn and redrawn in the context of changing tastes for the exotic, a tenuous balance between the familiar and strange, the banal and inedible, was sought at the colonial marketplace of the World's Fair.

Notes

1. See Van Troi Tran, *Manger et Boire aux Expositions universelles: Paris 1889, 1890* (Tours: Presses universitaires François Rabelais de Tours; Rennes: Presses universitaires de Rennes, 2012), p. 20; Aram Yengoyan, 'Culture, Ideology and World's Fairs', in *Fair Representations: World's Fairs and the Modern World*, ed. by Robert Rydell and Nancy Gwinn (Amsterdam: VU Press, 1994); James Gilbert, 'World's Fairs as Historical Events' in *Fair Representations* claims that the universal culture displayed in the World's Fairs is defined by the opposition of civilization and savagery.
2. Pavilions were constructed for Algeria, Angkor, Annam and Tonkin, Gabon, Guadeloupe, Guyana, Indochina, Martinique, Senegal, Serre and Tunisia; replica villages represented Cochin China, Java, Madagascar, the Kanak people of New Caledonia, the Pahouins of North Africa and the Alfours of New Guinea. See Burton Benedict, 'Rituals of Representation: Ethnic Stereotypes and Colonized People's at World's Fairs', in *Fair Representations*, and *Zoos humains*, ed. by Nicolas Bancel et al. (Paris: Découverte, 2004) for descriptions of pavilions and villages; for reports on agricultural displays, see *Reports of the United States Commissioners to the Universal Exposition of 1889 at Paris* (Washington, Government Printing Office, 1891).
3. See Tran, p. 192–4; Benedict argues that the Parisian Fair failed to distinguish between explicitly instructive colonial exhibitions and the 'amusement zone' (52); Turgeon, *Patrimoines Métissés: Contextes coloniaux et postcoloniaux* (Laval: Presses de l'université de Laval, 2003), p. 176. This translation and those following are my own.
4. See Tran, p. 207–8, for a discussion of exoticism expected of the products displayed at the Fair; Brincourt, *L'Exposition universelle de 1889* (Paris: Firmin-Didot, 1890), p. 212; Théophile Lindenlaub, 'La Tunisie', in *Revue de l'Exposition universelle de 1889*, ed. by François-Guillaume Dumas (Paris, Motteroz, 1890), VI, 169–176 (p. 172); Turgeon, p. 179.
5. Paul Rozin et al., 'Disgust, the cultural evolution of a food-based emotion', in *Food Taste and Preferences: Continuity and Change*, ed. by Helen Macbeth (Providence: Berghahn Books, 1997), p. 67, 72; Wulf

Schiefenhövel, 'Good Taste and Bad Taste', in *Food Taste and Preferences*, p. 62.
6. See Douglas (London, New York; ARK Paperbacks, 1966; repr. 1984), p. 2, p. 35–7; Bluysen, (Paris: Arnould, 1890), p. 117–8; for further consideration of contamination and contagion, see Rozin et al., p. 69.
7. See Rozin et al. for discussions of dirt and indiscriminate eating; for their association with colonial subjects, see Valérie Loichot, 'Introduction,' in *The Tropics Bite Back* (Minneapolis: U Minnesota P, 2013). For considerations of geophagy and pica, see Sarah L. Young, *Craving Earth: Understanding Pica* (New York: Columbia UP, 2011), and *Consuming the Inedible: Neglected Dimensions of Food Choice,* ed. by MacClancy et al. (New York: Berghahn Books, 2007).
8. *An Intellectual History of Cannibalism* (Princeton: Princeton UP, 2009), p. 166.
9. See Tran, p. 212, 228–32.
10. 'Le village javanais', (Paris: Motteroz, 1890), VI, 105–114 (p. 111).
11. See Bel S. Castro, 'Food, Morality, and Politics: The Spectacle of Dog-Eating Igorots at the 1904 St. Louis World Fair', in *Food and Morality: Proceedings of the Oxford Symposium on Food and Cookery 2007*, ed. by Susan R. Friedland (Totnes, Devon: Prospect Books, 2008).
12. Camille Debans, *Les coulisses de l'Exposition: guide pratique et anecdotique* (Paris: Kolb, 1889), p. 321–2, cited in Tran, p. 207–8.
13. 'The Culinary Triangle', *The Partisan Review*, 33 (1966), 586–596 (p. 587).
14. VI, 209–13 (p. 212–3).
15. Gaster (1889) vol. 14, p. 219, cited in Tran, p. 208.
16. See Benedict and Yengoyan in *Fair Representations*; Tran, p. 188.
17. Kilgour (Princeton: Princeton UP, 1990), p. 4, 7; Turgeon, p. 164.
18. For accounts of the Aïssaouas' performance, see Brincourt (p. 207–8); Henri Lavedan, 'Les Aissa-Ouas', in *Revue de l'Exposition*. For cannibalism as justification of colonialism, and colonialism as metaphoric cannibalism, see Avramescu; *Cannibalism and the Colonial World*, ed. by Barker et al. (Cambridge: Cambridge UP, 1998); *Eating Their Words: Cannibalism and the Boundaries of Cultural Identity*, ed. by Kristen Guest (Albany: State U New York P, 2001); Loichot.

Degrees of Freshness: The Contemporary International Market for Hyperfresh Seafood

Richard W. Shepro

The market for the highest-quality fresh seafood has been transformed in the last few decades into a complex, long-distance international network, at a time when many other types of markets are emphasizing the importance of local products.[1] Time and distance no longer define freshness. Characteristics of this market, including awareness of fishing techniques and technological change in refrigerated transport and handling, along with the challenges and opportunities of aquaculture, have changed market ideas of freshness and patterns of connoisseurship.[2]

Drying, smoking and preservation by chemical activity (generally salt) or fermentation allowed international markets in preserved seafood to develop on an enormous, international scale many centuries ago. The preserved seafood market has been well studied.[3] The international fresh market has been less studied and is characterized by very rapid change.

The romantic, vital and still viable old model

For fresh seafood, traditionally, restaurants and individuals interested in the highest quality needed to be near fishing docks. Although restaurants still often cluster at the waterfront their seafood is often not local, even at establishments concerned about quality.

The pure, romantic (and wonderful) ideal of an older local fresh-fish system continues at a very high quality in only a few places – for example, at Trattoria Piccolo Napoli near a very old fish market in Palermo, in Sicily. The restaurant, started in 1951, does not use this market.[4] Instead, two small boats sail every morning from the nearby fishing village of Terrasini and bring to the restaurant a mismatched assortment of just a few small fish, only enough for the number of reserved guests, exhibiting signs of freshness, such as a characteristic rigor-mortis curvature to one side, that are essentially unknown even in top-quality restaurants and seafood markets around the world.[5] By contrast, most of the Sicilian commercial catch now travels to Milan and enters an international distribution market. Before such a market existed, fish not sold to connoisseurs at Sicilian wharves went to the streets in wheelbarrows full of ice.[6] One can picture the arguments over quality as the wheelbarrows went farther inland, the price dropping as the ice melted and the quality declined.

The Contemporary International Market for Hyperfresh Seafood

On the Côte d'Azur in the south of France, there are a dwindling number of similar restaurants, such as Restaurant Bacon, in Cap d'Antibes, where the fish menu is a platter of just-caught fish from a syndicate of small boats, and by the end of the meal that menu has disappeared. The world of Le Petit Nice, in Marseille (three Michelin stars since 2008), revolves around exclusively local seafood, each dish identified by the fisherman or the boat, with a warning: *Tous nos plats peuvent varier selon la pêche, la Méditerranée est souveraine.*

By contrast, the trend is for restaurants to serve fish without regard for how far it has travelled. The frequency of *tartare de saumon* in waterside restaurants in the Vieux Port of Marseille is not the result of the Mediterranean suddenly becoming a hatchery for salmon (which do not exist in the Mediterranean) but of long distance fish travel. I've been visiting local seafood markets around the world since the mid-1970s. I became interested in the dwindling supply of high-quality seafood restaurants focusing on truly local seafood after I first visited Restaurant Michel ('Brasserie des Catalans'), on the outskirts of Marseille, in 1979, and realized how rare it was even in Marseille.

The modern world market

The extreme freshness of the fish at Piccolo Napoli, Bacon or Le Petit Nice presents tremendous gastronomic quality, and the local focus provides context, history and the pleasure of uniqueness, while allowing the cooks to become true experts in preparing local seafood varieties and adapting to local seasons. The guests can also take great pleasure in observing and participating in a deep level of connoisseurship that has been developed over generations.

Most of the world does not work that way, even when it pretends to. A restaurant with a serious tone in Amelia Island, Florida, in sight of working shrimp boats, has a menu touting local suppliers and boasting about having a supplier in Beaufort, North Carolina, which is more than 800 kilometres away.[7] In freshness terms, is that any closer than Washington State, the North Sea or Tokyo? In fact, it may well be farther.

The best restaurants participating in this modern international market do not pretend to be local. In the contemporary international market system, a tuna caught off Gloucester, Massachusetts, may be sold at the Gloucester pier auction, specially prepared and packed, refrigerated at a precisely controlled temperature, flown to Tokyo, sold for a high price in the fresh tuna auction at Tokyo's Tsukiji mammoth fish market, and then shipped, still in prize 'fresh' condition, often overseas again to another market intermediary and then delivered to its final destination, which might well be the restaurant Masa in New York or Clio in Boston. Tuna connoisseurs may appreciate this well travelled tuna as much or more than the travellers who seek out Piccolo Napoli or Restaurant Bacon in Cap d'Antibes and revel in their just-caught, truly local fish.

The celebrated seafood restaurant, Le Bernardin, acclaimed widely (essentially unanimously) for the quality of its literally raw materials, began in Paris in 1972 as a specialist in obtaining and cooking Breton seafood, shipped quickly from Brittany, and gained two Michelin stars.[8] The restaurant opened in New York in 1986 and closed in Paris. In New York, the founders, siblings Maguy and Gilbert Le Coze, became experts in local sourcing again. In the ensuing years under Chef Eric Ripert (now with three Michelin stars) the restaurant still takes advantage of local opportunities but the sources are more international, with a significant amount of fish coming from the North Sea and Japan. Freshness remains unquestioned.

Time and distance may no longer be the prime determinates of freshness, at least once you are past the remarkably short supply chains of Piccolo Napoli or Restaurant Bacon. Freshness is no longer a temporal concept.

Markets are usually necessary when distributing a variety of highly variegated products that need to be closely inspected by buyers or their representatives. Market participants engage in repeat transactions and develop trust and reliance. Traditional seafood markets had sea-oriented sources of supply, with sea connections as short as possible; local buyers bought for their own families or organizations or bought as intermediaries for buyers farther from the market. Most large cities around the world developed central markets of this type.

A first stage of internationalization – on the supply side only – is exhibited by the Rialto fish market in Venice, where you can buy seafood from a wide range of mostly European sources. Internationalization in this case is a result of connoisseurship outstripping local supply. For example, Venetians are connoisseurs of scampi (*Nephrops norvegicus*, also known as langoustine or Dublin Bay prawn) because it is historically an important local product from the Venetian lagoon. Though the lagoon is now overfished, hurt by pollution, and the fishery has collapsed, preferences and a desire for quality continue. At the Rialto market prime quality Sicilian scampi are available at a high price, lower quality langoustines from Norway at a lower price. This sort of import connoisseurship is seen in other markets, like the global distribution of (less perishable) fine and scarce wines around the world. But buyers outside the Veneto do not shop at the Rialto fish market.

The modern international market is more of a network web, with a few major fish markets functioning as central connectors, simultaneously importers, exporters and global intermediaries. These markets may sometimes be bypassed in favour of direct purchases from fishermen or, increasingly, aquaculture producers, who are experts in producing a uniform product and in the peculiarities of air freight.

As with the Venetian lagoon and many other small-boat fisheries worldwide, the fishing industry around Tokyo Bay almost completely disappeared in the 1950s and 1960s, beset by industrial development and pollution. The Rialto and Tokyo markets both date back at least four centuries, but by the 1970s Tokyo's Tsukiji market had become the central node in what Theodore Bestor has called a 'reconfiguration of the global fishing industry'.[9] Although the Venice market brought in supplies to satisfy existing connoisseurship, the wider world market encourages connoisseurship to develop in new places and may allow appreciation, rather than locale, to determine

The Contemporary International Market for Hyperfresh Seafood

where the highest quality products go.

Quality: the reasons for decay and putrefaction

With very few exceptions, great freshness is always a key goal.[10] Seafood is highly perishable. Fish protein and lipids degrade rapidly from the time of catch, and collagen deteriorates. Spoilage begins immediately with autolysis, a deterioration of tissue caused by the fish's own internal chemicals and enzymes, followed quickly by putrefaction, caused by a bacterial and enzymatic invasion of the previously sterile flesh of the fish after skin and membrane barriers lose their impermeability. Histamine levels rise and pH drops.[11] Microbial activity and fermentation increase on an exponential time scale that varies with temperature.[12] Unlike animals used for meat, fish have evolved while living in cold water (even the warmest spots where fish swim are usually well below animal body temperatures, with most fish used for food living in temperatures considerably below this level) with enzymes and bacteria that thrive at low temperatures, too. Highly unsaturated fatty acids in fish that remain fluid at low temperatures break down or become oxidized quickly.[13] All relevant microorganisms grow to some degree even at zero degrees C. It will be of little comfort to those obsessed with freshness to know that food scientists have ascertained that after the 'limited shelf-life with good quality' a later 'period with regular or even poor quality may follow, without [yet] introducing safety hazards to the consumer'.[14] (A fish in *rigor mortis* is extremely fresh; what seafood professionals simply call 'rigor' is a temporary condition lasting hours or a few days in which muscles stiffen until other deterioration processes cause them to relax and become more tender.)

In short, time has very significant effects on quality, but so do differences in methods of catch, processing and handling during transport and marketing (particularly temperature control).

That freshness is not a simple function of time after catch (or 'harvest,' the term used in aquaculture) comes as a surprise to most consumers. Survey data shows that in Germany, most consumers believe that a fish could be considered an acceptable, fresh purchase only if purchased less than forty-eight hours after catch. As a result, most retailers meet customer requirements by telling them that it is, but the retailers are lying, because most retail store's supply chains require longer periods for transport and handling.[15] I once visited a seafood shop where I heard customers keep asking, 'What came in fresh today?' The incessant answer was, 'Everything.' After a visit later in the week revealed to me what was left over and how quality had changed I decided not to return.

What, then, is freshness? It is essentially the absence of spoilage. This in one sense begs the question, and in countries, such as the United States, where most fresh seafood is sold as fillets rather than as whole fish, it can be difficult for retail customers to identify freshness without asking leading questions unlikely to lead to honest answers. (One good consumer strategy is to ask to buy fish bones for stock. It may be telling if there are none around or their quality is poor.)

There are many indices of quality in fresh seafood, both objective and subjective, varying by culture and geography. Although models of decay and scientific measurements are constantly being developed and tested, efforts to quantify freshness by measuring microbiological flora, pH or other specific attributes are still typically less successful than sensory inspection by a trained person. Large bacterial colonies may not have led to significant decay at the time of measurement but may set the stage for significant problems after all shipping and delivery stages are complete.[16] As a result, quality is evaluated mainly by the experience of the market through repeat transactions and reputation of sellers, whether at centralized markets like Tsukiji, Rungis in Paris, Santa Caterina in Barcelona or in direct sales. There is a hierarchy for most fish among the fifty or so central fish markets that serve as distribution nodes. For example, for tuna, Tsukiji is dominant, but it is one of thirty or more markets that compete for high-quality imported tuna. Mediterranean fishers often send their best tuna to Tsukiji, next best to Rungis, and so forth.[17]

In any case, freshness should not be assumed to be a straightforward function of elapsed time. As the expert and intellectual chef, Erling Wu-Bower, who has specialized in hyperfresh seafood, notes:

> One of the more revolutionary things that I realized […] is that time has nothing to do with freshness. It has something to do with it, but very little. So I can get identical species from California and Japan, and the Japanese product could be literally two days older, and it could be still in rigor mortis and perfect, and the stuff from California could be … not good.[18]

Technology: preserving and extending freshness

In much of the world it has been traditional for fishers and sellers of fish to judge their success based on quantity, not quality. Rules of the International Organization for Standardization (ISO) and preventative procedures prescribed by the International HACCP Alliance (Hazard Analysis and Critical Control Points), help develop safety and quality systems focused on preventing food poisoning in humans, which is a far less rigorous standard than those seeking hyperfresh seafood insist on.[19]

Practices aimed at hyperfreshness used in France and, especially, Japan, show how market internationalization affects the very idea of freshness. For example, when Le Bernardin moved to New York it brought ideas of freshness that required changes in fishing methods and distribution. It began to work with Rod Mitchell, a marine biologist who started Browne Trading Company in Portland, Maine, with sophisticated advice from Jean-Louis Palladin, another rising two-Michelin-star chef who had moved from France to the United States. Influenced by the standards of Palladin and Gilbert Le Coze, Mitchell, in turn, helped train his fishers, divers and transporters. Blue Ribbon Fish Company, a long-time vendor at New York's Fulton Street fish market (now at Hunts Point), had its business model transformed under the tutelage of Gilbert Le Coze, who insisted on extreme care being lavished on his fish, including special handling and packaging to assure the quality of each fish.[20] Le Coze even cooked dishes for the fishmongers to illustrate the results he wanted. 'When Gilbert first came down here we thought he was a joke,' the supplier noted. 'Nothing was good enough for him. He thought everything had to be fresher, better. But he knew more than we did.'[21] Practices that were new to Fulton Street may be normal other places, such as the extraordinary recently renovated Santa Caterina market in Barcelona.

I remember being surprised thirty-five years ago by the high price of a fish caught by hook and line at a Japanese fish market in Honolulu, compared to a fish that looked the same that was caught in a net. The difference was that the flesh of unbruised fish, handled individually and with reverence, would taste better and last longer than fish jostled and crushed by a thousand pounds of other fish writhing in the net. Bruising breaks down flesh, encouraging bacterial growth and hastening spoilage just as in ripe fruit. Not letting fish simply gasp, struggle and expire from exhaustion and asphyxiation when brought out of the water is also important. Careful Japanese techniques for killing, bleeding and storing fish at the time of catch, known as *ikijime*, are said to be humane and to diminish stress, reducing chemical changes that diminish eating quality and prolonging freshness.[22] *Ikijime* involves spiking the fish's ganglial mass, opening a hole to the spinal cord and passing a stiff nylon fibre down the cord. The fish is then bled and placed in an ice slurry for rapid chilling. This process, said to be hundreds of years old, delays the onset of and prolongs the period of *rigor mortis*, and is also said to increase the 'umami' quality of the fish, especially when served raw or lightly cooked.[23] *Ikijime* has spread to fishers across the world, partly because it is essential in order to receive the highest prices for fish exported to Japan. Once a subject for experts, the practice has spread to sport fishers and there are now do-it-yourself web sites, such as the Australian site ikijime.com promising 'Humane Killing of Fish: Maximum quality, minimum fuss' and including a search tool to 'Search for your fish and identify the spike point'.

Application of these techniques takes time and skill, and can result in substantially higher prices in a quest for quality, which Palladin, Le Coze and now Eric Ripert, like top Japanese restaurants (and their customers), are willing to pay. Practices spread. Regional seafood marketing organizations and local universities see prices rising elsewhere because of improved quality and train and teach fishers to improve 'attitudes and handling practices' that might otherwise 'hold back the market'.[24] Where traditionally most Alaskan salmon were left to die of asphyxiation on deck, merely kept more or less cool and then shipped after being processed on land, the Alaska Seafood Marketing Institute found in 2006 that 'a majority of fishermen (59%) now report they chill all their fish, up from 34% in 1991,' and 'the number of fishermen who now bleed their fish (49%) is up substantially from 27% in 2001'.[25]

Precise and constant temperature control facilitated by improved technology is vital to the international market, in which a fish may pass through multiple markets and customs inspections. Fresh fish requires a 'reserve of quality' to carry it to the consumer successfully. Perils abound, but can be controlled. A perfect temperature-controlled aeroplane ride will not yield a fresh fish if what the industry refers to as the 'cold chain' is broken; care must be taken to avoid contaminating packaging and equipment with the bacteria most detrimental to shelf-life. Once improper storage has occurred and the population of microorganisms has increased even the slower enzyme and bacterial activity at proper storage conditions may be devastating. The difference between the ideal storage temperature around zero degrees (fish freeze at a lower temperature than pure water, particularly fatty fish) and the four to five degrees C at which most refrigerators operate may not be particularly significant for meat but will be for fish. Advances in cold-chain technology that reduce the holding temperature from two degrees to zero have been shown to extend shelf-life by several days.[26]

The best shippers wrap or package each fish individually in special paper, with great care and concern for keeping it moist and unbruised, then wrap it again in strong polyethylene bags and surround it with specialized cooling gel packs. Insulation generally consists of expanded polystyrene inside corrugated cardboard. New insulating materials are constantly being developed.[27]

The massive air freight trade in fresh tuna, fish that can weigh 80 to even 560 kilos, began in the early 1970s.[28] Coolers for smaller fish had already been developed, but specialized equipment that could maintain a cool temperature for such a large fish – 'tuna coffins' – were developed by Japan Airlines and fishing intermediaries from Eastern Canada and New England eager to ship fresh tuna for sale at the Tsukiji market.[29] Japan Airlines cargo facilities now have a number of cargo holding rooms, set at different temperatures for different products.[30] Shipment of biotech and medical products also drive temperature control that can be useful in the seafood market. (In the Newark, New Jersey, airport in April 2014, I was surprised to see a number of insulated boxes marked, 'Live Human Organs, Handle with Care,' on the carousel with my suitcases.) In 2013, FedEx announced a new temperature controlled facility at its Memphis world hub, principally to move perishable biotech products that require temperature control.[31]

Without developments in communications technology, overseas customers would not be able to make purchases from Tsukiji brokers. Fax machines and, later, cell phones and the Internet sped communications but also reduced monopolies on information and made it possible for participants to have multiple, far-flung trading partners if they have the right expertise.[32] As chef Wu-Bower notes:

> You have to be educated about when it's going to come in, how it's going to arrive, and mastering all those channels that make sourcing what it is. I'm a FedEx expert. I'm an airline-schedule expert […] people don't realize that's an important part of being a chef, that you have to understand how shipping works

[…] especially with something as perishable as fish.[33]

One way to observe how the market has affected the concept of freshness through cooling technology, increased understanding of microbiology, improvement of fishing and general hygiene, is to smell fish markets. California seafood expert, Paul Johnson, reports a stink not so long ago around the San Francisco market, although he could buy fish that seemed fresh tasting and sweet-smelling, a paradox I have also experienced in the fish markets of Palermo.[34] In contrast, the culinary technology expert Dave Arnold exclaimed after a recent visit to Tsukiji:

> This place is extraordinarily clean. No part of it has any sort of off-smell. The only detectable aroma in the fish section was that of the ocean. Not the slightly rotting aroma of the beach, just the dead clean smell of floating at sea. … How could the whole market be that well ventilated? This lack of smell was just one indication that the folks at Tsukiji were playing the market game on a completely different level than I'd seen before.[35]

As with fine wines and other luxury products, there may sometimes be a fine line between improvement of quality and marketing. Saba, a Japanese mackerel sufficiently high in oil that it was rarely used in sushi, had a reputation for spoiling so rapidly that 'it starts stinking while it's still swimming'. It began to be marketed in the last decade by a Japanese cooperative as a luxury product reflecting ultra-careful handling: line caught, processed with *ikijime* and, 'to prevent excessive handling', never weighed or measured, simply observed by the buyer. The improvement in quality, together with a careful marketing campaign, was sufficient to generate prices more than six times the price of ordinary mackerel – and landing the brand Seki Saba a place in a leading textbook on marketing and consumer psychology.[36]

Aquaculture's tremendous advantage

The challenges and controversies surrounding worldwide aquaculture, like the debates over overfishing, make headlines, and are worth thinking about seriously. The gastronomic quality of wild fish and farmed fish cannot easily be compared, because both vary so widely.[37] In terms of freshness, however, there is no doubt that aquaculture is able to set new and exacting standards.[38] To begin with, raising a fish 'allows the producer unequalled control over the condition of the fish and the circumstances of the harvest'.[39] Aquaculture provides the vital opportunity to harvest the fish when its digestive system is empty, vastly reducing the opportunity for spoilage by digestive acids, bacteria and enzymes and eliminating a common spoilage pattern known as 'belly bursting'.[40] At the moment it is wrapped and boxed, even the most cared-for wild fish will have been deteriorating for considerable time, and it will likely continue to deteriorate at a more rapid rate than the best farmed fish.

The French government has established the Label Rouge as a sign of quality assurance for farmed salmon, turbot and other products produced in and outside of France. The fish is handled according to high standards: killed, bled, chilled and packaged within four hours from when it is selected. A tag is attached to the whole fish guaranteeing high freshness ('*Une fraîcheur suivie de très près*') for nine days from harvest for turbot and ten days for salmon.[41] Although, again, comparisons are difficult with such individualized products, wild turbot appears to cease seeming 'absolutely fresh' within forty-eight hours after catch.[42]

Aquaculture also can provide the international market with something consumers both fear and demand: a uniformity, standardization and constant supply that already bypasses traditional fish markets. Both the Label Rouge Atlantic salmon (*Salmo salar*) produced in Scotland by Loch Duart and the Ora King brand King salmon (*Oncorhynchus tshawytscha*) from New Zealand are known for arriving in hyperfresh condition after very long air journeys and are appreciated for their flavour in many countries by restaurants and fish stores with extremely high standards.[43] The New Zealand King Salmon Company, producer of Ora King, selects handling and distribution intermediaries after extensive shipping of test products, and finds it can deliver fresh fish to the United States with temperatures varying no more than two degrees Celsius from the time of packing, using specially designed foil-lined multi-layered recyclable corrugated cardboard boxes.[44]

Towards the future

Many of the developments in the international market related to handling and storing fresh fish can be applied locally as well, so it is possible that internationalization might actually improve local supplies in some places in the future. High-quality fish cannot be commoditized: the catch is too uncertain, and the individual characteristics of each fish can be attractive. Ranched and farmed fish, already more of a commodity, are far more likely to be sold in ways that bypass large fish markets. Farmed Mediterranean sea bass (*Dicentrarchus labrax*), under various names, can be obtained in precise sizes and quality levels, and are exhibited by sales representatives at the giant trade fair, Seafood Expo, held annually in Brussels, Barcelona, Boston and Hong Kong.[45] Other things being equal, no matter how restaurants and individuals buying seafood feel about farmed versus wild fish, comparisons of freshness that favour farmed fish will either lead to wild fish marketers catching up under competitive pressure with further improved technology and practices, or to consumers selecting the farmed fish. However, further developments in the market may well be shaped by entirely different factors, such as reduction in the availability of scarce wild fish and changes in aquaculture to deal with issues of disease or pollution.

The Contemporary International Market for Hyperfresh Seafood

Notes

1. Although some in the seafood industry emphasize the 'fresh' qualities of frozen and, especially, the often excellent 'super-frozen' (frozen at -60 degrees C) tuna, this paper follows the approach of the U.S. Food and Drug Administration by using the term 'fresh' to mean a product is 'in its raw state and has not been frozen or subjected to any form of thermal processing or any other form of preservation' (Code of Federal Regulations Title 21 Part 101.95(a)). The FDA, however, views freshness as a binary concept, not one of degree.
2. This paper focuses on transport, markets and fish quality. Tricky scientific and ethical questions about sustainability, travel distance, and fishing and aquaculture practices are written about in other places. The paper also does not address the market for live fish, which is important for many Asian cultures.
3. See, e.g., Harold Innis, *The Cod Fisheries: The History of an International Economy* (New Haven: Yale UP, 1940).
4. *Osterie d'Italia* (Br'a, Italy: Slow Food Editore, 2011), p. 780.
5. Inquiries and discussions with marine biologists and market experts have led to theories but no answers as to why these raw fish curl. One Sicilian simply said, 'that's how those fish are when really fresh.'
6. See the descriptions of old and new seafood markets in Giorgio Locatelli, *Made in Sicily* (London: HarperCollins, 2011), pp. 249–63.
7. Menu, Verandah restaurant, May 2014. Meanwhile, truly local wild caught seafood is served simply and rather elegantly at Timoti's Fry Shak, on the same island.
8. This Brittany-Paris supply chain remains the focus at the small La Cagouille, in the 14th arrondisement of Paris, where, because of the limited catch, as the evening progresses the names of most every fish are eventually wiped off the whiteboard menu. The chef-owner tells fascinating stories of the fishing that produced the restaurant's treasures (Gérard Allemandou, *De la mer à l'assiette* (Paris: Les Éditions du Pacifique, 2004).
9. Theodore C. Bester, *Tsukiji: The Fish Market at the Center of the World* (Berkeley, U California P, 2004), the absolutely indispensable work on the world's largest seafood market and its transformation from a sea-based to an air- and truck-based market, pp. 35–38. Quite apart from the distribution system, 'large scale trawler-factories [...] and the development of new technologies for [...] chilling fish on board propelled the Japanese fishing industry to a position as a global fishing power, operating fleets in most major fishing regions of the world's oceans' (p. 120).
10. *Solea solea*, 'Dover' sole, for example. See Alan Davidson, *North Atlantic Seafood* (London: Penguin). p. 158. There is a debate in both scientific and gastronomic literature about whether a fish can be too fresh when cooked and whether eating quality is better 'pre-rigor' or just after rigor mortis, but almost all consumption relevant here is 'post-rigor'.
11. Robert DiGregorio, *Tuna Grading and Evaluation: The Complete Tuna Buyer's Handbook* (Tom's River, NJ: Urner Barry, 2012), p. 37; B.T. Lunestad and J.T. Rosnes, 'Microbiological Quality and Safety of Farmed Fish', *Improving Farmed Fish Quality and Safety*, ed. by Øyvind Lie (Cambridge: Woodhead Publishing, 2008), p. 400–04.
12. Sandor Ellix Katz, *The Art of Fermentation* (Vermont: Chelsea Green, 2012), pp. 337–42.
13. Harold McGee, *On Food and Cooking* (New York: Scribner, 2004), p. 189.
14. Lunestad and Rosnes, p. 423. Please don't take this quotation as cooking advice or apply it to raw fish!
15. A. Dulsrud, H.M. Norberg and T. Lenz, 'Too Much or Too Little Information? The Importance of Origin and Traceability for Consumer Trust in Seafood in Norway and Germany', *Seafood Research from Fish to Dish: Quality, Safety and Processing of Wild and Farmed Fish*, ed. by J.B. Luten et al. (Wageningen, Holland: Wageningen Academic Publishers, 2006), p. 224.
16. See, e.g., Karen Bekaert, 'Development of a Quality Index Method Scheme to Evaluate Freshness of Tub Gurnard (Chelidonichthys lucernus)', in Luten, pp. 289–96.
17. Sasha Issenberg, *The Sushi Economy: Globalization and the Making of a Modern Delicacy* (New York: Gotham Books, 2007), p. 40.

18. Michael Gebert, 'Nico Osteria's Erling Wu-Bower Talks his World of Seafood,' *Chicago Reader* 25 February 2014.
19. Technology can also create an illusion of freshness. Treating tuna with carbon monoxide will preserve an appealing red colour. This procedure is prohibited in the EU and regulated in the US. Mysteriously, a tuna market expert describes the practice and then adds, 'This is not to say that the sole objective of CO tuna … is to deceive the public and sell them vastly inferior fish 'doctored up' to masquerade as fresh tuna' (DiGregorio, p. 76).
20. Taras Grescoe, *Bottomfeeder: How to Eat Ethically in a World of Vanishing Seafood* (New York: Bloomsbury, 2008), pp. 38–40.
21. Gael Greene, 'Starting Over,' *New York Magazine* 10 October 1994, p. 25.
22. Also sometimes rendered as *iki jime*, *ike jime*, or *ikejime*.
23. See, e.g., Ole G. Mouritsen and Klavs Styrbæk, *Umami: Unlocking the Secrets of the Fifth Taste* (New York: Columbia UP, 2014), pp. 71–72.
24. See, e.g., John P. Doyle, *Care and Handling of Salmon: The Key to Quality* (Fairbanks: University of Alaska School of Fisheries and Ocean Sciences, Marine Advisory Bulletin No. 45, June 1995).
25. *Alaska salmon quality survey 2006* <http://www.alaskaseafood.org/industry/qc/documents/2006ASMI SalmonQuality-mainreport.pdf>. A 2014 report from a smaller, highly successful Alaskan fishing region reported 'substantial improvement' but that 'on average, processors estimated that only half (55 percent) of the total raw product weight reported in 2012 was considered to be properly chilled by permit holders' (2012 Survey Prepared for Copper River Prince William Sound Marketing Association, April 2013 <http://copperrivermarketing.org/projects/quality-enhancement/pws-chilling-study/2013-pws-chilling-study/at_download/file>.
26. Thomas Ripen and Denise Skonberg, 'Handling of Fresh Fish', *The Seafood Industry: Species, Products, Processing and Safety*, ed. by Linda Ankenman Grenata et al. (Oxford: Wiley, 2012), p. 249–55.
27. An additional problem for retail stores is that display conditions are not the best storage conditions. Fish sitting on ice in an atmosphere warmer than the ice creates a temperature gradient encouraging spoilage, particularly on the top. I've often found that calmly noting that I would like some of 'that' but that the pieces on display don't look exactly like what I want leads to a fresher, better stored piece, or a new whole fish, emerging from the store's more precisely temperature-controlled storage area. This risk is also why sushi chefs don't precut their fish, and only keep small pieces in their display cases at a time.
28. DiGregorio, p. 52.
29. These developments are detailed in Issenberg, pp. 1–45. Outside of tuna transport there is a general seafood container size limit of 68 kilos (DiGregorio, p. 41).
30. Issenberg, p. 32.
31. Federal Express <http://www.fedex.com>, posted Oct. 10, 2013.
32. Bestor, p. 35.
33. Gebert.
34. Paul Johnson, *Fish Forever* (New York: Wiley, 2007), pp. 10–11.
35. Dave Arnold, 'Cooking Issues Goes to Tsukiji', *Cooking Issues: The International Culinary Center's Tech'N Stuff Blog*, 15 June 2012, <http://www.cookingissues.com/index.html%3Fp=5630.html>. Note also his 'The Practical Philosophy of Fish-Killing and The Ike-Jime Man,' posted 26 June 2012.
36. Mariko Mikami, 'The Moët of Mackerel: How a Japanese Fishermen's Co-op Turned Its Catch into a Luxury Brand', *CNN Money*, 20 April 2006 <http://money.cnn.com/magazines/business2/business2_archive/2006/05/01/8375947/>; described also in Delbert Hawkins and David Mothersbaugh, *Consumer Behavior: Building Marketing Strategy* (New York: McGraw Hill, 2010), p. 317.
37. The distinction between fishing for wild fish and aquaculture can blur: salmon farming is illegal in Alaska, but Alaskan salmon rivers are artificially stocked to produce more 'wild' salmon. In the tuna industry the situation is reversed: most tuna farming is really 'tuna ranching' where schools of fish are captured, transferred to pens and fattened before entering the international fresh market (DiGregorio, p. 75).

38. Standards are not always high, but can be. The market for low-quality wild and farmed seafood may be even more internationalized than the topic addressed by this paper.
39. McGee, pp. 181–83.
40. Withholding food for two weeks is often found optimal. Gunn Berit Olsson, Bjørn Gundersen and Margrethe Esaiassen, 'Pre-Slaughter Starvation of Farmed Atlantic Cod Fed Vegetable Proteins: Effects on Quality Parameters', in Luten, pp. 139–45.
41. L'Association des Produits Aquatiques Label Rouge, Aqualabel, <http://www.aqualabel.fr/web2/p275_turbot.html>.
42. Maider Nuin, Begoña Alfaro, Ziortza Cruz and Nevea Argarate, 'Time Temperature Indicators as Quality and Shelf Life Indicators for Fresh Turbot (*Psetta maxima*)', in Luten, pp. 521–23.
43. Loch Duart is the name of a business, not a Scottish lake; Le Bernardin often serves farmed salmon to its demanding clientele at lunch and wild salmon at dinner.
44. Meeting and emails with Gary Hooper, Chief Executive of Aquaculture New Zealand, May 2014.
45. Sea bass is also known as *bar*, *loup de mer*, *branzino*, *spigola* and *lubina*, just to name a few; for more on Seafood Expo, see: <http://www.seafoodexpo.com>.

The Hollywood Farmers Market: Gorgeous Produce, Beautiful People, a Remarkable Business Plan

Dan Strehl

Early Sunday morning, a block from the famous intersection of Hollywood and Vine, a large contingent of farmers and food producers set up booths along Ivar and Selma Avenues. One street is for farmers, the other for prepared foods and crafts. There's an alley of spice merchants as well. Soon, the first ardent shoppers of what will swell to over 10,000 flood the market, looking at some of California's finest produce. The people-watching is also excellent: beautiful young Hollywood, sprinkled with celebrities if you can recognize them.

Now in its twentieth year, the Hollywood Farmers Market is operated by Sustainable Economic Enterprises of Los Angeles (SEE-LA). The oldest Certified Farmers Market (CFM) in the LA area, it is highly regulated by the California Department of Food and Agriculture and covered by the rules of the Los Angeles County Public Health Department.

Most of this is invisible to the shoppers. Why is the mushroom guy on the corner? Because one street is for those who practise the agricultural arts and the cross street is for those who don't. Some of his mushrooms are wild gathered, and as such, don't qualify as agricultural. The mussel grower from Santa Barbara does grow his crop, but the fisherman from San Pedro doesn't. Fishing is gathering, not an agricultural practice. All the produce must be sold by the farmer, his family or his direct employees, and produce from another farm cannot be sold.

What also is not apparent is SEE-LA's agenda: SEE-LA's mission is a simple yet impactful one – to build sustainable food systems and to promote improved fresh food access that will benefit low-to-moderate income residents of Los Angeles County while also supporting California's small and mid-size farms. The market was founded by then Los Angeles City Council member Michael Woo, who represented the Hollywood area, as part of an effort to revitalize Hollywood. While well known for the glamour of the entertainment industry, Hollywood is also a highly diverse community of immigrants, with over thirty-five languages spoken by students at Hollywood High School. Income from the Hollywood market now supports the Watts Healthy Farmers Market, the Crenshaw Farmers Market, the Central Avenue Farmers Market, the new Glassell Park CFM and several others in economically challenged areas of Los Angeles.

The Hollywood Farmers Market

The farmers
The market has a current roster of about 120 producers.[1] Among these are old-timers such as Harry's Berries (home of the luscious Gaviota strawberry), Flora Bella, Kenter Canyon and McGrath Family Farm, as well as newcomers. While almost all the farmers practise organic farming, many are not federally certified as the amount of paperwork seems too onerous. They usually describe themselves as 'non-spray' or 'sustainable'.

There are about seventy-five vendors of prepared food (including pet food), and about forty artisans, including a knife sharpener and a guy who make bowls from LA's fallen trees. The new Spice Alley has spice and bulk food vendors, as well as prepared food vendors with spicy food.

Governance
SEE-LA is a 501(c)(3) non-profit corporation, and is governed by a Board of Directors made up of community leaders. One owns the Original Farmers Market at Third and Fairfax (nothing like this market), and the board includes four farmers.[2]

Regulation of the farmers markets
What distinguishes farmers markets in California from those in the rest of the United States is the amount of regulation designed to make sure that the produce on offer is in fact from a small farm. The California Department of Food and Agriculture is the primary regulator of Certified Farmers Markets. There are about 700 CFMs in California, with 152 in Los Angeles County. About one-half are year-round, and the others are seasonal. There are about 2200 certified producers. To become a certified producer, the farmer must complete an application which includes stating where his produce is grown and how much of it is planted. A state inspector verifies this information before a certificate is issued, which must be on display in the farmer's booth.[3] In addition, there are regulations from County Agricultural Commissioners and County Health Departments. In some cases, there are additional regulations from local municipal governments.

The California Administrative Code contains most of the relevant rules. These include the following: the farmer must obtain a Certified Producer's Certificate, indicating that he has produced the products through the practice of the agricultural arts; only the farmer's family or direct employees may sell the produce; the Certified Producer's Certificate must be displayed at the stand; they must use a 'sealed' scale; they can only sell the produce they have raised; they cannot sell products produced by another grower; food preparation is prohibited; processed foods must be prepared in a 'legal kitchen'; smoking is not permitted.

Once produce is on sale in a farmers market, the food is also examined by inspectors from the County Agricultural Commissioner's Office to ensure that the produce is actually grown by the local farmer and not commercially purchased.

Even with all these rules, some people feel compelled to cheat, which is one of the reasons the inspectors are needed. Actually cheating is quite rare at the Hollywood Market, as stalls there are so lucrative that few would risk being banned for such a small financial gain.

Economic equality

All the farmers in the SEE-LA markets are required to accept CalFresh benefits (formerly food stamps) and WIC (Women, Infants, Children) benefits. SEE-LA originally arranged it so the then SNAP/EBT dollars (food stamps) could be spent at all the farmers markets in Los Angeles County. 'Market Match' funds, which will be $80,000 next year, give up to $10/week to CalFresh/WIC users to purchase fresh produce. This money comes from a grant from First 5 LA.[4] There's also an educational programme to teach cooking skills and to provide nutrition education to low-income adults, which has reached nearly 7000 adult students during the past two years. SEE-LA also supports a 'Bring the Farmer to School' programme, which has brought farmers with their produce to 149,000 students during the same period

A Farmers Kitchen was established to serve as a small restaurant/café and to make produce available during the week. It also serves as a site for classes, and offers a 'legal' kitchen for small food entrepreneurs to manufacture their wares. It also prepares daily a from-scratch lunch for 260 students at the Larchmont Charter School, which is affiliated with Alice Water's Chez Panisse Foundation's Edible Schoolyard programme.

Entertainment

Aside from people watching, the market also includes a number of musicians and other events to enhance the community feel. There are regular book signings – David Lebovitz recently signed his new *My Paris Kitchen* and blogged about it – and the Culinary Historians of Southern California have an annual used cookbook sale there, a truly popular event.[5]

Celebrities

Yes, celebrities shop at the market. It is in Hollywood, after all, a community rife with celebrities, from 'A' listers to the 'do you know who I am?' type. I've seen a number of them at the market, such as Forrest Whitaker, Tim Curry and Julie Delpy. The late Huell Howser, a celebrity to Californians, used to insert himself in the market's management tent to greet his fans. (He lived nearby on Rossmore, the extension of Vine Street, in the Ravenswood Hollywood apartment building where Mae West had lived.) One day I saw my friend Russ Parsons, now the food editor of *The Los Angeles Times* (he lives in Long Beach, a thirty-mile drive from Hollywood) there with Joachim Splichal, a Los Angeles celebrity chef at the helm of the Patina Group. Some celebrities are not so fond of the market. At one board meeting, one of the neighbours, a music recording studio whose property fronted on the market, complained that his clients had a hard time getting their limos into his parking lot on Sunday mornings. When I inquired why they couldn't walk (a distance of about 200 feet), his response was 'we're talking Grammy talent here'.

What may look like an ordinary farmers market is actually much more. Far beyond the individual stalls, SEE-LA's innovative mission reaches into classrooms and out to farm fields.

Notes

1. For a current list of vendors, see <http://www.seela.org/our-vendors/>.
2. The author was on the Board of Directors of SEE-LA for over eight years.
3. California Department of Food and Agriculture, California Farmers Market Program <http://www.cdfa.ca.gov/is/i_&_c/cfm.html> [accessed 1 May 2014]
4. Russ Parsons, 'New $2.5 Million Grant Will Help Poor Buy Fresh, Locally Grown Produce', *Los Angeles Times* <http://www.latimes.com/food/dailydish/la-dd-calcook-new-25-million-grant-will-help-poor-buy-fresh-local-produce-20140507-story.html> [accessed 8 May 2014].
5. David Lebovitz, *L.A.* < http://www.davidlebovitz.com/2014/04/los-angelescalifornia/> [accessed 10 May 2014].

Markets Under Attack: Rioters and Regulators in Georgian England

David C. Sutton

Introduction: market forces

In the second half of the eighteenth century the 'free market' and *laissez-faire* ideas associated with the name of Adam Smith came into the ascendant. The actions of the working people of England in the period covered by this essay (roughly 1740–1840) present a wholly different (interventionist and morally-based) view of 'the market'.

Citizens were prepared to intervene when markets failed to meet their notion of a 'moral economy', especially when prices were forced upwards by adverse weather, bad harvests or profiteering. Popular attitudes gave more respect to justice than to law, and accepted that justice might require the breaking of the law.[1]

Our first two examples are paradigmatic. In 1766, lace-workers in Honiton went to the farmers' stores and seized sacks of corn. They then took the corn to Honiton Market and sold it for the fixed price which they considered fair, before going back to the farmers, handing over the money, and returning the sacks. The fixed price, naturally, was considerably lower than the free market price. The following year 200 colliers from Stourbridge descended upon Kidderminster Market, where they forced the trading farmers to reduce their wheat prices from seven shillings a bushel to five shillings a bushel and their butter from eight pence to six pence a pound.[2]

Reports of such events in newspapers or the Home Office archives regularly use the word 'mob' and phrases such as 'idle and disorderly persons'. Such insults are misplaced. Whilst actions such as those in Honiton and Kidderminster were illegal, they were clearly conducted with a strong sense of morality and justice. The return of the corn-sacks to the Honiton farmers is a compelling instance, which we find replicated in incidents elsewhere.

Other examples of goods being seized and sold at market at a lower price, and the money returned to the farmers, or of farmers being forced to go to market and accept reduced prices, can be found, in those years of 1766 and 1767 alone, in the market-towns of Abingdon, Beccles, Bewdley, Bromsgrove, Bungay, Cullompton, Ely, Evesham, Exeter, Gloucester, Halesowen, Leicester, Malmesbury, Redruth, St Austell, Salisbury, Silverton, Stourbridge itself, Stratford-upon-Avon, Stroud, Tetbury, Thame, Tiverton, Wallingford, Wincanton, Wolverhampton and Worcester.[3] Also in 1766 Berkshire witnessed actions by a group of price-arbiters who emphasized their moral rectitude by calling themselves The Regulators.

There were other examples of attacks on markets where the moral and regulating component disappeared and riotous behaviour, theft and violence took over. Examples include the Great Nottingham Cheese Riot and the Norwich 'insurrection', both in 1766.

Where the rioters retained their moral compass, however, they were likely to find support from some local corporations (such as those in Reading and Exeter) and magistrates. Progressive corporations and paternalist magistrates scandalized the national government by regarding arbiters such as The Regulators as less of a social problem than the hoarders and extortionists who sought to drive up prices in times of dearth. Reading Corporation several times intervened in the market to hold down the price of bread – voting the significant sums of £21 in 1757 and £30 in 1795. Similarly, some magistrates were accused by dealers of being sympathetic to rioters. A Bristol corn-factor in 1758 wrote bitterly of the JPs and 'your law-giving mob' preventing the export of corn from the Severn and Wye valley areas during the dearth years of 1756 and 1757 – despite repeated complaints to JPs.[4]

Daily bread

The importance of bread in the popular diet was paramount, with staple meals based on soup and cheese requiring very large quantities (typically over a kilogram) of bread per worker per day. The people's expectations, however, related not only to quantity of bread but also to its quality.

William Rubel has authoritatively described the hierarchy of breads during this period.[5] At the bottom was horse-bread, a coarse loaf full of bran, sometimes with straw and sweepings added, intended for horses but eaten in bad times by the poorest people. Boiled grains in various forms of porridge, not baked, then comprised the lowest form of food for humans. Next in the hierarchy came baked 'subsistence flatbreads', varying from region to region and ranging from pancakes and oat-cakes to rye-breads. At the top of the hierarchy were fully baked loaf-breads, but these also varied considerably – from mongrelized loaves, which might be made with branny flour and peas, through barley loaves and various categories of brown bread to the white loaf, reigning supreme.

In eighteenth- and nineteenth-century England, rich and poor alike sought access to the lightest and whitest bread. Poor people clearly believed that it was their right, their English entitlement, to have daily access not only to bread, but to white bread. Arthur Young was one of a number of contemporary observers to express dismay that 'even poor cottagers' expected to eat wheat bread and disdained rye and barley loaves.

The Assize of Bread

The price per weight of bread had been regulated for many centuries, notably by the Frankfurt Capitulare of 794. The Norman rulers of England resumed this practice under King Henry II, and consolidated the regulation under the first Assize of Bread in 1266. This continued in force, in various forms, until 1836.[6] For most of this time, the assumption in the legislation was that each batch of flour could be made into three categories of bread (known at first as wastell bread, bread of the whole wheat and bread treet, and later as white, wheaten and household), and that all aspects of bread-production needed to be overseen and regulated.

The purpose of the Assize of Bread was not to fix a maximum price for a loaf, but rather to establish a price and weight for loaves which would fairly reflect the price of wheat in any year. It aimed to prevent shortages and bad harvests from being used as a pretext for excessive price-rises or for providing loaves which were unacceptably small. The Assize created a unique relationship between bakers and the market, in that it did not allow them to set prices freely and thus make their livelihoods more profitable.

The legislation was consistently opposed, through century after century, by bakers and corn-factors, but it was renewed, and nominally strengthened, by a statute of 1710 which was designed to protect the poor from profiteers and to ensure a 'reasonable price of bread, and to prevent covetous and evil-disposed persons, for their own gain and lucre, from deceiving and oppressing Her Majesty's subjects, especially the poorer sort'.

The paternalist and anti-capitalist tone of the statute clearly ran counter to the free-market thinking which would soon become the new orthodoxy, and in many parts of England the Assize ceased to function. Sidney and Beatrice Webb suggest that the corporations of larger towns continued to set the Assize through the century, but 'it was evidently less and less observed'. The 1710 statute, however, provided a point of reference and legitimacy for the rioters and regulators in later decades – whether or not they knew what it said.[7]

Contemporary newspaper accounts indicate that the Webbs may have under-estimated the durability of the Assize. Here is one powerful example, from the *Oxford Gazette and Reading Mercury* (20 April 1767), concerning the City of London:

> Yesterday, a Baker was convicted before [...] the Lord Mayor in the sum of forty-five shillings, for selling a poor labouring man two quartern loaves nine ounces short of weight; half of which penalty is by law the property of the poor man; but his Lordship understanding that he had a wife and six small children [...] not only gave him the whole forty-five shillings, but as he was then out of employ, ordered him to be set to work immediately at the Mansion-house; and at the same time his Lordship was pleased to signify, that he was determined to do all in his power to lessen the price of bread; and that he would for the future publish in the daily papers the name and place of abode of all such Bakers as shall be convicted before him for short weight, in order effectually to deter them from defrauding the poor in these hard times.

The rioters knew that the profiteers were as likely to be farmers and millers as bakers. The bakers were squeezed between the millers, the Assize and the people, whereas farmers and millers were less regulated, and used their freedom to set higher prices and to mill flour in such a way as to subvert the expectations for the three grades of bread. Through the eighteenth century, the effect of this profit-driven milling was to make the bread of the rich finer and with a higher wheat content while the bread of the poor became coarser.

Writing in the *Annals of Agriculture* of 1788, Thomas Pownall, the former Governor of Massachusetts, described these changes: 'while the rich were pampered, the poor man's bread, made of stuff from which too great a proportion of the flour had been taken, and which had not the heart of wheat in it, had not the nourishment which it ought to have'. The situation was worsened by widespread adulteration. The use of alum to make bread appear whiter is often mentioned, but for most people a greater problem was the use of wheat which was diseased or rotten, or mixed with other grains, peas or potatoes. We find references where the rioters refer to 'stinking bread'.

Militant miners and the tinners' Law of the Maximum

The role of colliers and tinners in these market riots is distinctive. Like the men of Stourbridge who marched on Kidderminster Market in 1767, miners are often recorded as travelling to market towns in order to impose their sense of justice. Contemporary accounts convey a sense of awe and fear when the colliers or tinners come angrily to market. The traders knew that they would have either to hide or to reduce their prices.

During the Bristol food riots of 1740, there was a quasi-military stand-off, with the soldiers inside the city on full alert, while the colliers assembled outside the city and sent in unarmed delegates to discuss the price of bread and wheat with the Mayor. The colliers' riot at Shepton Mallet in 1753, involving some 700 miners, was an early example of corn being seized from warehouses, taken to the market and sold at 'fair' prices.

In 1756 the colliers of Shropshire marched from market to market, enforcing lower prices. At Bridgnorth the local landowners Sir Thomas Whitmore and Sir Richard Aston were so alarmed that they ordered their tenant-farmers to bring their wheat to market and sell it at the colliers' price – promising to reduce rents in compensation.[8]

In December 1756 the tinners of St Agnes marched to Padstow, where they believed that corn was being stored for export. They ransacked warehouses and attempted to board ships, and carried a significant amount of corn away with them. (Riots at ports and attempts to blockade corn-ships provide us with a closely related story. There were two such attacks on the port of Lyme Regis in 1766, and another in September 1767.)

In May 1757, a 'great number' of Welsh colliers attacked granaries at Kidwelly and seized oats, barley and oatmeal before marching on to Carmarthen. Five colliers were shot dead in these attacks, for which the Mayor of Carmarthen was tried and acquitted.

In the Wincanton market-riots of 1766, it is noteworthy that the authorities, fairly calm at first, became alarmed when the miners from the Somerset coalfield came to town and joined in.

On 27 September 1766, 200 colliers marched south to Coventry and forcibly opened a number of cheese warehouses. They then took the cheese to Coventry Market where they sold broken cheese 'by the lump' at either twopence or twopence-halfpenny per pound.

Certain towns had a reputation for frequent rioting. Truro was one of these. From the 1740s to the 1840s the tinners repeatedly attacked Truro Market and often had to be confronted by soldiers. On at least one occasion the soldiers refused to fire. There was serious rioting in Truro in 1789, 1791, 1793 and 1795. In 1789 John Wesley praised God that the tinners' riot had prevented his preaching at the Truro chapel, forcing him to move to outside the coinage hall, where he drew a bigger crowd.

The *Loi du maximum* is a celebrated feature of the most radical period of the French Revolution, being adopted in September 1793 and setting a price-ceiling for goods including flour, wheat, meat, onions and soap. This notion of a legitimate price-ceiling permeates many of the European food riots of the eighteenth century. The idea seems to have been especially strong in Cornwall, where it was enforced again and again by the tinners' arrival at market and where it continued longer than in other parts of the country, as Philip Payton indicates:

> Likewise, 'food riots' were an almost commonplace part of life in eighteenth century Cornwall, seen by both contemporary observers and modern scholars in the same light as smuggling and 'wrecking', and indeed remained a significant feature until at least May 1847 when hungry and angry miners forced 'fair prices' for corn at Callington market and miners and clayworkers looted shops in St Austell.[9]

In the riots which spread throughout the mining areas of Cornwall in 1796, Sir Francis Basset, MP for Penryn, suggested that the tinners were under the influence of the French Revolution and had terrorized the local corn-dealers into accepting their own Law of the Maximum.[10]

The Regulators

Between August and October 1766, a wave of riots swept through Berkshire, with attacks on grocers, mills and markets in Abingdon, Steventon, Drayton, Newbury, Shaw, Wallingford and Maidenhead. With extensive involvement (and leadership) by women, the Berkshire rioters seized flour, bread, cheese and bacon and resold it at their own fair price. They gave themselves the name of The Regulators.[11] The Regulators took wheat from Drayton to Abingdon, where they kept it in store before selling it at market the following Monday. The action may have begun when a group of road-builders responded to a call 'with one voice, come one & all to Newbury in a body to make the bread cheaper'. By the end of 1766 a large number of these regulators were confined in Reading Gaol, and many of them later suffered brutal punishments, notably 'burning in the hand'.

The Berkshire Regulators had a clear idea of prices and values. They 'would not suffer wheat to be sold for more than 10£ a load'. They confiscated overpriced goods, and resold them at market 'at a rate below their value'. There is something close to a Robin Hood bandit-hero morality here, which we find also in the plundering of Sudbury veal in 1767: 'As a waggon load of veal was coming to town from Sudbury in Suffolk, destined for the London markets, the mob seized and sold it for two pence per pound to the poor people, when they paid the owners the money received, returned them the cloths the veal was wrapped up in, and went quietly home to their habitations.'[12]

The Great Cheese Riot, Nottingham, 1766

The Great Nottingham Cheese Riot may have originated with ideas of moral economy, but it ended as a chaotic battle: a combination of overflowing violence and tragi-comic incident.[13] The abiding image is of the Mayor of Nottingham being knocked off his feet by a large cheese, as he sought in vain to restore order.

The annual Goose Fair opened in Nottingham on 2 October 1766, and it was noticed that there were more cheeses on sale than in previous years, although the prices were extremely high (up to 36 shillings a hundredweight, equating to almost fourpence a pound – double the price fixed by the colliers at Coventry Market only the previous week). Trouble began when traders from Lincolnshire bought large quantities of the cheese. It appears that the crowd became incensed both because the dealers could afford the extortionate price and because the Nottinghamshire cheese was to be taken away to Lincolnshire. In the violence which followed, full advantage was taken of the wheel-shape of the cheeses, which 'were rolled down Wheeler-gate and Peck-lane in abundance'. The Mayor sought to intervene in person to stop the violence, but was knocked to the ground by a fast-rolling cheese. Some rioters were arrested and brought before the justices, but this happened in a private house, not a secure building, and the crowd soon identified the place, smashed all the windows and liberated the prisoners. They then continued their march through the streets, and succeeded in seizing a boat laden with cheeses near Trent Bridge. The riot faded away with the arrival of a troop of soldiers. Some large quantities of cheese had changed ownership in the course of the riot, and the *Leicester and Nottingham Journal* felt able to accuse the rioters of causing the very scarcity against which they claimed to be protesting.

It is important to be clear that food riots were not always organized or regulated. Riots could dissolve into chaos and plundering, and people were often killed. Anger and hunger could lead to extremes of violence, and a simple pleasure in rioting can also be identified on occasion. This is a dramatic account of the riots in Norwich in 1766:

> At Norwich a general insurrection began, when the proclamation was read in the market-place, where provisions of all sorts were scattered about by the rioters in heaps; the new mill, a spacious building, which supplies the city with water, was attacked and pulled down; the flour, to the number of 150 sacks, thrown, sack

after sack, into the river; and the proprietor's book of account, furniture, plate, and money, carried off or destroyed; the bakers shops plundered and shattered; a large malt-house set fire to, and burnt; houses and warehouses pulled down; and the whole city thrown into the greatest consternation.[14]

The Norwich riots were of major significance. For many years until the early eighteenth century, Norwich had been the second-largest city in England and its strategic importance remained considerable. It also had a tradition of food riots. An unusual one had occurred in 1740, when riots about the high price of mackerel continued in the city for five days.[15]

The hanging of Thomas Spencer, Halifax, 1783

Popular support for attacks on markets, and popular contempt for the law, are illustrated in the behaviour of the crowds who attended the hanging and followed the cortege of Thomas Spencer, hanged at Beacon Hill near Halifax on 15 August 1783. Spencer had been singled out as the leader of the Halifax food riots of June 1783, and contemporary accounts leave little doubt of his leading role.[16]

The respectful observance of his execution and the accompanying of his coffin to his home village of Mytholmroyd by 'a Mass of people' constituted a characteristic form of dumb insolence and disrespect for authority.

On 7 June 1783, Spencer is said to have joined the rioters as they proceeded from Wadsworth to Halifax and to have set himself at their head. Drawing on his experience in the English army (he had been discharged, wounded, during the Seven Years War), he formed the protesters into double ranks and marched them in military order. One of his reported commands, slightly improbably, was 'Stop Mob!'; but it is said that the command was instantly obeyed. The crowd marched through the corn market to the Boar's Head Inn, where they believed that large quantities of corn were hoarded. There were numerous instances of raids on corn carts on their way to market:

> A very large quantity was sold by the Mob at Spencer's Price, and the owners suffered to receive the money where they could get it; this being done Spencer then commanded the Mob to go into the public roads leading to the town, and bring back such carriages loaded with corn as were returning home, and durst not enter the town for fear of having their grain sold at such prices as these desperadoes thought proper to fix, which they instantly obeyed and effected.

The military efficiency of the operation was probably one factor which led to a punishment as harsh as hanging. It was also unusual for a riot to have such a clearly identified leader, who appeared to be both popular and effective. In addition, Spencer was suspected of involvement in an earlier murder of a supervisor in Halifax, for which two of his friends had been hanged in 1769. This was a man whom the authorities saw as too dangerous to be allowed to live.

The East Anglian bankers and other regulators

In 1795 another wave of food riots spread across England. East Anglia was especially affected, and commentators noted the frequent involvement of itinerant workers who had come to the area to work on strengthening the banks of local canals and dykes. The bankers were especially blamed for the riots which in that year created havoc in the markets of Wisbech, Ely and Boston. As with the colliers and tinners, this was seen by the authorities as a dangerous action by an outside group marching to market. Other groups which were often associated with attacks on markets were clothworkers, road-builders, canal boatmen and weavers. The town of Frome in Somerset, home to communities of both coalminers and weavers, was noticed as especially riot-prone, and its market was attacked in 1757, 1766, 1795, 1810 and 1816.[17]

Another characteristic example of 'regulation' from this period was the riot of the Oldham weavers in 1800. The rioters had given the market traders notice that the price of corn-meal had to be reduced, otherwise action would be taken. The traders boldly ignored the warning, and so, on the appointed day, the crowd came to the market, seized all the meal, sold it at two-thirds of the asking price, gave the cash to the market-traders and returned the sacks.[18]

This returning of the sacks (Honiton in 1766, Oldham in 1800) or the Sudbury veal-cloths in 1767, and the similarities of approach between the Cornish tinners, the Stourbridge and Coventry colliers, the Berkshire Regulators and the Wisbech bankers raise questions about communication and shared information in an age of low literacy. It seems clear that rioters and market price-fixers in various parts of the country knew what had been happening elsewhere and were inspired to imitate. The role of travelling pedlars and chapmen in spreading news from town to town is often mentioned although difficult to quantify. The magistrates' and spies' reports in the Home Office archives are often written in a spirit of exaggeration or paranoia, but they do demonstrate how some dedicated radicals would travel the country speaking at secret meetings. Finally the wandering preachers, so characteristic of eighteenth-century England, were also a great source of news from market-town to market-town, and many of them (even some Methodists) were suspected by the authorities of a close sympathy with the ordinary people and their ideas of right and wrong.

Conclusions

Each side of a deep social divide had its own terminology. On the one side stand the self-styled Regulators, or the tinners enforcing their 'Laws of the Maximum'. On the other side, we have the dealers in food, widely suspected of adulteration, short measuring and profiteering. The names given to them in our original sources include hucksters, higsters, higglers, retailers, kidders, badgers, forestallers, stockjobbers of bread, laders, profiteers, broggers, regrators, engrossers, jobbers and hawkers. This can be contrasted with the official terminology which sets 'the mob' against 'honest tradesmen'.

Food and Markets

The terminology represents a widening social divide, which became a class divide with the emergence of the Industrial Revolution. Adam Smith's devotion to 'free market' thinking is often overstated, but his name became a symbol for a new market logic which overrode old expectations, rights and traditions.

The tipping-points for rioting in this period were easily reached. Hunger and under-nourishment were the constant burdens of poorer ranks of society. Roy Porter summarizes: 'Everyone below the income commanded by skilled craftsmen was undernourished.'[19] In such circumstances, one bad harvest or one report of profiteering could lead to revolt, in a society where public violence was commonplace. Benjamin Franklin wrote in 1769:

> I have seen, within a year, riots in the country, about corn; riots about elections; riots about workhouses; riots of colliers, riots of weavers, riots of coal-heavers, riots of sawyers; riots of Wilkesites; riots of government chairmen; riots of smugglers, in which custom house officers and excisemen have been murdered, the King's armed vessels and troops fired at.[20]

Public entertainments in this riotous society combined acceptable violence with an ever-present risk of escalation. Rough sports dominated at fairs and gatherings on common lands, including cock-fights, dog-fights and faction-fighting. Bear-baiting was not abolished in England until 1835.

Fairs were especially suspect to free-market thinkers, both as dangerous gathering places and as lost work-time. As a result, to take one example, Southwark Fair was reduced from a fortnight to three days in 1743, before being abolished in 1763.[21] Many other fairs suffered a similar fate in the eighteenth century (although the Nottingham Goose Fair survives to this day).

Both the conversion of popular anger into violence and the sheer pleasure of rioting have their importance in these attacks on markets. But the moral component was essential, and opposition to free-market thinking was a strong part of the moral economy.

Let us conclude with brief thoughts on four aspects of these attacks on markets: the sense of right and wrong, the role of women, the opposition to exporting local produce and the traditional market community.

The sense of right and wrong is a pervasive strand in these attacks on markets. Even publications such as the *Gentleman's Magazine* recognized this: 'The price was raised so high in the market at Barnstaple in Devonshire, that the poor joined in a body and compelled the farmers to sell it at 5s per bushel. Some of the farmers refusing to take the money, the poor were honest enough to tie it up for them in their sacks' (8 August 1766).

The rioters at Stroud the following month had the clearest possible sense of fair value. In reselling at a fairer price the cheese which they had confiscated, they set a rate of '3d a pound for old cheese, 2½ for other and 2d for new'.[22]

The role of women in the riots was widely noticed. On numerous occasions women are described as the leaders in the rioting. On other occasions (which are open to several interpretations) the leading role in a market attack would be taken by men wearing women's clothes.

In another Gloucestershire example from September 1766, an attack on the cheese-loft of one John Collett where the prodigious quantity of 'about 6 Ton weight of Cheese' (valued at £200) was carried away, the eight persons eventually identified and brought to trial for the seizure comprised six women and two men.[23]

The prevention of export (as in the riots at Bristol, Padstow and Lyme Regis) is a classic expression of loyalty to a sense of local economy against free-market trading. The popular view was that local corn should go to local markets.

The locations of the riots are telling. They are much more likely to occur in long-established market-towns with historic market traditions than in the recently expanding manufacturing towns. Manchester and Birmingham, for example, were much less affected than Oldham or Nuneaton. The attacks on markets show English women and men rejecting the harsh new free-market economic ideology (the forerunner of twentieth-century Reaganomics) and affirming a profound loyalty to an older and fairer version of 'the market'.

Notes

1. Among the secondary sources are Robert F. Wearmouth, *Methodism and the Common People of the Eighteenth Century* (London: Epworth Press, 1945); E. P. Thompson, *The Making of the English Working Class*, rev ed. (Harmondsworth: Penguin, 1968); Roger Wells, *Wretched Faces: Famine in Wartime England, 1793–1801* (Gloucester: Sutton, 1988) and E. P. Thompson, *Customs in Common* (London: Merlin Press, 1991). The principal primary sources are the *Annual Register* and *Gentleman's Magazine*, and the Home Office and Treasury Solicitor's papers in the National Archives.
2. R. B. Rose, '18th-Century Price-Riots, the French Revolution and the Jacobin Maximum', *International Review of Social History* 4 (1959), p. 435, citing *Annual Register*, 1766–1767.
3. *Annual Register*, 1766, 'Chronicle', pp. 137–40; Wearmouth, pp. 32–36.
4. Thompson, pp. 243 and 209.
5. William Rubel: *Bread: A Global History* (London: Reaktion Books, 2011), pp. 42–57.
6. Sidney and Beatrice Webb, 'The Assize of Bread', *Economic Journal* 14.54 (June 1904), pp. 196–218; Alan S. C. Ross, 'The Assize of Bread', *Economic History Review* 9.2 (1956), pp. 332–42.
7. Webb, p. 200.
8. John Bohstedt, *The Politics of Provisions: Food Riots, Moral Economy and Market Transition in England, c. 1550–1850* (Farnham: Ashgate, 2010), pp.136–38.
9. Philip Payton, *The Making of Modern Cornwall* (Redruth: Dyllansow Truran, 1992), p. 86.
10. John Rowe, *Cornwall in the Age of the Industrial Revolution* (Liverpool: Liverpool UP, 1953), pp. 104–05 for 1796; pp. 160–62 for 1847.
11. National Archives TS 11/995.
12. *Annual Register*, 1767, 'Chronicle', p. 85.
13. Valentine Yarnspinner, *Damn His Charity, We'll Have the Cheese for Nought!: Nottingham's Great Cheese Riot & Other 1766 Food Riots* (Nottingham: Loaf on a Stick Press, 2011), drawing extensively on *Leicester and Nottingham Journal*, 1766.

14. *Annual Register*, 1766, 'Chronicle', p. 139.
15. Roy Porter: *English Society in the Eighteenth Century*, rev. ed. (Harmondsworth: Penguin, 1990), p.100.
16. H. Ling Roth, *The Yorkshire Coiners* (Halifax: F. King & Son, 1906), especially pp. 107–09.
17. John Stevenson, *Popular Disturbances in England, 1700–1870* (London: Longman, 1979), p. 97.
18. Wells, p. 95.
19. Porter, p. 15.
20. Porter, p.17.
21. E. Boger: *Bygone Southwark*. London: Simpkin Marshall, 1895, p. 247.
22. National Archives TS 11/1128.
23. National Archives TS 11/1128.

Markets in Israel: Tradition and Transformations

Susan Weingarten

Looking through time at markets from ancient Palestine to modern Israel reveals both continuities and transformations that have taken place over the *longue durée*. There are both similarities and differences between old and new, and in this paper I hope to enlighten our understanding of the processes which caused them. While there is a literature on both ancient markets and modern ones, I think this is the first time they have been looked at together in this geographical and temporal context.

The Hebrew or Aramaic word for a market is *shuq* or *shuqa*. *Shuq* in the Talmudic literature also means a street, a square, a district: in some cases it is impossible to determine which of the above meanings is meant. This inherent ambiguity holds to the present day.

Early markets: organization and chaos

In the Greco-Roman world, the open space at the heart of the town, the agora or forum, was the meeting and discussion place par excellence of the local population. It was also often the place where they came to trade and barter and market produce, brought from near and far. Beginning as just an open space near road or river, the market gradually became more organized: earth gave way to paving stones to protect people from dust in the summer and mud in the winter. Usually square or rectangular, its shape became definitive of its function as the market square. Temporary stalls eventually became permanent. While most trade in Mediterranean countries took place in the open air, in many cases stoae or colonnades were built around the central space, open along one side, but roofed for protection from the elements, while some of the fora of Rome eventually boasted semi-circular purpose-built buildings. Because people congregated there, the space attracted public buildings around it: temples, assembly halls, law courts. Eventually the market itself was often re-sited some way away from the primary central forum to a secondary site, where its noise, smells and chaotic traffic were less likely to disturb the business of public life. The city of Rome, indeed, banned wagon traffic in the streets during daylight. The satirical poet Martial commends Germanus, who regulated marketing in Rome, saying that until his legislation Rome was one vast shop.[1]

Market trade came under the official control of the *agoranomos* (Greek) or *aedile* (Latin), charged with keeping the peace and inspecting weights, measures and prices. He often seems to have used violent methods to control the market, as we learn from the Talmudic literature, as well as from Apuleius, albeit satirical, who shows how buyers as well as sellers often suffered from his officiousness.[2] He appears in many papyri, and many of his official stamps have been found archaeologically.³ The fact that the town square was circumscribed made it easier to police, although trade also spread to the small streets leading off the official market.

In both parallel and contrast, highways and new settlements attracted informal trading spaces. The Romans constructed an empire-wide network of roads, with an official postal system, the *cursus publicus*, including inns and post-stations for changing horses. These way-stations needed to provide travellers with food and other necessities. Within a town, travellers could of course use the permanent market for this purpose, but outside towns we may surmise that local farmers came to these meeting points to sell their seasonal wares, just as today ad hoc market stalls appear along well-travelled routes and especially at cross-roads, selling seasonal fruit and fresh bread. Planned Roman legionary camps were set up all over the empire. Law and order appears often to have stopped at the walls of these camps, however, and *cannabae*, disorganized building of houses for local camp-followers with shops and stalls catering to army custom, grew up higgledy-piggledy around the camps, along twisted and winding streets quite unlike the neat right-angled grid inside. (A similar phenomenon can be seen today in the bazaars surrounding the American airbase at Inchirlik in southern Turkey.)

Markets in ancient Palestine

In the fourth century, a tax collector named Theophanes travelled from Egypt to Syria and back again via Palestine, using the *cursus publicus*. His daily shopping lists have been found in a stash of papyri from Hermopolis in Egypt, so we can see what food was available for the passing traveller in the smaller towns and cities of Palestine and Egypt, as opposed to the imperial centre of Antioch where Theophanes spent several months and clearly ate far better.⁴ Thus the market at Ascalon, a Hellenized city on the coastal plain, at the crossroads of the road to the sea and the highway between Egypt and Syria, provided him with a good selection of seasonal food at the end of July: fine loaves, grapes, fresh figs, peaches, apples, leeks, reduced wine, plums, ordinary wine, fish sauce, vinegar, gourds, vegetables, eggs and *exatilia* (maybe fish). In contrast, there was nothing to buy except bread and bean soup at Antipatris, a horse-changing station on the highway, so presumably there were not enough passing travellers there to warrant a varied market trade.

Apart from occasional markets, Late Roman Palestine clearly had permanent market streets in the larger settlements. Talmudic sources mention market stalls within a colonnade which could be locked up, and there was a market building with a cupola in Caesarea, the provincial capital.⁵ Stamps of *agoranomoi* have also been found in the province, so it is clear that the markets in Palestine were as organized as in other places in the Roman empire. The situation in the smaller settlements is less clear, and perhaps they were more on the level of the *cannabae*.

Following the second-century Bar Kokhba revolt, Jewish Jerusalem was re-founded as Roman Aelia Capitolina. The pattern of streets and markets established from then on into the Byzantine period has remained similar ever since, in spite of many changes of government. The sixth-century mosaic map found at Madeba across the Jordan shows a colonnaded street, the *cardo*, which is still there today, lined with shops. The Roman forum at the city centre is still the site of a market, although there have been changes to the layout, of which more presently.

In his 1985 paper, 'From Polis to Madina,' Hugh Kennedy describes the changes in structure of the cities of the Roman empire in the east after the seventh-century Moslem conquest.[6] Whereas urban life and economic activity continued, the physical forms of monumental buildings changed. Arab society had little use for many of the alien buildings of the classical city, such as pagan temples and theatres. The broad colonnaded streets, the large, paved open spaces such as hippodromes and amphitheatres, and the purpose-built market were invaded and encroached on by houses and shops. In Jerusalem three narrow *suqs* were built in parallel on the site of a single colonnaded street.

Kennedy has been criticized for stereotyping the Arabs as disorganized barbarians vis-à-vis the ordered classical world.[7] But his basic premise still holds, although it is now proposed that the encroachment on open spaces probably began in Christian Byzantine times and was often more organized than at first apparent. The process of domestication of the narrow linear markets in Jerusalem continued and they were eventually roofed by Queen Melisende in 1152 with stone vaults that survive to this day. The only large open markets were outside the city or in open spaces just inside the walls, selling livestock and produce from the city's hinterland.

A thirteenth-century description of Jerusalem, written by the conquering Crusaders, *L'estat de la citez de Hierusalem*, notes that the principal market, the Mauristan, sold cattle, cheese, chickens and other birds, as well as fish. Jerusalem is some 60 km from the sea, so these fish must have either been raised nearby in pools or salted. In the triple bazaar, one street sold vegetables and spices, and another was devoted to cloth. The middle one sold ready-cooked food to the many pilgrims to the city, and was called Malquisinat, the Street of Bad Cooking. Perhaps the Crusader rulers and foreign pilgrims did not like local food – or its smells. There is also a street in present-day Barcelona called Malcuinat, near the mediaeval port, and here the suggestion is that the 'bad' cooking was aimed at the sailors. There was also a butchers' market and a live animal market.[8]

Acre was the main port of Crusader Palestine at this time, and the various quarters of the city were built and inhabited by émigrés from different European cities: Pisa, Genoa, Venice and Marseilles.[9] These were like a collection of communes within the city. Lists of privileges demanded by the Italians always included a square, a *funda* or *fondaco*, i.e. a market-place. The *fondaco* appears to have formed the major economic centre of each quarter, like the market square of Italian towns. There was also a market on the quayside, the *catena*, called after the chain which protected the harbour at night. Each quarter had its own khan, or caravanserai, where people lodged and traded local and imported goods and produce, with a complex tax system. Unlike Jerusalem, the Crusader market spaces have not survived. Perhaps the model of several authorities each with its own market square was too alien an import into local society. The khans now extant in present-day Acre/Akko are from the Ottoman period, as is the market, which is linear in form.[10] International trade has now moved to the modern northern port of Haifa.

The market at the crossroads: *Sūq al-Khān*

With the defeat of the Crusaders, the Mamelukes and later the Ottomans took over the rule of Palestine. They too attempted to organize and control markets. Travellers between cities needed places to lodge, and Moslem charitable foundations provided khans along the major routes where travellers and their animals could rest.[11] In the case of Khan al-Tujjar, the Inn of the Merchants, in the mid-fifteenth century, the charitable founder, Shams al-Dīn b. al-Muzalliq, ensured that travellers received food for themselves and their animals.[12] Sited at the entrance to Galilee, this khan lay on the road from Gaza to Damascus at the crossroads with the Jerusalem-Damascus road. It included a well, a mosque, shops, stables and lodging for travellers. In Ottoman times, khans sometimes functioned as tax-collecting stations, with a military force stationed there for protection from marauding Bedouin. The structure of small rooms round a central courtyard would have added to the feeling of security. Khan at-Tujjar has a small fortlet built above it by the Ottoman authorities for the garrison stationed there. The combination of passing merchants and the crossroads site, together with the security provided by the permanent garrison must have been some of the factors which led to the holding of a large weekly market (*bazār*) at this khan, first recorded in 1582.[13] By the early nineteenth-century this Monday market – Sūq al-Khān – is recorded as specializing in livestock.[14] A local almanac lists all the major markets in the country: Gaza, Jenin, Hebron, Haifa, Jerusalem, Jaffa, Lod, Majdal, Safed, Ramla, Shechem [Nablus] as well as Sūq al-Khān, 'near Tiberias'. Jerusalem's weekly market was held in Birqat Sultan, outside the walls of the Old City 'where they bring between forty and eighty bulls and cows'.

The 1901 almanac notes that the Sūq al-Khān market has been discontinued, but apparently it did continue, presumably unofficially, until the 1920s.[15] What caused the death of this market after more than three centuries? The khan itself had fallen into disuse some years before the market was cancelled.[16] Did changing political factors mean travellers no longer used this route? Were there economic factors at work which made the market no longer viable? Or did it prove too difficult to protect people from attacks by marauders?

Modern markets in Israeli towns

Ancient survivals and modern goods: Jerusalem and Acre. Some of the ancient markets survive to this day. In the old city of Jerusalem, there is a walled enclosure within the sprawl of the nineteenth-century and modern city, the shops along the market-streets are open-fronted, displaying a variety of foods and goods, including holy and unholy souvenirs, as they must have done for centuries.[17] The market-streets slope downwards with a series of wide shallow paved steps which facilitate the movement of donkeys and carts, which are the main modes of transport of goods to the market still today. Merchandise is now often global – many of the shirts and robes once embroidered by local Palestinians are now imported from India, like the tea offered in tiny glasses on swinging trays. The glasses probably come from China now, although there was once a thriving glass industry in Hebron in the West Bank.

In the market in Acre/Akko, populated by both Arabs and Jews, many of the household goods are now international plastic. Biscuit-shapers (still found carved in wood in Nazareth's market) keep their traditional shape here, but are now made of plastic. *Narghile* (hubble-bubble) pipes now come from China. The tobacco used in them was an earlier import from the New World, like the now locally grown tomatoes, potatoes and sweet corn. Coffee arrived in the area from Mocca in the Yemen.

But there are still local Middle-Eastern products: carcasses of whole sheep hang at the butchers' stalls in Jerusalem, and local fish is on sale in sea-side Acre/Akko. Local olives are still called Suri, meaning that they either arrived originally from Syria or that they were specific to the city of Tyre (Tzur or Sur) in Lebanon. The trees themselves are a connection to the past, many of them being hundreds of years old. It is not by chance that the struggles between Israeli settlers and Palestinians in the West Bank often focus on olive trees. Olives can be bought in tins, but home curing is still widespread, so that it is normal here, as in any Israeli or Palestinian market, to taste all the different varieties offered before deciding which to buy. Both Arabs and Jews pickle their olives at home, and sell the surplus in the market, as must have happened from the earliest times. Fruit and vegetables come from small farms as well as commercial sources, and in season – during the winter rains – it is common for the markets to show a variety of green leaves foraged from the countryside, just as described in the Jerusalem Talmud.

Decline and transformation: Nazareth. Other markets are changing, due to the slow demise of traditional ways of life and modernization of transport, particularly among the Arab population. Nazareth, a hill-top town with mostly Christian Arabs, was a local market centre, where people from the villages all around came to sell surplus produce and buy what they needed. Most of the villages did not even have a grocer's. Nazareth market supplied their needs, including grinding their flour and sesame; cracking olives for salting and pressing them for oil; providing stalls to sell the produce of fields and gardens and the results of their foraging, as well as selling them food, clothing and household goods. Now the villages have more shops, and growing vegetables has become more centralized, so many of the food shops in the market stand empty most of the week.

However, this may not be the end of the story of this market. Modern transport now makes the town more accessible for tourists, and cake shops and souvenir stalls are flourishing. The town has traditionally attracted international Christian tourism, but there is now more local interest among Jews in the history of Christianity, which has led to an interesting syncretism in the souvenir stalls: Christmas cribs from local olive-wood side-by-side with Jewish prayer shawls. In parallel, in the food scene, increased interest in what are seen as 'authentic' methods of preparing food has led to local Jewish gastronomic tourism seeking home-made cheeses and home-cured olives (as well as a source of pork, often banned by local by-laws from sale in Jewish towns).

Market growth: Rosh HaAyin. Other markets are growing. Their site within a town may move, but the market remains. As centres of population shift and expand, land in the centre of town becomes too valuable or too difficult to access, and the market is moved further out, just as Roman markets were often held away from the main city forum to minimize the upheavals of market traffic. Rosh HaAyin in central Israel is near ancient Antipatris where Theophanes found only bread and beans. It was set up for Yemenite immigrants in 1948–50. When I first started visiting the market there, in the 1970s, the site was dusty and unpaved, and there was almost no car to be seen. People bought live chickens, or even lambs, to be slaughtered on the spot. Two or three stalls sold cheap clothing at the entrance, and a few vendors sold a small selection of household equipment, including special pans for Yemenite foods such as *kubbaneh* (a slow-baked, bread-like food with lots of fat), neatly stacked on the ground. But the main trade of the market was in seasonal fruit and vegetables sold from trestle tables. There was no protection from the heat in summer or the rain in winter. There are still similar local weekly markets in many small places around the country, although it is a long time since I have seen live chickens. Cars have proliferated, and unofficial trade is now carried on straight from the car boots.

The Rosh HaAyin market was moved some years ago and developed into a regional market, rather than a small local one. It now attracts not only sellers of food and household goods but also clothes vendors, haberdashery, toy and bookstalls (it is the only market I know where you can buy multi-volume sets of the Talmud) and local traditional Yemenite silversmiths. The market had always been held on a Friday to provide the traditional local community with fresh food for the Sabbath. The move in Israel to a five-day week, so that many people do not work on Fridays, meant that this market became a magnet not only for local people, but also for others who wanted to shop and have an 'ethnic' experience at the same time, and were prepared to travel. People from Yemenite families who no longer made their traditional foods in the old time-consuming ways now came to buy them in the market: *kubaneh*, *lahouh* (a pancake-bread with muffin-like holes), *hilbeh* (spiced fenugreek foam) and *samneh* (melted butter). Vendors from the Wednesday market at Ramle came to sell in this Friday market, while the same Druze women who made large soft pitta bread on an iron *saj* in neighbouring Arab Taiyybeh at their Saturday market now came to Rosh HaAyin's Jewish market on Fridays, bringing *labeneh* (yogurt cheese), olive oil and preserved vine-leaves from the village too.

Markets in Israel: Tradition and Transformations

Just as we saw with Khan at-Tujjar, this is a crossroads site, at the meeting of Highway 6 (which runs from the Negev in the south to Galilee in the north), with the major east-west highway from the mountains to Tel Aviv, including the border crossing with the Occupied Territories. A large car-park was set up, and eventually the new market-place was paved, awnings were erected to protect everyone from sun and rain, and electrical wiring was installed to enable setting up large fans, selling ready-cooked food and cooling drinks. Live animals were banned, and there were even unsuccessful attempts to ban the selling of sticky cakes and buns from large open trays. As with Ottoman Khan al-Tujjar, buyers were protected from the threat of terrorist attack by armed guards at the entrance, but here official regulation of the stalls by the authorities extended even to the appointment of a market rabbi, in charge of seeing that religious regulations were strictly kept.

Local and seasonal food

Most of the food sold in Rosh HaAyin, as in present-day Israeli markets in general, while sometimes originating in imports hundreds of years ago – like the potatoes from the New World we saw above, or those from the East such as aubergines, bananas and recently mangoes – is now locally grown, and changes with the seasons. Winter brings citrus fruits in plenty, spring is perfumed by huge piles of green garlic, summer is heralded by the all-too-short apricot season and autumn is marked by piles of olives and grapes. Modern agricultural techniques and marketing demands have extended some of the seasons (strawberries now begin in December) and changed some of the fruit (there are seedless watermelons and spineless sabra fruits) but there are still some very local specialities, particularly in the periphery. Thus the *faqqus*, or Arab cucumber, a hairy cucurbit mentioned by both Pliny and the Mishnah, is still sold in Safed in Galilee; ghat, a bitter-tasting, mildly narcotic but legal leaf chewed by Yemenites, is sold in Rosh HaAyin, as are giant *etrogim* (citrons), used on the festival of Sukkot.[18] Rue (used at traditional henna ceremonies before weddings for keeping away evil spirits) is popular there too, as is purple basil (used in Jewish houses in early twentieth-century Sanaa, in the Yemen, for keeping away flies). Cultivated varieties of greens which used to be gathered wild such as *za'atar*, hyssop, can be found in the market at Nazareth, and the *'aqub*, an edible wild thistle, can be found in the spring in the markets of Tiberias.

The mall and the market: complementary trends

The street encroaches on the mall. A very specific new site of 'street food' is to be found in shopping malls. The first purpose-built mall opened in Israel in 1985, and there are now hundreds all over the country, providing a shopping experience insulated from the outside world, with a security guard at the entrance. Oz Almog has identified one of the factors of this success in that the mall brought a shopping experience reminiscent of the magic of 'abroad' (or at least of North America and Europe) to a previously provincial economy.[19] Markets through history have often sold imported goods, but this feeling of actually experiencing being 'abroad' was particularly important in a country where crossing the border led to enemy territory. The shopper was no longer at the mercy of sun, rain, dust, mud, noise or the smells of decay outside, but enclosed in a new, clean, aseptic bubble, complete with gentle, piped music. However, whereas Israeli malls began as glittering marble-and-glass modern temples of consumerism, they are now showing signs of reverting to their street origins. Just as monumental Roman buildings enclosing much empty space were encroached on in the early Arab period, so here and now temporary stalls, often of the nature of a bazaar, are encroaching on the wide open spaces within the monumental malls. Noise levels have risen, and on Fridays many malls now host a new form of food market, selling cooked Sabbath foods, some of which are eagerly consumed on the spot by the buyers. However, unlike the open markets where the food is mostly Middle-Eastern or at least Sephardi Jewish, there is now a 'retro' trend in selling traditional Ashkenazi foods in city malls, particularly to young couples who no longer make these work-intensive foods themselves, but remember them from parents' or grandparents' homes. They stand and eat: *cholent*, long-cooked Sabbath stew; *kishka*, stuffed intestine; *latkes*, fried potato fritters; *kugel* (or *keegel*) *Yerushalmi*, sweet and peppery Jerusalem noodle-bake; and *krepelach*, ravioli-type dough pockets filled with potato or meat, served in chicken soup. Nostalgia in the midst of modernity – what could be a better recipe for success? A few Sephardi foods sometimes make an appearance: the Moroccan cigar, a roll with tucked-in ends, stuffed with chopped meat and onions; *briq*, a crispy fried pastry bundle surrounding meat or an egg yolk; and *pastellim*, little covered pies.

A similar alternative trend is the appearance of ethnic Arab foods in out-of-town malls, sited, like earlier khans, at the crossroads or entrance to regions such as Galilee. The mall at the Allonim junction, where the north-south highway meets the road west to Haifa and the sea, began as a coffee-stop in a petrol station. I remember stopping there twenty years ago for the simplest sort of *qafeh botz*, 'mud' coffee, sitting on plastic chairs outside a simple counter hoping to catch a breeze. The loos were better not described. This was replaced by a modern mall, with the usual marble-and-glass glitter, freezing air-conditioning, magnificently tiled loos and a number of upmarket cafés, pizzerias, and designer ice-cream shops. This mall has been so successful it is now building a third floor. Last time I visited, however, the street had invaded here too. On a Fridays the space in the centre of Allonim mall is host to an Arab market, providing ethnic food to local Jewish tourists to Galilee, and, perhaps, time-consuming home foods to local Arabs. Pitta bread is prepared on an electrically-heated *saj*, and you can buy a variety of *labeneh*, local olive-oil, home pickles, seeds, spices, *baklawa* (pastries in syrup) and hot *sahleb* drink (originally orchid root, now cornflour, with nuts and spices).

The experience of the mall as 'abroad' seems to have boomeranged. It is all very well to fly out of the country and shop until you drop in an aseptic foreign environment for a week or ten days. To do this all the time, I would suggest, produces a feeling of alienation. Wide spaces become threatening, just as they were, perhaps, to the Moslem population who took over and domesticated the Roman and Byzantine cities. Present-day Israelis, both Arabs and Jews, are similarly domesticating their alien malls, and they have done this in particular by filling them with nostalgic traditional food stalls.

The market moves towards the mall. A complementary trend can be seen most clearly in the heavily gentrified Mahaneh Yehudah market, situated in the new city of Jerusalem, which began in Ottoman times as a market for the very poor.[20] In the colonialist British mandatory plans for developing Jerusalem in the 1920s, C.R. Ashbee speaks of 'the miserable booths which ... disgrace the entrance to the modern city'.[21] Ashbee's re-development plans were never carried out, but recently the old market has grown more and more like a mall. It is now permanently roofed (like the Crusader market in the old city of Jerusalem or the Ottoman market in Acre). After terrorist bombs killed thirty-six people between 1968 and 2002, there are guards at all the entrances. In this originally working-class place, more and more expensive trendy shops, cafés and restaurants are opening up, with wines and cheeses from boutique Israeli wineries and dairies, or imported from France and Italy (and Georgia), designer ice-creams and sorbets, not to mention French pâtisserie, all mixed up with the old vegetable, meat, fish and cake stalls. The sophistication of food from abroad has arrived here and can be smelled and bought and tasted in the heart of Jerusalem. Israeli market shoppers now need feel no less sophisticated than their French or Italian counterparts, and they can still buy their *hallah* bread here for the Sabbath.

Tel Aviv's Carmel Market is developing in this direction as well. It too is now covered and protected from the elements, although not yet with a permanent roof. The main business remains fruit and vegetables in abundant Middle-Eastern profusion, meat and cheeses, as well as cheap and cheerful clothing. There are still old-fashioned stalls advertising food fashionable in the 1950s, listed on grubby white boards in red hand-painted lettering. Here you can buy the traditional drinks of the market: old-fashioned *qafeh botz* flavoured with *hel* (cardamom) and heavily sugared, or ice slushes in neon colours. Whether they actually sell all the foods advertised is unclear. Greasy *borekas* and pitta bread with a herb omelette filling are visible. But when I asked for the advertised *qrem Bavaria*, the local version of *crème Bavaroise*, I was told they had sold out. When had they sold out? Today, last week, years ago? This was a popular dessert in Tel Aviv of the 1980s. There are signs of the gentrification of this market too: new, glamorous imported foods, white-on-black signs with computer graphics and glittering stainless steel machines selling Italian coffee. But here too the new is being domesticated – *ciabatta* has become *ja-pitta* and the cheese in the rolls is local Safed cheese (similar to feta), not mozzarella. In the malls the space was domesticated by the encroachment of the food stalls: here the alien foods and ambience which have joined and sometimes replaced the local are now undergoing a process of domestication.

Conclusion

We have identified a number of often overlapping factors affecting markets, together with some contradictory trends through history: change from temporary to permanent followed by growth or decline and even death; attempts at regulation opposed by tendencies to the chaotic; trade at town sites and crossroads sites; open spaces and encroachment; and the import of foreign patterns and foods leading to alienation then domestication.

Notes

1. Martial 7.61.
2. Yalqut Shimoni, Numbers: Huqat 763; cf. Pesiqta deRav Kahana *Aser Te'aser* 2 and Apuleius *Golden Ass*, i, 0000.
3. For the *agoranomos* in the Roman world and particularly in the Talmudic literature, see D. Sperber, *The City in Roman Palestine* (Oxford: Oxford UP, 1998), pp. 32–47.
4. J. Matthews *The Journey of Theophanes: Travel, Business and Daily Life in the Roman East* (New Haven, CT: Yale UP, 2006).
5. Tosefta Moed Qatan, ii,13: *ib.* Demai i,11.
6. H. Kennedy, 'From Polis to Madina: Urban Change in Late Antique and Early Islamic Syria', *Past and Present* 106 (1985), pp. 3–27.
7. A. Walmsley, 'Byzantine Palestine and Arabia: Urban Prosperity in Late Antiquity', *Towns in Transition: Urban Evolution in Late Atiquity and the Early Middle Ages*, ed. by N. Christie and S.T. Loseby (Aldershot, UK: Scolar, 1996), pp. 126–58.
8. Ernoul, *L'estat de la citée de Iherusalem* (1231) and see in general A.J. Boas, *Domestic Settings: Sources on Domestic Architecture and Day-to-Day Activities in the Crusader States* (Leiden: Brill, 2010).
9. D. Jacoby, 'Crusader Acre in the Thirteenth Century: Urban Layout and Topography', *Studi Medievali* 3.20 (1979).
10. Khan al-Umdan, in its present form Ottoman, may have been built on Crusader foundations.
11. Khān al-sabīl; see K. Cytryn-Silverman, *The Road Inns (Khans) in Bilād al-Shām* (Oxford: Oxford UP, 2010), p. 12.
12. Cytryn-Silverman, pp. 144–53.
13. Cytryn-Silverman, p. 149.
14. A.M. Luncz, *Eretz Israel Almanac for the year 5656* [1896, in Hebrew] (Jerusalem, 1895), p. 19.
15. M. Lee, C. Raso and R. Hillenbrand, 'Mamluk Caravanserais in Galilee', *Levant* 24 (1992), p. 62.
16. Cytryn-Silverman, pp. 150–52.
17. *Ottoman Jerusalem: The Living City 1517–1917*, ed. by S. Auld and R. Hillenbrand (London: Altajir World of Islam Trust, 2000), p. 230.
18. H.S.Paris, 'Semitic-language Records of Snake-Melons (*Cucumis melo*, Cucurbitaceae) in the Medieval Period and the "piqqus" of the "faqqous"', *Genetic Resources and Crop Evolution* 59.1 (2011), pp. 31–38.
19. O. Almog, 'The Culture of Consumerism and Shopping in Israel', *People Israel: Your Guide to Israeli Society*, Samuel Neaman Institute for National Policy Research <http://www.peopleil.org/details.aspx?itemID=7870&searchMode=0&index=1> [in Hebrew, accessed January, 2014].
20. L. Meir, T. Arbel, R. Davosh *Shuq Mahaneh Yehudah* in *People Israel* (above, n. 19).
21. *Jerusalem 1920–22, Being the Records of the Pro-Jerusalem Council during the First Two Years of the Civil Administration*, ed. by C.R. Ashbee, preface by R. Storrs (London, 1924). On Ashbee's colonialist career in Jerusalem see S. Goldhill, 'The Cotswolds in Jerusalem: Restoration and Empire', *From Plunder to Preservation: Britain and the Heritage of Empire c1800–1940*, ed. by A. Swenson and P. Mandler (Oxford: Oxford UP, 2013).